THE HISTORIC HOUSES, CASTLES AND GARDENS OF FRANCE

The Official Guide to Sites Open to the Public

MINISTÈRE DE LA CULTURE
éditions de la
caisse nationale des
monuments historiques
et des sites
62 rue saint antoine
75004 paris

President : C.N.M.H.S.
Max QUERRIEN
Director : C.N.M.H.S.
Françoise SABATIER

This book is edited by
Bertrand DU VIGNAUD

assisted by
Sixtine de NAUROIS and Victoire BUFF,
Documentation
Colin BAILEY and Catherine HEALEY,
translation

Graphic Design : **Pierre DUSSER**
Cards : **La Coopérative de Création**

Inscription CPPP 30 301
ISSN 0242-830X
ISBN 2-85822-070-0

Cover :
Chambord (CNMHS-Archives
Photographiques)

7	**ALSACE**
8	Bas-Rhin
9	Haut-Rhin
11	**AQUITAINE — PÉRIGORD**
12	Dordogne
18	Gironde
23	Landes
27	Lot-et-Garonne
28	Pyrénées-Atlantiques
33	**AUVERGNE**
34	Allier
38	Cantal
41	Haute-Loire
44	Puy-de-Dôme
51	**BOURGOGNE**
52	Côte-d'Or
58	Nièvre
59	Saône-et-Loire
64	Yonne
71	**BRETAGNE**
72	Côtes-du-Nord
74	Finistère
76	Ille-et-Vilaine
82	Morbihan
87	**CENTRE — LOIRE VALLEY**
88	Cher
96	Eure-et-Loir
101	Indre
106	Indre-et-Loire
120	Loir-et-Cher
127	Loiret
133	**CHAMPAGNE — ARDENNES**
134	Ardennes
135	Aube
135	Marne
137	Haute-Marne
139	**CORSE**
141	**FRANCHE — COMTÉ**
142	Doubs
142	Jura
144	Territoire de Belfort
145	Haute-Saône

© Éditions de la Caisse Nationale des Monuments Historiques et des Sites, 1986

CONTENTS

ALPHABETICAL LIST OF FRENCH COUNTRIES

147	**ILE — DE — FRANCE**	275	**HAUTE — NORMANDIE**
148	Paris	276	Eure
150	Essonne	280	Seine-Maritime
152	Hauts-de-Seine	287	**PAYS — DE — LOIRE**
154	Seine-et-Marne	288	Loire-Atlantique
158	Seine-Saint-Denis	291	Maine-et-Loire
158	Val-de-Marne	299	Mayenne
159	Val-d'Oise	301	Sarthe
164	Yvelines	303	Vendée
171	**LANGUEDOC — ROUSSILLON**	309	**PICARDIE**
172	Aude	310	Aisne
173	Gard	314	Oise
178	Hérault	320	Somme
181	Lozère	325	**POITOU — CHARENTES**
182	Pyrénées-Orientales	326	Charente
185	**LIMOUSIN**	326	Charente-Maritime
186	Corrèze	329	Deux-Sèvres
186	Creuse	331	Vienne
187	Haute-Vienne	335	**PROVENCE — CÔTE D'AZUR**
191	**LORRAINE**	336	Alpes-de-Haute-Provence
192	Meurthe-et-Moselle	337	Hautes-Alpes
236	Meuse	337	Alpes-Maritimes
238	Moselle	341	Bouches-du-Rhône
239	Vosges	345	Var
243	**MIDI — PYRÉNÉES**	347	Vaucluse
244	Ariège	351	**RHÔNE — ALPES**
244	Aveyron	352	Ain
246	Haute-Garonne	354	Ardèche
247	Gers	358	Drôme
248	Lot	358	Isère
250	Hautes-Pyrénées	360	Loire
252	Tarn	362	Rhône
255	Tarn-et-Garonne	364	Savoie
257	**NORD — PAS — DE — CALAIS**	365	Haute-Savoie
258	Nord	367	**GUADELOUPE**
260	Pas-de-Calais	367	**MARTINIQUE**
261	**BASSE — NORMANDIE**	369	**INDEX**
262	Calvados		
266	Manche		
270	Orne		

The Caisse Nationale des Monuments Historiques et des Sites

The Caisse Nationale des Monuments Historiques et des Sites is a national agency, related to the Ministry of Culture, which has a wide range of activities :
— Restoration programs of historic monuments either for opening them to public visitors or for using them as cultural centers,
— Special grants to owners of privately held landmark buildings,
— Annual prizes for exceptionnal restoration programs of historic houses by young volunteers,
— Books, art magazines, guidebooks, posters... about historic monuments,
— Special guided tours in Paris and one hundred old cities in France,
— Financial support of cultural events taking place in historic buildings (exhibitions, lectures, concerts, theater and dance performances...),
— Exhibitions on historic monuments, old cities and architecture,
— Special programs for young people discovering France and its architecture,
— Touristic itineraries throughout historic châteaux and abbeys in France...

Hôtel de Sully
62, rue Saint-Antoine 75004 PARIS
Tél. : 42.74.22.22.

R. Jacques Archives Photographiques

PREFACE

This guide book is the product of a survey carried out on the owners, both public and private of the historical monuments of France. Each entry was compiled after informations provided by the owners themselves. For this reason the Caisse Nationale des Monuments Historiques must decline all responsibility for any changes in opening times, or other details which may occur. Furthermore some owners did not want their monument to appear in the guide which explains the ommission of some sites.

Photographs were also provided by the owners who were able to take out advertising space in black and white or colour. Although the Caisse Nationale des Monuments Historiques was anxious to give a lot of space to photographs it is not responsible for the choice of buildings photographed nor for the quality of the pictures.

Some historic sites requested the placing of an advertisement even though they do not fit in with the type of monument listed here (for example the town of Rocamadour, the salt mines of Arc et Senans or the Buffon forge at Montbard) or even though they are not open to the public on a regular basis (the case of numerous châteaux which take paying guests). These monuments not listed with the others but the Caisse Nationale des Monuments Historiques nevertheless felt that their readers would like to see them mentioned in the guide.

ALSACE
BAS-RHIN, HAUT-RHIN.

STRASBOURG
- ★ Musée de l'œuvre Notre-Dame
- ★ Barrage Vauban
- ▲ Jardin botanique
- ▲ Palais des Rohan
- ★ Musée Historique

RIQUEWHIR
- ■ Château des Würtemberg
- ★ Tour des voleurs
- ★ Tour Dolder

COLMAR
- ▲ Parc Schoppenwihr
- ★ Maison Berckheim

- ■ castle, château, manor house
- ● abbey, priory
- ▲ garden, park
- ★ town house, famous men house, farm, mill...
- ○ city

■ Wasigenstein
■ La Petite-Pierre
★ Bouxwiller
■ Grand Geroldseck
■ Saverne

STRASBOURG ○
■ Wangenbourg

■ Ortembourg
■ Haut-Koenigsbourg
○ Riquewhir
○ COLMAR

■ Hugstein

▲ Mulhouse Hôtel de ville

ALSACE

BAS-RHIN.

Bouxwiller (Chancellery-Museum).

Bouxwiller - 67330.
Saverne: 15 km.
Station: Obermodern - Bouxwiller.
Bus service.
Property of the Commune.
　The 13th century château de Bouxwiller, in ruins, was refurbished at the beginning of the 18th century by Jean Reinhard de Hanau-Lichtenberg. The Chancellery has kept its two Renaissance portals which bear coats of arms. Inside you can see three paintings of the school of Hyacinthe Gimignani and the museum's collection of polychromatic furniture.
Open April 4 to Dec. 31 : Weekdays 10 - 12, 2 - 4. Closed Sat.
Open 1st and 3rd Sundays of each month in season.
Parking.
Unaccompanied tours, leaflets available.
German — Guides.
Temporary exhibitions, lectures.
Lecture tours available for school parties only.
Tel.: (88) 70.70.16.

Grand Geroldseck (Castle).

Haegen - 67000.
Saverne: 4 km.
Property of the Commune.
　Built in the 12th century on a rocky plateau in order to protect the abbey of Marmoutier, the château came under the jurisdiction of the Bishop of Metz. A square keep, split by lightning in 1718, towers above the château walls which are surrounded by a ditch. Nearby are the ruins of little Geroldseck.
Unaccompanied tours.
Tel.: Mayor's Office: (88) 91.10.71.

Ortenbourg (Castle).

Scherwiller - 67750.
Sélestat: 7 km.
Station: Scherwiller: 3 km.
Bus service.
Property of the Commune.
　From the top of a rocky peak, at a height of 443 meters, the ruins of Ortensbourg castle tower above the town of Sélestat. Built at the beginning of the 13th century by Rudolph of Habsburg, the castle has preserved its pentagonal keep and seigneurial dwellings which nave Gothic windows. The castle is surrounded by protective walls.
Unaccompanied tours.
Parking for cars only.
Temporary exhibition: The Castles of Alsace.
Tel.: (88) 92.23.23.

La Petite-Pierre (Castle).

La Petite-Pierre - 67290.
Saverne: 25 km.
Station: Saverne or Wingen/s/Moder: 10 km.
Bus service.
Property of the Commune.
　Built in the 13th century, the castle sits on a steep rock. It was transformed first in the Renaissance by George-Jean de Veldenz, husband of the King of Sweden's daughter and again during the reign of Louis XV to accommodate a garrison. A water tank, dating from the 14th century, has been preserved. The Marshals d'Effiat and de Turenne stayed at the château as did Louis XIV. Today the château houses the Centre for Parkland of the Vosges du Nord.
Open April 1 to May 31 : 1 - 6, Sundays and holidays.
June 1 to Sept. 30 : 10 - 12, Mon.-Fri., 2 - 7 Sat., 11 - 7, Sun.
Oct., Sun. 1 - 6.
Nov. 1 and 11:1 to 6.
Open on request from October to Easter.
Unaccompanied tours.
Leaflets available, brochures, audiovisual programme.
Leaflets available in German.
Temporary exhibits, lectures.
Tours and lectures for teachers.
Tel.: (88) 70.46.55.

Saverne (Château).

Saverne - 67700.
Property of the Commune.
　Built on the site of an ancient fortress, the château de Saverne, called the château des Rohan, has undergone several transformations. First renovated in the 16th century, it was again worked on around 1670 by Bishop Furstenberg and then modified and refurbished for Cardinal Arnaud Gaston de Rohan Soubise by Robert de Cotte and Le Lorrain. The palace was completely destroyed by fire in 1779. At this time Cardinal Louis Réné de Rohan-Guéméné commissioned Salins de Monfort to build a neo-classical château nearly 140 meters in length. The north facade has been preserved, but was transformed by the architect Lejeune who remodelled the South facade and added two L shaped wings between 1852 and 1855 at the beginning of the Second Empire. Inside the château very little remains of either the uncompleted 18th century decoration or of the Second Empire renovations.
Museum only.
June 1 to Aug. 31 : 3 - 5.
Closed Tuesdays.
Parking.
Temporary exhibitions of paintings.
Tel.: (88) 91.06.28.

STRASBOURG

Palais des Rohan.

Strasbourg - 67000.
2, place du Château.
Property of the City.
　The Palais des Rohan is an excellent example of 18th century French architecture. Designed by Robert de Cotte, the king's architect, for Cardinal Rohan Soubise Prince Bishop of Strasbourg, the palace was built between 1730 and 1742. Today it houses the Museum of Fine Arts, the Museum of Decorative Arts and the Museum of Archeology. The interiors of the palace match the architecture and sculpture in their exceptionally high quality.
Open April 1 to Sept. 30 : 10 - 12, 2 6.; Oct. 1 to March 31, 10 to 12 : 2 - 6.
Closed Tuesdays Oct. 1 to March 31.
Parking
Unaccompanied tours.
Brochures, leaflets, guided tours available.
Theatre, concerts.
Tel.: (88) 32.48.95.

Botanical Gardens.

Strasbourg - 67083.
28, rue Goethe.
Station: Strasbourg 4 km.
Bus service.
Private property.
　The garden dates from 1619. was transfered in 1882 and an arboretum was added. Over 8° species are included in the 3 1/ hectare gardens which inclu greenhouses, rock gardens ar natural ponds.
Open Jan 1 to Dec. 31 : 8 - 11:45, 2 - 5
Closed Sunday afternoons.
Parking.

ALSACE
BAS-RHIN/HAUT-RHIN

Guided tours from May to Oct.: Sat. 3 pm.
Unaccompanied tours.
German - Guides.
Tel.: (88) 35.25.53.

L'Œuvre Notre-Dame (Museum).

Strasbourg - 67000.
3, place du Château.
Central Station: 2 km.
Property of the city.

Two buildings make up this edifice, one Gothic and the other Renaissance, constructed between 1579 and 1587 by one of the cathedral architects, Ulberger. The buildings first housed the body which administered the construction of Strasbourg cathedral, as well as the lodge of the masons and stone cutters. From 1459 it was the most important lodge of the Holy Roman Empire. The museum, founded in 1931, brings together sculpture and painting from the cathedral and other Alsatian monuments. It has an extremely rich collection.
Open Oct. 1 to March 30: 2 - 6.
April 1 to Sept. 30: 10 - 12, 2 - 6.
Closed Tuesdays Oct. 1 to March 30.
Parking.
Information in German.
Brochures.
Tel.: (88) 32.06.39.

Historical Museum.

Strasbourg - 67000.
3, rue du Vieux-Marché-aux-Poissons.
Property of the city.

This Museum is housed in the buildings of the former Butcher's Hall (built 1586) and contains all types of documents on the history of Strasbourg. Since its foundation in 1921 it has received several important donations and has a major collection of military art.
Open Oct. 1 to March 30: 2 - 6.
April 1 to Sept. 30: 10 - 12, 2 - 6.
Closed Tuesdays Oct. 1 to March 30.
Open each Sunday 10 - 12, 2 - 6.
Open out of season for groups on request.
Information in German.
Brochures, temporary exhibitions.
Lecture tours for school groups only.
Tel.: (88) 32.48.95.

Wangenbourg (Castle).

Wangenbourg - Engenthal - 67710.
Strasbourg: 38 km.
Station: Saverne 15 km.
Bus service.
Private property.

A circular keep erected on a quadrangular base with butresses is all that remains of this castle which probably dates from the 15th century. Hence the irregular shaped edifice, whose walls are at a sharp incline.
Unaccompanied visit.
Parking.
Tel.: (88) 87.30.24.

Wasigenstein (Castle).

Niedersteinbach - 67510.
Wissembourg: 24 km.
Station: Lembach 8 km.
Bus service.
Property of the commune.

Two castles, doubtless erected by the lords of Wasigenstein in the 13th century, rise above two rocky points separated by a deep fault. From the surrounding wall, a portal provides entry to a stairway hollowed out of the rock and leading to the château above. A pentagonal keep protects the main building. In the second castle the gemeled windows and the chapel of the main building have been preserved.
Tel.: (88) 09.25.53.

HAUT-RHIN

COLMAR
Schoppenwihr (Park). Berckheim (House).

Colmar - 68000.
Private property.

Schoppenwihr park was designed in the 19th century by a Scotsman who created a typically English landscape in the Alsatian plain at the foot of the Vosges mountains. The river with its small, romantic bridges, lakes and age old trees, water birds and deer makes this spot unique in the region. Typically Alsatian and still inhabited, the Berckheim house contains memorabilia of the Barons de Berckheim. It is the only house of this kind open to the public in Alsace.
Park open July 1 to Sept. 10, 10 to 12, 2 to 7.
Easter to July 1 and Sept. 10 to Nov.: afternoons only.
House: open afternoon the same dates.

Photo C. Meyer

Haut-Koenigsbourg (Castle).

Saint-Hippolyte - 68590.
Colmar: 28 km.
Property of the State.

Situated on the ridge of the Vosges, Haut-Koenigsbourg dominates the Alsatian plain below. This stunning reconstruction of a medieval « burg » was undertaken by Kaiser Wilhelm II who was given the ruins of a 15th century fortress by the town of Sélestat in 1899. The castle, which incorporates the most ancient remains, is itself enclosed by two powerful walls. You reach the castle by five gateways which are defended by portcullises, drawbridges, parapets and watchtowers. Inside, a collection of antlers are exhibited in the Hunt Room and below the main reception room, a drawbridge leads you to a terrace which has been laid out as bastion.
Open March 1 to 31: 9 - 12, 1 - 5.
April 1 to Sept. 30: 9 - 12, 1 - 6.
Oct. 1 to Oct. 31: 9 - 12, 1 - 5.
Nov. 1 to Feb. 28: 9 - 12, 1 - 4.
Parking.
Guided tour, brochure.
Tea room.
Tel.: (88) 32.11.46.

Hugstein (Castle).

Buhl - 68530.
Station: Mulhouse 25 km.
Property of the city.

The ruins of Hugstein castle rise above the promontory which dominates the Florival valley. The walls, the keep and the main building appear to date from the 13th century. The fully arched entrance gate dates from the 15th century.
Unaccompanied visit.
Tel.: Mayor's Office (89) 76.66.44.

MULHOUSE
Town Hall and Museum.

Mulhouse - 68100.
Place de la Réunion.
Property of the commune.

Mulhouse Town Hall is Rhenish

Renaissance building which was transformed into a museum in 1969. Only the Council room is still used. The town hall also houses the Mulhouse Historical Museum.
Open Jan. 1 to June 14 : 10 - 12, 2 - 5.
June 15 to Sept. 30 : 10 - 12, 2 - 6.
Thursdays : 8:30 - 10:30.
Oct. 1 to Dec. 31 : 10 - 12, 2 - 5.
Closed Tuesdays.
Parking.
Unaccompanied visits.
Guides on request, brochures available.
Facilities for handicapped. Temporary exhibitions.

RIQUEWIHR
Dolder Tower.

Riquewihr.
Rue du Général-de-Gaulle - 68340.
Bus services.
Property of the commune.

The Dolder tower, built in 1291, is part of the original site of Riquewihr. Today it houses a local museum whose four floors are devoted to historic memorabilia.
Open July 1 to Aug. 30 : 9 - 12, 1:30 - 6.
Easter to June 30 : Saturdays and Sundays.

Sept. 1 to Oct. 31 : 9 - 12, 1:30 - 6.
Parking.
Unaccompanied visits, brochures available.
Tel. : (89) 47.92.15.

Thieves Tower.

Riquewihr - 68340.
Rue des Juifs.
Bus services.

The Tieves Tower, abutting the surrounding walls of Riquewihr, has preserved its torture chamber.
Parking.

Wurtemberg
(Castle - Postal Museum).

Riquewihr - 68340.
Colmar : 11 km.
Station : Colmar.
Bus service.
Property of the commune.

Second residence of the Wurtenburg-Montbéliard family, this château built around 1540, sits at an angle to the city ramparts. The imposing gables, the mullioned windows of rose and yellow sandstone, the square tower and the arched porchway have all remained intact. The château has been transformed into a museum of the history of the Alsatian postal service.

Open March 31 to Nov. 11 : 10 - 12, 2 - 6.
Sundays and holidays : 10 - 12, 3 - 7.
Closed Wednesdays except in July and August.
Parking.
Unaccompanied visits (guided tours available).
Audiovisual programme, brochures.
German - English - Guide.
Leaflets available.
Temporary exhibitions, lectures.
Tel. : (89) 47.93.80.

HAUT-RHIN **HAUT-KOENIGSBOURG**

After being destroyed many times, this fortress overlooking the plain of Alsace, was finally rebuilt in the 19th century by Kaiser Wilhelm II of Germany. The castle has in part recovered its 15th century aspect but its furnishings are a testimony to the Neo-Gothic taste of the 19th century.

AQUITAINE

DORDOGNE, GIRONDE, LANDES, LOT-ET-GARONNE, PYRÉNÉES-ATLANTIQUES.

- ■ castle, château, manor house
- ● abbey, priory
- ▲ garden, park
- ★ town house, famous men house, farm, mill...
- ○ city

BORDEAUX
- ★ Hôtel Labottière

LIBOURNE
- ★ Hôtel de Ville - Musée
- ★ Tour du Grand Port

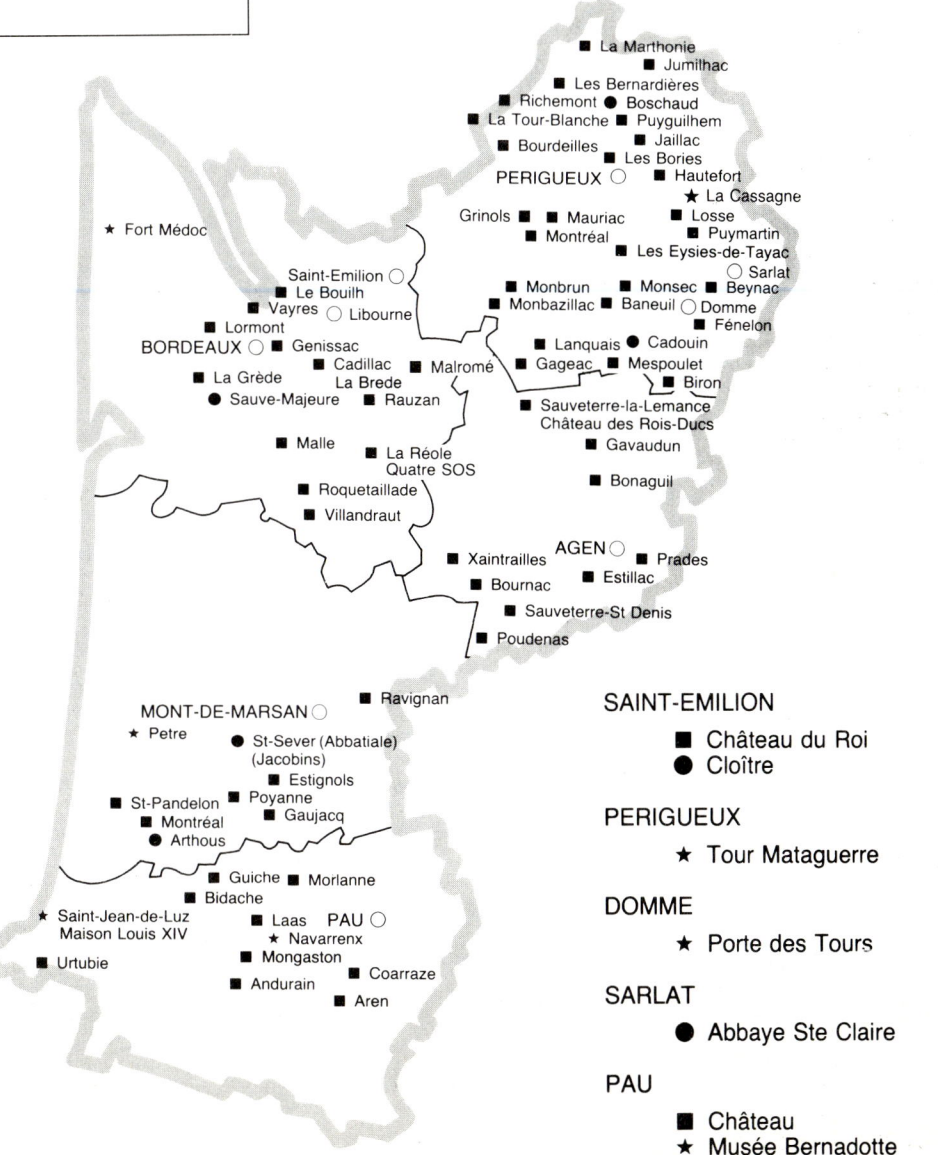

- ■ La Marthonie
- ■ Jumilhac
- ■ Les Bernardières
- ■ Richemont ● Boschaud
- ■ La Tour-Blanche ■ Puyguilhem
- ■ Bourdeilles ■ Jaillac
- ■ Les Bories
- PERIGUEUX ○ ■ Hautefort
- ★ La Cassagne
- Grinols ■ ■ Mauriac ■ Losse
- ★ Fort Médoc ■ Montréal ■ Puymartin
- ■ Les Eysies-de-Tayac
- ○ Sarlat
- Saint-Emilion ○ ■ Monbrun ■ Monsec ■ Beynac
- ■ Le Bouilh ■ Monbazillac ■ Baneuil ○ Domme
- ■ Vayres ■ Libourne ■ Fénelon
- ■ Lormont ■ Lanquais ● Cadouin
- BORDEAUX ○ ■ Genissac ■ Gageac ■ Mespoulet
- ■ La Grède ■ Cadillac ■ Malromé ■ Biron
- ■ La Brede ■ Sauveterre-la-Lemance
- ● Sauve-Majeure ■ Rauzan Château des Rois-Ducs
- ■ Malle ■ Gavaudun
- ■ La Réole ■ Bonaguil
- Quatre SOS
- ■ Roquetaillade
- ■ Villandraut
- ■ Xaintrailles AGEN ○ ■ Prades
- ■ Bournac ■ Estillac
- ■ Sauveterre-St Denis
- ■ Poudenas
- ■ Ravignan
- MONT-DE-MARSAN ○
- ★ Petre ● St-Sever (Abbatiale)
- (Jacobins)
- ■ Estignols
- ■ St-Pandelon ■ Poyanne
- ■ Montréal ■ Gaujacq
- ● Arthous
- ■ Guiche ■ Morlanne
- ■ Bidache
- ★ Saint-Jean-de-Luz ■ Laas PAU ○
- Maison Louis XIV ★ Navarrenx
- ■ Urtubie ■ Mongaston
- ■ Coarraze
- ■ Andurain
- ■ Aren

SAINT-EMILION
- ■ Château du Roi
- ● Cloître

PERIGUEUX
- ★ Tour Mataguerre

DOMME
- ★ Porte des Tours

SARLAT
- ● Abbaye Ste Claire

PAU
- ■ Château
- ★ Musée Bernadotte

AQUITAINE

DORDOGNE

Baneuil (Castle).

Baneuil - 24150.
Bergerac.
Station: Couze.
Private property.

In the 12th century Baneuil was known as the Tower of Vergt. The castle, with its Eastern and Southern facades at right angles to a 12th century oblong tower, also includes a 13th century round tower. Property of the Squire of Clerans, Baneuil was part of the French lines of defense against the English province of Guyenne.
Open July 1 to Sept. 20 : 10 - 12, 3 - 6.
Closed Sundays.
Guided tours.
Tel.: (53) 61.08.31.

Les Bernadières (Château).

Champeau - 24340.
Mareuil : 10 km.
Station : Angoulême 50 km.
Private property.

Laid to siege by Du Guesclin in 1377, Bernadières is surrounded by ditches and includes a 14th century keep with 15th century chimneys and dwellings transformed in the 17th century. The terraced formal gardens overlook the canals and the Nizonne river valley.
Open July 1 to Oct. 10 : 10 - 12, 2 - 6.
Open on request for groups.
Parking.
Guided tours.

Beynac (Castle).

Beynac - 24220.
Sarlat : 10 km.
Station : Sarlat.
Property of M. Lucien Crosso.

Beynac was one of the four baronies of Périgord. It is an imposing edifice dating from the 12th century. It was captured by Richard the Lionheart in 1184 and then by Simon de Montfort in 1214. Its defences are concentrated on the side which overlooks the plain and include double walls, a double moat and double barbicans. The side facing the sheer drop to the river is even more attractive in appearance.
Open daily March 1 to Nov. 15 : 10 - 12, 2:30 - 7.
Parking.
Guided tour.
Information in English - German - Spanish - Dutch.
Tel.: (53) 29.50.40.

Biron (Château).

Biron - 24540.
Monpazier : 8 km.
Station : Le Buisson-de-Cadouin 25 km.
Property of the Departmental Tourist Authority.

Built at the top of a hill, Biron, part of the barony of Périgord, is made up of a great variety of buildings, erected between the 12th and 18th centuries. The keep, the façades and the square tower date from the Middle Ages. The Gothic chapel was built between 1495 and 1515. The classical buildings of the North and West sides of the main courtyard were completed in 1730 but by the time of the Revolution the interior decoration was not yet completed. For several centuries the castle has belonged to the Gontaut-Biron family.
Open Feb. 1 to Dec. 15 : 9 - 11:30, 2 - 6.
Closed Tuesdays except July and August.
Parking.
Open by appointment for groups.
Guided tours.
English in Jult and Aug. - Guide.
Dance, Concerts.
Tel.: (53) 22.62.01.

Les Bories (Château).

Antonne-et-Trigonant - 24420.
Périgueux : 11 km.
Station : Périgueux.
Bus services.
Property of M. and Mme de Lary de Latour.

Built between 1497 and 1604 by the Saint-Astier family, who kept the château until 1892, the château des Bories is built in typical Renaissance style. The rectangular three storied main building is flanked by two imposing circular towers. The South facade boasts a square tower in which you can see a monumental staircase with rib vaulting. One of the rooms, also with rib vaulting, houses a huge fireplace with a basket handle arch. The mullioned windows are perfectly symmetrical.
Open daily July 1 to Sept. 30 : 10 - 12, 2 - 7.
Out of season on request.
Parking.
English - German - Guide.
Brochures available.
Tel.: (53) 06.00.01.

Notre-Dame-de-Boschaud (Abbey).

Villars - 24530.
Villars : 2 km.
Station : Périgueux 30 km.
Bus service.
Property of the department.

Founded in 1163, this Cistercian abbey was a centre of monastic life until it was severely damaged in the Wars of Religion. Successive restorations have uncovered three hectares of architecture which include cupolas, Romanesque arches, capitals and freizes both in the chapter house as well as in the monastery and cloisters.
Open July 15 to August 16 : 9 - 12, 2 - 7.
Parking.
Guided tours.
English - Guide.
Brochure available.
Photography exhibition (in the church).
Club du Vieux-Manoir restoration site.

Bourdeilles (Château).

Bourdeilles - 24210.
Brantôme : 10 km.
Station : Périgueux 25 km.
Property of the Departmental Tourist Authority.

Rising on a limestone spur which overlooks the Dronne, Bourdeilles castle was one of the four baronies of Périgord. Built by Jean

AQUITAINE — DORDOGNE

de Montbrond in honour of Catherine de Medicis, it consists of a fortress from the 13th and 15th centuries and a Renaissance palace furnished in high style. The château also possesses a collection of furniture.
Open Feb. 1 to Sept. 30 : 9 - 11:30, 2 - 6.
Oct. 11 to Dec. 15.
Closed Tuesdays except July - Aug.
Parking.
Groups by appointment.
Guided tours.
English in July - August. Guide.
Brochures available.
Concerts, temporary art exhibitions.
Tel.: (53) 05.73.36.

Cadouin (Abbey).

Le Buisson-de-Cadouin - 24480.
Station: 6 km.
Bus service.
Property of the departemental tourist authority.

Founded in 1115, the Cistercian abbey of Cadouin was for a long time guardian of a linen cloth (an 11th or 12 century Fatimid tapestry) considered to be the Holy Shroud. Hence the abbey's prosperity. The walls date as far back as the 11th century, but the cloisters, frescoes and sculpture are 15th century.
Open Feb 1 to Dec. 15 : 9 - 11:30, 2 - 6.
July and August, 9 - 6.
Closed Tuesdays except in July and August.
Groups by appointment.
Parking.
Guided tours.
English in July and August. Guide.
Brochures available.
Tel.: (53) 22.46.53.

La Cassagne (Tithe Barn).

La Cassagne-Terrasson - 24120.
Terrasson: 12 km.
Station: Le Lardin: 10 km.
Property of M. Choppin De Janvry.

Built in the 12th century by the Templars, this tithe barn which was transformed in the 15th century, has kept a fine vaulted room with a corner fireplace which served as a forge. The barn now houses exhibitions of the Perigordian cartoonist, Sem (1863-1934).
Open July 14 to Sept. 2 : 2:30 - 6:30.
Parking.
Information panels.
Information - English.
Guided tours.
Tel.: (53) 51.66.43.

Domme (Tower Gate).

Domme - 24250.
Sarlat: 10 km.
Property of the commune.

The tower gate, erected in 1282, was the major fortified gateway into the walled town. Consisting of two half towers which contain spiral staircases and guards' rooms, the building was used by the Templars from 1307 to 1318 as a prison.
Open from June 1 to Sept. 30 : 11 - 12, 5 - 6.
Open on request for groups all year.
Parking.
Guided tours, brochures.
Tel.: (53) 28.31.83.

Les Eyzies-de-Tayac (Château).

Les Eyzies-de-Tayac - 25620.
Sarlat: 20 km.
Station near by.
Property of the State.

This 15th and 16th century castle consists of two main buildings modified in the Renaissance and restored several times between 1914 and 1980. Since 1918 it has housed the National Museum of Prehistory, which has provided for the collection and exhibition of objects found in the region. You can see a collection of cut flint as well as paleontological and anthropological exhibitions.
Open March 1 to Nov. 30 : 9:30 - 12, 2 - 6.
Dec. 1 to Feb. 28 : 9:30 - 12, 2 - 5.
Closed Tuesdays.
Parking.
Guided tours on request 2 weeks in advance.
Information panels.
Brochures available.
Tel.: (53) 06.97.03.

Fénelon (Château).

Sainte-Mondane - 24370.
Salat: 18 km. Souillac: 16 km.
Station: Sarlat or Souillac.
Property of M. B. Roche.

Birthplace of the famous author, Fénelon, Archbishop of Cambrai and governor of the Duc de Bourgogne, the château is built on a succession of rocky terraces which form three walls overlooking the Dordogne river valley. Built in the 13th and 14th centuries it was transformed in the 16th and 17th centuries. The L shaped main building has large circular towers covered in grey stone. One room is devoted to Fénelon memorabilia and another part of the château houses a collection of vintage cars.
Open daily June 1 to Sept. 30 : 10 - 12, 2 - 7.
Oct. 1 to May 31 : 10 - 12, 2 - 6.
Parking.
Guided tours, brochures.
Tel: (53) 29.71.55 and 29.78.97.

Gageac (Château).

Rouillac - 24240.
Bergerac: 18 km.
Station: Gardonne 5 km.
Property of M. de la Verie de Vivans.

This medieval residence belonged to the English when it was besieged by Du Guesclin in 1370. The 12th century keep and the 15th century tower enclose the main buildings which were modified under Louis XIV. The Courtyard is closed off by a sentry way.
Opening hours not given.
Tel.: (53) 27.92.82.

Grignols (Fortified Castle).

Grignols Saint-Astier - 24110.
Neuvoc: 6 km.
Station: Périgueux 26 km.
Bus service.
Property of M. André Sagne.

Despite demolition, the fortress, with its 13th century towers and facades, still conveys the importance it once enjoyed. Used as a refuge by the Grimoärd and Talleyrand families, it was beseiged several times. Yet you can still admire its Gothic portal, its 15th century staircase, its 14th century keep and its sculptured chimneys.
Open June 1 to Sept. 30 : 2:30 - 7.
Open on request for groups.
Closed Mondays.
Guided tours.
Tel: (53) 54.25.40.

Hautefort (Château).

Hautefort - 24390.
Périgueux: 42 km.
Station: Condat-le-Lardin: 22 km.
Property of Mme de Bastard.

Overlooking the surrounding countryside, the present château was entirely rebuilt in the 17th century. The only remnant or the ancient fortress is the drawbridge. Hautefort is the largest classical château in Périgord. Two L shaped wings crowned by domed round towers flank the main building. Inside you find 16th and 17th century tapestries and 17th and 18th century furniture. The château is surrounded with terraced gardens. It has belonged to the troubadour Bertrand de Born and then to the Hautefort and Damas families. Burnt down in 1968, the château has been perfectly restored by the present owner.

Open from Palm Sunday to Sept. 15 : 9 - 12, 2 - 7.
Sept. 16 to Nov. 2 : 9 - 12, 2 - 6.
From Nov. 3 to Palm Sunday : Sun. and holidays, 2 - 5. For groups on request.
Parking.
Guided tours.
English - German - Dutch.
Leaflets available.
Concerts, temporary exhibitions.
Tel.: (53) 50.40.04.

Jaillac (Château).

Sorges - 24420.
Périgueux : 17 km.
Station : Négrondes 7 km.
Bus service.
Private property.

Built in the 12th century, Jaillac was much changed over the following centuries. It includes two entrance towers, linked by walls and topped by a fort as well as a main building. The remaining arrow slits testify to the castle's defensive role in the Middle Ages. A spiral grand staircase made of stone completes the decoration of the château's vast rooms, with their freizes, huge fireplaces and furniture dating from the reigns of Henri II to Louis-Philippe.

Open July 1 to Oct. 31 : 2 - 7.
Closed Tuesdays and Thursdays.
Parking.
Tel.: (53) 05.03.16.

Jumilhac (Château).

Jumilhac-le-Grand. - 24630.
Saint-Yrieix : 12 km.
Station : La Coquille 12 km.
Bus service.
Private property.

In 1579 the Chapelle de Jumilhac family acquired the 13th century fortress which dominates the Isle valley. They covered the château built in rough cut stone with a slate roof. The château consists of different sized turrets capped with embossed lead finials. Two wings were added in the 17th century and one of the towers boasts a fine spiral staircase. You can also see a fully panneled salon decorated with hangings by J. B. Oudry.

Open March 15 to June 30 : Sun. and holidays, 2 - 6.
July 1 to Sept. 15 daily 10 - 12, 2 - 6:30.
Sept. 15 to Nov. 15 : Sun. and holidays, 2 - 6.
Parking.
Guided tour, brochures.
Englsh - Guide.
Concerts, plays.

DORDOGNE

FÉNELON
Sainte-Mondane

Birthplace of the famous author, Archbishop of Cambrai and tutor to the duc de Bourgogne, the château de Fénelon is built on a group of rocky terraces which form three rows of fortifications overlooking the Dordogne. Built in the 13th and 14th centuries, it underwent transformations in the 16th and 17th centuries but has kept its original fortifications.

Open daily June 1 to Sept. 30 : 10 - 12 and 2 - 7.
Oct. 1 to May 31 : 10 - 12 and 2 - 6.
24370 Sainte-Mondane.

AQUITAINE — 15 — DORDOGNE

Lanquais (Château).

Lanquais - 24150.
Bergerac: 16 km.
Station: Saint-Capraise-de-Lalinde 4 km.
Bus service (from Bergerac).
Private property.

Built on a rustic? the château de Lanquais with its Gothic towers and parapets was enlarged in the 16th century with a four-storied wing in the Renaissance style. Entirely furnished inside, the château has fireplaces attributed to the Italian artists who worked on the Louvre. Ysabeau de Limeuil the most beautiful of Catherine de Medici's ladies in waiting lived in this château.
Open April 1 to Oct. 31 : 9:30 - 12, 2:30 - 7.
Closed Thursdays.
Parking.
Guided tours.
Concerts, theatre.
Tel.: (53) 61.24.24.

Losse (Château).

Thonac - 24290.
Montignac: 5 km.
Station: Les Eyzies 17 km.
Private property.

Perched on a cliff above the Vézère river, this château was built on the remains of a 13th century castle. Partly destroyed during the Wars of Religion, it was rebuilt in the 16th century by Jean de Losse, governor of Guyenne. The L shaped Renaissance buildings joined together by a circular tower are crowned by a sentry way. The fort is a fine example of military architecture. The entire edifice is made of the regional ochre stone. Inside you find fine examples of 16th and 17th century furniture and tapestries.
Open July 1 to Sept. 15 : 10 - 12:30, 2 - 6:30.
Open out of season for groups on request.
Guided tours, brochures.
English - German - Dutch depending on the guides, guides and information pannels.
Temporary art exhibitions.
Recorded Renaissance music.
Tel.: (53) 50.70.38.

La Marthonie (Château).

Saint-Jean-de-Cole - 24800.
Thiviers: 7 km.
Station: Thiviers.
Bus service.
Property of M. de Beaumont-Beynac.

Burnt down during the Hundred Years War, the old castle was rebuilt by Mondot de la Marthonie, Premier President of the Paris Parlement and councillor to François I. The château consists of two main buildings at right angles, a medieval wing with two 14th century towers and a 17th century wing built onto a gallery. During the 17th century one of the towers was embellished with a monumental staircase. The rooms below house an annex of the Historical museum of paper.
Open July 1 to Aug. 31 : 9 - 12, 2 - 7.
Parking.
Guided tours.
English. Guide.
Concerts, temporary exhibits (books on daily life/collections of farm tools).
Tel.: (53) 62.30.25.

Mauriac (Château).

Douzillac - 24190.
Mussidan: 10 km.
Private property.

Mauriac was built in the 16th century on the ruins of an 11th century castle overlooking the Isle river. Until the Revolution it belonged to the Talleyrand family. Montaigne stayed there in 1581. The main building, flanked by two large towers, is built on the site of the former battlements.
Open 10 - 12:30, 2:30 - 7.
Grounds only.
Parking.

Mespoulet (Château).

Saint-Pompont - 24170.
Sarlat: 27 km.
Station: Belvès 14 km.
Bus service.
Private property.

Mespoulet consists of assymetrical buildings with 14 to 18th century towers covered with slate, tiles and stone. It was built by the Templars.
Open June 1 to Sept. 30 : 2:30 - 6.
Parking.
Grounds only.
Interiors on request.
Unaccompanied visits.
Information pannels, leaflets, brochures.
English - Information.
Temporary art exhibits.
Tel.: (53) 28.45.39.

Monbazillac (Château).

Monbazillac - 24240.
Bergerac: 4 km.
Station: Bergerac 5 km.
Airport: Bergerac.
Bus service.
Property of the Monbazillac Wine Growers Cooperative.

Built by François d'Aydie, Vicomte de Riberac, the château has retained its Renaissance architectural style of the mid 16th century which contrasts with the more austere military features of drymoats, parapets and arrow slits. Based on a rectangular plan with circular towers, Monbazillac houses regional furniture, tapestries and two museums: a wine museum and a Protestant museum.
Open Nov. 1 to April 30 : 9:30 - 12, 2 - 5:30.
May 1 to Oct. 31 : 9 - 12, 2 - 6:30.
Parking.
Guided tour.
English July and August.
French - English brochures.
Tel.: (53) 58.30.27 and 57.06.38.

Monbrun (Château).

Verdon - 24520.Bergerac: 17 km.
Stations: Sainte-Capraise-de-Lalinde 6 km.
Private property.

This 18th century building is a perfect example of a perigourdian charterhouse. The single storey building is flanked by two pavilions which surround a terrace whose fourth side is closed off by a balustrade decorated with a stone sphinx. The covered well still has its original fittings.
Open on request only.
Parking.
Grounds only.
Tel.: (53) 23.21.51.

Monsec (Château).

Mouzens - 24220.
Saint-Cyprien: 5 km.
Station: Siorac-en-Périgord.
Bus service.
Private property.

Overlooking the Dordogne Monsec has retained a certain consistency despite the different periods during which it was built. The fort, erected during the reign of Louis XIII, abuts a Renaissance wing whichs itself continued by a 14th century wing. The other part of the main building, at right angles, consists of elements from the 14th to the 16th centuries. This residence has always belonged to the same family.
Open July 15 to Aug. 30: 10-12, 3-6.
Groups on request.
Parking.
Tel.: (53) 29.22.33.

Montréal (Château).

Issac - 24400.
Bergerac: 25 km.
Station: Mussidan 8 km.
Private property.

Ruined during the Hundred Years War, the fortress of Montréal with its double walls dating from the 12th century was finally turned into a sumptuous château in the 16th century. Its Renaissance facade includes highly decorated mullioned window framed by small columns. A rectangular chapel with tower and staircase was built in 1569 and contains a relic of the Crown of Thorns surrounded by statues. This château most probably gave its name to the Canadian city as Claude de Pontbriand known as « Montréal » was with Jacques Cartier when he named the site.
Grounds only.
Tel.: (53) 81.11.03.

PÉRIGUEUX
Mataguerre Tower

Périgueux - 24000.
Property of the commune.

Mataguerre is the last surviving tower of the 13th century city walls. Destroyed during the reign of Philip-Augustus, it was restored at the end of the 15th century. This round tower sits on a polygonal base and is crowned by a parapet. It bears the emblem of the kings of France.
Open on request.
Parking.
Guided tours.
English - German - Italian - Guides and information.
Lecture tours for school groups.

Puyguilhem (Château).

Villars - 24530.
Brantôme.
Station: Thivers.
Property of the state.

Built in the middle of the 16th century by the La Marthonie family, the château is the richest château in the region because of its sculpture. The main building is flanked to the North East by an imposing circular tower and to the South East by a pentagonal tower and a polygonal tower. Of the two pavilions that complete the edifice, the North pavilion was modified in the 17th century. The pentagonal tower's balustrade, the decoration of the dormer windowers as well as that of the interior all testify to the building's refinement.
Open Feb. 1 to Dec. 15: 9 - 11:30, 2 - 6.
Closed Tuesdays except July and August.
Open on request for groups.
Parking.
Guided tours, brochures.
English in July and August - Guide.
Temporary exhibits.
Tel.: (53) 54.82.18.

Puymartin (Château).

Marquay - 24200.
Sarlat: 8 km.
Station: Sarlat.
Private property.

The château de Sarlat, which witnessed a certain Captain Puymartin's struggle against the Huguenots, dates back to the 15th and 16th centuries but also includes some modern restoration. Enclosed by walls, the château consists of several main buildings joined together by round towers. Apart from Renaissance furniture, you can see Aubusson and Beauvais tapestries and a cabinet decorated in the style of the seventeenth century.
Open July 1 to Sept. 15: 10 - 12, 2 - 6.
Parking.
Guided tours (inside and outside).
English - Guide.

Richemont (Château).

Built between 1550 and 1580 by the historian Pierre de Bourdeille.
Richemont has two L shaped wings joined by a square tower with parapets. Inside you can visit the vaulted chapel where the first proprietor is buried and the panelled bedrooms. Which was built in 1610.
Open July 15 to Aug. 31, 10 - 12, 3 - 6.
Closed Fridays.
Parking.
Guided tour.
Tel.: (53) 05.72.81.

SARLAT

Sainte-Claire (Abbey).

Salat - 24200.
Côte de Toulouse, rue de La Boétie an rue J.J. Rousseau.
Bus service.
Property of the Association Paroissial du Sarladais.

LA TOUR BLANCHE

DORDOGNE

Built at the end of the 10th century on the site of a Gaulish oppidum, rising on a circular mound, the square keep of La Tour Blanche is considered the oldest in France. Constructed in the white stone of the region by a member of the de La Tour family it is the bithplace of Adhemar de La Tour, Bishop of Périgueux who was born in 1187. In 1265 it belonged to Marguerite, daughter of Hugues IV, king of Thessalonika and duke of Burgundy. By 1351 it was the property of Jean le Bon, king of France. After being occupied by the English, the castle was captured by Du Guesclin on March 9, 1356. In 1544, Marguerite de Valois d'Angoulême stayed at the castle with her husband King Henri II of Navarre. In 1613 Brantôme drew up his last will and testament here. Having gone over to the prince de Condé during the Fronde the castle was attacked in 1652 by Henri de Lorraine and occupied by the royal army. But when the comte d'Harcourt joined the Fronde the castle would once again be the site of further turmoil.

Occupied by the nuns of Saint Claire from 1621 until the Revolution, this 16th and 17th century abbey consists of an L shaped building which looks onto a garden in the heart of old Sarlat. It has retained the basket handle vaults and semi-circular vaults of the cloister and gallery. The Louis XIII facade on the garden side is decorated with shell-shaped windows, and the large rooms have fireplaces and panelling which date from the 16th century.
Open July 15 to Aug. 31, 9 - 12, 2 - 7.
Parking.
Guided tours, brochures.
Sarlat Theatre Festival.
Temporary exhibitions (photography, graphics).
Club du Vieux Manoir.

La Tour Blanche (Castle).

La Tour Blanche - 24320.
Périgueux or Angoulême : 38 km.
Station : Périgueux or Angoulême.
Bus service.
Property of Louis Soutoul.

La Tour Blanche, birthplace of Adhémar, bishop of Périgueux in 1187, belonged to Jean Le Bon, King of France. It was captured from the English by Du Guesclin and then inhabited by Marguerite de Valois. Built at the end of the 10th century on the site of a Gothic oppidum, this square keep made of white stone, was once surounded by a moat filled by the Buffebal river which still flows at the foot of the castle.
Open July 15 to Aug. 34 : 10 - 12, 3 - 6.
Closed Wednesdays.
Parking.
Guided tours.
English - German.

GIRONDE

BORDEAUX

Petit hôtel Labottière.

Bordeaux - 33000.
13, rue Saint-Laurent.
Private Property.

Built for Etienne Labottière on the site of the public gardens which the city of Bordeaux sold off in 1782, this small hôtel stands between a courtyard and garden and consists of a main building with two wings at right angles to it. The edifice forms a coherent whole. On the side facing the street, the garlands decorating the three arcatures were made by one of the sculptors who worked on the Bordeaux Theatre. The facade facing the courtyard is decorated and the garden facade is crowned with a balustrade. Victor Louis who built the Bordeaux theatre may also have built this Little hôtel.
Open on request.
Currently closed for restoration.
Parking.
Guided tours.
English - Spanish.
Lecture tours for school groups.
Tel. : (56) 52.31.55 or 44.85.10.

Le Bouilh (Château).

Saint-André-de-Cubzac - 33240.
Bordeaux : 25 km.
Station : Saint-André-de-Cubzac.
Bus service.
Proprety of M. Patrice de Feuilhade de Chauvin.

Built towards the end of the 18th century by Victor Louis on the site of a 14th century stronghold, this grandiose neo-classical edifice was never completed. Only one of the two buildings intended for the terrace was constructed. The French windows on the main facade set into arches support a balustrade. The out-buildings form a semi-circle below. The park is enlivened by a water tower and a dovecote with a pepperpot roof. Comte Frédéric de La Tour du Pin who created this huge estate to receive the king interrupted the construction so as not to be accused of squandering the State finances.
Open Thur., Sat., Sun., May 1 to Sept. 30 : 2:30 - 6:30. For groups on request.
Parking.
Guided tours, brochures.
Tel. : (57) 43.06.59.

CADILLAC
Château of the Ducs d'Epernon.

Cadillac - 33410.
Bordeaux : 35 km.
Station : Cérons 2 km.
Bus service.
Property of the State.

In 1598 the Duc d'Epernon, favorite of King Henri III, rased the fortress that occupied this site to build a château that would rival the royal residences. He commissioned the architects Pierre Souffron and Gille de La Touche Aguesse to build this sumptuous edifice, of which only the main building with its two wings remains. Inside you still see eight sculpted stone and marble monumental fireplaces, 17th century painted ceilings and tapestries woven testify to the splendour with which Charles IX, Henri IV Louis XIII, Louis XIV, Richelieu and Molière were entertained at the château.
Open April 11 to Oct. 31 : 10:45 - 12:4 7.
Nov. 1 to March 31 : 2:30 - 5:30.
Closed Mondays.
Parking.
Guided tours.
English - German - Guide.
Brochure available.
May Bordeaux Music Festival.
Theatre - Dance - Concerts.
Temporary exhibitions, Lectures.
Contemporary Art Show organised CADILLAC (Centre Contemporain Diffusion, d'Information et de Lectu pour l'art contemporain, tel. 62.13.03
Lecture tours for school groups.
Tel. : (56) 27.31.08).

GÉNISSAC
Le Vieux Château.

Génissac - 33420.
Libourne : 9 km.
Station : Libourne.
Private property.

In 1354 Edward II authorised the building of Genissac as a way ending the insecurity that reigne in the region. Part of the keep an the ramparts date from this perio while the remaining building were transformed in the 15th an 16th centuries or added thereafte
Open Aug. 1 to Sept. 9 : 2:30 - 6.
Parking.
Guided tours.
Tel. : (57) 24.48.41.

Labrède (Castle).

Labrède - 33650.
Bordeaux : 20 km.
Private property.

This large and many sided m dieval fortress, flanked by a rou tower and a rectangular keep, surrounded by a wide moat for e tra defence. Montesquieu w born here in 1689 and the cas remained his favorite residenc He created an English park arou the moat and this softened t otherwise austere character of t castle. The library still contai

CADILLAC
Ducs d'Épernon Castle

GIRONDE

This remarkable building which has survived the ravaged of history could easily be called « a Loire château built on the banks of the Garonne ». Visitors can enjoy a stroll through its fine vaulted rooms and lofty reception rooms with their monumental fireplaces, marble and stone mosaics and gilded ceilings.

over 7000 books collected by the celebrated philosopher.
Open Sundays March 6 to Easter and daily (except Tue.) from Easter to Nov. 1 : 2:30 - 5:30 (6:30 in summer).
Guided tours.
Tel. : (56) 20.20.49.

LIBOURNE
Town Hall
Princeteau Museum
Libourne - 33500.
Place Abel-Surchamp.
Bordeaux : 30 km.
Station.
Bus service.
Property of the commune.
Built in the 15th century and restored and extended at the beginning of the 20th, the Town Hall of Libourne was formerly the seat of the Town Council. It has kept its gabled facade with its mullioned windows as well as the bellfry and a monumental stone staircase. It is the home of the Princeteau Museum, the animal painter who was Toulouse-Lautrec's teacher, as well as of the Archeological Museum.
Town Hall :
Open Jan. 1 to Dec. 31 : 8:30 - 12, 1:15 - 5.
Museum :
Open Jan. 1 to Dec. 31 : 9:30 - 12:30, 2 - 5.
Closed Sat. Sun. Mon. and holidays.
Parking.
Unaccompanied visits.
Tel. : (57) 51.15.00.

Grand Port (Tower)
Libourne - 33500.
Bordeaux : 30 km.
Station : Bordeaux.
Bus service.
Property of the commune.
Set on the quay opposite the port and former royal causeway, two round towers frame this Gothic gateway which is all that remains of Libourne's ramparts. They played an important role in defending the port which was an active maritime centre until the 1850s.
Open all year.
Parking.
Unaccompanied visits.

LORMONT
Black Prince (Castle).
Lormont - 3310.
Bordeaux : 6 km.
Bus service.
Private property.

Once the residence of the kings of England and the Archbishops of Bordeaux, this castle was rebuilt by the Cardinal de Sourdis in the 17th century. Ruined in the Revolution it was restored in 1875. The main buildings which date from 1612 include bas-reliefs and vaults with grafitti from the same period as well as a seventeenth century fountain. The excavation of a 17th century château are being carried out in the large park.
Open Jan. 1 to Dec. 31 on request for groups.
Parking.
Guided tours, brochures.
Foreign language guides available with one month's notice.
Facilities for handicapped.
Lecture tours for school groups only.
Tel. : (56) 06.54.24.

Malle (Château).
Preignac : 4 km - 33210.
Langon : 4 km.
Preignac : 3 km.
Property of M. de Bournazel.
Built in the 17th century by Jacques de Malle, president of the Parlement of Bordeaux, the château de Malle owes its italianate appearance to changes carried out around 1700. The interior includes a small Italian theatre decorated with silhouettes of characters from the Commedia dell' Arte, and the garden and terraces are scattered with statues symbolising the vine. The château is a one story horseshoe shaped building flanked by two round towers.
Open March 27 to Oct. 16 : 3 - 7.
Closed Wednesdays.
Open on request at other times.
Parking.
Information in English, German, Dutch.
Acoustiguides, brochures.
Tel. : (56) 63.28.67.

Malromé (Château)
Saint-André-du-Bois - 33490.
Langon : 7 km.
Station : Langon.
Private property.
Built in the 12th century, transformed in the 19th, Malromé has had several illustrious owners including Leroy de Saint-Arnau Marshal of the Second Empi and the painter Henri de To louse-Lautrec who died here. T château has recently been cor pletely restored.
Open June 1 to Sept. 30 : 2 - 7.
Parking.
Indoor and outdoor vivits.
Brochures available.
Guided tours.
Tel. : (56) 61.14.47.

Fort Médoc.
Cussac-Fort-Médoc - 33460.
Bordeaux : 35 km.
Station : Moulis 5 km.
Bus service.
Property of the commune.
Fort Médoc is one of seve buildings designed by Vauban defend the city of Bordeaux. Wo began in 1690 : marshland w drained, dykes were construct and locks enabled the ditches be filled with water. The portico crowned by a pediment whi bears the royal sun emblem. T four strongholds overlook the ronde.
Open daily : May 15 to Sept. 15 : 9 - Oct. 16 to May 14, 10 - 5, Sat., St holidays.
Open on request for groups.
Guided tours on request.

RAUZAN
Ducs de Rauzan (Ch teau).
Rauzan - 33420.
Libourne : 23 km
Bus service.
Property of the commune.
Built mainly between the 1 and 17th centuries, this castle huge military and residential tate isolated by deep valleys was the seat of a powerful cour Law at the frontiers of the reg occupied by the English. The s rounding walls, flanked by square towers, contain a Go main building as well as a high cular keep, dating from the 1 century and modified in the 1 and 18th centuries.
Open July 10 to Aug. 20 : 8 - 12, 3 -

AQUITAINE — 21 — GIRONDE

Aug. 21 to july 9 : Sat., Sun., 10 - 12, 2 - ?.
Weekdays on request July 10 to Closed Mon. July 10 to Aug. 20.
Parking.
English - German - Guide (July and Aug.).
Brochures available.
Temporary exhibitions, archeological digs.
Lecture tours for school groups.
Tel. : (56) 84.13.04 (town hall).

LA RÉOLE
« Quatre SOS » (Castle).

La Réole - 33190.
Bordeaux : 60 km.
Station : La Réole.
Property of M. Viort.

This castle, built on a rocky spur in 1188, commanded entry to La Réole by both land and water. It was transformed first in 1224 and then again after the Hundred Years War when it had been laid to seige many times. Of the four towers (« The Four Sisters ») which gave the château its name, three still stand. The main tower is still lived in. The castle was demolished in the 17th century and its main building entirely rebuilt.
Open on request only, April 10 to Nov. 15.
Parking.
Guided tours.
Tel. : (56) 61.02.39.

Roquetaillade (Castle).

Mazères - 33210.
Bordeaux : 45 km.
Station : Langon 9 km.
Property of the Baritault family.
Built in 1306 by Cardinal Gaillard de La Mothe, nephew of the Gascon Pope, Clement V, Roquetaillade has undergone important restoration, first after the Wars of Religion and then after the Revolution. It now consists of two fortified castles : La Mothe, which dates from the 12th century and Roquetaillade, the « New Castle » which was partly restored, decorated and furnished in the 19th century by Viollet-le-Duc and his pupil, Duthoit. A 19th century Neo-Gothic staircase is to be found along with 17th century monumental fireplaces similar in style to those in the château de Cadillac.
Open Jan. 15 to April 30 : Sun. 2 - 5
May 1 to June 30 : 2 - 6.
July 1 to Sept. 30 : 9:30 - 12, 2 - 7.
Parking.
Guided tours, brochures.
English - German - Information.
Facilities for the handicapped.
Bordeaux May Music Festival.
Theatre.
Tel. : (56) 63.24.16.

LORMONT
Black Prince's Castle
GIRONDE

Built between the 12 and 19th centuries, former residence of the Dukes of Aquitaine, Kings of England and the Archbishops of Bordeaux. Destroyed during the Wars of Religion and rebuilt in 1612.
Open daily on request. Tel. : (56) 06.54.24.
Grounds. Prisons. Excavations. Beautiful views.

GIRONDE

MALLE
PREIGNAC - 33210 LANGON - Tel. : (56) 63.28.67

In the heart of the château country — there are 4 000 in the Bordeaux area — this authentic « wine château » is of interest both to lovers of wine and to lovers of art. The harmony of its proportions, the richness of its collections of paintings and furniture, the elegance of its terraced gardens and Italian theatre blend well with the château's association with the wine producing soils of Sauternes and Graves. In the grounds are several 17th century sculptures celebrating the art of wine producing.

GIRONDE

MALROMÉ

Built in the 12th century and transformed in the 19th, the château de Malromé has recently been completely restored. The painter Henri de Toulouse-Lautrec died here in 1901.

AQUITAINE — GIRONDE/LANDES

SAINT-ÉMILION

Château du Roi

Saint-Émilion - 33330.
Libourne : 8 km.
Bus service.
Property of the commune.

In 1224, while occupying the town of Saint-Émilion, Louis VIII planned the construction of this castle, whence its name. Work did not begin until 1237. The castle consists of an imposing square keep with two stories 32 meters high. Until 1720 it was the seat of the Town Hall. The upper parts were restored at the beginning of this century.
Open Jan. 1 to Dec. 31 : 9 - 12, 2 - 6.
Closed Christmas and New Year's Day.
Grounds only.
Unaccompanied visit.
Acoustiguides.

Chapter House Cloister.

Saint-Émilion - 33330.
Libourne : 8 km.
Bus service.
Property of the commune.

An inner courtyard, measuring 9 1/2 m in Length and 4 1/2 m in width, enclosed by four arcaded galleries with double columns is all that remains of the chapter house.
Open Jan. 1 to Dec. 31 : 9 - 12, 2 - 6.
Closes Christmas and New Year's Day.
Parking.
Grounds only.
Unaccompanied visits.

Sauve-Majeure (Abbey).

Léon - 33670.
Bordeaux : 25 km.
Property of the State.

Set in the Bordeaux vineyards of Entre-Deux-Mers, formerly called « Sylva Major » or the large forest, Sauve-Majeur was founded in 1079 and rebuilt in the 13th century. This Benedictine Abbey was on the pilgrimage route to Saint-Iago da Compostella and until the Renaissance was very prosperous. Now in ruins, the abbey church still bears witness to its former glory. Both the absidioles and the south aisle have kept their vaults. The latter is crowned by a high octagonal bell tower with gemeled openings. There are also fine Romanesque capitals.
Open April 1 to Sept. 30 : 9 - 11, 4:30 - 6.
Oct. 1 to March 31 : 10 - 11:30, 2:30 - 5.
Closed Tuesdays.
Guided tours, brochures.
Tel. : (56) 23.01.55.

Vayres (château).

Vayres - 33730.
Langon : 17 km.
Station : Langon.
Bus service.
Private property.

On the banks of the Dordogne rises this collection of buildings from different epochs. Laid to ruin during the Hundred Years War, rebuilt by the architect Louis de Foix only to be damaged again during the Fronde, Vayres was finally restored during the 18th century. Overall, Vayres still evokes the Middle Ages, but the East wing with its arcaded gallery brings to mind the lay out of Ancy-le-Franc. Terraces lead from the château to the Dordogne.
Open Oct. 1 to June 30 : Sundays only, 2:30 - 5.
July 1 to Sept 30 : 2:30 - 6.
Closed Tuesdays and Sunday mornings.
Parking.

Photo J. Feuillie

Villandraut (Castle).

Villandraut - 33730.
Langon : 17 km.
Station : Langon.
Bus service.
Private property.

Bertrand de Goth, the Archbishop of Bordeaux who became Pope Clement V in 1305, built this castle at his birthplace on the banks of the Ciron. It is a rare and successful combination of a palace and a fortress. The square walls are surrounded by a wide moat and are protected by six imposing towers, one of which was rased to the ground in 1592. They look down on the main courtyard and the remains of the papal residence.
Open June 1 to Sept. 30 : 10 - 12, 2:30 - 5:30.
Oct. 1 to Mays 30 : Sunday afternoons and on request.
Parking.
Marked itinerary.
Foreign Languages : guides.
Brochures available.
Tel. : (56) 25.87.57.

LANDES

Arthous (Abbey).

Hastingues - 40300.
Dax : 25 km.
Station : Puyoo, 17 km.
Bus service.
Property of the department.

Founded in 1167 by Premonstratensian monks, Arthous abbey which commands the surrounding plain, was damaged during the Wars of Religion in the 16th century and then rebuilt in the 17th century. Monastic buildings line the West, North and East sides of the cloister yard. The church dates from the Romanesque period.
Open Jan. 1 to Dec. 31 : 9 - 12, 2 - 6.
Parking.
Guided tours, brochures.
Information pannels or leaflets.
English - German - radio cassettes.
Abbey Festival : concerts, temporary art exhibits, lecture tours for school groups only.
Tel. : (58) 73.03.89.

Estignols (Château).

Aurice - 40500.
Mont-de-Marsan : 15 km.
Station : Saint-Sever, 3 km.
Bus service.
Property of M. de Spens d'Estignols.

The medieval fortress of Estignols was destroyed in 1615 by royal command since Paul de Spens had taken part in the prince de Condé's revolt against Louis XIII. In 1616 after the peace of Loudon which exonerated the rebels, the château was rebuilt. The present day building with its rectangular plan would appear to date from the 18th century with

only the brick columns that decorate the facade to remind us that this was indeed built in the 17th century. A fine belvedere crowns the tiled roof. The reception rooms, en enfilade, contain 18th century furniture and the entrance hall gives onto an oak staircase with balusters.
*Open July 1 to Sept. 31 : 3 - 6.
Closed Wednesdays.
Open during the rest of the year on request.
Parking.
Guided tours, brochures. English - Spanish-guide.
Tel. : (58) 76.01.60.*

Gaujac (Château)

*Gaujac - 40330.
Dax : 20 km.
Station : Orthez 15 km.
Private property.*

Built by the Escoubleau de Sourdis family on the same plan as a Gallo-Roman villa, Gaujac is a late 17th century charterhouse. Four single story buildings open onto an interior garden through a running gallery which recalls the entry to the Grand Trianon. The East and North facades both have porticos. Inside the ornamental marble floors and the 17th and 18th century pannelling and furniture have been preserved by the family which has lived in the château for 250 years.
*Open July 1 to Sept. 15 : 2:30 - 6:30.
Closed Thursdays.
Open during the rest of the year for groups on request.
Parking.
Guided tours.
Information pannels or leaflets.
Concerts.
Tel. : (58) 89.01.01.*

Montréal (Château)

*Peyrehorade - 40300.
Dax or Bayonne : 25 km.
Station : Peyrehorade.
Bus service.
Property of the commune.*

The vicomte d'Orthe began building the present day château around 1515-1520. Work was interrupted by the Spanish invasion and did not begin again until 1569. Imposing round towers mark the four corners of the main building which houses a spiral staircase. The ornate gateway and the panelling of the « Salon de Dyane » were added in the 18th century. The stables are set out in a semi-circle.
*Open July 13 to July 18 : 10 - 8.
July 20 to Aug. 15 : 2 - 7.
Parking.
Brochures available.
Temporary exhibitions.
Tel. : (58) 73.60.20.*

Pètre (Houses).

*Mézos - 40170 - Saint-Julien-en-Born.
Dax : 50 km.
Morcenx : 25 km.
Property of the Frèches family.*

These two half-timbered houses with their farm buildings formed the residence of the seigneur de Surgen under the Plantagenets

ROQUETAILLADE

GIRONDE

This Aquitaine fortress built by the English in the early Middle Ages has always been inhabited. In 1880 Viollet-le-Duc restored the castle in Medieval style but refurbished the interior with rare original furniture that reflects the taste of the Second Empire. « Nothing is as complete as the interiors of Roquetaillade. » (Philippe Julian.)

VAYRES

GIRONDE

Ghislaine and Philippe Barde have decided to make their cherished home come alive again. They personally take direct responsibility for organising your receptions, weddings, dinner dances and business functions and take great pleasure in providing exceptional service in the best of taste with the best cuisine.

Information and reservations call the château de Vayres - 33870 Vayres. Tel. : (57) 74.86.81.

LANDES — 26 — AQUITAINE

You can see the remains of a prison and a mill in the middle of an ancient pine forest.
Open year round.
Grounds only.
Information in English, Italian, Spanish, Portuguese.
Tel. : (58) 42.60.78.

Poyanne (Château).

Poyanne - 40380.
Dax : 25 km.
Station : Dax.
Private property.

The present day château was built on the site of a 12th century walled town in 1625 by Bernard de Poyanne, lieutenant general for Navarre and Béarn. It consists of five pavilions with different roofs placed side by side : the central pavilion has a dome with a Louis XIII lantern, the two buildings on either side have sloping roofs and those on the outside have pavilion roofs. The château which is similar to Cheverny was visited by Henri IV. The decoration of the « Gilded Room » formerly the salon, has been preserved : notice especially the fireplace and the coffered ceiling.

Open Jan. 1 to Dec. 31 : 2 - 5.
Closed Fridays.
Parking.
Unaccompanied visits.
Information panels or leaflets.
Tel. : (58) 98.40.46.

Ravignan (Château).

Perque - 40190.
Station : 30 km.
Bus nearby.
Private property.

This château which was built in 1663, was finally completed in the 19th century by Hippolyte de Ravignan. Inside you can see a series of rooms with large fireplaces and ceilings with exposed beams. The château also has a collection of costumes from the reign of Louis XVI, engravings relating to the reign of Henri IV and furniture of the 17th and 18th centuries.
Open May 1 to Sept. 30 : 3 - 7, every Sunday.
During the week on request only.
Parking.
Guided tours.
Information in English and German.
Concerts.
Tel. : (58) 58.22.04 and 45.26.44.

SAINT-PANDELON

Bishops' Château.

Saint-Pandelon - 40180.
Dax : 5 km.
Station : Dax.
Private property.

Ever since the fortified keep wa[s] erected at the beginning of th[e] 14th century, the bishops of Da[x] have constantly extended and re[-] furbished their residence. The la[st] bishop added a new building i[n] 1774 and was responsible for th[e] interior decoration of the châtea[u] that you see today. The presen[t] owners found the remnants of th[e] wall paper that was hung in th[e] late 18th century and have repro[-] duced it indentically, giving th[e] rooms the same appearance tha[t] they must have had on the eve o[f] the Revolution.

Open on request.
Parking.
Guided tours, brochures.
English - Spanish - Guide.
Tel. : (58) 74.85.69.

GIRONDE

LA SAUVE-MAJEURE

This Benedictine abbey was fouded in the 11th century and is situated on the pilgrimage route to Santiago da Compostella. The remains of the abbey — its towers and capitals — are of particular interest...

QUITAINE — LANDES/LOT-ET-GARONNE

AINT-SEVER

acobin's Abbey.

int-Sever - 40500.
e Lamarque.
u : 64 km.
ition : Mont-de-Marsan, 16 km.
operty of the commune.
Founded bu Queen Eleonor of
gland, the Dominican abbey of
e Jacobins was destroyed in
69 and then restored and partly
built in brick in the 17th century.
e chapter house has preserved
 14th century pulpit, frescoes
d a Gothic door. The Romanes-
e style cloisters date from the
h century.
en Jan. 1 to Dec. 31 all day (cloister).
apel and refectory open only on re-
est.
rking.
ided tours for groups of more than

accompanied visits, brochures.
oustiguides.
bey Festival, concerts, folklore.
nporary art, cultural and craft shows,
ures.
cture tours for school groups only.
. : (58) 76.01.38.

enedictine Abbey.

nt-Sever - 40500.
ce de la Tour-du-Sol.
u : 64 km.
nt-de-Marsan : 16 km.
operty of the commune.
Founded in 988 by Guillaume
ndre, duc de Gascogne, to
use the relics of Saint-Sever,
t actually built in the 11th cen-
y, this Benedictine abbey was
rtly destroyed by the Huguenots
1569. Rebuilt in the 17th cen-
y, it was restored in Gothic and
naissance style in the twentieth
ntury. The absidioles and tran-
ot chapels are all that remain of
 Romanesque period.
en Jan. 1 to Dec. 31 : 7am - 7pm.
rking.
ided tours for groups over ten.
accompanied visits, brochures.
oustiguides.
cture tours for school groups only.
. : (58) 76.00.02.

T-ET-GARONNE

onaguil (Castle).

nt-Front-sur-Lémance - 47500.
hors or Agen : 50 km.
tion : Monspempron-Libos, 15 km.
operty of the commune.
Built by the seigneurs de Ro-
efeuille at the end of the 15th
d beginning of the 16th centu-

ries Bonaguil is one of the last
great fortified castles to be built in
France. As such it offers the perfect example of French military
architecture of the period with its
system of defence designed spe-
cifically against the newly develo-
ped firearms. The castle has 104
gun emplacements and its prow
shaped keep was less vulnerable
to artillery fire. The castle is protected by six towers, seven turrets
and two surrounding walls, the largest of which is 350 m. in perime-
ter. The terraces were also designed to withstand a protracted
seige.
Open Palm Sunday to May 31 : 10:30 -
11, 2:30 - 4:30.
June 1 to Aug. 31 : 10 - 11:30, 3 - 6.
Sept. 1 to Sept. 30 : 10:30 - 11, 2:30 -
4:30.
Open on request Oct. 1 to March 31.
Parking.
Lecture tours, brochures.
English - German - Spanish - Tour
Guide and brochures.
Music, temporary exhibits.

Bournac (Château).

Nérac - 47600.
Private property.
Bournac was built in the 16th
century by Le Verrier, treasurer at
the court of Navarre, on the site of
an ancient fortress. It consists of a
large central pavilion with fortified
terraces, mullioned windows and
a fountain.
Tel. : (53) 65.02.64.

Estillac (Château).

Estillac - 47310.
Agen : 10 km.
Bus service.
Private property.
Estillac was greatly transformed
in the 16th century by Blaise de
Montluc who wrote his famous
« Commentaires » here. The round
tower to the West and the North
buildings date from the 13th cen-
tury. The edifice is protected by
fortified surrounding walls, a fea-
ture which would later be copied
by Vauban.
July 1 to Oct. 10 : Sundays and holi-
days, 2 - sunset.
Jan. 1 to Dec. 31 on request.
Guided tours.
Concerts, Dance.
Lecture tours for school groups only.
Tel. : (53) 67.81.83.

Gavaudun (Castle).

Gavaudun - 47150.
Fumel : 10 km.
Station : Monsempron-Libos 10 km.
Property of the commune.

The impressive ruins of the
castle of Gavaudun, rebuilt in the
13th century, rise from a rock that
overlooks the Lede valley. Gavau-
dun was an important military
stronghold during the Hundred
Years War and during the Wars of
Religion. The irregularly shaped
keep built six stories high has
been entirely preserved and now
houses a museum of Prehistory.
Open July 1 to Sept. 15 : 3 - 7.
Sept 16 to June 30 : Sundays and holi-
days, 3 - 7.
Open mornings on request.
Parking.
Guided tours, brochures.
English - German - Guide from July 1 to
Sept. 15.
Information panels or leaflets.
Tel. : (53) 36.45.79.

Poudenas (Château).

Poudenas - 47170.
Nérac : 17 km.
Station : Agen 47 km
Private property.
Built on the Plantagenet do-
main, Poudenas reached its peak
around 1580 when Henri IV came
and hunted there while his court
was at Nérac. The 13th century for-
tress was transformed into a 16th
century country residence with
mullioned windows to let in light.
The building was modernised in
the following century with the
construction of a new wing and an
Italianate facade with terraces bor-
dered by balustrades.
Open July 14 to Sept. 15 : 3 - 6.
May to Nov. 30 on request for groups.
Parking.
Guided tours.
English - Guide.
Tel. : (53) 65.78.86.

Prades (Manor House).

Lafox-Puymirol - 47270.
Agen : 8 km.
Private property.
Prades was built in the 16th century by the Cortete family and was
completely transformed in the
17th century. The mainbuilding is
flanked by round turrets with a
pentagonal tower in the middle.
The outbuildings make up the
fourth side of the courtyard. François de Cortete (1586-1667) lived
here and wrote the poems which
are still in the family's possession.
Open on request only.
Parking.
Guided tours.
Tel. : (53) 96.19.73.

SAUVETERRE-LA-LEMANCE
Rois Ducs (Castle).
Sauveterre-la-Lemance - 47500.
Sarlat or Cahors : 40 km.
Station : Sauveterre-la-Lemance.
Private property.

This castle was built around 1284 by the agents of Edward I of England and was modelled on his Welsh castles. This square shaped castle has kept its 13th century towers and facades, as well as the 15th century main building which overlooks the courtyard. The castle was captured by the Charles VII in 1432.
Open June 1 to Oct. 31 : 10 - 2, 7 - sunset.
Open on request the rest of the year.
Parking.
Guided tours.
English - Italian - German.
Tel. : (53) 71.67.17.

SAUVETERRE-SAINT-DENIS
Saint-Denis (Château).
Sauveterre-Saint-Denis.
Astaffort - 47220.
Agen : 12 km.
Station : Agen.
Private property.

Saint-Denis was built in 1850 by the de Bastard family in 18th century style. The long white stone facade consists of a double building flanked by two slightly projecting pavilions which are perfectly symmetrical. The main building also has an attic.
Grounds only. Times unspecified.
Horse-drawn carriages on request.
Tel. : (53) 87.02.21.

Xaintrailles (Castle).
Xaintrailles - 47230.
Station : Aiguillon 13 km.
Private property.

This castle belonged to Ponthon de Xaintrailles, one of Charles VII's captains and a companion of Joan of Arc. In the 18th century it came into the possession of the Lusignan family who transformed it. The square keep and the walls date from the 14th and 15th centuries. The entrance and the double staircase were rebuilt in the 18th century as was the North building. The South wing was added in the 19th century and decorated with Gothic and Renaissance style furniture.
Open on request only.
Parking.
Guided tours.
Tel. : (53) 65.41.49.

PYRÉNÉES-ATLANTIQUES
Andurain (Château).
Mauléon-Licharre - 64130.
1 rue du Jeu-de-Paume.
Property of M. d'Andurain de Maÿtie.

Andurain was begun in the 16th century by Pierre de Maÿtie and completed by three members of his family all bishops of Oloron : Arnaud I, Arnaud II and Arnaud-François. The square builing has towers at each corner and a wood and slate roof with a reversed hull shaped frame. Inside you can see 17th and 18th century furniture, original carved stone fireplaces and a Renaissance staircase.
Open July 1 to Sept. 15 : 11 - 12:30, 3 - 6.
Closed Thursdays and Sundays and holidays in the morning.
Open on request for groups Sept. 16 to June 30.
Parking.
Guided tours
English - German - Spanish - Guide.
Temporary exhibits.
Tel. : (59) 28.04.18.

Aren (Castle).
Aren - 64400.
Oloron - Sainte-Marie : 12 km.
Private property.

Built on the Left bank of the Oloron, Aren was among the castles of Béarn inventoried at the end of the 14th century. The seigneurs of Aren played an important role in the life of the château from the 11th century to the Revolution. As a result of numerous transformations there are now two buildings : a château and a fortress. The murals inside have been perfectly preserved. The grounds include the tower of the church which had a private entrance for the seigneurs of Aren.
Open June 1 to Sept. 15 : 2 - 6.
Closed Sundays.
Parking.
Guided tours.
Facilities for handicapped.
Lecture tours for school groups.
Tel. : (59) 39.58.62.

Coarraze (Château).
Coarraze - 64800.
6 rue des Pyrénées.
Pau : 48 km.
Station : 3 km.
Bus service.
Private property.

Coarraze has been one of the baronies of Béarn since the 12 century. All that remains from t medieval period is a five sid keep. The portal dates from t 16th century. The present day bu ding was erected in the 18th ce tury after being ravaged by fire 1684. This two story residen consists of a slightly project portico crowned by a triangu pediment. It was in this châte that Henri IV spent his childhoo the château is also mentioned Froissart's Chronicles.
Open July 1 to Aug. 15.
Parking.
Recommended itinerary.
English - Spanish.
Tel. : (59) 61.10.27.

BIDACHE
Gramont (Castle).
Bidache - 64520.
Bayonne : 32 km.
Station : Bayonne.
Private property.

The ruins of Gramont castle, f of the ducs of Gramont, soverei princes of Bidache, show the n merous transformations made the castle before it was aband ned. The towers and surroundi walls date back to the 14th ce tury, the main building to the 16 century, the pavilion to the 1 century and the archway of the e trance to the 18th centu Charles IX, Catherine de Medi Henri IV and Mazarin were amo the famous visitors to Gramont.
Open March 1 to Sept. 30 : 9 - 12, 2 - Closed Tuesdays.
Parking.
Unaccompanied visits, brochures.
Tel. : (59) 56.05.73.

Guiche (Castle).
Guiche - 64520.
Bayonne : 28 km.
Station : Guiche 2 km.
Private property.

Rebuilt in the 18th century the foundations of an ancie castle, the château de Guiche intimately connected to the histo of the ducs de Gramont, princes Bidache. After the region was vaded by the Spanish in 1523, t château was partially abandon

QUITAINE — PYRÉNÉES-ATLANTIQUES

...hich accounts for its present
...te of ruin.
...en March 1 to Sept. 30 : 9 - 12, 2 - 7.
...rking.
... accompanied visits.
... : (59) 56.05.73.

...as (Château).

...s - 64390.
...veterre-de-Béarn : 10 km.
...tion : Sauveterre-de-Béarn.
...perty of the department.
...he present day château de
...s was built by the Duclos fa-
...y in 1775. The main building
...h its perpendicular wings are in
...ghcast stone. The porch has an
...ra half story and is also distin-
...shed by a steep sloping roof.
... interior, completed in the pre-
...t century is decorated with fur-
...ire, tapestries, pictures and
...nce dating from various eras.
...n March 1 to June 30 : Sat., Sun.,
... 12, 3 - 6.
... 1 to Sept. 30 : 10 - 12, every day.
...ups by request.
...king.
...ded tours, brochures. Acoustiguides.
... : (59) 38.91.53.

...ngaston (Castle).

...re - 64190.
...rrenx : 8 km.
...on : Duyao.
...te property.
...ly a few walls remain of the
... of Mongaston which was
...ably built by Gaston VII of
...n in the 13th century. The
...-storied building itself dates
... the 16th century and is rec-
...ular in shape flanked by a tur-
...ith a hexagonal staircase on
... North-East side. This opens
... an arched doorway surroun-
...by pilasters.
... July 1 to Sept. 30 : 3 - 7.
...d Tuesdays in July, August and
...
...ng.
...d tours, brochures.
...h - German.
...ies for handicapped.
...orary exhibits, lectures.
...(59) 38.67.43.

Morlanne (Castle)

Morlanne - 64370.
Pau : 32 km.
Station : Pau.
Property of the department.

This brick and stone building erected around 1373 for the half-brother of Gaston Phoebus, belonged to Odet d'Aydie sénéchal and admiral of Guyenne in the 16th century and then in the 17th century to the maréchal de La Force, in whose arms Henri IV died. The seigneurial dwelling is surrounded by defensive walls with a rectangular towered gateway on the North side. Inside you can see a collection of furniture and pictures including a Canaletto, which show aspects of seigneurial life over the past 500 years.
Open March 1 to Oct. 31 : 2:30 - 6:30.
Parking.
Guided tours.
Tel. : (59) 81.60.27.

Navarrenx (Ramparts).

Navarrenx - 64190.
Oloron : 20 km.
Station : Pau 40 km.
Bus service.
Property of the commune.

In 1542 the King of Navarre decided to rebuild the town of Navarrenx on the right bank of the Oloron. He called upon the Italian architect, Fabrici Siciliano, to design the fortifications in the Italian style, then considered the most modern. The fortified town withstood many sieges and thus assured the defence of Béarn.
Unaccompanied visits.
Parking.
Brochures available.

PAU

Pau (Château).

Pau - 64000.
Property of the State.

Work on the castle was first started in the 12th century and it was enlarged by Gaston Phoebus in the 14th century as well as by the Kings of Navarre, especially Henri IV who was born here in 1553. Restored by both Louis-Philippe and Napoleon III, the castle has preserved its fine 19th century rooms. It also contains memorabilia from the time of Henri IV as well as an important collection of Flemish and Gobelins tapestries.
Open daily April 15 to Oct. 15 : 8:30 - 11:45, 2 - 4:45.
Parking.
Theatre, concerts.
Tel. : (59) 27.36.22.

Bernadotte Museum.

Pau - 64000.
8 rue de Tran.
Property of the commune.

The birthplace of Marshall Bernadotte, who was elected crown prince of Sweden in 1810 thus becoming the founder of the Swedish royal family, is a characteristic bourgeois dwelling of the 18th century. The two story building with its wooden galleries today houses furniture from the period of Louis XVI and of the Empire as well as documents, pictures, medals and sculpture relating to Bernadotte.
Open Jan. 2 to Dec. 31 : 10 - 12, 2 - 6.
Closed Mondays.
Parking.
Guided tours, information panels and leaflets.
English - German - Guide.
Brochures available.
Lecture tours for school groups.
Tel. : (59) 27.48.42.

SAINT-JEAN-DE-LUZ
Louis XIV House.

Saint-Jean-de-Luz - 64500.
Place Louis-XIV.
Private property.

When the young Louis XIV signed the Treaty of the Pyrenees and married the infanta Maria Theresa of Spain in 1660, he stayed in this house and held court here. The house was built in 1643 by the wealthy ship owner Johanais de Lohobiague whose descendants still live in the house. The Louis XIII stone facade and woo-

PAU — **BERNADOTTE MUSEUM** — PYRÉNÉES-ATLANTIQUES

Birthplace of J.-B. Bernadotte, marshal of France who was elected prince of Sweden in 1810 and king in 1818. This picturesque house offers a glimpse of life in Pau in the 18th century. Here you can discover the tempestuous story of a Bearnais family whose dynasty still reigns in Sweden.

monumental staircase as well
he furniture date from the 17th
tury.
n June 8 to June 30 : 10 - 12, 3 - 6.
1 to Aug. 31 : 10:30 - 12:30, 3:30 -
).
. 1 to Sept. 22 : 10 - 12, 3 - 6.
ed mornings Sundays and holidays.
n on request for groups out of sea-

ing.
ed tours, brochures.
ıstiguides, leaflets.
ish - German - Spanish.
: (59) 26.01.56.

ubie (Château).

gne - 64122.
-Jean-de-Luz : 3 km.
on : Saint-Jean-de-Luz.
service.
erty of M. de Coral.
ith the permission of Edward
of England, Martin d'Urtubie
a castle that was partly rased
e ground by his wife and then
ilt between 1505 and 1513. It
transformed for the last time
745. The fortified keep, the
r walls with their sentryway
the door flanked by two to-
s date from the 14th century.
Renaissance main building
the tower with its stone spiral
case were built in the 16th
ury. Extended once again in
18th century, the château's in-
or was also transformed. Inside
can see a collection of 17th
ury Flemish tapestries.
n July 13 to Sept. 5 : 3 - 7.
ed Tuesdays.
ing.
ed tours, brochures.
ish - Spanish - Recordings.
ure tours for school groups only.

AUVERGNE
ALLIER, CANTAL, HAUTE-LOIRE, PUY-DE-DÔME.

- ■ castle, château, manor house
- ● abbey, priory
- ▲ garden, park
- ★ town house, famous men house, farm, mill...
- ○ city

MOULINS
- ■ Pavillon
- ★ commanderie

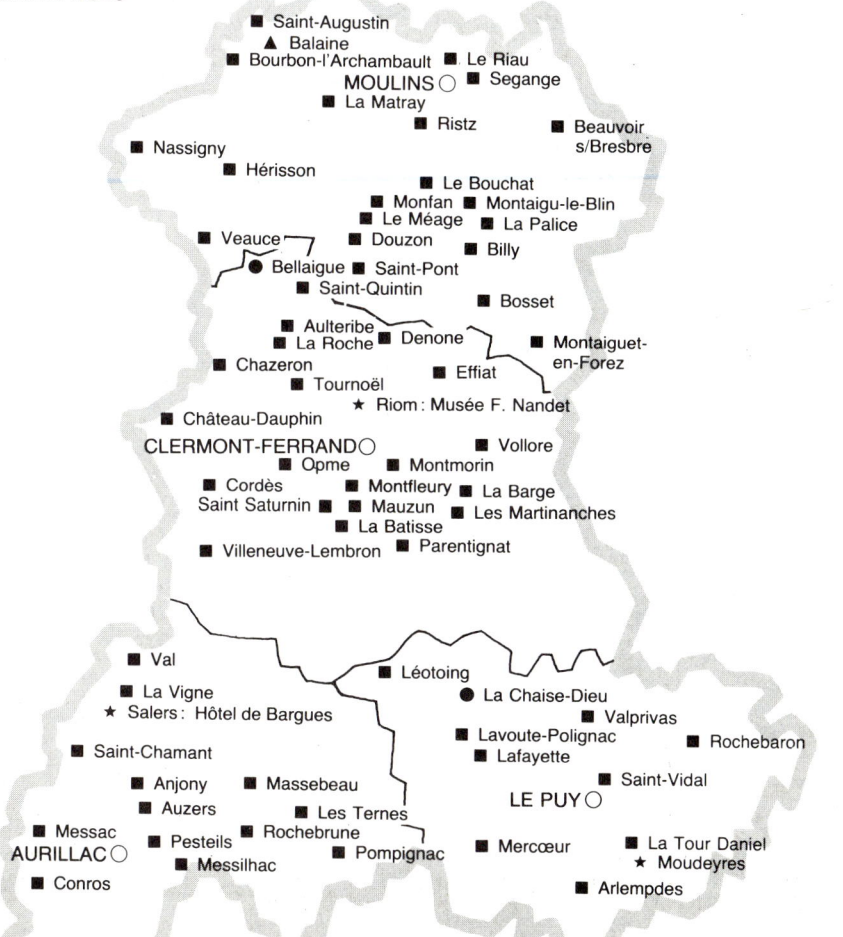

■ Saint-Augustin
▲ Balaine
■ Bourbon-l'Archambault ■ Le Riau
MOULINS ○ ■ Segange
■ La Matray
■ Ristz ■ Beauvoir s/Bresbre
■ Nassigny
■ Hérisson
■ Le Bouchat
■ Monfan ■ Montaigu-le-Blin
■ Le Méage ■ La Palice
■ Veauce ■ Douzon ■ Billy
● Bellaigue ■ Saint-Pont
■ Saint-Quintin
■ Bosset
■ Aulteribe
■ La Roche ■ Denone ■ Montaiguet-en-Forez
■ Chazeron
■ Tournoël ■ Effiat
■ Château-Dauphin
★ Riom : Musée F. Nandet
CLERMONT-FERRAND ○ ■ Vollore
■ Opme ■ Montmorin
■ Cordès ■ Montfleury ■ La Barge
Saint Saturnin ■ ■ Mauzun ■ Les Martinanches
■ La Batisse
■ Villeneuve-Lembron ■ Parentignat

■ Val
■ Léotoing
■ La Vigne ● La Chaise-Dieu
★ Salers : Hôtel de Bargues ■ Valprivas
■ Lavoute-Polignac ■ Rochebaron
■ Saint-Chamant ■ Lafayette
■ Anjony ■ Massebeau ■ Saint-Vidal
■ Auzers ■ Les Ternes LE PUY ○
■ Messac ■ Rochebrune ■ La Tour Daniel
AURILLAC ○ ■ Pesteils ■ Pompignac ■ Mercœur ★ Moudeyres
■ Conros ■ Messilhac
■ Arlempdes

AUVERGNE

ALLIER

Balaine (Arboretum).
Villeneuve-sur-Allier - 03460.
Moulins: 16 km.
Station: Villeneuve 4 km.
Private property.

This arboretum was created in 1804 by the daughter of the famous philosopher and botanist, Adanson, who had worked at the botanical gardens at the Petit Trianon during the reign of Marie-Antoinette. This park with its one thousand species of plants is typical of the gardens laid out in the 19th century. Among the spectacular azaleas and rhododendrons run streams and man made rivers with their footbridges and Japanese bridges.
Open April 1 to Nov. 15 : 2 - 7.
Closed Tuesdays and Fridays.
Parking.
Unaccompanied visits, brochures.
Temporary exhibits: paintings and engravings on botanical subjects.
Tel.: (70) 43.30.07.

Beauvoir-sur-Besbre (Castle).
Saint-Pourcain-sur-Besbre - 03290.
Moulins: 25 km.
Station: Dompierre-sur-Besbre 6 km.
Private property.

Originally a fort, this castle was occupied by the English during the Hundred Years War and then recaptured by Duc Louis de Bourbon in 1369. Built on a square plan at the end of the 14th century, the two buildings flanked by round towers are linked by high watch-towers. Surrounded by a moat, the building still contains seven large stone fireplaces dating from the 15th century, a Renaissance ceiling and a vaulted room.
Unaccompanied visit of the grounds.
Interiors on written request only.
Facilities for the handicapped.

Billy (Castle).
Billy - 03260.
Vichy: 13 km.
Property of the commune.

The hexagonal walls flanked by six round towers and a keep are all that survive of the ancient castle. From the sentry way you can look down on the Allier region. Billy was used as a royal prison until 1790.
Open on request only.
Guided tours, brochures.
Information in English and German.
Concerts, shows, temporary exhibits, lectures.
Other activities under study.
Tel.: (70) 43.52.19.

Bourbon-l'Archambault (Castle).
Bourbon-l'Archambault - 03160.
Moulins: 23 km.
Bus service.
Property of the State (Saint Louis Foundation).

Three round towers constructed by Louis I are all that remain of this huge fortress, fief of the lords and dukes of Bourbon who later became kings of France. Once 24 in number the towers were intended to protect the relics of the True Cross.
Open March 1 to Sept. 30 : 2 - 6 weekdays.
10 - 12, 2 - 6 sundays and holidays.
Open on request out of season.
Parking.
Guided tours.
Information panels, lectures.

Le Bouchat (Castle).
Lafeline - 03500.
Saint-Pourcain-sur-Sioule: 12 km.
Station: Moulins/Allier 25 km.
Private property.

At the end of the 14th century the fief belonged to the Condamine family who were to enlarge and transform the buildings in the 15th and 16th centuries. The inner walls still are impressive in size and the castle still has large stone fireplaces.
Open on request for groups.
Parking.
Guided tours.
Tel.: (70) 42.30.50.

Douzon (Château).
Etroussat - 03140.
Vichy: 25 km.
Bus service.
Private property.

All that remains of the original castle built in the 16th century are the keep and the round tower. The present day château was designed in 1730 by the Parisian architect Clément. The two story central building is surmounted by a triangular pediment and flanked by two perpendicular wings which give out onto a formal garden.
Open on request.
Parking.
Unaccompanied visits of the grounds.
Tel.: (70) 56.70.34.

Hérisson (Castle).
Hérisson - 03190.
Montluçon: 23 km.
Station: Vallon-en-Sully 11 km.
Property of the Touring Club of France.

The impressive ruins of Hérisson castle rise above the valley of the Aumance. The three towers, the façades, the keep and other buildings date from the 14th century. Hérisson was captured from the ducs de Bourbon by Louis X in the 15th century but won back two centuries later before it was demolished by Mazarin.
Unaccompanied visits.
Parking.
Brochures available.
Lecture tours for school groups.
Archeological dig and restoration site.

La Matray (Castle).
Souvigny - 03210.
Moulins: 12 km.
Station: Moulins.
Bus service.
Private property.

AUVERGNE — ALLIER

Formerly the stronghold and residence of the notables of the duchy of Bourbon and the generality of Moulins, Matray castle consists of a group of buildings laid out in the shape of a horseshoe. The buildings are dominated by a tower and surrounded by a wide moat with a stone bridge.
Unaccompanied visit of the grounds.
Interiors on request only for groups.
Parking.
Guided tours.

Le Méage (Castle).

Rongères - 03150.
Varennes-sur-Allier: 6 km.
Station: Saint-Germain-des-Fossés 7 km.
Private property.

Méage castle was built in the 15th century on the site of a fortress and transformed in the 18th century. The main courtyard has two outbuildings and a dovecote leads to the central building which is flanked on one side by a round tower and on the other by a square pavilion. The moat is still full of water. The garden, park and iron gate were added later.
Open daily all day long.
Grounds only.
Parking.
Unaccompanied visits.
Guided tours by the owner on request for groups.
Tel.: (70) 45.06.53.

Montaigu-le-Blin (Castle).

Montaigu-le-Blin - 03150.
Varennes-sur-Allier: 11 km.
Private property.

The castle was built in the 13th century on a rocky hill and now comprises a high walled building flanked by towers and protected by low surrounding walls. It was restored in the middle of the 15th century by Jacques de Chabannes and later became a hiding place for smugglers.
Open June 15 to Sept. 30: 2 - 6.
Open the rest of the year or request or groups or individuals.
Parking.
Set itinerary.
Information panels, brochures.
Shows: Medieval pageant.
Temporary exhibits, workshops for young pepople.

Montaiguet-en-Forez (Castle).

Montaiguet-en-Forez - 03130.
Moulins: 60 km.
Station: Saint-Martin-Sail-les-Bains 7 km.

Bus service.
Private property.

Montaiguet rises up like a fortress with its four towers. Although similar from the outside they are different inside; the East and South towers are round and the West and North are hexagonal. The castle is surrounded by a dry moat and a park.
Grounds only.
Parking.
Unaccompanied visit.
Tel.: (70) 55.20.01.

Montfan (Castle).

Louchy-Montfan - 03500.
Saint-Pourcain-sur-Sioule: 3 km.
Station: Moulins or Vichy 30 km.

This fortified castle is built on a hill which was a sacred site in the Gallo-Roman period (Monte Fanum). The castle walls are intact and the drawbridge is inside the building, a very unusual feature. Inside is a circular fireplace one of two to survive in France.
Open daily from Easter to Nov. 1 and closed Nov. 1 to Easter.
Open at other times on request for groups.
Parking.
Guided tours.
Information in English.
Tel.: (70) 45.40.31.

MOULINS
Anne de Beaujeu (Pavilion and Museum of Art and Archeology).

Moulins - 03000.
3, place du Colonel-Laussedat.
Property of the department and of the city.

The pavilion of Anne de Beaujeu, daughter of Louis XI, was built between 1488 and 1503 as an addition to the ducal palace. All that remains of the building is the entrance and the elegant facades. The museum has a picture collection which includes German primitives and academic French painters of the second half of the 19th century as well as a noteworthy collection of Nevers, Moulins and Rouen faience. It also houses artifacts from the prehistoric and Gallo-Roman periods.
Tel.: (70) 44.22.98.

Nassigny (Château).

Nassigny — 03190.
Montluçon: 18 km.
Station: Vallon-en-Sully 4 km.
Property of Mme P. Roux.

Built on a terrace overlooking the Cher valley, the château is surrounded by a park which has been transformed into a golf course. Rebuilt in the 16th century in Renaissance style, it is a typical Bourbonnais manor house of the period.
Open April 1 to Nov. 1: 10 - 6.
Parking.
Tel.: (70) 06.71.01.

La Palice (Château).

La Palisse - 03120.
Vichy: 22 km.
Station: La Palisse 2 km.
Bus service.
Property of M. G. de Chabannes La Palice.

La Palice was built in the 15th century on the site of a 13th century fortress on the banks of the Besbre. The rectangular main building is flanked by three towers, one crenellated, the others with pepper-pot roofs. The building was completed with the addition of a Renaissance wing erected by the maréchal de La Palice in the 16th century. The chapel, built in 1475 in High Gothic style contains the tombs of Jacques I de Chabannes and his wife. Renaissance ceilings and 15th century furniture and tapestries provided the setting for such illustrious visitors as Charles VII and Catherine de Medicis.
Open March 20 to Nov. 1: 9 - 12, 2 - 6.
Closed Tuesdays March to May and Sept. to Oct.
Parking.
Guided tours, brochures.
English - German - information panels or leaflets.
Historical pageant.
Temporary exhibits.
Tel.: (70) 99.08.51.

Le Riau (Château).

Villeneuve-sur-Allier - 03460.
Moulins: 31 km.
Station: Villeneuve-sur-Allier.
Private property.

Of the manor house built between the 15 and 17th centuries, Le Riau has kept its brick and stone fort made up of a brick and stone keep flanked by two towers. The half-timbered barn dates from 1548 and the wings of the main

building were added in the 17th century. The château contains a collection of painting by Emmanuel de La Villeon, an impressionist. Among those who have stayed here are Anne de Beaujeu, the connetable de Bourbon and Arthur Young.
Open April 1 to Sept. 30 : 3 - 6.
Closed Sundays and Tuesdays.
Parking.
Guided tours, brochures.
Recorded information at entrance.
German.
Facilities for the handicapped.
Tel. : (70) 46.30.74.

Ristz (Château).

Besson-Sauvigny - 03210.
Moulins : 15 km.
Station : Moulins.
Private property.

Built on a hill between 1307 and 1450, Ristz is on of several monuments to be found in this village. Its rectangular main building is flanked by two round towers and one hexagonal tower. The North side looks onto a moat and the West side onto a courtyard. The château belonged to the Bourbon-Parme family for many years.
Grounds only.
Unaccompanied visit.
Tel. : (70) 42.82.99.

Segange (Château).

Avermes - 03000.
Moulins : 4 km.
Station : Moulins.
Private property.

Built in 1517 on the site of a 15th century castle, Segange is on of the earliest Renaissance buildings in France. Erected by a courtier the château is decorated with the coats of arms of both the king François I and Charles III, duc de Bourbon, later notorious enemies. Anne de Bretagne stayed here in 1495 in the old castle whose tower and monumental fireplaces have survived.
Open June 15 to Sept. 15 : 9 - 12, 2-7.
Closed Mondays.
Parking.
Grounds only. Accompanied visits.
Information panels.
Tel. : (70) 44.06.63.

Saint-Augustin (Château).

Château-sur-Allier - 03320.
Nevers or Moulins : 35 km.
Station : Nevers or Moulins.
Property of Mme H. Villenave.

Saint-Augustin was built in the 18th century and still belongs to the same family. This coloured brick building of the Louis XV period consists of a main building and two wings. A belvedere was added to enable the women to follow the hunt from inside. The period rooms include the Louis XV salon, the trophy room, the dining room and the kitchen. The park contains domestic and wild animals from all parts of the world.
Open June 1 to Sept. 15 : 2-7.
Sept. 15 to May 31 Wed., Sat., Sun., school vacations and holiday 2-7.
Mornings on request.
Parking.

LE RIAU

ALLIER

Le Riau is a typical example of Bourbonnais architecture of the 15th to 17th centuries. The interiors contain paintings by the Impressionist Emmanuel de la Villéon.

Open April 1 to September 30 : 3 - 6. Closed Tuesdays.
October 1 to March 31 : 2 - 5. Closed Tuesdays and Sundays.

CHÂTEAU-SUR-ALLIER **SAINT-AUGUSTIN** ALLIER

Nature comes to Saint-Augustin...
Built in the 18th century on the site of an ancient fortress, Saint-Augustin, now a protected historical monument, is a polychrome brick château. A brickyard was actually created to make the bricks on the spot. The result is one of the marvels of Bourbonnais architecture. You can walk through the 35 hectare park planted with age old trees and admire the tame animals and the splendid water fowl on the lake. European and exotic animals. Lions in the courtyard.
Tel. : (70) 66.42.01.

Saint-Pont (Château).

Saint-Pont - 03110.
Vichy : 15 km.
Station : Vichy.
Bus service.
Private property.

Built in the 17th century on the site of a fortified castle, the present day Saint-Pont was transformed in 1745 for the marquise Begon de la Rouzière by the Prisian architect Clément. Set on terraces looking out on the Auvergne the château has brick and stone facades and a sloping tile roof. Close by you can see two dovecotes, the old bakery and two vaulted vats.

Open July 1 to Sept. 15 : 9 - 12, 3 - 7.
Grounds only.
Groups on request.
Parking.
Unaccompanied visits.

Veauce (Castle).

Veauce - 30450.
Vichy : 15 km.
Station : Gannat 15 km.
Bus service.
Private property.

Perched upon a rocky peak, the shape of Veauce castle are moulded with that of the landscape. The castle owes its commanding defensive position to the deep fault on the Ebreuil valley side and to the steep valleys all around. The edifice was originally built between the 13th and 15th centuries, remodelled in the Renaissance and then again more extensively in the 19th century. The main buildings around the courtyard underwent the same transformations and combine Medieval austerity and Romantic fantasy. A barony in the 15th century, the castle belonged to the Bourbon family. Inside you can see memorabilia relating to the duc de Morny and Napoleon III.

Open Jan. 15 to Dec. 15 : 10:30 - 12, 2:30 - 7.

Night visits 8 - 11 Aug. 1 to Sept. 15.
Parking.
Guided tours.
Audio-visual programme.
German - Russian - Guide.
Brochure available.
Festival of contemporary arts : painting, sculpture, stained glass, theatre, concerts.
Temporary exhibits : painting, sculpture, stained glass, weaving.
Lecture tours for school groups.
Tel. : (70) 58.53.27.

CANTAL

Anjony (Castle).

Tournemire - 15310.
Aurillac : 22 km.
Station : Aurillac.
Bus service.
Private property.

Built between 1439 and 1450 by the lords of Anjony, the castle rises from a rocky promontory towering above the Doire valley. The square keep with its four 40 meter towers is typical of a mountain fortress. It has remained intact. An adjacent building was erected in the 18th century. Inside are frescoes of various themes both sacred and profane as well as furniture, paintings and tapestries acquired over the years by the family which has always owned the castle.

Open April 1 to Oct. 31 : 2 - 6:30.
On request out of season.
Parking.
Guided tours, brochures.
English - German.
Facilities for handicapped.
Lecture tours for school groups.
Tel. : (71) 47.61.67.

Auzers (Castle).

Bort-les-Orgues or Mauriac : 20 km.
Station : Bort-les-Orgues.
Property of M. de Douet d'Auzers.

Auzer was built in the mountains during the Hundred Years War. Partially destroyed by fire in the 15th century, it was restored and extended shortly thereafter ane has remained unchanged ever since. It is surrounded by a sentry way and crowned by a stone roof. The oratory is decorated with paintings dating from the beginning of the 16th century.

Open daily July 1 to Sept 15 : 2 - 6:30.
On request for groups all year.
Parking.
Guided tours, brochures.
Information in English.
Potery workshop.
Tel. : (71) 78.62.59.

Conros (Castle).

Arpajon-sur-Cère - 15130.
Aurillac : 5 km.
Station : Aurillac.
Bus service.
Private property.

For nine centuries Conros was a fief of the Haute Auvergne protecting the Cère valley. The impressive feudal keep of the Astorg family who were seigneurs of Aurillac in the later Middle Ages, was transformed during the Renaissance into the residence which is still inhabited today and which has recently been restored. It now houses the Museum of Folk Art of the Cère valley.

Open July 14 to Aug. 31 : 2 - 7.
Parking.
Guided tours, brochures.
English - German - Spanish - Guide.
Concerts, temporary exhibits.
Lecture tours for school groups.
Tel. : (71) 63.50.27.

Massebeau (Castle)

Murat - 15300.
Station : Murat.
Private property.

The castle is located on land which belonged to the Armagnac family until the beginning of the 15th century. It comprises two buildings flanked by fortified towers with stone roofs.

Open July 16 to Aug. 24 : 10 - 12, 2 - 4.
Grounds only.
Parking.
Unaccompanied visit.

Messac (Château).

Le Roquebrou - 15150.
Aurillac : 25 km.
Station : La Roquebrou 2 km.

AUVERGNE — CANTAL

Bus service.
Private property.

Messac was remodelled in the 17th century. Its two perpendicular wings are linked by a round tower. The château has a spiral staircase and six Renaissance fireplaces.
Open on request.
Parking.
Tel.: (71) 62.00.54.

Messilhac (Castle).

Vic-sur-Cère - 15800.
Station: Vic-sur-Cère.
Private property.

Built on a rocky peak surrounded by mountains, Messilhac was the centre of a powerful seigneurie. Its two impressive 14th century square towers are linked by a Renaissance building which dates from 1531. Jean de Montamat was responsible for the carved facade. The castle still has its furniture and heraldic fireplaces.
Open July 4 to Sept. 8 : 2 - 6:30.
Parking.
Guided tours.
English - Guide.
Tel.: (71) 49.55.55.

Pesteils (Castle).

Polminhac - 15800.
Aurillac: 15 km.
Station: Polminhac 1 km.
Private property.

An imposing square keep, 35 meters high dating from the 13th and 14th centuries rises up on a rocky promontory overlooking the Cere valley. Pesteils also comprises a 17th century manor house which was extended in the 19th century. Inside the keep are 14th century frescoes and inside the main building are 17th century paintings. This fortress was partly rased in 1405 by bands of English and Gascon marauders and later invested by the Huguenots during the Wars of Religion.

Open daily : 2:30 - 5:30 July to Aug 30, 10-12, 4:30-6.00
Parking.
German - English - Literature.
Tel.: (71) 47.46.20.

Pompignac (Castle).

Loubaresse - 15390.
Saint-Flour: 18 km.
Station: Loubaresse 4 km.
Private property.

Pompignac was built by comte Jean d'Armagnac in 1345 and given to the Pompignac family in 1380. They still own it to this day. The basalt and granite keep overlooks the Arcomie valley and has preserved its monumental granite fireplaces and a spiral staircase.
Open July 15 to Sept. 8.
Grounds only.
Parking.
Tel.: (71) 73.70.02.

Ragheaud (Manor House).

Saint-Cernin - 15310.
Aurillac: 24 km.
Station: Aurillac.
Private property.

AUZERS — CANTAL

Half-way between Val and Salers.

Welcome to this historic monument where you can see :
— the salons with their Regency furniture ;
— the vaulted room with its Auvergnat furniture ;
— the monumental fireplaces ;
— the oratory with its 16th century murals.

Guided tours from 2:15 to 6:30, July 1 to September 15. Recommended itinerary.

This manor house which served as a place of refuge for villagers in case of attack, consists of a keep dating from the later Middle Ages which is attached to another tower, a chapel and two pavilions added in the 17th century.
Open daily by appointment only April 1 to July 31.
English - Spanish.
Tel.: (71) 47.60.17.

Rochebrune (Castle).

Oradour - 15260 Neuvéglise.
Saint-Flour: 20 km.
Station: Saint-Flour.
Bus service.
Private property.

Rochebrune served as a lookout point on the second line of defense for the town of Saint-Flour. Built in the 15th century on the site of a 12th century castle its five terraces dominate the valley below. In 1616 it acted as a meeting place for the noblemen who rebelled against Louis XIII. The ground floor rooms oven, cellar and store rooms are dug out of the rock. Lived in and furnished through a variety of periods the castle now houses a collection of blown glass, pictures and a display of Auvergnat folklore.
Open July 14 to Aug. 30 : 2:30 - 5:30.
Closed Tuesdays.
Parking.
Guided tours, brochures.
English - Langue d'oc.
Literary festival.
Temporary exhibits.
Lecture tours for groups only.
Tel.: (71) 23.82.72.

SALERS
Hôtel de Bargues.

Salers - 15410.
Mauriac: 20 km.
Station: Drugeac 10 km.
Property of M. de Bargues.

A vaulted Gothic passage leads into the inner courtyard of this town house still lived in by the Bargues family. Three buildings decorated with a Gothic balcony surround the courtyard. The West side was erected in the 17th century. Inside are two 17th century panelled bedrooms which include four-poster beds among the original furniture.
Open April 1 to Sept. 30 : 10 - 12, 2 - 7.
Oct. 1 to 31 : 10 - 12, 2 - 5.
Parking.
Guided tours.
Tel.: (71) 40.73.42.

Saint-Chamant (Château).

Saint-Chamant - 15140.
Aurillac or Maurillac: 29 km.
Station: Aurillac.
Private property.

A 15th century fortified tower stands out amidst the group of 17th and 18th century buildings erected on a platform overlooking the valley. It was probably built by Robert de Balsac, Sénéchal de Guyenne et d'Aquitaine, a comrade at arms of Charles VIII.
Open June 16 to Sept. 15 : 9 - 7.
Parking.
Grounds only.
Leaflets, brochures.
Tel.: (71) 69.22.01.

Les Ternes (Castle).

Les Ternes - 15100.
Saint-Flour: 10 km.
Station: Saint-Flour-Chaudesaigues 10 km.
Bus service.
Property of the commune.

After the old castle was destroyed during the Hundred Years War, the lords of Espinchal, one of whom was Queen Margot's Grand Chamberlain, rebuilt the castle in the 15th century. Designed to insure the defense of Saint-Flour it rises above the meeting point of three valleys. The three story square keep is flanked by a turret and a tower which were restored at the beginning of the 20th century. The nearby 15th century manor house was transformed in the 16th century.
Open July 1 to Aug. 30 : 2 - 7.
Closed Sundays.
Parking.
Guided tours, brochures.
Acoustiguides.
Folk dancing.
Temporary arts and crafts exhibits.

Val (Castle).

Lanobre - 15270.
Bort-les-Orgues: 7 km.
Station: Bort-les-Orgues.
Property of the city.
Management: O.T.S.I. Pays de Bort-Artense.

This fortress was built in 1440 on a rocky island in the middle of lake Bort by Guillaume IV d'Estaing. Its four wings are flanked with six fortified round towers with pepper pot roofs. The out buildings were added in the 15th and 18th centuries. The castle has some interesting polychrome fireplaces and a chapel dedicated to Saint Blaise. The interiors still have their Gothic and Louis XIII furnishings. After periods of glory and decline the family's descendants had the castle expropriated when the Bort-les-Orgues dam was built in 1951.
Open daily June 15 to Sept. 15 : 9 - 12 2 - 6:30.
Sept. 16 to June 14 : 9 - 12, 2 - 6.
Closed Nov. 2 to Dec. 15.
Closed Tuesdays Sept. 16 to June 14.
Parking.
Guided tours, brochures.
English - German - Dutch.
Temporary exhibits: painting, sculpture art, stamps.
Tel.: (71) 40.30.20 or (55) 96.02.49.

La Vigne (Château).

Ally - 15700 Pleaux.
Mauriac: 9 km.
Salers: 15 km.
Property of M. du Fayet de la Tour.

Built by Louis de Scorailles, sénéchal of Berry and Limousin 1450, La Vigne offers a spectacular view of the Auvergne mountains. The main building and towers are covered in stone. The vaults of the hall of justice and chapel were painted in the 16th century. Jean Jacques Rousseau is said to have stayed here in 1767.
Open daily July 1 to Aug. 31 : 2 - 7.
Other hours on request.
Groups received by appointment only.
Parking.
Guided tours.
Information in English - German Dutch.
Leaflets available.
Tel.: (71) 69.00.20.

AUVERGNE — 41 — HAUTE-LOIRE

HAUTE-LOIRE

Arlempdes (Castle).

Arlempdes - 43490.
Le Puy: 30 km.
Private property.

Built in the 12th century by the Lords of Montlaur, Arlempdes rises from a basalt plateau 30 meters above the Loire. The upper part consists of the main building, fragments of the ramparts and the chapel. Below is a huge courtyard enclosed by surrounding walls flanked by round towers. The castle was remodelled in the 15th century.
Open at all times (keys and tickets can be obtained from the Hôtel des Manoirs).
Parking.
Information panels and leaflets.

Lafayette (Château).

Chavaniac-Lafayette - 43230.
Le Puy-en-Velay: 40 km.
Station: Saint-Georges-d'Aurac 10 km.

Photo Velay

Property of the Association Mémorial Lafayette.

Born in this château on September 6 1757, Lafayette spent the first 11 years of his life here and returned many times, both before and after his American adventure, until 1829. The château was rebuilt in the 17th century on the ruins of a 14th century fort which had burnt down. A rose garden, park, wax museum and Lafayette memorabilia add to the château's, attractions.
Open Easter - Sept. 30: 9 - 12, 2 - 6.
Open on request in winter.
Parking.
Unaccompanied visit of the park.
Guided tours of the château.
Tel.: (71) 77.50.32.

Lavoûte-Polignac (Castle).

Lavoûte-sur-Loire - 43800.
Le Puy-en-Velay: 11 km.
Station: Lavoûte-sur-Loire 1 km.
Bus nearby.
Property of the duc de Polignac.

Lavoûte-Polignac sits above the waters of the Loire. Transformed throughout the centuries the castle has been the country residence of the Polignac family since 854. Inside are magnificent fireplaces, period furniture, a picture gallery of Polignac and royal family portraits and memorabilia of Louis XVI and Marie-Antoinette.
Open from Easter to Nov. 1: 9:30 12:30, 2 - 6:30.
On request out of season.
Parking.
Guided tours.
Information in English - German.
Tel.: (71) 08.50.02.

Léotoing (Castle).

Léotoing - 43410.
Brioude: 20 km.
Station: Arvant 10 km.
Private property.

The ruins of Léotoing rise on a rocky peak above the Allagnon

---

LES TERNES

15th century   CANTAL

Located on the D 921 10 km from Saint-Flour-Neuvéglise and 20 km from Chaudesaigues at Saint-Flour-Chaudesaigues.

Guided tours in July and August.
Rooms for receptions and conferences.
For information call (71) 73.01.39 or 73.00.51.

gorge. Erected in the 11th century by the Lords of Léotoing, the castle was rebuilt in 1255 by the dauphins of Auvergne. After becoming a hiding place for bandits it was finally demolished by Richelieu. The round keep, the main building, the farm-yard and a Romanesque chapel with 15th century paintings can still be seen today.
Unaccompanied visits.
Parking.

Mercœur (Castle).

Saint-Privat-d'Allier - 43460.
Le Puy-en-Velay: 20 km.
Station: Le Puy.
Private property.

A fief of the Mercœur family, vassals of the bishop of Puy, Mercœur is perched on the top of a mountain ridge. It withstood both Wars of Religion and subsequent invasions. The three-sided main building is flanked by a round on the enemy side and turrets on the other. The keep dates from the 12th and 14th centuries, whereas the mainbuilding was remodelled in the Renaissance.
Guided tours and unaccompanied visits.

MOUDEYRES

Le Bourg (Perrel brother's farm).

Moudeyres - 43150.
Le Puy-en-Velay: 23 km.
Station: Le Puy-en-Velay.
Property of the commune.

This farm built in 1730 is characteristic of the period with its thatched stables and barn. The main hall, chamber and kitchen are still preserved and much of the furniture has remained intact.
Open July 1 to Sept. 15: 9 - 12, 3 - 7.
Closed Wednesdays.
Open on request for groups.
Parking.
Guided tours.
Tel.: (71) 00.12.13.

Rochebaron (Castle).

Bas-en-Basset - 43210.
Between Saint-Etienne and le Puy.
Station: Bas-Monistrol 5 km.
Private property.

Rochebaron overlooks the gorges of the Loire. Built in the 11th century, the castle was remodelled in the 14th and 15th centuries before being abandoned under Louis XIV. The impressive ruins consist of the surrounding walls flanked by round towers and defended by a round keep facing the enemy side.
Unaccompanied visits.
Parking.

Saint-Vidal (Castle).

Saint-Vidal - Loudes - 43320.
Le Puy-en-Velay: 11 km.
Station: Saint-Vidal.
Private property.

Set on the slopes of the Borne valley, Saint-Vidal is a square building surrounding a courtyard bordered with 15th century ribbed vaulting. There are round towers on three sides of the castle and a keep to protect the fourth side. The fortress was built in the 14th century by the Lords of La Tour and was altered in the 16th century to face new methods of warfare. Inside the rooms have beamed ceilings and gothic fireplaces.
Open July 1 to Aug. 31: 2 - 6:30.
Parking.
Guided tours.
English - information panels or leaflets.

La Tour Daniel.

Coubon - 43700.
Le Puy: 8 km.
Station: Le Puy.
Property of M. and Mme de Franclieu.

La Tour Daniel, an outpost of the fortress of Bouzols has an imposing 14th century rectangular keep of uncut basalt. In the 16th century a Renaissance building was added with a facade carved with ball and diamond shapes. Another building was erected in the 17th century. Inside two carved fireplaces, probably the work of Spanish artists, show scenes from the life of Christ.
Open July 1 to Sept. 30: 2 - 6, Tuesday, Wednesday, Thursday.
Open on request for groups.
Parking.
Guided tours.
English - German.

Valprivas (Château).

Valprivas - 43210.
Saint-Etienne: 42 km.
Station: Bas-Monistrol 13 km.
Property of the Centre Culturel de Valprivas Association.

During the Renaissance, Antoine de Verdier, friend of the poets of the Pleiade group, lived in Valprivas. The doorway with its caryatids, the Italianate loggias and the main courtyard all date from this period. The chapel is decorated with two murals showing the Resurection and Hell painted in the style of the School of Fontainebleau.
Open daily: 10 - 12, 3 - 6.
Parking.
Guided tours.
German.
Concerts May-October.
Musical workshops and gatherings.
Tel.: (71) 66.71.33.

LA CHAISE-DIEU

Saint-Robert (Abbey church).

La Chaise-Dieu - 43160.
Le Puy: 43 km.
Property of the commune.

The severe appearance of the church is due to the grey granite of the region. Among the most famous tombs in the church is that of Pope Clement VI of Avignon. The choir walls are decorated with a fresco of the Danse Macabre where all mortals are led by death in an infernal dance. Above the choir stalls are tapestries of 84 scenes of the life of Christ and parallel episodes from the Old Testament. Behind the church is a huge courtyard dominated by a tower which includes a well and an oven for times of siege. Next to the courtyard are remains of a pretty cloister and monastic buildings.

LA CHAISE-DIEU

HAUTE-LOIRE

This massive abbey-fortress consists of a granite façade with two squat towers, the « Clementine Tower » (40 metres high), the 15th century cloister and library and monastic buildings dating from 1640. Beneath its Gothic vaults are a 17th century organ, a 15th century rood screen, a 144 stall choir, the tomb of Clement VI, tapestries dating from 1518 and the famous fresco of the Danse Macabre.

HAUTE-LOIRE/PUY-DE-DÔME — 44 — AUVERGNE

Open June 1 to Sept. 30 : 9 - 12, 2 - 7.
Oct. 1 to May 31 : 10 - 12, 2 - 5.
Closed Tuesdays Nov. 1 to June 1.
Parking.
Guided tours or unaccompanied visits.
Brochures in English and German.
Summer music festival.
Temporary exhibits.
Tel. : (71) 00.01.71.

PUY-DE-DÔME

Aulteribe (Château).

Sermentizon - 63120.
Thiers : 20 km.
Property of the C.N.M.H.S.

Set on the edge of a wooded ravine this fortified house is flanked by towers that were built in the 14th and 15th centuries. The castle was restored at the beginning of the 19th century in the Romantic style of the period and equipped to house the collections of its proprietors the composer Lord George Onslow and then the family of Pierre de Bernis. In 1954 the marquis Henri de Pierre bequethed the property to the Caisse Nationale des Monuments Historiques et des Sites which maintains the house thanks to the Onslow-de Pierre Foundation. The castle houses a remarkable collection of furniture and works of art including paintaings by Annibale Caracci, Hyacinthe Rigaud, Philippe de Champaigne and Hubert Robert and tapestries after Teniers.
Open May 1 to Sept. 30 : 9 - 12, 2 - 6.
Oct. 1 to April 30, 10 - 12, 2 - 5.
Closed Tuesdays.
Tel. : (73) 53.13.25.

La Barge (Castle).

Courpière - 63120.
Clermont-Ferrand and Vichy : 40 km.
Station : Clermont-Ferrand or Vichy.
Private property.

This 13th century fortress still has its original Moat. Terraces and a gallery were added in the Renaissance as well as the chapel. In the 18th century a perspective was added. Armand-Marc de Montmorin, one of Louis XVI's ministers was born here. The castle is still lived in by descendants of its original owners.
Open July 13 to Aug. 31 : 2 - 5:30.
On request for groups all yeqr.
Chapel and grounds only.
Guided tours, brochures.
English.

La Bâtisse (Castle).

Chanonat - 63450.
Clermont-Ferrand : 10 km.
Station : Clermont-Ferrand.
Private property.

La Bâtisse consists of a main building and two impressive 15th century round towers to which lanterns were added in the 17th century. The final transformations were carried out in the 18th century. The formal gardens, designed in the style of Le Nôtre are scattered with basins, rocaille grottoes and copses. The interiors

---

PUY-DE-DÔME

CHÂTEAU-DAUPHIN

Situated at the entrance to the Volcans d'Auvergne regional park near the Sioule bridge, Château-Dauphin is one of the only 12 and 13th century fortresses in Auvergne to have escaped the demolitions of Cardinal Richelieu.

The keep and six towers have been remarkably well preserved. The interiors, carefully restored in the 19th century and lived in since, contain historical and family memorabilia.

AUVERGNE — 45 — PUY-DE-DÔME

are decorated with frescoes 16th to 18th century furniture.
Open daily May 1 to Sept. 30 : 10 - 12, 2 - 7. Sat. - Sun. Oct. 1 to April 30 : 2 - 7.
Parking.
Guided tours, brochures.
English - German - Dutch - Leaflets.
Temporary exhibits (tapestries and carpets).
Tel. : (70) 79.41.04.

Bellaigue (Abbey).

Virlet - 63330.
Montluçon : 23 km.
Private property.
Founded on the orders of Louis in 1137, Bellaigue abbey was one of the last Cistercian abbeys to be established in Auvergne. The original church and tombs of the lords of Bourbon-Archambault have ben preserved. The monastery was remodelled in 1700 and has 17th century staircases and apartments.
Church open except in winter.
Guided tours in summer.
Monastery open on request.
Tel. : (70) 05.10.26.

Château-Dauphin (Castle).

Pontgibaud - 63230.
Clermont-Ferrand : 23 km.
Station : Pontgibaud 2 km.
Bus service.
Private property.
Built in 1190 by the troubadour Robert I of Auvergne, Château-Dauphin was completed in the 15th century by Gilbert III de La Fayette and restored in the 19th century. This medieval grey stone fortress has a main building and a 12th century round keep which occupies the centre of the courtyard flanked by six 15th century towers. The interiors, restored in the 19th century contain furniture from the 15th to 18th centuries as well as paintings, faience and 18th century miniatures.
Open July 14 to Aug. 31 : 2 - 6.
Closed Mondays.
Parking.
Guided tours, brochures.
English - German - Leaflets or information panels.
Tel. : (73) 88.73.39.

Chazeron (Castle).

Loubeyrat - 63410.
Riom : 8 km.
Bus service.
Property of M. R. Bruny.
During the second half of the 14th century Oudard de Chazeron built a mighty fortress on the ruins of an earlier castle whose armoury and oubliette still exist. The towers, the surounding walls and the large keep were demolished when François Monestay de Chazeron, lieutenant-general of Louis XIV's army transformed the castle to receive the king. He had the steps and gallery built and added two wings and a large wrought iron gate. He also enlarged the windows. Chazeron became a state prison in 1940 and housed political prisoners such as Leon Blum, Edouard Daladier and Paul Reynaud.
Open May 1 to Sept. 30 : 3 - 6.
Parking.
Unaccompanied visit, brochures.
Information panels and Leaflets.
English - German - panels or leaflets.
Music festival, coreography, theatre, temporary exhibits.
Tel. : (73) 86.66.12.

Cordès (Castle).

Orcival - 63210.
Clermont-Ferrand : 25 km.
Private property.
Built in the 14th century, Cordès was remodelled at the end of the 17th century by the maréchal d'Allègre who added windows to this square fortress flanked by towers. Le Nôtre is thought to have designed the gardens. The sumptuous interiors date from the 18th century.
Open all year : 10 - 12, 2 - 6.
Parking.
Guided tours.
Tel. : (73) 21.21.34.

Denone (Castle).

Effiat-Aigueperse.
Effiat - 63260.
Vichy, Riom : 16 km.
Clermont-Ferrand : 35 km.
Station : Riom 20 km.
Private property.
Birthplace of Saint Louise de Marcillac and later property of the famous financier John Law, Denone was rebuilt in 1550 on the site of a medieval castle.
Open daily June 30 to Sept. 2: 2 - 7.
Parking.
Guided tours, brochures.
Temporary exhibits.
Tel. : (73) 63.64.02.

Effiat (Château).

Effiat - 63260.
Vichy : 16 km.
Station : Aigueperse or Grannat : 10 km.
Bus service.
Property of M. G. de Moroges.
Effiat owes its present day appearance to the maréchal d'Effiat who transformed the older buildings between 1649 and 1632. The facade is divided by colossal pilasters of Volvic stone surmounted by a high slate roof. It was here that the famous Cinq-Mars, the maréchal's son was born. The majestic porch and the gardens designed by Le Nôtre's godfather, André Mollet are among the spectacular features of the residence. Inside are four rooms of documents and memorabilia relating to maréchal d'Effiat and his son. The salon has preserved its original ceiling, parquet floors and mantlepiece painting of the Forge of Vulcan by the Le Nain brothers as well as its Italian renaissance woodwork.
Open daily June 1 to Oct. 1: 9 - 12, 2 - 7.
Weekend and holidays Feb. 28 to June 1 : 9 - 12, 2 - 7.
Oct. 1 to Dec. 5 : 9 - 12, 2 - 6.
Open on request for groups of 20 out of season.
Parking.

Guided tours, brochures.
English - German - Guide.
Facilities for the handicapped.
Tel. : (73) 63.64.01.

Les Martinanches (Castle).

Saint-Dier-d'Auvergne - 65320.
Saint-Dier-d'Auvergne : 5 km.
Private property.

Built at the beginning of the 16th century on the remains of an 11th century edifice, Martinanches consists of facades and towers of white stone that are reflected in the waters of its wide moat. The period rooms offer examples of Louis XV, Louis XVI and Empire furniture and contain collections of bronzes, cristal, porcelain and paintings.

Open June 15 to Sept. 15 : 2 - 7.
Sept. 15 to June 15 : Sun. and holidays, 2 - 7.
Open out of season on request.
Parking.
Guided tours.
English - Dutch - Leaflets.
Tel. : (73) 70.80.02.

Mauzun (Castle).

Mauzun - 63160.
Billom : 9 km.
Station : Clermont-Ferrand 30 km.
Bus service.
Private property.

The ruins of Mauzon castle are among the most impressive of the Auvergne. Set on a basalt peak, the fortress consists of two protected areas the first with 15 towers, served as a refuge and the second with its keep and watch tower was the principal residence. Mauzon belonged to the Astorg family before becoming the property of the bishops of Clermont-Ferrand.
Parking.
Guided tours for groups on request.
Brochures available.
Theatre and music.
Workshops.

Montfleury (Château).

Laps - 63270.
Clermont-Ferrand : 24 km.
Station : Vic-le-Comte 3 km.
Bus service.
Property of M. Vinols de Montfleury.

This fine residence, set in a wooded valley on the edge of the Limagne has belonged to the same family for six centuries. Characteristic of Auvergnat architecture, it has fine furniture and attractive gardens.
Open April 15 to Sept. 30 : 10 - 12 2 - 7.
Parking.
Guided tours.
Facilities for the handicapped.
Tel. : (73) 69.02.55.

Montmorin (Château).

Billom - 63160.
Clermont-Ferrand : 25 km.
Station : Billom 3 km.
Bus service.
Private property.

Fief of the Montmorin family this 12th century castle consists of a central keep surrounded by defensive walls and towers forming several protected interior cour

---

PUY-DE-DÔME

CHAZERON

Throughout the centuries this castle has been a typical fortress from its construction to its restoration. Both residence and fortress Chazeron was used as a prison for political prisoners in 1940. Its inmates included Léon Blum, Paul Rénaud, General Gamelin, Édouard Daladier and Georges Mendel.

Open May-September : 3 - 6.

yards. Saved from ruin, the main building now houses the Auvergne Museum of Folk Art as well as a collection of arms and armour of the 14th to 17th centuries.
Open July 1 to Nov. 1 : 3 - 7.
Nov. 1 to June 30 : Sat. - Sun. 3 - 7.
On request for groups.
Parking.
Guided tours, brochures.
Germain - English - Dutch - Leaflets.
Temporary exhibits (archeology).

Opme (Castle).
Romagnat - 63540.
Clermont-Ferrand : 10 km.
Station : Clermont-Ferrand.
Private property.

A square keep is all that remains of the original fortress of Opme built between the 11th and 13th centuries. The rectangular surrounding walls built to protect the 15th century castle have round towers at each corner. Antoine de Ribeyre was responsible for the major construction work which transformed the castle into a residence in 1612: the large windows and the main courtyard, the terrace and the formal gardens, basins and Renaissance fountain.

Open July 1 to Sept. 30 : 9 - 12, 2 - 6.
Closed Wednesdays.
Open out of season on request.
Grounds only.
Parking.
Unaccompanied visits, brochures.
Information panels or leaflets.
Tel. : (73) 73.79.45.

Parentignat (Château).
Parentignat - 63500.
Issoire : 4 km.
Station : Issoire.
Property of Mme de Lastic.

Built between 1707 and 1720, Parentignat has been called « the Little Versailles ». The perfect symmetry of the U shaped building is due to the windows and the stable wings, a feature of Louis XIV domestic architecture. The interiors contain furniture, tapestries, and pictures from the 17th century to the Empire. The Lastic family has owned the château since its construction.
Open May-June Sundays and holidays : 2 - 6.
July 1 to Sept., 2 - 6.
Out of season on request.
Closed Wednesdays.
Parking.
Guided tours, brochures.
Temporary exhibits (family papers - balloons).
Tel. : (73) 89.06.55.

RIOM
Francisque Nandet Museum.
Riom - 63200.
Rue de l'Hôtel-de-Ville.
Near Clermont-Ferrand.
Property of the city.

This fine town house now contains a collection of stones from the region, an interesting picture collection including Northern artists as well as 18th century French paintings and works of contemporary regional artists. Another section of the museum is

MONTFLEURY
PUY-DE-DÔME

Set in a wooded valley on the edge of the Limagne, and typically Auvergnat in its architecture, Montfleury is a protected historic monument on the 13th to 18th centuries. It was given by Jean, duc de Berry to Jean d'Amarithon, ancestor of the family who still live in the château. Inside is a fine collection of 14th to 18th century furniture as well as a collection of carriages, unique in the Auvergne.

Open April 15 to the end of September from 10 to 12 and from 2 to 7.

devoted to medieval and ancient collections and Italian primitives. There is also a decorative arts collection with works from the Renaissance to the 18th century, a rich collection of gold and silver objects, fine faience and an armour collection.
Open April 1 to Sept. 30: 10 - 12, 2 - 5:30.
Oct. 1 to March 31: 10 - 12, 2 - 4:30.
Closed Tuesdays April 1 to Sept. 30 and Mondays and Tuesdays Oct. 1 to March 31.
Parking.
Unaccompanied visit.
Tel.: (73) 38.18.53.

La Roche (Castle).

Chaptuzat - 63260.
Aigueperse : 3 km.
Property of M. de Torcy.
Built by the dukes of Montpensier in the 12th and 13th centuries, La Roche was raised to a chatellenie by the conétable de Bourbon for the chancellor Michel de l'Hospital who transformed the castle in the 16th century. The 13th century fortress incorporates the 12th century keep and the main building has notable tapestries, armour and furniture.
Open Jan. 1 to Dec. 31: 9 - 12, 2 - 6.
Parking.
Guided tours, brochures.
English - Guide.
Lectures.
Lecture tours for school groups only.
Tel.: (73) 63.65.81.

Saint-Quintin (Castle).

Saint-Quintin-sur-Sioule - 63440.
Ebreuil : 4 km.
Station : Ebreuil.
Bus service.
Private property.
Saint-Quintin dates back to the 12th and 13th centuries. It has preserved a 10th century Romanesque chapel and reception rooms with Gothic fireplaces and 17th century paintings.
Open July and Sept.: 10 - 12, 2 - 4.
Parking.
Guided tours.
Tel.: (73) 90.72.54.

Saint-Saturnin (Castle).

Saint-Amant-Tallende - 63450.
Property of the Renaissance Association.
Built at the end of the 13th century and refurbished during the Renaissance, Saint-Saturnin was the residence of the barons de la Tour and one of the most opulent buildings of the Auvergne. Today it consists of surrounding walls rising on a rocky promontory, a remarkable example of 13th century military architecture.
Open daily Easter to Nov. 1: 2 - 6. (July and Aug. 2 - 7).
Off season : Sundays and holidays, 2 - 5.
Groups by appointment.
Guided tours.
Theatre.
Tel.: (73) 39.42.08.

Tournoël (Castle).

Volvic - 63530.
Clermont-Ferrand : 16 km.
Private property.

PUY-DE-DÔME

LA ROCHE
Open daily all year

La Roche castle offers you its medieval setting for your receptions, lectures and films.

Tel.: (73) 63.65.81 and (1) 574.18.50.

AUVERGNE — PUY-DE-DÔME

Perched on the top of a rocky spur, this impressive medieval fortress was damaged in the 16th century. The main building has been preserved with its 12th century square keep and round keep linked by 14th and 15th century buildings. A magnificent staircase leads from the main courtyard to the apartments which include fine fireplaces.
Open April 4 to Nov. 1: 9 - 12, 2 - 7.
Guided tours in season, unaccompanied visits out of season.
Information panels.
Brochures available.
Tel.: (73) 33.53.06.

Villeneuve-Lembron (Château).

Villeneuve-Lembron - 63340.
Issoire: 15 km.
Station: Le Breuil-sur-Couze 8 km.
Property of the State.

Villeneuve was built at the end of the 15th century by Rigaud d'Aureille, maître d'hôtel to several kings from Louis XI to François I. Constructed on a square plan it has towers at each corner and is surrounded by a wide ditch. 16th and 17th century frescoes decorate the gallery overlooking the courtyard and stables. They illustrate maxims and sayings and refer to literary themes.
Open April 1 to Sept. 30: 10 - 12, 2 - 4.
Oct. 1 to March 31 10 - 12, 2.
Closed Tuesdays in summer.
Parking.
Guided tours, brochures.
Tel.: (73) 96.41.64.

vives from this period. The 17th century granite château is flanked on its North side by 16th century tower, the remains of a 15th century edifice. Now the property of the descendants of General La Fayette, the château contains a collection of family memorabilia relating to La Fayette and the American War of Independence displayed in rooms decorated in 17th and 18th century style.
Open July 1 to Sept. 5: 2 - 4.
On request for groups all year.
Parking.
Guided tours.
English - Guide.
Concerts.
Lecture tours for school groups only.
Tel.: (73) 53.71.06.

Vollore (Château).

Vollore-Ville - 63120 Courpière.
Thiers: 18 km.
Station: Thiers.
Bus service.
Private property.

During the Middle Aged Vollore was the stronghold of the Vollore family. A Romanesque keep sur-

Photo J. Feuillie

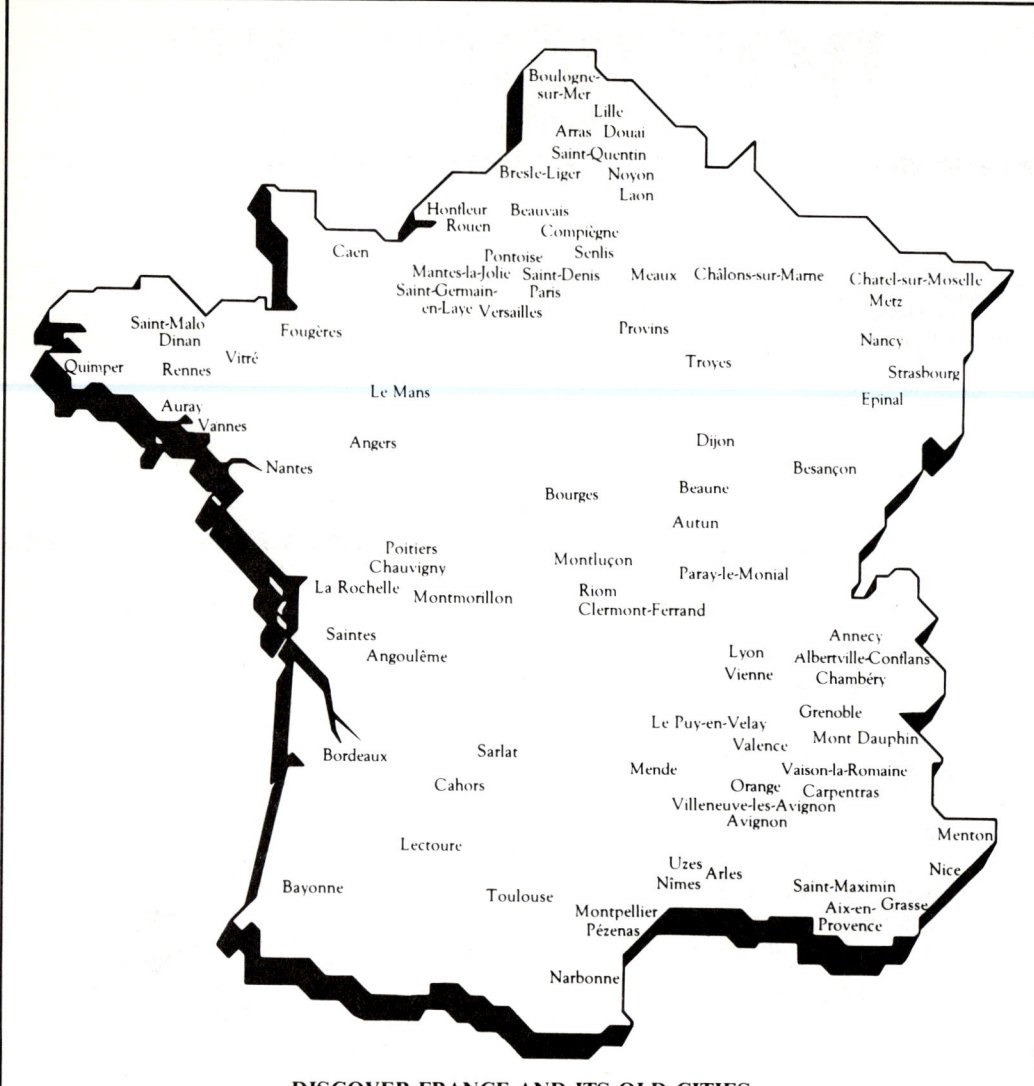

DISCOVER FRANCE AND ITS OLD CITIES
with the guided tours of the Caisse Nationale des Monuments Historiques

When travelling in France during your holidays, discover 100 Old Cities and their art treasures with the guided tours organised by the Caisse Nationale des Monuments Historiques. Daily tours are organised and last one hour or more. Ask for timetable and details in the Tourist Offices of cities like : AIX-EN-PROVENCE, ARLES, ARRAS, AVIGNON, BEAUNE, BEAUVAIS, LAON, LA ROCHELLE, LYON, METZ, MONTLUÇON, MONTPELLIER, NANCY, NANTES, ROUEN, STRASBOURG, VERSAILLES...

ENGLISH SPEAKING GUIDES.

Hôtel de Sully
62, rue Saint-Antoine 75004 PARIS
Tél. : 274.22.22.

BOURGOGNE

CÔTE D'OR, NIÈVRE, SAÔNE-ET-LOIRE, YONNE.

- ■ castle, château, manor house
- ● abbey, priory
- ▲ garden, park
- ★ town house, famous men house, farm, mill...
- ○ city

DIJON
- ▲ Jardin de l'Arquebuse
- ★ Palais des Etats
- ★ Musée Magnin

AUXERRE
- ● Abbaye Saint-Germain

BEAUNE
- ★ Hôtel des Ducs de Bourgogne
- ● Couvent des Ursulines (Hôtel de Ville)

■ Fleurigny
★ Sens : Palais Synodal
★ Villeneuve-sur-Yonne
■ Prunoy
■ Bontin
■ Tanlay
● Molesme
■ Grandchamp
■ Ancy-le-Franc
■ Jours
AUXERRE ○
■ Tremblay
■ Nuits
■ Ratilly
● Vausse
★ Salmaise
● Fontenay
■ Saint-Fargeau
■ Le Chastenay
■ Grignon
■ Epoisses
■ Fontaine-Française
● ▲ Boutissaint
■ Thizy
■ Courtivron
■ Druyes
■ Bourbilly
■ Frolois
■ Lux
■ Lantilly
■ Marigny
■ Corbelin
■ Bussy-Rabutin
■ Villemolin
■ Lantenay ○ DIJON
■ Chitry
■ Thil
■ Collonges
■ Lantilly
■ Commarin
■ Giry
■ Châteauneuf-en-Auxois
■ Clos-Vougeot
■ Menessaire
○ NEVERS
■ Besne
○ Beaune
■ Chatillon
■ Pierre-de-Bresse
■ Chevenon
■ Sully
■ Demigny
★ Autun : Hôtel Rolin
■ Rully
● Montambert
■ Couches
■ Saint-Aubin-sur-Loire
■ Le Creusot (ch. de la Verrerie)
■ Brandon
■ Germolles
■ Lavault
■ Cormatin
■ Sercy
■ Brancion
■ Lugny-les-Charolles
■ Digoine
■ Berzé-le-Châtel
■ Cypierre
■ Chevannes
● Cluny
● Berzé-la-Ville
○ MÂCON
■ Saint-Point
■ Tramayes
● Chevigné

BOURGOGNE

CÔTE-D'OR

BEAUNE
Hôtel des Ducs de Bourgogne

Beaune - 21200.
Rue d'Enfer.
Dijon : 30 km.
Station : Beaune.
Bus service.
Property of the commune.

The former residence of the Dukes of Burgundy is a 15th and 16th century building with a timbered gallery. Now home of the Museum of Wine which includes not only vats and presses, but Aubusson tapestries signed by Lurçat and Toutlière.
Open daily May 1 to Sept. 30: 9 - 12:30, 2 - 6:15.
Oct. 1 to April 30: 9 - 12, 2 - 5:45.
Parking
Guided tours or unaccompanied visits.
Information panels.
English - German for groups - Guides from the Tourist Authority.
Shows.
Rel. : (80) 22.08.19.

Hôtel de Ville

Beaune - 21200.
Dijon : 35 km.
Station : Beaune.
Property of the city.

This 17th century Ursuline convent has been the city hall since 1792. The chapel has been transformed into the Marey Museum and contains ancient and medieval sculpture, 16th to 20th century paintings including the works of local artists.
Open Easter to Nov. 30: 9 - 12, 2 - 5:30.
Closed Tuesdays.
Parking.
Guided tours, brochures.
English - German for groups - Guides from the Tourists Authority.
Tel. : (80) 22.20.80.

Bourbilly (Château).

Époisses - 21460.
Semur-en-Auxois : 10 km.
Private property.

Built in the Serein valley at the beginning of the 14th century and completely restored between 1867 and 1871 by Charles de Franqueville who saved it from complete destruction. Built on a horseshoe plan and flanked by whitewashed round towers with slate roofs. Sainte Jeanne de Chantal and Madame de Sévigné were among its famous visitors. Bourbilly has a modern chapel, dating from the middle of this century; its library, panelled in Neo-Gothic style has a collection of Venetian glass unique in France.
Open Easter to Oct. 31: 10 - 12, 3 - 6.
Closed Sunday mornings and Mondays.
Parking.
Guided tours, brochures.
Recorded information.
German - English - guides.
Lecture tours for school groups on request.
Tel. : (80) 97.05.02.

Bussy-Rabutin (Château).

Bussy-Rabutin - Les Laumes - 21150.
Dijon : 70 km.
Property of the State.

Nestled in wooded valley in the Morvan hills, Bussy-Rabutin owes its fame to Roger de Rabutin, warrior and writer who lived at the time of Louis XIV. Cousin to Madame de Sévigné, his taste for scandal led to his 17 year exile to his Burgundian estate. Here he spent his time extending and embellishing his residence, a square building flanked by towers and surrounded by a moat. He concentrated on decorating the reception rooms by adding a gallery of ancient and modern history, bringing together an impressive collection of portraits to which he added sarcastic captions.
Open April 1 to Sept. 30: 9 - 12, 2 - 6.
Closed Tuesdays.
Guided tours, brochures.
Tel. : (80) 96.00.03.

Châteauneuf-en-Auxois (Castle).

Pouilly-en-Auxois - 21320.
Property of the State.

Built on a commanding position on the road between Dijon and Autun, Châteauneuf has retained its irregularly shaped plan, as well as the main part of its defences : the 12th century square keep, the round towers and surrounding walls erected in the 13th and 15th centuries. In 1457 the castle was given by the Duke of Burgundy to his seneshal, Philippe Pot. It wa the latter who built the seigneuri residence in flamboyant Goth style. In the chapel are wall pai tings of Christs and the Apostle The castle has undergone sub tantial restoration since the com de Voguë gave it to the state 1936.
Open April 1 to Sept. 30: 9:30 - 11:3 2 - 7.
Oct. 1 to March 31: 10 - 12, 2 - 3.
Closed Tuesdays in summer, Wedne days in winter.
Guided tours.
Tel. : (80) 33.00.77.

Clos de Vougeot (Ch teau).

Vougeot - 21640.
Dijon : 20 km.
Station : Nuits-Saint-Georges 2 km.
Bus service.
Property of the Confraternity of the Cl valiers du Tastevin.

Clos de Vougeot is set in the neyeards planted by the monks Citeaux in the 12th century. T winery and cellars date from th period. The Renaissance wing w built in 1551 by Don Jean Loysi abbot of Citeaux. The wine contains four huge winepress and the cellars are used for me tings of the confraternity. The do mitory still has its original beam
Open Jan. 6 to Dec. 19: 9 - 11:30, 5:30.
Parking.
Guided tours, brochures.
Audiovisual programmes in conjuncti with the tours.
English - German - Dutch.
Acoustiguides ans recordings.
Tel. : (80) 62.86.09.

Collonges (Château).

Collonges-les-Bévy - 21220.
Nuits-Saint-Georges : 9 km.
Station : Nuit-Saint-Georges.
Property of M. de Haut de Sigy.

Louis Georges de Massol b Collonges on a hillside in 17 The mainbuilding and two perpe dicular wings date from this p riod. The château has a multic loured tile roof and a gallery w

CLOS DE VOUGEOT

CÔTE D'OR

Built in the 12th and 16th centuries.
Headquarters of the Confrateriny of the Chevaliers du Tastevin.

Guided tour and audio-visual presentation of the Confraterity of the Chevaliers de Tastevin.

added to the North side during the restoration of 1874. Inside the stairwell is decorated with bas-reliefs of the labours of Hercules. The little dining room has plasterwork and the large salon bas paintings, panelling and medallions. The château also contains much Empire memorabilia.
Open June 30 to Oct. 1 : 2 - 6, Sat., Sun., Easter Monday, Whitsunday, July 14, August 15.
Open on request all year (with one week's notice).
Parking.
Guided tours, brochures.
English - German - in July and August.
Concerts - Lectures.
Tel. : (80) 61.40.05.

Commarin (Château).

Commarin - 21320.
Dijon : 40 km.
Station : Dijon.
Bus nearby.
Property of M. de Vogüé.
   Commarin is a classical residence framed by medieval towers which look onto a wide moat. The decoration and furniture were chosen by Marie-Judith de Vienne, Talleyrand's grandmother and include 16th century armorial tapestries of exceptional quality.
Open April 1 to November 1 : 10 - 12, 2 - 4.
Closed Tuesdays.
Parking.
Guided tours, brochures.
Tel. : (80) 33.44.02.

Courtivron (Château).

Courtivron - 21120.
Dijon : 32 km.
Station : Is-sur-Tille 12 km.
Private property.
   Courtivron rises from a terrace surrounded by a moat at the edge of the Ignon river. Its square keep dates from the 15th whereas the main buildings were not erected until the 17th and 18th centuries. The river flows through the grounds.
Open July 14 to Aug. 21 : 9 - 6.
Grounds only.
Parking.
Tel. : (80) 95.00.50.

DIJON
L'Arquebuse (Botanical Gardens).

Dijon - 21000.
1, avenue Albert-I.
Property of the commune.
   The original botanical gardens, created by Lehouz de Gerland in 1773 soon became too small and was transfeed to the present site in 1833. The 18th century building was originally used by archers who used to practice in the grounds nearby. The garden contains over 3500 specimens of local flora and foreign plants. Morvan foxglove and Soane waterchesnuts can be seen alongside American hyacinth and peanuts.
Open March 1 to Sept. 30 : 6:45am - 7 pm.
Oct. 1 to Dec. 28 : 7:45 - 5:15.
Guided tours, brochures.
Lecture tours for school groups.
Tel. : (80) 43.46.39.

Palais des États de Bourgogne. Museum of Fine Arts.

Dijon 21000.
Place de la Sainte-Chapelle.
Property of the commune.
   Ever since the dukes of Burgundy transformed the medieval castle, the most famous architects of the 15th, 17th and 18th centuries have worked on this building : Jean Poncelet in 1448, Daniel Gittard in 1681 and Jules Hardouin-Mansart and Jacques Gabriel in the 18th century. The building is also one of France's oldest museums. Planned under Louis XVI it was finally opened in 1799 and has grown ever since. The Dijon Museum of Fine Arts if full of treasures : the remains of the charterhouse of Champol, a unique collection of German and Swiss primitives, Burgundian works of art, paintings and drawings by Old Masters and modern artists.
Open daily, 10 - 6.
Closed Tuesdays.

Magnin Museum.

Dijon - 21000.
4, rue des Bons-Enfants.
Property of the State.
   Since 1939, this town house built between 1652 and 1651 by a Burgundian official has been the home of the splendid collection of Maurice Magnin which includes French paintings of all periods, fine examples of works by foreign artists and sketches by David, Crodet and Gros. The museum is recognised as one of the major collections of France. Extensions the buildings were carried out the architect Auguste Perret who designed the new room in the style of a collector's picture gallery in accordance with Magnin's wishes.
Open daily : 9 - 12, 2 - 5.
Closed Tuesdays and holidays.
Tel. : (80) 32.12.64.

Epoisses (Château).

Epoisses - 21460.
Semur-en-Auxois : 13 km.
Station : Montbard 25 km.
Private property.
   Surrounded by two sets walls, Epoisses was both the royal residence of the Merovingians and then the home of the dukes of Burgundy. The 10th century walls have kept their tower and the 15 century walls enclose the main building. Remodelled between the 16th and 18th centuries, Epoisses was lived in by Brunehaut, Madame de Sévigné and Chateaubriand. In the 17th century painted beamed ceilings were added the main rooms which have kept their 18th century furniture.
Grounds : Jan 1 to Dec. 31 : 9 - 6.
Interiors : for groups of at least 10 from Easter to Nov. 1 : 10 - 12, 2 - 6. Individuals daily. Closed Tuesdays July and August.
Parking.
Guided tours of the interiors, brochures.
Leaflets for visit of the grounds.
English - German - Dutch - Italian - Spanish.
Tel. : (80) 96.40.56.

Fontaine-Française (Château).

Fontaine-Française - 21610.
Dijon : 40 km.
Private property.
   The name «Française» derives from the fact that this enclave the duchy of Burgundy was held directly by the French crown. But in 1754 the château numbers Voltaire, Rousseau, Madame de Staël among its better known visitors. Inside are fine Gobelin and Flanders tapestries. There is an ornamental pond in front of the façade that looks onto the park.
Open July 2 to Sept. 29 : 2 - 6.
Closed Tuesdays and Thursdays.
Parking.
Guided tours.
Tel. : (80) 95.80.24.

ontenay (Abbey).

ontbard - 21500.
ation : Montbard 6 km.
ivate property.

En 1119 the reformer of the Cistercian order, saint Bernard, founded Notre-Dame de Fontenay which enjoyed great prosperity. By the beginning of the 13th century the abbey boasted over 0 monks and lay brothers whose rming was responsible for the bey's prominence. Cistercian beys were always well located th regard to natural resources d Fontenay is no exception. Its neral lay-out and its austere but eticulous architecture are ually distinctive characteristics this order. A special building ting as forge and workshop was ilt to take advantage of the water that flows through the site and e monks were able to engage in portant industrial activity.

en daily : Sept. 16 to June 30 : 8 - 12, 30 - 6:30. Tours every hour.
y 1 to Sept. 15 : 9 - 12, 2 - 6:30. urs every half hour.
rking.
ided tours, brochures.

Information in English and German.
Nights of Burgundy Festival.
Tel. : (80) 92.15.00.

Frolois (Château).

Frolois par Les Laumes - 21150.
Les Laumes - Alésia : 16 km.
Station : Les Laumes 16 km, Thenissey 7 km.
Bus service.
Private property.

Built on a cliff overlooking the valley, this 15th century castle was transformed in the 17th and 18th centuries. It belonged to three dukes of Burgundy. From this period dates the pavilion with its decorated beams. The other 18th century buildings are arranged square plan. The interior walls are covered with tapisserie de Bergame and the rooms contain period furniture.

Open April 4 to April 18 and June 1 to Nov. 4 : 2 - 6.
April 18 to June 1 on Sat., Sun. and Mon. : 2 - 6.
On request for groups when otherwise closed.
Closed Tuesdays.
Guided tours, brochures.

English - German - panels and leaflets.
Annual concert.
Tel. : (80) 96.22.92.

Grignon (Castle).

Grignon - 21150.
Les Laumes - Alésia : 6 km.
Station : Les Laumes - Alésia. Bus service.
Private property.

Looking down onto the plain of Lumes from the top of a rocky hill, Grignon is a medieval fortress built by the dukes of Burgundy between the 12th and the 14th centuries. Of the original building all that remains is a fortified doorway and one building. In the 15th century the Chalon family built the central block whick was entirely restored in the 20th century.

Open July 1 to Sept. 1 : 2:30 - 6.
Groups on request.
Closed Tuesdays.
Parking.
Guided tours of the interiors.
Unaccompanied visits of the grounds - information provided.
Brochures available.
Tel. : (80) 92.03.48.

MONTBARD

BUFFON'S FORGE

CÔTE D'OR

Built in 1768 by the naturalist and writer G.L. Leclerc de Buffon, this large forge is an excellent example of the Enlightenment's preoccupation with rationalism and harmony. Carefully planned, this factory-farm is a model of industrial organisation of the Louis XV period. With its regional architecture, Buffon's forge appears as a model factory for its time.

Open June 1 to Sept. 30 except Tuesdays : 2:30 - 6.
Groups on request.
Tel. : (80) 92.40.30.

Jours (Château).

Jours-les-Baigneux - 21450.
Montbard : 22 km.
Station : Montbard.
Property of M. D. Jolly.

Jours is a Renaissance château built by the Anglure family between 1542 and 1566. The two story main building is flanked by a round tower and the attic has arched and pedimented dormer windows. The North face is decorated with Corinthian pilasters and niches. Inside the double staircase has kept its coffered ceiling decorated with stucco depicting scenes from the Legend of Hercules.

Open from the Easter holidays to Nov. 1 : 9 - 12, 2 - 5.
Closed Tuesdays.
Parking.
Guided tours.
English - information panels.
Tel. : (80) 96.54.90.

Lantenay (Château).

Lantenay - 21370.
Dijon : 15 km.
Station : Lantenay 2 km.
Private property.

Begun in 1665 by Jean Bouhier, member of the parlement of Burgundy, Lantenay was finally completed in 1740. It consists of two single story buildings arranged on an L-shaped plan and flanked to the North and South by two square pavilions, one with a spiral staircase the other with a square staircase. The square courtyard is framed on the North by a 17th century terrace.

Open April 1 to Sept. 15 : 2 - 6 the first and third Sundays of each month and every Thursday.
Interiors limited to the two staircases.
Parking.
Guided tours.
Tel. : (80) 33.63.22.

Lantilly (Château).

Lantilly - 21140.
Samur-en-Auxois : 7 km.
Station : Montbard 15 km.
Private property.

Lantilly overlooks the Laumes plain and faces the historic site of Alésia. It was rebuilt in 1709 by Charles de Chaugy on the site of an ancient stronghold. The main building consists of a semi-circular block flanked by two wings. The château's classical appearance is due largely to the many windows which give it the nickname « the château of 100 windows ». Inside are panelled room containing 18th century furniture.

Open April 15 to Oct. 1 : 10 - 12, 2 - 6.
Closed Tuesdays.
Parking.
Guided tours.
English.
Temporary art exhibits.
Tel. : (80) 97.11.57.

Lux (Château).

Lux - 21120.
Dijon : 25 km.
Private property.

Lux was built on the banks of the river Tile on the site of a 13th century fortress of which one round defensive tower still exists. Completely remodelled between 1749 and 1751 by Charles-Marie de Saulx-Tavannes, the present château has a two story main building of regular plan with an attic roof. The facade has an arched doorway and the interior was transformed at the beginning of the 19th century. There you can see Renaissance fireplaces, stained glass windows, murals of the Fontainebleau school and a 17th century staircase. The formal garden was replaced by a romantic English garden in the 19th century.

Open daily July 1 to Aug. 31 : 2:30 - 6:30.
Closed Saturdays.
Groups on request.
Parking.
Guided tours, brochures.
English - German - panels or leaflets.
Concerts.
Tel. : (80) 95.11.63.

Marigny-le-Cahouët (Château).

Les Laumes - 21150.
Montbard.
Station : Les Laumes.
Bus service.
Private property.

Built at the beginning of the 12th century Marigny-le-Cahouët became a powerful fortress by the 14th century. Thereafter is was successively transformed until the 19th century when it was restored to its 15th century appearance. It is a long rectangular building with square towers at each corner. The moat is crossed by a drawbridge and one of the main building has a 16th century timbered gallery.

Open June 1 to Oct. 31 : Sat., Sun. and Wed. : 9 - 12, 2 - 6.
Grounds only.
Unaccompanied visits.
Tel. : (80) 97.07.28.

Menessaire (Castle).

Mennessaire - Liernais - 21430.
Saulieu, Autun : 25 km.
Station : Saulieu and Autun 25 km.
Property of M. Mainçon

Boron de Menessaire, a 12th century Crusader, built this feudal castle whose large main building is flanked by four round towers and keep is encirled by a moat. The main room inside has a polychrome ceiling decorated with 18th century figures.

Open July 1 to Sept. 30, 2 - 6:30.
Parking.
Restoration workshops.
Tel. : (4) 771.82.94.

Molesme (Abbey).

Molesme - 21330.
Châtillon-sur-Seine : 25 km.
Property of M. Gelis.

The Benedictine abbey of Molesme was founded in 1075 by saint Robert and enjoyed a period of great prosperity. The remaining buildings include a variety vaults terraces surrounded by gardens. Several saints lived here.

Open April 1 to Nov. 2 : 2 - 7 and by appointement.
Closed Mondays.
Parking.
Guided tours.
Information panels and leaflets.
Tel. : (80) 93.44.47.

LUX

CÔTE D'OR

25 km from Dijon Lux is a living witness to the history of Burgundy.
Rising elegantly in the midst of its 9 hectare grounds Lux is a tranquil and dignified monument whose restoration began in 1979. Recently opened to the public, you can now visit the Renaissance mainbuilding which stands between two 12th century towers. Inside there are fine rooms with Renaissance fireplaces, a rare staircase dating from the reign of Louis XIII and most important of all the remains of murals attributed to the Italian artist Luca Penni, painted in 1540, the only ones of their kind in France.

Lux is available for your receptions. For information call (86) 88.81.01 or (80) 95.11.63.

Salmaise (Market Hall).

Salmaise - 21690.
Les Laumes - Alésia : 20 km.
Station : Verrey-sour-Salmaise 2 km.
Property of the commune.

Salmaise market hall was built by the villagers in 1265 after they obtained a royal charter. The low building measures 40 meters long and is made of stone pillars covered with a sloping lava roof. Situated in the heart of the historic village of Salmaise, the hall overlooks the Oze valley.
Unaccompanied visits.
Parking.
Accessible for the handicapped.

Thil (Castle).

Vic-sous-Thil - 21390.
Avallon - 30 km.
Station : Montbard 30 km.
Bus service.
Property of M. Guibert.

This feudal castle rises on a hill which dominates the valleys of the Armançon and the Serein. Its surrounding walls are protected by a ditch and enclose an early keep with buildings which date from the 9th and 11th centuries. The collegiate church with its single nave located to the North of the hill dates from th 14th century.
Open all year at all times.
Parking.
Guided tours and unaccompanied visits.
Facilities for the handicapped.
Brochures and guides available.
Shows, temporary exhibits, lectures, concerts, theatre, lights.
Tel. : (80) 64.53.00.

NIÈVRE

Besne (Château).

Saint-Péreuse - 58110.
Château-Chinon : 15 km.
Station : Nevers 60 km.
Bus service.
Property of M. de Saint-Péreuse.

Set on a solitary spur overlooking the plain of Bazois, Besne is a 15th century fortress consisting of three buildings arranged in a T — shape flanked by four towers and a dovecote. The buildings have lattice windows and the attics have lanterns. Besne was remodelled in the 19th century.
Open July 1 to Aug. 31 : 3 - 6.
Grounds only.
Tel. : (86) 84.42.14.

Châtillon (Château).

Châtillon-en-Bazois - 58110.
Nevers : 39 km.
Station : Nevers.
Bus service.
Property of M. Sribny.

The home of the lords of Châtillon rises on a rocky peak surrounded by a canal. The soldiers quarters, the 13th century store room and the 14th century round tower are all that remain of the ancient fortress. The vaulted ground floor rooms and the kitchen date from the 15th century. Both the exterior and interiors were remodelled in the 17th century.
Open July 1 to Aug. 31 : 3 - 6.
Closed Tuesdays.
Parking.
Lecture tours for school groups only.
Exhibits.
Concerts.

Chevenon (Castle).

Chevenon - 58160.
Nevers : 9 km.
Station : Imphy 3 km.
Property of M. J.-P. Bardin.

Between 1382 and 1406, Guillaume de Chevenon, captain of the « castles and towers of Vincennes », built this powerful fortress overlooking the Loire. The delapidated castle was saved from ruin the 19th century by Frédéric Girerd, friend of George Sand. Thanks to him the main building, both residence and keep, still exists. Its four stories are flanke by two huge towers and access the building is through a large s ral staircase. Inside the castle h preserved its medieval charac with its vaulted and domed roor its beamed ceilings and mor mental fireplaces.
Open Jan. 1 to 31 Dec. : 9 - 7.
Interiors open on request.
Parking.
Guided tours, brochures.
Recorded information.
English - German - Leaflets.
Tel. : (86) 68.70.73.

Chitry (Château).

Chitry-les-Mines - 58800.
Nevers : 60 km.
Station : Corbigny 3 km.
Private property.

An ancient fortress built on t site of a gallo-roman villa, Chi dominates the Yonne from t summit of a rocky peak. Its h seshoe shaped main building flanked by four 14th century wers. The complex was enlarg and remodelled in the 17th ce tury. Inside are Flanders a Aubusson tapestries and paintin from the Italian, Flemish a Dutch schools. There is also painted gallery called the Siby Gallery.
Open May 15 to Sept. 15 : 2 - 6 appo ment only.
Parking.
English.
Tel. : (86) 20.11.48.

Corbelin (Castle).

La Chapelle-Saint-André - 58210.
Varzy : 8 km.
Private property.

Built in the 14th century, Cor lin is situated between the fore of Couet and Arcy. Its four rou towers date from this period c in 1559 Etienne Le Muet adde terraced block linking the So towers. The building flanked parapets houses monumental f places with small columns beamed ceilings.
Grounds only.
Parking.
Tel. : (86) 29.13.96.

Giry (Château).

Giry - 58700.
Nevers : 35 km.
Private property.

Giry is a fortified dwell whose Renaissance style m block has a gallery with Go consoles unique in the region. side are beamed ceilings and thic and Louis XIII fireplaces.

BOURGOGNE

NIÈVRE/SAÔNE-ET-LOIRE

*pen July 1 to Sept. 30: 10 - 12, 2 - 5.
osed Tuesdays.
pen on request at other times.
rking.
ided tours.
l.: (86) 68.13.48.*

---

antilly (Castle).

*rbigny - 58800.
rbigny: 3 km.
tion: Corbigny 3,5 km.
s nearby.
perty of Mme Ramillon.*

On the site of an ancient villa longing to a Roman general called Lantins in the 7th century, this edieval castle was built surrounded by a moat. In the 14th century was used as a witches hiding ce.

*en July 1 to Sept. 2: 3 - 4, 5 - 6.
sed Tuesdays.
en on request out of season for ups.
king.
ded tours.
rmation in English.
nporary exhibits.
ture tours fort school groups only.
: (86) 20.01.22.*

---

ontambert (Priory).

*ntambert - 58250.
r Decize.
perty of M. de La Bruslerie.*

he ancient priory of Saint Peter tting the Romanesque church s rebuilt after a fire in the 17th tury. Once part of the priory of rity under the Benedictine rule Cluny, it has recently been restored.

*en April 1 to July 1: 10:30 - 6.
king.
: (86) 50.30.86.*

---

lemolin (Château).

*ien - 58800.
bigny: 7 km.
on: Corbigny.
perty of M. de Certaines.*

ved in by the Certaines family e 1528, Villemolin stands in a anding position over the ois valley. The main building h has been dated to the 15th ury is flanked by two 17th century round towers. The South building, erected in the 17 century has a 19th century tower, whereas the West building was entirely remodelled in the 19th century. In the entrance hall you see a 15th century monumental fireplace from the old castle. The stone staircase has an ironwork bannister and the panelling and furniture of the grand salon are Louis XVI. There is also a Neo-Gothic chapel.

*Open May 1 to Nov. 1: 10 - 12, 2 - 6.
Closed one day a week.
Parking.
Guided tours.
English - guide.
German - leaflets.
Lecture tours for school groups on request.
Tel.: (86) 20.09.86.*

SAÔNE-ET-LOIRE

AUTUN

Rolin (Town house).

*Autun - 71400.
5, rue des Blance.
Property of the commune.*

This 15th century town house was the property of th Rolin family. The three floors of rooms connected by a spiral stair case still have their original fireplaces. The building is now the home of the Rolin Museum.

*Open Jan. 1 to March 15: 10 - 12, 2 - 6.
March 16 to Sept. 30: 9:30 - 12, 2 - 6.
Oct. 1 to Nov. 15: 10 - 12, 2 - 5.
Nov. 16 to Dec. 30: 10 - 12, 2 - 4.
Closed May 1, July 14, Jan. 1, Nov. 1 and 11 Dec. 25 and Tuesdays.
Parking.
Unaccompanied visits, brochures.
English.
Concerts, temporary exhibits: sculpture.
Lectures, lecture tours for school groups only.
Tel.: (85) 52.09.76.*

Berzé-le-Châtel (Castle).

*Berzé-le-Châtel - 71960 Pierreclos.
Mâcon: 15 km.
Station: Mâcon-Loche T.G.V. 15 km.
Bus service.
Private property.*

In the 10th century the fortress of Berzé-le-Châtel defended the abbey of Cluny. Its surrounding walls with their twelve towers rise on a hillside and protect the main residence of which two blocks and two towers still exist. The edifice dates back to the 13th century. The interior, transformed during the 19th century is in Neo-Gothic style and the rectangular windows date from this period. The cut boxwood garden was laid out in the 20th century.

*Open daily May 1 to Nov. 1: 10 - 12, 2 - 5.
Parking.
Grounds only.
Tel.: (85) 36.60.83.*

BERZÉ-LA-VILLE

Chapelle aux Moines (Chapel).

*Berzé-la-Ville - 71112.
Mâcon or Cluny: 12 km.
Station: Mâcon.
Bus service.
Property of the Academy of Mâcon.*

Built at the end of the 11th century, this chapel was part of a country priory attached to the abbey of Cluny. It has preserved its barrel vaulting and wall paintings which date from the first quarter of the 12th century and show Christ with the Apostles and Martyrs.

*Open Palm Sunday to Nov. 1: 10 - 12, 2 - 6.
Closed Sunday mornings and Tuesdays.
Parking.
Unaccompanied visits, brochures.
English - German - panels or leaflets.*

Brancion (Château).

*Martailly-les-Brancion - 71700.
Tornus or Mâcon: 13 km.
Station: T.G.V. Tournus.
Property of M. de Murard.*

Built on a hill, the fortress of Brancion dominates the entire valley. It served as a ducal and then as a royal chatelleny. Its surrounding walls and towers encompass the present day village. A 10th century square keep abutts the main building which has huge fireplaces and the Beaujeu room.

*Open daily Holy Week to Nov. 11: 9 - 6,
Syndays, 10 - 12, 2 - 6.
Parking.
Unaccompanied visits, brochure.
Information pannels or leaflets.
English - German - Dutch.
Facilities for the handicapped.
Lecture tours for school children.
Tel.: (85) 47.63.63 and 51.11.41.*

SAÔNE-ET-LOIRE — 60 — BOURGOGN

Brandon (Castle).

Saint-Pierre-de-Varennes - 71670.
Le Creusot: 9 km.
Station: Le Creusot T.G.V. 10 km.
Private property.

Brandon, an ancient stronghold of the Dukes of Burgundy, was built on foundations which date from the Merovingians. Brandon has kept its five towers.
*Open July 1 to Aug. 30: 2 - 6.
Closed Wednesdays and Aug. 25.
Parking.
Guided tours.
Exhibition: Geneology.
Tel.: (85) 55.45.16.*

Chevannes (Castle).

Saint-Racho - 71800.
La Clayette: 4 km.
Station: La Clayette-Baudemont 4 km.
Bus service.
Property of M. de Noblet d'Anglure.

Given by Philip-Augustus to one lord d'Anglure, Chevannes now consists of a château with a Renaissance facade. The main building has two L-shaped whose round towers have cone-shaped roofs. The South wing has two superimposed galleries: a single carved column on the ground floor supports the wooden gallery above. The château has been undergoing restoration since 1970.
*Open daily June 1 to Aug. 2: 2:30 - 8.
Nov. 13 to Dec. 19: 2:30 - 6.
Parking.*
Unaccompanied visits, brochures.
Information panels or leaflets.
Craft show.
Temporary exhibits of contemporary arts and crafts.
Lecture tours on request for groups.
Sound and Light.
Tel.: (85) 28.17.74.

Chevigne (Priory).

Davaye - 71960.
Mâcon: 8 km.
Station: Mâcon.
Private property.

This priory was given by th king of France to the abbey Cluny in 932. It remained attache to the abbey until 1792. Its Rom nesque cloisters and 17th centu East facade still exist.
Grounds only.

Cluny (Abbey).

Cluny - 71250.
Property of the State.

The Benedictine abbey of Clu was the centre of reform that fected all of medieval Europ Founded in 909 and attached Rome, this abbey with its exce tional abbots controlled a group no less than 10 000 monks. prestige was such that it expa ded constantly reaching its heig under Saint Hugh and Peter Venerable. Unlike the new mon tery built in the 18th century th manesque abbey did not esca the ravages of the Revolution. T remains of the abbey church an model which you can see in monastery give some idea of appearance of the original, most important Christian inst

---

SAÔNE-ET-LOIRE

BRANDON

Formely a stronghold of the Dukes of Burgundy. Now a château belonging to the Montessus family.

Open July and August.
Geneology exhibit.
Tel.: (85) 55.45.16.

BOURGOGNE — SAÔNE-ET-LOIRE

on until the 16th century. Sculpture and other objects from the original site are on display in the chier Musuem and in the medieval granary.
Open April 1 to Sept. 30: 9 - 11:30, ... 6.
... 1 to.
... ided tours, brochures.
... : (85) 59.12.79.

...rmatin (Château)

...matin - 71460.
...ny: 12 km.
...tion: Le Creusot or Mâcon T.G.V.
... km.
... service.
...ate property.
...uilt between 1605 and 1608 on ... square plan of an earlier for...s, Cormatin has kept its main ...lding and one wing flanked by ...e large square pavilions. Cor...tin's mullioned windows and ...ets with their pepper pot roofs ... a medieval feeling to the fa...es that are classical in their ...position. In the middle of the ...n wing, the rose and white ...e staircase is one of the oldest ... largest of its kind. The main ...ns decorated in 1625, are ...wn as the Gilded Rooms. Here ... paneling, fireplaces, beamed ... coffered ceilings provide a ... example of a Louis XIII inte... Louis XIII, Richelieu and La...tine are among those who ...e stayed here.
...n Easter holidays: 10 - 12, 2:30 - Sat., Sun. and holidays in May and June: 10 - 12, 2:30 - 6:30.
July 1 to Oct. 31: 10 - 12, 2:30 - 7.
Parking.
Guided tours.
English - German - Italian - Dutch - Panels or leaflets.
Theatre and music festival in July and August.
Tel.: (85) 50.16.55.

Couches (Château).

Couches - 71490.
Private property.
Once Margaret of Burgundy's castle, Couches belonged to the Montagues (descendents of the Dukes of Burgundy) in the 13th century, then to the Rochechouart and Aumont families before being demolished in the 17th century. The main building was rebuilt in the 19th century in Neo-Gothic style. In 1946 the owners restored the keep and they have assembled a fine collection of objets d'art which is now on display.
Open daily July 1 to Aug. 31.
Open for groups on request April 1 to Oct. 31.
Tel.: (85) 49.68.02.

LE CREUSOT
La Verrerie (Château).

Le Creusot - 71200.
Chalon-sur-Saône: 35 km.
Station: T.G.V. Le Creusot-Montchanin 5 km.
Property of the commune.
Now the offices of the Cultural Centre for Research on Industrial Civilization, La Verrerie was previously a royal cristal works. Built in 1786, it was transformed into a private residence by the Schneider family. The Louis XVI block with its perpendicular wings has pediments and Mansard roofs. The concierge's lodge in the main courtyard in flanked by two conical forges, on of which has been turned into a theatre by the Schneider family.
Open all year: 10 - 2, 2 - 6.
Closed Sat. and Sun. mornings and all day Mondays.
Groups by appointment.
Parking.
Guided tours on request for groups and school children.
Slide shows.
Audio-visual programme on request.
English - panels of leaflets.
Permanent and temporary exhibits.
Tel.: (85) 55.01.11.

Cypierre (Château).

Volesvres - 71600.
Paray-le-Monial and Charolles: 6 km.
Station: Paray-le-Monial.
Bus service.
Private property.
Cypierre, home of the intendant of Orleans, M. de Cypierre then of general de Caulaincourt, duke of Vicenza, preserves the marks of its various stages of construction: the 14th century keep built on a fortified mound, a Renaissance loggia and a 19th century main building.
Parking.
Brochures.
Tel.: (85) 87.02.21.

Demigny (Château).

Demigny - 71150.
Beaune: 12 km.
Station: Chagny 6 km.
Private property.
Demigny was rebuilt after the Revolution by the Foudras family on the site of an earlier fortress. The main building, flanked by two pavilions has a portico with a pediment on its eastern side.
Open July 14 to Aug. 31: 2 - 6, and Sundays.
Grounds only.
Parking.
Unaccompanied visits.
Tel.: (85) 49.45.66

Digoine (Château).

Palinges - 71430.
Paray-le-Monial or Charolles: 12 km.
Private property.
Claude de Reclesme was responsible for the construction of Digoine in 1710 after demolishing the earlier fortress on the same site. The main building has a Louis XIV facade with two round towers; on the south side it has two perpendicular wings. The out buildings include a small 19th century theatre in which Sarah Bernhardt and Coquelin rehearsed L'Aiglon and where Offenbach had some of his works performed.
Open only on request for groups.
Grounds and little theatre.
Parking.
Tel.: (85) 70.20.27.

Germolles (Castle).

Mellecey - 71640.
Chalon-sur-Saône: 10 km.
Station: Chalon-sur-Saône.
Bus service.
Proprerty of M. Pinette.
At the end of the 14th century Philip the Bold commissioned the architects Drouet and Dammartin to build Germolles. The frescoes

were executed by Jehan de Beaumez and the sculpture by Jean de Marville and Claus Sluter. The residence was transformed into a fortification by Charles the Bold. The main building, the Gothic chapel and oratory facing the vaulted store room still exist. Inside are paintings from the 14th century school of Burgundy.
Open July 1 to Sept. 1: 10 - 12, 2 - 6:30.
Closed Tuesdays.
Parking.
Guided tours, brochures.
English sometimes - giude.
Lecture tours for groups.
Tel.: (85) 47.10.55.

Lavault (Château).

Neuvy-Grandchamp - 71130.
Paray-le-Monial: 30 km.
Station: Digoin 20 km.
Private property.

Lavault was built at the end of the 17th century in Charollais stone.
Open July 14 to Aug. 31: 9 - 12, 2 - 7.
Grounds only.
Tel.: (85) 85.24.46.

Lugny-lés-Charolles (Château).

Charolles - 71120.
Charolles: 6 km.
Station: Charolles.
Bus service.
Property of M. de Grammont.

Lugny was built at the end of the 18th century on the site of an ancient fortress standing on the top of a cliff overlooking the Arcone valley. It consists of a seven sided main building with two small perpendicular wings. These look onto a courtyard which is enclosed by two out-buildings and a gate. The complex is completed by an informal park and a kitchen garden.
Open on request by recommendation only.
Tel.: (85) 81.15.76.

Pierre-de-Bresse (Château).

Pierre-de-Bresse - 71270.
Chalon-sur-Saône/Dôle.
Property of the department.

In 1680 Claude Thyard built this château on the site of an ancient fortress. The main building is separated from the out buildings by a moat which is crossed by a drawbridge. This U-shaped brick building is framed by four round towers and its gate and balustrades are in fine iron work. One facade looks out on to formal gardens and an animal reserve. The château now houses the Economusee de la Bresse Bourguignonne.
Open June 16 to 30 Sept.: 2 - 6.
Closed Tuesdays.
Groups on request.
Parking.
Unaccompanied visits.
Temporary exhibits.
Lecture tours for school groups.

Rully (Castle).

Rully - 71150.
Chalon-sur-Saône or Beaune: 20 km.
Station: Chagny 5 km.
Private property.

Rully was originally a 13th century fortress with a square keep, three round towers and surrounding walls which commanded the entire region. By the 15th century the Saint-Leger family had constructed residential buildings on three sides of the inner courtyard. The castle and park still belong to the Rully family.
Open April 15 to Nov. 1: 10:30 - 12, 2 - 6, Sat.-Sun.
Interiors on request for groups of at least 15.
Grounds: guide.
Interiors shown by a member of the family.
English - German - short history.
Tel.: (85) 87.20.42.

Sercy (Château).

Sercy - 71460.
Châlon-sur-Saône: 27 km.
Station: Châlon-sur-Saône or Montchanin 30 km.
Bus service.
Private property.

Built in the 12th century, Sercy is one of the regions best preserved medieval fortresses. It was enlarged in the 15th century, and its residential buildings, flanked by various towers, enclose the inner courtyard. The 15th century wooden tower has remained intact.
Open April 1 to Nov. 1 by request.
Grounds only.
Parking.
Guided tours.
English - Spanish - German.
Tel.: (85) 47.67.68.

Saint-Aubin-sur-Loire (Château).

Saint-Aubin-sur-Loire - 71140.
Bourbon-Lancy: 7 km.
Private property.

A classic 18th century building constructed by Edme Vernique for Jean-Baptiste des Gallois de l Tour, Saint-Aubin occupies a commanding position on the Loire The cut stone facades both have peristyles with Ionic pilaster crowned by a pediment. Period tapestries and furniture can be seen inside the château.
Open July 8 to Sept. 1: 2 - 5.
Closed Tuesdays.
Parking.
English.
Tel.: (85) 53.91.96.

SAINT-POINT
Lamartine's house.

Saint-Point - 71630.
Near Cluny.
Station: Mâcon 25 km.
Private property.

The poet Lamartine inherite the château de Saint-Point in 18 and lived here until his death 1870. Between 1830 and 1845, built a main block with a terra which connected two Charolais wers, remnants of the former m dieval castle. This castle defend one of the valleys which provid access to the abbey of Cluny. T museum has a collection dedic ted to the famous poet includi his bedroom with its Spanish le ther hangings, books and curi A nearby Romanesque cha contains his tomb.
Open March 1 to Nov. 15: 10 - 12, 6.
Closed Sundays.
Parking.
Guided tours.
Tel.: (85) 50.50.30.

Sully (Château).

Sully - 71360.
Autun: 17 km.
Station: Autun.

ANCY-LE-FRANC

YONNE

An Italian palace in Burgundy.

This Renaissance château is attributed to the architect Serlio. Twenty-five sumptuously decorated and furnished rooms are open to the public.
Plus : a huge Romantic park, an automobile museum, exhibits of ancient arts and crafts.
Rooms can be hired for receptions.

Open daily April 1 to November 1.
Concerts in July and August.
Tel. : (86) 75.14.63.

BOIS-LE-ROI

YONNE

A perfect example of 17th century Burgundian architecture, Bois-le-Roi once belonged to the archbishops of Sens and then was given as a fief to Jean-Baptiste Couste, squire to King Louis XVI.
Rooms to rent receptions, weddings, seminars... in a Romantic and family atmosphere.

Located in Nailly (an hour and a half from Paris by motorway, 7 km from Sens).
Tel. : (86) 65.53.61 and (1) 354.45.91.
Open by appointment only.

SAÔNE-ET-LOIRE/YONNE — 64 — BOURGOGNE

Bus service.
Private property.
Nestled at the bottom of the Dree valley lie the four blocks and courtyard of Sully. Four towers at each corner and facades dating from different periods are surrounded by a moat. The West facade is Renaissance, the North is 18th century and the South and East facades were remodelled in the 19th century in Neo-Renaissance style. This large château was built by Gaspard de Saulx-Tavannes and has received numerous famous visitors including Madame de Sévigné. Marshal Mac-Mahon was born here.
Open daily Palm Sunday to Sept. 30: 9 - 6.
Grounds only.
Parking.
Unaccompanied visits, brochure.
Tel. : (85) 82.10.27.

Tramayes (Castle).

Tramayes - 71630.
Mâcon : 25 km.
Station : Mâcon T.G.V.
Private property.
Tramayes was built in the 14th century and fortified in the 16th. Its main building on a rectangular plan has three towers. Restored in the 19th century, the castle has undergone certain transformations: the moat has been filled in, the surrounding walls pulled down openings made and the interior decoration renewed. The park dates from the 19th century.
Open daily Jan. 1 to Dec. 31.
Parking.
Grounds only.
Tel. : (85) 50.50.85.

YONNE

Ancy-le-Franc (Château).

Ancy-le-Franc - 89160.
Tonnerre: 16 km.
Station : Ancy-le-Franc 2 km.
Property of M. Guyot.
Ancy-le-Franc is a veritable Italian palace set in the Armançon valley, built in 1546 for Armand de Clermont, comte de Tonnerre according to plans by Serlio. A suite of bedrooms, salons, and galleries is set around an inner courtyard richly decorated with sculpture. Many of these rooms were decorated in the 16th century by Primaticcio and his pupils. Henri III, Henri IV, Louis XIII and Louis XIV all stayed here. The château was once the property of Louis XIV's minister Louvois.
Open April 1 to Nov. 1: 10 - 12, 2 - 7.
Parking.
Guided tours in some parts of the château.
Information panels or leaflets.
Brochures available.
Automobile museum and exhibit of lost crafts in the attics.
Tel. : (86) 75.14.63.

AUXERRE
Saint-Germain (Abbey).

Auxerre - 89000.
Station : Auxerre 2 km.
Property of the commune.
Auxerre's Saint-Germain Abbey is one of the oldest in France. It was founded in the 6th century by Queen Clotilde, wife of Clovis. The crypt is the oldest part of the building dating from the 9th century and houses many sarcophagi, including that of Saint-Germain. These are of great interest both to the historian and archeologist. The crypt's fine frescoes depict the martyrdom of Saint Stephen are one of the few examples of Carolingian wall painting to have survived. The medieval church itself, clearly inspired by the cathedral of Saint Stephen of Auxerre, has a 17th century cloister. The 12th century cloister is currently being restored.
Open Jan 2 to Dec. 31: 9 - 12, 2 - 6.
Guided tours every half hour.
Closed Tuesdays and holidays.
Parking.
Panels, brochures.
Information in English and German.
Concerts, temporary exhibits.
Tel. : (86) 51.09.74.

Bontin (Château).

Les Ormes - 89110.
Auxerre : 30 km.
Station : Laroche-Mijennes 25 km.
Private property.
Bontin has a brick facade with a projecting portico crowned by a semi-circular pediment dating from the reign of Louis XIV. It is surrounded by a moat. Its L-shaped wings give onto the courtyard and have triangular pediments with windows. The marriage of Sully to Anne de Courtenay took place in the main salon here.
Open July 1 to Aug. 31: 10 - 12, 2 - 6.
Parking.
Guided tours.
English - Swedish - guides.

Boutissaint (Priory and Park).

Treigny - 89520.
Auxerre : 60 km.
Station : Cosne-sur-Loire 30 km.
Private property.
The ancient priory of Boutissaint founded in the year 1000 stands in the heart of the forest of Puisaye. With its two corner towers and its central tower it is characteristic of the Burgundian manor house. Its square courtyard is finished by tower pavilions on each corner. The edifice is covered with the flat tile roof typical of the region. The park of Saint Hubert contains regional fauna.
Open daily Jan. 1 to Dec. 31 : 7:30 am 8 pm.
Gorunds only.
Parking.
Information panels, brochures.
Photographic safaris, horn concerts and hunting shows in summer.
Tel. : (86) 74.71.28.

Chastenay (Manor).

Val-Sainte-Marie.
Arcy-sur-Cure - 89270.
Near Avallon and Vezelay.
Station : Arcy-sur-Cure 1,5 km.
Property of M. de la Varende.
Chastenay has belonged to the same family since its foundation 1080. It was the manor of the Arnays, the ill-fated lovers of the daughters-in-Law of Philip the Fair. The house then passed to the Huguenot David de Loron who pillaged the treasury of Saint-Germain-l'Auxerrois and hid its golden shrine which was never found. The building was fortified during the 13th century and its facade is decorated with 16th century carvings.
Open daily 10 - 12, 2 - 6, in season.
Off season for groups only.
Closed Sunday mornings.
Parking.
Lecture tour by the owner.
Panels, brochures.
Facilities for the handicapped.
Information in English.
Tel. : (86) 40.90.63 in season 40.92.24 out of season.

Druyes (Castle).

Druyes-les-Belles-Fontaines - 89560.
Auxerre : 33 km.

BOURGOGNE — 65 — YONNE

...ation: Coulanges-sur-Yonne 11 km.
...rivate property.

On a hill overlooking the valley and the ruins of Druyes castle, ...sidence of the comtes d'Auxerre ... de Nevers. The model for a se...es of castles built at the end of ...e reign of Philip-Augustus, this ...quare shaped castle was trans...rmed into a fortress. The main ...uilding has Romanesque decora...on. It was here that Pierre ...ourtenay, comte d'Auxerre et de ...evers received the ambassadors ...ho came to offer him the Impe...l crown of Constantinople in ...18.

...pen July 1 to Sept. 15 Sat., Sun. and ...olidays.
...arking.
...uided tours.
...mporary art exhibits.
...l.: (86) 41.57.86.

...leurigny (Château).

...eurigny - 89260.
...ns: 15 km.
...ation: Sens.
...operty of M. de Castellane Esparron.

Pulled down at the end of the ...undred Years War then partly re...ilt in the 16th century, Fleurigny still has its 13th century North facade. The inner courtyard has kept none of its medieval austerity: its Renaissance facades are decorated with coloured brickwork. The Renaissance chapel has sculptures and stained glass windows designed by Jean Cousin.

Open April 7 to Sept. 23: 2:30 - 5:30.
Sat., Sun. and holidays.
Every afternoon in August, except Wednesdays.
On request for groups of at least 30 the rest of the year.
Parking.
Guided tours, brochures.
English - German - Dutch - Spanish - leaflets.
Tel.: (86) 86.65.38.

Grandchamp (Château).

Grandchamp - 89350.
Auxerre: 35 km.
Bus service.
Private property.

Built on a rectangular terrace encircled by a moat by the Courtenay family in the 16th century, Grandchamp has both a forecourt and outbuildings. The main facade has an entry pavilion flanked by two round towers. The brick and flint decoration can be found on all facades from the main block to the wings and outbuildings.

Open year round.
Grounds only.
Parking.
Unaccompanied visits.
Tel.: (86) 45.71.21.

Nuits (Château).

Nuits-sur-Armançon - 89390.
Tonnerre: 27 km.
Station: Nuits-sous-Ravières 1 km.
Bus service.
Private property.

Built by Claude de Chenu in the mid-16th century, Nuits has a main block flanked by two pavilions. Of the two Renaissance fa-

CHASTENAY MANOR HOUSE — YONNE

You will be charmed by the unusual and unexpected lecture tour given by the owner.
You will come to understand the hidden meanings of the sculpture of this Templar residence and will be initiated into the Science of the Golden Number, key to the harmony of architecture in the Middle Ages.
You will be shown symbols of man and matter, and introduced to the search of the philosophers's stone and begin to reach a new level of knowledge thruogh the interpretation of these esoteric Burgundian sculptures.

cades, the West is decorated with Corinthian pilasters and arched pediments, the East is of more austere military style. The interiors still have their period fireplaces, panelling and tapestries.
Open May 15 to Oct. 31: 9 - 11:30, 4 - 6.
Parking.
Guided tours, brochures.
Information panels and leaflets.
Tel.: (86) 55.70.30.

Prunoy (Château).

Prunoy-Carny - 89120.
Joigny: 23 km.
Station: Joigny.
Property of M. Roumilhac.

This large 18th century construction has kept only one round tower form the old medieval manor house built in the 14th century. The main building is prolonged by two wings with two square towers attached looking onto the inner courtyard. The facade overlooking the park supports high pavilions flanked by square turrets with slate roofs. Guillaume de Crève-Cœur was given the fief when Burgundy was attached to France and he built the first château here in 1510. An 18th century tax collector decorated the ground floor rooms with wood panelling and installed the panels in the summer salon which show hunting scenes attributed to Oudry.
Open July 1 to Aug. 31.
Parking.
Brochures available.
Sound and Light.
Temporary exhibits.
Guided tours.
Tel.: (86) 63.66.91.

Ratilly (Château).

Treigny - 89820.
Auxerre: 45 km.
Station: Cosne 35 km.
Bus service.
Private property.

Ratilly was built in the 13th century. A perfect square in plan, it is made up of stone and sandstone buildings around a courtyard with round towers with cone shaped roofs at each corner. Entrance is through a forecourt surrounded by a moat with a draw-bridge. A 16th century keep towers above the bridge. The castle now houses a museum of regional pottery and a centre for contemporary art.
Open daily June 25 to Sept. 15: 10 - 6.
Sept. 16 to June 24: 2 - 5.
Closed Sundays.
Parking.
Recommended itinerary.
Information panels, leaflets.
English - Italian.
Brochures available.
Concerts, Contemporary Art Centre, Painting and sculpture June 25 to Sept. 11.
Pottery workshops July 15 to Sept 1.

Saint-Fargeau (Castle).

Saint-Fargeau - 89170.
Auxerre: 45 km.
Station: Auxerre.
Bus service.
Property of M. Guyot.

Fief of the bishops of Auxerre in th 10th century and property of Jacques Cœur in the 15th, Saint-Fargeau was the residence of the Grande Mademoiselle in exile in the 17th century. It with slate roofs and six monumental towers. Commissioned to rebuild the château in 1650, the architect Le Vau kept the 15th century towers and added a classical main block in the latest style.
Open April 1 to Nov. 1: 10 - 12, 2 - 7.
Parking.
Guided tours.
Information pannels, leaflets.
English - German - guides - panels o leaflets.
Temporary craft exhibits.
Tel.: (86) 74.05.67.

SENS
Palais Synodal

Sens - 89100.
133 bis, rue des Déportés-de-la-Résis tance.
Property of the State.

Since the earliest Christia times, Sens has been a majo episcopal centre. This palace buil at the beginning of the 13th cen tury by Archbishop Gautier Cornu housed the episcopal court. Loca ted next to the cathedral squar and archbishop's palace it still ha its court room above the jail. Th huge room has ribbed vaultin and is lit by high arcatures. Th building was restored by Violle le-Duc in 1849 and now houses collection of objets d'art from th 13th to the 17th century.
Open April 1 to Sept. 30: 9 - 12, 2 - Oct. 1 to March 31: 10 - 12, 2 - 4.
Closed Tuesdays.
Guided tours.
Tel.: (86) 65.05.30.

Tanlay (Château).

Tanlay - 89430.
Tonnerre: 9 km.
Station: Tanlay 1,5 km.
Property of M. de La Chauvinière.

This is one of the most impo tant châteaux in Burgundy, bo for its history — Admiral de Co gny and Particelli are associate with it — and for the beauty of i architecture — a fine example the integration of Renaissance an Louis XIII styles. It was complete by the architect Pierre le Mue one of the founders of the class cal style. After passing through th little château inspired by Flore tine palaces, you arrive at th moat and the main château whos splendid interiors date from th time of Particelli d'Emery wh made a fortune under Louis X Inside the Tower of the League a vaults decorated by artists fro the school of Fontainebleau.
Open Easter to Nov. 1: 9:15 - 11:5 2:15 - 5:15.
Closed Tuesdays.
Out of season open on request groiups.
Parking.
Information in English and German.
Brochures available.
Tel.: (86) 75.70.61.

SAINT-FARGEAU

YONNE

15th and 17th century.
Furniture, Horse Museum, Extensive grounds.

Rooms to hire for receptions.
Nightly historical history pageant in July and August.
Open daily April 1 to November 1.
Tel. : (86) 74.05.67.

TANLAY

YONNE

One of the finest examples of Renaissance architecture in Burgundy

Thizy (Castle).

Thizy - 89420.
Avallon: 15 km.
Station: Avallon.
Bus service.
Private property.

Formerly the priory of the abbey of Moutiers Saint Jean which was fortified in the 12th century, Thizy was damaged during the Hundred Years War and then rebuilt in the 15th century. The old priory storeroom with its ribbed vaulting still stands. The towers date from the 15th century and are joined by a sentryway.

Open on request.
Parking.
Unaccompanied visits, brochures.
German - English.
Temporary exhibits (sculpture).
Tel.: (86) 32.11.71.

Temblay (Château).

Fontenoy-en-Puisaye - 89520.
Auxerre: 30 km.
Station: Auxerre.
Bus service.

Built on the top of a hill the vast Louis XIII manor house of Temblay dominates the surrounding countryside. Characteristic of the 17th century is the use of brick and stone in the main block flanked by round and square towers and in the L-shaped wings of the outbuildings. For four centuries the château belonged to the du Deffand family whose most famous member Mme du Deffand held a famous literary salon in the 18th century. Today the château houses a collection of ancient tools.

Open April 1 to Nov. 1: 10 - 12, 2 - 7.
Parking.
Unaccompanied visit, brochure.
Temporary exhibits.
Tel.: (86) 44.02.18.

Vausse (Priory).

Châtel-Gérard - 89310.
Auxerre: 35 km.
Station: Avallon 30 km.
Private property.

Vausse was the first monastery attached to the priory of Val du Choux and was founded by Ansenic VI of Montreal and Nicolette de Vergy in 1220. The hostel has remained intact and the small Romanesque cloister has kept its water system. During the Revolution the priory was turned into a ceramics works and then bought by an individual in 1806.

Open April 1 to Sept. 31: 2 - 7, Wed., Sat., Sun.

THIZY

YONNE

15 km from Avallon.

Thizy is undergoing complete restoration and will soon recover its original appearance. Michel Roetzer has a Burgundian stone sculpture workshop in the castle.
Open on request. Tel.: (86) 32.11.71. Statues, fountains, monumental fireplaces.

Detail of the Renaissance Saint-Florentin foutain. This public fountain, once famous, has been entirely remade by Michel Roetzer in his workshop at Thizy based on an old engraving and pieces from the Cluny Museum in Paris.

Parking.
Guided tours.
Information panels or leaflets.
Tel.: (86) 55.86.84.

Villeneuve-sur-Yonne (Sens and Joigny Gates).

Villeneuve-sur-Yonne - 89500.
Sens: 13 km.
Station: Villeneuve-sur-Yonne.
Bus service.
Property of the commune.

In 1163 Louis VII created the fortified new town of Villeneuve to act as a defence against a possible attack from his powerful vassals. The horseshoe shaped surrounding walls opened onto a river and had five gates. Only two the gates of Sens and Joigny, still exist dating from the 12th century. The main block and the turrets were restored in the 16th century. The Louis le Gros tower is the only one of the seven towers of the walls to remain almost intact. This huge keep, measuring 17 meters in diameter with 4 meter thick walls consisted of three floors of vaulted rooms.

Open on request only.
Parking.
Guided tours or unaccompanied visits.
Information panels or leaflets.
Tel.: (86) 87.07.45.

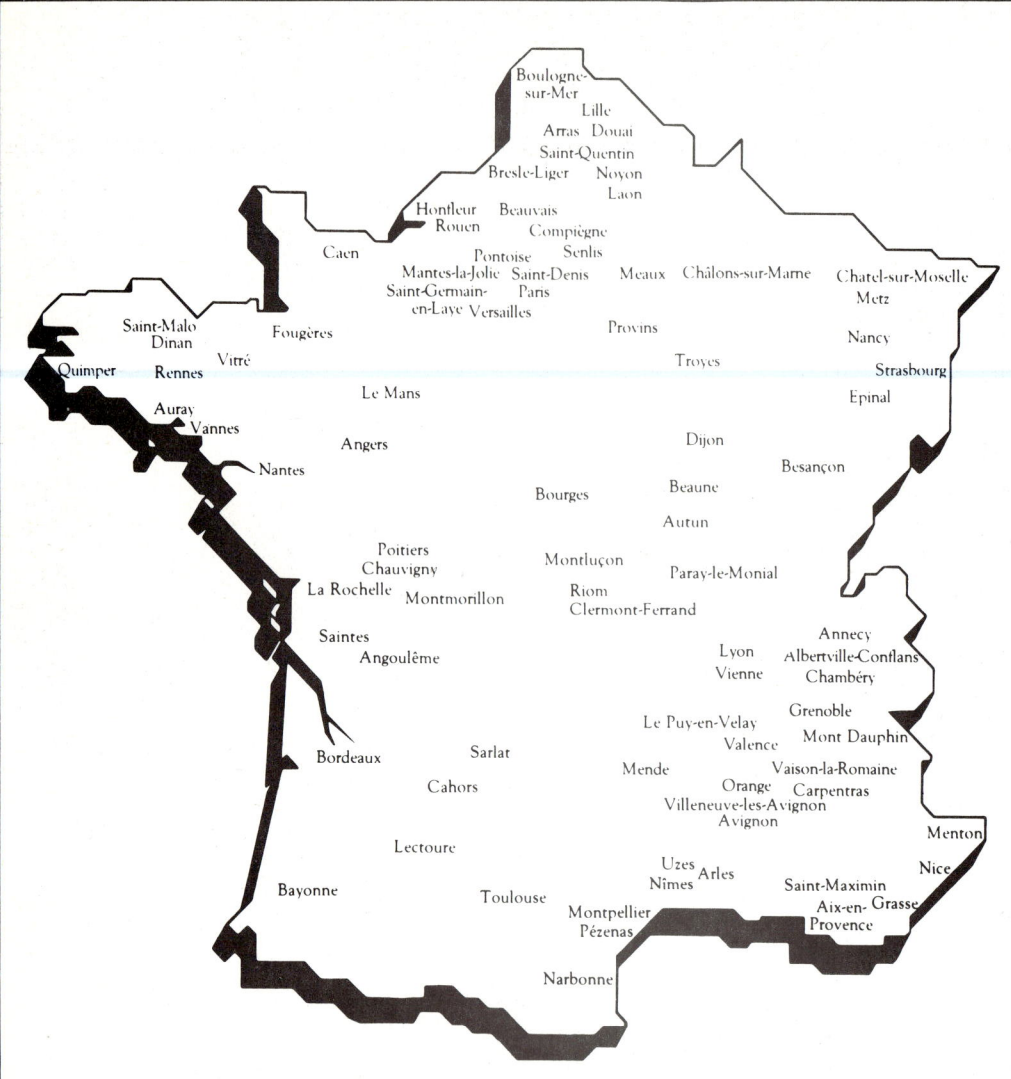

DISCOVER FRANCE AND ITS OLD CITIES
with the guided tours of the Caisse Nationale des Monuments Historiques

When travelling in France during your holidays, discover 100 Old Cities and their art treasures with the guided tours organised by the Caisse Nationale des Monuments Historiques. Daily tours are organised and last one hour or more. Ask for timetable and details in the Tourist Offices of cities like : AIX-EN-PROVENCE, ARLES, ARRAS, AVIGNON, BEAUNE, BEAUVAIS, LAON, LA ROCHELLE, LYON, METZ, MONTLUÇON, MONTPELLIER, NANCY, NANTES, ROUEN, STRASBOURG, VERSAILLES...

ENGLISH SPEAKING GUIDES.

Hôtel de Sully
62, rue Saint-Antoine 75004 PARIS
Tél. : 274.22.22.

CIVIS

BRETAGNE

CÔTES-DU-NORD, FINISTÈRE, ILE-ET-VILAINE, MORBIHAN.

- ■ castle, château, manor house
- ● abbey, priory
- ▲ garden, park
- ★ town house, famous men house, farm, mill...
- ○ city

SAINT-MALO

- ■ Château
- ■ Tour Solidor

VITRE

- ■ Château
- ● Monastère St Nicolas

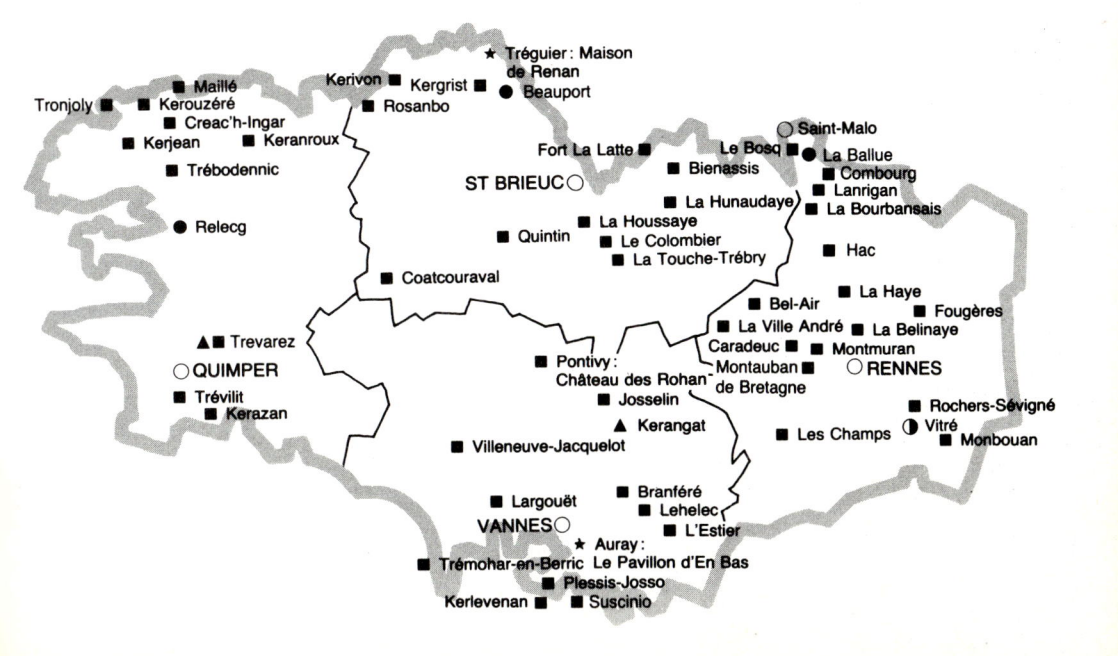

BRETAGNE

CÔTES-DU-NORD

Beauport (Abbey).

Kérity-Paimpol - 22500.
Perros-Guirec : 35 km.
Saint-Brieuc : 45 km.
Station : Guingamp-Paimpol 2 km.
Bus service.
Private property.

Beauport is a 12th century abbey founded by the Premonstratentians of Lucerne on land given by a local lord. The nave and transept give the church its striking appearance. Over the centuries the cloister has been transformed into a garden and is between the walls of the monks house and another building which has been completely preserved. The refectory has also kept its beauty and the whole complex looks out over the beach.

Open Easter weekend, Pentecost weekend, June 15 to Sept. 15 : 9:30 - 12:30, 2 - 7.
Grounds only.
Parking.
Brochures avalable.

Temporary exhibits.
Guided tours.

Bienassis (Château).

Erqy - 22430.
Saint-Brieuc : 25 km.
Station : Lamballe 17 km.
Bus service.
Property of M. de Kerjégu.

Of the original 15th century fortress Bienassis has kept its moat and crenelated walls flanked by two towers. The main building, destroyed during the Fronde was rebuilt in the 17th century : witness the high slate roofs and the classical pediments. The main courtyard and the formal gardens date from the same period as do the staircase, fireplaces and furniture.

Open June 6 to Sept. 17 : 10:30 - 12:30, 2 - 6:30.
Closed Sundays and holidays.
Open on request for groups all year.
Parking.
Guided tours.
English - German - Italian - panels.
English guides for groups by appontment.
Lecture tours for school groups on request.
Tel. : (96) 72.22.03.

Coatcouraval (Manor House).

Saint-Michel-en-Glomel - 22110.
Quimper : 65 km.
Private property.

Built towards the middle of the 15th century, Coarcouraval became the model for manor houses in the West of Brittany. Poulgi and Navez are modelled on this building. The main facade with its three asymmetrical windows i crowned by three imposing sculpted dormer windows. On the other side of the building the roof reaches further down and contain a watch tower with a pepper pot roof. In the garden are three springs.

Open July 1 to Sept. 1.
Tours by the owners.
Parking.
Tel. : (96) 29.09.61.

Le Colombier (Manor House).

Henon - 22150.
Saint-Brieuc : 16 km.
Property of M. de Lorgeril.

In the 15th century Le Colombier was built in a Romantic spo

CÔTES-DU-NORD

BEAUPORT ABBEY
13th century abbey.

35 km from Perros-Guirec and 45 km from Saint-Brieuc. Open at Pentecost and from June 15 to September 15 daily 9:30 - 12:30 and 2 - 7. Out of season on request.

on the edge of a three-sheltered ake. Certain sections were added n the 17th century.
Open on request.
Grounds only.
Parking.
Tel.: (40) 20.00.03.

Hac (Château).

Le Qiou-Evran - 22630.
Dinan: 15 km.
Station: Rennes 40 km.
Bus service.
Property of M. and Mme Deceneux.

This 15th century manor house consists of a rectangular building extended and flanked by 5 towers. Inside is Gothic and Renaissance furniture and in particular a collection of chests which date from the 15th and 17th centuries. At the beginning of the 15th century Hac was the residence of constable Arthur de Richemont.
Open April 22 to Sept. 30: 2:30 - 6:30.
Closed Mondays.
Parking.
Unaccompanied visits.
Information pannels, brochures.
Audiovisual programme.
Information: English - German - Italian.
Tel.: (90) 83.41.81.

La Houssaye (Château).

Quessoy - 22120.
Saint-Brieuc: 12 km.
Station: Saint-Brieuc 12 km.
Private property.

Built in the 18th century La Houssaye is classical in style. Over 50 meters long, the château is built in cut stone on a rectangular plan with Mansard roofs. It has an old granite dovecote and a chapel built in the 19th century with 15th century material. La Houssaye is set in extensive grounds.
Open July 20 to Aug. 31: 10 - 12, 3 - 7.
Closed August 15.
Parking.
Grounds only.
English - Spanish.
Tel.: (96) 42.30.04.

La Hunaudaye (Castle).

Pledeliac - 22270.
Lamballe : 15 km.
Station : Lamballe on Plancoët 15 km.
State property.

La Hunaudaye lies nestled in a valley. It was rebuilt in the 14th century by the lords of Tournemine. The granite walls are flanked by round towers, of which the largest acts a keep. The two smallest towers are part of the original 13th century castle. The castle which is said to have received royal visits from Anne of Brittany and Francois I was demolished during the revolution.
Open July 1 to Aug. 31: 10 - 1, 3 - 7.
Easter to Jund 30 and Sept. 1 to 30:Sundays and holidays, 3 - 7.
On request out of season.
Parking.
Guided tours, brochures.
Information panels, leaflets.
Dutch - German - pannels or leaflets.
Facilities for the handicapped.
Tel.: (96) 34.12.55.

Kergrist (Château).

Ploubezre - 22300.
Lannion: 8 km.
Station: Kerauzern 1 km.
Bus service.
Property of M. Huon de Penanster.

The oldest part of this château dates from the 15th century. The facade is spread out between asymmetrical turrets which have dormer windows and pinnacles. Transformed in the 18th century, the facade now has a classical pediment with a double escutcheon. The etage noble is connected to the terrace by a superb double staircase.
Open July 1 to Sept. 2, 2 - 6.
Close-Mondays and July 22.
Interiors and grounds.
Facilities for the handicapped.
Guided tours of the interiors.
Tel.: (96) 38.91.44.

Kerivon (Château).

Lannion - 22300.
Station: Lannion.
Bus service.
Private property.
Kerivon remains the property of one of the oldest families of the Tregor area. The 18th century château and stables are set in a 75 hectare park which has five artificial lakes and walks bordered by age old trees.
Open on request for groups (interiors).
Unaccompanied visits of the park.
Tel.: (96) 37.07.44.

La Latte (Fort).

Plevenon-Fréhel - 22240.
Dinan: 44 km.
Station: Lamballe 32 km.
Bus service.
Private property.

La Latte fort was founded by the lords of Goyon towards the middle of the 14th century. On a rocky crest overlooking the sea, the castle walls flanked by towers surrond a round keep. Two deep crevices separating the castle from the coast are crossed by drawbridges. Abandoned and pulled down during the 16th century, the fort was restored on the orders of Louis XIV who used it to protect the coast.
Open March 28 to April 25, week-end in May and June 1 to Sept. 30: 10 - 12:30, 2:30 - 6:30.
Groups on request.
Parking.
Guided tours, brochures, books.
Information panels, leaflets.
English - Spanish - pannels or leaflets.
Tel.: (96) 41.40.31.

Quintin (Château).

Quintin - 22800.
Saint-Brieuc: 18 km.
Station: Quintin or Saint-Brieuc.
Bus service.
Private property.

Begun in 1645 by the marquise de la Maussaye, sister of the marechal de Turenne, Quintin was never finished. Its impressive base dominates the valley and the grounds. The out-buildings built in the main courtyard in the 17th century were transformed into the château in the 18th century by the Choiseul-Praslin family.
Open daily (grounds only).

Rosanbo (Château).

Lanvellec-Plouaret - 22420.
Lannion: 17 km.
Private property.

The fortified terraces are all that remain of the ancient feudal castle which belonged to the Coskaer de Rosanbo family since 1050. The Renaissance château, arranged around a closed courtyard had its large pavilions remodelled in the 17th century and then restored in the 19th century. Renaissance and 17th century furniture, tapestries and a library of rare books fill the interiors. The formal garden has tree lined walks.

Open daily April 1 to April 8: 2 - 6.
Week-ends and holidays April 8 to june 30: 2 - 6.
Daily July 1 to Sept. 2: 10 - 12, 2 - 6.
On request for groups of at least 40 daily from April 1: 10 - 12, 2 - 6.
Parking.
Guided tours, brochures.
English - German - Dutch - panels of leaflets.
Tel.: (35) 41.01.00, 35.47.34 and (96) 35.18.77.

La Touche-Trébry (Château).

Trébry - 22510.
Saint-Brieuc: 30 km.
Station: Lamballe 15 km.
Private property.

Christophe de La Roche, governor of Moncontour, chose the site of an old manor house to build his château at the end of the 16th century. The gate with its parapets is framed by two large round towers with onion domes. The main building encloses the inner courtyard with its two perpendicular wings used for agricultural storage. It has onion domed turrets at each corner.

Open July 1 to Aug. 31: 2:30 - 6:30.
Closed Sundays and holidays.
Open on request out of season.
Parking.
Guided tours, brochures.
Leaflets.
English - German.
Tel.: (96) 42.78.55.

TRÉGUIER
Renan's House

Tréguier - 22223.
Paimpol: 15 km.
Property of the State.

Ernest Renan was born on February 28 1823 in a half-timbered Breton house which was built at the end of the 16th century. The facade that looks onto the street has two stories and is a corbelled construction. Althougt the writer only lived here for the first fifteen years of his life he always remained attached to his home and returned here for his holidays. The interior has been designed to evoke various stages in Renan's life: his childhood, adolescence and adulthood. You can see the writer's birthplace with its granite fireplace and closed bed, the schoolboy's room in the attic with its little desk and a replica of Renan's study at the College de France.

Open April 1 to Sept. 30: 10 - 12, 2 - 7.
Parking.
Tel.: (96) 92.45.63.

FINISTÈRE

Créac'h-Ingar (Manor House).

Tréflaouénan - 29225.
Saint-Pol-de-Léon: 8 km.
Private property.

Pillaged in the 16th century during the troubles of the League this manor house is now being restored.
Unaccompanied visits.

Keranroux (Château).

Ploujean-Morlaix - 29210.
Station: Morlaix 2 km.
Private property.

The main building of this château is made of the blue stone of the region. Inside the salon is decorated with large hunting scenes painted after Oudry. One room is furnished in typical Breton style.

Open July 15 to Sept. 1.
Guided tours of the interiors. Information in English.
Tel.: (98) 72.03.27.

Kerazan (Manor House).

Loctudy - 29125.
Quimper: 22 km.
Station: Quimper.
Bus service.
Property of the Institut de France.

Home of the lords of Loctudy, Kerazan has a 16th century perpendicular wing and an 18th century building. Inside is a collection of 18th and 19th century furniture and paintings and drawings from the 16th to 20th centuries, from the school of Fontainebleau to Maurice Denis.

Open June 1 to Sept. 15: 10 - 12, 2 - 6.
Closed Tuesdays.
Groups on request.
Parking.
Catalogues on loan for visitors.
English - German - catalogues.
Brochures available.
Temporary exhibits: crafts, paintings, scultpure, photography.
Tel.: (98) 87.40.40.

Kerjean (Château).

Plouzevède - 29225.
Morlaix: 30 km.
Station: Morlaix.
Property of the State.

Louis XIII considered Kerjean one of the most beautiful châteaux in his kingdom. It is an impressive Renaissance building, both granite fortress and elegant residence. Built in the 16th century, the château is protected by walls, the first acting as ramparts, the second formed by the three main blocks themselves.
Entrance is through an impressive gateway.

Open April 1 to Sept. 30: 9 - 12, 2 - 6.
Oct. 1 to March 31: 9 - 12, 2 - 5.
Closed Tuesdays.
Parking.
Guided tours, brochures.
Panels.
English - German.
Tel.: (98) 69.97.03.

KERAZAN MANOR

FINISTÈRE

To the West of the river Pont-l'Abbé, Kerazan manor house built in the 16th century and partially rebuilt in the 18th century, rises majestically in the heart of its spacious grounds. Its picture collection includes works from a variety of schools from Mabuse to Joseph Vernet. The paintings are hung in the setting of a home which is still inhabited.

KERJEAN

FINISTÈRE

Today a museum of Breton art, this Renaissance building once belonged to one of the most important families of the region who made it a château « worthy of a king ».

Kérouzéré (Castle).

Sibril - 29250.
Morlaix : 30 km.
Station : Saint-Pol-de-Léon 8 km.
Bus services.
Private property.

Built in 1425 by Jean de Kerouzéré cup bearer to duke Jean V, this is a good example of military achitecture of the 15 th century. Built on a rectangular plan, the granite complex has round towers at three of its towers and a square pavilion built in the 17th century after the wars of the League at the fourth corner. Inside is a collection of period furniture.
Interiors open by request only.
Unaccompanied visits of the grounds.
Parking.
Guided tours.
English - German - Leaflets.
Tel. : (98) 29.96.05.

Maillé (Château).

Plouvenez-Lochrist - 29221.
Morlaix : 30 km.
Private property.

Built around 1570 as an extension to a small manor house, Maillé consists of a square shaped Renaissance pavilion whose three stories are decorated by the three orders and a 17th century main building which has kept its Mansard roof. Inside are 16th and 18th century staircases and Louis XIII fireplaces and murals.
Open June 15 to Sept. 30 : 10 - 12, 3 - 5.
Closed Mon., Fri., Sat., Sun.
Parking.
Grounds unaccompanied.
Interiors on request only by appointment.
Guided tours.
Tel. : (98) 61.44.68.

Le Releg (Abbey).

Plounéour-Menez - 29223.
Morlaix : 18 km.
Station : Morlaix.
Private property.

Built on the site of an ancient monastery, Releg is one of the thirteen Cistercian abbeys founded in Brittany by Saint Bernard. Consecrated in 1132, its Romanesque church has survived despite the transformations of the 16th, 17th and 18th centuries. The Chapter house and refectory are ruined. The main court yard is preceded by two tall pillars.
Open daily 8 - 6.
Parking.
Celtic music festival in august.

Trébodennic (Manor House).

Ploudaniel - 29260.
Landerneau : 12 km.
Station : Landerneau.
Bus service from Brest airport : 15 km.
Property of M. P. Louboutin-Croc.

Built in 1580 by Alain de Poulpry, dean of the chapter of the collegiate church of Folgoat, Trebodennic has retained certain original features such as the outer doorway made of highly carved granite which matches its window. Inside is a huge columned fireplace.
Open April 1 to Sept. 20, 8 - 12.
Parking.
English.
Tel. : (98) 83.61.46.

Trevarez (Château and Park).

Saint-Goazec - 29163.
Châteauneuf-du-Faou : 6 km.
Quimper : 25 km.
Station : Rosporden 25 km.
Bus service.
Property of the département.

This château was built between 1894 and 1906 in rose Kernaston granite and brick. Situated on a rock dominating the entire region it has one hundred rooms. It was badly damaged during the Second World War. At that time the 75 hectares of grounds and the outbuildings were transformed and are today used for cultural activities. The Eastern section of the grounds were laid out in the English style and include camelias, azelias and rhododendrons unique in this part of France.
Open daily May 1 to Sept. 30 : 1 - 7.
April, Oct., Nov., Sat., Sun., holidays : 2 - 6.
Dec., Jan., Feb., March, Sun., holidays : 2 - 6.
Closed Tuesdays.
Parking.
Groups by appointment.
Guided tours, brochures.
Concerts, temporary exhibits.
Tel. : (98) 81.74.95.

Trévilit (Manor House).

Plonéour-Lanvern - 29120.
Pont-Labbé.
Station : Quimper 20 km.
Property of M. M. Le Tanneur de Rancourt.

Given by Saint Guénolé to the bishops of Quimper who used it as their summer residence until the 16th century, Trevilit dates from the 15th century. The fortified house and part of the second walls still exist. Inside are period firepalces, staircases and guards rooms.
Grounds only.
Parking.
Tel. : (98) 87.04.50.

Tronjoly (Château).

Cléder - 29233.
Saint-Pol-de-Léon : 10 km.
Station : Car 2 km.
Private property.

Tronjoly, built in 1535 by Christophe de Kergoët, lord of Tonjoly is a typical Breton Renaissance manor house. It consists of a main building flanked by two wings which enclose a square courtyard. A chapel and and an elegant pavilion were built on an esplanade which is bordered by balustrades. The door at the end of the courtyard is surmounted by a bull's eye window and a fine Gothic style dormer window. Inside is a mid-16th century granite spiral staircase. The main salon, repanelled at the end of the 17th century has fine period furniture.
Open all year : 10 - 12, 2 - 6.
Grounds only.
Parking.
Tel. : (98) 69.40.01.

ILLE-ET-VILAINE

La Ballue (Château).

Bazouges La Pérouse : 35560.
Dinard and Saint-Malo : 30 km.
Station : Combourg 13 km.
Property of Mme Cl. Arthaud.

Built on the site of two fortresses, dating from the 10th and 16th centuries, this rose granite classical style château was constructed between 1616 and

1620 by Gilles Ruellan, marquis de La Ballue, an adventurer ennobled by Henri IV. This was the headquarters of the Chouans, the Breton rebels during the Revolution when 7000 of them met here in 1793. Victor Hugo spent time here with Juiliette Drouet and gained inspiration for his novel « Quatre-vingt-treize ». The château was mentioned by Châteaubriand in his famous « Mémoires d'outre-tombe » and also inspired Balzac's « Les Chouans ». The Louis XIII and Renaissance gardens designed by Madame Claude Arthaud include more than 5000 trees and shurbs inciluting 60 rare species.

Open daily June 15, Sept. 15 : 11 - 12, 3 - 6 for the gardens and gardien museum.
« Salle des buffets » and hunt pavilion open by written request for 20 people minimum.
Guided tours on request.
Information panels, leaflets.
Information in English, Spanish.
Ancient and Modern music festival.
Temporary exhibits.
(Rooms for rent).
Tel. : (99) 73.13.93 and (4) 544.74.23.

La Belinaye (Château).

Saint-Christophe-de-Valins - 35140.
Fougères : 20 km.
Private property.

For five centuries this has ben the property of the La Belinaye family, a vicomté since 1682. Today's château is a Louis XIII granite building with a portico, Italian staircase and a central pavilion with a hull-shape roof.

Open on request only March 1 to Oct. 31 : 8 - 12, 2 - 6.
Closed Sundays Nov. 1 to Feb. 28.
Closed Saturdays and Sundays, March 1 to Oct. 31.
Parking.
Unaccompanied visits.
Tel. : (99) 55-35-41.

Le Bosq (Château).

Saint-Malo - 35400.
Route de La Passagère - Quelmer.
Property of M. Picard.

Built in 1717 by the Magon family, ship owners and privateers from Saint-Malo, Le Bosq is an elegant building with its slightly projecting portico crowned with a pediment decorating the principal facade. The garden side has projecting bays with slanting corners. The grounds have four 18th century Italian statues representing the four seasons. The dining room is decorated with Regency boiseries and the salon with Louis XVI boiseries. In the chapel is a painting of Saint Anne de Baziray.

Open July 1 to Aug. 31 : Visits at 3, 4 and 5 pm.
Open on request the rest of the year.
Parking.
Guided tours.
Information panels, Leaflets.
English - German - Italian - panels or Leaflets.
Tel. : (99) 81.40.11.

LA BOURBANSAIS

ILLE-ET-VILAINE

Half way between Rennes and Saint-Malo.
Don't leave Brittany without seeing La Bourbansais (16th and 17th century).

Formerly the residence of members of the Parlement of Brittany. « One of the loveliest great Breton châteaux. »
For information call : (99) 45.20.42.

ILLE-ET-VILAINE — 78 — BRETAGNE

La Bourbansais (Château).

Pleugeneuc - 35720.
Rennes : 30 km.
Station : Dol-de-Bretagne 18 km.
Bus service.
Private property.

Built in the 16th century on the ruins of an ancient Gallo-Roman villa, La Bourbansais was remodelled in the 18th century and the rooms inside decorated with panelling and wainscoating. Mansard roofs were added and formal gardens laid out. The château has never been sold and was for many years the summer residence of the magistrates of the parlement of Brittany. Zoo.

Open daily June 15 to Sept. 15 : Hourly visits in the afternoon. Sept. 15 to June 15 : Daily visits at 4 pm.
Sat.-Sun., 4 and 5 pm.
Morning on request for groups.
Parking.
Guided tours (45 min.), brochures.
English - German - guides.
The Bourbansais hounds on show on request on centian Sundays in summer.
Vintage car show second Sunday in June.
Tel. : (99) 45.20.42.

Caradeuc (Château).

Bécherel - 35190.
Dinan : 20 km.
Station : Rennes 30 km.
Bus service.
Private property.

Built in 1723 by Anne Nicholas de Caraduec, doyen of the parlement of Brittany and father of the procureur general La Chalotais, Caraduec is a purely classical style château. A columned peristyle in the middle of the main facade and a stone staircase on the garden side are the distinguishing features of the building, which is surrounded by extensive formal gardens. The terrace on the North of the château overlooks the Rance valley.
Open March 25 to Oct. 31 daily : 9 - 12:30, 1:30 - 8.
Nov. 1 to March 24 week-ends and holidays : 2 - 6.
Groups or request during the week.
Grounds only.
Parking.
Unaccompanied visits, brochures.
Tel. : (99) 66.77.76.

Champs (Château).

Guipry - 35480.
Redon : 35 km.
Station : Messac 6 km.
Property of M. de Guibert.

Home of Judith Picquet, comtesse de Maure, aunt of La Motte-Picquet, Champs was built in the 17th century and remodelled in the 18th. The main buildings, grouped around two courtyards are surrounded by a moat. The salon on the first floor has kept its original decoration.
Open July 10 - Aug. 20 : 9 - 12, 2 - 6.
Parking.
Tel. : (99) 34.03.04.

CÔTES-DU-NORD
ILLE-ET-VILAINE

CARADEUC

Known as the Versailles of Brittany, Caradeuc has the largest formal gardens in Brittany. You can enjoy its flower beds and its walks, its monuments and its garden buildings.

FOUGÈRES

ILLE-ET-VILAINE

Situated on the border between Brittany, Maine and Normandy, Fougères's strategic position made it one the region's most important fortresses. It was captured seven times in as many years, pillaged and held for ransom. Yet it always managed to rise from its ashes and grew more majestic every time. Fougères has preserved its impressive castle which dates from the 12th — 15th centuries and includes thirteen towers and covers almost two hectares.

Your entry ticket allows you to visit the fortress, the collection of footwear from the world over, the la Villeon museum with its impressionist pictures. During the holidays there are free guided tours of the floodlit castle and town monuments.

Combourg (Castle).

Combourg - 35270.
23, rue des Princes.
Station : Combourg 3 km.
Bus service.
Property of M. and Mme de La Tour du Pin Verclause.

Combourg was founded in 1016 by Junken, bishop of Dol but its earliest surviving parts date from the 14th and 15th centuries. The writer François-René de Chateaubriand spent his childhood here. With its gloomy walls, its crenelated sentry way and huge cut stone towers, Combourg has kept the austere appearance of a medieval fortress. In the 19th century its Romantic garden was designed by Buhler and a lake bordered by poplars adds to the charm of the grounds. The complex recalls the spirit of Châteaubriand. The interior, transformed in 1875 after the destructions of 1792 has Italian furniture and pieces form the reigns of Louis XV and Louis XVI.
Open March 1 to Nov. 30 : 9:30 - 12, 3 - 5:30.
Closed Tuesdays.
Grounds and interiors.
Parking.
English.
Audiovisual programme.
Brochures available.
Facilities for the handicapped.
Lecture tours for school groups.
Tea room.
Wild Life.
Guided tours.
Tel. : (98) 73.22.95.

Fougères (Castle).

Fougères - 35300.
Place Pierre-Simon.
Station : Fougères.
Bus service.
Property of the commune.

Built on a promontory this feudal castle consists of polygonal towers built between the 12th and 15th centuries. It is characteristic of Medieval military architecture with its towers facades, arrow slits and parapets. Stategically situated at the gateway to Britanny, it was besieged several times by both the English and the French which accounts for its many reconstructions.
Open daily 9 - 5, April 1 to April 15, Sept. 16 to Sept. 30.
9 - 6, April 16 to Sept. 15.
Closed December and January.
Parking.
Guided tours on the hour, brochures.
English - German - guides in summer, leaflets.
Tel. : (99) 99.18.98 and 94.12.20.

La Haye (Château).

Saint-Hilaire-des-Landes - 35140.
Fougères : 11 km.
Station : Vitré or Rennes 38 km.
Bus service.
Property of Colonel de La Haye Sainte-Hilaire.

The present day appearance of the château is due to Henri de La Haye Sainte-Hilaire, formerly the governor of Saint-Hilaire, who built the seigneurial dwelling at the end of the 17th century while preserving the 15th century fortified gateway and round tower. He joined the chapel to the main building by a granite balustrade which overlooks the moat. The property has never been sold and still belongs to his descendants.
Grounds only.

Lanrigan (Castle)

Lanrigan - 35270.
Station : Combourg or Dizé 5 km.
Private property.

This 15th and 16th century castle is flanked by polygonal and round turrets one of which contains the main staircase. The Renaissance facade includes à loggia with basket handle arcatures.
Open Wed., Thurs., Fri. June 1 to Sept. 30 : 8 - 12, 2 - 7.
Grounds only.
Parking.
Unaccompanied visits.

La Louverie (Manor House) Bel-Air (Castle)

Le Crouais - 3529.
Montfort-sur-Meu : 20 km.
Station : La Brohnière 5 km.
Private property.

In the 17th century La Louverie was an important seat of justice, in the following century it became the property of the missonaries of Saint Meen. It is a high rustic building with a Mansard roof and a watch tower. Some older features still exist, notably the Renaissance gate. Inside is a wooden Louis XI staircase.
Open July 1 to Aug. 31.
Closed Sundays and Holidays.
Grounds only.
Unaccompanied visits.
Tel. : (99) 09.67.54.

Monbouan (Château).

Moulins - 35680.
Vitré : 16 km.
Station : Vitré.
Private property.

Rebuilt in 1771, Monbouan is classical building set in spacious grounds. The format garden, embellished with a balustrade line with vases, is completed by a lake Since its construction the château has remained in the same family
Open July 15 to Aug. 31 : 9 - 12, 2 - 6.
Parking.
Guided tours.
English - German - Spanish.
Rel. : (99) 49.01.51.

Montauban-de-Bretagne (Castle).

Montauban-de-Bretagne - 35360.
Rennes : 53 km. Coast : 50 km.
Dinan : 32 km.
Station S.N.C.F.
Private property.

Montauban is an ancient Breton stronghold with parts dating from before the 12th century. The seigneurie belonged to the Montauban family and then passed to the Rohans. It was once a fortress surrounded by water, but this was destroyed during the Anglo French wars. The present castle has an imposing entrance tower which is almost a small castle itself. In the courtyard is the keep which lost its top two stories when the castle was captured by Charles VII in 1487. In the 18th century one of the two towers was used to construct a pavilion adjacent to the main building.
Open daily July 1 to Sept. 15 and weekends from May.
Closed Tuesdays.
Parking.
Guided tours.
Tel. : (99) 06.40.21.

Montmuran (Château).

Les Iffs - 35116.
Rennes : 27 km.
Station : Rennes.
Private property.

Montmuran is entered through 14th century gate preceded by drawbridge framed by two large towers with parapets. The chapel dates from the same period. The central building was erected in the

BRETAGNE

17th century and is classical in style with its pavilion crowned by a pedimaent remodelled in the 18th century. It was here that Bertrand du Guesclin was knighted in 1354 and married twenty years later.
*Open Easter to Nov. 1 : 2 - 7.
Nov. 1 to Easter, 2 - 6.
Groups on request.
Parking.
Guided tours, brouchures.
English - German - Leaflets.
Tel. : (99) 45.88.88.*

Les Rochers-Sévigné (Château).

*Vitré - 35500.
Rennes : 30 km.
Station : Vitré.
Bus service.
Private property.*

Rochers-Sévigné consists of two buildings at right angles linked by a round tower. Built at the beginning of the 16th century, this manor house was remodelled in the 17th century as attested by the vertical square paned windows and Louis XIII dormer windows. It was at this time that the gardens were laid out. Madame de Sévigné wrote many of her letters here and the interior are full of her memorabilia.
*Open all year : 9 - 12, 2 - 6.
Closed Sunday mornings.
Parking.
Guided tours.
Rel. : (99) 96.61.96.*

SAINT-MALO
Saint-Malo (Keep).

*Saint-Malo - 35400.
Bus service.
Property of the commune.*

The castle is set in the town ramparts and the small keep built in 1393 serves as a corner tower. The new castle built by the Duke of Britanny in 1424 has preserved its three story keep. The towers flanking the castle date from the 15th century. Vauban was responsible for finishing the edifice which is now the home of the town's historical museum.
*Open unaccompanied visits :
March 24 to April 15, June 1 to Sept. 30 : 9:30 - 12, 2 - 6.
Guided tours :
Oct. 1 to March 24, April 16 - May 31 : 10:45, 2, 3:15, 4:30.
Closed Tuesdays out of season.
Parking.
Tel. : (99) 56.41.36.*

Solidor (Tower).

*Saint-Malo - 35400.
Bus service.
Property of the State.*

The fortress of Solidor erected by Duke Jean IV from 1362 to 1369 allowed him to control the Rance. The edifice consists of three high towers linked by narrow walls. Once a state prison it has become a sailing museum.
Open with guided tours : March 24 to June 14, Sept. 16 to Sept. 30 : 10:30, 2, 3:30, 5.

MONTAUBAN DE BRETAGNE

ILLE-ET-VILAINE

Once a 12th century stronghold belonging to the Montauban and then to the Rohan family. Now consisting of an imposing entrance tower which is almost a miniature castle itself. In the courtyard you can still se the keep and inside you can enjoy a collection of medieval objects including arms and armour and portraits.

ILLE-ET-VILAINE/MORBIHAN — BRETAGNE

June 15 to Sept. 15 : 10:30, 11, 2, 2:30, 3:30, 4, 5.
March 16 to March 23.
Parking.
Tel. : (99) 56.41.36.

VITRÉ
Saint-Nicholas Monastery.

Vitré - 35500.
Rue du Rachat.
Rennes : 30 km.
Station : Vitré.
Bus service.
Property of the Association pour l'insertion sociale.

Built in the 17th century to lodge the Augustine nuns who cared for the sick at the nearby hospital, the monastery has retained its large buildings with Mansard roofs which surround a 17th century cloister.
Open Jan. 1 to Dec. 31 : 9 - 12, 2 - 6.
Parking.
Unaccompanied visits.
Tel. : (99) 75.32.59.

Vitré (Castle).

Vitré - 35500.
Rennes : 30 km.
Station : Vitré.
Bus service.
Property of the commune.

Set in the town of Vitré on the border of Brittany, this castle is a large fortress built in the 14th and 15th centuries on the site of an 11th century castle. Entering through a tower protected by a drawbridge you can see the triangular walls with their seven towers and imposing circular keep.
Open July 1 to Sept. 30 : 9:30 - 12:30, 2 - 6.
Oct. 1 to 30 : 10 - 12, 2 - 5:30.
Sat. - Sun : 2 - 5:30.
Nov. 1 to Easter : 2 - 5:30.

Groups on request in the morning.
Closed Tuesdays.
Parking.
Guided tours available, brochures.
Temporary exhibits : Photography.
Tel. : (99) 75.04.54.

La Ville-André (Manor House).

Dingé - 35440.
Rennes : 26 km.
Station : Dingé 5 km.
Property of M. Martin.

Seat of the lords of La Ville-André, this manor house, documented as early as 1390, is enhanced by a 16th century chapel. It is an oblong structure built from granite and slate flanked on its Southern face by two square turrets framing the terrace. The main facade has a monumental entry with two sculptured granite columns. Inside are impressive granite and terracotta fireplaces and a two story staircase which dates from the end of the 15th century.
Open : 8 - 12, 14 - 20.
Closed Sundays.
Grounds only.
Parking.
Unaccompanied visits.
English.

MORBIHAN

AURAY
Pavillon d'en bas (Inn) ·

Auray - 56400 Saint-Goustan.
51, rue du Château.
Station : Auray.
Private property.

At Saint-Goustan, in the port of Auray this old inn received such illustrious visitors as Madame de Sévigné and Benjamin Franklin when he arrived in France. The building consists of a main block flanked by gables. The cut stone facade is half-timbered and the large rooms inside are now used for exhibitions.
Open Jan. 1 to Dec. 31 : 11 - 12, 3 - 6.
Closed Tuesdays.
Parking.
Unaccompanied visits.
Temporary art exhibits.
Tel. : (97) 24.00.65.

Branféré (Château and zoo).

Le Guerno - 56190 Muzillac.
Vannes : 33 km.
Station : Questembert 15 km.
Property of M. Jourde.

Influenced in the 14th century by the architecture of the Breton Templars, Blanféré was entirely rebuilt at the beginning of the 17th century. After being destroyed during the Revolution it was purchased by the Jourde family who created a zoological park in the grounds.
Open March 24 to Sept. 22 : 9 - 12, 2 - 6:30.
Sept. 23 to Nov. 14 : 9 - 12, 2 - 5:30.
Parking.
Guided tours - recommended itinerary.
Panels or leaflets.
English - guides (during vacations) - panels or leaflets.
Special transportation for the handicapped.
Brochures available.
Audio-visual programme.
Temporary art exhibits about nature.
Tel. : (97) 41.69.21.

L'Estier (Castle).

Béganne - 56350.
Redon or La Roche-Bernard : 15 km.
Station : Redon.
Private property.

This important manor house dates from the end of the 14th century consists of two wings at right angles joined by a turret in which you can see a stone spiral staircase. During a 17th century restoration the main facade was extended. The interior is decorated by sculpture and a large number of granite fireplaces.
Open July 1 to Sept. 15 : 2 - 7.
Closed Tuesdays.
Groups on request.
Parking.
Guided tours.
English - Spanish.
Lectures.
Tel. : (99) 91.80.79.

Josselin (Château).

Josselin - 56120.
Station : 40 km.
Bus service.
Property of M. de Rohan.

This imposing 11th century fortress was rebuilt by Olivier de Clisson in the 14th century. In the 15th it was embellished by Alain de Rohan and Jean II, who were responsible for the flamboyant facade, a precious example of Breton Renaissance architecture and a remarkable contrast to the military towers and defensive walls. The interior was restored in the 19th century and has some valuable pieces of furniture. The château has always belonged to the Rohan family.
Open Easter to June 1, Wed. Sun. holidays : 2 - 6.
Daily June 1 to June 30 : 2 - 6.

L'ESTIER

MORBIHAN

A 14th century castle: large medieval rooms with fine granite sculpture qnd mullioned windows. One of the main features of this castle is its many large fireplaces (16 large and 8 small). It also has a large cutstone tower and a 15th century spiral staircase. The history of the castle is closely linked with that of Brittany...

JOSSELIN

MORBIHAN

Built on a rocky peak, Josselin is a superb example of feudal architecture and Renaissance art. Inside the castle which has belonged to the Rohan family since it was built, you can see fine pieces of furniture.

MORBIHAN 84 BRETAGN

July 1 to Aug. 31 : 10 - 12, 2 - 6.
Groups on request from Sept. 1 to Easter.
Parking.
Guided tours, brochures.
English - German - guide.
Tel. : (97) 22.22.50.

Doll Museum Rohan Collection

Écuries du Château.
Josselin - 56120.
3, rue des Trente.

Photo L. Levier

You cas visit the Rohan doll collection in its new home, a museum recently established in the stables of Josselin castle. Among the treasures of this unusual collection are a superb 17th century wooden doll, 18th century dolls and a large number of dolls in traditional costume exhibited in a huge attic on the first floor. There are dolls in Breton dress, and dolls from other French provinces as well as dolls in Dutch, German and English costumes. Africa, Asia and America are also represented. There is also an exhibition of accessories an doll's furniture.
Open daily May 1 to Sept. 30 : 10 - 12, 2 - 6 except Mondays.
Feb. 1 to April 30, Oct. 1 to Nov. 15 : Wed., Weekends and holidays, 10 - 12, 2 - 6.
Groups by appointment Nov. 15 - Jan. 31.
Tel. : (97) 22.36.45.

Kerangat (Arboretum).

Plumelec - 56420.
Vannes : 28 km.
Station : Vannes.
Private property.

Designed in 1866 by the vicomte de Bellevue, an enthusuastic cellector, the arboretum can be considered one of the finest. The Atlantic climate is favorable to the growth of several varieties of trees which come from the world over.

Open or request only (M. Joyeux, Chambre Agriculture, boulevard de la Résistance, 56009 Vannes cedex).
Parking.
Guided tours.
Tel. : (97) 60.31.14.

Kerlevenan (Château).

Sarzeau - 56370.
Vannes : 19 km.
Bus service.
Private property.

In the heart of the Rhuys peninsula overlooking the Gulf of Morbihan is the white stone castle of Kerlevenan built at the end of the 18th century. The notable neoclassical elements of the building are its ionic pilasters on the garden side and its Corinthian portico. The balustrade which highlights the sloping roof are reminiscent of Italian terraces. The grounds are enhanced by a temple of love and a Chinese pavilion.
Open July 1 to Sept. 15 by writen request.
Parking.

Largouet (Towers).

Elven - 56250.
Vannes : 15 km.
Station : Vannes.
Private property.

Built by the Malestroit family in the 13th and 14th centuries, this fortress served as a prison for the future Henri VII d'Angoulême between 1474 and 1476. Later it was owned briefly by the minister Fouquet. A keep, a tower, a postern with a drawbridge and connecting walls are all that remain of the original structure which was surrounded by a moat. The 14th century eight-sided keep standing at 44 metres is one of the highest in France. The semi-circular tower, built at the beginning of the 15th century, was restored in 1905.
Open Jan. 1 to Nov. 12 : 9 - 6.
Grounds only.
Unaccompanied visits, brochures.
Sound and light.

Léhélec (Château).

Beganne - 56350.
Redon : 19 km.

Station : Redon.
Private property.
Property of the Le Minitier Léhélec family since 1580, the cl teau has kept its austere gran and red schist facade. It was us as a hiding place by the Breton bels during the French Revoluti The Southern facade overloc courtyards lined with buildin which date from the 16th and 1 centuries. The interiors are deco ted with period furniture and c jets d'art and have kept their or nal layout.

Open July 1 to Aug. 31 : 2 - 7.
Closed Tuesdays.
Parking.
Guided tours, brochure.
English.
Facilities for the handicapped.
Concerts.
Tel. : (99) 91.81.14.

Le Plessis-Josso (Ch teau).

Theix - 56450.
Vannes : 15 km.
Station : Vannes.
Private property.

Built between the 14th and 1 centuries, Le Plessis-Josso is large manor house consisting Gothic and Renaissance buildin The facade is interuped by a pc gonal stair tower. During the re of Louis XIII a pavilion was add The château is still protected ramparts and towers protecti the manor house, mill lake a woods.
Open July 10 to Aug. 30 : 2 - 7.
Parking.
Guided tours.
English.
Temporary art exhibits.
Tel. : (97) 43.16.16.

PONTIVY

Rohan (Castle).

Pontivy - 56300.
Rue du Général-de-Gaulle.
Private property.
This fortress was built in 1485 and still dominates the Blaret. It is surronded by ditches and outer walls.
Open Wed. - Sun. : 2 - 6.
Open daily in summer : 10 - 12, 2 - 6.
Parking.
Unaccompanied visits, brochures.
Temporary exhibits.
Tel. : (97) 25.12.93.

Suscinio (Castle).

Sarzeau - 56370.
Vannes : 21 km.
Station : Vannes.
Property of the département.
This fortress built by Pierre de Dreux in the 13th century was one of the dukes of Brittany's favorite summer residences. Fortified after the War of the Breton succession in the 14th century, the castle was abandoned between the 16th and 19th centuries. All that remains of the original buildings are two towers and their connecting wall (13th and 14th centuries), the East Tower, the West main building linked to the « New Tower » and the stronghold known as Mercœur (15th century). On the first floor of the fully restored main building are fragments of 14th century pavement discovered in 1976.
Open Oct. 1 to March 31, Tue., weekends and holidays : 9:30 - 12, 1:30 - 7.
April 1 to Sept. 30 daily : 9:30 - 12, 1:30 - 7.
Closed Wednesday mornings.
Parking.
Unaccompanied visits.
Brochures.
Festival.

Tremohar-en-Berric (Château).

Berric - 56230.
Vannes : 18 km.
Station : Vannes.
Private property.
Built in the 14th and 15th centuries, Tremohar was pillaged and then rased during the wars of the League. The fortified outbuildings still stand and the classical château was added during the first half of the 17th century.
Open July 1 to Sept. 15 : 9 - 12, 2:30 -
On request.
Parking.
Guided tours.
Tel. : (97) 43.03.24.

La Villeneuve-Jacquelot (Château).

Quisitnic - 56310.
Pontivy : 25 km.
Private property.
Built at the beginning of the 16th century, La Villeneuve-Jacquelot was transformed during the 17th century. The main building, flanked by a horse shoe shaped tower, has an arched gateway crowned by a seigneurial coat of arms. On the North side, a square tower houses a sculpted staircase and the dormer windows are decorated with finials. The main rooms have Renaissance fireplaces.
Open Jan. 1 to Dec. 31.
Parking.

DISCOVER FRANCE AND ITS OLD CITIES
with the guided tours of the Caisse Nationale des Monuments Historiques

When travelling in France during your holidays, discover 100 Old Cities and their art treasures with the guided tours organised by the Caisse Nationale des Monuments Historiques. Daily tours are organised and last one hour or more. Ask for timetable and details in the Tourist Offices of cities like : AIX-EN-PROVENCE, ARLES, ARRAS, AVIGNON, BEAUNE, BEAUVAIS, LAON, LA ROCHELLE, LYON, METZ, MONTLUÇON, MONTPELLIER, NANCY, NANTES, ROUEN, STRASBOURG, VERSAILLES...

ENGLISH SPEAKING GUIDES.

Hôtel de Sully
62, rue Saint-Antoine 75004 PARIS
Tél. : 274.22.22.

CIVIS

CENTRE

CHER, EURE-ET-LOIR, INDRE, INDRE-ET-LOIRE, LOIR-ET-CHER, LOIRET.

- ■ castle, château, manor house
- ● abbey, priory
- ▲ garden, park
- ★ town house, famous men house, farm, mill...
- ○ city

ORLEANS
- ★ Hôtel Groslot

VENDOME
- ● La Trinité

CHARTRES
- ▲ Jardin d'Horticulture

BOURGES
- ★ Hôtel Jacques-Cœur
- ☆ Hôtel Cujas
- ★ Hôtel Lallemand

BLOIS
- ■ Château

TOURS
- ★ Hôtel Mame
- ★ Hôtel Goüin

VALLUAU
- □ Château
- ● Anc. prieuré Saint-Laurent

ISSOUDUN
- Musée Saint-Roch

Map locations:
- ■ Anet
- ■ Sorel
- ■ Montigny-sur-Avre
- ■ Maillebois
- ■ Maintenon
- CHARTRES ○
- ■ Blanville
- ■ Frazé
- ■ Denonville
- ■ Alluyes : Fondation Chevallier Debeausse
- ■ Saint-Agil
- ■ Bondaroy
- ■ Reverseaux ■ Rouville ■ Malesherbes
- ★ Arville
- ■ Ville-Prevost ■ Denainvilliers
- ■ Châteaudun
- ■ Les Radrets
- ■ Yevre-le-Châtel
- ■ Bonaventure
- ■ Bellegarde
- ■ Lavardin ● Vendôme
- ● Chevilly
- ■ Sully-sur-Loire
- ■ La Poissonnière
- ○ ORLEANS
- ■ Talcy
- ■ Meung-sur-Loire
- ■ Châteauneuf-sur-Loire
- ■ La Roche Racan
- ■ Cour-sur-Loire
- ▲ Les Grandes Bruyères
- ○ Gien
- ■ Vaudésir
- BLOIS ○ ■ Chambord
- ■ Le Plessis-sur-Thilouze
- ■ Saint-Denis- ■ Villesavin
- ★ Meslay
- sur-Loire ■ Troussay
- ■ Chatigny ● St-Cosme ■ Amboise
- ■ Beauregard ■ Cheverny
- ■ Langeais TOURS ○
- ■ Clos-Lucé ■ Chaumont-
- ■ Petit Château
- ■ Cinq-Mars
- ■ Chenonceaux sur-Loire ■ Chemery
- ■ Les Pêcheurs
- ■ Bourgueil ■ Azay-le- ■ Villandry ■ Nitray
- ■ Fougères-sur-Bièvre
- ■ Blancafort ■ Pont Chevron
- ■ Chinon Rideau ■ Saché ■ Montpoupon ■ Le Gué-Péan
- ■ La Verrerie
- ■ Turpenay ■ Grillemont ■ Montrésor ● Pontlevoy
- ★ Grenier de
- ★ La Devinière ■ Loches
- ■ Le Moulin ■ La Ferté- Villatre-Nançay
- ■ Le Rivau ● Le Liget
- Imbault
- ■ Champigny-sur-Veude ■ Bridoré
- ■ Valençay ■ Chapelle d'Angillon
- ■ Veuil
- ■ Maupas
- ● Bois-Aubry
- ■ Bouges
- ■ Apremont
- ■ Notre-Dame
- ■ Mehun-sur-Yevre :
- ■ Menetou-Salon
- ■ Grand- du Landais ○ Issoudun Charles VII
- ★ Hôtel Mame
- Pressigny ○ Palluau ■ Villegongis BOURGES ○ ■ Tour-de-Vevre
- ★ Hôtel Goüin
- ■ La Guerche ■ Argy
- ■ Jussy-Champagne
- ■ Diors
- ■ Sagonne
- CHATEAUROUX ○
- ■ Bouchet-en-Brenne
- ■ Le Chatelier ■ Lys Saint-
- ● Noirlac
- □ Château
- ■ Guillaume Georges
- ■ Meillant
- ● Anc. prieuré
- ■ Breuil-Yvain
- ■ Thaumiers
- Saint-Laurent
- ★ Nohant :
- ■ Ainay-le-Vieil
- ■ Sarzay Domaine de
- Georges Sand
- ■ Varennes ■ Culan

CHER

Ainay-le-Vieil (Castle).

*Ainay-le-Vieil - 18200.
Saint-Amand-Montrond : 9 km.
Station.
Property of Mme d'Aligny.*

With its Renaissance mainbuilding which has a fine spiral staircase at the centre of its eight-sided surrounding walls, Ainay-le-Vieil is a perfectly preserved castle flanked by 9 towers and surrounded by water. You can visit its sentry way, its towers and its apartments which contain memorabilia relating to Colbert, Marie-Antoinette and Napoleon. The chapel is decorated with 15th century painting. The castle has remained in the same family since 1467.

*Open Feb. 5 to Dec. 1 : 10 - 12, 2 - 7.
Parking.
Guided tours, brochures.
Leaflets in English, German, Spanish, Japanese, Dutch, Italian.
Tel : (48) 96.14.39.*

Apremont-sur-Allier (Château and park).

*La-Guerche-sur-l'Aubois - 18150.
Nevers : 16 km.
Station : Neveers.
Private property.*

Apremont was originally a medieval fortress that served as a prison under the Dukes of Burgundy. It was partially destroyed after the Hundred Years War and rebuilt at the end of the 15th century. The castle was turned into a summer residence in the 19th century and is fully furnished. Since 1722 Apremont has belonged to the same family and now includes a carriage museum. A floral park created ten years ago at the foot of the château includes trees, flowers, lawns, waterfalls, lakes and aquatic birds.

*Open daily April 15 to Sept. 23 : Carriage museum : 2 - 7; Floral park : 10 - 12, 2 - 7.
Closed Tuesdays.
Parking.
Unaccompanied visits recommended itinerary.
English - German.
Tel. : (48) 80.41.41.*

Blancafort (Château).

*Blancafort - 18480.
Aubigny-sur-Néré : 10 km.
Gien : 26 km.
Private property.*

This lovely brick building has hardly been touched since the 15th century. Set on the right bank of the Sauldre, Blancafort is a rectangular château with two wings terminated by square pavilions. In the inner courtyards is a gallery which was restored in the 16th century. The interior is furnished and the château has formal gardens.

*Open April 1 to Oct. : 10 - 12, 2 - 7.
Oct. 1 to Nov : 10 - 12, 2 - 5.
Parking.
Facilities for the handicapped.
English leaflets.
Tel. : (48) 58.60.56.*

CHER
AINAY-LE-VIEIL

With its eight sided surrounding walls flanked by towers and protected by a moat, its elegant Renaissance main building, its main salon decorated to receive Louis XII and Anne of Brittany which opens onto a delightful oratory... This historic castle also has memorabilia of Colbert, Marie-Antoinette and Napoleon.

BOURGES

Palais Jacques-Cœur

Bourges - 18000.
Property of the city.

This palace is one of the finest examples of late Gothic domestic architecture with details in Renaissance style. Charles VII's great minister of finance Jacques Cœur held several different official and entrepreneurial positions during the first half of the 15th century. His success was such that his enormous wealth made him many enemies and he was arrested in 1453 and his property confiscated.
Open Nov. 1 to Palm Sunday : 9 - 11:15, 2 - 4:15.
Palm Sunday to Nov. 1 : 9 - 11:15, 2 - 5:15.
Closed Jan. 1, May 1, Nov. 1 and 11, Dec. 25.
Guided tours.
English and German.
Brochures.
Tel. : (48) 24.06.87.

Hôtel Cujas (Berry Museum).

Bourges - 18000.
4-6, rue des Arènes.
Property of the city.

Two elegant corbelled turrets rise from a fine facade framed by a corner pavillion. The building dates from 1515 and inside are ancient artefacts, 13th century figures of prophets and mourners from the duc de Berry's chapel, local arts and crafts, a ceramics collection. 
Open daily Museum : 10 - 12, 2 - 6.
Special exhibits : 10 - 6.
Closed Tuesdays, Jan. 1, May 1, Nov. 1 and Dec. 25.
Unaccompanied visits.
Tel. : (48) 70.41.92.

Hôtel Lallemant (Museum).

Bourges - 18000.
Rue Bourbonnoux.
Property of the city.

The Gothic plan, the sculptures which decorate the facade, the staircase and the main rooms make this town house one of the most striking examples of French Renaissance architecture. Its coffered ceilings have 30 heraldic emblems. The house also contains an important collection of decorative arts from the 16th to 19th centuries.
Open April 1 to Oct. 15 : 10 - 12, 2 - 6.
Guided tours at 10:15, 11:15, 2, 3, 3:15, 4:15, 5:15 from Oct. 16 to March 31.
Closed Mondays, Jan. 1, May 1, Nov. 1, Dec. 25.
Guided tours.
Tel. : (48) 70.19.32.

LA BEUVRIÈRE

A castle dating back to the 11th century and recently restored. It has five guest rooms (reservations : (48) 75.08.14 or 75.14.63..
Buffet supper available on request. Reception rooms : 300 square meters. Available for receptions, seminars. Fishing, walking, tennis.
Property of A. and Ch. de Brach.

La Chapelle d'Angillon (« Béthune » Castle).

La Chapelle d'Angillon - 18380.
Bourges : 30 km.
Station : Bourges, Vierzon, Gien, 30 km.
Private property.

Bethune was the residence of the prince de Boisbelle. As a small sovereign state it was exempt from taxes. Among the famous visitors were the princesse de Cleves and the duc de Sully. You can visit the keep with its staircase set in the walls, the tennis court, the king's room, the chapel, etc. One of the rooms devoted to the work of the novelist Alain Fournier, has an audiovisual programme. To commemorate the centenary of his birth a centre with books and exhibits is planned for 1986.
Open Palm Sunday to Oct. 30 : 10 - 12, 2 - 7.
Closed Sunday mornings.
Tel. : (48) 73.41.10.

Culan (Castle).

Culan - 18270.
Saint-Amand : 24 km.
Montluçon : 30 km.
Private property.

Situated on a commanding position above the river with its three towers, Culan once defended the Arnon valley. It was built on the site of a medieval fortress captured by Philip-Augustus in 1188 and then rebuilt in the 15th century by the admiral de Culan a comrade of Joan of Arc who came to the castle in 1429. In 1600 Sully became the owner succeeded by the prince de Condé. The present owner of Culan has restored the castle and won a prize for his work in 1966.
Open July 1 to Sept. 30 : 9 - 11:30, 2 - 6:30.
Oct. 1 to Dec. 30 : 9 - 11:30, 2 - 5.
March 1 to June 30 : 9 - 11:30, 2 - 6.
Closed Wednesdays and is February.
Parking.
Guided tours, brochures, Temporary exhibits.
Tel. : (48) 96.22.72 and 56.64.18.

Jussy-Champagne (Château).

Jussy-Champagne - 18130.
Bourges : 22 km.
Station : Avord 6 km.
Private property.

Jussy-Champagne was built o an H-shaped plan between 15 and 1650 by members of the G maches family who were part the king's household for gener tions. The interiors include furn ture, paintings and tapestries fro the 16th to 18th centuries.
Open March 25 to Nov. 15 : 9 - 11:45 - 6:30.
Parking.
Guided tours, brochures.
Information in English, Spanish, Italia Flemish.
English speaking Guide on request.
Leaflets.
Exhibits (historical costumes).
Tel. : (48) 25.00.61.

CHER LA CHAPELLE-D'ANGILLON

Many famous figures have visited this historic château : Sully and Henri IV and Louis XIV who spent a night here during the Fronde. You will leave here pondering the dramatic story of the princesse de Clèves and captivated by the adventures of the Grand Meaulnes, a young man haunted by the mysterious domain in which the perfect Yvonne de Galais lived. A furnished residence with Old Master paintings / Audio visual programme on Alain Fournier and Le Grand Meaulnes, the château and its history, the principality of Boisbelle.

chesse de Berry and to the comte de Chambord who was tutored by Maupas as well as a remarkable collection of 887 plates and tapestries etc.

Open daily July 1 to Sept 8 mornings. Sundays and holidays from Easter to Oct.
Parking.
Audiovisual programme.
Temporary exhibits.
Tel. : (48) 64.41.71.

Jacques Cœur built in Bourges in the mid-15th century. At Meillant Italian Renaissance ornamentation appears at its most discrete. The interiors are as sumptuous as the building itself with a large collection of furniture and objects which reflect the taste of the château's various owners.

Open April 1 to Oct. 15 : 9 - 11:30, 2 - 6:30.
Oct. 15 to March 31 : 9 - 11:30, 2 - 5.
Parking.
Guided tours, brochures.
Leaflets in English.
Tel. : (48) 96.16.51.

Maupas (Castle).

Morogues - 18220.
Bourges : 25 km.
Station : Bourges
Property of M. de Maupas.

This castle over looking a large lake in the middle of a forest was the residence of the duchesse de Berry. Built in the 15th century on the site of a property once belonging to the Sully and Rochehouart families, Maupas has buildings which date from the Louis XV period. The rooms have memorabilia relating to the du-

Meillant (Château).

Saint-Amand - 18200.
Bourges : 35 km.
Saint-Amand : 6 km.
Private property.

Meillant is the most famous château in the Berry. Originally a 14th century castle similar to Ainay-le-Vieil, it was transformed into a luxurious residence for Charles II d'Amboise by the cardinal of Amboise who had built Gaillon. These major transformations are obvious in the extravagant decoration modelled on the Hôtel de

Mehun-sur-Yèvre Charles VII Castle.

Mehun-sur-Yèvre - 18500.
Property of the commune.

This castle was transformed at the end of the 14th century by Jean, duc de Berry one of the three « great princes of the West », a great patron, collector and builder. All that is left of the original castle is the North tower at the

CULAN

Culan rises proudly from a rocky spur, keeping its military appearance and looking like a fortress ready for a seige. It was captured by Philip Augustus in 1188. From the 10th to the 16th centuries it belonged to the seigneurs then barons of Culan before becoming the property of Sully, the prince de Condé, Michel Le Tellier (Louvois' father) and finally of the princes d'Harcourt and de Croÿ. Joan of Arc stayed here in 1429, Louis XI in 1465 later followed by Sully, Condé and Louvois.
Inside are fine 15th century fireplaces. You can see Joan of Arc's room which is furnished.
Of special interest are the 15th century chests the French and Flemish tapestries and French and Spanish paintings. Notice especially the Ribera Saint Peter and the Luca Giordano Mary Magdelene.

CHER

juncture of the Yèvre and Annain rivers and the North-West tower which is half ruined. The Charles VII tower is now the home of a small museum with historic documents, furniture, ceramics and archeological exhibits from the reign.
Open Easter weekend.
June 1 to 30 : Sundays and hollidays : 10 - 12, 2:30 - 5.
July 1 to Aug. ; 31 daily except Tuesdays and Sept. 1 to 30, Sundays : 10 - 12, 2:30 - 5:30.
Parking.
Guided tours.
Tel. : (48) 57.30.25.

Menetou-Salon (Château).

Menetou-Salon - 18510.
Station : Bourges 18 km.
Private property.

Menetou-Salon is a translation of the Latin Monastelum-Salonis, literally the Monastery of Salon. This huge château belonged to Jacques Cœur in the 15th century and was restored by prince Auguste d'Arenberg four centuries later. It was therefore one of the princely residences of the Belle Epoque. Inside is a collection of vintage cars and carriages dating from the turn of the century. There are also period tapestries and furniture.
Open March 2 to Dec. 4 : 2 - 6.
Closed Tuesdays.
Parking.
Guided tours, brochures.
English - Spanish - German.
Panels.
School activities on request.
Tel. : (48) 64.80.54.

Noirlac (Abbey).

Bruère-Allichamps - 18200.
Bourges : 30 km.
Property of the department.

Set in a valley on the banks of the Cher, the Cistercian abbey of Noirlac, founded in 1150, has kept its original plan as established by the rule of Saint Bernard. The church and the chapter house built in the 12th and 13th centuries surround a 13th to 15th century cloister. Except for the large dormitory which was made into apartments in the 17th century, the structure has been preserved despite transformations after the Revolution. The abbey has recently been completely restored by the Monuments Historiques.
Open daily April 1 to Sept. 30 : 10 - 12, 2 - 6.
Oct. 1 to March 31 : 10 - 12, 2 - 5.
Closed Tuesdays in October.
Guided tours.

CHER

MEILLANT

A fine example of late 15th / early 16th century architecture, Meillant was restored by Charles I of Amboise and his son Charles II who completely transformed the medieval fortress. The cardinal d'Amboise supervised the work. The South façade is still very medieval in appearance but the North façade is an example of flamboyant Gothic with Renaissance elements. Inside are numerous sumptuously furnished rooms.

...gonne (Castle).

...gonne - 18600.
...coins : 8 km.
...urges : 45 km.
...vate property.

...agonne has been lived in by
...rielle d'Estrées and by Jules
...douin-Mansart, the architect of
...sailles. It is separated from a
...dieval village by walls and a
...at. Its enormous keep has a
...pel and two painted rooms as
... as armour and memorabilia
...hose who have resided at Sa-
...ne.
...n July 1 to Sept. 30 : 2 - 6.
...ups on request off season.
...ed tours, brochures.
...rded information.

Notices in English and German.
Shows.
Tel. : (44) 733.59.25 and
(48) 74.62.13.

Thaumiers (Château).

Charenton-sur-Cher - 18210.
Bourges : 35 km.
Saint-Amand-Montrond : 18 km.
Property of M. de Bonneval.

This ancient fortress was remodelled in the 18th century. Madeleine de l'Aubespine whose beauty was celebrated by Ronsard lived here.
Open July 1 to Aug. 31 : 10 - 7.
Groups on request out of season.
Parking.
Unaccompanied visits.
Information in English and Spanish.
Tel. : (48) 60.87.62.

Tour-de-Vèvre (Castle)

Neuvy-Deux-Clochers - 18520.
Near Bourged (Station).
Property of the commune.

Built in 1170 by descendants of the Norman invaders, this square shaped keep is four stories high and has an impressive 15 meter high roof.
Open for groups on request.
Guided tours.
Brochures.
Tel. : (48) 54.23.00.

La Verrerie (Château).

Oizon - 18700.
Bourges : 45 km.
Private property.

NOIRLAC

CHER

the heart of the Berry countryside, his Abbey was founded in 1136. emarkably well restored, Noirlac has preserved all the features of a Cistercian abbey : church, chapter house, cloister and storeroom.

ROUTE JACQUES-CŒUR

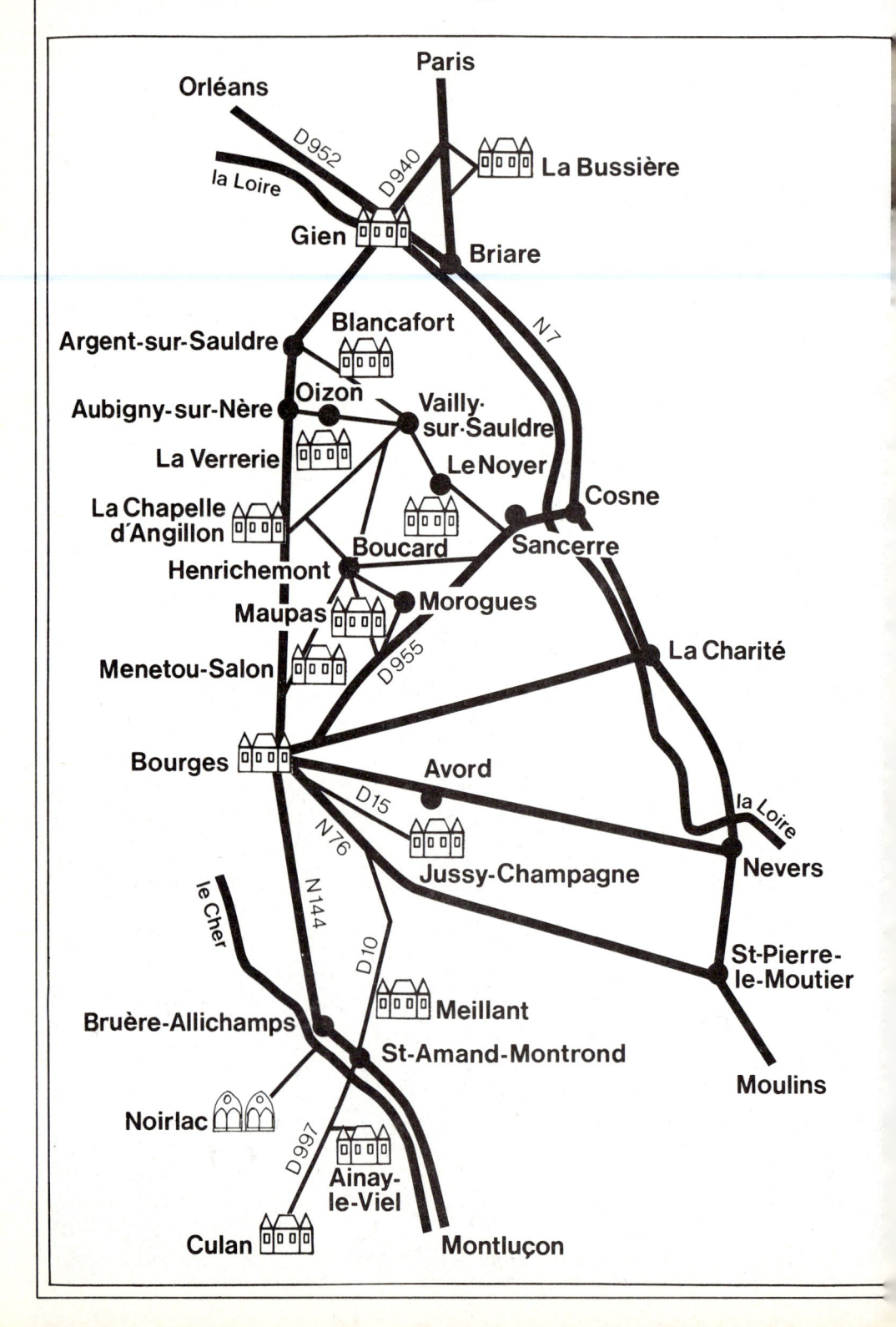

THAUMIERS

CHER

Paying Guests.

Whether you are just passing through or staying for a quiet holiday, you will be welcome at Thaumiers.

Thaumiers is located 36 km South of the medieval town of Bourges near the Berry châteaux on the Jacques Cœur route, in the middle of the Sancerre vineyards, near George Sand's home at Nohant.

For further information write to:
Madame la Vicomtesse de Bonneval
Château de Thaumiers
18210 Charenton-du-Cher.
Tel.: (48) 60.87.62.

CHER/EURE-ET-LOIR

In 1423, Charles VII gave this site to John Stuart, the youngest son of the Scottish royal family in recognition of his assistance against the English. The main building, the chapel decorated with frescoes and the entryway were built during the first Italian Wars. Later, Robert Stuart finished the château in 1525. Its style is that of the early Renaissance decorated with medallions and marble busts. In 1684, following the extinction of the French Stuart line Louis XIV gave La Verrerie to Louise de Kerouaille, Duchess of Portsmouth, favorite of Charles II. In 1842 the château was sold to the Vogüe family. The excellent state of the château enables the visitor to fully appreciate the quality of the works of art that are to be seen there.

Open Feb. 15 to Nov. 15 : 10 - 12, 2 - 7.
Off season on request.
Parking.
Guided tours.
Concerts.
Tel. : (48) 58.06.91.

Villatre (Granary). Sophie and Gerard Capazza Gallery.

Nançay - 18330.
Bourges : 35 km.
Station : Vierzon 18 km.
Bus service.
Private property.

Formerly a 17th century barracks built in local brick and flat slate, Villatre is now a contemporary art gallery.

Open March 20 to Jan. 16 : 9:30 - 12:30, 2:30 - 7:30.
On request Fridays and Saturdays and for groups daily out of season.
Closed Tues., Wed., Thurs.
Parking.
Unaccompanied visits, panels.
English - German - Spanish.
Guided tours available.
Shows.
Lecture tours for school groups.
Tel. : (48) 51.80.22.

EURE-ET-LOIR

Alluyes (Castle). Chevallier-Debeausse Foundation.

Alluyes - 28800.
Station : Bonneval 6 km.
Private Property.

The 12th and 13th century keep and a building flanked by two towers are all that remains of this ancient castle on the banks of the Loir. The castle still has its surrounding wall, moat and Renaissance chapel.

Open on request.
Parking.
Unaccompanied visits, brochures.
Tel. : (37) 47.20.32.

Anet (Château).

Anet - 28260.
Private property.

In 1550 the architect Philibert Delorme built Anet on the order of Henri II for Diane de Poitiers. The greatest artists of the French Renaissance worked here : there are fine bas-reliefs by Jean Gou

---

CHER

LA VERRERIE

This Stuart château is set in fine grounds with lakes and ponds. The chapel is deconrated with frescoes and there is a Renaissance gallery. Inside are works of art and Vogüe family memorabilia.

..., statues by Germain Pilon and tapestries after cartoons by Jean Cousin. The Italian Renaissance is also represented with works by Benvenuto Cellini (the figure of Diana), Primaticcio and Andrea della Robbia. During the reign of Louis XIV the duc de Vendôme continued to embellish the château adding a grand staircase by Claude Desgots and a basin by Le Nôtre. Badly damaged during the Revolution, the château was not restored until 1840.

Open Nov. 1 to March 31 Saturdays : 2 - 5; Sundays and holidays : 10 - 11:30, 2 - 5.
April 1 to Oct. 31 Daily : 2:30 - 6:30; Sundays and holidays : 10 - 11:30, 2:30 - 6:30.
Closed Tuesdays.
Tel. : (37) 41.90.07.

Blanville (Château).

Fourville-sur-Eure
28190 Saint-Luperce.
Private property.

This Louis XIII building set among boxwood and trees once belonged to François de Cluzel, intendant of the city of Tours, town planner and builder of renown. Inside is 17th, 18th, and 19th century furniture.

Open daily Jan. 1 to Easter, Oct. 1 to Dec. 31 : 10 - 12, 3 - 6.
Groups on request.
Guided tours and brochures.
English and German.
Tel. : (37) 26.85.22
and (4) 705.57.36.

CHARTRES
Botanical Gardens.

39, avenue d'Aligre.
Chartres - 28000.
Property of the Eure et Loire Horticultural Society.

Located to the North of the city, the gardens cover some two hectares and have age old trees among which is a ginko. The gardens are kept up by the local horticultural society. It has a pavilion which used to serve as a leper house.

Open April 1 to Nov. 1 : 8:30 - 6.
Unaccompanied visits.
Tel. : (37) 21.39.15.

Châteaudun (Château).

Châteaudun - 28200.
Property of the State.

Thanks to its comanding position on the Loir valley, Châteaudun occupied an important strategic position on the Beauce plain. It was the property of the Orléans family from 1391 to 1710. The feudal castle was replaced by a comfortable and airy residence. The courtyard still has two loggia staircases, one decorated in High Gothic style, the other in Renaissance style. Remarkably well preserved, the interiors include huge kitchens with ribbed vaulting and three large fireplaces. In the Gothic chapel are statues of Saints and a 16th century fresco of the Last

GRENIER DE VILLATRE
GALLERY
SOPHIE AND GERARD CAPAZZA

CHER

You are invited to visit the permanent exhibitions of painting, engraving, sculpture, tapestry, textiles, murals, stained glass and contemporary art in Sophie and Gérard Capazza's gallery. Their selection also includes jewellery, ceramics, wood carvings, tooled leather, painted silk, patchwork, lacquer (furniture, screens). Hand made clothing, silk clothing, wrought iron furniture, blown glass etc.

130 different artists from all over France.

Open weekends and holidays : 9:30 - 12:30, 2:30 - 7:30.
Mondays and Fridays by appointment.

EURE-ET-LOIR

ANET

In 1550 Philibert Delorme was ordered by King Henri II to build Anet for the beautiful Diane de Poitiers. The greatest artists of the French Renaissance worked here. You can see fine bas-reliefs by Jean Goujon, Germain Pilon's statues, tapestries designed by Jean Cousin. The Italian Renaissance is also represented by Benvenuto Cellini's Diana and works by Primaticcio and Andrea della Robbia. During the reign of Louis XIV the ducs de Vendôme added the impressive staircase by Claude Desgots and commissioned Le Nôtre to design the basins.

Anet is within easy reach of Paris by the Autoroute de l'Ouest (75 km).

MAINTENON

EURE-ET-LOIR

This famous brick and stone château was given to Madame de Maintenon by Louis XIV who later married her. With its furnishings intact, Maintenon offers a unique image of the Seventeenth Century, of Madame de Maintenon and of the Noailles family who have owned it since 1698. The grounds laid out by Le Nôtre and the avenues in the park evoke the memory of Racine, author of « Esther » and « Athalie ». Vauban's acquaduct designed to bring water to Versailles but never finished is another impressive reminder of the age of Louis XIV.

Judgement. The château was restored in 1930 and has kept its fine tapestry collection.
Open daily April 15 to Oct. 31 : 9:30 - 11:45, 2 - 6.
Nov. 1 to April 15 : 10 - 11:45, 2 - 6.
Parking.
Guided tours, brochures.
Tel. : (37) 45.22.70.

Denonville (Château).

Denonville - 28700.
Anneau : 3 km.
Private property.

The château was transformed in the 16th century after it was pillaged by the Huguenots. Flanked by four crenellated towers, it has a stone wing with a fine staircase whose wrought iron bannister is of particular interest. The main rooms still have their period panelling.
Open July 3 to Sept. 15 : 2 - 6.
Closed Tuesdays.
Parking.
Guided tours, brochures.
Acoustiguides.
Tel. : (37) 99.63.00.

Frazé (Château).

Frazé - 28160.
Chartres : 40 km.
Station : Brou 8 km.
Private property.

Fraze was rebuilt in 1493 and its fortified gate, ground floor buildings and keep are all that remain of the 15th century castle. The residence that was built at the end of the 16th century and beginning of the 17th century has been very much restored. In the grounds is an ancient Roman mound. Formal gardens.
Open Sundays and holidays : 3 - 6.
Parking.
Unaccompanied visits.
Tel. : (37) 49.46.76.

Maillebois (Château).

Maillebois - 28170.
Dreux : 23 km.
Chartres : 33 km.
Private property.

François d'O, minister of Finance under Henri III and owner of the château d'O in the Orne, transformed Maillebois. The fireplace, bed and paintings come from Madame de Pompadour's Château at Crécy.
Open on request April 4 to Sept. 9.
Parking.
Guided tours.
English and German.
Tel. : (37) 48.17.01.

Maintenon (Château).

Maintenon - 28130.
Chartres : 18 km.
Park : 500 m.
Private property.

On December 27 1674, Françoise d'Aubigné, the future marquise de Maintenon, purchased this estate and added a wing to the château. She transformed the main rooms, the most remarkable of which is an antechamber hung with gilt-leather. She also had the main building joined to the church of St. Nicholas. The Racine path in the garden designed by Le Nôtre commemorates the playwright who worked on his tragedies « Esther » and « Athalie » while staying at Maintenon. The acquaduct designed by La Hire and Vauban to carry water from the Eure to Ver-

---

CHATEAUDUN

EURE-ET-LOIR

Towering over the Loir, Chateaudun is a feudal castle which belonged to the Orléans family.

Its Gothic and Renaissance façades house a fine collection of Flemish and Parisian tapestries.

sailles, is still to be seen, unfinished in the château grounds.
*Open Nov. 1 to March 31, week-ends: 2 - 5:30.
April 1 to Oct. 31, daily 2 - 6:30.
Sundays and holidays: 11 - 12:30, 2 - 6:30.
Closed Tuesdays.
Closed Christmas day and January.
Open or request for groups.
Parking.
Guided tours or unaccompanied visits.
Leaflets in English, German, Spanish, Italian, Portuguese, Japanese, Russian.
Brochures.
Helicopter tours on request.
Lecture tours on request.
Lectures, temporary exhibits.
Concerts, arts and crafts.
Tel.: (37) 23.00.09.*

Montigny-sur-Avre (Château).

*Montigny-sur-Avre - 28270.
Station: Verneuil-sur-Avre, 8 km.
Private property.*
A treelined avenue leads to two 18th century brick and stone pavilions with Mansard roofs and turrets at each corner. The château belonged to the Montmorency-Laval family.
*Open on request.
Parking.
Guided tours.
Tel.: (37) 48.28.25.*

Sorel (Château).

*Sorel-Moussel - 28520.
Anet: 5 km.
Dreux: 14 km.
Private property.*
Built on a rock spur on the Eure river, Sorel occupies a commanding position in a Normandy valley which was controlled by the English for four hundred years. Many castles were built on this site but apart from scattered medieval remains, all that can be seen today is the east wing of a building of the Louis XIII period, destroyed during the Revolution. This brick and stone building consisted of a main block flanked by two wings and an armorial portal decorated with allegories which can still be seen today.
*Open week-ends.
Grounds only.
Parking.
Unaccompanied visits.
Tel.: (37) 41.80.92.*

Reverseaux (Château).

*Rouvray-Saint-Florentin - 28150.
Chartres: 25 km.
Jouves: 5,5 km.
Private property.*

This Louis XIII château flanked by Louis XIV turrets, was acquired by general de Gouvion-Saint-Cyr in 1807. In 1870 it served temporarily as a hospital.
*Open for groups on request.
Tel.: (4) 503.41.78.*

Ville-Prévost (Château).

*Tilly-en-Péneux - 28140.
Chartres, Orléans: 40 km.
Artenay: 15 km.
Property of M. Fougeron.*
Ville-Prévost is a perfectly maintained example of an 18th century Beauce country seat.
*Open Saturdays and holidays: May 20 to Oct. 1: 10 - 12, 2 - 6:30. Sundays, May 20 to Oct. 3: 2 - 6:30.
Parking.
Open for groups on request.
Guided tours, brochures.
English and German.
Tel.: (37) 99.45.17.*

INDRE

Argy (Château).

*Buzançais - 36500.
Châteauroux: 30 km.
Buzançais: 6 km.
Property of the Club du Vieux Manoir.*
This square Renaissance structure is flanked by three towers which are joined by a fine gallery with basket handle arches and floral motifs. There is also a 15th century keep and 18th century outbuildings.
*Open Jan. 1 to Dec. 31: 8 - 12, 2 - 6.
Parking.
Guided tours, brochures.
English.
Temporary exhibits.
Lecture tours.
Camps, restroration sites.
Environmental studies group.
Tel.: (54) 84.04.98.*

Azay-le-Ferron (Château).

*Azay-le-Ferron - 36290.
Loches: 40 km.
Property of the city of Tours.*
The buildings which make up this château date from the 15th to the early 18th centuries, including towers with parapets, a 17th century wing, a François I pavilion and the Breteuil pavilion completed in 1714. Azay-le-Ferron is situated at the crossroads of Touraine and the Berry. Inside are twenty rooms decorated with works of art and furniture dating from the 15th to the 19th centuries.
*Open April 1 to Sept. 30: 10 - 12, 2 - 6, except Tuesdays.
Oct. 1 to Oct. 31 and March 1 to March 31: 10 - 12, 2 - 5, Wed., Sat. and holidays.
Nov. 1 Feb. 28: 10 - 12, 2 - 4:30, Weds. Week-ends and holidays.
Closed Nov. 1, Nov. 11, Dec. 25, Jan. 1 - Jan. 31.
Groups Wed., Thurs., Fri.
Guided tours, brochures.
Tel.: (54) 39.20.06.*

Le Bouchet-en-Brenne (Château).

*Rosnay - 36300.
Le Blanc: 15 km.
Station: Châteauroux, 45 km.
Private property.*
Captured by the English during the Hundred Years War, this fortress was completed at the end of the 15th century and then demolished in the 16th. The Mortemart family who owned the château from the 16th century to 1808 added two wings during the 17th century.
*Open July 1 to Sept. 15: 9:30 - 12, 2:30 - 7.
Groups on request the rest of the year.
Closed Tuesdays and Sunday mornings.
Parking.
Guided tours, brochures.
Temporary exhibits.
Tel.: (54) 37.80.14.*

Bouges (Château).

*Bouges - 36110 Levroux.
Châteauroux: 20 km.
Property of the C.N.M.H.S.*
Located near Valençay, this Ita-

...lianate pavilion was built in the 18th century for Charles François Leblanc de Marnaval on an estate once belonging to Catherine de Medici. Set in the middle of terraces and framed by balustrades Bouges is reminiscent of the Petit Trianon and is thought to have been built by the same architect, Gabriel. Its rectangular façades are surrounded by formal gardens and a large park. Although stripped of its original furnishings, Bouges recovered its former splendour through the efforts of M. Henri Viguier, the proprietor who left the château and all its works of art to the Caisse Nationale des Monuments Historiques in 1967.
Open daily April 1 to June 30, Oct. 1 to 30 : 10 - 12, 2 - 6.
July 1 to Sept. 30 : 9 - 12, 2 - 6.
Nov. 1 to March 30 : 10 - 12, 2 - 5.

Week-ends and Wed. afternoon only.
Closed Tuesdays.
Rooms for hire.
Floodlighting for receptions.
Tel. : (54) 35.88.26.

Breuil-Yvain (Château).

Orsennes - 36190.
Châteauroux : 40 km.
Private property.
This fortified house has an entry tower which dates from the 15th century. You pass through this tower into the main building and out buildings which date from the 18th century.
Open Aug. 1 to Sept. 15.
Grounds only.
Parking.
Unaccompanied visits.
Tel. : (54) 47.22.14.

Château-Guillaume (Château).

Lignac-Belabre - 36370.
Argenton-sur-Creuse : 35 km.
Le Blanc : 24 km.
Private property.
This castle was built by William X, father of Eleonor of Aquitaine who was born here. From the 13th to the 16th centuries the castle belonged to the La Tremoïlle family. It has a large Romanesque keep which is surrounded by four towers and ramparts.
Open July 1 to Aug. 30 : 2:30 - 6, Wed Thurs., week-ends : 2:30 - 6.
Aug. 20 - 30 : 2:30 - 6, daily.
Sept. week-end except 29 and 30.
Parking.
Guided tours.

Le Châtelier (Château).

Pommiers — 36190.
Station : Argenton-sur-Creuse, 15 km.
Private property.
You enter Le Châtelier through Renaissance building, in front of which you see a courtyard with well and a keep. This keep was built on three stories in the 15th century and is of remarkable design. Built as a means of defence Le Châtelier was a residence as well as a military stronghold which is why Richelieu did not destroy it.
On the eve of the Revolution belonged to the Lusignan family.
Open Jan. 1 to Dec. 31 : 9 - 12, 2 - 5
Parking.
Unaccompanied visits.
Tel. : (54) 47.85.95.

INDRE

AZAY-LE-FERRON

Fifteenth century tower, 17th century d'Humière wing.

Renaissance pavilion façade from 1600 and Breteuil wing from 1700.

PALLUAU-SUR-INDRE

INDRE

Built in the 11th century, Palluau witnessed many bloody battles : its underground passages alone were capable of housing an entire army. Rebuilt in the 15th century, the château now offers guided tours, musical entertainment and sound and light shows. Guest rooms are available and the château can also be used for receptions, parties and filming. The medieval village has all amenities and there is a beach and camping site on the banks of the Indre.

DIORS

Trois Guerres (Château and Museum).

Diors-par-Déols - 36130.
Châteauroux : 10 km.
Property of M. de La Rochefoucauld.

Diors which dated from the 16th and 18th centuries was destroyed by bombing in 1944. The outbuildings which survived now house a museum devoted to the wars of 1870, 1914 and 1939, with 30 000 objects displayed in 30 rooms.
Open Feb. 5 to Jan. 5 : 9 -12, 2 - 6.
Closed Tuesdays.
Parking.
Brochures.
Tel. : (54) 26.02.16.

ISSOUDUN

Saint-Roch (Museum).

Issoudun - 36100.
Station : Issoudun.
Property of the commune.

The main museum of Issoudun, founded in 1864, was installed in a 16th century vicarage which was destroyed in 1940. The collection that was saved was then displayed in the hospital and chapel of Saint Roch, a hospice dating from the 13th to 16th centuries. Among the many exhibits are a large dispensary with pots of Nevers faience and a library noted for its collections of books relating to pharmacology and medecine of the 16th to 19th centuries.
Open Jan. 1 to Dec. 31 : 10 - 12, 2 - 7.
Closed Tuesdays.
Parking.
Unaccompanied visits, brochures.
Information in English and German.
Tel. : (54) 21.01.76.

Notre-Dame du Landais (Abbey).

Fredille - 36500.
Station : Châteauroux, 26 km.
Property of M. Pécherat.

This Cistercian abbey, founded in 1140, was restored in the 17th century, sold during the Revolution and then used as a quarry in 1830. Of the original abbey you can now see the choir, two chapels of the South transept and the sacristy.
Open Jan. 1 to Dec. 31.
Closed Sunday mornings.
Groups on request at other times.
Guided tours.
Panels.
Information in English - German.
Lecture tours for school groups.
Tel. : (54) 34.70.49.

Le Lys Saint-Georges (Castle).

Le Lys Saint-Georges - 36230.
Station : Châteauroux, 25 km.
Private property.

This medieval fortress with its interior Renaissance courtyard once housed Ludovico Sforza, il Moro, whom Louis XII imprisoned here during the Italian wars. The walls are surrounded by a moat and you can also see the foundations of the impressive keep.
Open all year.
Grounds only.
Concerts.
Tel. : (54) 30.81.51.

NOHANT

George Sand's Residence

Nohant-Vicq - 36400 La Châtre.
La Châtre : 6 km.
Châteauroux : 30 km.
Property of the State.

George Sand described her country home at Nohan as « set on the edge of a forest and as simple as a villager's cottage ». In fact this building is set in courtyard surrounded by outbuildings. It was built at the end of the 18th century for the governor of Vierzon and then acquired by Madame Dupin de Francueil, the author's grandmother in 1793. She was responsible for the huge grounds and gardens, greenhouses and walks. It was here that the young Aurore Dupin spent her childhood years and later on she wrote many of her novels here and received a stream of celebrated guests : Liszt, Balzac, Chopin, Flaubert. Delacroix had an studio here. The interiors have been preserved exactly as George Sand had known them in the last years of her life. You can see her dining room, theatre, puppet theatre and blue room.
Open daily April 1 to Oct. 31 : 10 - 12, 2 - 6.
Nov. 1 to March 31 : 10 - 12, 2 - 4.
Parking.
Guided tours.
Brochures, audiovisual.
Festival.
Tel. : (54) 31.06.04.

Palluau (Château).

Palluau-sur-Indre - 36500.
Loches : 35 km.
Private property.

Palluau was built in the 11th century and was the scene of many bloody battles. The underground passages alone could house an entire army. Rebuilt in the 15th century, the château has Renaissance furnishings and a chapel decorated with frescoes.
Open Jan. 1 to Dec. 31 : 10 - 12, 2 - 6.
Closed Tuesdays.
Parking.
Guided tours, brochures.
Panels.
English - German - Spanish.
Facilities for the handicapped.
Sound and Light.
Temporary exhibits.
Crafts workshops.
Tel. : (54) 38.47.49.

Saint-Laurent (Priory).

Palluau-sur-Indre - 36500.
Near Châteauroux.
Station : Saint-Genou, 2 km.
Private property.

In this Romanesque church are fragments of 12th century wall paintings representing the Virgin, the Annunciation, Christ in Majesty and the martyrdom of Sai

SARZAY

INDRE

A feudal castle built in 1300 by the lord of Barbancois.
Five round fortified towers.

VALENÇAY

INDRE

Sound and Light Festivals

The famous home of the prince de Talleyrand.
Completely furnished.

Vintage car museum. Nature park.
Group visits and lectures on request.
Information : Tel. : (54) 00.10.66.

INDRE/INDRE-ET-LOIRE — CENTRE

Lawrence dating from the 15th century. The Romanesque crypt has recently been excavated. The priory is currently being restored.
Open daily.
Unaccompanied visits.
Information on other abbeys in the region.
Tel. : (54) 05.66.58.

Sarzay (Castle).

Neuvy-Saint-Sépulcre - 36230.
La Châtre : 7 km.
Station : Châteauroux - La Châtre : 35 km.
Private property.

Built in 1300 by the lords of Barbancois, this feudal castle has 38 surrounding towers. Today you can see five of these each with parapets. The four storied castle has fragments of Romanesque and Gothic murals.
Open April 1 to Sept. 30 : 10 - 12, 2 - 6.
Parking.
Guided tours.
Lectures - Guides - Brochures.
Tel. : (54) 48.33.52.

Valençay (Château).

Valençay - 36600.
Station : Valençay.
Private property.

Built during the Renaissance and extended in the 17th and 18th centuries, Valençay was purchased by Talleyrand who was minister of Foreign Affairs under Napoleon and Louis XVIII. It then became a political centre and was used as a prison for the princes of Spain during the Empire. The interior is decorated in Louis XVI and Empire styles and now houses a vintage car museum. The grounds are also full of many different kinds of animals.
Open March 15 to Nov. 15, 9 - 12, 2 - 6.
Grounds and museum open all year.
Parking.
Guided tours of the château.
Unaccompanied visits of the museum.
English - German - Spanish - Italian.
Guided tours in English and German by written request.
Brochures.
Festivals, temporary exhibits.
Lecture tours by the curator on request.
Nature park.
Tel. : (54) 00.10.66.

Varennes (Abbey).

Fougerolles - 36230.
Station : Châteauroux, 35 km.
Private property.

Varennes is a Cistercian abbey which was founded in 1155 by Henry II of England. The church has a single vaulted nave typical of the Western Gothic style in France. At the beginning of the 20th century the abbey acted as a literary salon ; André Maurois and Romain Rolland were among its habitués.
Open July 7 to Aug. 19, Sept. 1 to 16 : 10 - 12, 2 - 6.
Closed Fridays.
Parking.
Panels.
Tel. : (4) 527.73.83.

Veuil (Château).

Veuil-Valençay - 36600.
Station : Valençay, 6 km.
Private property.

Louis XV erected Veuil to a comté. It had formerly been the property of Jacques Hurault member of the Paris parlement in the 16th century and then passed to Talleyrand who neglected it. All that remains of the original building is the West front with its Renaissance gallery, two towers and the kitchens.
Open April 1 to Sept. 30 : 9 - 6.
Parking.
Unaccompanied visits.
Panels.
Tel. : (54) 40.32.77.

Villegongis (Château).

Villegongis-Levroux - 36110.
Station : Châteauroux, 15 km.
Property of M. de Montesquieu.

Villegongis was built in the Renaissance by Pierre Trinqueau, on of the master builders responsible for Chambord. The decoration is rather surprising : cut slate ornamentation, monumental fireplaces sculpted as if in silver and gold.
Open April 1 to Sept. 30 : 11 - 12, 2 - 5:30.
On request out of season.
Guided tours, brochures.
Information in English.
Tel. : (54) 36.60.51.

INDRE-ET-LOIRE

Amboise (Château).

Amboise - 37400.
Tours : 25 km.
Blois : 35 km.
Property of the Saint-Louis Foundation.

Rebuilt after the first Italian wars by Italian designers and painters, Amboise, with its thick walls decorated with balustrades and carved dormer windows, was the scene of many important events. Leonardo da Vinci organised many elaborate entertainments here but Amboise was also used as a prison and witnessed many conspiracies the most famous of which, the Amboise Conspiracy, ended in a bloody defeat for the Protestants. Thereafter, the kings of France rarely returned to the château which became a state prison before being sold. Restoration began at the end of the 19th century.
Open daily Nov. 1 to Palm Sunday : 9 - 12, 2:30 - 5:30.
Palm Sunday to Oct. 31 : 9 - 12, 2 - 6:30.

Azay-le-Rideau (Château).

Azay-le-Rideau - 37109.
Tours : 28 km.
Property of the State.

Built on piles on an island in the Indre, Azay-le-Rideau was erected between 1518 and 1527 on the site of and old stronghold. Originally the residence of Gilles Berthelot, royal treasurer, the château has survived without any major remodelling. Its uneventful history contrasts with its brillant architecture which sums up the aspirations of the Renaissance. With their towers and turrets the two perpendicular wings present a harmonious mixture of traditional motifs and elements from Italian art. The rooms have been furnished with the help of the Monuments Historiques and the Cluny museum. You can see a fine collection of Flanders tapestries of the 16th and 17th centuries.
Open daily April 1 to Sept. 30 : 9:15 - 12, 2 - 6:30.
Oct. 1 to Nov. 15 : 9:15 - 12, 2 - 5.
Nov. 15 to palm Sunday : 9:30 - 12, 2 - 4:45.
Parking.
Guided tours.
Brochures.
Sound and Light in summer.
Tel. : (47) 43.32.04.

VILLEGONGIS

INDRE

Built by Avoye de Chabannes and her husband, Jacques de Brizay. Construction supervised by Pierre Trinqueneau, one of the master builders of Chambord. The château has never been sold and has changed hands through marriage only. Inside are period rooms of the 16th to 19th centuries.
For visits call (54) 36.60.51.

Bois-Aubry (Abbey).

Luze - 37120.
Richelieu : 15 km.
Châtellerault : 28 km.
Private property.

Founded in 1118, this abbey was the home of the Tiron Benedictines until 1791. It was built along Cistercian lines. Its church and 40 meter bell tower, the dormitory, the chapter house and the scriptorium still exist. Today Bois-Aubry belongs to the monks of the order of Saint Benoit.
Open daily Jan. 1 to Dec. 31 : 10 - 12, 2 - 6.
Parking.
Guided tours.
English - German - Spanish.
Lectures.
Lecture tours for school groups.
Tel. : (47) 58.34.48.

Bourgueil (Abbey).

Bourgueil - 37140.
52, avenue Le Jouteux - 37140.
Chinon : 17 km.
Port-Boulet : 5 km.
Private property.

This large abbey was founded in 990 by Emma, daughter of Thibault le Tricheur, comte d'Anjou and was enlarged in the 18th century. The Eastern section still preserves some of the original buildings. The church was destroyed in the Revolution but you can still visit the main building, the refectory, the barns and the storeroom. The corbelled staircase, an architectural feat leads to the monks cells where works of art are displayed.
Open Easter to Sept. 30 and holidays : 2 - 6.
July 1 to Aug. 31 : Fri., Mon. and weekends : 2 - 6.

Groups on request out of season.
Guided tours.
English and German.
Panels.
Tel. : (47) 97.72.04.

Bridoré (Château).

Bridoré-Loches - 37600.
Loches : 14 km.
Private property.

This 14th and 15th century fortress was built by Imbert de Bastarnay, Louis XI's Chamberlain. With its network of defences, it was the most highly fortified site in the region. The public can visit the upper and lower courts, the kitchens, the heating system and the rustic furnished rooms typical of the Middle Ages.
Open daily June 15 to Aug. 31 : 2 - 6.

Photo J. Gachet

INDRE-ET-LOIRE

AZAY-LE-RIDEAU

Built under François I, Azay-le-Rideau bears witness to the wealth and luxury displayed by the great financiers of the 16th century. Its exterior was inspired by Blois, and the courtyard staircase, a real piece of bravura design, leads to a lavishly decorated interior.

CHENONCEAU

INDRE-ET-LOIRE

A masterpiece of the Renaissance, Chenonceau, with its noble elegant architecture, bears witness to the finest and surest feminine taste. Diane de Poitiers and the Catherine de Medici left their mark on this château building first the bridge and gallery over the Cher and the embellishing this residence with the gardens than can still be admired today. It is thanks to these two women that Chenonceau has the grace and charm which has made it world famous.

Guided tours, brochures.
Panels in English and French.
Temporary exhibits.
Tel. : (47) 94.72.63.

Champigny-sur-Veude (Château and Chapel).

Champigny-sur-Veude - 37120.
Station : Chinon 15 km.
Bus service from the station.
Private property.

Built by the duc de Montpensier in 1508, the château was burnt to the ground by Richelieu in 1635 following the rebellion by Gaston d'Orléans. The Holy Chapel so called because it contained a relic of the True Cross, was saved through the intervention of Pope Urban VIII thanks to whom the important stained glass windows can still be seen. You can also visit the gardens and the courtyards and see the facades of the out buildings which became the seigneurial residence when Champigny was handed back to Anne Marie de Montpensier, the Grande Mademoiselle. They have been completely restored.
Open April 1 to Oct. 15 : 9 - 12, 2 - 6.
Parking.
Guided tours, brochures.
Leaflets in English and German.
High Mass on Saint Louis day August 28.
Tel. : (47) 95.73.20.

Chatigny (Château).

Fondettes - 37230.
Station : Fondettes-Saint-Cyr, 4 km.
Tours : 10 km.
Private property.

Chatigny was built in the 15th century on the site of a Gallo-Roman villa. The grounds still contain remains of the original structure. The brick and stone château itself dominates the Loire with its three main towers. Inside you can see a dozen rooms, most of which were decorated during the Second Empire. There is also a chapel.
Open on request.
Parking.
Unaccompanied visits.
Information in English.
Tel. : (47) 55.20.05.

Chenonceau (Château).

Chenonceau - 37150.
Tours : 34 km.
Amboise : 12 km.
Private property.

In 1547 Henri II gave Chenonceau to Diane de Poitiers but on his death she was forced to give the property to Catherine de Medici. It was only then that the château became the centre for lavish entertainments where the Italian style was triumphant. The château had been designed for women by women hence the altogether Eexceptional charm of the site. Beside the 15th century keep and the square main building whose facade was inspired by François I's wing at Blois, Philibert Delorme decided to link the château to the left bank of the Cher. Thus followed the two storied wing, sixty meters long which spans the river supported by five arches.
Open daily March 16 to Sept. 15 : 9 - 7.
Sept. 16 to Sept. 30 : 9 - 6:30.
Oct. 1 to 31 : 9 - 6.
Nov. 1 to 15 : 9 - 5.
Nov. 16 to Feb. 15 : 9 - 12, 2 - 4:30.
Feb. 16 to 28 : 9 - 5:30.
March 1 to 15 : 9 - 6.
Parking.
Unaccompanied visits.
Panels.
Information in English, German, Spanish, Italian, Dutch, Japanese.
Brochures.
Boat rides in July and August.
Tel. : (47) 23.90.07.

Chinon (Castle).

Chinon - 37500.
Station : 2 km.
Bus nearby.

Three medieval fortresses were built here on this ancient Gallo-Roman site. They were from East to West, the fort of Saint George, the Middle Castle, and the Coudray castle. The defence network of this group of castles was reinforced by their successive proprietors, the comtes de Blois, Henry Plantagenet, Philip Augustus. It was in this powerful complex that Joan of Arc met the future king Charles VII in 1429. By the end of the 15th century, the fame of Chinon was gradually eclipsed and the castle was left to ruin. This process was accelerated by the demolitions carried out under Richelieu.
Open March 15 to Sept. 30, July 1 to Aug. 31 : 9 - 12, 2 - 6.
Oct. 1 to March 14 : 9 - 12, 2 - 5.
Closed Wednesdays Oct. to March 14.
Closed December and January.
Parking.
Unaccompanied visits or guided tours brochures.
Panels.
Notices in English, German, Italian.
Tel. : (47) 93.13.45.

Le Clos-Lucé (Leonardo da Vinci's Residence).

Amboise - 37400.
Tours : 24 km.
Amboise : 2 km.
Private property.

Leonardo da Vinci settled in a Clos Lucé on his arrival from Ital and worked here until his death i 1519. The house contains a fabulous collection of models of fort of his inventions including the firs airplane, tank and automobile a well as his room, kitchen, orator with ceilings painted by his wor shop and a mysterious under ground passage that leads to th château at Amboise.
Open May 1 to 30, Sept. 1 to Oct. 1 : 9 12, 2 - 7.
June 1 to Aug. 30 : 9 - 7.
Closed Dec. 25 and Jan. 2 to 31.
Parking.
Guided tours available.
Panels.
Information in English, German, Italian Spanish, Japanese.
Concerts, plays, temporary exhibits.
Lectures.
Tel. : (47) 57.62.88.

Cinq-Mars (Castle).

Cinq-Mars-la-Pile.
Langeais - 37130.
Tours : 17 km.
Langeais : 4 km.
Property of Mme Untersteller.

This is the birth place of Hen Coeffer de Ruzé, marquis de Cinq Mars, the favorite of Louis XI who was beheaded in 1642 at the age of 22 for having conspire with the Spaniards for the down

fall of Richelieu. The latter had the castle seized and dismantled. All that remains are the two towers and the moat.
Open April 1 to Oct. 1 : 10 - 12, 2 - 6.
Oct. 1 to Nov. 11 : 10 - 12, 2 - 5.
Closed Mondays except holidays.
Parking.
Guided tours, brochures.
Panels.
Information in English, German, Spanish, Italian, Dutch.
Facilities for the handicapped.
Tel. : (47) 96.40.49.

La Devinière (Rabelais' House and Museum).

Seuilly.
Chinon - 37500.
Property of the department.
Tradition has it that François Rabelais was born in this house in 1494. The house is a good example of a Renaissance bourgeois country house and contains a variety of documents relating to the importance of the region in the author's work. Much of the surrounding countryside is described by Rabelais and La Devinière is the model for the house of Grangousier.
Open March 15 to Sept. 30 : 9 - 12, 2 - 6.
Oct. 1 to March 14 : 9 - 12, 2 - 5.
Closed Wednesdays Oct. 1 to March 14.
Closed Dec. and Jan.
Parking.
Guided tours available, brochures.
Panels.
Information in English, German, Italian.
Tel. : (47) 95.91.18.

La Guerche (Castle).

Le Grand-Pressigny - 37350.
Loches : 40 km.
Châtellerault : 20 km.
La Roche-Posay : 14 km.
Private property.
La Guerche is an ancient stronghold built on the site where a Roman road crossed the Creuse river. The castle was rebuilt in the 15th century with massive towers, guardroom and drawbridge. There are two floors of vaulted cellars, one containing ancient canons the other was a grain silo.
Open July 1 to Aug. 31 : 10 - 12, 2 - 6:30.
Closed Sunday mornings.
Sept. 1 to June 30 : 2 - 6.
Closed Tuesdays.
Open on request out of season.
Tel. : (47) 94.92.61 or (4) 527.72.72.

Le Grand-Pressigny (Castle).

Le Grand-Pressigny - 37350.
Tours : 60 km.
Station : Tours.
Bus near by.
Property of the département.
The remains of Grand-Pressigny castle are among the most important medieval architectural sites : one of the first Romanesque keeps of the Loire valley with fortifications added in the 15th century and the octagonal « Vironne tower ». The castle was transformed in the 16th century and its arcaded gallery leads to the Museum of Palentology and Prehistory.
Open daily March 15 to Sept. 30 : 9 - 12, 2 - 6.
Oct. 1 to March 14 : 9 - 12, 2 - 5.
Closed Wednesdays from Oct. 1 to March 14.
Closed Dec. and Jan.
Parking.
Guided tours.
Temporary exhibits.
Prehistory workshops.
Tel. : (47) 94.90.20.

Grillemont (Castle).

La chapelle Blanche.
Ligueil - 37240.
Tours : 40 km.
Loches : 22 km.
Private property.
This major castle was built around 1470 by Bertrand de Lescouet, grand veneur under Louis XI who stayed here. It was turned into a pleasure château by the fermier général Dange d'Orsay in the middle of the 18th century when the keep was torn down and the gardens redesigned.
Open on request.
Parking.
Unaccompanied visit.
Information in English.
Guided tours available.
Tel. : (47) 59.62.03.

Langeais (Château).

Langeais - 37130.
Tours : 25 km.
Station : Langeais.
Property of the Institut de France.
Langeais is the work of Louis XI who wanted both a fortress and a residence. It is a rather severe construction lacking the pleasant qualities of most Loire valley châteaux. The marriage between Charles VIII and Anne of Brittany which brought the duchy under the crown took place here in 1431. The interiors have been refurnished with a large collection of Flemish tapestries of the 15th and 16th centuries. In the park are the oldest remains of a stone keep to be found in France.
Open March 15 to Jund 30 : 9 - 12, 2 - 6.
July 1 to Aug. 31 : 9 - 12, 2 - 6:30.
Sept. 1 to Nov. 2 : 9 - 12, 2 - 5:30.
Nov. 3 to March 15 : 9 - 12, 2 - 5:30.
Closed Monday mornings except holidays.
Parking.
Guided tours, brochures.
Recordings in English, German, Spanish, Italian.
Leaflets.
Information in the above languages plus Russian, Dutch, Japanese.
Tel. : (47) 96.72.60.

Le Liget (Charterhouse).

Montrésor - 37460.
Private property.
This charterhouse was founded in 1176 by Henri II Plantagenet perhaps to atone for having ordered the murder of Thomas à Beckett, archbishop of Canterbury. It was completely transformed in the 18th century. On the far side of the monumental gate are two pavilions, one for ladies to the right. Below are the out buildings where the community's lay labourers worked.
Open Jan. 1 to Dec. 31 : 9 - 7.
Parking.
Tel. : (47) 94.20.02.

Leonardo da Vinci spent the last four years of his life at Clos-Lucé and died here on May 2, 1519. At Clos-Lucé you can still enjoy the informal atmosphere of a 16th century home, fully furnished with Leonardo's bedroom, kitchen, large Renaissance rooms, the chapel with his frescoes and the gardens where he used to walk. Here you will also encounter Leonardo the engineer, whose genius was four hundred years in advance of his time. You will find 40 machines including the first airplanes, automobile, helicopter, tank, machine

CHÂTEAU OUVERT TOUS LES JOURS.

AU CLOS LUCÉ D'AMBOISE LÉONARD DE VINCI INVENTE L'AN 2000.

Venez voir ses fabuleuses machines.

gun and swing bridge. You can also see reproductions of 80 of the master's drawings.
Clos-Lucé 37400 Amboise, Val-de-Loire. 2 hours from Paris by motorway or train, 10 km from Chenonceau, 25 km from Tours.

Open daily 9 - 12, 2 - 7.
Summer 9 - 7.
Tel. : (47) 57.62.88.
Seminars - Conferences - Receptions - Film Locations.

INDRE-ET-LOIRE

LANGEAIS
Louis XI Castle. Foulques Nerra keep

In the heart of the Loire valley, Langeais provides a fine example of medieval architecture. Louis XI had this mighty fortress built between 1465 and 1467. In 1491 the marriage between Charles VIII and Anne of Brittany which brought the duchy into the kingdom was celebrated here. The exterior is a typical fortified castle, the interior courtyard heralds the Renaissance. Jacques Siegfried assembled the 15th and 16th century furnishings and gave them with the castle to the Institut de France in 1904. The prize of this museum is an admirable collection of medieval and Renaissance tapestries. The Foulques Nerra keep built in 944 by the comte d'Anjou the terrible Black Falcon, Foulques Nerra dominates the inner courtyard and the gardens.

Loches (Castle).

Loches - 37600.
Property of the département.
In the Middle Ages Loches was one of the most important fortresses of France. The Royal Gate is cut through a 15th wall and bears a plaque recording the meeting which took place here in May 1429 between Joan of Arc and Charles VII. The complex contains two museums : a local history museum and the Lansyer Museum in the house of the 19th century painter Emmanuel Lansyer. You can also visit the Anne of Brittany oratory and the tomb of Agnes Sorel.
Open March 15 to Sept. 30 : 9 - 12, 2 - 6.
Oct. 1 to March 14 : 9 - 12, 2 - 5.
July 1 to Aug. 31 : 9 - 6.
Closed Dec. and Jan.
Closed Wednesdays Oct. 1 to March 14.
Parking.
Guided tours available, brochures.
Information in English, German, Italian.
Panels.
Concerts.
Tel. : (47) 59.01.32.

Loches (Keep).

Loches - 37600.
Property of the departement.
This fortress was begun around the year 1000. The guard room, the New Tower and the Martelet tower were built in 1450. Ludovico Sforza in 1500, and Jacques Hurault were prisoners here.
Open March 15 to Sept. 30 : 9:30 - 12:30, 2:30 - 6:30.
July 1 to Aug. 31 : 9:30 - 6:30.
Oct. 1 to March 14 : 9:30 - 12:30, 2:30 - 5:30.
Closed Dec. and Jan.
Closed Wednesdays from Oct. 1 to March 31.
Parking.
Guided tours available, brochures.
Panels.
Information in English, German, Italian.
Tel. : (47) 59.07.86.

Meslay (Farm).

Parcay-Meslay - 37210.
Station : Tours, 7 km.
Bus near by.
Private property.
This is one of the oldest and largest fortified farms of the 13th century. It once belonged to the monks of Marmoutier and includes a magnificent barn with an oak roof of over three thousand square meters.
Open April 2 to Nov. 1 : 3 - 6:30, weekend and holidays.
Groups on request in the week.
Parking.
Recommended itinerary, brochures.
Information in English.
Guided tours available.
Facilities for the handicapped.
Music festivals, shows.
Tel. : (47) 51.31.21.

Montpoupon (Château).

Montrésor - 37460.
Blois and Tours : 45 km.
Station : Saint-Pierre-des-Corps, 40 km.
Private property.
Montpoupon was an important defensive position between Loches and Montrichard. The turreted Renaissance entrance gate is reminiscent of Chenonceaux. The king's bedroom has kept its 15th century decoration. Memorabilia of Louise de Prie the governess of Louis XV's children are kept here. Part of the residence, the chapel, the kitchen, the tack room, the carriages and a hunting museum are open to the public.
Open during spring vacation : 2 - 6.
June 15 to Sept. 30 : 10 - 12, 2 - 7.
Easter to June 14 and october, weekends and holidays : 10 - 12, 2 - 7.
Groups on request out of season by calling the numbers below.
Parking.
Guided tours.
English - German - Spanish.
Panels.
Temporary Exhibits.
Tel. : (47) 94.23.62. and 94.30.77.

Montrésor (Château).

Montrésor - 37460.
Loches : 15 km.
Private property.
Montrésor was built by Imbert de Bastarnay, councillor of Louis XI who in the 15th century also built the nearby castle of Bridoré. Montrésor then belonged to the Joyeuse, Brantôme and Beauvilliers families before being purchased by a Polish aristocrat in 1834. The latter restored the castle and left a large collection of works of art including gold objects once belonging to the Polish royal family. The Renaissance paintings belonged to the collection of cardinal Fesch.
Open daily April 1 to Oct. 31 : 9 - 12, 2 - 6:30.
Parking. Guided tours, brochures.
Panels.
Tel. : (47) 94.20.04.

Nitray (Château).

Athée-sur-Cher - 37270.
Tours : 10 km.
Saint-Martin-le-Briau : 3 km.
Private property.
Nitray is set in a huge park and once belonged to Enery Lopin, an official of Louise de Savoie, mother of François I. The château and the two towers were built in the 16th century, the forge and dovecote in the 15th.
Open July 1 to Aug. 10 : 10 - 12, 3 - 6.
Parking.
Unaccompanied visits.
Information in English.
Tel. : (47) 50.68.07.

Le Plessis-sur-Thilouze (Château).

Thilouze - 37260.
Tours : 25 km.
Private property.
The history of the residence is well known thanks to its archives which have been kept since it was built. Its first owner was a Scots archer in the service of Charles VII. The main building flanked with a stair tower was erected in 1440 by the architect Jean de la Porte. The two wings were added in the 18 th

INDRE-ET-LOIRE — 116 — CENTR

century. Balzac was a frequent visitor.
Open on request only.
Parking.
Tel. : (47) 26.87.72.

Le Rivau (Château).

Lemère - 37120.
Richelieu and Chinon : 10 km.
Station : Chinon.
Private property.

Charles VII gave permission to his High Chamberlain Pierre de Beauvau to fortify his castle whose origin remains unknown. The keep abutts the main building which is flanked by two towers, one containing the stair case the other the chapel. A pavilion to the North contains a postern. The guardroom, cells, king's room, the 13th century white stone floors and the Gothic furniture are all of interest.
Open March 15 to Oct. 10 : 10 - 12:30, 2 - 7.
Parking.
Guided tours, brochures.
Temporary art exhibits.
Tel. : (47) 95.71.03.

La Roche-Racan (Château).

Saint-Paterne-Racan - 37370.
Tours : 35 km.
Station : Saint-Paterne-Racan 2 km.
Property of M. Brackers de Hugo.

La Roche-Racan was built for the baron de Racan (1589-1670), poet and member of the Académie Française, by Jacques I Gabriel first in the dynasty of architects who built the Rouen Town Hall. Racan spent the last years of his life at the château which is entirely furnished.
Open daily Aug. 5 to Sept. 15 : 10 - 12, 3 - 5.
Groups on request out of season.
Parking.
Guided tours, brochures.
Information in English and Spanish.
Tel. : (4) 577.57.77.

Saché (Château).

Saché - 37190.
Azay-le-Rideau : 6 km.
Property of the département.

This 16th century manor hou was transformed in the 19th ce tury when Balzac used to spe time here writing several of his n vels. Today it houses a Balzac m seum.
Open March 15 to Sept. 30 : 9 - 2 - 6.
July 1 to Aug. 31 : 9 - 6.
Oct. 1 to March 14 : 9 - 12, 2 - 5.
Closed Dec. and Jan.
Closed Wednesdays from Oct. 1 March 14.
Parking.
Guided tours, brochures.
Panels.
English, German, Italian.
Tel. : (47) 26.86.50.

LES RÉAUX

INDRE-ET-LOIRE

Guest rooms and meals year round. Come share the graceful charm of this historic house located in the heart of the Loire valley.

Le Port-Boulet 37410 Bourgueil.
Tel. : (47) 95.14.40. (Michelin map number 64).

VILLANDRY

INDRE-ET-LOIRE

Completed in 1536, Villandry is the last of the great Renaissance châteaux built along the Loire. It was built by Jean Le Breton, Minister to François I and marks an important step in the evolution of architectural style. There is a fine main courtyard, and the interiors which were refurbished in the 18th century are open to the public. The gardens which combine the practical with the beautiful are unique in Europe. They have been adapted to the site and the climate and are separated into three levels separated by hedges.

Saint-Cosme (Priory).

La Riche
Tours : 3 km.
Property of the département.
Pierre de Ronsard was prior here from 1565 to his death in 1585. The famous poet is buried in the choir of the church. Despite the destructions of the 18th century and the bombardments of 1944, a part of the church, the 12th century refectory and the 15th century lodgings have been preserved.
Open March 15 to Sept. 30 : 9 - 12, 2 - 6.
Oct. 1 to March 14 : 9 - 12, 2 - 5.
Closed Wednesdays from Oct. 1 to March 14.
Closed Dec. and Jan.
Parking.
Guided tours, brochures.
Panels.
English, German, Italian.
Tel. : (47) 20.99.29.

TOURS
Hôtel Gouin.

Tours - 37000.
25 Rue du Commerce.
Property of the département.
This town house was built on Roman foundations and transformed during the Renaissance. Acquired by the banker Goüin in 1738, it was transformed in the 19th century and restored after a fire in June 1940. It houses the Touraine archeological Museum. The basement is devoted to prehistory, the ground floor and the first floor to the Middle Ages and Renaissance.
Open March 15 to Sept. 30 : 9 - 12, 2 - 4.
Oct. 1 to March 14 : 9 - 12, 2 - 5.
Closed Fridays Oct. 1 to March 14.
Closed in Dec. and Jan.
Unaccompanied visits, brochures.
Panels.
Information in English and German.
Concerts.
Tel. : (47) 66.22.32.

Hôtel Mame.

Tours - 37000.
19 Rue Emile Zola.
Station : Tours.
Property of M. Mame.
This town house built in 1771 by Meugnier, a pupil of Jacques-Ange Gabriel is witness to the prosperity of Tours which was then a center for the production of silk and velvet. The « Fortune on her Ship » of the façade is a symbol of that of the owner. The staircase with a wrought iron railing leads to rooms which contain exhibits on the different crafts of the city. In 1870 the house was acquired by the publisher Mame.
Open April 15 to Nov. 4 : 2:30 - 6:30.
Parking.
Unaccompanied visits, brochures.
Panels..
Information in English.
Tel. : (47) 05.60.87.

Turpenay (Abbey).

Saint-Benoit-la-Forêt.
Chinon : 10 km.
Station : Rivarennes 4 km.
Private property.
This Benedictine abbey founded in 1127 in the middle of the forest of Chinon by the comte d'Anjou was pillaged at the Revolution. All that remains are the 15th to 17th century lodgings, the South wing of the cloister, an 18th century pavilion and a ruined hostellry.
Open July 15 to Aug. 31 : 10 - 12, 2 - 6.
Closed Sundays and July 14, Aug. 15.
Parking.
Guided tours, brochures.
Information in English.
Tel. : (47) 58.01.47.

Ussé (Castle).

Rigny-Ussé - 37420.
Avoine
Tours : 40 km.
Private property.
Built during the 15th and 16th centuries and located on the bank of the Indre, Ussé is a typical French château of the Middle Ages. It is said to have been the model for the castle in Perrault's famous story « Beauty and the Beast ». The house has belonged to different families and today is the property of the marquis de Blacas. Of particular interest are the Renaissance chapel and the reception rooms decorated in the 18th century.
Open March 15 to Sept. 30 : 9 - 12 2 - 7.
Nov. 1 to 5 and 10 to 11 : 9 - 12, 2 - 6.
Guided tours.
Exhibitions.
Tel. : (47) 93.13.65.

Vaudésir (Manor House).

Saint-Christophe-sur-le-Nais - 37370.
Tours : 34 km.
Station : Saint-Paterne or Château d Loir.
Bus near by.
Property of M. Amiot.
Vaudésir is a 16th century complex surrounded with a moat with a bridge leading to the main courtyard which has the cut-stone main building to the East linked to the North-West pavilions by a gallery.
Grounds only.
Parking.
Unaccompanied visits.
Tel. : (47) 29.24.53.

Villandry (Château).

Villandry - 37510.
Tours : 17 km.
Station : Savonnières 4 km.
Property of M. Carvallo.
Built from 1532 by Jean Le Breton, Secrétaire d'Etat under François I, Villandry has kept some of its older building, in particular the 14th century keep and the outer façade of the far wing. Its architecture is typical of the region. The famous gardens were restored in the early 20th century in Renaissance fashion with vegetable combined with flowers. Inside is collection of Spanish paintings.
Château : March 20 to Nov. 11 : 9 - 6
Gardens : Jan. 1 to Dec. 31 : 8:45 - 8p. or nightfall.
Parking.
Guided tour of the Château (French English).
Facilities for the handicapped.
Tel. : (47) 50.02.09.

ROUTE DES DAMES DE TOURAINE

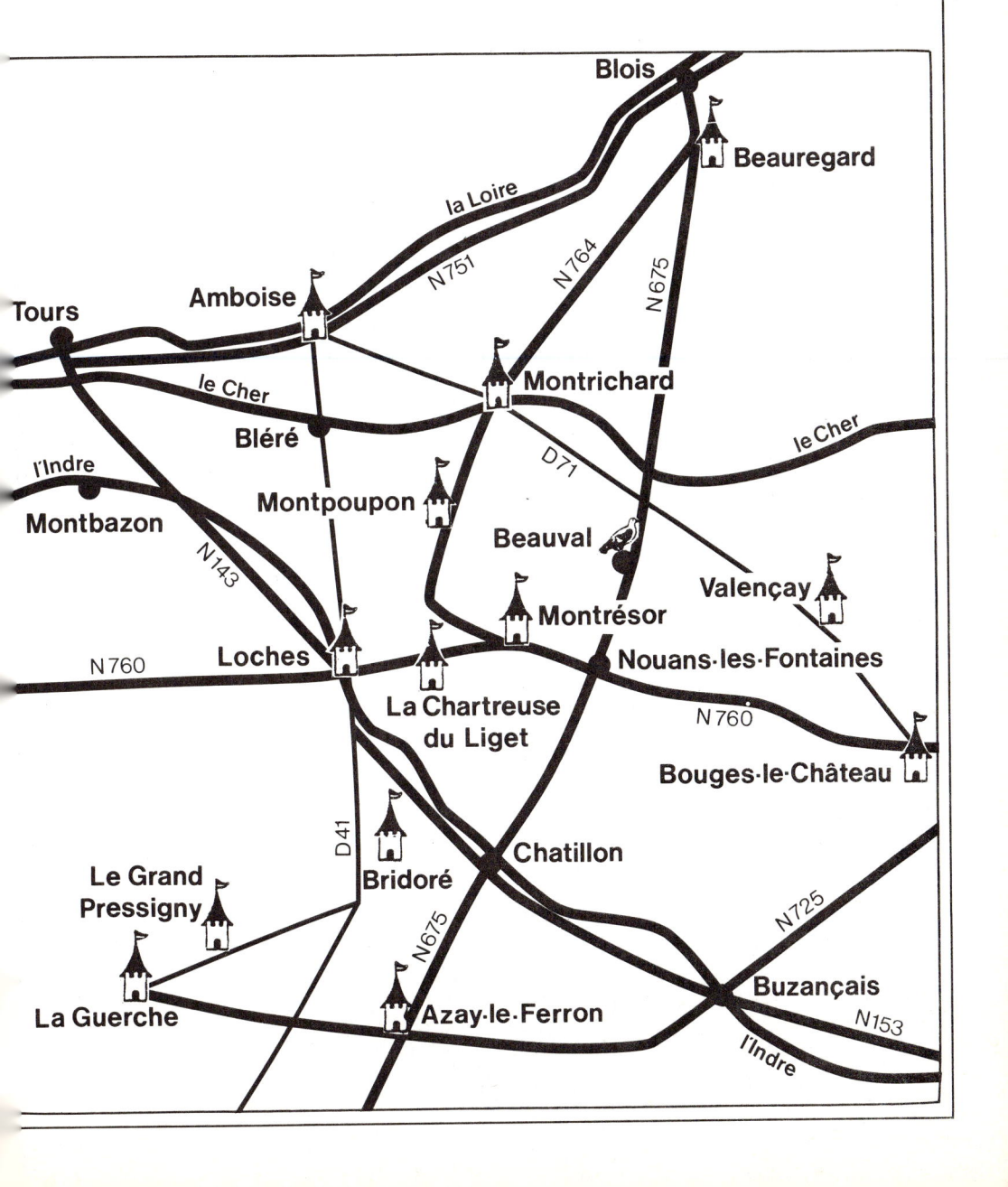

LOIR-ET-CHER

ARVILLE
Les Templiers.

Arville - 41170.
Vendôme : 40 km.
Station : Saint-Agil 3 km.
Property of the Syndicat Intercommunal de la Commanderie d'Arville.

This building was erected between 1125 and 1150 and has a remarkable roof. The dovecote, barn, turetted porch and church have survived.
Open on request.
Parking.
Unaccompanied visits, brochures.
Panels.
Tel. : (54) 80.86.38.

Beauregard (Château).

Cellettes - 41120.
Station : Blois 6 km.
Property of M. du Pavillon.

Formerly one of François I's hunting lodges, Beauregard was enlarged and decorated when it became the residence of ministers who were patrons of the arts. The renowned gallery of famous men was completed under Louis XIII and has kept its remarkable portraits and Delft tile floor. From the 16th century are the « Bell Closet », the kitchens and a fine collection of furniture. The 17th century orangery has been arranged for receptions.
Open Feb. 5 to April 1, Oct. 4 to Dec. 1 : 9:30 - 12, 2 - 5.
April 2 to Oct. 3 : 9:30 - 12, 2 - 6:30.
Closed Wednesdays Oct. 1 to March 31.
Parking.
Guided tours, brochures.
Information in English, German, Italian, Spanish, Japanese.
Panels or leaflets.
Concerts, temporary exhibits.
Tel. : (4) 747.05.41.

Blois (Château).

Blois - 41000
Station : 500 m.
Property of the city.

Blois is far too rich to describe in any detail. Its history begins with the comtes de Blois who built a fortress in the 13th century which survives at the Hall of the Estates General. Later Louis XII built the entrance block and perpendicular wing, the chapel of Saint Calais and commission the magnificent gardens.

When François I made Blois principal residence his Italian st wing became the glory of the c teau. The interior façade with spiral staircase is the most fam part of the building but the exte façade is more innovative. The l round of construction began 1634 when François Mansart b the Gaston d'Orléans wing. D pite destruction and transforr tions Blois is still associated w the tragic memory of the death the duc de Guise.
Open Oct. 1 to March 15 : 9 - 12, 2 -
March 16 to May 31 : 9 - 12, 2 - 6:3
June 1 to Aug. 31 : 9 - 6:30.
Sept. 1 to 30 : 9 - 12, 2 - 6:30.
Closed Dec. 25 and Jan. 1 in the n ning.
Parking.
Guided tours all year. Unaccompan visits March 15 to Nov. 1.
Audio visual programme.
Guided tours in English, German, Sc dinavian languages, Dutch.
Panels.
Facilities for the handicapped.
Brochures.
Concerts, Shows, exhibits.
Tel. : (54) 78.06.62. and 74.16.06.

CHAMBORD

This, the largest of the Loire valley châteaux, was built by François I. Constructed on a medieval plan the château shows a sense of symmetry and splendour typical of the Renaissance. The double spiral staircase is proof of the genius of the anonymous architect.

Bonaventure (Manor House).

Azangé - Vendôme - 41100.
Station : Vendôme 9 km.
Private property.
Formerly the property of the Musset family, Bonaventure dates from the Renaissance. It has recently been restored. An erroneous tradition names it as property of the father of Henri IV, King of Navarre.
Open on request.
Parking.
Grounds only.
Guided tours.
English and German.
Tel. : (4) 661.29.28. and (54) 72.07.43.

Chambord (Château).

Bracieux - 41250.
Property of the State.
Construction began on Chambord in 1519 and was completed by the death of its builder François I in 1547. The château is in the midst of a closed game park of 5 342 hectares. Its plan resembles that of a medieval castle with its surrounding wall, corner towers and keep. Its architecture however is one of the gems of the early French Renaissance with its famous double staircase, the Royal Gate and its roof with the fine chimneys. Chambord is one of the largest of the Loire valley châteaux and its history is full of famous names : François I, Henri II, Louis XIV, the maréchal de Saxe, etc. The château houses a hunting museum.
Open daily except Jan. 1, May 1, Nov. 1 and 11, Dec. 25.
April 1 to June 19, Sept. 1 to Oct. 30 : 9:30 - 12, 2 - 6.
June 20 to Aug. 31 : 9:30 - 12, 2 - 7.
Nov. 1 to March 31 : 9:30 - 12, 2 - 5.
Lecture tours daily July 1 to Sept. 15 and on request at other times for groups. Unaccompanied visits at other times.
Sound and Light Easter weekend and May 1 to Sept. 30 at 9:30 or 10:45 according to season.
Tel. : (54) 20.31.32.

Photo J. Feuillie

Chaumont-sur-Loire (Château).

Chaumont-sur-Loire - 41150.
Blois : 20 km.
Property of the State.
Overlooking the Loire from a cliff top, Chaumont was first a fortress dismantled by Louis XI in 1465 and rebuilt by the Amboise family in 1510. The château lost some of its military aspect in the 18th century when the building en-

CHAUMONT
LOIR-ET-CHER

Diane de Poitiers, Madame de Staël and Madame Récamier all stayed in this medieval fortress whose architecture includes Renaissance features. The château's magnificent salons were the scene of lavish receptions at the beginning of this century and remind the visitor of the life of the princes de Broglie the last owners of the château who also built the stables.

LOIR-ET-CHER — 122 — CENTR

closing the courtyard on the valley side was torn down. The defensive buildings contrast with the Renaissance style interior façades. The history of Chaumont is told on its walls with the emblem of Diane de Poitiers who was forced to take over the château by Catherine de Medici. Inside are Aubusson tapestries, 17th and 18th century furniture, a collection of terracotta medallions made in the castle workshop in the 18th century. Prince de Broglie built the luxurious stables in the 19th century.

Open : Park : April 1 to Sept. 30 : 9:15 - 11:30, 2 - 5:30.
Oct. 1 to March 30 : 9:30 - 11:45, 1:45 - 3:45.
Castle : Daily : April 1 to Sept. 30 : 9:30 - 11:45, 2:15 - 5:45.
Oct. 1 to March 31 : 9:45 - 12:15, 2 - 4:30.
Stables : Daily : April 1 to Sept. 30 : 9:30 - 12:15, 2:15 - 6:15.
Oct. 1 to March 31 : 9:45 - 12:30, 2 - 4:30.
Closed Jan 1, May 1, Nov. 1 and 11, Dec. 25.
Parking.
Guided tours, brochures.
Tel. : (54) 46.98.03.

Chemery (Château).
Chemery - 41700.
Blois : 30 km.
Property of M. Fontaine.

The archives of this château were burnt at the Revolution. Research has shown that the main part was built in the Renaissance on the side of a 13th century castle (some remains survive) which had replaced a 12th century fortress. The complex is surrounded by a moat.

Open Jan. 1 to Dec. 31 : 10 - 12, 2 - 6.
Closed Tuesdays.
Parking.

Guided tours.
English, German, Spanish.
Sound and Light Saturdays at 9:45 fr June 9 to Sept. 1.
Weaving workshops.
Tel. : (54) 71.82.77.

Cheverny (Château).
Contres - 41700.
Station : Blois 14 km.
Private property.

Cheverny is marked by the R naissance although its beauti white façade already heralds t classical age by its unity. The in rior decoration is contempora with the construction, and forr one of the finest Louis XIII bu dings. The out buildings contair trophy collection of over two tho

---

LOIR-ET-CHER

CHEMERY

This Renaissance château is being restored by the owners themselves. Its beautiful reception rooms are perfect for your business lunches, parties, dances. Service rooms for caterers, rest rooms and cloak rooms available, over 300 square meters in all. The courtyard is also available. Your rent will help save the building from ruin.

CENTRE — 123 — LOIR-ET-CHER

and antlers and a kennel with seventy hounds.
Open daily Nov. 1 to Feb. 28 : 9:30 - 12, 2:15 - 5.
March 1 to 31 : 9 - 12, 2:15 - 5:30.
April 1 to May 15 : 9 - 12, 2:15 - 6.
May 15 to June 14 : 9 - 12, 2:15 - 6:30.
June 15 to Sept 15 : 9:30 - 6:30.
Sept. 16 to Oct. 31 : 9 - 12, 2:15 - 6.
Parking.
Guided tours available, brochures.
Leaflets in foreigh languages.
Tel. : (54) 79.96.29.

Cour-sur-Loire (Château).

Cour-sur-Loire - Mer - 41500.
Station : Blois 10 km, Mer 9 km.
Private property.

Built in the 16th century by Jacques Hurault and linked to Ménars in the 17th and 18th centuries, Cour-sur-Loire was decorated by the marquise de Pompadour. The mullioned windows look out on to the Loire.
Open on request.
Ground only.
Guided tours.
Information in English.
Tel. : (54) 46.81.04.

La Ferté-Imbault (Château).

La Ferté-Imbault - 41300.
Romorantin : 17 km.
Private property.

After being destroyed in the Hundred Years War then burnt down, this castle was rebuilt by Jacques d'Etampes, marshal of France in 1630. It includes an out building which served as a barracks in the 17th century, two pavilions and a main building with four towers.
Open July 1 to Sept. 30 : 2 - 5; weekends and holidays.
On request at other times for groups.
Parking.
Guided tours.
Information in English and Spanish.
Tel. : (4) 622.47.26.

Fougères-sur-Bièvre (Château).

Fougères-sur-Bièvre - 41120.
Blois : 18 km.
Station and bus nearby.
Property of the State.

Fougères-sur-Bièvre is an ancient stronghold which still has its 11th century keep. The castle was built by Pierre de Refuge a financier under Louis XI in 1470. It has the traditional elements of a medieval castle : turrets, machicolations, sentry way. It is exceptional in its arches, octagonal pillars, and covered gallery reminiscent of Blois. It was much transformed in the 16th century but still has its magnificent beams.
Open April 1 to Sept. 30 : 9 - 11:15, 2 - 6.
Oct. 1 to March 31 : 10 - 11:15, 2 - 3:30.
Closed Tuesdays and Wednesdays.
Parking.
Guided tours, brochures.
Show and exhibits.
Tel. : (54) 46.27.18.

FOUGÈRES-SUR-BIÈVRE LOIR-ET-CHER

One of Louis XI's financiers took a medieval keep and in the 15th century built a castle reminiscent of Blois. A textile mill in the 19th century Fougères-sur-Bièvre was admirably restored in 1932.

Le Gué-Péan (Château).

Monthou-sur-Cher - 41400.
Montrichard : 11 km.
Station : Thésée-la-Romaine 4 km.
Property of M. de Kerguelin.

Le Gué-Péan is an old hunting lodge and one of the least known châteaux of the Loire valley. Two fine Renaissance pavilions surround a main block which is full of paintings by David, Andrea del Sarto etc. and tapestries. Outside is a chapel, guardroom and sentry way. There is also an autograph collection.
Open Jan. 1 to March 31 : 9 - 6.
April 1 to Dec. 31 : 9 - 7.
Guided tours, brochures.
English, German, Spanish, Italian, Dutch, Japanese.
Facilities for the handicapped.
Tel. : (54) 71.43.01.

LASSAY-SUR-CROISNE
Le Moulin (Château).

Lassay-Mur-de-Sologne - 41230.
Romorantin : 10 km.
Station : Romorantin.
Private property.

Located in the heart of the Sologne this castle was built in 1492 by the court architect J. de Persigny. It is proof of the rapid ascension of Philippe du Moulin, companion and captain of Charles VIII. The moat, keep, two entrance towers and a part of the covered court flanked by a tower remain of the original building. The salon has its original painted ceiling and a statue of Saint Catherine attributed to the school of Michel Colombe (15th century). Sixteenth and seventeenth century tapestries. Furnished and inhabited.
Open March 1 to Nov. 15:9 - 11:30, 2 - 6:30.
Parking.
Guided tours.
English, German.
Tel. : (54) 83.83.51.

Lavardin (Castle).

Montoire - 41800.
Lavardin : 2 km.
Station : 30 km.
Private property.

Lavardin was extremely important in the 12th century and then found itself in the midst of the Wars of Religion when it was destroyed by Henri IV. Its vast ruins look down over the Loire valley and have been restored. Fine Gothic architecture.

Open July 5 to Sept. 9 and April 1 to 10: 9 - 12, 2 - 7.
On request from the mayor of Lavardin at other times.
Parking.
Guided tours, brochures.
Information in English when the Club du Vieux Manoir is present.
Cut stone work shops, camps, restoration sites.
Tel. : (4) 508.80.40.

Pontlevoy (Abbey).

Pontlevoy - 41400.
Montrichard : 7 km.
Blois : 25 km.
Station : Montrichard.
Bus service.
Private property.

Pontlevoy abbey was founded in 1034 by the seigneur of Chaumont-sur-Loire who had been miraculously saved in a ship wreck. The chapel and the Charles VII tower are fine example of 15th century architecture. The main building was erected by Richelieu and later buildings bear witness to the abbey's continuing prosperity. For nine centuries Pontlevoy was a great place of learning and became a royal military college in 1776.
Open daily April 15 to May 1 and June 16 to Aug. 17 : 10:30 - 12, 2:30 - 6:30.
May 2 to June 15 : 2:30 - 6:30 except Mondays and Tuesdays.
Parking.
Guided tours, brochures.
Information in English.
Concerts.
Tel. : (54) 32.00.19.

La Possonnière (Manor House).

Couture-sur-Loir - 41800.
Vendôme : 33 km.
Station : Pont-de-Braye 3 km.
Private property.

The poet Pierre de Ronsard was born and spent his childhood this fief acquired by his father the 16th century. The manor hous looked much as it does today main building overlooking the va ley with an octagonal turret to th back. The inside is decorated wi sculptures and inscriptions.
Open on request Jan 1 to Dec. 31.
Parking.
Guided tours.
Concerts.
Tel. : (4) 651.41.45.

Les Radrets (Château).

Sarge-sur-Braye - 41170.
Vendôme : 25 km.
Bus service.
Private property.

Built on the side of a hill ov looking two valleys, Les Radre has its original moat and three c ner bastions. A draw bridge links to the service court which is t old 14th century manor comp sing a square pavilion and tv long perpendicular buildings, o a tax barn with a vaulted wo roof. The complex was built b ween the 14th and 15th centuri the castle was in part remodelle It belonged to a grand daughter Jean Racine.
Open July 14 to Sept. 15, weeken 2:30 - 6:30.
Other days on request.
Tel. : (54) 23.73.10.

Saint-Agil (Château).

Saint-Agil - 41170.
Vendôme : 30 km.
Private property.

This castle set in a deep, w moat has a fine entrance pavil built 1510 to 1529.
Open all year 9 - 5.
Ground only.
Parking.
Tel. : (54) 80.94.02.

Saint-Denis-sur-Loire (Château).

Saint-Denis-sur-Loire - 41000.
Blois : 8 km.
Private property.

This 18th century château ov looks a wide moat surrounded

ASSAY-SUR-CROISNE # CHÂTEAU DU MOULIN LOIR-ET-CHER

A furnished, inhabited château 25 km from Cheverny.
Guided tours March 1 to November 15.
Personalised visits with drinks.

Receptions for 50 to 80 people.
Weddings.
Locations for photography or films.

LOIR-ET-CHER — CENTRE

ramparts on the North bank of the Loire. Remains of an ancient chapel.
Open June 1 to Sept. 30 : 9 - 12, 2 - 4.
Closed Sundays.
Grounds only.
Tel. : (54) 78.31.02.

Talcy (Château).

Talcy - 41370.
Blois : 26 km.
Property of the State.

In the 15th and 16th centuries Talcy was a simple stronghold. It became famous only after its purchase by Bernard Salviati a relative of the Medici family. Although it has lost one block Talcy still looks much as it did when Cassandre and her niece Diane, beloved of Ronsard and Agrippa d'Aubigné lived here. The « Catherine de Medici » and « Charles XI » rooms are reminders of the Talcy conference which was the last meeting between Protestants and Catholics before the Wars of Religion in 1562. In 1932 the château was purchased by the State in order to preserve its fine collection of furniture.

Open April 1 to Sept. 30 : 9:30 - 11:15, 2 - 6.
Oct. 1 to March 31 : 10 - 11:15, 2 - 4:30.
Parking.
Closed Tuesdays and Jan. 1, May 1, Nov. 1 and 11, Dec. 25.
Guided tours, brochures.
Shows.
Tel. : (54) 81.03.01.

Troussay (Château).

Cheverny - 41700 Contres.
Blois : 15 km.
Private property.

This 15th and 16th century manor house was embellished in the last century by the historian L. de La Saussaye with fine pieces from monuments of the region which have now disappeared. Inside a carved wood chapel door, Renaissance stained glass window, Louis XII tile floor and a painted ceiling attributed to Jean Mosnier a regional painter of the 17th century. The Sologne Museum contains agricultural tools and household utensils from bygone years.
Open daily March 24 to April 15, Su

TALCY

LOIR-ET-CHER

Built in the 16th century by a relative of the Medici, Talcy was the setting for some famous love affairs (Ronsard and Cassandre, Agrippa d'Aubigné and Diane Savalti). This medieval castle has miraculously kept its 17th and 18th century furniture.

ys and holidays April 16 to June 29 :
- 12:30, 2:15 - 6:30.
ily June 30 to Sept. 9 : 10 - 12:30,
5 - 7.
ndays and holidays Sept. 10 to
v. 11 : 10 - 12:30, 2 - 4.
rking.
oups on request.
ided tours, leaflets.
glish, German, Italian.
. : (54) 79.96.07.

ENDÔME
oître de la Trinité
bbey-Monastery).

ndôme - 41100.
urs : 50 km.
tion : Vendôme 2 km.
perty of the commune.
This Benedictine abbey was nded in 1033 by the comte de ndôme. The church is one of finest in the region with its les ranging from the 11th to the h centuries. The bell tower and transept are Romanesque, the ade is a masterpiece of flam-yant Gothic. In the cloister garth the entrance to a regional ar-eological museum.

Open Jan. 1 to Dec. 31, except Jan. 1 and Dec. 25.
Closed Tuesdays.
Parking.
Guided tours on request.
Recorded information and audiovisual programme.
English and German.
Temporary exhibits.
Tel. : (54) 77.26.13.

Villesavin (Château).

Tour-en-Sologne - 41250.
Bracieux : 3 km.
Chambord : 9 km.
Station : Blois 17 km.
Bus service.
Property of M. de Sparre.
 Villesavin was built in the 16th century on the site of an ancient seigneurie by Jean Le Breton, seigneur de Villandry and Villesavin, secretary of François I. It was the work of the same Italian and French artists who were building the great royal residences of the time. This Renaissance château has come down to us almost intact.
Open daily March 1 to Sept. 30 : 10 - 12, 2 - 7.

Oct. 1 to Dec. 20 : 2 - 5.
Parking.
Guided tours.
Panels, leaflets.
Facilities for the handicapped. Lectures.
Lecture tours for school groups.
Tel. : (54) 46.42.88.

LOIRET

Arch. Phot. Loiret

AUTRY-LE-CHÂTEL
Le Petit Château.

Autry-le-Châtel - 45500.
Station : Gien 12 km.
Private property.
 This rectangular building has three assymmetrical towers and a

---

VILLESAVIN
Between Chambord and Cheverny

LOIR-ET-CHER

 jewel of the Renaissance in the heart
f the Loire valley (1537).
ine marble fountain.
rescoed chapel.
are 16th century dovecote.

Pediments with sculpted windows.
Medallions of the Caesars.
Renaissance furnished rooms.
Vintage car museum.

stone spiral staircase on the façade. Madame de Sévigné was a visitor here.
Open on request for groups.
Grounds only.
Guided tours.
Tel. : (4) 705.22.14.

Bellegarde (Château).
Bellegarde - 45270.
Montargis : 23 km.
Property of the commune.
Two pavilions are situated on either side of the entrance gate. Madame de Montespan's son the duc d'Antin received some of the great thinkers of the 18th century here. The 14th century keep has survived.
Grounds only.
Brochures.
Tel. : (38) 90.10.03.

Bondaroy (Manor House).
Bondaroy - 45300.
Pithiviers : 2 km.
Pithiviers bus station : 2 km.
Private property.
This fortified farm was rebuilt in cut stone after the Hundred Years War by a camarade at arms of Joan of Arc, Martin de La Taille.
Open Jan. 1 to June 24 and Sept. 16 to Dec. 31 on request.
June 25 to Sept. 15 : 10 - 12, 2 - 5.
Closed Tuesdays, Wednesdays, Thursdays except between Aug. 15 and Sept. 15.
Parking.
Guided tours. Panels.
Shows.
Tel. : (38) 30.49.34.

La Bussière (Château des Pêcheurs).
Gien : 12 km.
Station : Gien 12 km.
Private property.
This 17th century château set in a Le Nôtre park houses the owner's family furniture and his own collection which makes this a fishing museum complete with aquariums.
Open March 15 to Nov. 15 : 9 - 12, 2 - 6.
Nov. 15 to March 15, Sundays and holidays : 9 - 12, 2 - 5.
Closed Tuesdays.
Parking.
Open on request in winter.
Guided tours, brochures.
English, German, Italian.
Tel. : (38) 35.93.35.

Châteauneuf-sur-Loire (Château, museum and park).
Châteauneuf-sur-Loire - 45110.
Orléans : 25 km.
Property of the commune.
The 17th century château was destroyed in 1803, except the four pavilions of the forecourt, the vaulted stables and the orangery with the formal gardens. The 40 hectare park is planted with exotic species. The town hall situated next to the 17th century rotunda house

Photo Delanoë

LOIRET

CHEVILLY

Château that once belonged to Monsieur de Silhouette, minister to Louis XV.

A collection of statues of the five continents in the grounds.

MEUNG-SUR-LOIRE

LOIRET

12th, 13th and 18th centuries.

The first Loire valley château on the way down from Paris (130 km).
Former residence of the bishops of Orléans. Entirely furnished. Cellars, oubliettes and François Villon's prison.

Headquarters of the English troops in the 15th century until they were expelled by Joan of Arc.
Fine Hall with kitchen which can be used for receptions, weddings and lectures.

four rooms of the Loire naval museum.
Open 2 - 6 : April 1 to May 31, Sept. 1 to Oct. 2, weekends and holidays.
June 1 to Aug. 30, Daily except Tuesdays.
Groups on request 10 days in advance.
Parking.
Guided tours for groups.
English, German, Spanish, Italian.
Tel. : (38) 58.41.18.

Chevilly (Château).
Chevilly - 45520.
Orléans - 15 km.
Private property.
All that remains of the original 1631 château are the out buildings. The intendant, M. de Cypierre had the chapel rebuilt and decorated by Desfriches. Chevilly belonged to the famous M. de Silhouette, minister of finance in 1759 who invited famous guests like the philosopher Condillac to the château. The château is approached along a fine paved avenue and the park contains a set of statues representing the five continents.
Groups by appointment all year.
Grounds, chapel and out buildings.
Tel. : (38) 80.10.10.

Denainvilliers (Château).
Dadonville - 45300.
Pithiviers : 3 km.
Bus station : 3 km.
Private property.
This Louis XIII château was inhabited by Duhamel de Monceau, inspector general of the Navy in the 18th century. The interior contains wood panneling.
Open July 1 to Sept. 30 : 2 - 5:30, Mondays, Fridays and weekends.
Parking.
Guided tours.
Concerts.
Tel. : (38) 30.10.38.

Gien (Château).
Gien - 45500.
Orléans : 60 km.
Station SNCF.
Bus service.
Property of the département.
A gift from Louis XI to his daughter Anne de Beaujeu, Gien was completely rebuilt between 1484 and 1500. Here François I signed over the regency to his mother Louise de Savoie before setting off for Italy. Today it houses the International Hunting Museum which includes a fine collection of paintings by François Desportes (1661-1743) and J.-B. Oudry (1686-1755), as well as hunting horns and buttons.

LOIRET

MALESHERBES
An historic house in a natural setting.
An hour from Paris by the Autoroute du Sud ; Ury exit.

Tax barn, dovecote.
Chapel.
Châteaubriand's house.
Rentals for : concerts, lectures,

receptions (50 to 600 people).
Locations for filming indoors and outdoors.

Open daily Palm Sunday to Nov. 1 :
9:15 - 12:15, 2:15 - 6:30.
Nov. 1 to Palm Sunday : 9:15 - 12:15,
2 - 5:30.
Parking.
Guided tours available.
Information in English.
Information panels, brochures.
Exhibitions.
Tel. : (38) 67.24.11.

Grandes-Bruyères (Park).

Ingrannes - 45450 Fay-aux-Loges.
Orléans : 25 km.
Private property.
   This fairly new park covers several hectares with a fine collection of a wide variety of plants including one hundred varieties of ancient roses, ninety varieties of clematis and three hundred varieties of heather as well as various trees and bushes.
Open June 10, July 15, Aug. 19, Nov. 3 and April 11 : 9 to 7.
Open out of season on request.
Unaccompanied visits.
Tel. : (38) 59.56.68.

Malesherbes (Château).

Malesherbes - 45330.
Fontainebleau : 25 km.
Station : Malesherbes.
Private property.
   Malesherbes is made up of two 17th century brick and stone wings and three medieval corner towers. Inside are seven panelled, furnished rooms. Fine 14th to 18th century out buildings are situated next to the château which was visited by three kings of France and belonged to Malesherbes, philosopher and defender of Louis XVI.
Open Nov. 2 to March 24 : 2 - 5:30.
March 24 to Nov. 1 : 10 - 11:30, 2:30 - 5:15.
Closed Mondays and Tuesdays.
Parking.
Guided tours, brochures.
Horse shows, concerts.
Tel. : (4) 553.86.00.

Meung-sur-Loire (Château).

Meung-sur-Loire - 45130.
Orléans : 17 km.
Station : Meung-sur-Loire 3 km.
Private property.
   This was the residence of the Bishops of Orléans from the 12 th century to the Revolution. Louis XI, Joan of Arc, François I stayed here. The château has twenty-one furnished rooms open to the public.
Open April 1 to Nov. 1 : 8:30 - 6:30, daily.

Nov. 2 to March 31 : 9 - 5, weekends and holidays.
Guided tours, brochures.
English, German, Spanish.
Tel. : (38) 44.36.47.

ORLÉANS
Hôtel Groslot.

Orléans - 45000.
Place de l'Etape.
Property of the city.
   This Renaissance building was erected for Jacques d'Orléans possibly by the architect du Cerceau. Mary Queen of Scots husband François II died here in 1560. The interiors have been reconstituted as close as possible to the originals. Today the hôtel serves as the Town Hall.
Open Jan. 1 to Dec. 31 : 10 - 12, 2 - 5.
Parking.
English, German, Spanish, Italian.
Brochures, temporary exhibits.
Tel. : (38) 42.22.22.

Pont-Chevron (Château).

Ouzouère-sur-Trézée.
Briare - 45250.
Gien : 10 km.
Property of M. de La Rochefoucauld.
   This 18th century style château received the visit of queen Amelia of Portugal. Inside are paintings by Oudry and antique furniture. The out buildings contain a collection of Gallo-Roman artefacts.
Open April 1 to Sept. 15 : 2 - 6.
Closed Tuesdays.
Open on request Sept. 15 to April 1.
Parking.
Guided tours of the château.
Recommended itinerary of the mosaics.
Information panels for the Gallo-Roman exhibits.
Tel. : (38) 31.92.02.

Sully-sur-Loire (Château).

Sully-sur-Loire - 45600.
Orléans : 40 km.
Station : Gien 24 km.
Property of the departement.
   This medieval castle was built in the 14th century and transformed in the 17th and 18th centuries. It is a square building comprising a main block flanked by four towers, a keep and sentry way, surrounded by a moat. Inside are the guard room, the Hall with numerous portraits of the Bethune family, the king's room and 18th century apartments, as well as fine chesnut beams dating from the end of the 14th century. The castle belonged to the Sully family until 1360 and then to the Trémoille family until 1602 when it was purchased by Maximilien de Béthune, marquis de Rosny. It remained in the Béthune family until it was sold to the departement in 1962. Visitors to the castle included Joan of Arc, Charles VII, the young Louis XIV, Voltaire during his exile and La Fayette on his return from America.
Open March 1 to April 31 : 10 - 11:45, 2 - 4:45.
May 1 to Sept. 30 : 9 - 11:45, 2 - 5:45.
Oct. 1 to 30 : 10 - 11:45, 2 - 4:45.
Nov. 1 to 11 : 10 - 11:45, 2 - 4:45.
Parking.
Guided tours.
Tel. : (38) 36.25.60.

Rouville (Château).

Malesherbes - 45330.
Malesherbes : 1,5 km.
Private property.
   This ancient castle was restored in 1863 by Magne, a pupil of Viollet-le-Duc.
Open for groups only on request.
Parking.
Grounds and Chapel.
Guided tours.
Tel. : (4) 553.25.05.

Yèvre-le-Châtel (Castle).

Yèvre-le-Châtel - 45300 Pithiviers.
Pithiviers : 7 km.
Property of the commune.
   The imposing ruins of this castle that was rebuilt in the 13th century comprise a postern and the surrounding walls flanked with four towers linked by the sentry way. Chapel and Saint Crault parish church.
Open only on request.
Guided tours available in summer.
Tel. : (38) 30.17.05.

CHAMPAGNE ARDENNES

ARDENNES, AUBE, MARNE, HAUTE-MARNE.

REIMS
- ★ Palais du Tau
- ★ Hôtel de la Salle
- ★ Hôtel le Vergeur
- ★ Salle de Guerre

LANGRES
- ★ Maison Renaissance
- ★ Hôtel du Breuil

CHÂLONS-SUR-MARNE
- ● Notre-Dame-en-Vaux

Legend:
- ■ castle, château, manor house
- ● abbey, priory
- ▲ garden, park
- ★ town house, famous men house, farm, mill...
- ○ city

- Forteresse de Charlemont ■
- ■ Remparts de Rocroi
- ▲ Parc de Belval
- ■ Montcornet
- CHARLEVILLE-MÉZIÈRES ○
- ■ Bazeilles
- ■ Sedan
- ■ Tassigny
- ★ Moulin de Charleville-Mézières
- ■ Mouzon
- ■ Villy-la-Ferté
- ■ Grandpré
- ○ REIMS
- Braux Sainte Cohière ■
- CHÂLONS-SUR-MARNE ○
- ● Le Reclus
- ● Trois Fontaines
- ■ Esternay
- ● Le Paraclet
- ■ La Motte-Tilly
- ■ Barberey
- TROYES ○
- ■ Tremilly
- ○ CHAUMONT
- ■ Les Tourelles
- ■ Parnot
- ○ Langres

CHAMPAGNE-ARDENNES

ARDENNES

Bazeilles (Château).

Bazeilles - 08140.
Sedan : 3 km.
Bus nearby.
Private property.
   Built as a summer residence in the 18th century, Bazeilles is surrounded by a park with an orangery, a pavilion and a dovecote.
Open all year : 10 - 12, 2 - 6.
Closed Mondays.
Parking.
Information in English.
Lecture tours.
Temporary exhibits.
Tel. : (24) 27.09.68.

Belval (Nature Park).

Belval-Bois-des-Dames - 08240.
Private property.
   This recently created park has as its speciality the fact that it contains only local animals (wild boar, deer, bison) which have been in the region for the past 1500 or 2000 years.
Open Feb. 15 to Oct. 15 : Wed. weekends and holidays.
Daily during school holidays at Easter and in the summer.
On request for groups out of season.
Parking.
Guided tours on request, brochures.
Tel. : (29) 30.01.86.

Charlemont (Fortress).

Givet - 08600.
Givet station : 1 km.
Property of the State.
   Overlooking the Givet valley, this fortress was built by Charles V in 1555 to counter the fortress of Rocroi. In 1678 it was captured by Louis XIV who had it remodelled by Vauban. Charlemont was also used during the last two World Wars.
Open July 1 to Aug. 31 : 10 - 2.
Parking.
Guided tours, brochures.
Panels.
Information in English and German.
Lecture tours for school groups.
Tel. : (24) 55.06.62.

CHARLEVILLE-MÉZIÈRES

Vieux-Moulin (Museum).

Charleville-Mézières - 08000.
Quai Rimbaud.
Property of the city.
   Built on a bridge spanning the Meuse, this old brick and stone mill dates from the same period as the city and ducal palace. It now houses the Artur Rimbaud Museum and the Ardennes Museum.
Open all year : 10 - 12, 2 - 6.
Closed Mondays.
Unaccompanied visits.
Exhibitions.
Tel. : (24) 33.31.64.

Grandpré (Castle Gate).

Grandpré.
Vouziers : 15 km.
Station : Rethel 45 km.
   From the 15th to the 18th centuries the ancient stronghold of Grandpré belonged to the comtes de Joyeuse who built a magnificent castle here. The remaining gate gives some idea of the size of the fortress which unfortunately was destroyed by fire in 1834.
Open at all times.
Grounds only.
Parking.

Montcornet (Château).

Montcornet-en-Ardenne - 08100.
Charleville-Mézières : 10 km.
Property of M. Lussigny.
   Montcornet has belonged to many illustrious people. Originally a hunting lodge belonging to Louis the Debonnaire, it was fortified by the de Croÿ family before passing to Charles Gonzaga, duke of Mantua in 1613. It was then acquired by Hortense Mancini. The castle is a good example of the adaptation of medieval architecture to fire arms. It houses a museum of the history of life in the castle until it was dismantled in 1790.
Open July 1 to Sept. 15 : 2 - 6.
Easter to Nov. 1 : weekends 2 - 6.
Closed Mondays.
Parking.
Groups on request.
Panels, brochures.
Shows.
Tel. : (24) 54.93.48.

MOUZON
Burgundy Gate.

Mouzon - 08210.
Sedan : 18 km.
Bus nearby.
Property of the commune.
   This entrance gate to the town of Mouzon is the principal remains of the walls that once surrounded it. The gate is crowned with a 16th century square belfry. On either side are remains of cellars and walls with ditches and battlements. Several rooms are devoted to collections of local historical and archeological interest.
Open weekends June 1 to Aug. 31 : 3 - 6.
Parking.
Guided tours, brochures.
Tel. : (24) 26.10.01 and 26.13.80.

Rocroi (Ramparts).

Rocroi - 08230.
Bus nearby.
Property of the city.
   Rocroi has defended the marches of the kingdom of France since the Renaissance. Its chief fame comes from the battle of the Thirty Years War in which the prince de Condé won a great victory over the Spanish giving the French infantry its reputation. The fortifications were started in 1555 and finished by Vauban at the end of the 17th century.
Open all year.
Parking.
Guided tours, brochures.
Panels, films.
Shows.
Tel. : (24) 54.17.93.

Sedan (Fortified Castle).

Sedan - 08200.
Station : Sedan 500 m.
Bus service.
Property of the commune.
   This fortified castle covering 35 000 square meters of seven levels is built on a rocky spur between two streams. Evrard de Marck began building in 142 using the remains of a 13th century monastery. The triangular plan, the twin towers, the East tower and the ramparts all date from this period. At the end of the 15th century the fortress was transformed into a fortified town with surrounding walls. Corner bastions were added in the 16th century and the princes palace built at the beginning of the 17th. Further work was carried out in the 18t

nd 19th centuries. Local history museum.
Open daily April 1 to Sept. 9 : 10 - 5:30.
Sept. 10 to Oct. 28 : 1:30 - 5:30.
Closed Mondays.
Groups on request out of season.
Parking.
Guided tours, brochures.
Unaccompanied visit of the museum.

Tassigny (Château).

Tassigny-Margut - 08370.
Sedan : 33 km.
Private property.
This fortified house comprises two blocks flanked with four corner towers. In the Renaissance it was embellished by mullioned windows and carved doorways. Until the Thirty Years War Tassigny belonged to the duchy of Luxembourg.
Open daily April 1 to Nov. 15 : 9 - 12, 2 - 6.
Groups on request.
Grounds only.
Unaccompanied visits.

Villy-la-Ferté (Fort and Arms Museum).

Villy-la-Ferté - 08370.
Carignan : 8 km.
Property of the commune.
This fort comprising two blocks linked by an underground passage played a part in World War II by trying to resist the German advance. A commemorative monument was erected in 1950.
Open Sundays and holidays from Palm Sunday to Oct. 30.
Daily June 30 to Sept. 1 : 1:30 - 5.
Parking.
Guided tours, brochures.
Projector.
Facilities for handicapped.
Tel. : (24) 22.06.72.

AUBE

Barberey-Saint-Sulpice (Château).

Barberey-Saint-Sulpice - 10600.
Troyes : 6 km.
Private property.

This pure Louis XIII style brick and stone château was built in the 17th century by Jean Le Mairat. It has since been surrounded by a fine formal garden.
Open Aug. 1 to Sept. 15 : 10 - 12, 2 - 6.
Parking.
Grounds only.
Unaccompanied visits, brochures.
Tel. : (25) 43.36.13.

La Motte-Tilly (Château).

La Motte-Tilly - 10400.
Troyes : 50 km.
Fontainebleau : 66 km.
Property of the C.N.M.H.S.
This large 18th century château is situated on a domain a few kilometers from Nogent-sur-Seine. Abbé Joseph Terray became seigneur of La Motte-Tilly in 1748 and had the old château rased to the ground in order to build his château according to plans by François Lancret, nephew and godchild of Louis XV's painter. The château was damaged by the Revolution and the Tsar's troops. The property was saved by the comte de Rohan-Chabot who acquired it in 1910 and set about restoring both the building and the formal gardens. His daughter the marquise de Maillé continued his work by recreating the interiors of the château. She collected the finest furniture signed by the greatest cabinetmakers of the Ancien Régime. At her death in 1972, both château and grounds were left to the Caisse Nationale des Monuments Historiques et des Sites.
Open daily April 1 to Sept. 30 : 10 - 11:30, 2 - 6:15.
Weekends Oct. to Nov. 30 : 2 - 5.
Groups on request.
Closed Tuesdays.
Parking.
Brochures.
Tel. : (25) 25.84.54.

Le Paraclet (Abbey).

Nogent-sur-Seine - 10400.
Nogent-sur-Seine : 6 km.
Troyes : 45 km.
Private property.
Abelard was the founder of this abbey and Heloise its first abbess.

An obelisk has been raised on the site of their tomb. The remains of the abbey include the cellar which is the oldest part with its remarkable stone lantern, the farm, mill and lodgings.
Open July 1 to Sept. 9 : 2 - 6.
Closed Sundays.
Groups on request out of season.
Grounds only.
Unaccompanied.
Information leaflets.
Tel. : (25) 25.80.22.

Les Tourelles (Manor House).

Rumilly-les-Vaudes - 10260.
Troyes : 22 km.
Property of the commune.
This manor house was built in the 16th century by a merchant from Troyes. The four corner towers and the stairtowers are linked by wooden galleries. Some rooms still have their carved beams. The monumental fireplaces are decorated with medallions. It was purchased by the commune and turned into the town hall in 1902.
Open for groups on request.
Parking.
Guided tours, brochures.
Sound and light shows.
Tel. : (25) 40.92.14.

MARNE

Braux-Sainte-Cohière (Castle).

Braux-Sainte-Cohière - 51800.
Sainte-Menhould : 4 km.
Private property.
This large square building surrounded by a moat and flanked with corner towers is a former military command comprising officers quarters, stables and drinking trough built by Philippe Thomassin governor of Châlons-sur-Marne. The « Champagne-Argonne » organizes a variety of activities here.
Open June 2 to Sept. 4 : 9 - 12, 2 - 7.
Closed Tuesdays.
Acoustiguides, brochures.
Panels, films.

English - German.
Facilities for the handicapped.
Concerts, shows, exhibits, lectures.
Tel. : (26) 60.83.51.

CHÂLONS-SUR-MARNE
Notre-Dame-en-Vaux (Cloister).

Châlons-sur-Marne - 51000.
Rue Nicholas-Durand.
Property of the State.

The cloister of Notre-Dame-en-Vaux was built in the 12th century and entirely destroyed in the 18th century. Excavation of the site began in 1963 and magnificent examples of early Gothic sculpture have been uncovered. The sculpted figures emerge from the columns, the first full length statue columns. Three quarters of the cloister have been uncovered and a museum has been set up for the collection of finely carved faces, the Foolish Virgins with their lanterns, demons and prophets with swirling draperies.
Open April 1 to Sept. 30 : 10 - 12, 2 - 7.
Oct. 1 to March 31 : 10 - 12, 2 - 5.
Closed Tuesdays.
Tel. : (26) 64.03.87.

Esternay (Château).

Esternay - 51310.
Sézanne : 10 km.
Bus nearby.
Property of M. de La Rochelambert.
Esternay was built in 1525 by the Raguier brothers, financiers under François I, in Italian Renaissance style. It comprises fine sculpture. Although partially destroyed by baron d'Aurillac on the eve of the Revolution, a handsome main building flanked by towers and surrounded by a moat, still survives. Esternay was the scene of a glorious episode of the Battle of the Marne in 1914.
Open on request for groups.
Grounds only.
Parking.
Guided tours.
Information in English and German.
Concerts.
Tel. : (26) 42.50.92.

Le Reclus (Abbey).

Montmort - 51270 Talus-Saint-Prix.
Epernay : 35 km.
Private property.

Notre-Dame du Reclus was founded in 1142 on the instigation of Saint Bernard of Citeaux. Its name derives from Hugues le Reclus who came here in 1128 to live

---

MARNE
BRAUX-SAINTE-COHIÈRE

Located an hour and a half from Paris, 4 km from the Sainte-Menehould exit of the Autoroute de l'Est (A 4).
Braux-Sainte-Cohière is a seventeenth century light-cavalry headquarters, a characteristic example of military architecture of the period.
Summer festival June-September.
Concerts each Saturday in July 9 pm.
Exhibits of contemporary art and of folk art.

Regional Orientation Museum.
December 24 : Christmas of the shepherds of Champagne.
Large rooms for groups of 600 to 800.
Facilities for the organization of cultural activities in this pleasant woodland setting.
Locations for filming.
Tel. : (1) 651.41.64.

CHAMPAGNE-ARDENNES — MARNE/HAUTE-MARNE

...s a hermit. The abbey prospered ntil the 18th century when it was sed as a place of detention for ne religious or people under ouse arrest. It was sold at the Re- olution. Since 1972 excavation as been going on and the chap- er house has been uncovered. ome of the stonework has been ut back in place and some of the estoration is at an advanced tage.
)pen July 1 to Aug. 31 : 3:30 and 4:30.
)ther hours on request.
:losed Tuesdays.
'arking.
uided tours, brochures.
formation in English and German.
el. : (26) 80.36.11.

RHEIMS (REIMS).
La Salle (Town House).

ïeims - 51100.
bis Rue de l'Arbalète.
'roperty of the La Salle Foundation.
 This Renaissance town house vas built in 1545. Jean-Baptiste de a Salle, founder of the brothers of ne Christian Schools, was born ere in 1951. A museum includes ocuments commemorating the oundation. The façade and nterior tower are of particular in- erest.
)pen all year.
:losed Tuesdays.
uided tours.
el. : (25) 47.73.21.

au (Palais).

ìeims - 51100.
'roperty of the State.
 The episcopal palace of Rheims as a history that goes back to the eginnings of Christianity. Its si- ation next to the cathedral has ade it the site of numerous his- oric events as the kings of France tayed here prior to their corona- on. In 1690 the medieval palace as transformed by François Man- art and Robert de Cotte. The two rchitects left the 13th century chapel untouched but shortened the great hall built between 1497 and 1507 which had been the scene of so many royal occasions. In the other rooms restored since 1950 are tapestries, sculptures from the cathedral and the Royal Treasure.

Open April 1 to Sept. 30 : 10 - 12, 2 - 6.
Oct. 1 to March 31 : 10 - 12, 2 - 6.
Unaccompanied visits.
Brochures.
Tel. : (26) 47.74.39.

Le Vergeur (Town House).

Reims - 51100.
36 Place du Forum.
Station and bus nearby.
Property of the Société des Amis du Vieux-Reims.
 In the 16th century this town house belonged to a local patron of the arts Nicholas le Vergeur. Its three stories contain fine 18th and 19th century furniture and docu- ments relating to the history of Rheims. The house is situated in a large garden near the cathedral.
Open Jan. 2 to Dec. 23 : 2 - 6.
Closed Mondays.
Parking.
Guided tours, brochures.
Information in English and German.
Temporary exhibits.
Lectures, archeological walks.
Tel. : (26) 47.20.75.

War Hall.

Reims - 51100.
12 Rue Franklin-Roosevelt.
Station and bus nearby.
Property of the city.
 Formerly the Hall of the profes- sors of the Rheims technical col- lege. General Eisenhower made his headquarters here and the room witnessed the signature of the German surrender in 1945.
Open March 15 to Nov. 11 : 10:30 - 12, 2 - 6.
Closed Tuesdays.
Parking during school holidays.
Information in English and German.
Panels.
Brochures.
Tel. : (26) 47.28.44.

Trois-Fontaines (Abbey).

Trois-Fontaines - 51250.
Saint-Dizier : 8 km.
Private property.
 Trois-Fontaines abbey was founded in 1118 by Saint Bernard. The buildings which were rebuilt in the 18th century are linked by an arcaded gallery. The imposing ruins of the abbey church stand near by. A 1911 cross marks the site of the monks' cemetary. The large park is planted with hundred year old lime trees and contains 18th century statues.
Open June 15 to Sept. 15 : 2:30 - 7 Sun- days.
Grounds all year.
Parking.
Guided tours on request for groups.
Information in English and German.
Facilities for the handicapped.
Brochures.
Sound and Light Saturdays July 1 to Aug. 15.
Crafts exhibits.
Tel. : (26) 41.14.04.

LANGRES
Breuil de Saint-Germain (House).

Langres - 52200.
2 Rue de Chambrulard.
Private property.
 This 16th century town house was enlarged in the 18th century. The building comprises two wings, one Renaissance with de- corated windows and doors, the other 18th century with larger win- dows and a baroque interior. The du Breuil de Saint Germain family gave it to the local historical so- ciety to be transformed into a mu- seum in 1923.
Open Oct 1 to Feb. 28 : 10 - 12, 2 - 5.
March 1 to Sept; 30 : 10 - 12, 2 - 6.
Closed Tuesdays.
Guided tours available.
Information English/German.
Exhibits (Egyptian, paleontology, numis- matics).
Tel. : (25) 85.08.05.

Renaissance House.

Langres - 52200.
20 Rue du Cardinal-Morlot.
Property of the city.
 This house mis-named Diane de Poitier's house was in fact built in the 16th century for a rich local family. The charming courtyard fa- çade contains two stories of mul- lioned windows. The ground floor gives out onto a small terrace which has a cupola covered well. The inner staircase leads up to fine Renaissance rooms.
Open all year : Exteriors 8 - 9pm.

Interiors : guided tours for groups on request.
Information in English and German.
Tel. : (25) 85.03.32.

Parnot (Château).

Parnot-en-Bassigny - 52400.
Bourbonne-les-Bains : 11 km.
Property of M. de La Bruslerie.

Parnot is one of the few seigneurial dwellings left in Southern Lorraine near the source of the Meuse on the ancient borders of France and the Holy Roman Empire. In the 19th century it belonged to marshal Pélissier, duc de Malakoff, who brought back many souvenirs from Sebastopol and Algeria.

Open April 1 to July 1 : 10:30 - 6.
Parking.
Grounds only.
Tel. : (25) 90.80.25.

Tremilly (Château).

Tremilly - 52110.
Brienne-le-Château : 20 km.
Property of M. Dacier.

The first château was destroyed by fire in 1593. The present 18th century building still has Renaissance doors and a well.

Open July 24 to Sept., 7 : 10 - 12, 2 - 5.
Closed Mondays.
Parking.
Groups on request.
Information in English.
Facilities for the handicapped.
Brochures.
Tel. : (25) 55.40.72.

CORSE

CORSE-DU-SUD

ALÉRIA
Matra (Fort).
Aléria - 20270.
Property of the départment.

Matra was built in 1572 at the time of the Genoese occupation. It comprises a main block with a square tower and interior patio. The fort was the residence of the first and only king of Corsica. Today it houses a collection of prehistoric and ancient artifacts from Aléria.
Open May 16 to Sept. 30 : 8 - 12, 2 - 7.
Oct. 1 to May 15 : 8 - 12, 2 - 5.
Unaccompanied visits.
Panels, brochures.
Information in Italian.
Music festival.
Tel. : (95) 57.00.92.

HAUTE-CORSE

AJACCIO
The Bonaparte House (National Museum).
Ajaccio - 20000.
Rue Saint-Charles.
Property of the State.

This house belonged to the Bonaparte family from 1743. It is located in the heart of the old city of Ajaccio and is full of Bonaparte family memorabilia including portraits, his mother's furniture, as well as information on Corsican history. The house was restored by the Historical Monuments authorities.
Open June 21 to Sept. 30 : 9 - 12, 2 - 6.
Oct. 1 to June 20 : 10 - 12, 2 - 5.
Closed Sunday afternoons and Monday mornings.
Tel. : (95) 21.43.89.

FRANCHE-COMTÉ

DOUBS, JURA, TERRITOIRE-DE-BELFORT, HAUTE-SAÔNE.

- ■ castle, château, manor house
- ● abbey, priory
- ▲ garden, park
- ★ town house, famous men house, farm, mill...
- ○ city

BESANÇON

- ★ Hôtel de ville
- ■ Citadelle
- ★ Palais Granvelle

■ Luxeuil-les-Bains

○ VESOUL
■ Ray   ■ Filain   ■ Villersexel
■ Belfort
■ Gray
■ Belvoir
■ Malans   ■ Moncley
■ Pesmes   ○ BESANÇON

★ Salins-les-Bains-Salines
★ Arbois : Hôtel Sarret de Crozon
■ Frontenay
■ Arlay   ● Baume-les-Messieurs
○ LONS-LE-SAUNIER
Le Pin
■ Syam

FRANCHE-COMT[É]

DOUBS

Belvoir (Castle).
Belvoir - 25430.
Near Montbéliard.
Private property.

Belvoir was built on a peak around 1150 and became a fief of the vassals of the Dukes of Burgundy. Béatrice de Cusance, princesse de Cantecroix and duchesse de Lorraine was its principal heroine. The medieval fortress overlooking the Sancey valley still has its three towers and two main blocks separated by two coutryards. The interiors contain 16th and 17th century furniture, arms, paintings and faience collections.
Open Easter to Nov. 1, Sundays and holidays : 10 - 12, 2 - 7.
July 1 to Sept. 31, daily 9 - 12, 2 - 7.
Parking.
Guided tours in season - unaccompanied visits.
Brochure.
Tel. : (81) 91.06.40.

BESANÇON
Citadel.
Besançon - 25000.
Rue des Fusillés.
Property of the commune.

Besançon still has remains of its medieval fortifications which were transformed by Vauban after the French conquest in 1674. He built the citadel which now houses the Resistance Museum, the Folklore Museum, the zoo and the aquarium.
Open daily 9:30 - 6.
Closed Tuesdays;
Parking.
Temporary exhibits.
Tel. : (81) 82.16.22.

Granvelle Palace.
Besançon - 25000.
96 Grande Rue.
Bus service.
Property of the commune.

The Granvelle palace belonged to Nicholas Perrenot, seigneur de Granvelle, chancellor under Charles V and then to Cardinal de Granvelle, councillor under Philip II. It is a fine example of regional Renaissance architecture. The main hall is decorated with a serie of 17th century Bruges tapestries. The buiding now houses the city's historical museum.
Open Jan. 1 to Dec. 31 : 9 - 12, 2 - 6.
Closed Tuesdays.
Parking.
Guided tours available.
International music festival Summer shows.
Temporary exhibits.
Lecture tours for school groups.
Tel. : (81) 81.45.14.

Moncley (Château).
Moncley-Recologne - 25170.
Besançon : 16 km.
Private property.

Moncley is a Neo-classical château built by the architect Bertrand for the marquis de Terrier-Santans, president of the Besançon parlement. It still belongs to his descendants. The façade shows a palladian influence (columns and pediment). The vestibule occupies the whole height of the building. The building also comprises a gallery mounted on Corinthian capitals. The specially designed furniture is still in place as is the extraordinary 18th century painted wall paper.
Open Sundays May 15 to Sept. 15 : 2:30 - 6:30.
Weekends July and August : 2:30 - 6:30.
On request all year.
Parking.
Guided tours, brochures.
Lecture tours for school groups.
Facilities for the handicapped.
Tel. : (81) 55.04.05.

JURA

Arlay (Château).
Bletterans - 39140.
Lons-le-Saunier : 12 km.
Station : Dôle 35 km.
Private property.

In 1774 the comtesse de Lau[ra]gais used an old 17th cent[ury] convent to create her château [at] Arlay. This purely classical st[yle] building comprises a main blo[ck] with two perpendicular wings. T[he] façade has columns and a pe[di]ment. The Gallo-Roman rema[ins] of the ancient fortress of t[he] princes of Orange were used [in] the creation of the Romantic pa[rk]. The interiors contain fine Char[les] X furniture.
Open July 1 to Sept. 15 : 10 - 12, 2 -[*]
Closed Sunday mornings.
Parking.
Guided tours of the château.
Unaccompanied visits of the grounds
Lecture tours for school groups.
Tel. : (84) 85.04.22.

ARBOIS
Sarret de Grozon
(Town House).
Arbois - 39600.
9 Grande Rue.
Property of the commune.

This house was built in the 17[th] and 18th centuries and bought [by] the Sarret de Grozon family whi[ch] left it to the town. It comprises[s a] fine staircase leading to apa[rt]ments containing collections [of] arms, faience, porcelain, silver a[nd] paintings. It is now an art m[u]seum.
Open June weekends and July 1 [to] Sept. 6 : 3 - 7.Closed Tuesdays.
Parking.
Guided tours.
Lectures.
Tel. : (84) 66.07.45.

Baume-les-Messieurs
(Abbey).
Baume-les-Messieurs - 39210.
Lons-le-Saunier : 17 km.
Station : Domblans-Voiteur 9 km.
Private property.

Founded in the 6th century [in] one of the loveliest Jura valley[s] this Benedictine abbey wa partic[u]larly prosperous under abbot Be[r]non who went on to found Clu[ny] in 910. After its decline it remaine[d] a noble chapter until the Revolu[ ]tion. The numerous 15th and 16[th]

ARC ET SENANS

Royal Salt Mines

DOUBS

Located in the Doubs, between Dôle and Besançon.
The Arc et Senans Royal Salt Mines comprise a series of buildings designed by the eighteenth century architect C. N. Ledoux.

The complex was designated by UNESCO as part of the World Heritage in 1983.
Open daily : Winter : 9 - 12, 2 - 5.
Summer : 9 - 6.
Guided tours for groups on request.
Regular guided tours from May to September.

JURA/TERRITOIRE DE BELFORT — 144 — FRANCHE-COMTÉ

century buildings house 15th century Burgundian sculpture, a Flemish altar-piece of the early 16th century.
Open July 1 to Aug. 31 : 11 - 12, 2:30 - 6.
Parking.
Guided tours available.
Brochures.
Tel. : (84) 44.61.41.

Frontenay (Castle).

Voiteur - 39210.
Lons-le-Saunier.
Station : Domblans 5 km.
Private property.

A 12th century keep remains from the old castle which was supposed to protect the salt route. A main building was added in the 18th century and the façade was transformed in the 19th century.

Here, in 1400, Saint Colette was received by Blanche of Geneva and founded her first religious order. In 1638 under Captain Flamand, the Castle withstood a siege by the French.
Open daily.
Grounds only.
Parking.
Concerts, theatre, cabaret.
Tel. : (84) 85.23.36.

Le Pin (Castle).

Le Pin - 39120.
Lons-le-Saunier : 5 km.
Private property.

Built on the foundations of a 13th century fort the castle now comprises a surrounding wall flanked by five towers and a large square keep built in the 15th century to protect the salt route from Lons-le-Saulnier.
Open daily all day.
Parking.
Grounds and Keep.
Unaccompanied visits.

Syam (Château).

Syam - 39300.
Champagnole : 5 km.
Private property.

Syam is a large country house built in 1818 for Jean-Emmanuel Jobez, member of the Jura parlement, master of the iron works and poet. Its Palladian style is due largely to Lapret, a pupil of the architect Paris, who had lived in Italy. It has a perfect square plan with four symmetrical façades and a central portico with Ionic columns. The rotunda has balconies and a peristyle to match the Empire style interiors.
Open July 1 to Sept. 30, weekends and Mondays : 2 - 6.
On request for groups at other times.
Parking.
Guided tours.
English - German - guide.
Tel. : (84) 52.03.63.

TERRITOIRE DE BELFORT

Belfort (Castle).

Belfort - 90000.
Colmar : 80 km.
Station : Belfort 3 km.
Bus service.
Property of the commune.

A few foundation walls remain of the castle built by Thierry

JURA

SYAM

Italian style villa reminiscent of those of Andrea Palladio, built at the end of the Empire (1815) by Lapret a pupil of Pierre-Adrien Paris.
Central rotunda 16 meters high with a painted ceiling, peristyle and colonade with three circular balconies.
Empire and Restoration interiors including original wall paper, furniture and objets.
Fine out buildings in the style of Claude-Nicholas Ledoux in an English style park with age old trees.
Near by the 1813 iron works still in use are worth a visit.

FRANCHE-COMTÉ   145   TERRITOIRE DE BELFORT/HAUTE-SAÔNE

comte de Montbéliard. The Bourgeois tower dated from the 14th and 15th centuries. The immense ditch carved into the rock was begun in the 17th century and completed by the Brisach gate designed by Vauban. The fortress was transformed in the early 19th century by General Haxo and withstood the siege of 1813-1815 and the Prussian invasion of 1870-1871.

Open daily May 1 to Sept. 30 : 8 - 12, 2 - 7.
Nov. 1 to March 31 (except Tuesdays) : 10 - 12, 2 - 5.
Weekends : 8 - 12, 2 - 6.
Oct and April (except Tuesdays) : 10 - 12, 2 - 6.
Parking.
Brochure.

Museum of Fine Arts and Military Museum.
Natural history and ethnography collections.
Festivals.
Opera, exhibits.
Tel. : (84) 28.52.96.

HAUTE-SAÔNE

Filain (Castle).

Montbozon - 70230.
Vesoul : 15 km.
Station : Vesoul.
Private property.

The oldest parts of the castle date from the 15th century. They are the wing to the right of the main courtyard which was once part of the fortified house with its round towers remodelled in the 16th and 18th centuries. The other part was built at the end of the 16th century on an L-shaped plan with an arcaded façade with Tuscan and Ionic columns. General Marulaz, baron d'Empire, the defendor of Besançon added 18th century apartments including à Louis XVI salon with signed Jacob furniture.

Open weekends and holiday : May 1 to July 14 and Sept. 1 to Oct. 11 : 2 - 7.
Daily July 15 to August 30 : 2 - 7.
On request for groups out of season.
Guided tours, brochures.
Tel. : (84) 78.30.66.

Gray (Château)
Baron Martin Museum.

Gray - 70100.
Rue Pigalle.
Station : Dijon or Besançon 45 km.

This 18th century edifice once belonged to the comte de Provence Louis XVI's brother. It was erected on the site of the old castle of which the entrance tower, foundations and cellars re-

VILLERSEXEL   HAUTE-SAÔNE

As a lived in historical monument, the château de Grammont is now looking towards the future. The out buildings were rebuilt by Nicholas Ledoux. Garnier worked on the plans of the château.

Restaurant, rooms, swimming pool, tennis courts.
Private guests or groups of 20 to 400.
20 km from the Autoroute A 36 (Baume-les-Dames exit) - 70110 VILLERSEXEL. Tel. : (84) 20.51.53.
Open all year.

main, the latter housing the museum's archeological collection. Some of the rooms still have their original panelling and furniture and contain a fine collection of works by Prud'hon who stayed in the region between 1794 and 1796 as well as works by other Western schools from the 14th century to the present.
Open April 1 to Sept. 30 : 9 - 12, 1 - 6.
Oct. 1 to March 31 : 9 - 12, 2 - 5.
Closed Tuesdays.
Parking.
Guided tours on request.
Acoustiguides.
English - German.
Brochures.
Concerts, temporary exhibits.
Lecture tours.
Tel. : (84) 65.02.57.

Luxeuil-les-Bains (Echevins tower).

Luxeuil-les-Bains - 70300.
Rue Victor-Genoux.
Besançon : 77 km.
Property of the city.

This tower was built in the 15th century by Perrin Jouffroy and for many years was the center of municipal authority. It has retained its medieval air with its fortifications, turrets and gargoyles. It houses the oldest museum in France (collection of funerary stele and the Jules Adler Museum).
Open all year : 2 - 5:30.
Closed Tuesdays.
Parking.
Unaccompanied visits, brochures.
Panels.
Temporary exhibits.
Tel. : (84) 40.00.07.

Malans (Château).

Mans - 70140.
Dôle : 25 km.
Besançon : 35 km.
Dijon : 45 km.
Property of M. Hoyet.

Once a medieval fortified house, Malans was turned into a Renaissance residence in the 16th century and restored by an ambassador of Napoleon III. The main building is flanked by two perpendicular wings and an octagonal stair tower. The double staircase is a product of the 19th century as is the Second Empire furniture.
Open June 6 to Sept. 15 : 3 - 5.
Closed Tuesdays.
Parking.
Guided tours, brochures.
Engliosh - German - Spanish - guide.
Temporary exhibits.
Tel. : (84) 31.23.19.

Pesmes (Château).

Pesmes - 70140.
Gray : 18 km.
Station : Auxonne 16 km.
Bus service.
Private property.

Pesmes castle overlooks the Ognon and the fortified village. It was first mentioned in 937 and transformed many times over the centuries. It was partially destroyed except for part of the stables and the entrance pavilions. The fortress changed hands frequently during the Franco-Spainish wars. Henri IV and Louis XIII stayed here.
Open July 1 to Sept 30 Mon., Thurs., Sun. : 2:30 - 6:30.
Parking.
Guided tours, Concerts.

Ray (Castle).

Ray-sur-Saône - 70130.
Gray and Vesoul.
Property of Mme de Salverte.

Built in the Middle Ages on the site of a Roman fort Ray castle has been in the same family since 1080. Otton de la Roche de Ray, Duke of Athens participated in the Fourth Crusade in 1204. The castle was partially destroyed during the Hundred Years War and rebuilt in the 17th and 18th centuries.
Open Sundays and holidays, Easter to Oct. 1 : 2:30 - 6:30.
Guided tours available, brochures.
Recordings.
Panels or leaflets.
Tel. : (84) 78.42.44.

Villersexel (Château).

Villersexel - 70110.
Vesoul : 26 km.
Station : Vesoul.
Private property.

Guy de Granges built the first castle here in 1308 on land granted by Henri de Bourgogne to h brother Renaud comte de Mor béliard. The castle was bur down at the victory of Villersexel 1870 and only the farm built by M cholas Ledoux remained. Recor truction of the château took fro 1884 to 1887 and was carried o by Danjoy and Garnier, architect the Paris Opera House. Today t château is a museum containi Aubusson and Gobelins tape tries, Ming vases and a collecti of ivories.
Open Nov. 1 to Dec. 31 : 3 - 5.
April 1 to Oct. 31 : 10 - 12, 3 - 6.
Closed Monday afternoons.
Groups on request.
Parking.
Guided tours.
Information in English and Spanish.
Lecture tours.
Facilities for the handicapped.
Sound and Light.
Temporary exhibits.
Lectures.
Lecture tours for school groups.
Tel. : (84) 20.51.53.

PARIS, ESSONNE, HAUTS-DE-SEINE, SEINE-ET-MARNE,
ILE DE FRANCE
SEINE-SAINT-DENIS, VAL-D'OISE, VAL-DE-MARNE, YVELINES.

- ■ castle, château, manor house
- ● abbey, priory
- ▲ garden, park
- ★ town house, famous men house, farm, mill...
- ○ city

PARIS et ses environs

HAUTS-DE-SEINE
- ★ ▲ St-Cloud
- ■ Sceaux
- ★ Sèvres
- ★ Clamart

YVELINES
- ■ Maisons-Laffitte
- ■ Rambouillet
- ● Saint-Germain-en-Laye

VAL-DE-MARNE
- ■ Vincennes

SEINE-SAINT-DENIS
- ● Saint-Denis

MEAUX
- ★ Palais Episcopal
- ▲ Jardin Bossuet

FONTAINEBLEAU
- ★ Hôtel d'Orléans
- ★ Le Vieux Logis
- ■ Château

MORET-SUR-LOING
- ■ Donjon
- ★ Maison Clémenceau

■ Guiry
● Moussy ■ Gadancourt
■ Montgeroult ■ Villette
■ Thoiry ■ Cœuilly   ○ Meaux ● Jouarre
■ Maudetour ● Taverny ● Royaumont ■ Champs
■ Neuville ■ Tilly ■ Nointel ■ Gros-Bois
■ Malmaison ■ Ecouen ■ Guermantes
■ Medan PARIS ○ ■ La Grange
▲ ■ Versailles ● Port-Royal ■ Ferrières ★ Choix
■ Gran' Maisons ■ Montlhéry
■ Mauvières ▲ Chevreloup ■ Vaux-le-Vicomte
■ Breteuil ■ Vauboyen
■ Saussay ■ Blandy-les-Tours
Sainte ■ Courson ○ MELUN ● Le Lys
■ Mesme ■ Le Marais ★ Barbizon ○ Moret-sur-Loing
■ Dourdan ■ Mesnil-Voisin ■ Bourron
■ Courances Fontainebleau ○
■ Jeurre
■ Dommerville ■ By

○ Nemours

The architectural riches of Paris are such that it is impossible to list them all in a work of this scope. Only the most important monuments, open to the public or visible from the outside, are listed below.

PALACES

La Conciergerie
Le Palais de Justice
1, quai de l'Horloge - 75001
Tel. : (1) 42-72-86-43 (Conciergerie)
43-29-12-55 (Palais de Justice)

Hôtel de Ville
Place de l'Hôtel-de-Ville - 75004
Tel. : (1) 42-76-40-40

Palais de l'Institut
23, quai Conti - 75006
Tel. : (1) 43-29-55-10

Palais de Justice
4, boulevard du Palais - 75001
Tel. : (1) 43-29-12-55

Palais du Louvre
Place du Carrousel - 75001
Tel. : (1) 42-60-39-26

PARKS AND GARDENS

Jardin de Bagatelle
Bois de Boulogne
Intersection of the allée de Longchamp and the allée de la Reine-Marguerite

Bois de Boulogne
Boulogne-Billancourt - 92200.

Parc des Buttes-Chaumont
Rue Botzaris - 75019

Jardin du Champ-de-Mars
Quai Branly - Place Joffre - 75007

Jardin du Luxembourg
Rue de Vaugirard - Rue Auguste-Comte 75006

Parc Monceau
Boulevard de Courcelles - 75008
Tel. : (1) 42-27-39-56

Parc Montsouris
Avenue Reille - 75014

Jardin d'Albert Kahn
1, rue des Abondances
Boulogne - 92100
(open March 15 to Nov. 15)
Tel. : (1) 46-03-31-83.

Bois de Vincennes
Vincennes - 94300

Jardin du Palais Royal
Palais Royal - 75004

Jardin des Plantes
57, rue Cuvier - 75005

Jardin des Tuileries
Rue de Rivoli - 75001

Parc Floral de Vincennes
Route de la Pyramide - 75012

MANSIONS AND TOWN HOUSES

Hôtel d'Aumont
Administrative Court
1, rue de Jouy - 75004

L'Arsenal
1, rue de Sully - 75004
Tel. : (1) 42-77-44-21

Hôtel de Beauvais
(Courtyard and staircase)
68, rue François-Miron - 75004

Hôtel de Béthune-Sully
Caisse Nationale des Monuments Historiques et des Sites
62, rue Saint-Antoine - 75004
Tel. : (1) 42-74-22-22

Hôtel Biron
Rodin Museum
77, rue de Varenne - 75007
Tel. : (1) 47-05-01-34 and 45-55-17-

Hôtel de Bouillon
School of Fine Arts
17, quai Malaquais - 75006
Tel. : (1) 42-60-34-57

Palais Bourbon
National Assembly
Quai d'Orsay - 75007

Hôtel de Bourienne
58, rue de Hauteville - 75010
Tel. : (1) 47-70-51-14

Hôtel Carnavalet
Museum of the History of Paris
Madame de Sévigné's House
23, rue de Sévigné - 75003
Tel. : (1) 42-72-21-13

Hôtel de Chalons-Luxembourg
16, rue Geoffroy-l'Asnier - 75004

Hôtel de Chaulnes
Academy of Architecture
9, place des Vosges - 75004
Tel. : (1) 48-87-85-74

Hôtel de Choiseul-Prasli
Postal Museum
34, boulevard de Vaugirard - 75015
Tel. : (1) 43-20-15-30

Hôtel de Cluny
Roman Baths and Medieval Art Muse
6, place Paul-Painlevé - 75005
Tel. : (1) 43-25-62-00

Hôtel d'Ennery
Museum of Oriental Art
59, avenue Foch - 75116
Tel. : (1) 45-53-57-96

Hôtel de Fieubet or la Rozière
10, rue des Lions Saint-Paul - 75004

Hôtel Galliera
Costume Museum
10, avenue Pierre-Ier-de-Serbie - 751
Tel. : (1) 47-20-85-23

ÎLE-DE-FRANCE — PARIS

Hôtel Guénégaud des Brosses
Hunting and Nature Museum
60, rue des Archives - 75003
Tel. : (1) 42-72-86-43

Hôtel de Gallifet
Italian Cultural Institute
50, rue de Varenne - 75007
Tel. : (1) 42-22-12-78

Hôtel des Invalides
Army Museum
Museum of the Order of the Liberation
Museum of Maps and Plans
Place des Invalides - 75007

Hôtel Jacquemart-André
Art Museum
158, boulevard Hausmann - 75008
Tel. : (1) 45-62-39-94

Hôtel de Jaucourt
National Archives
1, rue des Francs-Bourgeois - 75003
Tel. : (1) 42-77-11-30

Hôtel Lamoignon
Library of the History of Paris
24, rue Pavée - 75003
Tel. : (1) 22-74-44-44

Hôtel de Lauzun
17, quai d'Anjou - 74004
Tel. : (1) 40-33-27-14

Palais de la Légion d'Honneur
Museum of the Legion of Honour
2 rue de Bellechasse - 75007
Tel. : (1) 45-55-95-16

Hôtel Le Peletier de Saint-Fargeau
(In restoration)
29, rue de Sévigné - 74004

Hôtel Libéral Bruand
Museum of Locks and Iron Work
1 rue de la Perle - 75003
Tel. : (1) 42-77-79-62

Hôtel de Marle
Swedish Institute
11, rue Payenne - 75003
Tel. : (1) 42-72-87-50

Hôtel Marmottan
Marmottan Museum
2 rue Louis-Boilly - 75016
Tel. : (1) 42-24-07-02

Hôtel de Massa
38, rue du Faubourg-Saint-Jacques
75014

Hôtel Miramion
Museum of Public Services
47, quai de la Tournelle - 75005
Tel. : (1) 46-33-01-43

Hôtel de Montmorency
Ministry of the Economy
5, rue de Montmorency - 75003
Tel. : (1) 42-71-96-26

Hôtel de la Monnaie
11, quai de Conti - 75006
Tel. : (1) 43-29-12-48

Hôtel Nissim de Camondo
Museum
63, rue Monceau - 75006
Tel. : (1) 45-63-26-32

Maison d'Ourcamp
Association for the Preservation of Historic Paris
44, rue François-Miron - 75004
Tel. : (1) 48-87-74-31

Cour de Rohan
Former Town hous of the Bishops of Rouen
Rue du Jardinet - 75006

Hôtel de Rohan
National Archives
60, rue des Francs-Bourgeois - 75003

Hôtel de Rohan-Guéménée
Victor Hugo's House
6, place des Vosges - 75003
Tel. : (1) 42-72-16-65 and 42-72-10-16

Hôtel de Saint-Aignan
ICOMOS
71-75, rue du Temple - 75003
Tel. : (1) 45-55-95-16

Hôtel Saidiné
15, rue Scipion - 75005

Hôtel des Archevêques de Sens
Forney Library
1, rue du Figuier - 75004
Tel. : (1) 42-78-14-60 and 42-78-17-34

Hôtel de Soubise
Museum of the History of France
60, rue des Francs-Bourgeois - 75003
Tel. : (1) 42-77-11-30

Hôtel de Toulouse
Banque de France
39, rue Croix-des-Petits-Champs
75001
Tel. : (1) 42-61-56-72

Hôtel Tubeuf
National Library
8, rue des Petits-Champs - 75001
Tel. : (1) 42-96-36-21

HOUSES OF FAMOUS MEN

Balzac's House
47, rue Rayouard - 75016
Tel. : (1) 42-24-56-38

Henri Bouchard's House and Studio
25, rue de l'Yvette - 75016
Tel. : (1) 46-47-63-46

Antoine Bourdelle's House
16, rue Antoine-Bourdelle - 75014
Tel. : (1) 45-48-67-27

Constantin Brancusi's Studio
Place Beaubourg - 75004
Tel. : (1) 42-77-12-33

Clemenceau's House
8, rue Franklin - 75008
Tel. : (1) 45-20-53-41

Auguste Comte's House
10, rue Monsieur-le-Prince - 75005
Tel. : (1) 43-26-08-56

Eugène Delacroix's Studio
6, place Furstenberg - 75006
Tel. : (1) 43-54-04-87

Gustave Eiffel's Apartment
Eiffel Tower — Champ-de-Mars - 75007
Tel. : (1) 45-50-34-56

Victor Hugo's House
6, place des Vosges - 75004
Tel. : (1) 42-72-16-65 and 42-72-10-16

Lenin's Apartment and Museum
4, rue Marie-Rose - 75014

Gustave Moreau's House and Museum
14, rue de La Rochefoucauld - 75009
Tel. : (1) 48-74-38-50

Louis Pasteur's House and Museum
25, rue du Docteur-Roux - 75015
Tel. : (1) 43-06-19-19

Rodin's House and Museum
Hôtel Biron
7, rue de Varenne - 75007
Tel. : (1) 47-05-01-34 and 45-55-17-61

Renan Scheffer House
(part of the Carnavalet Museum)
16, rue Chaptal - 75009
Tel. : (1) 42-72-21-13 and 42-78-60-39

ILE-DE-FRANCE — PARIS/ESSONN

Madame de Sévigné's House
Hôtel Carnevalet - 75003
Tel. : (1) 42-72-21-13 and 42-78-60-39

Adolphe Thiers' House
Frédéric Masson Museum
27, place Saint-Georges - 75009
Tel. : (1) 48-78-14-33

Zadkine's Studio
100 bis, rue d'Assas
2, avenue Vavin - 75006
Tel. : (1) 43-26-91-90

ABBEYS

Former Refectory of the Bernardins
(visible from the street)
Rue de Poissy - 75005

Former Carmelite Convent
70, rue de Vaugirard - 75006

Former Cordelier Convent
(Monk's dormitory visible from the courtyard of the Ecole Pratique de Médecine)
Rue de l'École de Médecine - 75006

Former Priory of Saint-Martin-des-Champs
Library of the School of Applied Arts
Refectory
Rue Saint-Martin - 75004

Val-de-Grâce Abbey
Val-de-Grâce Museum
277 bis, rue Saint-Jacques - 75005
Tel. : (1) 43.29.12.31.

ESSONNE

Courances (Château).
Courances - Milly-la-Forêt - 91490.
Boutigny : 10 km.
Melun : 18 km.
Private Property.

This Louis XIII château surounded by water has a horse-shoe shaped staircase inspired by the one at Fontainebleau. The garden contains ornemental lakes, canals and basins. The grounds of Courances are among the largest and finest in the Ile de France. The château has also kept most of its interior decoration.

Open April 1 to Nov. 4 : 2 - 6, Weekends and holidays.
Guided tours of the château.
Unaccompanied visits of the park.
Pannels.
Information in English.
Concerts in June.
Tel. : (6) 550.34.24.

Courson (Château).
Courson-Monteloup - 91680.
Paris : 35 km.
Station : Breuillet 4 km.
Station : Bruyère-le-Châtel 4 km.
Private property.

The buildings of Courson are typical of 17th century rural architecture. They include a hamlet of traditional houses clustered around a well, the farm and its outbuildings, a vicarage and an old school house. The château was built by a pupil of Le Vau in 1676 for Lamoignon. Both architecture and decoration are typical of the establishments that the dignitaries of the court of Louis XIV built for themselves in the Ile de France. The main reason for doing so was the proximity to Versailles. Among the Napoleonic memorabilia preserved in the château is the duke of Padua's gallery of Spanish paintings. The English gardens designed by the Empress Josephine's landscape architect, Bertault, have been restored to their original state.
Open weekends and holidays, March 15 to Nov. 15 : 2 - 6.
On request for groups at other times.
Parking.
Guided tours of the château.
Information in English, German, Spanish.
Pannels, brochures.
Visits for the handicapped on request.
Concerts.
Tel. : (6) 491.90.12.

Dommerville (Château).
Angerville - 91670.
Étampes : 17 km.
Angerville Station : 1 km.
Private property.

This château was built between 1777 and 1782 and consists of a main building and two perpendicular wings. Inside is a rare faience stove. Transformed into farm in 1868, Dommerville ha been in the process of restoratio since 1972.
Open on request Sundays and holida May 1 to Sept. 30 for groups of 20 more.
Parking.
Guided tours.
Tel. : (6) 495.20.23.

Dourdan (Castle and Museum).
Dourdan - 91410.
Place du Général-de-Gaulle.
Station : Dourdan.
Property of the commune.

This square shaped fortres with its nine towers was built b Philip Augustus in 1222 and wa used by the kings of France as hunting lodge and resting place Today it houses a museum o painting, sculpture, furniture an armour.
Open July 1 to Sept. 30 : 10 - 12, 2 - (5 on Fridays).
Oct. 1 to June 30 : 2 - 6.
Closed Mondays and Tuesdays.
Parking.
Guided tours.
Audio-visual programme.
Temporary exhibits.
Tel. : (6) 459.66.83.

La Grange (Château).
Yerres - 91330.
Paris : 20 km.
R.E.R. : Boissy-Saint-Léger : 4 km.
Station : Yerres 3 km.
Bus nearby.
Property of M. Gourgaud.

This Louis XIII château has gallery decorated with stucco ar busts. The salons are decorated Louis XV style and have old ma

COURANCES

ESSONE

In the 17th century Le Nôtre or one of his pupils designed one of the lovliest gardens in the world just 50 km south of Paris.
Today with its 15 hectares of lawns and greenery, its 17 basins and its Japanese gardens the park, of the château de Courances is the perfect place for a relaxing walk. The Louis XIII château and its park are open to the public weekends and holidays in the afternoon from April 1 to November 1.

Tel. (6) 498.41.18.

DOMMERVILLE

ESSONNE

Tel. (6) 495.20.23

Located 68 km South-West of Paris (55 m off the R.N. 20), Dommerville was built at the end of the 18th century. Its right wing has been recently restored and has reception rooms for up to 200 people. Clients can choose their own caterer.

ter paintings along with works by Winterhalter.
Open July 10 to Aug. 22 : 2 - 6.
Parking.
Guided tours.
Information in English.
Tel. : (6) 948.12.00.

Jeurre (Château).

Morigny-Champigny-Étampes - 91150.
Étampes : 3 km.
Station : Étrechy 2 km.
Private property.

Jeurre comprises six monuments. Four of these, known as « fabriques », were designed in the 18th century by Hubert Robert for the embellishment of the park at Méréville. At the end of the 19th century they were dismantled and brought to Jeurre. At the edge of the grounds is a pediment from the château at Saint Cloud, now destroyed. The château of Jeurre itself is made up of bits of 18th century Paris town houses.

Open 10 and 3 except holidays and holiday weekends.
Closed Wednesdays and Saturday mornings.
Garden buildings only.
2 hour guided tour.
Tel. : (6) 494.57.43.

Le Marais (Château).

Saint-Chéron - Val-Saint-Germain 91530.
Dourdan : 11 km.
Private property.

Le Marais was built by the architect Barré in 1770 and is one of the finest buildings to have survived from this period. It combines elegant decoration with simple large spaces showing early traces of neo-classicism. The main building has a peristyle and a pediment crowning the first floor which is embellished with a cupola. The garden facade is decorated with pilasters. During the 19th century Le Marais was a literary centre and in the out buildings you can see memorabilia relating to Talleyrand.

Open Sundays and holidays March 15 to Nov. 15 : 2 - 6:30.
Groups on request during the week.
Park and museum only.
Unaccompanied visits.
Recorded information.
Temporary exhibitions.
Tel. : (6) 491.91.26.

Mesnil-Voisin (Château).

Bouray-sur-Juine - 91850.
1, rue Lardy.
Near Arpajon.
Private property.

Saved from ruin only ten years ago, this château is a large sandstone building from the Louis XIII period. The two pavilions on either side of the main block seem to date from the 16th century. The dovecote is one of the largest in France.

Open Sundays Jan. 1 to Dec. 31 : 2 - 6.
Closed in August.
Parking.
Unaccompagnied visits.
Tel. : (6) 456.47.46.

Montlhéry (Tower).

Montlhéry - 91310.
Property of the State.

The strategic position of Montlhéry was soon put to good use. At the beginning of the 11th century comte Thibaud File-Etoup surrounded the town with ramparts and built an imposing castle to control the Paris-Orléans road. In the 12th century Montlhéry was taken by the king who was combatting the feudal lords of the Ile-de-France. It was dismantled and all that is left is the pentagonal foundation and a tower which rises from what was once the keep. During the 18th and 19th centuries, the tower was used as an observatory.

Open 10 - 12, 2 - 6 ; Weekends : 10 - 1, 2:30 - 7:30.
Closed Thursdays and Fridays.
Parking.

Le Saussay (Château).

Ballancourt - 91610.
Corbeil : 15 km.
Ballancourt : 2 km.
Private property.

This château is divided into two 17th century buildings which face each other across the grounds. The entry pavilion dates from the directory and the chapel is 18th century.

Open March 15 to Oct. 15 : 2 - 6. Sundays and holidays.
Groups on request Thursdays.
Parking.
Guided tours.
Recorded information.
Tel. : (6) 493.20.10.

Vauboyen (Château).

Bièvres - 91570.
Paris : 15 km.
Station : Vauboyen 300 m.
Private property.

Vauboyen is a neo-classical building inspired by the Palladian style. It was built in 1815 by Bernier who was assisted by Napoleon's architects Percier and Fontaine. Its elegant interiors include a collection of neo-classical furniture and works of art.

Open on request only.
Parking.
Tel. : (6) 941.89.24.

HAUTS-DE-SEINE

Clamart
Abbé Delille' House.

Clamart - 92140.
26, avenue du Président-Roosevelt.
Property of M. Boell.

This Directory house includes Directory and Empire furniture. The Abbé Delille wrote some of

35 Km SOUTH OF PARIS

domaine de courson

Discover this seventeenth century château, its Romantic 40 hectare park and its traditional Hurepoix village

A personal welcome in an inhabited château
A variety of visits
Groups on request
A unique gallery with a collection of Spanish paintings
An original site with a variety of locations for filming
Receptions, lectures, seminars in the restored stables

DOMAINE DE COURSON - 91680 - BRUYERES-LE-CHATEL
Tel. : 9 - 12 (6) 458.90.12 or (1) 555.41.74.

his work and Stendhal was a guest here.
*Open on request preferably for groups.
Parking.
Guided tours.
Tel. : 46.42.14.68.*

Malmaison Museum and châteaux of Malmaison and Bois-Préau.

*Rueil-Malmaison - 92500.
Avenue du Château.
Property of the State.*

Renovated by Percier, Fontaine and the landscape architect Bertault, Malmaison was the favorite residence of the First Consul and as such witnessed the great political events of 1800 to 1804. It was embellished by the Empress Josephine and became her residence after the divorce. She died here in 1814. The main rooms have been restored and contain many works of art from the Napoleonic period, including pictures by the leading artists of the period and memorabilia of the Imperial family.
*Open 10 - 12:30, 1:30 - 5:30.
Tel. : 47.49.20.07.*

Saint-Cloud Park and Historical Museum.

*Saint-Cloud - 92210.
Property of the State.*

Located at the edge of Paris the verdant grounds of Saint-Cloud stretch along the banks of the Seine. Designed by Le Nôtre for Louis XIV's brother in 1670, the park replaced the Italianate gardens of the château's original owners the Gondi family. Today the grounds are all that remain of the estate which belonged to the Orléans family and then to the Crown. It was from this official residence that Napoleon chose to proclaim the Empire in 1804. The palace was demolished after a fire in 1870. All that remains are the outbuildings and two 17th century pavilions. The history and architecture of this important site are explained in the historical museum.
*Grounds open March 1 to April 30 : 7 am - 9 pm.
May 1 to Aug. 31 : 7 am - 10 pm.
Sept. 1 to Oct. 31 : 7 am - 9 pm.
Nov. 1 to Feb. 28 : 7 am - 8 pm.
Historic Museum open Wed. weekends and holidays : 2 - 5.
Lecture tours on request.
Tel. : 46.02.70.01.*

Sceaux (Château).

*Sceaux - 92330.
Paris : 15 km.
Property of the department.*

There was already a 15th century castle at Sceaux when Colbert purchased the estate in 1670. He brought some of the greatest artists of his day to work on his new residence : Le Nôtre, Perrault, Coysevox and Tuby. Although the château itself was replaced by a Louis XIII style edifice in the 19th century, the other buildings and the grounds have remained intact thanks to extensive restoration projects. Besides the beautiful gardens with their basins and waterfall, you can see the entry pavilion, with its sculpture by Coysevox, the Dawn pavilion designed by Perrault with its cupola decorated by Le Brun as well as the little château. The Orangery was designed by Jules Hardouin-Mansart for Colbert's son Seignelay in 1685. The Hanover pavilion, built by Chevoter for one of the new boulevards in Paris was moved to Sceaux in 1930. The statues of the Nations by Desjardins come originally from the Place des Victoires in Paris. The château is now the home of the museum of the History of the Ile-de-France.
*Park open all year sunrise to sunset.
Museum open daily except Tuesdays : 10 - 12 (except Mon. and Fri.), 2 - 5, 6, or 7.
Tel. : 46.61.06.71.*

Sèvres (Gambetta's House).

*Sèvres - 92310.
14, rue Gambetta.
Near Paris.
Property of the State.*

Forty years after Balzac, Gambetta became the owner of the little house in Sèvres. Apart from adding one room the politician did not change this simple house where he died unexpectedly in 1882. Since then the house has been a monument to his memory with many of his personal belongings kept here. In the garden is a monument designed by Bartholdi in 1891.
*Open April 1 to Sept. 30 :
Closed Tuesdays and Wednesdays.
Guided tours.
Tel. : 45.34.61.22.*

SEINE-ET-MARNE

Blandy-les-Tours (Castle).

*Blandy-les-Tours - 77115.
Place des Tours.
Melun : 12 km.
Bus service.
Property of the commune.*

Originally a fief belonging to Aurelien, one of the companions of Clovis, Blandy-les-Tours was rebuilt in the 16th century by François d'Orléans who transformed into a country residence. The princesse de Clèves was married here in 1572 in the presence of Henri IV. After being restored again in the 17th century, the castle was demolished and turned into a farm. The imposing keep set inside the polygonal walls still survives as do the round towers dating from the 14th century. In the courtyard you can also see a Merovingian crypt.
*Open March 1 to Oct. 31 : 9 - 12, 2 - (except Wed.). Nov. 1 to Feb. 28 : 9 - 12 - 5:30 weekends and holidays.
Open other times on request.
Parking.
Guided tours available on request.
Information pannels, brochures, leaflets English, German.
June music festival, temporary exhibits
Tel. : (6) 066.90.23 and 066.96.75.*

Bourron (Château).

*Bourron-Marlotte - 77780.
14 bis, rue Maréchal-Foch.*

...ontainebleau : 8 km.
...tation : Bourron-Marlotte.
...rivate property.
This simple Louis XIII brick and ...tone château received both king ...tanislas and Louis XV. It has a ...re stairway with a swing bridge, ...7th, 18th and Directory furniture ...elonging to Madame Récamier.
...pen March 25 to Nov. 1, weekends ...nd holidays : 2 - 6.
...pen at other times on request.
...arking.
...uided tours, brochures, pannels.
...udio-visual programme.
...uided tours in English.
...el. : (6) 070.79.03.

...y (Château).
...osa Bonheur Museum.

...omery - 77810.
..., rue Rosa-Bonheur.
...ntainebleau : 6 km.
...ation : Thomery 2 km.
...ivate property.
Once a hunting lodge this pro...rty was acquired by the great ...th century animal painter Rosa ...nheur. She built a huge studio ...re in 1859. The museum now al-lows you to see the environment in which the artist worked for over forty years.
Open all year Wednesdays and Saturdays : 2 - 6.
Groups on request on other days.
Parking.
Guided tours.
Tel. : (6) 070.06.19.

Champs-sur-Marne (Château).

Champs-sur-Marne - 77420.
Paris : 20 km.
Property of the State.

Champs-sur-Marne was part of a huge estate created by the financier Poisson de Bourvallais near Paris at the end of the reign of Louis XIV. The château was built at the beginning of the 18th century and restored by comte Louis Cahen d'Anvers at the end of the 19th century. The château has a fine view down to the Marne. Its interiors reflect the changing taste of its owners : the original paintings in the Oval salon, the Chinese room created for the duc de la Vallière and the refined panelling of Madame de Pompadour's bedroom. In 1935 the château and its fine furniture were given to the State by M. Cahen d'Anvers's son.
Open March 21 to Sept. 30 : 10 - 12, 1:30 - 5:30.
Nov. 1 to 30 : 10 - 12, 1:30 - 4:30.
Dec. 1 to Feb. 20 : 10 - 12, 1:30 - 4.
Feb. 21 to March 21 : 10 - 12, 1:30 - 5.
Closed Tuesdays.
Parking.
Tel. : (6) 005.24.43.

Choix (Mill).

Gastins - 77370.
Near Nangis.
Private property.

This stone mill has kept its mechanism intact. You can see its wings and the cogs and wheels. It replaced a windmill built in 1267 and was restored to working order in 1977.
Open April 30 to Sept. 30 : 3 - 6 Sundays.
Closed holidays.
Groups on request during the week.
Parking.
Guided tours, brochures.
Tel. : (6) 068.71.73.

BLANDY-LES-TOURS — SEINE-ET-MARNE
7 km from Vaux-le-Vicomte

Castle of the vicomtes of Melun.
A medieval fortress (contemporary with the Bastille in Paris).
The finest preserved example of 14th century military architecture in the Paris area.
Available for private or public receptions.
Open daily except Wednesdays.
Guided tours on request.

Ferrières (Château).

*Ferrières - 77164.
Lagny : 6 km.
Station : Torcy 6 km.
Bus service.
Property of the University of Paris.*

Built in 1865 for baron de Rothschild by the English architect Paxton, Ferrières is one of the finest examples of the English country house style in France. For over a century it was the Rothschilds' family home. They decorated and furnished in a style that has become associated with their name. The château has very fine gardens with rare plants.

*Open Oct. 1 to April 30 : 2 - 5 Sundays only.
May 1 to Sept. 30 : 2 - 7.
Closed Mondays and Tuesdays.
Groups on request during the week.
Parking.
Guided tours.
Guides, brochures, lectures.
Lecture tours for school groups only.
Tel. : (6) 430.31.25.*

FONTAINEBLEAU.

Castle and Museum.

*Fontainebleau - 77300.
Station : 3 km.
Property of the State.*

Fontainebleau was entirely rebuilt by François I who kept only one Medieval building, the keep erected by Saint Louis. The magnificent interior decoration was carried out by a team of Italian artists under Il Rosso and Primaticcio. The château also housed the king's famous art collection. Enlarged by Henri IV, transformed by his successors and badly damaged during the Revolution, Fontainebleau was refurbished by Napoleon. Louis-Philippe and Napoleon III continued the restoration of the château whose superb collection offers an overview of pain-

ting, furniture and objects from the 16th century on.
*Open Oct. 1 to March 31 : 10 - 12:30, 2 - 5.
April 1 to Sept. 30 : 10 - 12:30, 2 - 6.
Closed Tuesdays.
Concerts.
Tel. : (6) 422.27.40 and 422.34.39.*

Le Vieux Logis.

*Fontainebleau - 77300.
7, boulevard Magenta.
Private property.*

To appreciate old Fontainebleau you must visit this delightful house. Formerly the château's building office, situated across the park, it is a simple house in the typical Ile-de-France style, surrounded by a garden.

*Open April 1 to Sept. 30 on request.
Closed Sundays.
Guided tours by the owners.
Information in English and Spanish.
Tel. : (6) 422.35.52.*

Hôtel d'Orléans.

*Fontainebleau - 77300.
83, rue de France.
Private property.*

This small town house which belonged to the duc d'Orléans in 1766 includes three rooms painted by students of Boucher.

*Open on request.
Guided tours.
Tel. : (6) 422.30.58.*

Guermantes (Castle).

*Guermantes Lagny-sur-Marne - 77400.
Paris : 27 km (A4 Lagny exit).
Private property.*

Guermantes is a brick and stone edifice begun in 1630 and completed and decorated in 1700. The work was directed by Robert de Cotte and Perrault who designed the formal gallery called « la belle inutile » which is over 30 m long adn which has kept its 1705 pannelling, painting, mirrors and floors. Proust immortalised Guermantes by giving its name to one of the main characters in his work « Remembrance of Things Past ».

*Open weekends and holidays March to Nov. 15 : 2 - 6.
Parking.
Guided tours, brochures.
Information pannels, leaflets.
Information in English.
Tel. : (6) 430.00.94.*

JOUARRE.

Abbey.

*Jouarre - 77640.
6, rue Montmorin.
Private property.*

In 603 Saint Adon founded double monastery of both me and women according to a princ ple established by the order Saint Colomban which then dom nated the north of France. The a bey later thrived under the order Saint Benoit but was sold at th Revolution. It was bought back Benedictine nuns in 1837. You c visit the Romanesque tower, th buildings with their 16th centu vaulted rooms containing doc ments relating to the history of t abbey. The abbey is located ne the famous Merovingian crypts.

*Open all year 10 - 12, 2:30 - 5.
Closed Tuesdays.
Guided tours available.
Pannels, brochures.
Audio-visual programme.
Information in English, German, Du and Polish.
Temporary exhibits.
Picnic area.
Tel. : (6) 022.06.11.*

Crypts.

*Jouarre - 77640.
6, rue Montmorin.
Meaux : 15 km.
La Ferté-sous-Jouarre : 3 km.
Property of the commune.*

The crypts of Jouarre are a lar funerary oratory founded in 630 the order of Irish monks w came to convert Merovingi Gaul. They are a rare example early Christian building in Franc The sarcophagi of the founders the order are decorated in a sty reminiscent of Antiquity.

en Jan. 1 to Dec. 31 : 10:30 - 12,
'0 - 5.
sed Tuesdays.
king.
ded tours, brochures.
ormation in English, German, Polish
Dutch.
. : (6) 022.06.11.

Lys (Royal Abbey).

nmarie-lès-Lys.
tion : Melun 3 km.
perty of the commune.
his abbey was founded in 1244
Saint Louis and Blanche de
stille for the monks of the Cis-
cian order. From the ruins you
still make out the choir, the
all-columned piers and the
e windows. A staircase goes
as far as the vaults of the North
nsept.
: (6) 439.06.82.

EAUX.

shop's Palace
ossuet Museum).

ux - 77100.
lace de Gaulle.
perty of the city.
Now used as the Bossuet Mu-
m and library, the former bis-
's palace is an imposing 17th
tury building with rooms that
back even farther. In the
dle of the façade which gives
o the courtyard is a 16th cen-
tower which has a ramp and
ch served as access for the
keys bringing corn to the pa-
. The museum's collection is
palyed in Medieval, 17th and
century rooms. Louis XVI and
family spent a night in this pa-
on ther way back from Va-
nes.
n daily : 10:30 - 12, 2 - 6.
sed Tuesdays and holidays.
king.
ccompanied visits, brochures.
ded tours on request Sundays May 1
ec. 31 at 3:30.
rmation in German from the tourist
rmation office.
lities for the handicapped.
certs, temporary exhibits.
: (6) 434.84.45.

rdin Bossuet

ux - 77100.
épiscopale.
r the Station.
perty of the city.
hese gardens of the former
op's palace were designed by
Le Nôtre in the shape of a Bishop's mitre. They are enclose by
Gallo-Roman and Medieval ramparts. Bossuet, one of the most
active defenders of Catholicism,
was one of the most respected
and controversial polemicists of
his time.
Open Jan. 1 to Dec. 31 : 9 - 6 Daily.
Guided tours on request Sundays, May
1 to Dec. 31 at 3:30.

MORET-SUR-LOING.

Keep.

Moret-sur-Loing - 77250.
Rue du Donjon.
Fontainebleau : 10 km.
Station : Moret/Veneux-les-Sablons.
Private property.
This is all that remains of a 12th
century fortress which was the
property of the commune of
France. All the kings of France
stayed here at some point and
Fouquet was imprisoned here for
two months before his transferal
to the fortress of Pignerolo. Inside
are Flanders and Aubusson tapes-
tries as well as period furniture.
*Open April 21 to Sept. 9, Sundays and
holidays : 3 - 6.*
*During the Moret-sur-Loing Festival in
July and Aug. open Sat. 3 - 7.*
Parking.
Guided tours, brochures.
Unaccompanied visits of the park.
Information in English and German.
Leaflets.
Tel. : (6) 070.50.39.

Clemenceau's House.

Moret-sur-Loing - 77250.
Fontainebleau : 10 km.
Station : Moret-Sablons.
Bus service.
Property of Mme Clemenceau.
President Georges Clemenceau
designed the plans for the house
himself un 1928. This thatched
roofed building, set on the banks
of the Loing, received some of the
most prominent politicians and artists of the day. Inside the furniture
and collections are reminders of
the life of the President. The
grounds of over five hectares include waterlilies which symbolise
the gardens of Claude Monet, a
friend of Clemenceau's.
Open April 1 to Oct. 14 : 2:30 - 6.
Oct. 15 to Nov. 30 : 2 - 5.
Parking.
Guided tours by Mme Clemenceau.
Brochures.
Lectures on the life of Georges Clemenceau.
Tel. : (6) 070.51.21.

Nemours
(Castle-Museum).

Nemours - 77140.
Rue Gautier-Ier.
Bus service.
Property of the city.
Built in 1130 by the seigneur of
Nemours, the castle has maintained its austere fortress like appearance, despite the transformations
carried out by Jacques d'Armagnac in the 15th century and the
duc d'Orléans in the 17th. It is a
four sided building with round towers at each corner linked to a
square watch tower by a narrow
gallery. In 1715 a chapel was added and since 1903 the castle has
housed an archeological museum
and a collection of local art.
Open all year Wed. to Fri. : 2 - 5:30.
Sat. to Mon. : 10 - 12, 2 - 5:30.
Closed Tuesdays.
Parking.
Brochures, temporary exhibits.
Tel. : (6) 428.40.37.

Vaux-le-Vicomte
(Château).

Maincy - 77950.
Melun : 6 km.
Private property.
Next to Versailles, Vaux-le-Vicomte is the most beautiful and
complete 17th century château. Finance Minister Nicholas Fouquet
brought the most talented artists
of the time to work on Vaux : Le
Vau directed the architecture, Le
Brun the decoration and Le Nôtre
the gardens. The buildings make
up a carefully planned complex
and reflect Baroque taste in their
grandeur and depth. Inside, the
rooms are arranged around an Italianate salon crowned by a dome.
Le Nôtre's gardens served as a
model for classical French gardens. Sadly, Fouquet, did not be-
nefit from this syptuous residence. After the entertainment given to the king on August 17 1661,
Fouquet was imprisoned, the furniture sold off and the statues
transfered to Versailles. Today the
magnificent interiors and extensive gardens make Vaux-le-Vi-

comte one of the most splendidly resored châteaux in France.
Open Daily April 1 to Oct. 31 : 10 - 6.
Weekends Nov. 1 to 30, Feb. 1 to March 30 : 2 - 5.
Parking.
Unaccompanied visits, brochures.
Information in English and German.
Pannels.
Tel. : (6) 066.97.09 and 066.97.11.

SEINE-SAINT-DENIS

Saint-Denis (Abbey Church).

Saint-Denis - 93200.
Near Paris (Metro).
Property of the State.

For 12 centuries Saint-Denis was the burial place of the kings of France and its history is closely linked to that of the monarchy. King Dagobert was the first monarch to be buried here near the relics of Saint Denis. In the 12th century Abbot Suger began the reconstruction of the 8th century church and by the time it was consecrated in 1144 the choir of Saint Denis had become one of the earliest examples of Gothic art in France. The main part of the building is the 13th century work of the great architect Pierre de Montreuil. Its luminosity and structure make it a Gothic masterpiece which has not been deminished by the 19th restorations. The tombs make up a very important collection of French funerary sculpture from the Middle Ages to the Renaissance. 12th century stained glass and 16th century choir stalls.
Open April 1 to Sept. 30 : 10 - 5:30.
Oct. 1 to March 31 : 10 - 3:30.
Sundays 12 -
Guided tours available, brochures.
Concerts.
Tel. : 48.20.15.57.

VAL-DE-MARNE

Cœuilly (Château).

Champigny-sur-Marne - 94500.
6, rue de l'Abreuvoir.
Champigny : 2 km.
R.E.R. and Bus 208.
Property of MM. Poujade and Vichy.

This 17th century building be longed to Louis XIII's private se cretary. It is a massive buildin with a pilastered pediment. Th first floor windows are decorate with smiling fauns. Inside are fin Regency firepalces and a gran staircase.
Grounds only.
Parking.
Tel. : 48.80.73.42.

Grosbois (Château).

Boissy-Saint-Léger - 94470.
Créteil : 5 km.
R.E.R. Boissy-Saint-Léger : 2,5 km.
Property of the Société d'encourag ment à l'élevage du cheval français.

Grosbois was built around 161 by Charles de Valois, son c Charles IX and Marie Touchet. Th present building is set around courtyard whose perspective he ralds the design of Versailles. Th inner facade is semi-circular brick and stone. The great hall c the first floor has kept its Louis X style but the other rooms were r decorated by Berthier a marshal Napoleon's army. The gallery h sconces by Thomire, works by C

SEINE-SAINT-DENIS

ABBAYE DE SAINT-DENIS

Abbé Suger's 12th century church transformed by Pierre de Montreuil in the 13th century.
Royal burial place from the Middle Ages to the Revolution.
Near Paris (direct Metro line).

va, Prudhon and Gérard and memorabilia of the Empire.
en Sundays and holidays all year.
oups on request.
rking.
ided tours, brochures.
: 45.69.03.47.

ncennes (Château).

cennes - 94300.
r Paris : Bus or Metro.
perty of the State.
'incennes is the most complete dieval royal residence surviving. The keep was built in the h century not far from a Cape- castle which has since disappared. It surrounded by a huge l with nine towers built by arles V. The chapel was begun under Saint Louis in the same style as the Sainte-Chapelle in Paris. In the 17th century Anne of Austria and Mazarin remodelled the fortress and had the two pavilions built. After the court moved to Versailles a royal porcelain factory (the future Sèvres) was installed in the château before it became a state prison which held the Marquis de Sade and Diderot. Restoration was begun by Viollet-le-Duc in 1852 and is still going on.
Open daily April 1 to Sept. 30 : 10 - 6.
Oct. 1 to March 3 : 10 - 5.
Historical Museum.
Brochures.
Tel. : 43.28.15.48.

VAL-D'OISE

Écouen (Château). Renaissance Museum.

Écouen - 95440.
Property of the State.
Écouen was built for the connétable Anne de Montmorency in the middle of the 16th century by several architects including Jean Bullant. It is a square plan building surrounded by wide ditches, reminescent of the Middle Ages although its corner pavilions and sculpted dormer windows, fireplaces and doorways are examples of French Renaissance art. The museum comprises 20 rooms filled with Renaissance artifacts installed in the house of a 16th century patron of the arts.
Open 9:45 - 12:30, 2 - 5:15.
Closed Tuesdays and holidays.
Tel. : (3) 990.04.04.

GROSBOIS

VAL-DE-MARNE

rosbois appears at the end of a long lée entered through a wrought iron ate flanked by two Empire pavilions. It a 17th century brick and stone esidence. Two wings flanked with avilions and surrounded by à dry moat urround the main courtyard. The main ock has a semi-circular façade on the ourtyard side and has survived the transformations carried out by the duc d'Angoulême.
Magnificently furnished and decorated by marechal Berthier during the First Empire it is now an art and history museum of the period as well as one of the loveliest residences of the Paris area both in style and interior decoration.

VAUX-LE-VICOMTE

Masterpiece created for Nicholas Fouquet by the architect le Vau, the painter Le Brun and the landscape architect Le Nôtre. The model for Versailles which has preserved its architecture, interiors and gardens.

A private residence open to the public daily from April 1 to October 30, from 10 to 6. Fountains the second and last Saturdays of each month. Candlelight visits each Saturday at 9 pm from June 1 to September 30.

5 km East of Melun
Road Autoroute A4 or A6 (Melun-Sénart or Melun exit) R.N. 6 or R.N. 36.
Train From Paris Gare de Lyon to Melun.

Information
Tourist Service
Domaine de Vaux-le-Vicomte
77950 Maincy
Tel. : (6) 066.97.09.

The King's Chamber

Furniture, paintings, Savonnerie carpets, Gobelins tapestries, sculptures decorate the State rooms which precede the Servant's Rooms of the huge cellars : kitchens, pantry, wine cellar and now an Archive room.

Carriage museum

The art of the great carriage makers relives in the Fouquet's stables.

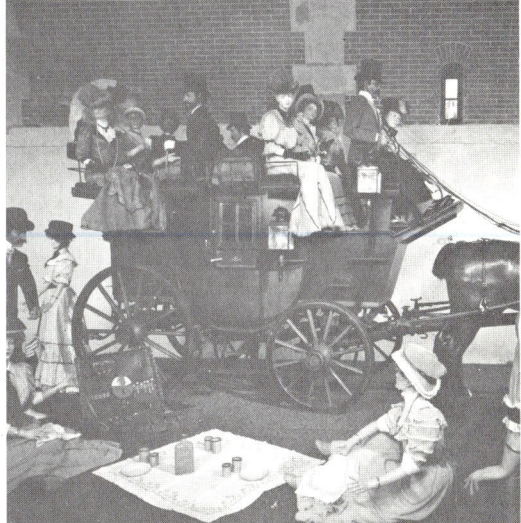

␣'Ecureuil

In the château's outbuildings meals and refreshments are served on the terrace or inside during opening hours.

VAL-D'OISE — 162 — ILE-DE-FRANCE

Gadancourt (Château).

Vigny - 95450.
Magny-en-Vexin : 6 km.
Station : Cergy 12 km.
Private property.
 The château comprises two 17th century pavilions and a main block rebuilt after a fire at the end of the 18th century.
Open on written request only.
Parking.
Tel. : (3) 39.20.02.

Guiry (Château).

Guiry.
Vigny - 95450.
Private property.
 The cut stone building is attributed to François Mansart and was completed in 1665. Its facade has a large sculpted pediment. Inside is memorabilia of Joseph de Maistre. The village of Guiry is an archeological centre. Exhibition of paintings by Henri de Maistre, painter of the Nabis school.
Open on request for groups.
Open on a regular basis July 23 to Aug. 31.
Guided tours available.
Tel. : (3) 476.40.71 and 704.31.73.

Maudetour (Château).

Maudetour-en-Vexin - 95420.
Magny-en-Vexin : 8 km.
Mantes-la-Jolie : 15 km.
Property of M. Durand.

 This building begun at the beginning of the 18th century was never completed for an unknown reason. It is an irregular shaped construction, with the outbuildings on one side and the chapel and the « Audience », a building which served as court and prison on the other. The ice-house in the park allowed things to be kept cold in July and August. In restoration.
Open July 1 to August 10 : 10 - 12, 2 - 6.
Groups on request at other times.
Unaccompanied visits.
Tel. : (3) 467.15.93.

Montgeroult (Château).

Boissy-l'Aillerie - 95650.
Pontoise : 8 km.
Station : Mongeroult-Courcelles.
Private property.
 This Classical cut-stone château is composed of a pedimented main building and a perpendicular wing on the North side. The large stables border the forecourt. Inside is fine 18th century panneling.
Open July 5 to Sept. 15 : 10:30 - 12:30 3 - 6:30.
For groups only on request.
Closed Thursdays and Fridays from Aug. 10 to 20.
Guided tours.
Tel. : (3) 039.11.03.

VAL D'OISE

GUIRY-EN-VEXIN

Guiry is one of the gems of the Ile de France.
It was built in 1665 by François Mansart and it offers you only 50 km from Paris (between Pontise and Magny-en-Vexin) its :
— vaulted cellars and salons for your dinners, luncheons or receptions from 50 to 80 people.

— the outbuildings remodelled for receptions of 100 to 150 persons as well as for conferences, exhibits, concerts, etc.
— its incomperable setting for photography locations or other cultural activities.

Tel. : (3) 467.40.31 and 704.31.73.

NOINTEL

VAL D'OISE
30 km from Paris

Prince Murat Museum and centre for contemporary art

Located between Presle and Beaumont-sur-Oise.

A prestigious historic setting. A 17th and 18th century château enlarged during the Second Empire, surrounded with statues by Coysevox and a famous park designed by Mansard and Fragonard. Fine Second Empire rooms.

ACCESS
By Road Autoroute du Nord then R.N. 1, Presles or Beaumont-sur-Oise exit.
By Rail Nointel Station from the Gare du Nord, Persan-Beaumont via Montsoult train.
Tel. : 034.66.88 and 470.09.52.

Forward looking Collections. 600 recent hundred paintings, sculptures, drawings, gouaches, illustrations, engravings, water colours, comic strips : New Realism, Figurative Criticism and Narrative, Metarealism, Superhumanism, Commercial Art, Fantastic art, Science Fiction, Popular Art.

OPEN
daily March 15 to Nov. 15 : 2 - 6.
Weekends and holidays : 11 - 6:30.
Parking.
Amusement park for children.
Picnic area.
30 ha park.
Open Nov. 15 to March 15 for groups by appointement.

Moussy (Priory).

Moussy-en-Vexin - Marines - 95640.
Pontoise and Gisors nearby.
Station : Chais 5 km.
Private property.

This Renaissance fortified manor house has towers of either side of its entrance. It belonged to Jean Gisors the king's Falconner.
Open on request May 1 to Oct. 15 : 9 - 11:30, 2 - 6.
Grounds only.
Guided tours available.
Tel. : (3) 467.40.95.

Nointel (Château).

Nointel-par-Presles - 95590.
Presles-Beaumont-sur-Oise : 1 km.
Station : Nointel (500 m).
Private property.

This 17th and 18th century château was enlarged under the Second Empire and is surounded by statues by Coysevox and a famous park designed by Mansard and Fragonard. Many famous people have stayed here : Voltaire, Balzac, the princes de Conti, Fragonard, Hubert Robert, Boucher... Today the château has fine Empire rooms and a museum of contemporary art founded by the Prince Murat.
Open daily : 2 - 6.
Weekends and holidays : 11 - 6.
Parking.
Unaccompanied visits.
Information pannels, leaflets.
Brochures.
Temporary exhibits, concerts.
Tel. : (3) 034.66.88 and 470.09.52.

Royaumont (Abbey).

Asnières-sur-Oise - 95270.
Viarmes : 3 km.
Private property.

Royaumont was founded in 1228 by Saint Louis who buried five of his children here. The king and his successors richly endowed the abbey which accounts for the fine buildings. It flourished until the Revolution. The South transept remains from the church. The cloister set around a pretty garden has survived. The refectory where Saint Louis served the monks, the chapter house, the guest quarters and store rooms are all open to the public. Today Royaumont houses a Cultural Institute.
Open Jan. 12 to Oct. 1 : 10 - 12, 2 - 6.
Closed Wednesdays.
Parking.
Guided tours.
Concerts, workshops, exhibits.
Tel. : (3) 727.70.18.

Taverny (Priory).

Taverny - 95150.
Parvis de l'Église.
Montmorency : 10 km.
Station : Taverny.
Property of M. Martin.

This Benedictine priory was founded in 1120 by the Montmorency family. Several kings of France visited it and George Sand stayed here. The garden is planted with age old trees (chesnuts, cedars and tropical plants...).
Open weekends May 5 to July 25.
Saturdays Sept. 5 to Oct. 31 : 2 - 6.
Nov. 1 to April 30 : 2 - 5.
Closed Dec. 24 and 25, Jan. 1 and 2, Easter Sunday, May 1 ane July 15 and 15.
Parking.
Guided tours of the interiors.
Tel. : (3) 960.05.03.

Villette (Château).

Condecourt - 95450 Vigny.
Meulan : 4 km.
Private property.

Nestled between two hills Villette was built in 1663 acording to plans by François Mansart for Jean Dyel, ambassador to Venice and then finished by J. Hardouin-Mansart. The main block is flanked by two wings. Two 17th century pavilions guard the entrance. The classical sobriety of the forecourt contrasts with the fine ornementation of the gardens. Vases and Spinhxes from Marly. The interiors have kept their original decoration. A colossal statue of Neptune presides over the « River » and the view which once ressembled that of Marly.
Open April 1 to May 10 : 3 - 6 on request for groups of at least twenty.
Parking.
Recommended itinerary.
Brochure.
Tel. : (4) 359.77.77.

YVELINES

Breteuil (Château).

Choiseul-Chevreuse - 78460.
Paris : 35 km.
Gare : Saint-Rémy-lès-Chevreuse 7 km.
Property of M. de Breteuil.

Set in a huge 70 hectare park Breteuil rises above the Chevreuse valley. Begun under Henri IV and Louis XIII the complex comprises a main block flanked with two brick and stone wings. The 18th century interiors include a rich collection of laquer furniture, Gobelins tapestries, Swedish porcelain and paintings by Rigaud, de Troy Boilly... The château has always belonged to the Breteuil family.
Open daily Park : 10 am.
Château : 2:30, except Sundays and holidays, and July and August : 11 am.
Groups on request.
Guided tours, brochures.
Audio-visual programmes.
English, German guides.
Childrens activities.
Concerts from Easter to November Sundays 5 pm.
Tel. : (3) 052.05.11.

Chevreloup (Park).

Rocquencourt - 78150.
30, route de Versailles.
Station : Versailles 3 km.
Property of the Museum of Natural History.

This hunting ground belonged to Louis XIV before Louis XV incorporated it into the Trianon gardens. It now forms a branch of the Paris botanical gardens, with 200 hectares devoted to the enrichment and conservation of the country's botanical heritage.
Open Jan. 21 to Dec. 31, Saturdays : 10 - 2:30.
Groups on request except Sundays.
Parking.
Guided tours.
Pannels.
Tel. : (3) 955.53.80.

BRETEUIL

YVELINES

35 km from Paris in the Chevreuse valley
Château and Park of Breteuil

Three centuries of European History. Waxworks from fron the Musée Grévin of Marie-Antoinette, Louis XVI, Louis XVIII, Edward VII, Gambetta, Marcel Proust and their guests.
Your day at Breteuil can include a visit of the château, its waxworks and « the table of Europe »,
— the grounds with its picnic areas and playgrounds,
— the arts centre (exhibits and concerts),
— receptions in the château and the orangery.

Open daily.
Choisel 78460 Chevreuse.
Tel. : 052.05.11 and 052.05.02.

Past meets present at Breteuil : Edward VII and Henri Marquis de Breteuil having tea with Henri's grandson Henri-François and his wife Sévrine.

Dampierre (Château).

Dampierre - 78720.
Versailles : 18 km.
Station : Saint-Rémy-lès-Chevreuse.
Private property.

Built for the duc de Chevreuse by Jules Hardouin-Mansart in the 17th century, Dampierre is one of the most important château in the famous « vallée de Chevreuse ». The park was designed by Le Nôtre and acts as a superb setting for the château and its outbuildings. Inside you can see important memorabilia and works of art relating to the Luynes family who still live in the house. In the great hall is the « Age d'Or » painted by Ingres and a unique antique decorative scheme painted in the 19th century.
Open April 1 to Oct. 15 : 2 - 6.
Closed Tuesdays.
Guided tours.
Tel. : (3) 054.52.83.

Grand'Maisons (Château).

Villepreux - 78450.
Versailles : 10 km.
Parc de Villepreux : 3 km.
Private property.

This château was built at the beginning of the 18th century by Jean-Baptiste Leroux for the Francinis, Louis XIV's fountain builders. This elegant and harmonious residence still has its period decoration.
Open on request only.
Parking.
Guided tours.
Information in English, Italian, Spanish.
Temporary exhibits.
Tel. : (3) 056.20.05.

Maisons-Lafitte (Château).

Maisons-Lafitte - 78600.
Paris : 20 km.
Property of the State.

Built between 1642 and 1651 by François Mansart Maisons is one of the finest examples of French classical architecture. On completion it received a visit from the young Louis XIV and his mother Anne of Austria and a century later many famous scientists, philosophers and men of letters, including Voltaire came here. The rooms are arranged around the fine grand staircase, one of Mansart's masterpieces. Since 1967 the château has been restored by the French government in conjunction with various museums who contributed paintings by Van Loo, Hubert Robert, Patel... The exterior grand staircase leads down to a formal garden which is all that remains of the huge park sold off in lots at the beginning of the 19th century by the banker Jacques Lafitte. State property since 1905.
Open all year : 10 - 12, 2 - 6.
Closed Tuesdays and Sunday mornings.
Groupes on advance request.
Guided tours.
Brochures.
Architecture workshops for school children (by appointment).
Tel. : (3) 962.01.49.

Mauvières (Château).

Saint-Forget-les-Sablons - 78720.
Station : Saint-Rémy-lès-Chevreuse 4 km.
Private property.

The present day Mauvières was built in the 18th century on the site of an ancient manor house which was the property of the Cyrano family and the birth place of the famous Cyrano de Bergerac. The main building is flanked by a dove cote and a service courtyard built in the 17th century. This white stone Louis XV building is as refined as its fine painted wood pannelled interiors. It is surrounded by an English garden.
Open daily, sunrise to sunset.
Groups on request.
Parking.
Guided tours on request.
Pannels, brochures, leaflets.
Facilities for the handicapped.
Concerts, temporary exhibits.
Tel. : (3) 052.54.76.

Médan (Château).

Médan - 78670.
43, rue Pierre-Curie.
Poissy : 7 km.
Station : 2 km.
Private property.

This former hunting lodge dates from the 15th century. In the 16th century it received Ronsard and the Pléiade poets. In 1924 it became the residence of Maurice Maeterlinck and in 1967 the newspaper « Combat » set up its presses here. Three hundred meters away is Emile Zola's house.
Open Aug. 1 to 31 and Sept. 15 to 30 9 - 12, 2 - 5.
Parking.
Unaccompanied visits.
Tel. : (3) 975.86.59.

Neuville (Château).

Gambais - 78950.
Station : Houdan 5 km.
Property of M. de Labriffe.

Neuville was built in the 16th century in the midst of a large land and then transformed in the 17th century. It is a one-story horseshoe shaped building with 18th century interiors. In 1965 the owners undertook an extensive restoration programme.
Open on request only for groups.
Parking.
Guided tours.
Acoustiguides in the chapel.
Information in English.
Tel. : (3) 227.27.10.

Port-Royal (Granges - Museum).

Magny-les-Hameaux - 78470.
Versailles : 12 km.
Property of the State.

The museum is installed in th

THOIRY

YVELINES

Thoiry is an historic monument dating from the Valois period surrounded by a famous game park ; Built in 1564 by Delorme and continuously embellished for the past 400 years by the family of the Comte de la Panouse who still lives here.

Receptions, meetings, seminars, film locations. Call the Vicomtesse de la Panouse — Tel. : (3) 487.40.67 and 487.40.06.

building erected in 1652 to accomodate the students of the school set up by the scholars attached to the famous abbey of Port-Royal; Racine was a student here from 1656 to 1658. The building has been restored and the expanded collection of documents, paintings and engravings tell the story of the Jansenist movement in the 17th and 18th centuries.
Open Oct. 15 to Feb. 28 : 10 - 11:30, 2 - 5.
March 1 to Oct. 15 : 10 - 11:30, 2 - 5:30.
Closed Monday, Tuesday and holidays (except Easter and Pentecost).
Tel. : (3) 043.73.05.

Rambouillet (Château).

Rambouillet - 78120.
Property of the State.
Château : Rambouillet is set in the heart of 20 000 hectares of woodland, all that is left of the Yvelines forest. The château has kept its medieval contours and its 14th century keep despite the alterations carried out by its successive owners. Numerous kings were attracted to this hunting residence conveniently located near Paris; François I died here and Charles X abdicated here. In the 17th century the marquise de Rambouillet and her daughter Julie d'Angennes held a brilliant literary salon here. The château has kept its function as royal residence dating from Louis XVI and Napoleon.
The Shell Pavilion : The two garden buildings erected by the duc de Penthièvre are good examples of the 18th century's taste for nature. One of them, the Shell Pavilion looks like a simple thatched cottage from the outside but the interiors are decorated with shells, mother of pearl and marble.
The Queen's Dairy : Louis XVI created an experimental farm and had one of the elaborate dairies so favoured by the ladies of the court, built here for Marie-Antoinette in 1785. This little sandstone temple in the Neo-classical style has a rustic artificial grotto nearby.

Open April 1 to May 30 : 10 - 12, 2 - 4.
Closed Tuesdays and Wednesdays.
Parking.
Guided tours, brochures.
Tel. : (3) 483.34.54.

Saint-Germain-en-Laye (Château and Museum of Antiquities).

Saint-Germain-en-Laye - 78103.
Place du Château.
R.E.R. Saint-Germain-en-Laye.
Property of the State.
The château was built under Charles V, remodelled under François I and Louis XIV who was born here. It was restored at the end of the 19th century to accomodate the museum. The collection includes archeological collections dating from the Paleolithic age to the reign of Charlemagne. The finest prehistoric, Gallo-Roman and Merovingian artifacts found in France are displayed on three floors.
Open all year : 9:45 - 12, 1 - 5:15.
Closed Tuesdays.
Children's workshops.
Tel. : (3) 451.53.63.

Saint-Germain-en-Laye Priory (Museum).

Saint-Germain-en-Laye - 78100.
2, rue Maurice-Denis.
R.E.R. Saint-Germain-en-Laye.
Property of the department.
Originally, this was a hospice for the poor founded by Madame de Montespan. The oldest vault in the priory bears the date 1692. This simple imposing building comprises a chapel, common rooms, a double grand staircase and pantries. The priory has not been a hospice since 1803 and was sold in 1816 to become artists' studios. After the Franco-Prussian war it was used as a retirement home by the Jesuit order until 1902. Maurice Denis acquired the property in 1912 and built a studio on plans by the architect Auguste Perret. Today the Museum is devoted to receating the Symbolist atmosphere of the period thanks to the collection donated by Maurice Denis's family.
Open all year Wed. to Sun. : 10:30 5:30.
Closed Mondays and Tuesdays.
Parking.
Guided tours available.
Information in English, German, Spanish.
Lectures, brochures.
Facilities for the handicapped.
Temporary exhibits.
Tel. : (3) 973.77.87.

Sainte-Mesme (Manor House).

Sainte-Mesme - 78730.
1, rue de Legaignena.
Dourdan : 4 km.
Station : Dourdan R.E.R.
Property of Colonel and Mme de Lanbilly.
The foundations of this 16th century hunting lodge date back to Romanesque times. The Eastern Gothic facade has an octogonal tower with a spiral staircase. The South facade has large mullioned windows dating from the 16th century. The interiors have beamed ceilings. Restoration has been going on since 1981.
Open only on request.
Parking.
Guided tours.
Information in English, Spanish, German.
Brochures, lecture tours on request.
Concerts, temporary exhibits.

Thoiry (Château).

Thoiry - 78770.
Versailles : 25 km.
Station : Montfort-l'Amaury 8 km.
Property of M. de La Panouse.
In 1564, Philibert Delorme built Thoiry. The collection of Gobelin tapestries were all gifts of the kings of France to their minister. The formal gardens date from 1727 but were partially destroyed in the 18th and 19th by Chatelain and Varé who repalced them with English gardens. All the gardens were restored in the 19th century

The park includes a large game reserve.
Open all year : 9:45 - 5:15 and Sundays 9:45 - 5:45.
Parking.
Unaccompanied visits, brochures.
Recorded information.
Information pannels, leaflets.
Temporary exhibitions.
Archival Museum : 1050 to the present.
Tel. : (3) 487.40.67.

Tilly (Château).

Tilly - 78790.
Mantes : 18 km.
Station : Bréval or Houdan 12 km.
Private property.
This Louis XIII manor house is set in a 7 hectare park. Here you can see copies of the cannons given by George Washington to admiral de Grasse, marquis de Tilly.
Open on request.
Brochures.
Tel. : (3) 651.98.76.

VERSAILLES

Château-Museum-Trianons.

Versailles - 78000.
Property of the State.
Louis XIII's hunting lodge was greatly enlarged by Le Vau and Mansart under Louis XIV and by Gabriel under Louis XV. After 1660 it replaced the Louvre as the principal residence of the crown. The huge park designed by Le Nôtre continued to be embellished until the Revolution. After the destruction of the Revolution, Louis-Philippe created the first museum of the history of France. Ever since, restoration has been carried out to return the apartments to their original state. The State and Private apartments, the Museum of the history of France, the Royal Opera House, the Grand and the Petit Trianon and Marie-Antoinette's « Hameau » and the gardens are open to the public.
Open 9:45 - 5.
Closed Monday.
Tel. : (3) 950.58.32 and 950.41.47.

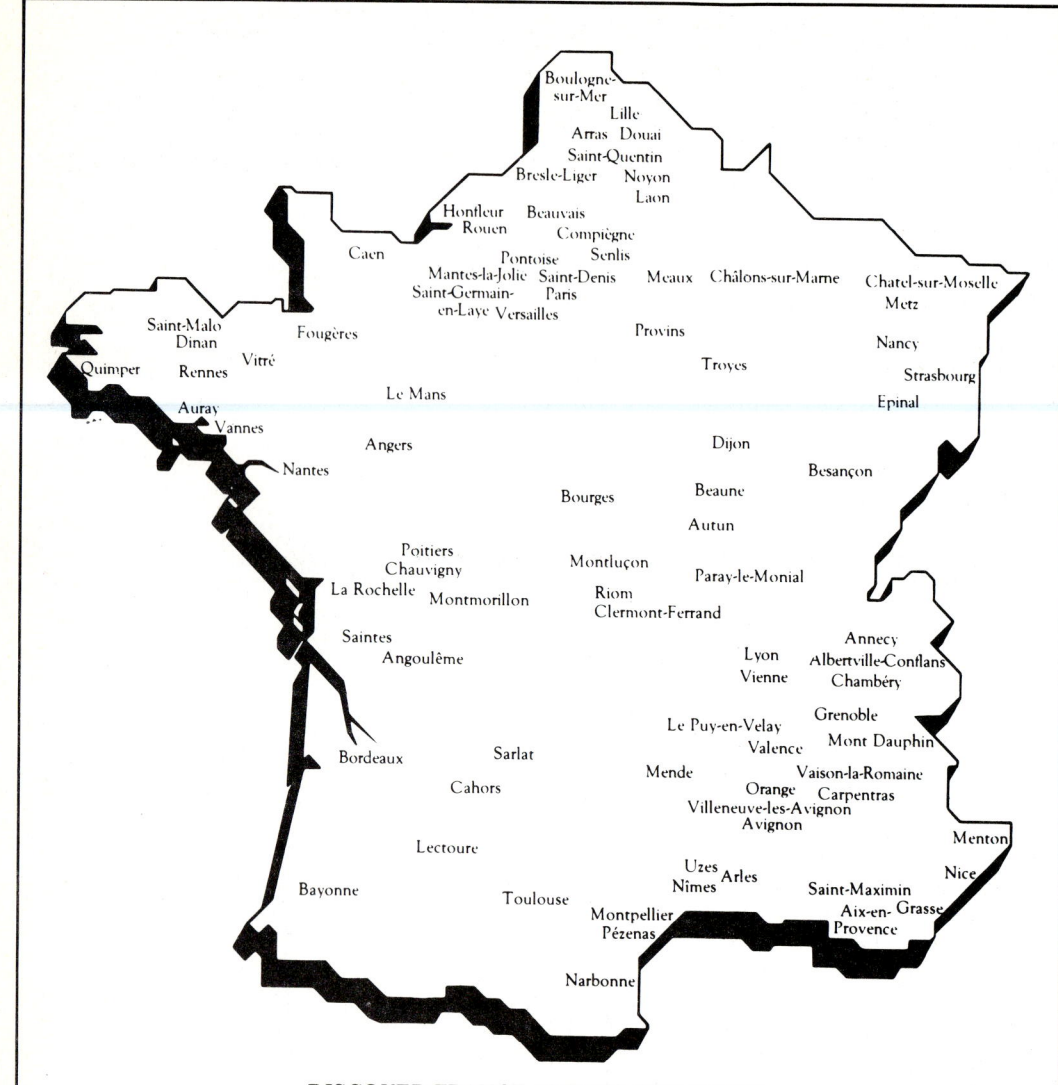

DISCOVER FRANCE AND ITS OLD CITIES
with the guided tours of the Caisse Nationale des Monuments Historiques

When travelling in France during your holidays, discover 100 Old Cities and their art treasures with the guided tours organised by the Caisse Nationale des Monuments Historiques. Daily tours are organised and last one hour or more. Ask for timetable and details in the Tourist Offices of cities like : AIX-EN-PROVENCE, ARLES, ARRAS, AVIGNON, BEAUNE, BEAUVAIS, LAON, LA ROCHELLE, LYON, METZ, MONTLUÇON, MONTPELLIER, NANCY, NANTES, ROUEN, STRASBOURG, VERSAILLES...

ENGLISH SPEAKING GUIDES.

Hôtel de Sully
62, rue Saint-Antoine 75004 PARIS
Tél. : 274.22.22.

CIVIS

LANGUEDOC ROUSSILLON

AUDE, GARD, HÉRAULT, LOZÈRE, PYRÉNÉES-ORIENTALES.

- ■ castle, château, manor house
- ● abbey, priory
- ▲ garden, park
- ★ town house, famous men house, farm, mill...
- ○ city

NIMES
- ▲ La Fontaine
- ● Jésuites (couvent des)
- ● Palais épiscopal
- ■ Tour Magne

BEAUCAIRE
- ● Saint-Roman
- ■ Château

NARBONNE
- ★ Hôtel Poulhariez
- ★ palais des archevêques
- ★ donjon

PEZENAS
- ★ Hôtel d'Alfonce
- ★ Hôtel de Saint-Germain

CASTELNAUDARY
- ■ Présidial
- ★ Moulin

VILLENEUVE-LES-AVIGNON
- ■ Fort
- ● Abbaye
- ■ Tour
- ● Chartreuse

■ Condres
■ La Baume
■ Castanet
MENDE ○
★ Pouget
■ Prades
■ Portes ■ Valbonne
● Saint-Enimie
■ Calberte ■ Rousson
■ Uzès
▲ L'Hort de Dieu ▲ Prafrance ○ Villeneuve-les-Avignon
▲ La Foux
■ Castellas
NIMES ○ ○ Beaucaire
■ Londres ■ Villevieille
■ Montlaur
■ Saint-Michel de Grandmont ■ Castries ■ Teillan
■ Flaugergues
■ Cazilhac MONTPELLIER ○ ■ L'Engarran
■ La Mogère ■ Aigues-Mortes
● Saint-Félix de Montceau
○ Pézenas
● Valmagne
● Fontcaude
★ BEZIERS Hôtel de Sarret
■ Saissac
● Saint-Papoul
○ Castelnaudary ○ Narbonne
CARCASSONNE ○ ● Fontfroide
■ Pennautier ● Sainte-Marie d'Orbieu
■ Caudeval
■ Couiza ● Salses
PERPIGNAN ○
■ Villefranche-de-Conflent ● Marcevol
● Saint-Michel-de-Cuxa ■ Collioure
● Saint-Martin-du-Canigou ● Arles-sur-Tech

LANGUEDOC-ROUSSILLON

AUDE

Carcassonne (Old City).
Carcassone - 11000.
Station and bus nearby.
Property of the State.

The original walls were fortified thoughout the centuries until the Crown gave the city its final set of ramparts in the 12th century. They have arrow slits and fortifications and surround the high walls of the count's castle whose main building, outbuildings and chapel are set around a courtyard. The North-West front has a watch tower and two habitable keeps one of which was remodelled by Viollet-le-Duc. inside is an historical museum.
Open daily April 1 to Sept. 30 : 9 - 12, 2 - 6:30.
Oct. 1 to March 31 : 9 - 12, 2 - 5.
Guided tours, brochures.
Exhibits.
Tel. : (68) 25.01.66.

CASTELNAUDARY

Présidial.
Castelnaudary - 11400.
Rampe du Présidial.
Property of the commune.

The presidial court created by Catherine de Medicis in 1554 houses a local archeological museum on its first floor.
Open on request from the town hall.
Guided tours.
Pannels.
Information in English and Spanich.
Lecture tours for school groups on request.
Tel. : (68) 23.11.16.

Moulin Cugarel.
Castelnaudary - 11400.
Property of the commune.

This mill is set on the side of the hill and was used until 1919 and restored in 1961. It is a round structure with turning sails and a dwelling attached.
Open on request.
Guided tours.
Information in English and Spanish.
Lecture tours for school groups on request.
Tel. : (68) 23.11.16.

Caudeval (Château).
Chalabre-Caudeval - 11230.
Carcassonne : 47 km.
Mirepoix : 9 km.
Station : Limoux 22 km.
Private property.

Caudeval is one of the ancient fiefs of the Levis-Mirepoix family. It was involved in the Albigensian Crusade and beseiged and captured in 1209 and again in 1575. The château houses a Roman museum, an artillery museum and a document collection. The rooms decorated with plasterwork, the guard room, the prison and the orangery are also open to the public.
Open April 1 to July 22 and
Parking.
Guided tours.
Pannels.
Information in English and German.
Temporary exhibits.
lacture tours for school groups.
Tel. : (61) 25.40.28.

Couiza (Château of the ducs de Joyeuse).
Couiza - 11190.
Carcassone : 40 km.
Station : Couiza.
Property of the commune.

The château of the ducs de Joyeuse is situated on the banks of the Aude in the heart of the Cathar country. Built in the 16th century, its exteriors are still medieval in aspect. The grand staircase leads up to the spacious first floor rooms with beamed ceilings.
Open all year : 9 - 6.
Parking.
Grounds only.
Unaccompanied visits, brochures.
Tel. : (68) 74.02.80.

Fontfroide (Abbey).
Narbonne - 11100.
Private property.

Fontroide abbey was part of the Cistercian movement in 1143. Its medieval buildings set in a wild gorge are reminiscent of the Cistercian abbeys of Provence : Senanque, Silvacane and Le Thoronet. The cloister is one of the finest in the Midi. The 12th century church, the chapel, the dormitory, the refectory etc. are open to the public. Pierre de Castelnau was a monk here ; it was his murder in 1208 when he was Papal legate at the court of Raymond de Toulouse that led to the Albigensian crusade.
Open April 1 to Sept. 30 : 9:30 - 12, 2:30 - 6.
Oct. 1 to March 31 : 9:30 - 12, 2 - 5.
Closed Tuesdays Oct. to March 31.
Parking.
Guided tours.
Brochures in English, German, French.
Concerts.
Tel. : (68) 45.11.08.

NARBONNE
Hôtel Poulhariez.
Narbonne - 11100.
17, rue Rouget-de-Lisle.
Property of M. Lelu de Brach.

LANGUEDOC-ROUSSILLON — AUDE/GARD

This 18th century town house has a porch and staircase with a fine wrought iron balustrade. An inscribed marble Roman funerary stele is set into the wall across from the entrance.
Exteriors only.
Tel. : (68) 32.06.90.

Bishop's Palace.

*Narbonne - 11100.
Place de l'Hôtel-de-Ville.
Property of the city.*
The bishop's palace of Narbonne served as Viollet-le-Duc's model for his restoration of the Papal Palace of Avignon. The building once dominated both the town and the port with its military fortifications. The Old Palace and the New Palace are separated by a passage and house an archeological museum and an art and history museum. The palace was enlarged and embellished as the power of the bishops increased.
*Open May 16 to Sept. 30 : 10 - 11:50, 2 - 6.
Oct. 1 to May 15 : 10 - 11:50, 2 - 5.
Museums closed Mondays.
Parking.
Guided tours for groups by contacting the city hall. Tel. : (68) 32.31.60 ext. 379.
Guided tours available July 1 to Sept. 15.
Leaflets.
Documentation in French, English, German, Spanish.
Sound and Light, concerts, temporary exhibits, lectures, colloquia.*
Tel. : (68) 32.31.60.

Gilles Aycellin Keep.

*Narbonne - 11100.
Place de l'Hôtel-de-Ville.
Property of the city.*
This large square tower was built by bishop Gilles Aycellin around 1300 on Roman foundations. From the top is a fine view of the city.
*Open July 1 to Sept. 30 : 10 - 11:50, 2 - 5:30.
Groups on request out of season.
Parking.
Unaccompanied visits.*
Tel. : (68) 32.31.60.

Pennautier (Château).

*Carcassonne - 11100.
Private property.*
Pennautier is a château built in 1620, flanked with two 18th century wings, in which Louis XIII spent July 14, 1642. The château has been in the same family since its construction. The interiors have kept their 17th century furniture.
*Open July 1 to; Oct. 30 : 10:30 - 12, 12:30 - 5:30.
Closed Tuesdays and Sundays.
Parking.
Guided tours.*
Tel. : (68) 25.02.11.

Sainte-Marie-d'Orbieu (Abbey).

*Lagrasse - 11220.
Carcassonne : 35 km.
Station : Lézignan-Corbières 19 km.
Private property.*
This abbey was founded by Charlemagne in 778 and survived until the Revolution. Its numerous buildings dating from the 10th to the 18th centuries are set on the banks of the Orbieu. In the 11th century, this huge Benedictine domain stretched from the dioceses of Toulouse and Beziers to those of Urgel and Gerone and unlike many monasteries of the period flourished until the Revolution. Today the buildings are used for charity. They show the evolution of a monastic life throughout the Ancien Régime.
*Open June 1 to Sept. 14 : 9 - 12, 4 - 7.
Sept. 15 to May 31 : 11:30 - 4:30.
Closed Sunday mornings.
Parking.
Information in English, Spanish, Italian.*
Tel. : (68) 43.13.97.

Saint-Papoul (Abbey).

*Saint-Papoul - 11440.
Castelnaudary : 7 km.
Station : Castelnaudary.
Property of the commune.*
Saint-Papoul was founded in the century by Pepin the Short on the foot hills of the Montagne Noire. Its cloister was rebuilt in the 14th century. The Romanesque church was pillaged and burned at the end of the 13th century and reconstructed in the 14th on the remains of the choir and belfry. The interior decoration was redone in the 18th century. The 18th century bishops palace is private and not open to the public.
*Open all year : 7 am - 7 pm.
Closed at times for maintenence.
Parking.
Unaccompanied visits, brochures.
Information pannels or Leaflets.*
Tel. : (68) 60.92.83.

Saissac (Tower).

*Saissac - 11310.
Carcassonne : 25 km.
Station : Carcassonne.
Property of the commune.*
The tower houses a museum of the crafts of the Montagne Noire.
*Open June 15 to Sept. 30 : 10 - 12, 3 - 6.
Parking.
Unaccompanied visits.
Pannels, brochures.*
Tel. : (68) 24.40.22.

GARD

Aigues-Mortes (Ramparts).

*Aigues-Mortes - 30220.
Montpellier : 32 km.
Property of the State.*
Saint Louis created the city of Aigues-Mortes in the marshy Montpellier plain. In 1242 work began on the fortifications which

were at first limited to the Constance tower which acted as light house for the port before becoming a prison under Louis XIV. Thirty years later Saint Louis's son Philip the Bold, continued the work in the walls which were finally finshed at the end of the 13th century. The ramparts are almost perfectly preserved with their 5 towers and 10 gates.
Open April 1 to Sept. 30 : 9 - 12, 2 - 6:30.
Oct. 1 to March 30 : 10 - 12, 2 - 5.
Guided tours, brochures.
Theatre festival.
Tel. : (68) 51.01.55.

BEAUCAIRE

Saint-Roman (Abbey).

Beaucaire è 30300.
Route de Nîmes.
Station : Beaucaire 5 km.
Bus nearby.
Private propermty.
The chapel, cells, cisterns, and press of this monastery were carved into the rock which is unique in France. The site has been occupied since the 5th century and has a fine view over the Rhône valley.
Open Oct. 16 to June 30 : 2 - 6 weekends and school holidays.
July 1 to Oct. 15 : 10 - 7.
Closed Thursdays.
Parking.
Recommended itineraty.
Pannels, brochures.
Information in English, German, Dutch.
Lecture tours for school groups.

La Vignasse (Castle and Museum).

Beaucaire - 30300.
Near Tarascon.
Property of the city.
This fortress is one of the largest in France and was built by Saint Louis in 1229 after the Languedoc was incorporated into the realm. It overlooked the Rhône which at the time was the border between Fance and Provence. The castle was destroyed by Richelieu. All that remains is a fortified gate, a triangular tower, the chapel and a round tower. The Vignasse museum is being installed in the castle.
Open daily except Fridays.
Parking.
Recommended itinerary.
Brochures.
Temporary exhibits.
Tel. : (66) 59.25.20.

Castellas (Castle).

La Chapelle - Saint-Bonnet de Salendrique - 30460.
Nîmes : 50 km.
Montpellier : 60 km.
Station : Alès 37 km.
Private property.
This L-shaped structure has two round towers and a square Romanesque keep. It fell into the hands of Saint Louis at the outcome of the Albigensian Crusade. The castle has two stories on a vaulted ground floor and has 17th century sculptures.
Open July 14 to August 26 : 1:30 - 6:30.
Groups on request out of season.
Parking.
Guided tours, brochures.

La Foux (Arboretum).

Lanvejols - 30120.
Le Vignan : 45 km.
Property of the State.
Like the neighbouring arboretum of Hort de Dieu, La Foux contributes to the rich plant life of the Aigoual mountains. The collection of trees spreads over 10 hectares and provides precious information for local forestation. There are varieties of red oak with trunks measuring 1.5 m round and numerous pines.
Continuously open to the public.
Recommended itinerary.
Brochures from the Vigan Touris Office.
Tel. : (67) 81.00.83.

L'Hort de Dieu (Arboretum).

L'Espérou.
Valleraugue - 30120.
Le Vigan : 45 km.
Property of the State.
This arboretum is part of the same forest as the above arboretum of La Foux.
Open continuously except in winter.
Unaccompanied visits, brochures from the Tourist Office in Le Vigan.
Labeled trees.
Tel. : (67) 81.00.83.

NÎMES

Bishop's Palace.

Nîmes - 30000.
Place aux Herbes.
Property of the city.
Built in the 17th century by Alexis de La Feuille de Merville, the palace now houses the historical museum of the city of Nîmes, the school of fine arts and the conservatoire.
Open April 1 to Oct. 30 : 9 - 12, 2 - 5.
Oct. 1 to March 31 : 9- 12, 2 - 6.
Closed Tuesdays Oct. 1 to March 31, Jan. 1, May 1, Nov. 1 and 11, Dec. 24 and 25 and Sunday mornings.
Parking.
Unaccompanied visits.
Pannels.
Temporary exhibits.
Tel. : (66) 36.00.64.

Former Jesuit Convent.

Nîmes - 30000.
13, boulevard Amiral-Courbet.
Property of the city.
This 17th century Jesuit college houses the municipal library, a museum of natural history and prehistory, an archeological museum with important prehistorical and Gallo-Roman artifacts.
Open April 1 to Sept. 30 : 9 - 12, 2 - 7.
Oct. 1 to March 30 : 9 - 12, 2 - 6.
Closed Tuesdays from Oct. 1 to March 30, Jan. 1, May 1, Nov. 1 and 11, Dec. 24 and 25 and Sunday mornings.
Unaccompanied visits. Temporary exhibits.
Lecture tours for school groups.
Tel. : (66) 67.25.57.

LANGUEDOC-ROUSSILLON — GARD

Jardins de la Fontaine.

Nîmes - 30000.
Property of the city.
   In the 18th century the engineer Mareschal laid out a formal garden on the site of some ancient ruins that had just been uncovered. The graceful setting includes vases, balustrades, statues mingling with the local specimens of plants planted in the 19th century. One of the finest parks in the Midi.
Open all year.
Parking.
Unaccompanied visits, brochures.
Information in English and German.
Guided tours on request from the Tourist Office.
Facilities for the handicapped.
Theatre, concerts, folk dancing.
Tel. : (66) 67.25.57.

Tour Magne.

Nîmes - 30000.
Place Stéphane-Mallarmé.
Property of the city.
   This 112 meter tower was part of the Roman fortifications of the city. It was built on pre-Roman foundations as a watch tower and a symbol of strength. The interiors were torn out under Henri IV in search of treasure. In 1843 it was consolidated and restored. Mistral heralded this as the beacon of the Renaissance of the Midi. Its summit offers a fine view of Nîmes and its surroundings.
Open Oct. 1 to March 31 : 9 - 12, 2 - 5.
April 1 to Sept. 30 : 9 - 12, 2 - 7.
Closed Tuesdays from Oct. to March 31 and May 1.
Parking.
Unaccompanied visits.
Information in English and German.
Guided tours on request from the Tourist Office.
Tel. : (66) 67.25.57.

Portes (Castle).

Portes - 30530.
Alès : 21 km.
Station : Chambrigaud 7 km.
Private Property.
   Portes is a square plan medieval fortress, protected by towers with a Renaissance addition jutting out from the South East corner.
Open daily July 1 to Sept. 30 : 9 - 12, 2 - 7.
Weekends and holidays April 1 to June 30, Oct. 1 to Nov. 30 : 2 - 5.
Closed Mondays.

Open on request out of saison.
Pannels.
Information in English, German (generally in summer).
Brochures, lecture tours.
Temporary exhibits, concerts.
Volonteer restoration projects.
Tel. : (66) 34.51.66.

Prafrance (Bamboo Grove).

Anduze - 30140.
Private property.
   Prafrance enjoys a microclimate thanks to its vegetation which protects it from the wind. This unique bamboo grove offers the visitor 10 hectares of tropical forest with giant bamboo, green houses full

---

PRAFRANCE — **BAMBOO GROVE** — GARD

A Unique Tropical Garden.

Located at Anduze in the Cévennes half an hour from Nîmes and an hour from Montpellier.
Open daily March 1 to Oct. 31.

of flowers and a reconstructed Asian village.
Open daily March 1 to June 30, Sept. 1 to Nov. 1 : 9 - 12, 2 - 7.
July 1 to Aug. 30 : 9 - 7.
Parking.
Guided tours, brochures.
Pannels.
Information in English.
Facilities for the handicapped.
Tel. : (66) 61.7047.

Rousson (Château).

Rousson-Salindres - 30340.
Station : Alès 10 km.
Bus nearby.
Private property.

Rousson, built between 1600 and 1615 by Jacques d'Aquelhac de Beaumont, is typical of the square Languedoc castle with towers at each corner and a flat tile roof. The interiors include remarkable ceilings, floors and Louis XIII fireplaces. The terrace overlooks the Ventoux and the Cévennes.
Open daily July 1 to Aug. 31 : 10 - 7.
Groups on request from Easter to June 30 and from Sept. 1 to Nov. 1.
Parking.
Guided tours, brochures.
Information in English.

Theatre.
Tel. : (66) 85.60.31.

Teillan (Château).

Aimargues - 30470.
Station : Lunel 5 km.
Private property.

Once the property of the Abbey of Psalmody, this château was linked to Aigues-Mortes by an underground passage which was used for supplies. The château was later bought by a royal magistrate. The final building projects were carried out under Henri IV and Louis XIII makinging this one of the largest buildings of the king in Languedoc. The interiors include the «Richelieu Room» and a room decorated for the visit of Napoleon's sister Pauline in 1805.
Open July 1 to Aug. 31 : 2 - 6.
On request April 1 to Oct. 10.
Closed Mondays.
Parking.
Guided tours of the interiors.
Recommended itinerary for the park.
Pannels.
Information in English and German.
Tel. : (66) 88.02.38.

Uzès (Château).

Uzès - 30700.
Nîmes : 20 km.
Private property.

Local tradition calls this complex of buildings erected around the 11th century square keep «The Duchy». Uzès was hottly disputed during the Wars of Religion. The 16th century wing of the castle with its inside façade attributed to Philibert Delorme is a fine example of Provençal Renaissance architecture. The château has always belonged to the Cruso d'Uzès family.
Open Winter 10:30 - 12, 2 - 4:30.
Summer 9:30 - 12, 2 - 6:30.
Hours change at Palm Sunday.
Tel. : (66) 22.18.96.

GARD

CHARTERHOUSE OF VILLENEUVE-LÈS-AVIGNON

This 600 year old fortified charterhouse is the largest in France.
Today it is a cultural centre, its three cloisters full of art treasures and used for a variety of events.

LANGUEDOC-ROUSSILLON — GARD

Valbonne (Charterhouse).

Saint-Paulet-de-Caisson - 30130.
Pont-Saint-Esprit : 10 km.
Private property.

Valbonne is a remarkable example of a Classical monastery built on the same plan as a Medieval charterhouse. Before visiting the chapels and cloister, you can see the interior of a cell reconstructed to give some idea of the life of the Carthusian monks.
Open Feb. 1 to Nov. 30 : 9 - 12, 2 - 6.
Parking.
Guided tours, brochures.
Information in English and German.
Tel. : (66) 89.68.32.

VILLENEUVE-LES-AVIGNON

Val de Bénédiction Charterhouse.

Villeneuve-lès-Avignon - 30400.
Rue de la République.
Avignon : 5 km.
Station : Avignon.
Property of the State.

This charterhouse was founded in 1356 across from Avignon by Pope Innocent VI. Its three cloisters make it the second largest charterhouse after that of Grenoble whose palan it ressembles. The buildings include the church, refectory and chapter house set around a cloister and the cells set around two cloisters. The Innocent VI chapel is decorated with frecoes attributed to Matteo Giovanetti, the Italian painter who also worked at the Papal Palace in Avignon. Most of the art treasures of the monastery were scattered during the Revolution. The charterhouse in undergoing extensive restoration and is an international design research centre.
Open daily April 1 to Sept. 30 : 9 - 12, 2 - 6:30.
Oct. 1 to March 31 : 10 - 12, 2 - 5.
Parking.
Unaccompanied visits, brochures.
Concerts, dance, theatre, litterary gatherings.
Various workshops, temporary exhibits, lectures.
Tel. : (90) 25.05.46.

Photo Ch. Robin

Fort Saint-André.

Villeneuve-lès-Avignon - 30400.
Property of the State.

Philip Augustus's new city built across from Avignon is dominated by the walls of the Saint André fort. Erected in the 14th century the walls once protected a village and an abbey that have since disappeared. Its major role was to act as a citadelle to reinforce the defense of the Saint Bénézet Bridge. Three fortified towers and a fortified gate remain. The entrance vault still has traces of the gates and their mechanisms.
Open April 1 to Sept. 31 : 9 - 12, 2 - 6:30.
Oct. 1 to March 31 : 10 - 12, 2 - 5.
Closed Tuesdays and Wednesdays.
Parking.
Guided tours, brochures.
Tel. : (90) 25.45.35.

VILLENEUVE-LÈS-AVIGNON — GARD

Philip the Fair's Tower
Built on the orders of Philip the Fair in 1292 the tower was used as a prison from the 15th to the 19th centuries.
Exhibition halls.
Open Oct. 1 to March 31 : 10 - 12, 2 - 5.
April 1 to Sept. 30 : 10:30 and 3 - 7:30.

GARD/HÉRAULT — 178 — LANGUEDOC-ROUSSILLON

Abbaye Saint-André.

Villeneuve-lès-Avignon - 30400.
Fort Saint-André.
Station : Avignon.
Private property.

Inside the Saint-André fort lies the remains of a 17th century Benedictine abbey. All that is left are the entrance porch and a block with Italianate terraces over looking the Rhône valley, Avignon, the Mont Ventoux and the Lubéron.

Open all Year : 9 - 12:30, 2 - 6.
Parking.
Unaccompanied visits.

Villevieille (Castle).

Sommières-Villevieille - 32025.
Montpellier : 30 km.
Arles : 38 km.
Station : Nîmes 25 km.
Bus service.
Property of M. de David-Beauregard.

This castle was built on the foundations of a 12th century keep by the Bermond d'Anduze family. Some parts of the building go back to the 13th century but the castle was later radically transformed. Louis XIII fought here in 1622. The main building was erected at the end of the 16th century by François II de Pavée and restored in the 18th century as were the buildings around the inside courtyard. Inside is a collection of faiance and period furniture.

Open daily July to Sept. 10 : 3 - 7:30.
Palm Sunday to Nov. 1 : 2 : 30 - 6 : 30.
Parking.
Guided tours.
Facilities for the handicapped.
Concerts, temporary exhibits.
Tel. : (80) 01.62.66.

HÉRAULT

BÉZIERS

Hôtel de Sarret.

Béziers - 34500.
23, rue des Balances.
Private property.

The first building on this site was probably the early 16th century residence of the governors of Béziers. A pert of it remains around the entrance to the main courtyard where the 17th century building is located. In 1759 the baron de Sarret, mayor of Béziers and member of the French naval expedition in the American war of Independence was born here. Here he received the duc d'Angoulême who had come to the Midi to stop the reprisals after the Revolution.

Open all year.
Closed Sundays.
Parking.
Unaccompanied visits.
Litterary lectures.
Vaulted cellars can be used by local cultural groups.
Tel. : (67) 28.88.10.

Castries (Château).

Castries - 34160.
Montpellier : 12 km.
Station : Castries.
Property of M. de Castries.

Castries is an austere Renaissance building which was enlarged by a long gallery in 1674 to receive the Estates of Languedoc. At the same period the façade of a wing which had been destroyed by fire served as a backdrop for the terraced gardens whose waters are provided by an acqueduct built by Riquet the engineer of the Canal du Midi. The château has been in the same family since 1495. Period furniture and family portraits.

Open daily April 1 to Dec. 15 : 10 - 1, 2:30 - 6.
Weekends Jan. 15 to April 1 : 2 - 6.
Closed Mondays except holidays and Dec. 15 to Jan. 1.
Parking.
Guided tours, brochures.
Concerts in July.
Tel. : (67) 70.11.83.

Cazilhac (Castle).

Le Bousquet-d'Orb - 34260.
Béziers : 50 km.
Montpellier : 70 km.
Station : Bousquet d'Orb 2 km.
Property of M. Leroy-Beaulieu.

This ancient fortified residence perched on a rocky spur near the Abbey of Joncels was transformed several times, most notably during the Renaissance. To the North the massive main building overlooks a wood of century old trees. On the other side, terraces go down to the vineyards in the plain. The building is surrounded by fine basins in a garden which includes the largest cedar of Lebanon in France.

Open July 10 to Sept. 20 : 2:30 - 6:30
Closed Tuesdays, Wednsedays, Thursdays (except holidays).
Guided tours of the interiors.
Tel. : (67) 23.81.10.

L'Engarran (Château).

Laverune - 34430.
Montpellier : 5 km.
Private property.

This Regency « folie » was built into a hunting lodge by a local magistrate. It is surrounded by a formal garden with three basins, « rocaille » fountain and enclosed by a large gate.

Open for groups on request.
Parking.
Guided tours.
Information in English and Spanish.
Tel. : (4) 261.11.20.

Flaugergues (Château).

Montpellier - 34000.
Station : Montpellier 4 km.
Bus nearby.
Property of M. Henri de Colbert.

In 1690 Étienne de Flaugergues gave his château the harmonious unity of style that it has today. The Mediterranean garden and the simple façade give the building its Italian air. Inside an unusual stairway is hung with Brussels tapestries. The fine furniture adds to the charm of this residence where

LANGUEDOC-ROUSSILLON — 179 — HÉRAULT

ch successive generation has
ft its mark.
pen daily Jule 1 to Aug. 31 : 2:30 -
30.
osed Mondays.
pt. 1 to June 30 Open on request.
arking.
uided tours.
de show.
formation in English.
ctures on local history and agriculture.
l. : (67) 65.79.64 or 65.51.72.

ontcaude (Abbey).

azedarnes-Cessenon - 34460.
éziers : 15 km.
s nearby.
ivate property.

Founded in 1154, then turned over to the Premonstratention order, this monastery was ruined during the Wars of Religion and then saved by the Friends of Fontcaude in 1969. All that is left of the monastery is the apse of the church, the ruins of the monks wing and the lay brothers wing. The building now houses a sculpture museum.
Open all year on Sundays 2 - 5.
Parking.
Unaccompanied visits.
Concerts.
Tel. : (67) 37.01.46.

Londres (Castle).

Notre-Dame de-Londres - 34380.
Property of M. de Wisches.
This medieval fortified castle belonged to the Roquefeuil family for over three centuries. The interiors include painted beamed ceilings, a picture collection and some 16th century furniture.
Open daily March 1 to June 30.
Sundays and holidays Oct. 1 to Dec. 1 : 2 - 6.
Parking.
Guided tours.
Information in English and German.

Theatre.
Temporary exhibits.
Tel. : (67) 55.01.29.

La Mogère (Château).

Montpellier - 34000.
Route de Vauguières.
Montpellier : 4 km.
Property of M. de Saporta.
This « folie » built in 1716 has been passed down through the same family ever since. The fine park includes a huge fountain and an acqueduct. The salon is decorated with plaster work.

FLAUGERGUES
HERAULT

The only site in the region which comprises :
- a coteaux de la Méjanelle and coteaux du Languedoc vineyard ;
- a fine location with a flowering park ;
- a château with its beautiful staircase, quality furniture, objets d'art and books and documents relating to the history of the region ;
- the wine cellars where you can taste and buy the wines and products of this and other regions.
You can spen your time doing a variety of things in this living château.

Open daily from Pentecost to Sept. 30 : 2:30 - 6:30.
Weekends and holidays or on request from Oct. 1 to Pentecost : 2:30 - 6.
Parking.

Montlaur (Castle).

Montaud - 34160.
Station : Montpellier 18 km.
Property of M. de Montlaur.
Ruins of a military fortress with three surrounding walls which was first mentioned in the year 1000 and continued to play an important role until the 17th century. At the centre the remains of a 16th century residence, chapel and watch tower with a view to the sea.
Open all year.
Parking.

PEZENAS
Hôtel Vulliod-de-Saint-Germain.

Pezenas - 34120.
Rue A.-P.-Alliès.
Station : Béziers 20 km.
Property of the commune.
This historic 18th century town house now houses a museum of local history and collections of Aubusson tapestries, faience from the old hospital, engravings and paintings from the 16th to the 20th centuries.
Open July 1 to Aug. 31 : 10 - 12, 2 - 6.
Sept. 1 to June 30 : 10 - 12, 2 - 5.
Closed Mondays and Tuesdays and June 30, July 1, Aug. 31 and Sept. 1.
Parking.
Unaccompanied visits.
Audiovisual programme.
Temporary exhibits.
Tel. : (67) 54.45.14.

Hôtel d'Alfonce.

Pézenas - 34120.
32, rue Conti.
Béziers : 23 km.
Station : Béziers.
Private property.
It was here that the prince of Conti received the delegates from the Estates of Languedoc in 165. A few days later Molière is alleged to have given the first performance of the « Médecin volant ». The garden façade has two stories of loggias and an odd spiral staircase.
Open all year Tuesdays and Fridays :
12, 2 - 6.
Concerts.
Theatre.

Saint-Félix-de-Montceau (Abbey).

Sète - 34200.
Station : Sète 12 km.
Private property.
This Benedictine convent is situated the km from Gigean. It was founded in 1091 and abandoned in 1514. Since 1970 it has been the subject of a massive restoration

Guided tours.
Brochures in French, English, German.
Tel. : (67) 65.72.01 and 65.77.51.

HÉRAULT SAINT-FÉLIX-DE-MONCEAU

11 th and 12 th centuries.
A Prestigious setting in the wilderness.
A Gothic church, a Romanesque chapel and its outbuildings rise from the thyme covered hillside.
A magnificent award winning Sound and Light show brings all this to life each July.
Volonteer restoration since 1970.
A Museum opened since April 1983.
A monument and site not to be missed.
Reservations fot shows and tours :
Tel. : (67) 53.11.00.

LANGUEDOC-ROUSSILLON — 181 — HÉRAULT/LOZÈRE

oject carried out by a volonteer oup.
en daily 9 - 12, 2 - 6.
rking.
ided tours Wed., Sat., Sun.
nnels, brochures.
ormation in Spanish.
uth programmes.
ening masses.
ormation on restoration, the environ-nt and religious life.
l. : (67) 53.11.00.

aint-Michel--Grandmont riory).

umont - 34700.
dève : 8 km.
ivate property.
This 11 and 12th century priory s remained intact with its clois-r, church, chapter house, etc. It set in the midst of a park full of ifacts from the last 5000 years : nding stones, carvings, sarco-agi, etc. Grandmont has been a iritual centre for seven centu-s.
en daily, except Mondays, June 15 to pt. 30 : 3 - 6.
t. 1 to 31 and March 15 to June 14, n. and holidays at 3.
oups on request all year.
rking.
ided tours, brochures.
aflets in English and German.
mporary exhibits.
l. : (67) 44.09.31.

almagne (Abbey).

leveyrac-Mèze - 34140.
ontpellier : 30 km.
ivate property.
This Cistercian abbey is one of e finest medieval complexes in e Languedoc. The church which the size of a cathedral shows. The influence of Northern ench Gothic on the Midi. The rch has two square towers in ntradiction to the rules of the or-r which makes it unique in ance. The 14th century cloister is moniscent of that of Fontfroide ude). The octagonal washing vilion is the result of 1768 trans-rmations.
pen daily (except Tues.) June 15 to pt. 15 : 2:30 - 6:30.
ct. 15 to June 14, Sun. and holidays : - 6.
ornings for groups on request.
rking.
cture tours.
formation in English.
ochures.
ncerts.
l. : (67) 78.06.09.

LOZÈRE

La Baume (Château).

Prinsvejols-Marvejols - 48100.
Rodez : 100 km.
Mende : 45 km.
Station : Aumont-Aubrac 15 km.
Private property.
This château, built between 1630 and 1706 has kept memorabilia of Mademoiselle de Fontanges one of Louis XIV's favorites. The grey granite walls and the dark stone roof give La Baume a somber aspect which belies the elegant 18th century interior decoration. Memorabilia of Las Cases, Napoleon's companion on Saint Helena.
Open June 15 to Sept. 15 : 10 - 12, 2 - 6.
Sept. 16 to June 14 : 2 - 5.
Closed Tuesdays Sept. 15 to June 14.
Parking.
Guided tours, brochures.
Concerts, temporary exhibits.
Lecture tours for school groups.
Tel. : (66) 32.51.59.

Calberte (Castle).

Saint-Germain-de-Calberte - 48240.
Alès, Anduze : 40 km.
Property of M. Darnas.
Calberte is a very ancient castle built from the 9th to the 12th centuries. The round tower, square keep and rectangular building still survive. The Romanesque chapel has recently been restored by the Owner.
Open July 15 to Sept. 15 and during Easter school holidays : 3 - 7.
Parking.
Unaccompanied visits.
Temporary exhibits.
Tel. : (66) 45.90.30.

Castanet (Castle).

Villefort - 48800.
Station : Villefort 5 km.
Bus nearby.
Private property.
This square granite edifice flanked with three round towers was built by Jacques d'Isarn in 1578. It was saved from destruction when the area was floded by a dam and restored since 1964. It now contains a collection of period furniture and receives contemporary art exhibits.
Open July 1 to Sept. 2 : 10 - 7.
Grounds only.
Parking.
Information in English.
Temporary exhibits.
Tel. : (66) 46.81.11.

Condres (Castle).

Condres (Near Grandieu).
Saint-Bonnet-de-Montauroux - 48600.
Langogne : 15 km.
Station : Chapeauroux 2 km.
Private property.
Condres was built on the site of an ancient Roman city by a family related to Urban V, last Avignon Pope. The massive granite exteriors have corner towers and a sentry way. Four rooms are vaulted and certain have 18th century wood pannels.
Open daily July 1 to Aug. 31 : 2:30 - 7.
Parking.
Guided tours, brochures.
Pannels.
Temporary exhibits.
Tel. : (66) 46.32.21.

SAINT-MARTIN-DU-CANIGOU
PYRÉNÉES-ORIENTALES

Founded in 1005, abandonned in 1783, partially restored between 1902 and 1932 by Monseigneur de Carsalade and completed between 1952 and 1982 by Father Bernard de Chabannes, a Benedictine monk from En-Calat abbey, Saint-Martin-du-Canigou has become a spiritual centre to be visited all year round at any time of day.

SALSES FORT
PYRÉNÉES-ORIENTALES

Built in the 16th century on a rectangular plan with four towers and a particulary impressive defense system, this fort is closely linked to the ward betwen Spain and France fought in Roussillon. It was restored by Vauban just as its military use was coming to an end.

LANGUEDOC-ROUSSILLON — LOZÈRE/PYRÉNÉES ORIENTALES

e Pouget (Village).

 Pouget-Pourcharesse - 48800.
ation : Villefort 3 km.
ivate property.
 Le Pouget is a hamlet of ancient anite stone covered farms. Every chitectural feature both inside d out has been carefully preser- d. The furniture, utensils and ols are all original.
en all year : 8 - 12, 3 - 5.
ormation in English, German and tch.
storation sites.
afts.
l. : (66) 46.80.40.

rades (Castle).

inte-Enimie - 48210.
ende : 33 km.
operty of M. Gourraud.
 This ancient fortress is built on a cky spur overlooking the village Prades in the Tarn gorges. It as the property of the priors of e abbey of Sainte-Enimie until e Revolution. In 1581 it withs- od an attack by the Protestant my of Mathieu de Merle. Inside e furnished vaulted rooms.
en daily July 1 to Aug. 31 : 10 - 12, 30 - 6:30.
arking.
uided tours.
nnels.
l. : (42) 26.60.75.

ainte-Enimie (Abbey).

inte-Enimie - 48210.
ende : 28 km.
ation : Mende 55 km.
operty of the commune.
 The abbey was founded in the h century. The buildings were estroyed by fire during the Revo- tion. All that remains is the chap- r house where the pilgrims to antiago da Compostella gathe- d and the crypt. Two rooms have een set up to house the collec- on of carvings.
pen June 15 to Sept. 15 : 10 - 12, 2 -
arking.
nnels, brochures.
udiovisual programme.
ound and Light.
el. : (66) 48.50.14.

YRÉNÉES-ORIENTALES

rles-sur-Tech
Abbey of Sainte Marie).

rles-sur-Tech - 66150.
erpignan : 41 km.
tation and bus nearby.

 The first abbey on this site was founded in the Carolingian period. The present buildings date from the 11th century with later addi- tions which have survived. The tympanum cross is an early exam- ple of monumental sculpture. In the apse is a rare marble alter cha- racteristic of early Mediterranean Romanesque art. 12th century frescoes.
Parish church open at all times.
Parking.
Unaccompanied visits.
Tel. : (68) 39.18.58.

Collioure (Castle).

Perpignan : 23 km.
Station : Collioure 1 km.
Property of the department.
 This fort overlooking the sea at the entrance of the port measures over 1000 square meters on five levels. The ramparts, cellars, and collections of Catalan art and local flora are open to the public. The fortress played a part in the strug- gle between the kingdoms of Ma- jorca and Aragon and was once the residence of the rulers of Ma- jorca Peter the Catholic and Marie de Montepllier.
Open daily April 10 to 13 : 10 - 6.
Aug. 12 to Sept. 30 : 2:30 - 7:30.
Parking.
Unaccompanied visits, brochures.
Pannels.
Information in German, English and Spanish.
Shows, temporary exhibits, theatre workshops.
Tel. : (68) 82.06.43.

Marcevol (Priory).

Arboussols - 66320.
Perpignan : 45 km.
Station : Vinça 9 km.
Private property.
 Marcevol priory was founded in the 12th century by the military or- der of the Holy Sepulchre. The for- tified church contains the remains of a frescoe of Christ Pantocrator on a starry background.
Open daily June 30 to Sept. 30 : 3 - 7.
Jan. to.
Parking.
Unaccompanied visits.
Shows.
Tel. : (68) 96.54.03.

PERPIGNAN

Palace of the Kings of Majorca.

Perpignan - 66000.
Rue des Archers.
Property of the department.

Tyis fine huilding was erected at the time of the capital of the kings of Maiorque. It used to be a pa- lace for the kings, then for the knigts of Saint-John of Jerusalem and of Maltie. In the chapel one cau sec frescoes dahinx from the 13d century. In the out brilduigs a Museum is organized.
Open May 1 to June 30 : Sundays and.
Days off : 2 - 6.
July 1 to August 31 : daily 2 - 6.
September 1to October 20 : Sundays 2 - 6.
On request for groups other times.
Parking.
Guided tours.
Exhibitions.
Tel. : (55) 65.07.62.

Saint-Martin du-Canigou (Abbey).

Casteil - Vernet-les-Bains - 66500.
Prades : 10 km.
Perpignan : 60 km.
 This abbey was founded in 1001 and abandonned after the Revolu- tion. Its magnificent ruins were an inspiration to Romantic artists. The walk up to the abbey makes the vi- sitor appreciate its extraordinary location, its historic significance and its austerity which was saved from total ruin by a more or less successful restoration at the be- ginning of the century. The church is a complex building of great ar- cheological interest. It is one of the earliest completly vaulted Ro- manesque churches and its capi- tals herald 11th century French sculpture.
Open daily all year : 10 - 12:30, 2 - 5.
Half an hour on foot or by rented jeep from Vernet or Prades.
Guided tours on request.
Tel. : Prades Tourist Office (68) 96.27.58. Perpignan (68) 34.29.94.

Saint-Michel de Cuxa (Abbey).

Codalet - 66500.
Station : Prades.
Private property.
 In the Carolingian period Saint- Michel de Cuxa was the most im- portant religious centre in Roussil- lon. Around the year 1000 the ab- bey acquired international renown that was accompanied by a flurry of building activity. The austere fortified church with its Visigothic arches was rebuilt. The main cloi- ster was built in the 12th century. But then the abbey lost its impor- tance before its final decline in the 18th century. At the beginning of the 20th century parts of the abbey were dismantled and taken to the

United States. Since 1919 the Cistercian monks of Fontfroid and then the Benedictines of Montserrat since 1965 have returned the abbey to prominence.
Open May 1 to Sept. 30 : 9:30 - 11:30, 2:30 - 6.
Oct. 1 to April 30 : 9:30 - 11:55, 2:30 - 5.
Closed Sunday mornings.
Parking.
Guided tours available.
Information in English, German, Dutch, Catalan, Italian.
Leaflets, brochures.
Facilities for the handicapped.
Music festivals.
Romanesque festival July 10 to 20.
Tel. : (68) 96.02.40.

Unaccompanied visits, brochures.
Pannels.
Information in Spanish, Italian.
Temporary exhibits.
Nature classes and restoration sites.
Summer programmes, folk dancing.
Tel. : (68) 96.10.78.

Salses (Castle).

Rivesaltes - 66600.
Perpignan : 17 km.
Property of the State.

The history of Salses is closely linked to the wars between France and Spain both fought in and over Roussillon. The fort was built by the Spaniards in the 15th century on the site of an ancient castle. Its system of fortifications was very advanced for the period : external fortifications preceded by a huge dry moat, a square rampart around a sunken courtyard. The austere aspect of the fort conceals the complexity of the interiors with their labyrinthine corridors, parapets and traps. The forts military history came to an end in 1659 with the Treaty of the Pyrénées bringing peace between France and Spain. It bearely escaped destruction and was made a protected dite as early as 1886.
Open Oct. 1 to March 30 : 10 - 11, 2 - 5:30.
April 1 to Sept. 30 : 9:30 - 11, 2 - 5:30.
Parking.
Guided tours, brochures.
Tel. : (68) 38.60.13.

Villefranche-de-Conflent (Remparts)

Villefranche-de-Conflent - 66500.
Perpignan : 50 km.
Prades : 7 km.
Station : 500 m.

Once part of the kingdom of Aragon, the capital of the Conflent has ben a part of France only since 1659. Its ramparts were remodelled in the 17th century and still have their covered sentry way, gates and the « Devil's Tower ».
Open daily June 1 to, Sept. 30 : and during Easter weekend : 9-7.
Oct. 1 to May 30 : 2-6.
Parking.

LIMOUSIN

CORREZE, CREUSE, HAUTE-VIENNE.

- ■ castle, château, manor house
- ● abbey, priory
- ▲ garden, park
- ★ town house, famous men house, farm, mill...
- ○ city

ULLE

- ● Musée du cloître

MOGES

- ● Musée de l'ancien Evêché
- ▲ Jardin de l'ancien Evêché
- ★ Maison traditionnelle de la Boucherie
- ★ Maison natale du Maréchal Jourdan
- ▲ Jardin d'Orsay
- ● Crypte de l'ancienne Abbaye Saint-Martial

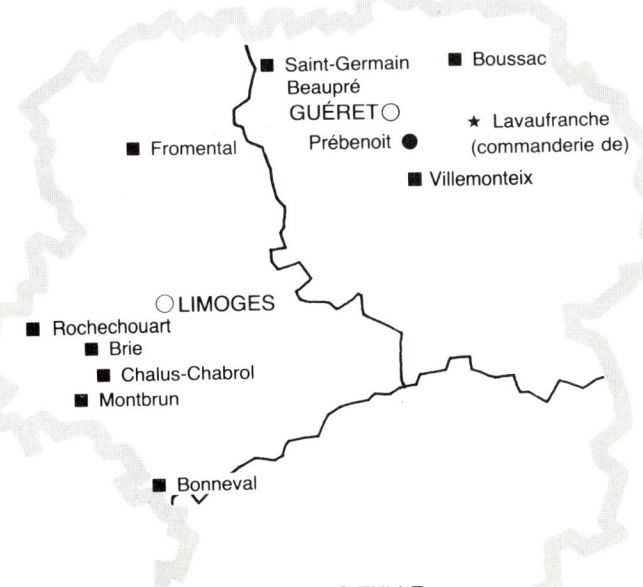

■ Saint-Germain Beaupré
■ Boussac
GUÉRET ○
★ Lavaufranche (commanderie de)
■ Fromental
Prébenoit ●
■ Villemonteix

○ LIMOGES
■ Rochechouart
■ Brie
■ Chalus-Chabrol
■ Montbrun

■ Bonneval

○ TULLE
● Aubazines
■ Tours de Merle
Ragheaud ■
■ Turenne

CORRÈZE

Aubazine (Abbey).
Aubazine - 19190 Beynat.
Brive-la-Gaillarde : 14 km.
Station : Aubazine 4 km.
Private property.
 This Cistercian abbey was founded in 1130 by Saint Stephen of Aubazine. The monks were expelled at the Revolution. For 100 years after that it was inhabited by nuns and since 1965 by Greek Catholic nuns. The Cistercian abbey comprises a church, chapter house, Romanesque scriptorium; a 17th century corridor with a decorated floor, the old fountain and cistern fed by a 12th century canal.
Closed Mondays except Easter and Pentecost.
Variable opening hours.
Parking.
Guided tours, brochures.

Merle (Towers).
Saint-Geniez-ô-Merle - 19220.
Brive : 60 km.
Station : Tulle 35 km.
Property of the commune.
 These towers, built in the 11th ant 13th centuries, were beseiged by the English and the Huguenots but never captured. Protected by a bend in the Maronne river this powerful fortress was abandoned after the Wars of Religion.
Open June 1 to Sept. 30 : 10 - 7.
Parking.
Unaccompanied visits, brochures.
Pannels, leaflets.
Temporary crafts exhibits.
Tel. : (55) 28.21.86.

Tulle (Cloister Museum)
Tulle - 19012.
Place Monseigneur-Berteaud.
Brive : 26 km.
Station : Tulle 1 km.
Bus service.
Property of the State.
 A Benedictine abbey in the 12th century that became the seat of the bishop in 1317, secularised in the 16th century before being dismantled, the building has served as local court and Revolutionary tribunal; All that is left are two cloister galleries, a vaulted chapter house with rare murals and the remains of abbey buildings. The collection is varied including prehistorical, archeological artifacts, arms, ethnographic artifacts, objets d'art...
Open April 1 to Sept. 30 : 9:30 - 12, 2 - 6.

Oct. 1 to March 31 : 10 - 12, 2:30 - 5.
Closed Tuesdays Sept. 16 to June 15.
Parking.
Unaccompanied visits.
Pannels or leaflets.
Temporary exhibits, lectures.
Lecture tours for school groups only.
Tel. : (55) 26.22.05.

Turenne (Castle).
Meyssac - 19500.
Brive : 16 km.
Station : Meyssac 3 km.
Private property.
 The two towers of Turenne castle overlook the city. The 12th century tower has an orientation map and the 14th century tower « the clock tower » includes the guard room. Seat of a countyn that remained independent until 1738, the castle belonged to Henri I, father of the maréchal de Turenne.
Open April 1 to Nov. 30 : 9 - 12, 2 - 7, daily.
Nov. 30 to April 1 : 9 - 12, 2 - 7, weekends.
Parking.
Grounds only.
Unaccompanied visits, brochures.
Tel. : (55) 85.40.66.

CREUSE

Boussac (Castle).
Boussac - 23600.
Montluçon : 40 km.
Station : Lavaufranche 5 km.
Bus service.
Private property.
 Built on a rock spur, the site of successive buildings since Antiquity, the current castle dates from the 14th century and incorporates 12th and 13th century elements such as the suite of rooms with monumental fireplaces. In the 18th century the interiors were remondelled with panelling, furniture and ancient tapestries in the taset of the period. George Sand discovered the « Dame à la Licorne » tapestries here. The castle is in the course of restoration.
Open all year 9 - 12, 2 - 6.
Parking.
Guided tours, brochures.
Bellac Theatre Festival.
Temporary tapestry exhibits.
Tel. : (55) 65.07.62.

Lavaufranche
Lavaufranche - 23600.
Montluçon : 35 km.
Station Lavaufranche near Boussac.
Private property.
 This fortified complex includes a 12th century keep, a 12th and 13 century chapel and a 15th centu castle built by the Hospitaliers the Order of Saint John of Jerus lem. It was the property of t Knights of Malta until the Revo tion when it was turned into farm. The chapel has 13th centu frescoes and the out buildin house a folk art museum.
Open May 1 to June 31, Sundays a holidays : 2 - 6.
July 1 to Aug. 31 : 2 - 6, daily.
Sept. 1 to Oct. 20, Sundays : 2 - 6.
Parking.
Groups on request out of season.
Temporary tapestry exhibits.
Tel. : (55) 65.07.62.

Prébenoît (Abbey).
Bétête - 23270.
Guéret : 25 km.
Station : Guéret.
Bus service.
Property of the Centre d'Animation de Tourisme.
 In 1140 the lords of Malval a the monks of Geraud de Sa founded this abbey which was taced to the Cistercian order af 1164. After four peaceful cen ries, in 1590 the abbey was cap red by the Huguenots who pi ged and burned the buildings. T church was rebuilt in 1622, t monastic buildings in 1715. Pie de Gesne, the last monk left 1790. Today the monastic b dings are being restored by vol teers.
Open July 1 to Sept. 15.
Pannels, brochures.
Temporary exhibits and activities.
Sound and Light.
Tel. : (55) 80.78.91.

Saint-Germain-Beaupré (Château).
Saint-Germain-Beaupré - 23160.
La Souterraine : 10 km.
Station : La Souterraine.
Property of M. Cambessedes.
 This moated castle was built the 15th century and restored the 17th when dome covered w dows with lanterns were add Partially destroyed by local riv ries, it did however keep three

s towers. Henri IV stayed here nd la Grande Mademoiselle was xiled here.
Open July 1 to Sept. 30 : 9 - 12, 2 - 6.
Parking.
Guided tours, brochures.
Tel. : (55) 63.52.01.

Villemonteix (Castle).

hun - 23150.
henerailles : 2 km.
ubusson : 20 km.
tation : Cressot 2 km.
rivate property.

This very ancient seigneurie was art of the comté de la Marche. Its 5th century castle is a precursor f the Renaissance. During the Revolution it was the seat of a major oyalist plot. It has remained almost intact despite 18th century transformations and has been partially refurnished and inhabited since 1982.
Open June 1 to Oct. 31 : 10 - 12, 2 - 7.
On request.
Parking.
Guided tours.
Tel. : (55) 62.33.92.

HAUTE-VIENNE

Bonneval (Castle).

Cousac-Bonneval - 87500.
Limoges : 42.
Station : Coussac-Bonneval 1 km.
Private Property.

The current castle was built in the 14th century on 11th century foundations. The entrance façade remains intact with its towerflanked portal. The keep overlooks the complex. The other buildings were remodeled in the 18th and 19th centuries. The interiors were redecorated in the 18th century and include fine furniture and tapestries from the late Middle Ages to the 18th century.
Open all year/ 2 - 6.

Parking.
Guided tours.
Concerts.
Tel. : (55) 75.20.11.

Brie (Château).

Champagne-Oradour - 87150.
Limoges : 35 km.
Chalus : 7 km.
Private property.

Jean de Brie had a fortified house built here around 1500. It is overlooked by a 25 meter high square keep which includes a spiral staircase supporting a flamboyant Gothic vault. Period furniture fills the interiors.
Open from the first Sunday in April to Oct. 1, Sundays and holidays : 2 - 7.
Parking.
Guided tours.
Tel. : (55) 78.17.52.

Chalus-Chabrol (Castle).

Chalus - 87230.
Limoges : 36 km.
Station : Bussière-Galant 8 km.
Bus service.
Private property.

Chalus-Chabrol was built between the 11th and 13th centuries overlooking the valley. The Roma-

---

BOUSSAC

CREUSE

The Home of the « Lady with the Unicorn » 15th century guard room and kitchens. 18th century rooms. George Sand's bedroom. Furnished and Inhabited. Exhibitions of ancient and modern tapestries. Open daily all year.

nesque keep is surrounded by two towers, a chapel and a main building. Richard the Lionheart died here in 1199 before being buried a Fontevrault.
Open April 1 to June 30, Sundays and holidays : 10 - 12, 3 - 7.
July 1 to Sept. 15, daily : 10 - 12, 3 - 7.
Sept. 16 to March 31 : on request.
Parking.
Guided tours.
English, German, Dutch.
Leaflets.
Lecture tours for school groups.
Tel. : (55) 78.43.40.

Fromental (Castle).

Fromental - 87250.
Limoges : 35 km.
Station : La Souterraine 12 km.
Private property.
This complex surrounded by a moat and dominated by a keep belonged to Guy de Saint-Martial, seigneur de Fromental in 1356. The main block was remodelled in the Renaissance and restored in 1642 by Jean Morel, baron de Fromental and a magistrate od the city of Limoges.
Open June 15 to Sept. 15.
Grounds only.

Parking.
Tel. : (55) 76.07.76.

LIMOGES
(Bishop's Palace Museum).

Limoges - 87000.
Place de la Cathédrale.
Station : Bénédictins 2 km.
Bus service.
Property of the commune.
Built between 1766 and 1786 by the architect Broussaud for Monseigneur de Plessis d'Argentré ; bishop of Limoges ; the grey granite residence has been a museum since 1910. It includes collections of ennamels, precious stones, minerals, paintings, and Egyptian and Gallo-Romen artifacts.
Open June 1 to Sept. 30 : 10 - 11:45, 2 - 6.
Oct. 1 to May 31 : 10 - 11:45, 2 - 5.
Closed Tuesdays except July 1 to Sept. 30.
Parking
Guided tours available.
Facilities for the handicapped.
Brochure.
Tel. : (55) 33.70.10.

Bishop's Garden.

Limoges - 87000.
Place de l'Évêché.
Station : 2 km.
Property of the city.
This terraced garden overlooking the Vienne was created at the same time as the Bishop's Palace in the 18th century. It includes botanical garden and an orangery
Open daily all year 9 - 7.
Parking.
Unaccompanied visits.
Facilities for the handicapped.
Tel. : (55) 33.70.10.

Orsay Garden.

Limoges - 87000.
Place des Carmes.
Station 2 km.
This garden was created in the 18th century by the intendant Orsay on the site of the partially restored Roman arena. Renovated 1967, the garden includes aged trees and play grounds.
Open daily 8 - 7.
Parking.
Facilities for the handicapped.
Tel. : (55) 33.70.10.

HAUTE-VIENNE

CHALUS-CHABROL

11th, 13th and 17th centuries.
Owes its fame to the siege of 1199 in which Richard the Lionheart, king of England, was mortally wounded by a crossbow. The keep, tower, chapel and 11th and 13th century rooms are open to the public.

Maréchal Jourdan's Birthplace.

Limoges - 87000.
, rue de Pont-Saint-Etienne.
Station : 2 km.
Bus service.
Property of the city.

Jourdan was born in this three-story 16th century half-timbered house in 1762. The interiors include much memorabilia of the Maréchal as well as the first figurine museum in France.
Parking.
Tel. : (55) 33.70.10.

Butcher's House.

Limoges - 87000.
, rue de la Boucherie.
Station : 2 km.
Property of the city.

The butchers of Limoges used to reside in this old neighbourhood grouped in their guild which was placed under the protection of Saint Aurélien. The shop with its utensils and the house with its period furniture reflect the lifestyle of the guild members in the 16th century. Now in restoration.
Parking.
Tel. : (55) 33.70.10.

Crypt of Saint Martial Abbey.

Limoges - 87000.
Place de la République.
Station : 2 km.
Bus service.
Property of the commune.

In 1960 excavations of the crypt of the former abbey of Saint Martial unearthed the bodies of Saint Martial and two of his followers Alpinien and Austriclinien who were buried here in the 4th century. A ditch had been dug in the 9th century to protect them from the Viking pillagers.
Open July 1 to Sept. 30 : 9:30 - 12, 2:30 - 7.
Parking.
Guided tours, brochures.
English, leaflets.
Tel. : (55) 33.70.10.

Montbrun (Castle).

Dournazac - 87230.
Limoges : 42 km.
Station : Bussière-Galant 12 km.
Private property.

Built by the side of the water. Montbrun has a 12th century keep and four 15th century round towers. The interior courtyard leads onto the sentry way. Pierre Brun, seigneur de Montbrun was commander of Chalus when Richard the Lionheart was mortally wounded there in 1199. The castle was carefully restored in the 19th century.
Open April 1 to Sept. 30 : 9 - 12, 2 - 7.
Oct. 1 to March 30 : 10 - 12, 2 - 5.
Parking.
Guided tours, brochures.
English, leaflets.
Lectures.
Lecture tours for school groups.
Tel. : (55) 78.40.10.

Rochechouart (Castle).

Rochechouart - 87600.
Saint-Junien : 10 km.
Limoges : 42 km.
Bus service.
Property of the commune (museum) and of the department (castle).

This fortress was built to insure the defense of Aquitaine in the 10th century, a 13th century tower

---

MONTBRUN
HAUTE-VIENNE

On the road to Périgord lies Montbrun, a true medieval castle of the 12th to the 15th century with keep, four massive round towers, sentry way and interior courtyard with portals with coats of arms. 40 km from Limoges, 70 km from Périgueux and Angoulême. Open daily.

still survives. The castle's present day apperance was the work of Anne de Rochechouart and her husband J. de Pontcille. The main façade rising from the rock has numerous windows on four stories. The fine double staiecase leading up to the reception rooms is an 18th century addition. The hunting hall still has interesting 16th century interiors. At the death of the vicomte de Rochechouart in 1832 the castle was acquired by the department who turned it over to Viollet-le-Duc for restoration. In 1894 Albert de Masfrand established museum of pre-historic artifacts mainly from the Gallo-Roman site at Chassenon. It also includes furniture, portraits and memorabilia of Lazare and Sadi Carnot as well as original letters from Turgot.

Museum : Open daily July 1 to Sept. 15 : 10 - 11:30, 3 - 6.
Palm Sunday to July 1 and Sept. 15 to Nov. 11, weekends and holidays : 10 - 11:30, 3 - 6.
Nov. 11 to Palm Sunday, Sundays : 3 - 5.
Parking.
Guided tours.
Guides, brochures.
Tel. : (55) 03.60.15.

LORRAINE
MEURTHE-ET-MOSELLE, MEUSE, MOSELLE, VOSGES.

- ■ castle, château, manor house
- ● abbey, priory
- ▲ garden, park
- ★ town house, famous men house, farm, mill...
- ○ city

NANCY
- ▲ Jardin botanique Ste Catherine

Cons-la-Granville
■ Montmédy
★ Rodemach
■ Sierck-les-Bains
■ La Grange
Entrange ■
■ Veckring
■ Luttange
Rarecourt ★   Bouzonville ▲   ○ Pange
de La Vallée
Maison forte
○ METZ
■ Bitche

Mardigny ■
Alteville ■
■ Bidestroff
○ BAR-LE-DUC
● Pont-à-Mousson
■ La Varenne ■ Bazincourt-   Abbaye des Prémontrés
sur-Saulx
■ Lenoncourt
Sexey ■   ○ NANCY   Villers-les-Nancy :
■ Montaigu   Jardin botanique du Montet
■ Fleville ▲
■ Lunéville
■ Haroué   ■ Gerbeviller

Chamagne ★ ● Autrey Abbaye Notre-Dame
▲ Moyenmoutier
■ Châtel-sur-Moselle   Forteresse des sires
Saint-Maur-de ●   de Neufchâtel
Bleurville   Sainte Marguerite ★
Deuilly-les-Morizecourt ▲   EPINAL ○
■ Lichecourt   ■ Fontenoy
Les Thons ▲   ○ ▲ Le Haut-Chitelet
Bains-Les-Bains   Jardin d'altitude
Châtillon sur Saône   Col de la Schlucht

MEURTHE-ET-MOSELLE

Cons-la-Grandville (Château).

Cons-la-Grandville - 54870.
Longwy : 6 km.
Station : Longwy 6 km. Longuyon 12 km.
Bus service.
Private property.

Despite the remains of the 12th century fortress, Cons-la-Grandville is essentially a château erected in 1572 by Martin de Custine. The right wign on the courtyard has kept its Renaissance decoration included the fine columned doorway and allegorical figures. The left hand wing and the main block were rebuilt in the 18th century. Several famous people have stayed here including king Stanislas Leczinski.
Open daily July 15 to Aug. 26 : 2 - 6.
Groups on request in the morning.
Parking.
Facilities for the handicapped.
Guided tours.
Tel. : (8) 244.90.86.

Fléville (Château).

Fléville-Devant-Nancy - 54710.
Nancy : 8 km.
Bus service.
Property of M. de Lambel.

Next to the feudal 14th century keep a Renaissance residence was erected in 1533 comprising thre corner towers. Besides 18th century furniture the château includes the « Galerie des États de Lorraine » created between 1853 and 1855 to tell the story of the dukes. King Stanilsas's room is another reminder of the past glories of Lorraine. The château has belonged to the Lambel family since the Empire.
Open daily July 1 to Aug. 31 : 1:30 -
Parking.
Guided tours.
English, German.
Concerts, folk dancing.
Temporary art exhibits.
Tel. : (8) 354.64.71.

Gerbeviller (Château).

Gerbeviller - 54830.
Luneville : 10 km.
Bus service.
Private property.

The present day château was rebuilt in 1920 by Laprade on the remains of an early 18th century château burned down in 1914. The Louis XIII pavilion is a brick and stone construction with a two storied pedimented front. The nymph pond in the park dates back to the 18th century.
Open on request.
Parking.
Recommended itinerary.
Information pannels or leaflets.
English, German, Spanish, pannels leaflets.
Tel. : (8) 342.70.15.

MEURTHE-ET-MOSELLE

FLEVILLE

Six centuries of Lorraine history at the gates of Nancy. This elegant and graceful inhabited residence invites you to visit its memorabilia of the life of the duchy of Lorraine. Tours, receptions, lectures, conferences.

Between Brive and Périgueux.

HAUTEFORT
(see page 13)
The Chambord of Périgord

DORDOGNE

Set high above the surrounding hills, this castle was once the residence of Bertrand de Born, the famous troubadour warrior of the 12th century. A main block joins the two wings with their 17th century domed round towers. The inner court looks over superb gardens. The interiors include the 17th century chapel, main gallery, tapestry hall and a grand staircase reminiscent of one at Versailles. The complex has been remarkably restored since the fire of 1968.

ANJONY
(see page 38)

CANTAL

Located in the heart of the Auvergne mountains, Anjony is open to the public every afternoon from Easter to November 1.

A furnished inhabited residence. Impressive 16th century frescoes.

ALLIER

LA PALICE
(see page 35)

La Palice is not a dead museum. It is alive with furniture and the mementoes of the family which has lived here for five centuries. The out-buildings date from 1613 and now house a bar, tea-room and reception hall. Meals served in July and August. Information available on the summer entertainment.

VAL
(see page 40)
Near Bort-les-Orgues

CANTAL

Can you picture a more Romantic fortress? Built in the 15th century, it is flanked by six fortified towers and is set on the edge of the Bort dam lake.

Guided tours all year. Closed Tuesdays from Sept. 9 to June 15. Closed for holidays Nov. 2 to Dec. 15.
Tel. : (71) 40.30.20.

PUY-DE-DÔME

AULTERIBE
(see page 44)

This medieval fortress has Neo-Gothic 19th century interiors. Inside is fine 16th and 18th century furniture.

PUY-DE-DÔME

TOURNOËL
(see page 48)

VOLVI

An imposing fortress damaged during the Wars of Religion.
The castle still has its main courtyard and Flamboyant Gothic staircase, several rooms with fine fireplaces, the chapel, a square keep which has remained intact and a mighty round keep.

Open Easter to Nov. 1 daily except Tuesdays : 9 - 12, 2 - 7.
In winter call (73) 33.53.06 for information of visits

CRAON

(see page 300)

MAYENNE

These days it is rare to find an estate comperable the château and park of Craon. The building is a pearl of 18th century architecture with fine wood panelled interiors and period furniture. It is surrounded by formal gardens and a landscape park of over 40 hectares. There is also a stable and an orangery built at the beginning of the 19th century as well as an ice-house and laundry.

The château has guest rooms open to the public in July and August.

Tel. : (43) 06.11.20.

APREMONT

(see page 303)

VENDÉE

9th century château rebuilt by admiral de Chabot in the 16th century. Restoration work.

Tower and sentry way, chapel, hall open to the public.

AISNE

FÈRE-EN-TARDENOIS
(see page 311)

Royal castle of the ducs de Montmorency.
13 th and 16th century.
Historic Monument since 1843.

Unacompanied visits all year round. For all gatherings, films or use of photographs contact the owner and restorer of the monument :

R. de La Tramerye
6, rue Quentin-Bauchart
Paris 75008
Tel. : 723.93.62 mornings

OISE

VERDERONNE
(see page 319)

On the banks of the pond, at the foot of the château, a 17th and 18th century theatre which houses exhibits and art shows.

20 km from Senlis and Chantilly on the D 59.

Verderonne - 60140 Liancourt
Tel. : (4) 473.10.67.

GOURDON
(see page 338)

ALPES-MARITIMES

Fortified castle built in the 12th century on the foundations of a 9th century Sarasin fortress, restored in the 17th century overlooking the Loup valley. It includes a collection of antiquities, furniture, arms, documents and paintings from the 16th, 17th and 18th centuries and a collection of contemporary naïve art.

The ground offer a spectacular view of the coast from the mouth of the Var to Nice and Cap Roux.

Tel. : (93) 42.50.13.

GRIGNAN
(see page 358)

DRÔME

One of the finest Renaissance châteaux of the south-east built by the Adhémar de Monteil family. It owes its fame to the letters of Madame de Sévigné whose daughter was the comtesse de Grignan. It still has some of its original furniture. Now the property of the department, it is the setting for musical, theatrical, literary and audio-visual events all year long.

Photo C. Trézin

HIGH PERFORMANCE

High Technology: We fly the Concorde between New York and Paris in just 225 minutes.
Efficiency: A leading record for on-time performance worldwide.
Cargo Leadership: One of the world's 3 largest cargo carriers.
Business Sense: We make your mileage count through our partnership in United Airlines Mileage Plus and Continental's TravelBank.

AIR FRANCE

TARASCON
Château of King René
(see page 345)

BOUCHES-DU-RHÔNE

This important medieval residence belonged to King René of Anjou who was also established in Provence. Inside one can see now a very fine collection of tapestries « L'histoire de Scipion ».

MONTMAJOUR
Abbey
(see page 343)

BOUCHES-DU-RHÔNE

Close to Arles, this 12th century abbey still stands in its unique site. One of the old abbeys in the heart of Provence.

L'AIR DU TEMPS

NINA RICCI
Paris

LE BEC HELLOUIN
Abbey
(see page 276)

EURE

Established around 1035, this abbey was rebuilt during the 17th and 18th centuries. The park, the refectories, the tower are interesting...

CASTELNAU-BRETENOUX
(see page 248)

LOT

A living relic of the past thanks to its fine furnishings, this might fortress of the Lot still has a keep dating from the year 1000.

Executive Car
CAREY LIMOUSINE
★★★★★

CAREY INTERNATIONAL LIMOUSINE SYSTEM

THE UNIQUE WORLDWIDE CHAUFFEUR DRIVEN CAR SYSTEM
- 200 CITIES
- 55 COUNTRIES
- 5 CONTINENTS

CALL IN PARIS:
- Executive Car - CAREY FRANCE
  (1) 265.54.20
- Your Travel Agent
- AIR FRANCE

TELEX TO:
- 650 265-F Reineco

WRITE TO:
- 25, rue d'Astorg
  75008 Paris - France

- Immediate confirmation
- Fully air conditioned cars
- Limousines - Sedans - Minibus
- Multilingual Drivers-Guide
- 24 hour service
- Central billing
- Major credit cards accepted

UNITED STATES AND CANADA: 140 CITIES IT'S
CAREY LIMOUSINE SYSTEM
4545-42nd Street, N.W.
Washington D.C. 20016

US TOLL FREE: (800) 336.46.46

LE THORONET
(see page 346)

VAR

This Cistercian monastery was built in 1146 in the Var Valley.
The cloister and the church are among the jewels of Provence.

DE VENOGE

LE CHAMPAGNE DES PRINCES

MAISON FONDÉE EN 1837

30, AVENUE DE CHAMPAGNE — 51204 EPERNAY — Tél. (26) 55.01.01

Visite des Caves : jours ouvrables 10H - 12H, 14H - 18H
week-end : sur R.V.

les 5 de la Villette

A TRADITIONAL CULINARY COOKING
DELICIOUS UNUSUAL MEAT

A LA FERME DE LA VILLETTE
46.07.60.96 closed on Sunday

AU BŒUF COURONNÉ
46.07.89.52 closed on Sunday

au Cochon d'Or
46.07.23.13 open on week days

La Mer
42.08.39.81 open on week days

Dagorno
Sweet musical dinner atmosphere
46.07.02.29 closed on Saturday

from N° 184 to N° 192 Avenue Jean Jaurès. 75019 PARIS
Open all the summer long
Easy parking from "Parc de la Villette" to "Porte de Pantin"

Haroué (Château).

Haroué - 54740.
Nancy: 28 km.
Bus service.
Property of the Beauvau-Craon family.

In the 18th century Boffrand used the plans and foundations of the old 14th century castle to build Haroué. The château is arranged in a horse-shoe plan, flanked by towers and surrounded by a moat. There is a distinctive ionic peristyle supperting a terrace surrounding the courtyard. The ironwork is by Jean Lamour, the frescoes by Pillement, the tapestries byn Malrange and the furniture belonged to Louis XVIII. The château belonged to Bassompierre, maréchal under Henri IV and then the Princes of Beauvau.

Open daily March 15 to Nov. 11 : 2 - 6.
Groups on request in the morning.
Parking.
Guided tours, brochures.
English, German, in July and August, guides.
Lecture tours for school groups.
Tel.: (8) 352.40.14.

Lenoncourt (Château).

Lenoncourt - 54110.
43 Rue de l'Église.
Nancy: 12 km.
Station: Lenoncourt 3 km.
Bus service.
Private property.

The Lenoncourt family played an important role from the Middle Ages to the 18th century thanks to its alliances with the Nancy family. This 16th century château set in a huge park has two powerful round towers. The interiors have been remodelled several times. The vaulted main kitchens with the monumental fireplace, the ground floor reception room with beamed ceilings and fine 18th century salons still survive.

Open each Sunday: 2 - 5.
Parking.
Grounds only.
Guided tours.
Tel.: (8) 348.60.29 and 348.48.51.

Lunéville (Château).

Lunéville - 54300.
Nancy: 30 km.
Station: Lunéville.
Bus service.
Property of the city.

Built between 1730 and 1720 by duc Léopold Ier of Lorraine according to plans by Germain Boffrand, Lunéville recalls the splendour of Louis XIV's Versailles. The main building has a peristyle with Corinthian columns surmonted by a pediment and crowned by a dome. The park facade is mirrored by the large basins of the formal garden. The chapel and the « salon des Trophées » still have their original 18th century decoration. King Stanislas lived here between 1737 and 1766.

Open Jan. 1 to March 31. Oct. 1 to Dec. 31: 10 - 12, 2 - 5.
April 1 to Sept. 30: 10 - 12, 2 - 6.
Closed Tuesdays.
Parking.
Brochure.
Facilities for the handicapped.
Temporary exhibits.
Sound and Light.
Concerts, lectures.
Nature Park.
Guided tours on request.
Tel.: (8) 373.18.27.

HAROUÉ
MEURTHE-ET-MOSELLE

The Versailles of Lorraine built by the 18th century architect Boffrand. Private collections of the Princes of Beauvau-Craon including Louis XVIII's furniture.

A magnificent setting for your receptions and conferences.

Open daily March 15 to Nov. 15 : 2 - 7.
Tel.: (8) 352.40.14.

Montaigu (Château).

Laneuville-devant-Nancy - 54410.
167 Rue Lucien-Galtier.
Nancy: 5 km.
Station: Nancy.
Bus service.
Property of the city.

Montaigu was originally a country house built by the tax collector Bon Prévost in 1757. Around 1869 it became the property of the marquis de Vaugiraud who turned it into a real château with the assistance of the architect Jasson. Ravaged by fire in 1921, it was restored by Edouard Salin who left it to the city of Nancy in 1975. The château is set in a park full of statues, basins and rocaille fountains. Inside is fine period furniture.

Open Jan. 1 to March 24: 8 - 5, weekends and holidays.
March 25 to Sept. 23: 12 - 7, during the week and 8 - 7 on weekends and holidays.
June 15 to Aug. 15 until 9 pm.
Closed Tuesdays.
Guided tours.
Tél.: (8) 351.25.63.

NANCY
Sainte Catherine (Botanical Gardens).

Nancy - 54000.
Property of the Syndicat Mixte des Jardins Botaniques de Nancy.

This garden was founded in 1758 by King Stanislas Leczinski, last duc de Lorraine. Its collections of annuals, perennials, bulbs and rock plants merited a visit by the Empress Josephine and by Émile Gallé.

Open Jan. 2 to Dec. 31: 8 - 12, 1 - 5.
Closed Jan. 1, May 1, Dec. 25 and Sunday mornings.
Parking.
Tel.: (8) 351.57.42.

PONT-À-MOUSSON
Premonstratensian Abbey.

Pont-à-Mousson - 54700.
Rue Saint-Martin.
Nancy and Metz: 30 km.
Station: Pont-à-Mousson.
Bus service.
Property of the commune.

Built between 1705 and 1735 the abbey has been destroyed and rebuilt several times in the course of its history, most recently in 1944 and then restored between 1960 and 1980. The main façade flanked with two pavilions and two perpendicular wings offers a fine exemple of Baroque monastic architecture of the period. The church is remarkable for its volume, luminosity and now for its stage which make it a good place for conerences, dance and musioc concerts and exhibits. The complex is set on the banks of the Mosell with a landing place for boats. Since 1964 the abbey has been an art centre with its own collectior of exotic and contemporarary art.

Open Jan. 15 to Feb. 20: 9 - 12, 2 - 7
Guided tours available on Sunday after noons and on request.
English, German.
Tel.: (8) 381.10.32.
Telex: 850.066. F.

Sexey (Château).

Sexey-aux-Forges - 54550.
4 Rue du Château.
Nancy: 15 km.
Station: Pont-Saint-Vincent 3 km.
Property of J. F. and N. Soligot.

The village of Sexey used to belong to the abbey of Saint-Mansu

---

MEURTHE-ET-MOSELLE # LENONCOURT

Residence of the Lenoncourt family who were important from the Middle Ages to the 18th century. The 16th century château is set in the midst of a huge park.

PONT-À-MOUSSON MEURTHE-ET-MOSELLE

PREMONSTRATENTIAN ABBEY
CULTURAL CENTRE

For you meeting, colloquia, seminars, conferences, film locations: modern facilities in a magnificent 18th century setting on the banks of the Mosell in the heart of Europe.

All year long tours and cultural programmes: dance, theatre, concerts, cinema, exhibits, art clases.
Comtemporary and exotic art collection.

A model of restoration used by 60 000 visitors a year
Complete documentation on request
54700 Pont-à-Mousson
Tel.: (8) 381.10.32.

which owned forges here since the 15th century. A Château was built in 1502. In the 17th century important remodelling was carried out. Sexey is flanked to the South side by a turret with spiral staircase. The North face has interesting windows. The Moor's head pierced with eyeholes enabled the access of the château to be watched.

Parking.
Grounds only.
Tel.: (8) 347.21.11.

VILLERS-LES-NANCY
Le Montet (Botanical Garden).

Villers-les-Nancy - 54600.
100 Rue Jardin-Botanique.
Station : Nancy 5 km.
Bus service.
Property of the Conservatoire des Jardins Botaniques de Nancy.

This garden was created in 1977 in a valley of the grounds of the château du Montet. It is modern in its concept and contains 3 800 varieties of tropical plants in hot houses and scientific, cultural and educational collections as well. It provides a haven for plants threatened with extinction in France and its overseas territories.

Open 2 - 5, Wednesdays to Sundays.
Groups on request.
Parking.
Guided tours, brochures.
Facilities for the handicapped.
Tel.: (8) 351.57.42.

MEUSE

Bazincourt-sur-Saulx (Château).

Bazincourt-sur-Saulx - 55000.
Bar-le-Duc : 14 km.
Private property.

Origianlly a 13th century fortified house, Bazincourt was transformed in the Renaissance by the private secretary th the ambassador of the dukes of Lorraine and Anjou. In 1774 Louis XV gave it to his minister Choiseul. The spiral staircase enclosed in a turret leads up to the first floor where a surprinsing 1534 chimney is decorated with busts of the owner and his wife.

Open June 1 to Sept. 30. Sundays and holidays.
July 23 to Sept. 3 daily 2:30 - 6.
Grounds from 11.
Parking.
Guided tours.
German, guide.
Tel.: (8) 798.15.44 and 798.45.89.

Hattonchatel (Castle).

Hattonchatel - 55210.
Verdun : 32 km.
Station : Metz 48 km.
Private property.

A fortress was built here in 850 by Haton. It was given to the duc de Lorraine in 1546 and dismantled by Swedes and French. At the beginning of the century a Neo-Romanesque castle was built on the site.

Open Jan. 1 to March 31.
Parking.
Guided tours.
German, English.
Guide, recorded information.
Tel. (29) 89.31.79.

MEURTHE-ET-MOSELLE

RARECOURT DE LA VALLÉE

Museum of Argonne Art through the Centuries
5 km from Clermont-en-Argonne

One of the oldest fortified houses of the Argonne dating from the 17th and 18th centuries with tower and rooms full of faience, pottery, artifacts, autographs and coins.

Open daily July 1 to Aug. 31 : 10 - 12, 2 - 6:30.

Montmédy (Citadel).

Montmédy - 55600.
Verdun: 50 km.
Station: Montmédy.
Bus service.
Property of the commune.

The 13th century fortress in the Ardennes forest was fortified further after the Treaty of the Pyrenes. Charles V made it one of the strongholds of his Empire. In 1657 it was captured by the French in the presence of Louis XIV and then transformed by Vauban. This fine example of 16 and 17th century military architecture houses the Bastien Lepage art museum.
Open March 1 to Oct. 31: 9:30 - 6:30.
Nov. 1 to Feb. 28: by appointment.
Parking.
Guided tours on request.
Recorded information.
Pannels of leaflets.
English, German, Dutch, pannels of leaflets.
Brochure.
Horse show.
Lecture tours for school groups.
Tel.: (29) 80.15.90.

Rarecourt de la Vallée (Fortified House).

La Vallée - 55120.
Verdun: 20 km.
Station: Clermont-en-Argonne 5 km.
Private property.

In the 14th century this fortified house surrounded by a moat and farm buildings belonged to the Pimodan de Rarécourt de La Vallée family. A new cut stone fortified house with tower, porch and central courtyard was built on the site of the old one probably in the 18th century. It houses archeological artifacts and collections of faience, pottery and coins as well as the Argonne art museum.
Open July 1 to Aug. 31: 10 - 12, 2 - 6:30.
Parking.
Recommended itinerary.
Pannels of leaflets.
Facilities for the handicapped.
Brochure.

La Varenne (Château).

Haironville - 55000.
Bar-le-Duc: 12 km.
Bus service.
Private property.

The main building of the current château was built in 1506 in French Renaissance style. It is flanked with two turrets set into the building. The two wing and the dovecote date from 1574. The guard room is vaulted. The main courtyard is surrounded by 18th century balustrades. Inside is a rare coffered ceiling and a staircase with a wrought iron bannister.
Open July 15 to Sept. 1.
Groups on request out of season.
Parking.
Guided tours, leaflets.
English, Spanish.
Facilities for the handicapped.
Tel.: (29) 70.21.45.

LA GRANGE
MOSELLE

On this site was an ancient fortress belonging to the lords of Luxembourg during the Middle Ages which served as an out post to the fortifications of Thionville until the 17th century; Christian Gomé des Hazards had the present château built by Robert de Cotte. Although it was badly damaged in the cours of several wars, the château has been carefully restored in recent years. Inside is a fine collection of 17th and 18th century furniture.

Open weekends: 2:30 - 6.
Tel.: (8) 253.25.40.

MOSELLE

Alteville (Château).
Taquimpol - 57260.
Nancy: 50 km.
Bus station: Dieuze 7 km.
Bus service.
Private property.
 In the midst of the Lorraine lake district, these two châteaux face each other across a square court. One dates from 1565 the other from 1698 was remodelled in 1968. The poet and philosopher, friend of Barrès, Syanislas de Guaita (1861-1897) lived here.
Open on request.
Closed Fridays, Mondays and weekends.
Information in German.
Brochures.
Temporary exhibits, lectures, workshops.
Tel.: (8) 786.92.40.

Bidestroff (Château).
Bidestroff - 57260.
Dieuze: 6 km.
Property of M. Vagost.
 This square plan castle is flanked by four towers and surrounded by a ditch. A fief of the ducs de Lorraine since the 13th century, it was purchased by the Schneider family after the Revolution;
Open for groups on request.
Parking.
Open Mondays and Fridays.
Guided tours, brochures.
English, German.
Tel.: (8) 786.57.72.

Bitche (Citadel).
Bitche - 57230.
Strasbourg: 50 km.
Station: Bitche.
Bus service.
Property of the commune.
 Bitche citadel was built by Vauban on a rock in the Basses Voges. Although it was partially destroyed in the Franco-Prussian war the Saint Louis chapel has survived to become a history museum. Bitche was the only town behind the peace treaty lines to hold out to the Prussians in 1870. The huge cellars are intact and open to the public.
Open April 1 to Oct. 31: 9 - 12, 2 - 6.
Groups on request.
Parking.
Guided tours of the cellars.
Leaflets, brochures.
German, English.
Bitche festival in July.
Tours on request.
Tel.: (8) 796.18.82.

Bouzonville (Abbey).
Bouzonville - 57320.
Cour de l'Abbaye.
Bouzonville station.
Bus service.
Property of the city.
 This Benedictine abbey was founded by Adalbert de Lorraine and his wife Judith and dedicated to the Holy Cross. Its Romanesque church dating from 1033 was rebuilt in Gothic style in the 14th century.
Open all year.
Parking.

ENTRANGE Zeiterholz (Maginot Line Fort).
Entrange - 57330.
Rue de la Forêt.
Station: Thionville 12 km.
Property of the commune.
 This two story structure built in 1934 still has all its original fittings in perfect working order. It was part of the Maginot Line series of fortifications.
Open afternoons the first and third Sundays in June, July and August.
Groups on request all year.
Audiovisual programme.
Brochures.
Information in German.
Carnival and concerts in June.
Guided tours.
Tel.: (8) 253.10.46.

La Grange (Château).
Manom-Thionville - 57100.
Metz: 30 km.
Station: Thionville.
Private property.
 Robert de Cotte built La Grange in 1714 in the classical style surrounded by a moat. I contains 17th and 18th century furniture, a porcelain stove made locally in 1760, a large ceramic collection and paintings by Van Dyck, Tiepolo and Vigée-Le-Brun. In 1750 it was acquired by a branch of the Fouquet family who still own it.
Open weekends: 2:30, 3:30, 4:30, 5:30.
On request during the week.
Parking.
Guided tours, brochures.
English, Italian, guides.
Horse and driving shows.
Tel.: (8) 253.25.40.

Luttange (Castle).
Luttange - 57144.
Metz: 25 km.
Station: Thionville 17 km.
Bus service.
Property of the commune.
 Once fought over by the lords of Metz and Luxembourg, this might fortress still has remains of round towers and a square keep. An elegant 18th century facade was added to the North wall. It was practically abandoned after the Second World War but it is now being restored by local volunteers.
Open for groups on request.
Parking.
Guided tours.
Tel.: (8) 283.51.92.

Pange (Château).
Pange - 57530.
Metz: 12 km.
Private property.
 This large elegant residenc was built between 1753 and 175 by Louis for Thomas; marquis d Pange on the site of an ancien fortress. The main block and tw wings house fine 18th century fu niture and paintings. Emperes Marie-Louise stayed here in 1812
Open July 1 to Aug. 31: 2 - 6.
Groups on request.
Closed Mondays and Tuesdays.
Parking.
Guided tours.
Tel.: (8) 777.04.41.

Rodemack (Bailli's House).
Rodemack - 57570.
46 Place des Baiili.
Thionville: 15 km.
Station: Thionville.
Bus service.
Property of M. and Mme Delvecchio.
 The original château was bui around 1570 by Christophe d Bade and destroyed in th 18th century and repalced by th main guard block. In the 19th cen tury baron Charles de Gorgan ac quired the ruins of the châtea and converted them into a res dence. Inside are period woo pannels.
Open Oct. 1 to June 30.
Closed Mondays and Tuesdays.
Parking.
Temporary exhibits.
Tel. (8) 283.43.76.

LORRAINE

Sierck (Castle).

Sierck-les-Bains - 57480.
Thionville : 20 km.
Bus service.
Property of the commune.

Once the property of the ducs de Lorraine Sierck was remodelled in the 17th and 18th centuries. Remains include important towers and walls.

Open May 1 to Sept. 30 : 9 - 12, 2 - 7.
Closed Monday mornings.
Parking.
Facilities for the handicapped.
Brochures.
Tel. : (8) 283.83.23.

Veckring Hackenberg Maginot Line Fort.

Veckring - 57920.
Thionville : 18 km.
Bus service.
Property of the commune.

Nicknamed the Monster of the Maginot line this fort was built between 1929 and 1935. It comprises galleries that stretch for 10 km over an area of 160 hectares. It could house 1 200 men with enough supplies for three months and fire four tons of shells per minute. An electric train takes visitors from the blockades to the kitchens, hospitals and barracks which are now a museum.

Open april 1 to Oct. 31, weekends : 2:00.
Groups on request.
Information in German, English.
Guides, brochures.
Facilities for the handicapped.
Guided torus.
Tel. : (8) 291.31.22.

VOSGES

AUTREY Notre-Dame (Abbey).

Rambervilliers - 88700.
Épinal : 25 km.
Station : Rambervilliers 8 km.
Bus service.
Private property.

Founded in the 12th century by Étienne de Bar, bishop of Metz, the abbey was restored in the 16th century. Burned down during the Thirty Years War, it was partially rebuilt in the 18th century. It was transformed into a metal works in 1789 it has regained its original vocation by becoming a pilgramage site for Saint Hubert.

Open on request.
Closed Fridays.
Parking.
Guided tours.
English, German, guide.
Facilities for the handicapped.
Tel. (8) 29.65.10.12.

Bains-les-Bains Château de la Manufacture.

Bains-les-Bains - 88240.
Station : Bains-les-Bains 3 km.
Private property.

This is an 18th century master forgers château set in the middle of an industrial area which gives it a special interest.

Open all year.
Parking.
Grounds only.

Chamagne (Claude Gellée's Birthpalce).

Chamagne - 88130.
Épinal-Nancy : 30 km.

PANGE

MOSELLE

Between 1753 and 1756 the Thomas, marquis de Pange had these elegant main block and two pavillions built by the architect Louis on the site of an ancient fortress. Inside are 18th century paintings and furniture. Empress Marie-Louise stayed here in 1812.

Open July 1 to Aug. 31 : 2 - 6.
Closed Mondays and Tuesdays. Groups on request. Parking. Guided tours . Tel. : (8) 777.04.41.

Station: Charmes 5 km.
Bus service.
Property of the département.
This labourers house was enlarged in the 18th century. Claude Gellée, le Lorrain, was born here in 1600.
Open Aptil 15 to Oct. 14: Wednesdays and weekends: 2:30 - 6.
Groups on request.
Parking.
Unaccompanied visits.
Brochures.

CHÂTEL-SUR-MOSELLE

Photo Y. Cleuvenot

Fortress of the Lords of Neufchâtel.

Châtel-sur-Mosell - 88330.
Épinal: 16 km.
Station: Châtel-Nomexy 4 km.
Bus service.
Property of the commune.
In the 14th century this fort changed hands by marriage and came into the possession of the lords of Neuchâtel-Comté. It then went to the ducs de Lorraine before being dismantled by Louis XIV in 1670. The remains of the fort cover 5 hectares surrounded by impressive walls, a fine example of 11th to 15th century military architecture. The convent of Notre-Dame was built inside the walls in 1710. A museum including stone collections, and artifacts and documents on daily and military life in the Middle Ages is houses here.
Open 3 - 6 Sundays and holidays all year.
Groups on request during the week.
Parking.
Guided tours, brochures.
Audiovisual programme.
English, German, guides.
Facilities for the handicapped.
Ramparts Festival, Musical walks.
Danse, temporary exhibits, lectures, lecture tours for school groups.
Tel.: (29) 67.14.18.

Châtillon-sur-Saône (Renaissance Town).

Châtillon-sur-Saône - 88140.
Bourbonne: 12 km.
Station: Bourbonne.
Private property.
Châtillon-sur-Saône was entirely rebuilt after its destruction in 1484. Charles III, duc de Lorraine was probably born here in 1543. A dozen Renaissance houses with French style facades and Italian style doors (1540-1560) line the streets leading up to the church and the castle that was rebuilt in the 19th century. The large tower at the entrance of the town is open to the public.
Open July 1 to Sept. 1: 8 12, 2 - 7.
Parking.
Guided tours.
Guides, brochures.

Photo CIM

Deuilly-les-Morizecourt (Priory).

Morizecourt - 88320.
Lamarche: 6 km.
Station: Vittel 18 km.
Private property.
As early as the middle of the 11th century a priory was built near Deuilly castle. Destroyed by the Châtelet family at the end of the 16th century, it was rebuilt in the 17th century with the ruins of Deuilly castle. Remaining buildings include a large deambulatory, a chapter house, pannelled cells, the Prior's chapel, a monumental gate and a school room.
Open July 1 to March 31 and
Out of season on request.
Closed Wednesdays Sept. 1 to 25.
Parking.
Guided tours.
Tel.: (29) 09.32.65.

Fontenoy (Castle).

Fontenoy-le-Château - 88240.
24 Grand-Rue.
Épinal: 38 km.
Station: Bains-les-Bains: 9 km.
Bus service.
Property of the city.
Fontenoy was first mentionned in the 11th century when it belonged to the comtes de Toul. It then went the to comtes de Lorraine and then to the house of Bourgogne-Neufchâtel. The castle bombarded, burned and reduced to ruins in 1635. A 1768 pla shows walls, round towers and th remains of a mighty keep datin from 1019. One round tower re mains.
Open April 1 to Oct. 15 on request onl
Ground only.
Parking.
Information in German.
Cross-bow, competition, volonteer rest ration sites and excavations.
Guided tours.

Lichecourt (Castle).

Relanges - 88260.
Darney: 4 km.
Station: Vittel 16 km.
Property of M. Labarge.
Lichecourt still has one Medie val block and round towerflanke by an 18th century chapel and pa villon. To the West lies the currer château which was probably bui in the 16th century. It has a rectar gular main building flanked by tw round towers with an 18th centur red stone facade. It is one of th few remaining residences of th Lorraine gentlemen glass-blower
Open on request for groups.
Parking.
Unaccompanied visits.
Tel.: (29) 09.35.83.

Moyenmoutier (Saint Hydulphe Abbey).

Moyenmoutier - 88420.
Daint-Dié: 15 km.
Station: Moyenmoutier.
Bus service.
Property of the departement.
This huge Benedictine abbe built in the 7th century was rebu between 1765 and 1776. The Bu dings were turned into a factor but the church was saved fror ruin and is a fine example of Barc que architecture and decoration.
Open all year: 10 - 6.
Parking.
Information pannels, brochures.
Temporary exhibits.

Sainte-Marguerite. Soyotte house.

Faing de Sainte-Marguerite.
Sainte-Marguerite - 88100.
Saint-Die: 1 km.
Station: Saint-Die.
Bus service.
Property of the Soyotte de Saint-D Folk Group.
This farm reconstitues 18th ar 19th century peasant life with collection of furniture and artifact
Open April 1 to Oct. 30: 3 - 6.
Other days on request.
Parking.

Guided tours.
Information in German.
Guides, brochures.
Exhibits.
Lecture tours.
Craft work shops.
Tel.: (29) 50.00.96.

Saint-Maur-de-Bleurville (Abbey).

Bleurville - 88410.
Vittel: 20 km.
Station: Contrexéville 15 km.
Bus service.
Private property.

The 9th century parish church was a Romanesque church built on it in the 11th century to serve the convent. Burnt down in the 16th century its vaults and stained glass were then restored un Gothic style. It was originally conserated by Pope Leo IX in 1045. A few Romanesque arches remain. Inside is a 16th century Pieta by Mansuy Gauvin.

Open July 1 to Sept. 4: 9 - 11, 1 - 7.
Parking.
Guided tours, brochures.
German, English, guides.
Facilities for the handicapped.
Cultural and musical evenings.
Temporary exhibits.
Tel.: (29) 09.01.78.

La Schlucht (Haut Chitelet Garden).

Gérardmer - 88400.
Gérardmer: 20 km.
Munster: 17 km.
Station: Gérardmer.
Bus service.
Property of the Conservatoire des Jardins Botaniques de Nancy.

This garden was created in 1966 to repalce a previous garden which had been opened on July 4 1914 but which was quickly destroyed by the war. It includes 2200 species of mountainous plants from the world over... There is a 10 hectare peat field and a garden of Vosges flowers.

Open June 1 to Aug. 31: 8 - 6.
Sept. 1 to Oct. 15: 8 - 5.
Parking.
Guided tours on request, brochure.
Tel.: (8) 351.57.42.

Les Petits Thons (Convent).

Les Thons - 88410.
Lamarche: 12 km.
Private property.

This convent was founded in 1452 by Guillaume de Saint-Loup. The church was built in 1483 on the same plan as the basilica at Assissi. Its longs nave and lateral chapels are fine examples of flamboyant Gothic.

Open June 15 to Sept. 15: 10 - 6.
Church Only.
Weekend the rest of the year.
Parking.
Brochures.
Unaccompanied visits.
Tel.: (29) 09.03.41.

DISCOVER FRANCE AND ITS OLD CITIES
with the guided tours of the Caisse Nationale des Monuments Historiques

When travelling in France during your holidays, discover 100 Old Cities and their art treasures with the guided tours organised by the Caisse Nationale des Monuments Historiques. Daily tours are organised and last one hour or more. Ask for timetable and details in the Tourist Offices of cities like : AIX-EN-PROVENCE, ARLES, ARRAS, AVIGNON, BEAUNE, BEAUVAIS, LAON, LA ROCHELLE, LYON, METZ, MONTLUÇON, MONTPELLIER, NANCY, NANTES, ROUEN, STRASBOURG, VERSAILLES...

ENGLISH SPEAKING GUIDES.

Hôtel de Sully
62, rue Saint-Antoine 75004 PARIS
Tél. : 274.22.22.

CIVIS

MIDI-PYRÉNÉES

ARIÈGE, AVEYRON, HAUTE-GARONNE, GERS,
LOT, HAUTES-PYRÉNÉES, TARN, TARN-ET-GARONNE.

- ■ castle, château, manor house
- ● abbey, priory
- ▲ garden, park
- ★ town house, famous men house, farm, mill...
- ○ city

TOULOUSE
- ■ La Reynerie
- ● Jacobins (couvent des)
- ★ Maison Calas

LOURDES
- ★ Moulin de Boly

■ Castelnaux-Bretenoux
★ Martel La Raymondie
■ Assier
● Conques
■ Roussillon
CAHORS ○
■ Cenevières
● La Ramière
RODEZ ○
● Loc Dieu
● Villefranche-de-Rouergue
■ Cas
■ Najac
■ Le Bosc
■ Sainte-Eulalie de Cernon
■ Brassac
● Beaulieu-en-Rouergue
★ Caussade Hôtel de Maleville
■ La Couvertoirade
Flamarens ■
MONTAUBAN ○
★ Hôtel L. de Pompignan
■ Le Cayla
■ Montaigut
● La Romieu
■ Mauriac
ALBI ○
★ Maison Natale de Toulouse-Lautrec
■ Gramont
▲ Gaillac Foucaud
■ Avezan
■ Saint-Géry
■ Ferrières
★ Pimbat Cruzalet
★ Lavaur
▲ ★ Castres Evêché et Jardins
■ Montgey
■ Caumont
TOULOUSE ○
■ Aguts
■ Le Gua
AUCH ○
■ Saint Géniès
■ Saint-Felix-Lauragais
★ Revel Halle
■ Lastours

○ TARBES
■ Maison Foch
■ Gaudies
■ Tour Sainte-Foy
■ Mauvezin
FOIX ○
■ Montsegur
○ Lourdes
■ Arcizan-Avant Ch. du Prince-Noir

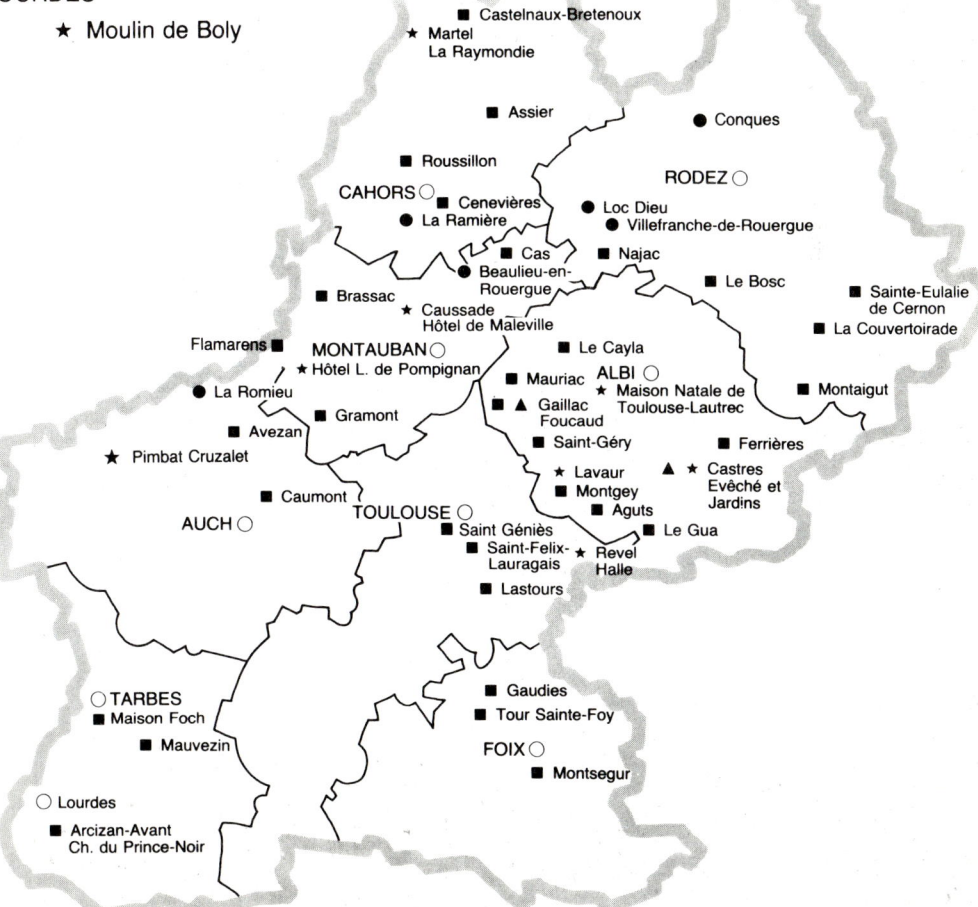

MIDI-PYRÉNÉES

ARIÈGE

Gaudiés (Château).

Gaudiés - 09700.
Pamiers : 14 km.
Belpech : 4 km.
Station : Pamiers.
Property of M. P. Duffaut.

All that is left of the 13th century castle are the ruins of the walls and a façade with 17th century mullioned windows. The draw bridge dates from the same century. The other façade was built between 1700 an 1740. The château belonged to the bishops of Toulouse until 1569 and to the marquis de Levis-Gaudiés from 1620 to 1840.
Open May 1 to Aug. 31 : 2:30 - 6:30.
Parking.
Guided tours, brochures.
English.
Lecture tours for school groups.
Tel. : (61) 67.10.23.

MIREPOIX
Sainte-Foy (Tower).

Mirepoix - 09500.
Mirepoix : 6 km.
Station : Pamiers or Castelnaudary 30 km.
Bus service.
Private property.

Built on a hill across from Montségur castle his fortification was used to enforce the authority of the Levis-Mirepoix. It is one of the rare 12th and 13th century buildings to have survived in the area.
Unaccompanied visits.
Parking.
Tel. : (61) 68.20.86.

MONTSÉGUR
Cathar Castle.

Montségur - 09300.
Lavelanet : 2 km.
Foix : 37 km.
Toulouse : 100 km.
Station : Foix.
Bus service.
Property of the commune.

This ruined Cathar castle was built on a peak at the beginning of the 13th century. The last bastion of Cathar resistence in the Albigensian crusade (1242-1244) it was taken by assault and 210 Cathars were captured and burnt at the stake. All that remains are the surrounding walls and the keep.

Open May 1 to Sept. 30 : 9 - 7.
Parking.
Unaccompagnied visits, brochures.
Tel. : (61) 01.10.27.

AVEYRON

Le Bosc (Château).

Camjac - 12800.
Albi : 45 km.
Station : Naucelle 3 km.
Private property.

Henri de Toulouse Lautrec used to spend his holidays in this ancient medieval fortress built in 1180 and remodelled at the end of the 15th century. Besides the furniture and tapestries, the interiors contain family mementos. The

---

AVEYRON — SAINTE FOY DE CONQUES
ABBEY CHURCH

An exceptional Romanesque church with a carved tympanum and a cloister in a protected site. Fine treasury of precious religious objects. 10th century gold statue of Saint Foy.

château has been inhabited by the same family since the 12th century.
Open March 28 to Nov. 11 : 9 - 12, 2 - 7.
Parking.
Guided tours.
English, German, Flemish, guide, leaflets.
Exhibits.
Tel. : (65) 69.20.83.

Conques Sainte-Foy (Abbey).

Conques - Saint-Cyprien-sur-Dourdou - 12320.
Rodez : 38 km.
Bus service.
Station : Rodez.
Property of the commune.

At the end of the 8th century the hermit Dadon retired to this spot near the waters of the Plô. Thus was founded the Benedictine abbey that was to become one of the major stops on the pilgrimage route from Puy-en-Velay to Santiago da Compostella. The monastery was destroyed by the Protestants in 1561. It was saved from demolition in the last century by Prosper Merimée. It has fine 11th and 12th century carved capitals and a marvellous Last Judgement over the West door. One arcade of the cloister survives and gives onto the refectory and a serpentine basin. The treasury houses the famous 10th century statue of Sainte Foy made of gold and encrusted with gems givien by pilgrims.
Open daily 9 - 12, 2 - 6 (7 in season).
Unaccompanied visits.
Recorded information, brochures.
Information pannels, leaflets.
Information in English, German. Musical programmes.
Temporary exhibits.
Slides.
Tel. : (65) 72.85.00 and 69.85.11.

La Couvertoirade (Ramparts).

La Couvertoirade - 12230.
La Cavalerie.
Millau : 40 km.
Bus service.
Property of the commune.

La Couvertoirade is an example of late medieval urban architecture. The ruined church and castle were built in the 12th century by the Templars. In the 15th century the knights of Saint John of Jerusalem built the ramparts which have been perfectly preserved.
Open March 1 to Dec. 31 : 8 - 6.
Parking.
Unaccompanied visits, brochures.
Recordings.
Tel. : (65) 62.25.81.

Loc-Dieu (Abbey).

Martiel - 12200.
Villefranche-de-Rouergue : 10 km.
Station : Villefranche-de-Rouergue.
Private property.

This abbey was founded in 1123, a grand daughter of Citeaux. Only the Romanesque church with its Gothic choir survives from this period. After their destruction by the English in the Hundred Years War, the cloister and chapter house were rebuilt. They were restored by Paul Gout in 1880. The most famous abbot was Claude Fleury, tutor to the royal children in 1716.
Open July 1 to Sept. 10 : 10 - 12, 2 - 6.
Closed Tuesdays.
Parking.
Guided tours, brochures.
Music festival.
Tel. : (65) 45.00.32.

MARTIEL

LOC-DIEU

AVEYRON

This ancient Cistercian abbey called Locus Dei was founded in 1123. The 12th century Romanesque church has a Gothic choir. The cloister and chapter house were rebuilt in the 15th century after their destruction in the Hundred Years War. The buildings were restored in the 19th century by Paul Goüt to be used as a residence. Open July 1 to September 10 every day but Tuesday.

Montaigut (Castle).

Gissac - 12360.
Saint-Affrique : 10 km.
Station : Tournemire-Roquefort 20 km.
Bus service.
Private property.

Montaigut was built on its 600 m perch in 1100 to insure the defense of the comté de Millau. During the Wars of Religion it was held by the seigneurs de Blanc. The rectangular main building had baulted rooms, Gothic fireplaces and a spiral staircase. Tombs carved into the Roch are to be found under the guard room.
Open daily July 1 to Aug. 31 : 8 am - 8 pm.
Sundays April 1 to June 30 and Sept. 1 to Nov. 1 : 1 - 7.
On request Nov. 2 to March 30.
Parking.
Guided tours, brochures.
Audiovisual programme.
Temporary exhibits.
Lecture tours for school groups.
Tel. : (65) 99.81.50.

Najac (Castle).

Najac - 12270.
Villefranche-de-Rouergue : 20 km.
Station : Najac 1 km.
Bus service.
Private property.

Najac castle rises above a loop in the Aveyron. It was built in 1100 by the comte de Toulouse as part of a chain of castles that stretch to Rodez. Partially destroyed by the Cathars and the English it was rebuilt in 1263 by Alphonse de Poitiers, Saint Louis's brother. This fine example of South western military architecture was unfortunately damaged in the 19th century.
Open April 1 to Sept. 31 and Sundays in October : 10 - 12, 12:30 - 6.
Guided tours, brochures.
Concerts.
Lecture tours for school groups.
Tel. : (65) 65.76.46.

VILLEFRANCHE-DE-ROUERGUE
Hospital Charterhouse.

Villefranche-de-Rouergue - 12220.
Avenue Viezan-Valette.
Station : Villefranche-de-Rouergue.
Bus service.

Built between 1451 and 1459, this charterhouse was occupied until 1791 when it was tuned into a hospital by the municipality. It comprises a chapel with a polygonal porch, a vestibule with Renaissance stained glass, a chapter house, a refectory and a Flamboyant Gothic cloister.
Open July 1 to Aug. 31 : 9:30 - 12, 2:30 - 6:30.
Parking.
Guided tours in July and August.
Brochure.
Festival : piano recitals.

Sainte-Eulalie-de-Cernon. Templar Castle.

Saint-Eulalie-de-Cernon - 12230.
Millau : 25 km.
Bus service.
Property of the commune.

The complex comprises ruins of the 13th and 14th century castle, of the 12th century Romanesque church and the 15th century ramparts. Some precious objects are kept in the castle.
Parking.
Brochure.
Tel. : (65) 62.72.99.

HAUTE-GARONNE

Lastours (Château).

Baziège - 31450.
Toulouse : 20 km.
Station : Baziège 1 km.
Private property.

This Renaissance château built at the beginning of the century received Catherine de Medici. It comprises twenty rooms with a fine monumental brick fireplace in the hall. The rooms contain period furniture. The château is surounded by a moat.
Open daily 2 - 7.
Unaccompanied tours.
Tel. : (61) 81.81.60.

REVEL
Central Market.

Revel - 31250.
Toulouse : 52 km.
Bus service.
Property of the commune.

This is one of the largest and oldest covered markets in France built in 1342 by Philippe VI de Valois. It is surrounded by covered galleries containing shops. The tile roof is supported by 79 wooden pillars. There is a two storied watch tower in the centre which was replaced during the Revolution. Used as a municipal building and prison until the 19th century, the wooden tower was rebuilt after a fire in 1829. Today it houses the Tourist Office.
Tourist Office open April 1 to Sept. 30 10 - 12, 3 - 6.
Sundays : 10 - 12. Closed Mondays.
Nov. 1 to March 31 : 2 - 5. Saturdays 10 - 12, 2 - 5.
Closed Sundays and Mandays.
Parking.
Unaccompanied visits, brochures.
Temporary exhibits.
Tel. : (61) 83.50.06.

Le Reynerie (Château).

Toulouse - 31300.
160, chemin de l'Estang.
Bus service.
Private property.

This «du Barry folly» is attributed to Nicholas Ledoux. It belonged to Guillaume du Barry, the husband of Louis XV's favorite and the protector of the architect who was then working for Louis XVI. This 18th century folly has a jutting North façade and a South Façade with a rotunda with a porch and Italianate roof. The rooms are decorated in Louis XVI style with gilt pannelling, cherry floors and period furniture.
Open June 1 to Sept. 30 : 3 - 5.
Groups on request.
Parking.
Unaccompanied visits.
Tel. : (61) 40.46.76.

Saint-Félix-Lauragais (Castle).

Saint-Félix-Lauragais - 31540.
Toulouse : 42 km.
Bus service.
Private property.

The castle comprises a main block flanked by two wings, a 14th century keep, and three square towers. The imposing façade faces the Montagne Noire. The vaulted rooms have remained intact.
Open July 1 to Sept. 30 : 9 - 11:30, 2 - 6.
Closed Wednesdays.
Parking.
Guided tours.
Foreign languages, guide.
Dance, music.
Temporary art exhibits.
Tel. : (61) 83.02.06.

Saint-Geniès (Château).

Saint-Geniès-l'Union - 31240.
Toulouse : 9 km.
Bus service.
Private property.

The château was built in the middle of the 16th century and acquired by one of the notables of Toulouse in 1742. The château is entirely made of brick. Inside is a typical Languedoc Renaissance straight staircase and a hall with a carved brick fireplace.
Open July 10 to Aug. 31 : 10 - 12, 2 - 4.
Closed Tuesdays.
Parking.
Leaflets.
Information in English.
Guided tours.
Tel. : (61) 74.26.45.

TOULOUSE
Calas House.

Toulouse - 31000.
50, rue Filatiers.
Bus service.
Private property.

This 15th century half timbered house was plastered in the 19th century. It comprises a Gothic door, 16th century carving and a 17th century door. It was rented to Jean Calas in 1730 who lived here until the death of his son Marc-Antoine on October 13 1761. Its name recalls the famous Calas affair.
Open all year 9 - 7.
Parling.
Interiors on request.
Guided tours with the city.
Tel. : (61) 53.14.00.

Jacobins (Convent).

Toulouse - 31000.
Parvis des Jacobins.
Property of the city.

This convent was founded in 1216 by Saint Dominic when he was combatting the Cathar heresy. The double naved church, the cloister. chapter house, refectory and Chapel were built in the 13th and 14th centuries. 14th century frescoes embellish the cloister.
Open daily except Sundays : 10 - 12, 2:30 - 6.
Guided tours available.
Pannels, leaflets.
Brochures.
Music festival.
Lecture tours for School groups.
Tel. : (61) 22.21.92.

GERS

Avezan (Castle).

Avezan - 32380.
Fleurance : 12 km.
Station : Agen or Auch 45 km.
Property of M. P. Cournot.

This 13th century Gascon castle overlooks the Arratz valley. It origi-

---

LASTOURS

HAUTE-GARONNE

Open daily all year, afternoons 2 - 7.
31450 Baziège. Tel. : (61) 81.81.60.
20 km from Toulouse on the Carcassone road.
Private entrance through the village at Baziège.

nally belonged to the Manas family and then to the Larocan family in the 17th century. Its austere aspect was softened by the large windows, staircase and huge chimneys added in the 17th century.
Open March 15 to Oct. 15 : 10 - 6.
Parking.
Guided tours.
Brochures.
Various shows.
Tel. : (61) 64.45.93.

Caumont (Château).

Cazaux-Savés - 32130 Samatan.
Toulouse or Auch : 40 km.
Station : L'Isle-en-Jourdain 17 km.
Private property.
　　Built at the beginning of the 16th and 17th centuries Caumont is the birthplace of Henri III's favorite the duc d'Epernon. This large brick and stone Renaissance château contains a staight Renaissance staircase and a main salon decorated in 19th century Troubadour style.
Open daily July 13 to Aug. 21 : 3-6.
Parking.
Pannels, leaflets, foreign languages.
Tel. : (62) 62.37.01.

Flamarens (Castle).

Flamarens - 32340.
Agen : 31 km.
Station : Valence d'Agen.
Motorway exit : Valence d'Agen 19 km.
Private property.
　　Despite its ruined state this 13th and 15th century castle is one of the finest examples of Gascon feudal architecture. A 16th century church survives inside the walls. Pierre Benoît wrote one of his novels « Flamarens » here.

Open July 1 to Aug. 31 : 10 - 7.
On request at other times.
Parking.
Guided tours.
Brochures.
Temporary exhibits.

Pinbat-Cruzalet (Château).

Vic-Fezensac - 32190.
Vic-Fezensac : 4 km.
Private property.
　　This little château is typical of the local Renaissance style. In 1628 it belonged to the consul of Vic-Fezensac and in the 18th century it was acquired by a Breton gentleman. All that remains is a long single storied building flanked by a round tower with a spiral staircase. Inside are beamed ceilings and fine Renaissance style fireplaces.
Open on request June 23 to July 7 and July 21 to Aug. 12 : 10 - 12, 3 - 6.
Closed Fridays.
Parking.

LA ROMIEU

Saint-Pierre (Collegiate).

La Romieu - 32480.
Property of the commune.
　　Saint-Pierre de La Romieu was founded by cardinal Arnaud d'Aux, a cousin of Pope Clement V of Avignon and built between 1312 and 1321. The Southern Gothic church is flanked by an octogonal tower embellished with frescoes. There is a Gothic cloister situated to the North of the church. There are remains of the Cardinal's palace as well.
Open July 1 to Dec. 31 : 8 - 7.
July 1 to Aug. 31 : 9 - 12, 2 - 7.
Special schedule for the Octagonal tower on request.
Guided tours in summer.
Brochures.
Concerts and plays.
Tel. : (62) 28.03.17.

LOT

Assier (Château).

Assier - 46320.
Bus service.
Property of the State.
　　Galiot de Genouillac, hero of the battle of Marignan had this château built in the 16th century. He was grand master of the king's artillery under Louis XII, Charles VIII, François I. All that remains are the ruins of the four wings and the West block. The façade on the

court still has its carved freizes and its portico with an early Renaissance staircase. The whole complex is a fine example of local Renaissance architecture.
Open March 15 to Sept. 30 : 10 - 12, 2:30 - 6:30.
On request at other times.
Closed Tuesdays.
Guided tours.
Concerts, festivals.
Temporary exhibits.
Tel. : (65) 40.57.31.

Castelnau-Bretenoux (Castle).

Castenau-Bretenoux - 46130.
Souillac : 38 km.
Property of the State.
　　The 11th century keep of Castenau-Bretenoux rises from its site on the border between Auvergne Guyenne and Languedoc. For nine centuries this fortress was the fief of the Castelnau family. Its triangular surrounding walls and round towers have survived. In 1851, fire raged through the 17th century part of the castle. The property of the Luynes family in 1715, the castle was purchased at the end of the 19th century by the singer Jean Mouliérat who restored it, refurnished it and gave it to the State in 1932. Today the Jean Mouliérat foundation has a fine collection of pewter objects and religious pieces, furniture and a small gem collection.
Open April 1 to Sept. 30:9 - 12, 2 - 6.
Oct. 1 to march 31 : 10 - 12, 2 - 5.
Closed Tuesdays.
Guided tours, brochures.
Tel. : (65) 38.52.04.

Cenevières (Castle).

Cenevières - 46330.
Cahors and Villefranche-de-Rouergue 36 km.
Station : Cahors.
Private property.
　　Once a fortified grotto and 8th century retreat of the duc d'Angoulême, captured by Pepin the Short, Cenevières belonged to the seigneurs de Gourdon for several centuries. Flotard de Gourdon transformed the fortress into a

CASTELNAU-BRETENOUX

LOT

A living relic of the past thanks to its fine furnishings; this might fortress of the Lot still has a keep dating from the year 1000.

CENEVIÈRES

LOT

13TH AND 14TH CENTURIES

763 : Pepin the Short captured Cénevières
1580 Henri IV stopped here
Why not you ?

13th century castle
— gard room, kitchen.
— chapel, oubliettes...
Open daily from April 1 to November 1.

Renaissance Palace
— Gallery, Salon (Painted ceiling)
— Alchemy room 5frescoes)
Parking for cars and buses. Tel. : (65) 31.27.33.

Renaissance château : windows, fireplaces, frescoes, furniture, library, alchemy room and columned gallery remain. The 13th century guard room and chapel have remained intact. The castle was visited by Henri de Navarre in 1580 and belonged to the marquis de la Tour du Pin, miniter under Louis XVI.
Open April 1 to Nov. 11 : 10 - 12, 2 - 6.
Groups on request out of season.
Guided tours, brochures.
English, German, Spanish (summers), guides.
Concerts, temporary exhibits.
Tel. : (65) 31.27.33.

MARTEL
La Raymondie (Palace).

Martel - 46600.
Souillac : 15 km.
Station : Saint-Denis 8 km.
Bus service.
Property of the commune.

The medieval fortress built by Bernard Raymondi, the son of Raymond IV was turned into a Gothic palace and belonged to the vicomtes de Turenne. The huge building has a belfry and rose windows. Two carved wood fireplaces and a Renaissance bas-relief embellish the first floor and the Uxellodunum museum occupies the keep.
Open all year.
Closed Sturday afternoon and Sundays.
Unaccompanied visits, brochures.
English.
Concerts, theatre, temporary art exhibits.
Tel. : (65) 37.30.03.

La Ramière (Priory).

La Ramière - 46260.
Station : Villefranche-de-Rouergue 16 km.
Property of M. Touvet.

Founded in the 12th century and built in the 13th century, the priory was severely damaged during the Wars of Religion. It was restored in the 17th century and transformed in the 19th century. From the 13th century remain three wings built over a cavern with a stream flowing through it. The keep, a part of the chapel, and the chapter house frescoes still remain.
Open all year : 10 - 12, 2 - 6.
Parking.
Guided tours.
Tel. : (65) 31.50.46.

Rousillon (Castle).

Saint-Pierre-de-la-Feuille - 46000.
Cahors : 12 km.
Property of Mme Hourriez.

Rousillon was built in the 12th century and transformed until the 15th. Its ruined towers and three main blocks are a reminder that it was one of the defenses of Cahors and one of the major Protestant strongholds in the region in the 16th century. Louis XIII was a visitor here in 1632. The fortress was dismantled in the 19th century and is now being restored.
Open July 1 to Aug. 8, Mondays : 2 - 7.
Groups on request at other times of the year.
Parking.
Guided tours, brochures.
Theatre, temporary exhibits.
Tel. : (65) 36.87.05.

HAUTES-PYRÉNÉES
ARCIZANS-AVANT

Castle of the Black Prince.

Arcizans-Avant - 65400.
Lourdes : 16 km.
Station : Argelès-Gazost 4 km.
Private property.

A fortified tower dominated the passage between the Saint-Savin and Auzun valleys since the 12th century. In the 16th century the lords of Arcizans builk a block flanked by two towers. The building was abandoned after the Revolution and is now being restored.
Open daily July 1 to Sept. 21 : 2:30 - 7.
Sundays and vacations April 4 to Oct. 30 : 3 - 6.
Parking.
Unaccompanied visits, brochures.
Pannels or leaflets.
Audiovisual marterials.
English, German, acoustiguides or recorded information.
Temporary excibits.
Tel. : (62) 97.02.79.

LOURDES
Lourdes (Castle).

Lourdes - 65100.
Tarbes : 20 km.
Bus service.
Property of the commune.

The seigneurial residence of the comtes de Bigorre until the 12th century, Lourdes was often besieged during the Wars of Religion. The castle was greatly transformed between 1820 and 1880 by the army which used it as a prison the 15th century keep stille survives. The Pyrénées museum housed in several of the buildings
Open April 1 to June 19 : 9 - 11, 2 - June 20 to Sept. 15 : 9 - 11, 2 - 6.
Sept. 16 to March 31 : 9 - 11, 2 - 4.
Parking.
Recommended Itinerary.
Pannels or leaflets.
English, Italian.
Facilities for the handicapped.
Brochures.
Temporary exhibits.
Lecture tours for school groups.
Tel. : (62) 94.02.04.

Moulin de Boly.

Lourdes - 65100.
Rue B.-Soubirou.
Station : Lourdes 1 km.
Bus service.
Property of the commune.

In this house where Bernadett Soubirou was born the period fu niture and objects evoke the life the Saint.
Open Easter to Oct. 10 : 9 - 11:45, 2: - 6:45.
Closed Saturdays.
Parking.
Unaccompanied visits.
Information pannels, brochures.
Information in English, German, Sp nish, Italian, Dutch.

Mauvezin (Castle).

Capvern-les-Bains - 65130.
Station : Capvern-les-Bains 3 km.
Bus service.
Private property.

The first restorations were ca ried out on this fortress in 190 and continue today. It once belon ged to the comted de Bigorre, th king of France, to the Black Prince th Gaston Phoebus and t Henri IV. Six rooms house a fo and history museum. The heraldr room has the mysterious inscrip tion « J'ay belle dame ».
Open daily May 1 to Sept. 30 : 9 12:30, 2 - 7.
Groups on request out of season.
Parking.

GRAMAT

ROCAMADOUR

LOT

One of the most famous picturesque sites in the South of France.

TARBES

Maréchal Foch's Birthplace.

Tarbes - 65000.
2, place de la Victoire.
Property of the State.

In 1951 Foch's birthplace was turned into a museum to celebrate the centenary of his birth. The ground floor has portraits of the marechal. Upstairs is the room where he was born, a study and the battle room show his committment to recapturing Alsace and Lorraine which was shared by so many of his generation and which he made a reality. Another room is full of the gifts presented to this great World War One hero.
Open July 1 to Sept. 15 : 8 - 12, 2 - 5:15.
Sept. 16 to June 30 : 8 - 12, 1:30 - 5:45.
Closed Tuesdays and Wednesdays.
Guided tours.
Tel. : (62) 93.19.02.

TARN

ALBI

Toulouse-Lautrec's Birthplace.

Albi - 81000.
14, rue Toulouse-Lautrec.
Bus service.
Private property.

On November 24 1864, Henri de Toulouse-Lautrec was born in this pink brick town house which had been built in the 17th century by the du Bosc family on the ancient walls of Albi. It was in the main salon here that he broke his left leg leading to his handicap. The stuccoed staircase dates back to the 18th century. Besides period furniture and much memorabilia of the painter and his family, the house also contains a collection of the painter's work. It overlooks a formal garden. The hôtel du Bosc still belongs to the painter's family.
Open July 1 to Sept. 15 : 9:30 - 1:00, 2:30 - 7.
Groups on request out of season.
Parking.
Guided tours, brochures.
English, German, Spanish, Dutch, guides, pannels or leaflets.
Lecture tours for school groups.
Tel. : (63) 54.21.81.

Aguts (Castle).

Aguts - 81470.
Puylaurens or Revel : 15 km.
Bus service.
Private property.

Aguts occupied by the Protestants in the Wars of Religion and was the childhood home of Léotine de Villeneuve who inspired Châteaubriand. Aguts is a closed square building surrounded by à moat, facing the Montagne Noire. The vaulted kitchen and the maine stone staircase have remained intact. The castle is being restored.
Open July 5 to Aug. 30 : 9 - 7.
Parking.
Guided tours.

CASTRES

Bishop's Palace and Garden.

Castres - 81100.
Toulouse : 80 km.
Station : Castres.
Bus service.
Property of the commune.

This former bishop's palace was begun in 1669 and designed by Jules Hardouin-Mansart. Le Nôtre laid out the fine formal gardens in 1676. Now the city all it also houses the Goya and Jaurès museums.

Open March 20 to Sept. 23 : 9 - 12, 2 - 6.
Sept. 24 to March 19 : 9 - 12, 2 - 5.
Daily in July and August.
Sundays opened at 10.
Closed Mondays.
Parking.
Unaccompanied visits.
Guitare festival.
Temporary exhibits July to end of September.
Tel. : (63) 59.12.43 and 59.62.63.

Le Cayla (Château).

Castelnau-de-Montmiral - 81140.
Gaillac : 16 km.
Station : 8 km.
Bus service.
Property of the department.

Built in the 15th and the 16 centuries and remodelled in th 17th, Cayla is a gentleman's res dence with a tower with a peppe pot roof. Access is by a doub staircase. The South side ove looks a terrace. The rooms ar furniture are Romantic in style a evoke the memory of the broth and sister poets, Maurice ar Eugénie Guérin who lived here the mid-19th century.
Open daily : 10-12, 2-6.
Closed Fridays.
Parking.
Guided tours, brochures.
Pannels, leaflets.
Foreign languages : guide on request.
Literazry festival.
Temporary art exhibits.
Lectures.
Tel. : (63) 33.90.30.

Ferrières (Château).

Ferrières - 81260.
Castres : 20 km.
Bus service.
Property of M. O Cébe.

Ferrières was built on the ban of the Agoût in the 15th century. was a military stronghold of a Pr testant leader during the Wars Religion and transformed into Renaissance château in the 16 century. In the 18th century it b came a State prison. The sculptu of the court façade with the freizes, pannels and medallior are Renaissance in style. Insic are caryatid fireplaces and loc period furniture. A museum of l cal Protestant history and a cent for stringed instrument makers a housed here.
Grounds open all year.
Interiors June 30 to Sept. 16.
Museums : June 15 to Sept. 15, dai Sept. 16 to June 15 on request.
Guided tours.
Foreign languages, guide.
Brochure.
Concerts, temporary exhibits, lectures
Lecture tours for school groups.
Tel. : (63) 74.03.53.

Unaccompanied visits, brochures.
English, Spanish.
Tel. : (62) 36.10.27.

ALBI

TOULOUSE-LAUTREC'S HOUSE

TARN

Located on the edge of the old quarter of Albi, on the city ramparts, Henri de Toulouse-Lautrec's birthplace has belonged to the painter's family since the seventeenth century.
Toulouse-Lautrec was born and spent his early years in this house. This Southern style pink brick town house was built different periods overlooking terraced gardens which give it special charm. Inside it has kept its period decoration and furniture as well as mementoes of the Toulouse-Lautrec family and of the painter himself, including early drawings and paintings.

GAILLAC
Foucaud
(Château and Park).

Gaillac - 81600.
Station : Gaillac.
Property of the commune.

This pink brick main building flanked with two wings was built in the 17th century by a member of the Parlement of Toulouse. Inside is a museum of painting and local history. To the North of the château is a formal gardens leading to the out buildings. To the South the terraces have fountains which go down to the river. Fragonard and Liszt were guests here.

Open April 1 to Oct. 30 : 3 - 7.
Nov. 1 to March 31 : 5 - 6.
Closed tuesdays.
Parking.
Guided tours available.
Foreign languages on request.
Festivals, Concerts.
Temporary art exhibits.
Lecture tours for school groups.
Tel. : (63) 54.14.65.

Le Gua (Château).

Lescout - 81110.
Castres : 15 km.
Bus service.
Private property.

Built in 1728 by Timoléon de Bonnemain, a member of the Parlement of Toulouse, Le Gua is a charterhouse flanked by two out buildings. It is original in its building materials which are alternately bricks and thick stones, a fine example of Louis XIII architecture.

Grounds only.
Groups on request.
Tel. : (63) 54.13.90.

LAVAUR
Vieux Lavaur (House).

Lavaur - 81500.
7, rue Père-Colin.
Toulouse : 37 km.
Station : Lavaur.
Bus service.
Private property.

Built at the beginning of the 16th century, this Renaissance dwelling is set around an arcaded courtyard. Fireplaces, furniture and regional pieces embellish the interiors.

Open July 15 to Aug. 30 : 3 - 7.
Parking.
Guided tours.
Tel. : (63) 58.02.65.

Mauriac (Château).

Senouillac - 81600.
Gaillac : 7 km.
Station : Tessonnière 2 km.
Bus service.
Private property.

This castle was built in the 15th century and became a major site

---

TARN

MAURIAC
7 km from Gaillac, 20 km from Albi

After 20 years of restoration work the painter Bistes has renewed the cultural vocation of this fortress and invites you to discover his work as painter, decorator and host for receptions, lectures and concerts.

Photo B. Bistes

Protestant resistance in the re-
on during the Wars of Religion.
ie stronghold was attached to
e crown in 1596. The fortress-
e appearance contrasts with the
enaissance courtyard.
pen daily May 1 to Oct. 30 : 3 - 7.
l year Sundays and holidays : 3 - 7.
arking.
uided tours.
panish, English, guides.
oncerts.
emporary exhibits.
ctures.
ecture tours for school groups.
l. : (63) 57.16.56.

longey (Castle).

uq-Toulza - 81470.
oulouse : 50 km.
ation : Toulouse.
ivate property.
An ancient Roman road leads to
lontgey, built on a rocky spur
verlooking the Revel plain. The
edieval fortress belonged to the
ourdain de Roquefort family until
e Albigensian Crusade. It was
aptured by Simon de Montfort in
211. There is a Romanesque to-
er and buildings with windows
several periods as well as a Re-
aissance door and an Italianate
allery with a view of the Pyré-
es. A fireplace of the school of
ontainebleau presides over the
ain hall.
pen Sundays all year : 2 - 6.
arking.
uided tours, brochures.
nglish, Spanish.
ecture tours for school groups.
l. : (63) 75.72.37.

aint-Géry (Château).

abastens - 81800.
oulouse and Albi : 40 km.
us service.
ivate property.
A monumental entrance guar-
ed by stone sphinxes leads to the
ree main blocks which surround
e main court of Saint-Géry built
the 14th century, remodelled in
e 15th and enlarged in the 18th.
urrounded by a park with an
angery, the château is filled with
7th and 18th century furniture,
Chinese objects and Wedgewood
style pieces fill the Ancient style
dining room. Cardinal de Rabas-
tens was born here in the 14th
century and Richelieu came as a
guest.
*Open April 1 to Nov. 11, Sunday and
holiday afternoons.
Every afternoon in July and August.
Parking.
Guided tours.
English.
Tel. : (63) 33.70.43.*

TARN-ET-GARONNE

Beaulieu-en Rouergue (Abbey).

*Ginals-Lexos - 82330.
Villefranche-de-Rouergue : 30 km.
Mantauban : 50 km.
Property of the C.N.M.H.S.*
Adhémar III, the bishop of Rodez who founded this Cistercian
abbey in 1144 in a wooded hollow
called the site Bellus locus or
Beau lieu. The buildings surrounding the cloister were reconstructed in the 13th and 14th centuries
and partially remodelled in the
17th and 18th centuries. In the
19th century the monastery was
turned into a farm which added to
the deterioration of the buildings
which had begun with the Revolution. The abbey was saved by the
work carried out by Monsieur and
Madame Brache rom 1960. It was
donated to the Caisse Nationale
des Monuments Historiques et
des Sites in 1973. Continuing restoration has returned the abbey to
its original Cistercian Gothic architecture. A contemporary art centre
has opened around the collection
donated by Madame Bonnefoi-
Brache.
*Open daily from Palm Sunday to Sept.
30 : 10 - 12, 2 - 6.
Closed Tuesdays.
Groups on request out of season.
Parking.
Modern music festival.
Modern art exhibits.
Tel. : (63) 30.76.84.*

Brassac (Castle).

*Brassac - 82190.
Station : Moissac, Valence d'Agen 18 km.
Private property.*
Brassac castle was founded in
1180 by Raymond V, comte de
Toulouse. Despite the destruction
of the Wars of Religion and two
fires in the 18th century the fortress is a rare example of regional
military architecture. The building
is surrounded by a moat and flanked by towers. Large armories
with firing holes are located under
the terrace. The complex is surrounded by age old pines and cedars of Lebanon.
*Open from Easter to Nov. 1 : 2 - 6:30.
Closed mornings.
Parking.
Acoustiguides.
Foreign languages, pannels, leaflets.
Temporary exhibits.
Tel. : (63) 94.23.82 or 94.25.32.*

Cas (Castle).

*Espinas - 82160.
Caylus and Saint-Antonin-Noble-Val : 6 km.
Station : Caussade or Villefranche-de-Rouergue.
Property of M. de Lastic Saint-Jal.*
Built in the 12th century, trans-
formed in the 14th and 16th centu-
ries, Cas was a Templar fort fefore
belonging to the Powerful Car-
dailhac family. It survived the Hun-
dred Years War and the Wars of
Religion but was never sold. The
ruins have recently been restored
to their original aspect including
furnished rooms.
*Open weekends and holidays, May 1 to
Sept. 30 : 2 - 7.
Daily in August.
Parking.
Guided tours.
English, German.
Festival, Concerts.*

CAUSSADE (Hôtel de Maleville).

*Caussade - 82300.
Montauban : 22 km.
Station : Caussade.
Bus service.
Private property.*
Built in the 17th century by
Pierre and Bernard inside the ancient walls of Caussade, the façades and the dovecote roof of
this town house have recently
been restored. The Louis XVI staircase with the wrought iron balustrade, the restored vault, the Flemish tapestries and Louis XV pan-

nels of the dining room embellish the interiors.
Open on request April 1 to Nov. 15.
Closed Sundays and Mondays (Market day).

in the 18th century. Paintings embellish the interiors.
Open on request by the Tourist Office.
Parking.
Brochure.
Tel. : (63) 63.15.90.

Gramont (Château).

Gramont-Lavit - 82120.
Lectoure : 15 km.
Property of the State.

Gramont is situated on the border of Languedoc and Gascogne. In 1215 Simon de Montfort gave it to Eudes de Montaut. All that remains of this first edifice is the « Simon de Montfort tower » which shoulders the entrance way. In the 16th century it was owned by the Voisins family who built the perpendicular wing flanked by two pavilions in Renaissance style. In 1961 it was purchased by Monsieur and Madame Dichamp who restored the property to its original state before giving it to the Caisse Nationale des Monuments Historique et des Sites. The castle includes period furniture. A large space has been set up to receive exhibitions.
Open April 1 to June 30 and Sept. 15 to Nov. 11 : 2 - 7.
July 1 to Sept. 15 : 9 - 12, 2 - 7.
Closed Tuesdays.
Parking.
Guided tours, brochures.
Festivals.
Exhibitions.
Tel. : (63) 94.05.26.

MONTAUBAN

Hôtel Lefranc de Pompignan.

Montauban - 82000.
10, rue Armand-Cambon.
Private property.

This town house was built in the 17th century by Vicose a friend of Henri IV. The poet Pompignan was born here in 1709 the painter Armand Cambon was a frequent visitor. A main building flanked by two pink brick wings surround a classical style main courtyard. The staircase with the wooden bannister dates from the original buiding but the brick door way was added

NORD PAS-DE-CALAIS

NORD, PAS-DE-CALAIS.

- ■ castle, château, manor house
- ● abbey, priory
- ▲ garden, park
- ★ town house, famous men house, farm, mill...
- ○ city

ARRAS
  ● Saint Vaast

■ Le Klap Houck
■ Esquelbeck
■ Vert-Bois
★ La Hamayde
■ La Villeneuve
■ Denacre
○ LILLE
● Vieil Hesdin Ancien couvent des Sœurs Noires
■ Olhain
ARRAS ○
■ Esnes
■ Barly
● Vaucelles

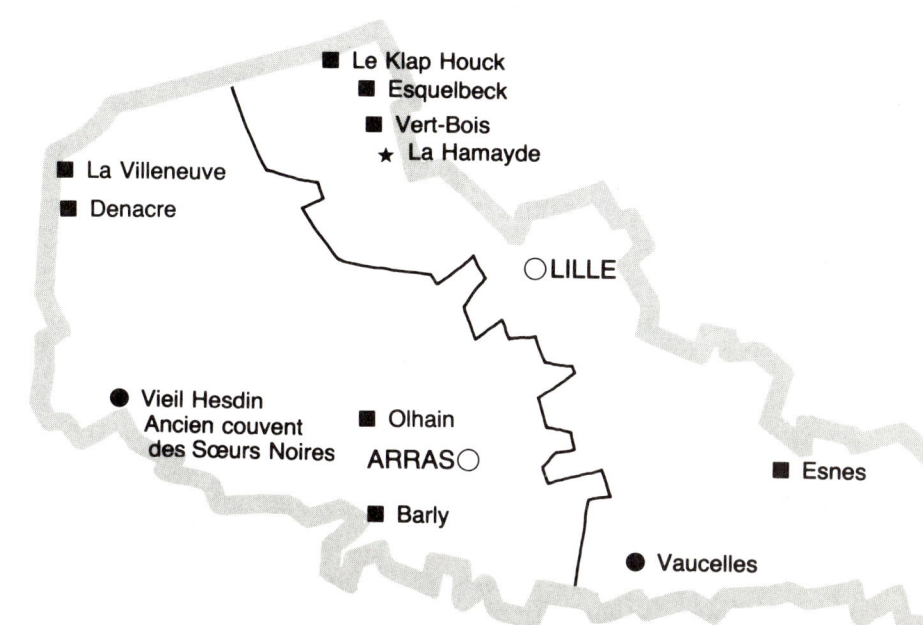

NORD/PAS-DE-CALAI[S]

NORD

Esnes (Château).

Walincourt - Selvigny - 59127.
Cambrai : 10 km.
Station : Cambrai.
Bus service.
Private property.

Tucked away in a small valley Esnes is on of the few remaining remains of this size in the area. The four towers which survive from the medieval fortress built in the 14th and 15th centuries are examples of military architecture of the period. They provide a contrast to the main brick and stone building constructed in 1735 by the architect Playez. The 18th century interiors have survived.
Open Sept. 1 to June 30, every 4th Sunday : 10 - 12, 2 - 6.
July and August, every 2nd and 4th Sundays : 10 - 12, 2 - 6.
On request on other days.
Parking.
Guided tours, brochures.
Historical pageant, May 1 (games, jugglers, music and dancing).
Temporary exhibits : architecture.

Esquelbecq (Castle).

Esquelbecq - 59248.
10, Grand-Place.
Dunkerque : 15 km.
Station : Esquelbecq.
Private property.

Saint Folquin, Charlemagne's nephew died in the original castle in 800. The existing castle with its austere brick facade was rebuilt at the beginning of the 17th century by Valentin de Pardieu in the style if a fortified castle. The castle is surrounded by a moat fed by a branch of the Yser river. Three of the tapestries inside were woven at Aubusson in the 17th century and tell the story of Esther. A French Renaissance garden and espaliered fruit trees surround th[e] castle.
Open daily July 1 to Sept. 17 : 2:3[0-]6:30.
Weekends April 1 to Oct. 31 : 2:3[0-]6:30.
Parking.
Guided tours, brochures.
English, Flemish, German.
Festival, temporary exhibits.
Tel. : (28) 62.89.84.

La Hamayde (House).

Chereng - 59152.
Lille : 12 km.
Station : Tressin 0,5 km.
Bus service.
Property of M. and Mme R. Meillasso[n] Pollet.

Once the property of the La H[a]mayde family, this old residen[ce]

ESQUELBECQ

NORD

15 km from Dunkerque and 30 km from Calais, 1 hour and a half from Great Britain, Esquelbecq invites you to its lecture tours, its school programmes and art programmes.

Esquelbecq offers a magnificent setting for lectures, conferences, seminars and film locations.

Tel. : (28) 62.89.84 and (5) 260.07.82.

was used as a coaching inn from 1670 to 1860. Its brick and white stone facade is based on the Flemish Renaissance style. The decorative scheme includes a sun carved over the doorway and lions between the windows.
Open or request, all year : 9:30 - 12, - 7.
Parking.
Unaccompanied visits.
Tel. : (20) 34.39.53.

Le Klap Houck (Château).

Socx - 59380.
Bergues and Dunkirk : 15 km.
Bus service.
Private property.

Klap Houck is set in an attractive park and dates from the early part of the 19th century. The main building is flanked by two pavilions which include pediments and pilasters. The château still belongs to descendants of General Desticker and was visited by Marshal Foch.
Open on request.
Grounds only.
Unaccompanied visits.
Tel. : (28) 68.63.59.

Vaucelles (Abbey).

Crèvecœur-sur-Escaut - 59258.
Cambrai : 12 km.
Station : Cambrai.
Bus service.
Private property.

Vaucelles abbey was founded by Saint Bernard in 1132. It is one of the oldest monuments in the North of France and one of the purest examples of Cistercian architecture. The monestary includes four rooms : the monk's room built in 1145, the parlour dating from 1155, the sacred passage where the monks gathered before services and the chapter house built in 1170, the jewel of the abbey. Ruins of a 17th century abbots palace remain. The church was destroyed at the end of the 18th century.
Open the last Sunday of every month from April to September : 3 - 7.
On request at other times for groups.
Parking.
Guided tours, brochures.
Tel. : (27) 82.11.58.

Le Vert-Bois (Château).

Bondues - 59910.
N. 352.
Lille : 9 km.
Bus services.
Private property.

Vert-Bois was built in 1743 on the site of an ancient fortified farm. It is approached through a turretted pavilion. The 1743 monumental gate is decorated with pilasters and a pediment. Partially surrounded by moat, the château is a typical folly of the period in its use of carved stone and brick, large windows separated by pillasters and pedimented façade. The courtyard is flanked by two brick and stone pavilions, one of which was used as a chapel. The 18th century wood pannelled interiors house a collection of impressionist and Modern paintings as well

NOTRE-DAME-DE-VAUCELLES NORD

The 12th century Cistercian abbey of Notre-Dame-de-Vaucelles, located near Cambrai in the Escault valley was founded by Saint Bernard in 1132. The chapter house, sacred passage, monk's room, oratory and 17th century ruined abbot's palace are in course of restoration.

Guided tours on request.
Tel. : (27) 82.11.58.

Photo A. Lagoutte

as Delft and Persian ceramics. 500 meters from the château an old farm is now the « Anne and Albert Prouvost Septentrion » Foundation.
Foundation : Open daily Aug. 15 to July 15 : 2 - 6, except Mondays.
Château : Open Sundays and holidays Aug. 15 to July 15 : 4:30 - 6, except Tuesdays.
Parking.
English, German, Dutch, guides on request.
Concerts, temporary exhibits.
Tel. : (20) 46.23.16.

PAS-DE-CALAIS

Arras (Saint Vaast Abbey).
Arras - 62000.
Rue Paul-Doumer.
Station : S.N.C.F.
Bus service.
Property of the city.

A monestary was built here in the 7th century in hommage to Saint Vaast who had been sent by Clovis around 500 A.D. to evangelize Northern Gaul. It was destroyed in the 9th century by the Vikings and then burned down three times before it was rebuilt in its present form in the 11th century. Redesigned on a uniform plan in the 18th century, the Abbey today houses the Arras Museum of Fine Arts and the Municipal Library.
Open daily : 10 - 12, 2 - 5 (5:30 in summer), Sundays : 10 - 12, 3 - 5 (5:30 in summer).
Closed Tuesdays.
Parking.
Brochures.
Temporary exhibits.
Guided tours on request.
Tel. : (21) 21.26.43 or 71.26.43.

Barly (Château).
Avesne-le-Comte - 62810.
Arras : 18 km.
Station :
Private property.

Begun in the 1780's, this elegant château was probably finished during the French Revolution. It incorporates some of the purest elements of Louis XVI architecture :

the use of white stone ; a main building flanked by two slightly protruding pavilions and the four fluted columns of the façade surmounted by a pediment. The eighteenth century wood pannelling, the 1786 golden staircase and the pillastered drawing room are the main features of the interior decoration.
Open on request April 1 to Sept. 30.
Parking.
Guided tours, brochures.
E,glish.
Facilities for handicapped.
Musical evenings in July.
Tel. : (21) 48.41.20 and (1) 288.79.74.

Le Denacre (Château).
Wimille - 62126.
Boulogne-sur-Mer : 4 km.
Station : Boulogne of Wimille 4 km.
Bus service.
Owner M. F. Dubly.

Le Denacre was built between 1777 and 1778 and occupied by the Germans during the Second World War. This small grey stone château has kept its Louis XV wood panelling as well as its 17th and 18 th centuries furniture and paintings.
Open on request.
Parking.
Unaccompanied visits.
Tel. : (21) 31.86.14.

Olhain (Castle and Farm).
Fresnicourt-le-Dolmen - 62150.
Arras : 25 km.
Station : Béthune 14 km.
Owner : M. Dutoit.

Built by Jean de Nielles around 1405 on the site of an ancient fort, Olhain is one opf the major medieval fortresses in Artois. The castle is divided into two distinct parts : the oval service court and the castle proper both surrounded by a pond and connected by a draw-bridge. The castle has retained its medieval aspect with its keep flanked by a watch tower.
Open Sundays and holidays from April 1 to Oct. 31 : 3 - 6:30.
Parking.
Unaccompanied visits, brochures.
Tel. : (21) 27.94.76.

Vieil Hesdin (Convent).
Le Parcq - 62770.
Hesdin : 8 km.
Private property.

Only a few bits of wall remain of the castle of Hesdin which once belonged to the comtes d'Artois and the ducs de Bourgogne. However a larged slate covered brick and stone edifice surrounding a

vaulted brick cloister survives fro the 18th century convent.
Open on written request.
Guided tours available.
Tel. : (21) 04.87.21.

La Villeneuve (Château).
Bellebrune - 62142.
Boulogne-sur-Mer : 14 km.
Bus service.
Private property.

François de Villeneuve, se gneur de Chambourg, built th château in 1668. It has a grey f çade, dormer windows cut in blue slate roof and a Classic door.
Open on request June 1 to Sept. 3 9 - 2.
Guided tours.
English.
Facilities for the handicapped.
Tel. : (21) 33.31.87/5.

BASSE-NORMANDIE

CALVADOS, MANCHE, ORNE.

- ■ castle, château, manor house
- ● abbey, priory
- ▲ garden, park
- ★ town house, famous men house, farm, mill...
- ○ city

CAEN

▲ Jardin des Plantes

HONFLEUR

★ Musée « Le Vieux Honfleur »

LISIEUX

★ Les Buissonnets

■ Nacqueville ■ Saint-Pierre-Eglise
Dur-Ecu ■ ○ Cherbourg
■ Martinvast ■ Gonneville
★ Valognes : Hôtel de Beaumont
● Sainte-Marie
Saint-Gabriel- en-Brecy
■ Coigny ■ Brecy ● Longues-s-Mer ○ Honfleur
■ Mondaye ■ Fontaine-Henry ■ Bonneville
● Cerisy-La-Forêt ■ Balleroy ■ Lantheuil ■ Ducs de Normandie
■ Pirou ST-LO○ ■ Canon
CAEN ○ ■ Mont de la Vigne
■ Gratot Outrelaise Aubichon ■ ○ Lisieux
■ Cerisy Vendœuvre ■ Fervaques ■ St-Germain- de-Livet
● Hambye La Motte ■ Courson St-Hyppolyte
● La Lucerne ■ Falaise
■ Rabodanges
■ La Bérardière
● Mortain
● Mont-St-Michel ■ Saint-Sauveur ■ Champobert
Sassy ■ ■ Argentelles ● Chêne-Gallon
■ Médavy ■ Pontgirard
■ Carrouges ○ ○ Courcy ■ Lavove
○ ALENÇON
■ Letertre

CHERBOURG

▲ Jardin de la Roche- Fauconnière
● Abbaye du Vœu

BASSE-NORMANDIE

CALVADOS

Aubichon (Manor House).
Lisieux - 14100.
Chemin de Colendon.
Lisieux : 3 km.
Station : Lisieux.
Private property.

This half-timbered manor house was built in 1520 by Cardinal Jean le Veneur, bishop and count of Lisieux. It includes unusual carved armorial posts and polychromatic effects.
Open on request.
Parking.
Tel. : (31) 62.16.07.

Balleroy (Château).
Balleroy - 14490.
Bayeux : 17 km.
Station : Bayeux.
Private property.

François Mansart designed Balleroy in 1646 for Jean de Choisy. The central pavilion is crowned by a lantern and flanked by two lower buildings. The out-buildings are on either side of the garden designed by Le Nôtre. Two pavilions are set at the entrance to the courtyard. A ceiling painted in the French style, portraits by Mignard and objets d'art, decorate the interior. One of the out-buildings contains a museum of the history of baloons from the time of the Montgolfier brothers.
Open daily 9 - 12, 2 - 6.
Closed Wednesdays from Nov. 1 to Feb. 28.
Guided tours available.
English, pannels or leaflets.
Brochures.
Baloon festival.
Tel. : (31) 21.60.61.

BONNEVILLE-SUR-TOUQUES

Dukes of Normandy Castle.
Bonneville-sur-Touques - 14800.
Route D 284.
Deauville : 4 km.
Bus service.
Private property.

Built on a site overlooking the Touques estuary which was once a busy cross Channel port, the castle provided the Dukes of Normandy with a stronghold that remained fortified until the end of the 16th century. The 13th century fortress was captured and freed five times between 1203 and 1449. Its remains include a deep circular ditch surrounding an outer wall flanked by five towers, a keep and a Gothic fort. Bonneville was the residence of William the Conqueror, Eleonor of Aquitaine and Philippe Egalité.
Open weekends and holidays, March 20 to Nov. 14 : 2 - 6.
Parking.
Grounds only.
Guided tours on request.
English, German.
Brochure.
Tel. : (31) 88.00.10.

Brécy (Château).
Brécy-Saint-Gabriel - 14480.
Bayeux : 12 km.
Property of M. and Mme Jacques de Lacretelle.

Nestled in the Seulles valley, the 16th century manor house was transformed in the 17th century. It belonged to the Le Bas family who were friends of François Mansart the supposed architect. The main classical style building is situated at the end of a courtyard flanked by two out-buildings. The splendid gardens are scattered with carved stone lions, vases and acanthus leaf balusters. The entrance gate is the work of Issac Geslin. The stone fireplaces inside have remained intact. The property also includes a 13th century church.
Open daily, April 16 to Nov. 1 : 2 - 6.
On request Nov. 2 to April 15 : 2:30 - 5.
Closed Wednesdays.
Parking.
Guided tours.
Tel. : (31) 80.11.48.

CAEN
Botanical Gardens.
Caen - 14000.
5, place Blot.
Bayeux : 50 km.
Station : Caen.
Bus service.
Property of the commune.

This park was purchased in 180 and added to the Botanical Garden which had existed since 173 Three hectares are covered with variety of both ancient and modern species. The greenhouse contain rare exotic plants as we as cacti and succulents. Rock gardens, flowers, medicinal and utilitarian plants all have their place here along with an orangery and beech grove.
Open Nov. 1 to Feb. : 8 - 5.
March 1 to May 31 : 8 - 7:30.
June 1 to Aug. 31 : 8 - 8.
Sept. 1 to 30 : 8 - 7.
Oct. 1 to 31 : 8 - 6.
Greenhouses open to the public Su days, Wednesdays and holidays : 2 -
Open on request for groups. Closed ring icy or freezing weather.
Parking.
Guided tours on request for groups.
Temporary exhibits.
Tel. : (31) 84.81.25 ext. 263.

Canon (Château).
Mézidon - 14270.
Caen or Lisieux : 25 km.
Bus service.
Property of the Delom de Méze family.

Canon owes its fame to its cre teo Elie de Beaumont, the famo lawyer and friend of Voltaire w built the square plan château the 18th century. Its false terrac and balusters are proof of its l lian inspiration. The vast symet cal out-buildings are sheltered linden trees. The château is s ounded by an Anglo-French pa with Carrac marble statues, a te ple, a Chinese kiosk and Ne Classical ruins scattered betwe the allées and ound the orn mental lake. Canon also boasts famous « Chartreuses », a uniq set of enclosed flower garder This preserved ensemble is architypical 18th century re dence.
Open daily July 1 to Sept. 31 : 2 - 6.
Weekends and holidays, Easter to Ju 30 : 2 - 6.
Groups on request out of season.
Closed Tuesdays.

ASSE-NORMANDIE — CALVADOS

rking.
uided tours, recommended itinerary.
nnels or leaflets.
glish, German, pannels or leaflets.
oncerts.
l. : (31) 20.02.72 or 20.05.07.

ourson (Manor House).

otre-Dame de Courson-Livarot
140.
sieux : 20 km.
rbec-Livarot : 10 km.
ation : Lisieux.
ivate property.
Courson was built at the end of e 15th century and at the beginng of the 16th century by Jean Neufville, seigneur de Courson. e manor house was enlarged d restored after 1663.
en May to Sept.
ounds only.
rking.
ided tours.
l. : (31) 32.30.69.

alaise (Castle).

aise - 14700.
ce Guillaume-le-Conquérant.
en : 30 km.
s service.
operty of the city.

There nas been a castle in Falaise since the 10th century. It saw the birth of William the Conqueror who spent his childhood here. The surviving edifice dates from the time of Henri I de Beauclerc who had it rebuilt around 1125. The heavily butressed main keep, the minor keep and the Talbot tower date from the 12th and 13th centuries. Captured by the English in 1418 and retaken by Charles VII in 1450, the fortress was also attacked in the Wars of Religion. After being partly destroyed and then abandoned restoration work was begun in 1864 under the supervision of Ruprich-Robert.
Open daily : 9 - 12, 2 - 6.
Closed Tuesdays and Sunday mornings, Mondays and Tuesdays from Oct. 1 to Palm Sunday.
Parking.
Information in English and German.
Guides and brochures.
Fireworks.
Guided tours.
Tel. : (31) 90.13.57.

Fervaques (Château).

The château comprises a postern and a 15th century manor house attached to a 17th century château of Classical proportions. It was the property of Delphine de Custine, a friend of Châteaubriand who stayed at the château. It is now a leisure and culture centre.
Open on request.
Parking.
Guided tours, brochures.
Facilities for the handicapped.
Concerts.
Temporary exhibitions.
Tel. : (31) 32.33.96.

Fontaine-Henry (Château).

Fontaine-Henry - 14610.
Caen : 13 km.
Property of M. J. d'Oilliamson.
Fontaine-Henry was built by the d'Harcourt family on the remains of a fortress inherited by the Tilly family. The 11th century vaults and the 12th and 13th century cellars

---

BRÉCY — CALVADOS

7th Century
Attributed to François Mansard. Fine carved gate. Terraced gardens embellished with vases, lions and 17th century stone balusters. At the top of the garden a wrought iron gate seems to open to the sky.
Beautiful 13th century church next to the garden. A spring which was once a pilgrimage site.

are left from the original building. The present château was begun under the reign of Charles VIII and finished under Henri II. It includes a richly sculptured Gothic pavilion which was completed during the Renaissance. The East face was completely remodeled under Louis XV. The exceptionally high pointed roof complete a château which houses important collections of paintings, furniture and objets d'art. The 13th century chapel had its nave transformed in the 16th century. The château has never ben sold and has belonged to the same family since its construction.
Open Easter to May 31, Wed. weekends and holidays : 2:30 - 6:30. June 1 to Sept. 15 : 2:30 - 6:30, daily except Tue. and Fri. Sept. 16 to Oct. 15 : Wed. and weekends : 2:30 - 6:30. Oct. 16 to Easter : Sun. and holidays : 2 - 6.
Groups on request.
Parking.
Guided tours.
English, German.
Concerts, Exhibitions.
Tel. : (31) 80.00.42.

HONFLEUR
Museum of Old Honfleur.

Honfleur - 14600.
Bus service.
Property of the Vieux Honfleur Society.
  The old half-timbered housed near the fromer gaol house a museum of Norman ethnography and folk art. There are twelve rooms full of a variety of collections including arms, ceramics, costumes, furniture and iconographic and historical mementoes of Honfleur. Reconstructed interiors show aspects of Norman daily life. A wooden 16th century manor house was brought from Lisieux and errected in the courtyard.
Open July 1 to Sept. 15 : 10:30 - 12, 2:30 - 6.
Groups on request from Jan. 1 to June 30 and Sept. 16 to Dec. 31.
Parking.
Guided tours.
Lectures.
Guided tours of Norman Monuments.
Tel. : (31) 89.14.12 or 89.05.38.

Lantheuil (Château).

Creully - 14480.
Bayeux : 14 km.
Station : Caen 19 km.
Private property.
  Lantheuil was built by Antoine Turgot de Saint-Clair in the second quarter of the 17th century. It is set in a fine parke of flower beds scattered with topiary, vases and sculpture, an 18th century terrace overlooks the garden. The château houses memorabilia of the Turgot family and their relatives. The main drawing room still has its 18th century portraits, furniture and decoration. The library was redecorated in Louis XIII style in the 19th century. Portraits of Franklin and Fénelon as well as of family members are part of this remarkable collection.
Open Easter to Oct. 15 : 2:30 - 6:30.
Oct. 16 to Easter, Sundays and holidays : 2 - 6.
Closed Tuesdays and Fridays in summer.
Parking.
Information in English.
Guided tours.
Tel. : (31) 80.11.12.

LISIEUX
Les Buissonnets (Saint Theresa's House).

  This is the family where Therese Martin, the girl who was to become Saint Theresa lived between 1877 and 1888. It comprises a main building constructed at the beginning of the 19th century which contains furniture dating from the second half of the century. Saint Theresa's life is traced throughout the visit.
Open July 1 to Oct. 3 : 9 - 12, 2 - 6.
Oct. 3 to Nov. 3 : 10 - 12, 2 - 5.
Nov. 3 to April 3 : 10 - 12, 2 - 4.
April 3 to July 1 : 9 - 12, 2 - 5:30.
Groups on request.
Parking.
Guided tours, brochures.
Pannels or leaflets.
English, Spanish, Portuguese, German, pannels or leaflets.
Lecture tours for school groups.
Tel. : (31) 62.08.70.

LONGUES-SUR-MER
Sainte-Marie (Abbey).

  Founded by Hugues Wac in the 11th century, Sainte Marie was at its height during the 13 and 14th centuries. The monk finally left in 1780. Among the remains of the Benedictine abbey are the choir of the church, the refectory with the gravestones and a rare collection of 13th century enamelled tiles. The abbot's quarters were remodelled in the 18th century.
Open Thursdays all year : 2 - 6.
Other days on request.
Parking.
Grounds only.
Guided tours, recommended itinerary.
Booklet.
English, German.
Tel. : (31) 21.78.41 and 21.92.72.

Mondaye (Abbey).

Juaye-Mondaye - 14250.
Station : Bayeux 6 km.
Private property.
  Founded at the beginning of th 13th century by canons of the Pre monstratensian order, Mondaye now a series of classical building remodelled in the 18th century b father Eustache Restout, architec painter and interior designer. Th sacristy, cloister, refectory, th Eastern façade, the main staircas and the library are all examples (Classical style and are in perfe(harmony with the abbey churc decorated with wood pannels an paintings.
Open Sundays 2 - 6. One hour tour wi an organ recital at the end.
Groups during the week by request.
July and August visits from 3 - 5.
Brochure.
Parking.
Tel. : (31) 92.58.11.

Mont-de-la-Vigne (Castle

Monteille - 14270.
Lisieux : 17 km.
Station : Mézidon 12 km.
Private property.
  Mont-de-la-Vigne is an old fc tress with three 14th century t wers and one from the 17th ce tury. The building materials are t pically Norman : pink brick, whi stone and half-timber. The chap dates from the 18th century. Pa tially destroyed during the la war, the castle was rebuilt by th present owner.
Open Sundays April 1 to Sept. 30 : 3 - Mondays Oct. 1 to March 30 : 3 - 6.
Parking.
English.
Tel. : (31) 63.02.22.

La Motte (Château).

Acqueville - 14220.
Caen : 28 km.
Property of M. Thibault.
  This fine 1660 château is set in beautiful park.
Open all year : 10 - 6.
Parking.
Grounds only.
Tel. : (31) 78.31.73.

Outrelaise (Château).

Bretteville-sur-Laize - 14680.
Caen and Falaise : 18 km.
Bus service.
Private property.
  Outrelaise has retained its 16 century entrance postern, its ou buildings and its main buildin flanked by a brick and stone wi

built in the 16th and 17th centuries.
Open May 1 to Oct. 31 : 3 - 6.
Grounds only.
Parking.
English.
Tel. : (31) 23.50.81.

Saint-Germain-de-Livet (Château).

Lisieux - 14100.
Lisieux : 10 km.
Station : Lisieux.
Property of the commune of Lisieux.

Saint-Germain-de-Livet was built in the 16th and 17th centuries by the Tournebu family. It is surrounded by a moat and owes its particular charm to the checkered pattern of its white stone and green varnished bricks, its pink, red, yellow and green tiles and red brick visible on the round tower and arcaded gallery. The interior is furnished with 18th and 19th century furniture and paintings by Léon Riesener, a cousin of Delacroix.

Open April 1 to Sept. 30 : 10 - 12, 2 - 7.
Oct. 1 to March 31 : 10 - 12, 2 - 5.
Closed Tuesdays.
Parking.
Guided tours, brochures.
English, German, pannels or leaflets.
Temporary exhibits.
Lecture tours for school groups.
Tel. : (31) 31.00.03.

Saint-Gabriel (Priory).

Saint-Gabriel-Brécy - 14480.
Bayeux : 10 km.
Station : Bayeux or Caen 20 km.
Bus service.
Private property.

Founded in 1058 by the Benedictine abbey of Fécamp, this priory played an important part in the reconversion of the area after the Viking invasions. It has retained its monastic buildings and in particular the gate house, refectory, ecclesiastic court and choir of the 12th century church.

Open June 1 to Aug. 31 : 2 - 7.
Sept. 1 to May 31 : 2 - 5.
Grounds only.
Unaccompanied visit.

JUAYE-MONDAYE

CALVADOS

In a tranquil green setting on the side of a hill, the Abbey of Mondaye, founded at the beginning of the 13th century by canons of the Premonstratensian order is now a remarkable collection of Classical buildings created in the 18th century by father Eustache Restout, prior of the abbey, architect painter and interior designer assisted by the Flemish sculptor Melchior Verly.
The abbey church has unusual vaults, an organ by Parizot and a Lady Chapel with the most beautiful Assomption in France carved by Verly.
Premonstratensian Fathers still occupy the buildings built by and for them. The community welcomes all those who wish to share a bit of their life.

CALVADOS/MANCHE

English, German, recorded commentary, leaflets.
Temporary exhibits.
Tel. : (31) 80.10.20.

Saint-Hippolyte (Manor House).
The manor house was built on the bank of the Touques in Flamboyant Gothic style in the 16th century. It includes a main building of limestone surmounted by brick and two half timbered dormer windows. The dovecote dates from the same period.
Unaccompanied visits.
Tel. : (31) 31.03.52.

Vendeuvre (Château).
Saint-Pierre-sur-Dives - 14170.
Lisieux or Caen : 30 km
Station : Saint-Pierre-sur-Dives 5 km.
Property of M. G. de Vendeuvre.

Alexandre le Forestier, comte de Vendeuvre, built the château in 1750 according to plans by Blondel. It has remained in the family ever since. The château is surrounded by a park and its white stone fore-part is surmounted by a pediment. The salons still have their Louis XV wood panelling. The 18th century orangery houses a unique collection of miniature furniture and presentation pieces from all over Europe.
Open daily May 1 to Sept. 2 : 2 - 7.
Parking.
Unaccompanied visits, brochures.
Pannels or leaflets.
Tel. : (31) 40.93.83.

MANCHE

Cerisy (Château).
Cerisy-la-Salle - 50210.
Saint-Lô - Coutance : 15 km.
Station : Carantilly-Marigny 5 km.
Private property.

Cerisy is built on the site of an 11th century castle destroyed during the Wars of Religion when had been one of the most important Protestant strongholds in th region. The current château date from 1605 and the reign o Henri IV. It includes a central bui ding flanked by four pavilions an a staircase. Although its moat i old fashioned, the peaked roc and narrow Renaissance stly wi dows are typical of the taste of th period. The château is now a cu tural centre which hosts colloqui seminars and workshops.
Open on request Thursdays in Augus 2:30 - 5.
Parking.
Brochures.
Concerts.
Temporary exhibits.
Tel. : (33) 46.91.66.

Cerisy-la-Forêt (Abbey).
Cerisy-la-Forêt - 50680.
Saint-Lô : 18 km.
Bayeux : 22 km.
Station : Lisieux 10 km.
Property of the commune.

The charter of Cerisy-la-Forê was granted by Robert the Magn ficent Duke of Normandy, in 103 Built between 1035 and 1110, th

---

VENDEUVRE

CALVADOS

Hundreds of 18th to 20th century miniature pieces of furniture, presentation piesces, models, and childrens furniture from the world over are presented among the orange trees. Each miniature is unique and combines originality and perfect craftsmanship.

bbey has retained its church with its three tiered apse and its Romanesque buildings which include a hall of justice, cell and gatehouse. The monk's furniture, manuscripts and ancient documents can be seen in the museum housed in the hall of justice.
Open Sundays and holidays, March 15 to June 30 : 2 - 6.
July 1 to Sept. 15 : 10 - 12, 2:30 - 6:30 and 2 - 6 on Sundays and holidays.
Open on request the rest of the year.
Parking.
Guided tours available.
Pannels of leaflets, brochures.
English, German, Dutch, pannels and leaflets.
Concerts, temporary exhibits.
Tel. : (33) 56.10.01.

CHERBOURG
Vœu or Chantereyne Abbey.
Cherbourg - 50108.
Rue de l'Abbaye.
Bus service.
Property of the commune.

Empress Mathilda, William the Conqueror's grand daughter founded the Abbey in 1087 after being spared in a storm. Remains include the foundations of the sacristy, part of the church, the chapterhouse, the refectory, a gallery and the ruins of the d'Harcourt house all in cours of restoration.
Grounds only.
Parking.
Tel. : (33) 44.55.20.

Coigny (Château).
Coigny - 50250.
Carentan : 15 km.
Cherbourg : 50 km.
Property of M. Ionckheere.

This seat of the Coigny family whose members included several marshals of France was built at the beginning of the 17th century then abandoned in 1670. The Louis XIII building contains a polychrome monumental fireplace and is flanked by a brick stair tower built at the end of the 19th century and by a modern building in Louis XIII style. The château is surrounded by a moat except on the side of the out buildings which are now a farm.
Open July 1 to Sept. 30 : 2 - 5.
Out of season on request.
Closed Tuesdays.
Parking.
Guided tours, brochures.
Lecture tours for archeological groups and tourist groups.
Tel. : (33) 42.10.79.

Courcy (Château).
Fontenay-sur-Mer.
Montebourg - 50310.
Valognes : 12 km.
Station : Valognes.
Private property.

Courcy dates from the 17th century as its little pointed pediment, small wings and slate roof clearly show. Large Second Empire cast iron vases decorated with children and garlands are situated on either side of the gate leading into the main courtyard giving a pleasing

CERISY-LA-FORÊT
MANCHE

An Abbey built by Robert the Magnificent, Duke of Normandy.

An abbey church of pure Romanesque style with three remaining bays.
The apse contains three stories of windows.
Fourteenth century stalls. Abbots chapel accessible through the old gateway.
The hall of justice which houses furniture, reliquaries, parchment and vestments.
The cell with walls covered in grafitti houses pieces of pottery and sculpture.
Guided tours or unaccompanied visits.

Baroque note to the comfortable friendliness of the residence.
Interiors open on request March 1 to Nov. 30 : 2 - 7.
Closed Sundays.
Parking.
Tel. : (33) 41.14.56.

Dur-Écu (Manor House).

Urville-Nacqueville - 50460.
Cherbourg : 12 km.
Private property.

Although it was seriously damaged in 1944, Dur-Écu has retained several buildings divided by 15th and 16th century granite towers. Situated high above the sea and surrounded by trees the complex is now being restored.
Open April 1 to Sept. 30 : 11 - 6.
Closed Mondays and Tuesdays.
Parking.
Grounds only.

Gonneville (Château).

Gonneville-Fermanville - 50480.
Cherbourg : 14 km.
Station : Cherbourg.
Property of M. de Barthes de Montfort.

Built in the 16th century, Gonneville is surrounded by a moat and includes a main building, two older service wings and a watch tower. A square postern once defended the drawbridge.
Open June 1 to Oct. 15 : 9 - 12, 2 - 7.
Closed Sunday mornings.
Parking.
Lecture tours.
Nature park.
Guided tours available.
Tel. : (33) 22.90.92.

Gratot (Château).

Gratot - 50200.
Coutances : 4 km.
Bus service.
Private property.

Gratot is medieval fortress surrounded by a moat. Although it was built in the 14th century transformations continued until the 18th century. For four centuries i was the property of the d'Ar gouges family. Restoration was begun in 1968. The octagonal to wer « the Fairy Tower » is the architectural and legendary centre of the château.
Open all year.
Parking.
Unaccompanied visits.
Pannels or leaflets.
Audiovisual programmes in summer.
English, German, Dutch.
Festivals, exhibits.
Tel. : (31) 85.25.93.

Hambye (Abbey).

Hambye - 50650.
Saint-Lô : 30 km.
Station : Villedieu 11 km.
Property of the department and privat property.

Founded by Guillaume Paynel i 1145, this Benedictine abbey situa ted in the Sienne valley has reta ned many of its original building The chapter house in unusual its double vaulted nave. Althoug the cloister has disappeared, th mortuary, werming-room and pa lour survive. The farm building house paintings furniture, tapestr

---

MANCHE

MARTINVAST

A château protected by the Monuments Historiques.
Its classified English park.
Its stud farm.

Its out-buildings converted into rented residences.
Its classified 18th century obelisk.
Its Norman Romanesque church.

Photo C. de Pourtalès

d sculpture is to be seen in the brothers' dwellings.
en Feb. 1 to April 1 and Sept. 30 to c. 31 : 10 - 12, 2 - 5:30.
ril 1 to Sept. 30 : 10 - 12, 2 - 6.
ups on request.
sed Wednesdays.
king.
ded tours, leaflets.
lish, German, Flemish, Spanish, Italian, Danish.
rmation pannels, brochures.
ture tours.
ncerts, exhibits.
: (50) 61.76.92.

Lucerne (Abbey).

Lucerne d'Outremer - 50320.
nville : 12 km.
ion.
service.
ate property.
ounded in 1143 by Premonstrasian monks, La Lucerne is sited on the edge of the Thar val
The monastic buildings date n the 12th century but were sformed in the 17th century. cloister was rebuilt between 0 and 1712. The abbot's palace ated on the far side of a basin, es from the 17th century and statues from the 12th and 17th. abbey was turned into a textile ory at the Revolution. It has n in course of restoration since 9. The Cistercian style church been reconsecrated.
en all year : 9 - 12, 2 - 6:30.
ing.
ded tours in July and August.
mation pannels or leaflets.
lish, German, Dutch, Danish.
hure.
certs, exhibits.
: (33) 48.83.56.

artinvast (Château).

invast - 50690.
aine de Beaurepaire.
rbourg : 7 km.
service.
te property.
artinvast has retained its 11th tury which is now linked to the century by a 19th century addition. The west wing and the terrace with its Gothic cloister are all that remain of the château built by Barthole de Moncel. Between 1867 and 1870 baron Schickler transformed it in the Neo-Gothic style.
Open all year, sunrise to sunset.
Parking.
Grounds only.
Unaccompanied visits.
English, German.
Tel. : (33) 52.02.23.

Mont-Saint-Michel (Abbey).

Le Mont-Saint-Michel - 50112.
Property of the State.
The Benedictine abbey of Mont-Saint-Michel was a major pilgrimage site between the 8th and 16th centuries. Today it is one of the finest examples of Medieval religious and military architecture. For lack of space the buildings had to be errected on top of each other ; their grandeur attest to the continued importance of the chapel dedicated to the archangel Michael by the bishop of Avranche in 708. Aubert, the most brilliant of the builders surpassed his predessors by constructing « the Marvel », an ingenious conglomeration of guest and knights quarters and a cloister which combines monumentality and elegant ornementation. In the 15th century the High Gothic choir completed the pyramid of structures built around the pre-Romanesque church of Notre-Dame-sous-Terre. Mont-Saint-Michel became a powerful fortress during the Hundred Years War and a prison from the 15th to the 19th centuries. Protected as an historic monument since 1874, restoration has taken almost a century.
Open daily from Palm Sunday to Sept. 30 : 9:30 - 5:30.
Oct. 1 to Palm Sunday : 10 - 12, 2 - 4:30.
Parking.
Lecture tours, brochures.
Information rooms.
Tel. : (33) 60.14.14.

MORTAIN
Blanche Abbey.

Mortain - 50140.
Station : Vire 25 km.
Bus service.
Property of the Fathers of the Holy Spirit.
This Cistercian abbey has a history closely linked to that of the county of Mortain. The convent was founded by Saint Vital's sister Adeline and was very important from the 12th century to the Revolution. In accordance with the Cistercian plan the chapter house, church and refectory are arranged around a 12th century cloister. 15th and 17th century stalls remain.
Open all year : 10 - 12, 2 - 6.
Closed Tuesdays.
Parking.
Guided tours from July 1 to Sept. 15.
English, German.
Brochure.
Music festival of Mont Saint Michel.
Concerts.
Tel. : (33) 59.00.21.

Nacqueville (Château).

Urville-Nacqueville - 50460.
Cherbourg : 6 km.
Bus service.
Private property.
Located in a green valley near a river and a basin, Nacqueville was built by Jean II de Grimaville under François I and completed by his son. The château is entered through a drawbridge surmonted by a postern flanked by two towers. The main building is made of granite and has been transformed throughout the centuries. It is surrounded by a square pavilion and a round tower. The château is set in an English garden.

Open April 1 to Sept. 30 : 2 - 3, 4 - 5.
On request for large groups.
Closed Tuesdays and Fridays except holidays.
Parking.
Guided tours.
Tel. : (33) 03.56.03.

Pirou (Castle).

This imposing 12 the century fortress is located on a hill surrounded by an artificial pond, a site fortified since the time of the Norman invasions. Its high shale and sandstone walls date from the 12th century. Inside the inner court are two separate dwellings : the older was built under Henri IV and the more recent under Louis XIV in 1708. There is also and 18th century chapel and a tapestry of the conquest of Puglia and Sicily.
Open daily March 1 to Sept. 30 : 9 - 12, 2 - 7.
Oct. 1 to March 1 : 9 - 12, 2 - 5:30.
Closed Dec. 15 to Jan. 15.
Closed Tuesdays.
Parking.
Guided tours available.
English, German, Dutch, Danish.
Leaflets or information pannels.
Brochures.
Exhibits.
Tel. : (33) 48.83.56.

Saint-Pierre-Église (Château).

Saint-Pierre-Église - 50330.
Cherbourg : 17 km.
Bus service.
Private property.
This granite château was built in the 18th century and comprises three classical style pavilions. A long avenue leads to a building with a beautiful staircase with an unusual balustrade an Louis XV wood pannelling. It is surrounded by a walled park.
Open on request for groups.
Parking.
Tel. : (33) 54.31.38.

VALOGNES
Hôtel de Beaumont.

Valognes - 50700.
Rue Barbey-d'Aurevilly.
Cherbourg : 18 km.
Station : Valognes.
Bus service.
Private property.
Built in the mid-18th century the comte de Beaumont in pur Classical style, this private to house has remained intact. T monumental staircase domina the hall and Louis XV furniture f the dining room, drawing roo and library. The gardens and races have been restored.
Open July 1 to Sept. 15 : 2:30 - 6.
Closed Wednesdays.
Parking.
Guided tours.
English.
Tel. : (33) 40.12.30.

ORNE

Argentelles (Manor House).

Villebadin - Exmes - 61310.
Argentan : 14 km.

NACQUEVILLE

MANCHE

Situated only a few kilometers from Cherbourg, Nacqueville is a typical Cotentin manor house with its granite walls and stone roof. Nestled in a green valley, the château is surrounded by an English garden in full bloom from May to October. It is the ideal destination for lovers of fine houses and beautiful gardens.

tion : Argentan.
ate property.
Argentelles was built at the be-
ning of the 15th century by
illot d'Ouilly. Dating from the
ndred Years War, this little for-
ss with its slit windows and
g walls is more reminiscent of
architecture of the Loire valley
n of the Auge. The manor today
uses a museum.
en April 1 to Sept. 30 : 4 - 7, Sun-
s aon on request.
king.
: (33) 67.93.61.

Bérardière
(Manor House).

t-Bomer-les-Forges - 61700.
s : 16 km.
perty of M. Roulleaux Dugage.
a Bérardière is made up of a
n building, two entrance pavi-
s and a chapel built in 1697. A
h century pavilion remains from
old manor house. One wing
s added in 1920. The interior in-
des a large staircase and wood
nelled rooms.
unds open on Sundays.
riors on request.

Parking.
Guided tours of the interiors.
English, Spanish, guide.
Tel. : (33) 37.60.56.

Carrouges (Château).

Carrouges - 61320.
Alençon : 30 km.
Property of the State.
 The successive owners of Carrouges have managed to keep the
military aspect of this ancient fortress situated on the border between Maine and Normandy. The
main courtyard is surrounded by
brick and granite walls which rise
above the moat. Next to the Medieval keep and 15th century building, the Le Veneur family who
owned the château until 1936, added wings in the 16th century. The
complex was completed by a
small fortified entrance gate. The
State has faithfully reconstructed
the 17th and 18th century interiors.
The out-buildings house the headquarters of the Normandy-Maine
regional park.

Open April 1 to Sept. 30 : 9 - 12, 2 - 6.
Oct. 1 to March 31 : 10 - 12, 2 - 4.
Closed Tuesdays.
Parking.
Guided tours, brochures.
Pannels.
Tel. : (33) 27.20.32.

PIROU

MANCHE

s the lords of Pirou were the allies of
e 11th century Norman conquerors of
icily and Southern Italy, in July and
ugust of each year a piece of
mbroidery in the style of the Bayeux
pestry is exhibited at the castle. The
ool embroidery on linen is a colourful
humouristic account of the Viking
conquest of Normandy (including the
legend of the defenders of Pirou changing into geese to escape the invaders)
and then of Calabria, Puglia and Sicily.

The castle is open from Jan. 15 to Dec. 15.

ORNE

CHÂTEAU D'O
15 th - 17th centuries
A furnished inhabited residence

The château d'O is a page in the seigneurial and architectural history of France. It rises out of a pond which forms its natural moat and has beautiful carved Gothic façades and a high pointed slate roof. Each generation has done its best to embellish it. The O family has had many famous members from Crusaders to the minister of finance and favorite of Henri II, François d'O. The interiors, including salons with 17th and 18th century murals and a beautiful 30 meter long gallery are open to the public. The inner courtyard shows the appearance of Renaissance style in its fine arcades carved with Italian style motifs.

Cinema. Television. Theatre. Music. Advertising. Exhibitions. Trade Fairs. Conferences. Receptions. Crafts. La Ferme d'O Restaurant.

Open all year.
Tours every morning on request, except Tuesdays
Mortrée, 61570.
Tel. : (33) 35.33.56.

Photo S. Peignot

BASSE-NORMANDIE — 273 — ORNE

Champobert (Château).

Sillebadin - Exmes - 61310.
Argentan : 13 km.
Property of M. du Mesnil du Buisson.
Champobert was built in 1850 according to two 18th century plans. It is surrounded by a park. A nearby chapel contains a 14th century stone statue of the Virgin, a great crucifix attributed to Jean Goujon and a piece of embroidery made by the Carmelites of Bourges for Louis XIV.
Open by request, written or telephoned.
Parking.
Tel. : (33) 67.93.61.

Chêne-Galon (Abbaye).

Perrais - 61400.
Bellême : 4,5 km.
Sellavilliers : 3 km.
Private property.
Founded in the 11th century on the orders of Grand-Mont, Chêne Galon Abbey became the country property of the bishop of Sées in the 18th century. The large building was errected in the 14th century and transformed in the 17th.
Open July 1 to Aug. 25 : 3 pm and om.

Closed Tuesdays.
Parking.
Guided tours.

Médavy (Château).

Médavy - 61570.
Argentan : 12 km.
Station : Almenesches 0,5 km.
Private property.
The moat and watch towers of Médavy survive from the 12th century fortress. Built at the beginning of the 18th century by the maréchal de Médavy-Grancey, the château is made up of a slightly protruding central pavilion whose two wings end in massive edifices. One was rebuilt in the 19th century. Both château and outbuilding have Manxsard roofs. Formal garden.

Open daily July 14 to Sept. 9 : 10 - 12, 2 - 6:30.
On request out of season.
Parking.
Guided tours, brochure.
English, German, Italian, short descriptions.
Tel. : (33) 35.34.54.

Photo S. Peignot

O (Château).

Mortée - 61500.
Sées : 8 km.
Station : Surdon 6 km.
Private property.
The château was built in the 16th century by Jean d'O on the site of a fortress destroyed in the Hundred Years War. The collection of pavilions and turrets with

SAINT-SAUVEUR

ORNE

Saint-Sauveur, the jewel of the Norman countryside rebuilt in 1641 on the remains of a 13th century castle, is reflected in the wide free running moat : the formal garden and 16th century chapel add to its charm. The Louis XIII wood pannelled interiors are decorated with furniture and paintings from the 17th to 18th century with all the charm of an inhabited residence.

Open all year.
Easter to May 31 : weekends and holidays : 2:30 - 6:30.
June 1 to August 31 : afternoons (except Tuesdays and Wednesdays) 2:30 - 6:30.
Oct. 1 to Easter : Sundays and holidays (except February) : 2:30 - 4:30.
Open on special request for groups.
Sainte-Honorine-la-Chardonne
61430 Athis-de-l'Orne.

Photo A. Bouchard

their high ponted roofs are typical of late Gothic and Renaissance style. The Château is surrounded by a large moat. The Renaissance gallery decorated with marble paint matches the salon with its paintings of Apollo and the Nine Muses. François d'O, Henri II's minister of finance led a luxurious, ostentatious life here. By the time he died he had lost his fortune and the château was sold. The buildings have been remarkable well restored over the past few years.
Open Nov. 1 to April 15 : 2:30 - 5.
April 16 to Oct. 31 : 10 - 12, 2 - 6.
Closed Tuesdays.
Parking.
Guided tours.
Foreign languaged.
Guide.
Pannels of leaflets.
Concerts.
Folk dancing and singing.
Exhibitions, music festivals.
Tel. : (33) 35.33.56.

Pontgirard (Manor House).

Monceaux - 61290.
Longny-au-Perche : 5 km.
Station : Condé-sur-Huisne 17 km.
Property of M. P. Siguret.
    Pontgirard was built in the 16th century by a family of iron masters, the Chouets, who were related to the marechal de Catinat and to Juchereau, who were responsible for the Percheron emigration to Canada. The gabled main building is entered via a horseshoe-shaped staircase. To the back, the wing comprises a square tower with a pavilion roof. It opens onto a terraced garden.
Grounds only.
Tel. : (33) 73.61.49.

Rabodanges (Château).

Rabodanges - 61120.
Near Falaise.
Station : Briouze 15 km.
Private property.
    Built in the 17th century on the site of an ancient castle, Rabondanges is set in a park enclosed by a wrought iron fence. The pedimented chaplain's house, the moat and the terraced garden are intact.
Open weekdays in July and September : 10 - 12, 2 - 4:30.
Groupes on request out of season.
Closed weekends.
Grounds only.
Parking.
Guided tours.
Tel. : (33) 35.04.76.

Saint-Sauveur (Château).

Sainte-Honorine-la-Chardonne - 61430 Athis-de-l'Orne.
Flers : 13 km.
Caen : 50 km.
Station : Flers.
Private property.
    Saint-Sauveur was built in 1641 on the remains of a 13th century castle destroyed in the Wars of Religion. It is granite with curved slate roofs. The moat is surrounded by a balustrade. The interior houses old paintings and furniture.
Open weekends June 1 to Aug. 31 : 2:30 - 6:30.
Sundays and holidays, Oct. 1 to May 31 : 2:30 - 6:30.
Closed Tuesdays and Wednesdays.
Parking.
Guided tours, brochures.
English, Spanish, guide.
Lecture tours for school groups.
Tel. : (33) 66.40.13.

Sassy (Château).

Argentan - 61200.
Argentan : 10 km.
Station : Argentan.
Property of M. d'Audiffret Pasquier.
    Sassy was built in 1760 at the top of a hill on the site of an ancient castle. In 1850 Chancellor Pasquier enlarged it in the same brick and stone style to house his library of 30 000 volumes which he brought from Paris. The long perpendicular wing which separates the main courtyard from the stables dates from the beginning of the 20th century. A pond is set in the formal garden.
Open daily July July 1 to Aug. 31 : 3 - 6 sta. and Sunday March to November.
Other times on request.
Parking.
Guided tours, brochures.
English, Spanish, German.
Facilities for the handicapped.
Tel. : (33) 35.32.66.

Le Tertre (Manor House).

Sérigny - 61130.
Nogent-le-Rotrou : 20 km.
Private property.
    Built under Louis XIII by Gilles Bry de la Clergerie, historian of La Perche, Le Tertre is a fine bri... and stone dwelling. Roger Mart... du Gard was so fond of this rema... kable site that he made it his pr... ferred residence and wrote man... of his books here. The quiet se... ting is full of literary memories.
Open only on request.
Grounds only.
Guided tours.
Organised lecture tours.
Tel. : (33) 73.18.30.

La Vove (Manor House).

Corbon - 61400.
Mortagne-au-Perche.
Station : Condé-sur-Luisne 10 km.
Private property.
    Built in the 16th and 17th cent... ries by the seigneurs de la Vov... the manor later belonged to t... marquis de Langan et de Glapio... It became a farm at the Revol... tion. The keep, octagonal tow... chapel and interior court still s... vive. Its main building is filled w... peasant furniture.
Open daily April 1 to Oct. 30 : 10 - 1 2 - 7.
Parking.
Guided tours.
Concerts.
Tel. : (33) 83.80.01.

HAUTE-NORMANDIE
EURE, SEINE-MARITIME.

■ castle, château, manor house
● abbey, priory
▲ garden, park
★ town house, famous men house, farm, mill...
○ city

ROUEN
- ★ Petite Couronne Maison de Pierre Corneille
- ★ Tour Jeanne d'Arc
- ● Abbatiales St-Ouen
- ▲ Jardin des plantes

ST-MARTIN-DE-BOSCHERVILLE
- ● Abbaye St-Georges
- ★ Ferme des Templiers

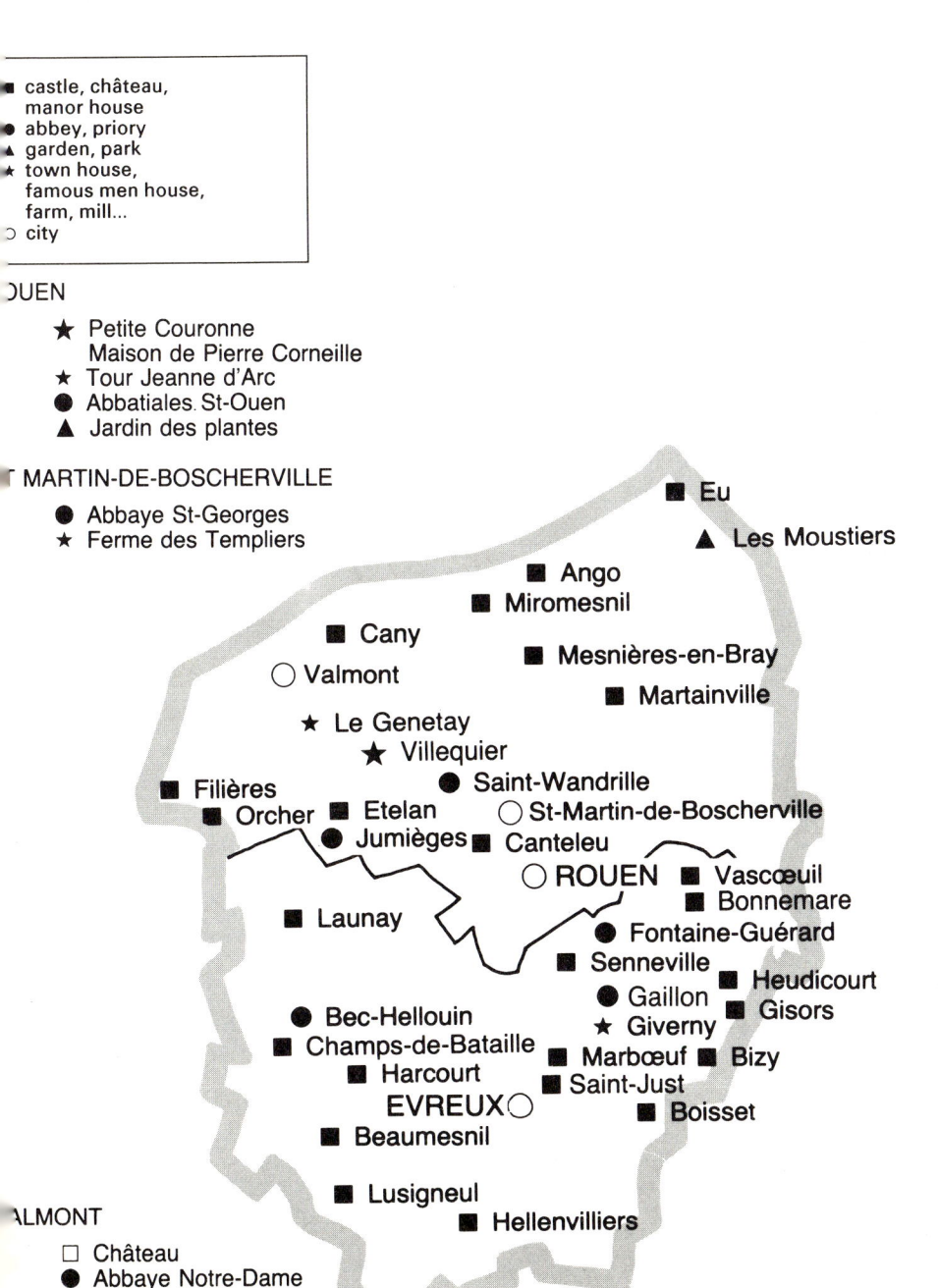

VALMONT
- □ Château
- ● Abbaye Notre-Dame

■ Eu
▲ Les Moustiers
■ Ango
■ Miromesnil
■ Cany
■ Mesnières-en-Bray
○ Valmont
■ Martainville
★ Le Genetay
★ Villequier
● Saint-Wandrille
■ Filières
○ St-Martin-de-Boscherville
■ Orcher ■ Etelan
● Jumièges ■ Canteleu
○ ROUEN ■ Vascœuil
■ Bonnemare
■ Launay
● Fontaine-Guérard
■ Senneville
■ Heudicourt
● Gaillon
● Bec-Helouin ★ Giverny ■ Gisors
■ Champs-de-Bataille
■ Marbœuf ■ Bizy
■ Harcourt ■ Saint-Just
EVREUX○ ■ Boisset
■ Beaumesnil
■ Lusigneul
■ Hellenvilliers

EURE

Beaumesnil (Château).
Beaumesnil - 27410.
Bernay : 10 km.
Private property.

The Rouen architect Jean Gaillard was comissioned to build Beaumesnil for Marie Dauvets des Marets, marquise de Nonant. One of the finest examples of Louis XIII brick and stone architecture, it is mirrored by a large moat. The staircase is the focal point of the edifice : it occupies one quarter of the building. The Louis XIII furniture and ancient objects of the dining room are placed next to the grand salon. The château contains a museum of book binding.
Open May 15 to Sept. 15 : 2 - 6.
Groups on request.
Parking.
Leaflets.
Recorded commentary.
Brochure.
Tel. : (32) 44.40.09.

Le Bec Hellouin (Abbey).
Notre-Dame-du-Bec/Brionne - 27800.
Property of the State.

Established at its present site by the Chevalier Hellouin around 1035, the abbey had a great intellectual influence in the 11th century thanks to the theologians Lanfranc and Saint Anselme. The current monastery was rebuilt in the 17th and 18th centuries by the community of Saint Maur. It surrounds a vast courtyard adjoining the cloister and comprises two remarkable rooms, the new and the old refectories. The high Saint Nicholas tower survives from the 15th century. Since 1948 Le Bec Hellouin has housed a community of Olivetan minks who have been able to give new life to the buildings which had been damaged by their previous use as Army stables.
Open daily 9 - 11, 3 - 5.
Tel. : (32) 44.86.09.

Bizy (Château).
Vernon - 27200.
Private property.

The first château was built 1720 by Constant d'Ivry for Fouquet, the surintendant's grandson. It belonged to the duc de Penthièvre and Louis XV before being

---

BEAUMESNIL

EURE

Beaumesnil is one of the finest Louis XIII château in France. Built between 1633 and 1640, it is also the most important Baroque châteaux in the country.

Its park and gardens have been reconstructed according to the originals plans and its museum of bookbinding is unique in France.

Open May 15 to Sept. 15 : Mon., Fri., and weekends : 2:30 - 6.

HAUTE-NORMANDIE — EURE

zed at the Revolution. The famous stables modelled on Versailles and the fountains and cascade were spared. Baron Schickler had the present edifice built in 1858 in Italian style. The grandiose façade comprises a ground floor with a Doric central portal and Ionic Columns on the two stories. The fountains and cascades of the garden are Italian in inspiration. In 1909 the duke of Albufera inherited the property and restored the 18th century buildings. The château, still belongs to his family and contains Empire memorabilia.
Open April 1 to Nov. 1.
Parking.
Tel. : (32) 51.00.82.

Boisset-les-Prévanches (Château).

Pacy-sur-Eure - 27120.
Évreux : 17 km.
Pacy-sur-Eure : 7 km.
Station : Boisset 1 km.
Property of the de Mézières family in 1499 and then of the Lespinasse-Langeac family since 1776. The complex is grouped around a brick and stone château built in 1580. The façades and the roof are or equal height. Next to the château and park is a large traditional Norman farm. Across from these two buildings is an English style house built in 1891. The 120 seat theatre built in 1912 has been recently restored and reopened.
Open May 1 to Sept. 30.
Groups of at least 20.
Parking.
Guided tours.
English.
Tel. : (32) 36.80.05.

Bonnemare (Château).

Radepont - Fleury s/Andelle - 27380.
Rouen : 25 km.
Paris : 97 km by the N. 14.
Private property.
Bonnemare is situated in Radepont overlooking the Andelle valley. It is a fine picturesque Renaissance complex including a fortified entrance on the road, château and round chapel attributed to Philibert de l'Orme or to one of his pupils. It was built around 1570 for a magisdtrate of the Normandy parlement. The original interiors date from the 16th, 17th and 18th centuries. In the 1660 farm buildings are apple presses.
Open for groups of 20 by appointment June 1 to July 31 and Sept. 1 to Dec. 15.
Tel. : (32) 49.03.73.

Champ-de-Bataille (Château).

Sainte-Opportune - Le Neubourg - 27110.
Evreux, Lisieux : 28 km.
Private property.
On the site of the 17th century château, a terrible battle had been fought in 935. The building's unusual plan comprises two identical wings, one for the masters and one for the servants. The architect is unknown. The interiors include original Louis XVI coloured stucco decoration and 18th century salons.
Open April 15 to Dec. 11, daily except Tuesdays : 10:30 to sunset.
Dinner and candlelight visits weekends 9:30 pm to 11:30 pm.
Parking.
Guided tours, brochures. English.
Temporary exhibits.
Cultural activities.
Golf.
Video games and computer centre.
Tel. : (32) 35.03.72.

Fontaine-Guérard (Abbey).

Radepont - 27380.
Rouen : 25 km.
Property of the Salvation Army.
This Cistercian abbey was begun in 1132 by Robert-White-Hands, Earl of Leicester. It was completed in 1198. The early Gothis style is visible in the remains of the church, chapter house, parlour and work room. The abbey enjoyed the protection of John Lackland, Saint Louis, Philip Augustus, Philip the Bold and others.
Open April 1 to Oct. 31 : 2 - 6.
Closed Mondays.
Parking.
Unaccompanied visits, brochures.
Tel. : (32) 49.03.82.

Gaillon (Château).

Gaillon - 27600.
Paris : 85 km.
Former residence of the Archbishops of Rouen, this sumptuous Renaissance residence built in the Italian style dominates the town of Gaillon with its old Norman houses along the banks of the Seine. The château has recently been restored.
Tel. : (32) 52.65.98.

Gisors (Castle).

Gisors - 27140.
Rue de Penthièvre.
Paris : 70 km.
Station : Gisors 1 km.
Property of the commune.
Gisors reflects Franco-English history through the different phases of its construction. William Ruffus, William the Conqueror's son was responsible for the keep built in 1096. Henry Plantagenet fortified it and built the outer wall. The second keep, the « Prisoners Tower » was the work of Philip Augustus. The vaulted cellars date from the 12th century. The fortress is surrounded by a large park.
Open daily April 1 to Sept. 30.
Park : 8 am to 8 pm. Guided tours : 10 - 12, 2 - 6 except Tuesdays.
Oct. 1 to March 31 : 8 - 6. Guided tours weekends 11 - 12, 2 - 5.
Guided tours.
English, German, pannels.
Festivals.
Temporary art exhibits.
Tel. : (32) 55.20.28.

Giverny (Claude Monet's House).

Giverny - 27620.
Vernon : 3 km.

Station : Vernon 7 km.
Property of the Institut de France.
It was in this comfortable house that Claude Monet received Clemenceau, Renoir, Manet, Siseley, Pissaro... He lived here between 1883 and 1926. His furniture remains as does his collection of Japanese prints. His famous gardens and lily pond have been completely restored.
Open April 1 to Oct. 31 : 10 - 6 for the gardens and 10 - 12, 2 - 6 for the house.
Closed Mondays.
Parking.
Unaccompanied visits, brochures.
Tel. : (32) 51.28.21.

Harcourt (Château and Arboretum).

Harcourt - 27800.
Brionne and Le Neubourg : 6 km.
Station : Evreux, Honfleur.
Property of the Académie d'Agriculture de France.
Harcourt was given by Rollon to one of his companions, an ancestor of the Harcourt family which stretches over nine centuries. Harcourt is a fine example of medieval military architecture with its fortifications and deep moat, its service court, fort and residence « modernized » in the 17th century. Today Harcourt is surrounded by a famous arboretum which includes 1000 rare species.
Open daily June 15 to Sept. 15.
Sundays and holidays out of season.
Groups of 40 by appointment.
Parking.
Recorded information.
Pannels or leaflets.
Labeled trees.
Temporary exhibits.
Tel. : (32) 35.00.01.

Hellenvilliers (Manor house).

Le Mesnil-Jourdain - 27400.
Louviers : 6 km.
Private property.
This manorial dwelling was essentially built by the lords of Hellenvilliers between 1420 and 1580. The three main buildings are placed around a square courtyard next to the church. The first was built in the 15th century in stone and flint. The second, built in the 16th century is half-timnered and has a stair tower, the third is 17th century cut stone.
Open school holidays and weekends.
Groups on request.
Parking.
Grounds only.
English.
Tel. : (32) 50.53.00.

Heudicourt (Château).

Heudicourt - 27860.
Gisors : 12 km.
Station : Gisors.
Private property.
This Louis XIII brick and stone château set in formal gardens is reached by an avenue and esplanade. Inside is a collection of 17th century furniture and some very interesting Flemish and French paintings as memorabilia of Madame de Maintenon who was a friend of Madame de Heudicourt in the 17th century.
Open March 25 to Nov. 1.
Groups on request.
Parking.
Guided tours, brochures.
Recorded information.
Camping.
Tel. : (32) 55.86.06.

Launay (Château).

Saint-Georges-du-Vièvre - 27450.
Bernay : 20 km.
Station : Bernay.
Private property.
Launay is Regency château surrounded by typically Norman 16th century out-buildings and dovecote. The interiors and wood pannelling have remained intact.
Grounds only.
Open all year.

Lusigneul (Château).

Montreuil-l'Argilé - 27390.
Bernay : 20 km.
Station : Bernay.
Bus service.
Private property.
Built in the 13th century when France and England were fighting over Normandy, the château was extensively remodelled in 1600 when it acquired its T- shape plan. The final transformations were carried out in 1800. Its brick and stone façade is in Louis XIII style.
Open only on request.
Parking.
Guided tours, brochures.

Marbeuf (Château).

Marbeuf - 27110.
Louviers : 17 km.
Station : Évreux 20 km.
Bus service.
Private property.
Marbeuf is a Louis XIII château, with its one wing and a tower rebuilt after a fire. It is set in the middle of a park. The original stables are now restored and in use. Gui d'Arche, one of the lords of Marbeuf wounded at the seige of Arras was buried in the church ; his funeral monument depicts him in full armour.
Open only on request.
Parking.
Guided tours.
English, German, Spanish.
Tel. : (32) 35.21.01.

Saint-Just (Château).

Saint-Just - 27950.
Vernon Station.
Private property.
Built at the end of the 16th century by the Croismaine family, in 1652 Saint-Just became the residence of the Savary family. In 1776 the duc de Penthièvre transformed it into a residence for his old servants. The château was sold at the Revolution and in the 19th century the duc d'Albufera remodelled the interiors which contain memorabilia of the poet Casimir de la Vigne and the painter Henri de Maistre. The château is surrounded by a Romantic park with hundred year old trees, basins, out-buildings and an ice-house.
Open for groups by request.
Guided tours.
Tel. : (1) 727.73.60.

Senneville (Manor House).

Amfreville-sous-les-Monts - 27380.
Rouen : 27 km.
Station : Le Vaudreuil 20 km.
Property of M. de Cournon.
This 16th century brick and stone manor house has remained unchanged since it was built. Its high slate roof and façade have stone frame windows. The dovecote dated from the same period. The interiors are 17th century and include two sculpted fireplaces, one with a figure of Louis XIV. Senneville belonged to the Alorge

MARBEUF

EURE

A center of cross-country horseback riding in Normandy only one hour from Paris. This comfortable sized Louis XIII château has beautiful period stables which have been restored to receive riders and their friends from the world over. Riding ring and jumping courses. Holidays. Seminars. Receptions.

family for four centuries before passing to the marquis d'Aligre in the 19th century.
Open all year : 9 - 7.
Parking.
Unaccompanied visits.
Concerts and exhibits.
Tel. : (32) 49.75.24.

Vascœuil (Manor House).

Vascœuil - 27910.
Rouen : 20 km.
Station : Rouen.
Property of M. Papillard.

Today Vascœuil appears exactly as it did on its original 1774 plans with its octagonal tower, main courtyard and formal gardens. It has belonged to such illustrious persons as Charles Henault, president of the Paris parlement and friend of Louis XV. From 1842 to 1862 it was the home of the historian Jules Michelet who lived and wrote here. Much memorabilia remains of his time here. Outside is a permanent exhibit of ceramics, sculptures and mosaics by contemporary artists such as Braque, Carzon, Folon, Léger, Vassarely and Dali.
Open daily April 1 to Nov. 11 : 2:30 - 6:30.
Weekends and holidays : 10:30 - 12:30, 2:30 - 6:30.
Parking.
Unaccompanied visit of the park.
Pannels, audiovisual programme.
Facilities for the handicapped.
Brochures, catalogues.
Temporary art exhibits of major 20th century painters.
Tel. : (32) 23.62.35.

SEINE MARITIME

Ango (Manor House).

Varengeville-sur-Mer - 76119.
Dieppe : 8 km.
Station : Dieppe.
Bus service.
Private property.

Ango was built in the 16th century as the summer residence of Jehan Ango, vicomte de Dieppe. Diane de Poitiers stayed in this elegant manor house built around a 16th century dovecote. The sea front is the best preserved façade. The dovecote was a gift from the king and is one of the largest in Normandy.
Open daily March to November : 10 - 12, 2 - 7.
In winter weekends and holidays : 10 - 5.
Parking.
Guided tours available.
English, guide.
Tel. : (35) 85.15.20.

Canteleu (Château).

Canteleu - 76380.
Route de Sahurs.
Rouen : 5 km.
Station : Rouen 7 km.
Bus service.
Private property.

Canteleu has been remodelled since it was built in the 17th century. Two pavilions were torn down and the roof changed in 1780. The interior decoration and furniture date from the Empire. The château houses a rare collection of exotic stuffed birds from Brazil and the Carribean dating from 1820.
Open July 5 to Sept. 10 on written request.
Closed weekends.
Parking.
Guided tours.
English.
Tel. : (35) 36.00.96.

Cany (Château).

Cany - 76450.
Dieppe : 40 km.
Station : Yvetot 18 km.
Bus service.
Private property.

Cany was built between 1640 and 1646 by the architect François Mansart, uncle of the builder of Versailles. The Louis XIII château surrounded by a moat overlooks the main courtyard and the out buildings. It is one of the earliest examples of Classical architecture. It has a large part of its original furniture and still belongs to the descendants of the man who had it built.
Open July 1 to Sept. 30 : 10 - 12, 2 - 6.
Closed Fridays and the fourth Sunday in July.
Parking.
Guided tours.
English, German, guide.
Tel. : (35) 97.70.32.

Ételan (Château).

Saint-Maurice d'Ételan - 76330.
Caudebec-en-Caux : 15 km.
Station : Yvetot.
Bus service.
Private property.

Built in 1493 on the ruins of a castle, Etelan is a late Gothic residence with a Renaissance stair-tower. The chapel contains 16th century stained glass windows and statues; Etelan belonged to the Cossé-Brissac and Epinay Saint-Luc families whose guests included Louis XI, François I, Catherine de Medici, Michel de l'Hospital, Charles IX who came of age at the château, Voltaire who enjoyed its walks and André Capelet who composed here.
Open July 15 to Aug. 31 : 2 - 6.
Groups on request.
Closed Tuesdays.
Parking.
Pannels or leaflets.
English, Spanish.
Brochures.
Seine-Maritime festival.
Temporary exhibits.
Lecture tours for school groups.
Tel. : (35) 39.91.27.

Eu (Château).

Eu - 76260.
Bus service.
Property of the commune.

Eu was built at the end of the 16th century on the site of William the Conqueror's castle. It was extensively remodelled by the « Grande Mademoiselle » and by the Orleans family (especially by Louis Philippe and his grandson the comte de Paris). The main brick and stone pilasteres building dates from the 17th century. Louis Philippe added the stained glass windows and Viollet-le-Duc was put in charge of the interiors in the 19th century. The château is closely linked to Orleans family history.
Open April 2 to Oct. 31 : 10 - 12, 2 - 6.
Closed Tuesdays.
Parking.
Guided tours, brochures.
Audiovisual programme.
English, German, pannel or leaflets.
Facilities for the handicapped.
Concerts.
Lecture tours for school groups.
Tel. : (35) 86.44.00 ext. 57.

HAUTE-NORMANDIE — 281 — SEINE-MARITIME

Filières (Château).

Saint-Romain-de-Colbosc - 76430.
Le Havre : 20 km.
Station : Bréauté-Beuzeville 8 km.
Private property.

Filières was rebuilt in the 18th century on the site of an older castle whose dry moat and wing survive. It is a classical 18th century building with a central pavilion and sculpted pediment and suite of rooms lit from both sides. The interiors are decorated with 18th century wood work, furniture and sculptures by Ingres (the painter's father). The park is famous for its beech trees known as « the cathedral ».

Open from Easter to Nov. 1 : 1 - 7.
Closed Mon., Tue., Thurs., Fri.
Parking.
Guided tours.
English, guide.
Tel. : (35) 20.53.30.

Le Genetay (Templar Farm).

Saint-Martin-de-Boscherville.
Rouen : 10 km.
Private property.

Built in 1214 for the Templars of Sainte-Vaubourg, the farm became attached to the abbey of Saint George de Boscherville. This is a fine example of Gothic civil architecture with its main building of cut stone and sculpted chimneys. Other buildings are in stone, rough cast or half timbering. 17th century paintings decorate the chapel.

Open all year : 9 - 6.
Parking.
Unaccompanied visits.
Tel. : (35) 32.02.71.

Jumièges (Abbey).

Jumièges Duclair - 76480.
Property of the State.

The history of Jumièges spans a period of prosperity and decline from its foundation by Saint Philibert in 654 to its destruction in 1802. Today all that remains of the great monastery which once housed 900 monks and 1500 servants is the impressive ruin of its church consecrated in 1067. This Romanesque complex is surprising in its monumental size : the Western end with its two octagonal towers, the nave, once the highest in Normandy and the lantern tower rising into the open sky. Other ruins show that there was once an adjoining cloister with its surrounding buildings and a second church. Once restored the abbots house will house a museum of sculpture found at Jumièges.

Open April 1 to Sept. 30 : 9 - 12, 2 - 6.
Oct. 1 to March 30 : 10 - 12, 2 - 4.
Parking.
Guided tours, brochures.
Tel. : (35) 91.84.02.

Photo Arch. Phot.

MARTAINVILLE
SEINE-MARITIME

Set in the midst of a large park in the Normandy countryside, Martainville is a particularly fine château both in its exterior and interior decoration.

Photo E. Revault

CANY

SEINE-MARITIME

Nestled in the green Durdent Valley, Cany offers the visitor the majesty of its courtyard and out-buildings. It is a reminder of the austere splendour of the Louis XIII period. Built between 1640 and 1646 by François Mansart, uncle of the architect of Versailles for Pierre Le Marinier, this beautiful residence has been in the family ever since.

Cany still retains much of its original furniture thanks to Armande de Becdelièvre who managed to save the château from confiscation during the darest days of the Revolution.

Martainville (Château).

Martainville-Épreville - 76124.
Rouen : 12 km.
Property of the State.

Martainville was built around 1485 by Jacques Lepelletier, a rich Rouen merchant. Although it still has the square court, towers and fortifications, they are more decorative than defensive as are the coloured brick and stone walls, gothic chimneys and delicately carved loggia of the 16th century entrance. The State saved the château from destruction by purchasing it in the early 20th century. Since 1961 the department has used it to house a museum of Folk Art.

Open April 1 to Sept. 30 : 10 - 12, 2 - 6.
Oct. 1 to March 30 : 10 - 12, 2 - 5.
Closed Tuesdays in summer and Tuesdays and Wednesdays in winter.
Parking.
Guided tours, brochures.
Tel. : (35) 23.40.13.

Mesnières-en-Bray (Château).

Mesnières-en-Bray - 76270.
Neufchâtel-en-Bray : 6 km.
Bus service.
Private property.

Situated at the crosroads of the feudal rads between Paris, Dieppe, Rouen and Eu, the first Mesnières castle was dismantled by the English around 1415. Louis de Boissay built the present château between 1500 and 1550. Tow round towers similar to those of Chaumont-sur-Loire open onto the main staircase built in 1735. 17th century painted ceilings and 19th century paintings decorate the main room. The 16th century chapel contains statues and stained glass windows; the 19th century chapel includes period wood panelling.

Open weekends Easter to Nov. 1 : 2 - 6.
Parking.
Guided tours.
Temporary exhibits.
Lecture tours for school groups.
Tel. : (35) 93.10.04.

Miromesnil (Château).

Offranville - 76550.
Dieppe : 8 km.
Station : Dieppe.
Private property.

Built shortly after 1589 in one of the prettiest woods in the Caux region, Miromesnil was the birthplace of Guy de Maupassant. The simplicity of the Southern façade with its ancient round towers contrasts with the court façade whose sculpted ornementation is typical of the Louis XIII style. In the salons are mementoes of the marquis de Miromesnil, Louis XVI's minister and of Maupassant and Albert de Mun. In the middle of the wood a sober stone and flint chapel contains wood panelling, statues and stained glass windows.

Open May 1 to Oct. 15 : 2 - 6.
Groups of 20 on request, mornings.
Closed Tuesdays.
Parking.
Guided tours.
English, German.
Tel. : (35) 04.40.30.

Les Moutiers (Park and Manor House).

Varengeville-sur-Mer - 76119.
Route de l'Église.
Dieppe : 5 km.
Bus service.
Private property.

Guillaume Malet acquired this property set high on the cliffs of Dieppe in 1879 and asked the young British architect Lutyens to build him a house, one of his first and his only commission in France. He chose the English pre-Raphaelite « arts and crafts » style. The flowering park wanders from clearing to clearing each devoted to a different theme, scent, colour or sound. The garden and park are laid out in 18th century English style.

Open March 15 to Nov. 15 : 9 - 12, 2 - 7.
Closed Sunday mornings.
Parking.
House in summer only.
Exhibits on old roses.
Concerts.
Temporary art exhibits.
Lecture tours.
Tel. : (35) 85.10.02.

Orcher (Château).

Gonfreville-l'Orcher - 76700.
Le Havre : 10 km.
Bus service.
Private property.

Set on a wooded cliff 100 meters above the Seine estuary, Orcher is made up of a rectangular fortress flanked by four 11th and 12th century towers. It was transformed into a residence in the 17th century when three sides were razed and the interiors transformed, furnished and panelled in Louis XV style. During the Hundred Years War, the castle belonged to Falstaff, then duc of Bedford and finally to John Law in the 18th century.

Open Mon., Wed., Fri., Sun., July 4 to Sept. 26 : 2 - 6.
Parking.
Guided tours, brochures.
English guide.
Facilities for the handicapped.
Tel. : (35) 45.45.91.

PETIT-COURONNE
Pierre Corneille's Country House.

Petit-Couronne - 76000.
62, rue Pierre-Corneille.
Rouen : 10 km.
Bus service.
Property of the departement.

This 16th century half-timbered house which Pierre Corneille inherited from his father has just been renovated. The furniture, documents and prints evoke the author and his family. The surrounding orchard and the thatched bread oven preserve a note of authenticity on the property.

Open all year : 10 - 12, 2 - 5:30.
Closed thursdays and November.
Parking.
Guided tours on request.
Information pannels.
Guides.
Brochures.
Tel. : (35) 68.13.86 and 98.55.10.

ROUEN
Joan of Arc's Tower.

Rouen - 76000.
Rue du Donjon.
Station : 200 m.
Property of the departement.

Joan of Arc's tower is the only remaining part of the castle rebuilt by Philip Augustus after his reconquest of Normandy in 1204. It rises above a little garden surrounded by a moat. It has three stories : a vaulted room on the ground floor, an exhibit telling the story of the castle and of its restoration on the first floor and another of photographs and texts relating the tale of Joan of Arc on the second floor.
Open all year : 10 - 12, 2 - 5:30.
Closed Thursdays.
Unaccompanied visits, brochures in French and English.
Information pannels or leaflets English, pannels and leaflets.
Tel. : (35) 98.55.10.

Saint-Ouen
(Abbey Church).

Rouen - 76000.
Place du Général-de-Gaulle.
Bus service.
Property of the commune.

All that remains of the abbey founded in 535 is the church, a wing of the cloister and the mon's dormitory now occupied by the mayor's office. The 14th century Flamboyant Gothic style building is surmounted by a crowned tower, the « Ducal Crown of Normandy ».
Open April 1 to Sept. 30 : 9 - 12, 2 - 6.
Oct. 1 to March 31 : 10 - 12, 2 - 3.
Parking.
Guided tours on request by callong (35) 71.41.77.
Brochures.
Concerts.

Botanical Garden.

Rouen - 76100.
114 ter, avenue des Martyrs-de-la-Résistance.
Station : Touen Rive Droite 5 km.
Property of the commune.

The Rouen Botanical Garden was transplanted many times from its founding in 1735 until 1838. The public garden, botanical garden, hothouses and orangery cover 10 hectares. They include a wide variety of species from pine trees rhododendrons, from camelias a giant Amazon water lily.

Saint-Georges-de-Boscherville (Abbey).

Saint-Martin-de-Boscherville - 76840.
Rouen : 10 km.
Station : Rouen R.D.
Bus service.
Property of the commune.

This abbey was founded in 10 by William the Conqueror's Gra Chamberlain. Benedictine mo were installed at the abbey wher was completed in 1120. The gre Romanesque church survives p fectly with its two towers, lante

---

SEINE-MARITIME

ORCHER

Originally Orcher was a fortified castle with four 11th and 12th century towers built on a cliff 100 meters above the Seine estuary. Three sides of the castle were razed around 1740 and the fourth was remodelled and furnished in Louis XV style. The dovecote dates from the 15th century. Formal gardens with beeches and oaks.

Photo E. D'Harcourt

tower and three naves. The capitals of the chapter house are richly sculpted with numerous different scenes.
Open April 1 to Oct. 1 : 10 - 12, 2:30 - 6:30.
Groups on request all year.
Closed Tuesdays.
Parking.
Guided tours with one week's notice.
Brochure.
Seine-Maritime festival.
Lecture tours for school groups.

Saint-Wandrille (Abbey).

Caudebec-en-Caux - 76490.
Rouen : 35 km.
Station : Yvetot 12 km.
Bus service.
Private property.

Founded in 649 by Wandrille, a minister of King Dagobert, the abbey had a great deal of influence throughout the region until monastic life was interrupted by the invading Vikings. Disruption occured again at the time of the Revolution and again in the 20th century with the law of expulsions. The abbey includes the ruins of the 13th and 14th century church, the present church built at the same period on an old barn, the 14th and 15th century cloister and the 17th and 18th century buildings still occupied by the monks.
Open all year 3 and 4 pm and mornings on request.
Sundays 11:30, 3, 4.
Parking.
Guided tours, brochures.
English, German.
Tel. : (35) 96.23.11.

VALMONT
Notre-Dame (Abbey).

Valmont - 76540.
Fécamp : 10 km.
Station : Fécamp 10 km and Yvetot 20 km.
Bus service.
Private property.

Founded in 1169 by Nicholas d'Estouteville, this Benedictine abbey is closely linked to his family's history. The Gothic church was rebuilt in the 14th century and the choir in the Renaissance. The monastic buildings were rebuilt at the reform of Saint Maur at the end of 17th century. Although the monks left at the time of the French Revolution. The abbey still contains the tombs of the founder and his family as well as the Announciation mantlepiece attributed to Germain Pilon.
Open daily 10 - 12, 2 - 6.
Closed Sundays and Wednesdays.
Open Sundays May 1 to Oct. 1.
Parking.
Guided tours.
English.
Festival.
Lecture tours for school groups.
Tel. : (35) 29.83.03.

Valmont (Castle).

Valmont - 76540.
Fécamp : 10 km.
Bus service.
Private property.

Both site and building are typical of the Caux region. This complete medieval fortress in part dismantled in the 19th century, was once a part of the defenses of Normandy between Arques and Tancarville. The keep dating from the First Crusade (1100), a fortified brick and stone building and a Renaissance wing (1537-1550) were remodelled in the 19th century. As residence of the Estouteville family who counted companions of William the Conqueror, a defendor of Mont-Saint-Michel and an archbishop of Rouen, it has witnessed the major event of Norman history.
Open weekends March 15 to Oct. 31 : 2 - 6.
Weekends and Wednesdays July 1 to Aug. 31 : 2 - 6.
Groups on request out of season.
Parking.
Guided tours on request.
Brochures.
Summer festival.
Music, theater, dance, folk singing, puppets.
Temporary exhibits.
Lectures.
Lecture tours for school groups.
Tel. : (35) 29.84.36.

VILLEQUIER
Victor Hugo Museum.

Caudebec-en-Caux - 76490.
Rouen : 40 km.
Station : Yvetot 11 km.
Property of the departement.

This museum is installed in the house of the Vacquerie family, Leopoldine Hugo's in-laws. The house and its garden along the banks of the Seine are full of memorabilia of both families and of the great author himself. There is also a growing collection of Victor Hugo's drawings.
Open March 16 to Sept. 30 : 10 - 12, 2 - 7.
Oct. 1 to March 15 : 10 - 12; 2 - 5.
Closed Tuesdays (and Mondays in Winter).
Parking.
Guided tours on request.
Information pannels.
Guides.
Brochures.
Tel. : (35) 56.78.31.

PAYS DE LOIRE

LOIRE-ATLANTIQUE, MAINE-ET-LOIRE, MAYENNE, SARTHE, VENDÉE.

- ■ castle, château, manor house
- ● abbey, priory
- ▲ garden, park
- ★ town house, famous men house, farm, mill...
- ○ city

ANGERS
- ★ Logis Barrault : Musée des Beaux-Arts
- ■ Château du Roi René
- ▲ La Maulévrié

LAVAL
- ■ Vieux Château

NANTES
- ■ Château des Ducs de Bretagne
- ▲ Grand Blottereau
- ▲ Jardin des Plantes
- ▲ La Chantrerie
- ▲ Parc Procé
- ▲ La Beaujoire
- ▲ La Gaudinière

SAUMUR
- ■ Château des Ducs d'Anjou

■ Goué
■ Bois de Maine
■ La Roche Pichemer
■ Foulletorte
LAVAL ○
■ Le Rocher
■ Sainte-Suzanne ● Le Boucq ■ Saint-Aignan
■ Les Arsis (Chateau-l'Hermitage)
■ La Motte-Glain ■ Craon ■ Ballon ■ Montmirail
■ Magnanne ■ Balluère ○ LE MANS
■ Ranrouet ■ Bouillé-Ménard ■ L'Escoblère
■ Pouancé ■ Moyre
★ La Marmite ■ Raguin ■ La Hamomière
■ Plessis-Bourré ■ Bazouges
■ Plessis-Macé ■ Venevelles ■ Ponce
■ La Thibaudière ■ Le Lude
■ Serrant ■ Montgeoffroy
■ La Baronnière ○ ANGERS ■ Sancé
NANTES ○ ● La Noe de ★ La Roche ★ Les Quatre Croix
Goulaine ■ Bel-Air ■ La Colaissière ■ La Haute Guerche
■ Clisson ■ Brissac
■ Boumois
★ Le Gué-Robert ○ Saumur
■ La Vérie ■ Bois-Chevalier ■ Le Coudray-Montbault ● Asnières
■ La Preuille ■ Montreuil-Bellay ● Fontevraud
■ Apremont
■ Beaumarchais ■ La Chabotterie ■ Tiffanges
■ La Métairie ■ Les Essarts ■ La Bonnelière
○ LA ROCHE SUR YON ● Grainetière
★ Puy-du-Fou
★ Mouilleron-en-Pareds :
Maison Maréchal de Lattre
■ Sigournais
■ Saint-Juire
■ Pierre Levée ■ Court d'Aron
■ Talmont
■ Notre-Dame ● Nieul sur Autisse : St Vincent
de Lieu-Dieu ■ Terre-Neuve
St Vincent-sur-Jard : ★ ● St Michel en Herm
Maison de Clemenceau ● St-Pierre-de Maillezais

PAYS-DE-LOIRE

LOIRE ATLANTIQUE

Bois-Chevalier (Château).

Légé - 44650.
Nantes : 39 km.
Bus service.
Property of Mme de Lépinay.

Built in 1653 by Olivier du Bois-Chevalier, Mayor of Nantes and head of the courts, this château is comprised of a central domed building flanked by six pavillion. In gratitude for services rendered Louis XIV authorised the building of a drawbridge across the moat. The vaulted granite three-storied stairwell, the wood panelling, the Aubusson tapestries and the Regency furniture are original. The château served as a refuge for royalists during the French revolution.

Open April 1 to Nov. 1.
Parking.
Guided tours.
English.
Lecture tours for school groups.
Tel. : (40) 26.62.18.

Clisson (Château).

Clisson - 44190.
Nantes : 27 km.
Station : Clisson.
Property of the Département.

Surrounded by a double moat and fortified walls overlooking the Sèvre, this medieval fort was erected in the 14th century in its eastern part. The monumental entrance with its twin towers also dates from the same period. The remainder was built by François II of Brittany in the second half of the 15th century. Olivier IV, Constable of France and a friend of the Guesclin was the most famous Lord of Clisson.

Open Jan. 1 to 31 Dec. : 9:30 - 12, 2 - 6.
Closed Tuesdays, December and school holidays from 1 Jan. to 28 Feb.
Parking.
Guided tours and brochures.
English.
Festivals : medieval pageants.
Sound and light.
Tel. : (40) 78.02.22.

Goulaine (Château).

Haute-Goulaine - 44115.
Nantes : 18 km.
Station : Nantes.
Bus service.
Property of M. R. de Goulaine.

The central building dating from the end of the 15th century constructed entirely of chalk, makes Goulaine an authentic Loire château. The interior, decorated at the beginning of the 17th century, houses a fine collection of 17th and 18th century furniture. Since its foundation during the High Middle Ages, the château has belonged to the same family. Its guests included Henri IV and Louis XIV.

Open daily June 18 to Sept. 16. 2 - 6:30.
April 4 to June 17, Sept. 17 to Nov. 4, weekends, 2 - 6:30.
Closed Tuesday.
Parking.
Guided tours.
Information panels, leaflets.
Information in English, German, Spanish.
Lecture tours.
Concerts, temporary exhibitions.
From June 15 to Sept. 15, collection of live tropical butterflies.
Tel. : (40) 54.91.42.

LOIRE-ATLANTIQUE

BOIS-CHEVALIER

Built in 1655

Daily tours from April 1 to Oct. 31
from 9 - 12 and 2 - 7. Tél. : (40) 26.62.18.

GOULAINE
LOIRE-ATLANTIQUE

This château has remained in the same family since it was built in the High Middle Ages. The main building dates from the 15th century. Luxurious interiors decorated in the 17th century. 17th and 18th century furniture.

LA MOTTE-GLAIN
LOIRE-ATLANTIQUE

Summer festival. Hunting Museum

Facilities for filming and for receptions. Unspoilt country setting with woods and lake.
Cultural centre, variety of exhibitions.

Open Saturdays, Sundays, Holidays from Easter; from June 15 to Sept. 15; open 2:30 - 6:30.

Open all year for groups upon request.
Tel. : (40) 81.52.01.

La Motte-Glain (Château).

La Chapelle-Glain - 44670.
Châteaubriand : 18 km.
Station : Angers or Nantes 55 km.
Bus service.
Property of M. de Lézardière.

Rebuilt in 1495 by Pierre de Rohan, Marshall de Gié, La Motte-Glain was visited by Anne of Brittany and Charles VII and later on by Catherine de Medici and Charles IX in 1565. The entrance to the château is protected by a parapet walk flanked by two towers. The main building and outbuildings, made of local stone, form a closed courtyard. To the north lies a pond. Inside are furnished rooms and hunting trophies from Africa.

Open weekends and holidays from Easter.
Daily except Tuesday, June 15 to Sept. 20, 2:30 - 6:30.
By appointment for groups during rest of year.
Parking.
Guided tours, brochures.
English, German.
Theatre, ballet, concerts.
Temporary exhibitions.
Tel. : (40) 81.52.01.

NANTES
Château of the Dukes of Brittany.

Nantes - 44000.
1, place Marc-Elder.
Property of the commune.

Begun in 1466 for François II the castle was completed by his daughter Anne who was born in 1477. Surrounded by a moat, its military style architecture contrasts with the Renaissance interiors. It now houses the Museum of Breton folk art, the Salorges Museum and the Museum of Decorative Arts.

Open all year, 10 - 12, 2 - 6.
Closed holidays and Tuesdays, except in July and August.
Parking.
English, German.
Acoustiguide, audiovisual.
Festivals, theatre.
Temporary exhibitions.
Tel. : (40) 47.18.15. and 47.02.42.

Parks (City Property).
Beaujoire Floral Park.

Nantes - 44000.
Route Saint-Joseph.

34 hectares of greenery, 18 of floral park. This park stretches along the left bank of the Erdre with its gardens of iris, heather, perennials and magnolias. Facilities for the handicapped.

La Chantrerie Park.

Nantes - 44000.
Gachet Route.

Designed by Noisette at the beginning of the 19th century, the 37 hectares of the park stretch along the banks of the Erdre. Century old oaks, spruce, beach and tulip-trees are to be found alongside the collection of bamboos.

La Gaudinière Park.

Nantes - 44000.
Boulevard Robert-Schumann.

This park was laid out on the side of a picturesque hill in the 18th century by wealthy garden lovers. The Val d'Or river flows through this park which is rich in its variety of trees.

Procé Park.

Nantes - 44000.
44, rue de Dervallières.

Laid out by Antoine Noissette in 1883 and acquired by the city in 1912, this 16 hectare park has a large collection of rhododendrons and oaks, as well as one of the finest tulip trees in the West of France.

Grand Blottereau Park.

Nantes - 44000.
Boulevard A.-Perreau.
Station : Nantes, 3 km.
Bus service.
Property of the city.

This 38 hectare park includes a formal garden surrounding the château, an amusement park and hot housses of tropical plants such as spices, perfumes, medicinal plants, edible plants, exotic woods and textiles Rebuilt in 1762 the château was bequeathed to the city in 1905 by Thomas Dobrée.

For all five parks :
Open, Oct. 15 to Mar. 31 : 8 - 6.
Apr. 1 to Apr. 30 : 8 - 8.
May 1 to Aug. 30 : 8 - 9:30.
Sept. 1 to Oct. 14 : 8 - 8.
Entry free.
Unaccompanied tours.

La Noê de Bel-Air (Château).

Vallet - 44330.
Nantes : 24 km.
Private property.

The château of La Noê de Bel-Air has the appearance of a Palladian villa whose interior loggia is supported by doric columns. It was built in 1836 at the same time as its English gardens which have also remained unspoilt.

Open on request only.
Grounds only.
Unaccompanied tours - brochures.
Tel. : (40) 78.20.59.

Ranrouët (Château).

Herbignac - 44410.
Saint-Nazaire.
Bus service.
Private property.

Built during the 11th and 12th centuries by the lords of Asserac and Rochefort, the fortress of Ranrouët was transformed many time until it was finally abandoned in 1793. The castle is entered through a 13th century gateway, protected by a half-moon shaped bastion. Semi-circular in form, it has six towers joined by a connecting wall. You cross the double moats by means of a drawbridge.

Open daily June 15 to Sept. 15 on request, sundays and holidays.
Lecture tours for groups only.
Preservation sites.
Information : Friends of the Château de Ranrouët.
Tel. : (40) 53.53.04.

Saint-Philibert de Grand-Lieu (Abbey).

Saint-Philibert de Grand-Lieu - 44310.
Nantes : 25 km.
Bus service.
Property of the commune.

Remains of the ancient abbey which dates to the merovingian period. Founded in the 7th century

by Saint-Philibert who withdrew to the island of Noirmoutier after establishing the abbey of Jumièges. The walls of the church of alternately stone and brick. You can also see an eleventh century sarcophagus and capitals.
Open daily April 1 to Sept. 30 : 8 - 8.
Oct. 1 to March 31 : 9 - 5.
Parking.
Guided tours.
English, German, Italian.
Brochures, exhibitions.
Tel. : (40) 78.78.79 and 78.70.15.

MAINE-ET-LOIRE

ANGERS
(Château of the Roi René).

Angers - 49000.
Walk to World's End.
Access by bus.
Property of the State.

As a means of consolidating his control over the ancient fief of the Plantagenets, Saint-Louis decided to erect a monumental fortress on the site of one their former castles, situated on a rocky and impenetrable promontory. Ten years in the making (1220-1230). The castle is surgrounded by seventeen towers and is shaped as a pentagon. From the 14th century onwards it became the favourite residence of the Dukes of Anjou, and the castle was then transformed into a charming complex. With the exception of the chapel in the centre, this was all due to the 15th century monarch, King René, who built the palm vaulted staircase, the surrounding gallery which served as a tribune for court festivities, and the hanging gardens. Woven for the castle in the 14th century, the famous Apocalypse tapsetry can now be seen in the castle's interior, where it is displayed thanks to the Monuments Historiques.
Open Oct. 1 to Palm Sunday : 9:30 - 12, 2 - 5:30.
April 1 to June 30 : 9:30 - 12:30, 2 - 6.
July 1 to March 31 : 9:30 - 12, 2 - 5.
Closed Jan. 1, May 1, May 8, Nov. 1, Nov. 11, 25 Dec.

Guided and unaccompanied tours.
Acoustiguides.
Information in English, German.
Brochures.
Shows, exhibitions.
Lecture theatre for school groups only.
Tel. : (41) 87.43.47.

La Maulévrie (Arboretum).

Angers - 49000.
Chemin d'Ogremont.
City Property.
Situated to the south of the town, this garden was created by the avid botanist, Gaston Allard. It passed to the Pasteur Institute after he died and then became the property of the city of Angers, which was responsible for its restoration. You enter the arbor through a majestic avenue of exotic oak which dates from 1875.
Open June 1 to Oct. 1, 8 - 8.
Parking.
Tel. : (41) 88.98.92 (Town Hall).

Logis Barrault (Museum of Fine Arts).

Angers - 49000.
10, rue du Musée.
Property of the commune.
This hôtel, where such eminent visitors as Ceasar Borgia, Mary Stuart and Catherine de Medici were lodged, was built at the end of the 15th century and then enlerged in the 17 th. The sculpture gallery which displays David d'Angers work was a gift from the artist himself. Transformed into a museum as early as 1804, the Logis Barrault has paintings from the 14th to the 20th century and objetcs from the Medieval and Renaissance periods.
Open all Year, 10 - 12, 2 - 6.
Closed Mondays.
Unaccompanied tours, brochures.
Leaflets available.
Concerts, lectures.
Temporary exhibitions.
Lecture tours for school groups only.
Tours for teachers.
Tel. : (41) 88.64.65.

Asnières (Abbey).

Cizay-la-Madeleine - 49700.
Saumur : 16 km.
Doué-la-Fontaine : 6 km.
Property of the Department.
The abbey of Asnières dates from the beginning of the 13th century. Although the nave of the abbatial church has disappeared, the choir and the transept are both fine examples of High Gothic in the west of France. The beauty of the vaults is complemented by the sculpted and painted decoration of the keystones. Asnières has kept its varnished paving stones which constitute a further decorative element.
Open July 1 to Aug. 30 : 10 - 12, 2 - 6.
Closed Tuesdays.
Parking.
Grounds only.
Accompanied tours, pamphlets.

La Baronnière (Château).

La Chapelle-Saint-Florent : 49410.
Angers or Nantes : 45 km.
Property of M. de Bodard-Grandmaison.
Built during the Renaissance, the château de La Baronnière was destroyed at the time of the Vendée. Its restauration was undertaken by the architect René Hoé, Viollet-le-Duc's teacher, and by 1850 it was transformed into a neogothic structure in troubadour style. Inside you can see a monumental spiral staircase made of stone: there are also fireplaces, panelling and furniture mainly of Empire style. The 16th century enclosed courtyard has been preserved.
Open April 1 to Oct. 1. 10-12. 3-7.
Closed Tuesday
Guided tours, pamphlets.
English, German.
Facilities for the handicapped.
Tel.: (41) 78.53.49.

Bouillé-Ménard (Château).

Bouillé-Ménard - 49720.
Segré: 10 km.
Station:Segré.
Private property.
Entering the château of Bouillé-Ménard through a gateway, you reach a four-sided structure surrounded by cylindrical towers attached to the walls. Initially a defensive castle built in the 14th century, it was enlarged in the 16th and the large wing and staircase date from this epoch. The salons have 18th century panelling.
Open by request only.
Parking.
Guided tours.
English.
Tel. : (41) 92.52.08.

Boumois (Château).

Saint-Martin-de-la-Place.
Saumur : 6 km.
Station : Saumur.
Bus service.
Private property.

A rectangular shaped château, enclosed by a moat, Boumois exterior appearance still reminds us that it was a 15th century fortress, with its fortified surrounding walls and its parapets and turrets. The main building is decorated in transitional style and the chapel was added in the 17th century. Apart from the collection of paintings, you can see arms and armour dating from the 15th century.
Open from Palm Sunday to All Saints, 10 - 12, 2 - 6.
July 1 to Sept. 1 : 10 - 12, 2 - 7.
Closed Tuesday.
Parking.
Guided tours.
Concerts.
Tel. : (41) 38.43.16.

Brissac (Château).

Brissac-Quincé - 49160.
Angers : 19 km.
Station : Angers.
Bus service.
Property of M. de Brissac.

In 1606 Charles de Cossé, Duke of Brissac, peer of France, built the present day château between two large round towers which date from the 15th century. Both a fortress and a palace, this building has seven floors and 150 rooms. The influence of the Baroque can be seen in the dome, the niches, the pilasters of all orders, the pediments and the ornaments in general. Inside, the rooms are decorated with Flanders, Brussels and Gobelin tapestries, and you can see a fine collection of porcelain, paintings and period furniture. The château has remained in the possession of the Cossé-Brissac family to this day.
Open April 1 to June 30, July 1 to Aug. 30, Sept. 1 to Nov. 11 : 9:30 - 11:30, 2:15 - 5:15.
Closed Tuesday from March 31 to June 30 and Sept. 15 to April 11.
Parking.

Guided tours, pamphlets.
Leaflets available.
English, German.
Concerts, theatre.
Tel. : (40) 91.23.43.

Colaissière (Château).

Saint-Sauveur-de-Landemont - 49270.
Nantes : 30 km.
Station : Ancenis 15 km.
Private property.

In 1522 the count de la Poëze built this Renaissance château on his fief of La Colaissière. It is a four-sided building surrounded by a moat. Inside you can see Gothic, Renaissance and 17th century furniture, as well as an important collection of religious objects.
Open Jan. 1 to July 15 : 10-12, 3 - 7.
Aug. 15 to Dec. 31 : 10 - 12, 3 - 6.
Parking.
Guided tours.
Tel. : (40) 83.70.96.

Coudray-Monbault (Château).

Saint-Hilaire-du-Bois - 49310.
Cholet : 25 km.
Angers : 48 km.
Saumur : 43 km.

LA BARONNIÈRE

MAINE-ET-LOIRE

Château built in 1840 by René Hodé around a 16th century courtyard. General Bonchamps, hero of the Vendée army, lived in this historic site.
A part of the park — the courossé with its panorama — is open to the public at no charge.
You can drink the local wines — Cabernet, Gamay, Cuvée — in the 16th century cellars.
La Baronnière is also available for receptions, lectures and conferences.

BRISSAC

MAINE-ET-LOIRE

Brissac, with its seven floors and 150 rooms, is one of the highest châteaux in France. It has preserved its collection of tapestries, pictures and furniture which date from the reign of Louis XIII. For over five centuries the château has been owned by the Brissac family, and it is the Marquis de Brissac who, with the help of his wife, will do all to make your visit a memorable one.
Dining facilities are available in the vaulted rooms which date from the 17th century.

Upon request :
— luncheon for coach parties
— hiring of main salons and theatre (200 seats) for parties, seminars and evening entertainment.

MAINE-ET-LOIRE

LES BRIOTTIÈRES

25 km north of Angers

We look forward to welcoming you to this château situated in the heart of the Loire valley. Discover Anjou and all its charms while staying in this old family house which offers :
— bedrooms and table d'hôtes ;
— hiring of rooms for seminars, marriages (up to 400 people) ;
— films, cinema.

For information and reservations write to :
Château des Broittières
49330 Champigné
Tel. : (41) 42.00.02.

tion : Cholet.
ate property.
Built in the 15th and 16th centu-
s, the château of Le Coudray-
ntbault is surrounded by a
at and consists of a main buil-
g flanked by three large round
vers. The facade is decorated
h dark green lozenge-patterned
ckwork. Near the formal gar-
ns are the ruins of the 12th and
h century church and priory, as
ll as a 16th century chapel.
en July 15 to Sept. 15 : 3 - 7.
king.
ded tours.
: (40) 64.80.47.

ntevraud (Abbey).

ntevraud - 49590.
mur : 15 km.
perty of the State.
n 1099 the reforming preacher
ert d'Arbrissel founded a mo-
stery in a valley at the borders
Anjou, Poitou and la Touraine,
led Font Evraud (the Evraud
untain). A royal abbey, attached
h to the Crown and to the Pa-
cy. Fontevraud abbey reflects
special character of an order
ich brought together several
erent communities of monks
d nuns. The high birth of the
ther-abbesses ensured that the
bey would be well patronised :
only were the Plantagenets bu-
d there, but the daughters of
uis XV were educated at Fonte-
ud. The various buildings,
ich date from the 12th to the
h centuries, show that the ab-
y did not decline in the interve-
g centuries. From the majestic
olas of the abbatial church to
spacious romanesque kit-
ens, one finds an opulence that
also present in the huge refec-
y and the chapter house which
decorated with paintings from
16th century. In 1963 the pri-
built by Napoleon in 1804 was
roughly restored and now acts
a centre for artists.
en April 1 to Sept. 30 : 9 - 12, 2 -
0.
. 1 to March 31 : 9:30 - 12, 2 - 6.
sed Tuesday, Jan. 1, May 1, Nov. 1,
. 25.

Parking.
Guided tours, pamphlets.
Acoustiguide.
Tel. : (41) 51.71.41.

Gué-Robert (Windmill).

Gonnord-Valanjou - 49670.
Angers : 37 km.
Station : Chemillé 11 km.
Private property.
Built at the end of the war of the
Vendée to replace the windmill
burnt down in 1794, Gué-Robert
has wooden strets, a double mill
and a 19th century grain sorter.
Open July 1 to Sept 15 : 9 - 12, 2-7.
Parking.
Unaccompanied tour.
Tel. : (41) 92.15.33.

La Haute-Guerche (Château).

Saint-Aubin-de-Luigné.
Angers : 25 km.
Station : Chalonnes 10 km.
Private property.
Built in the 15th century on the
site of a 12th century building, La
Haute-Guerche stands in a commanding position overlooking the
valley of the Layon, famous for its
vineyards. It has preserved its
large round towers charactéristic
of fortified castles, whereas successive additions transformed La
Haute-Guerche into an elegant residence. In one wing you can see
its celebrated attics, underground
rooms and vaults. Rased during
the Vendée, the château is still
being restored, and its owners
were awarded first prize for saving
Masterpieces in danger in 1971.
Open June 15 to Sept. 15 : 9 - 12, 2 - 6
by request for groups during rest of year.
Parking.
Unaccompanied tours.
Leaflets available.
Tel. : (47) 78.33.46.

La Marmite (Windmill).

Angrie - 49440.
Condé : 2 km.
Station : Angers 40 km.
Bus service.
Property of M. H. Gauguet.
Built during the reign of
Louis XIV, the La Marmite wind-
mill was restored to working order
in 1980. Its tower has preserved
the original mechanism, and has
two double mills that are operatio-
nal.
Open April 1 to Oct. 31 : 9 - 8.
Parking.
Guided tours, pamphlets.
Tel. : (41) 92.04.28.

Montgeoffroy (Château).

Mazé - 49250.
Angers : 25 km.
Private property.
The château of Montgeoffroy
was built between 1772 and 1775
by the architect Barré for the Marshall de Contades, Governor of
Strasbourg. The interior, which
has remained in tact, has furniture
by Gourdon, Blanchard, Garnier
and Durand. The picture collection
includes works by Rigaud, Desportes and Van Loo.
Open March 26 to Nov. 1 : 9:30 - 12,
2:30 - 6:30.
Parking.
Guided tours, pamphlets.
Tel. : (41) 80.60.02.

Montreuil-Bellay (Château).

Montreuil-Bellay - 49260.
Saumur : 10 km.
Fontevraud : 10 km.
Station : Saumur.
Bus service.
Private property.
The feudal castle of Montreuil,
built by Foulques Nerra in 1025
and given to his vassal, Berlay,
was continually beseiged by the
Plantagenets and the Kings of
France. From this period date the
barbican, the moat, the fortified
ramparts, the underground rooms
and the kitchen. The new château
and the collegial buildings, the canon's residence, the oratory with
its frescoes all date from the 15th
century. The salons, decorated
with furniture of the 17th and 18th
centuries, bear witness to the history of the Dukes of Orléans-Lon-
gueville and La Trémoille.
Open April 1 to Nov. 1 : 10 - 12, 2 - 6.
July and Aug. : 10 - 12, 2:30 - 6:30.
Guided tours of the interior, unaccompanied tours of the gardens. Acoustiguide
in English, German, Spanish, Italian,
Dutch, Japanese.
Leaflets available.
Tel. : (41) 52.33.06.

Moyre (Château).

Sœurdres - 49330.
Route de Marigné.
Angers : 30 km.
Private property.
Built in 1810 on the site of older
château, Moyre is a classical château, at the centre of whose three-
storied facade there is a triangular
pediment enclosed by a balustrade. The trees are particularly
old, the avenue of oaks dating to
before the 17th century. The terrace is enclosed by a moat.

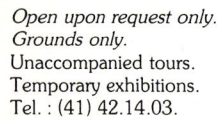

MAINE-ET-LOIRE — 296 — PAYS-DE-LOIRE

Open upon request only.
Grounds only.
Unaccompanied tours.
Temporary exhibitions.
Tel. : (41) 42.14.03.

Le Plessis-Bourré (Château).

Cheffes-sur-Sarthe.
Angers : 15 km.
Station : Angers.
Property of M. Reille-Soult de Dalmatie.

Le Plessis-Bourré was built in a single session lasting five years (1468-1473) by Jean Bourré, silversmith and chief adviser to Louis XI. You enter the château by a drawbridge which crosses the moat. The richly furnished interior is a fine example of seignorial dwellings of the period. The wooden ceiling of the Guards room, painted at the end of the 15th century, has allegorical figures representing humorous themes. The library has an important fan collection.

Open Jan. 1 to March 31 : 10 - 12, 2 - 5.
April 1 to Sept. 30, 10 - 12, 2 - 7.
Closed wed, thurs am.
Annual closing, 15 nov. to 15 Dec. (open by request).
Guided tours, pamphlets.
English, German, Italian leaflets available.
Temporary exhibitions.
Tel. : (41) 32.06.72 and 32.06.01.

Le Plessis-Macé Château).

Le Plessis-Macé - 49220.
Angers : 15 km.
Property of the Département.

Built in the 12th century by the du Plessis family in a position dominating the fortified town, the fortress was transformed in the 15th century by Louis de Beaufort, favourite of Louis XI. The initial building has kept only the outer walls and the towers. The main courtyard is enclosed by buildings whose facades are decorated with balconies sculpted in the 15th century. This château, which received Louis XI, Charles VIII, François and Henri IV, contains an important collection of chests.

Open March 1 to June 30, Oct. 1 Nov 30 : 2 - 6.
July 1 to Sept. 30 : 10 - 12, 2 - 6:30.
Parking.
Guided tours.
Tel. : (41) 91.64.08.

Pouancé (Castle).

Pouancé - 49420.
Allée Louis-Bessière.
Châteaubriand : 16 km.

MAINE-ET-LOIRE **MONTREUIL-BELLAY** VAL DE LOIRE

Open April 1 to November 1 from 10 to 12 and from 2 to 6. Closed Tuesdays. Guided tours in French, English, Spanish, Italian, Dutch and Japanese.

For information : Château de Montreuil - 49260.
Tel. : (41) 52.33.06.

tation : Châteaubriand or Laval,) km.
roperty of the commune.
 Following the example of Brittany, Pouancé was one of the first ortified towns in Anjou. The earest defences date back to Foulues Nerra in the 11th century. he importance of this castle can e judged by its impressive reains : nine towers, vaulted corriors, underground rooms still xist. It was here that Du Guesclin urrendered to Jean of Brittany after a protracted seigne. The enemble offers an excellent idea of ilitary architecture from the beinning of the 13th to the end of e 15th centuries.
pen July 2 to Aug. 20 : 9:30 - 12, 2 - 6. y request for groups off season.

Quatre-Croix (Windmill).

Saint-Saturnin-sur-Loire - 49320.
Angers : 15 km.
Bus service.
Private property.
 The Quatre-Croix windmill was used in the 17th and 18th centuries to grind corn for the baking of bread. It was restored in 1980.
Open by request only, July 1 to Sept. 30 : 2:30 - 7.
Parking.
Guided tours, pamphlets.
Temporary exhibitions, grounds available.
Tel. : (41) 91.93.03.

Raguin (Château).

Chaze-sur-Argos - 49500.
Angers : 35 km.
Private property.
 Surrounded by a moat and protected by towers, Raguin was built on ancient foundations by three generations of the Du Bellay family at the end of the 16th and beginning of the 17th centuries. Walls were erected later on, as was a turret surmonted by a dome. On the first floor the two gilded chambers' are covered with paintings of vases of flowers, antique figures and landscapes where the predominant colours are blue and grey. This is the work of Italian artists, inspired by the example of Italian Renaissance decoration. The château was owned by the Marshall of Contades during the 18th century.
Open May 1 to Sept. 30: 3 - 6.
Parking.
Guided tours.
Tel. : (41) 92.13.62.

La Roche (Windmill).

La Possonière - 49170.
Angers : 20 km.
Station : La Possonière 4 km.
Private property.

LE PLESSIS-BOURRÉ MAINE-ET-LOIRE

15th century private residence

We are delighted to offer you guided tours around this architectural masterpiece which has been used as both fortress and sumptuous residence. You will see suites of fully furnished salons and bedrooms which date from different periods, as well as the Library, the Law Courts, the Prison and the Chapel. The most famous room in the château is the Guards room with its extraordinary ceiling, painted in the 15th century.
You can also hire this dream-like setting for parties, seminars, film shows and receptions.

The La Roche windill has kept its Berton system blade mechanism, its wooden interior mechanism and its double mill that dates from 1860. It is still used to grind cereals and rye.
Open sundays and holidays from March 14 to Dec. 12 : 3 - 7.
Parking.
Guided tours, pamphlets.
Temporary exhibitions : the windmills of Anjou.
Tel. : (41) 41.14.40.

Sancé (Château).

Saint-Martin-d'Arcé - 49150.
Baugé : 5 km.
Private property.
Built in the 17th and 18th centuries, the classical château of Sancé consists of a main building flanked by two wings at right angles. Four rooms, including an 18th century dining room, have been classified. The complex is surrounded by a wide moat.
Open July 14 to Aug. 31 : 9 - 7, and sundays throughout the year.
Parking.
Accompanied tours.
English

Lecture tours available for school groups.
Tel. : (41) 89.29.72.

SAUMUR

Château des Ducs d'Anjou.

Saumur - 49400
Property of the commune.
Rebuilt on the site of a 13th century fortress in the following century by Louis of Anjou, the château des Ducs was fortified at the end of the 16th century on the orders of the Governor Duplessis-Mornay when Saumur became a Protestant refuge. During the Empire it was transformed into a state prison. In a commanding position over the Loire, this residence has collections of furniture, enamels, sculpted wood and ceramics, as well as medieval tapestry from the church of Notre Dame de Nantilly. The château also houses the Museum of Decorative Arts.
Open April 1 to June 30, Jan. 1 to Oct. 31 : 9 - 11:30, 2 - 6.
July 1 to Sept. 30 : 9 - 6:30, 8:30 - 10:30.
Nov. 1 to March 31 : 9:30 - 11:30, 2 - 5.
Parking.
Guided tours.
English - German - Italian - Guides and brochures (July - Sept).
Tel. : (41) 51.30.46.

Serrant (Château).

Saint-Georges-sur-Loire - 49170.
Angers 17 km.
Bus service.
Private property.
Begun in the mid 16th century and completed at the end of the 17th century. Serrant owes its harmony to the fact that the initial plans were followed over this long period of time. The 16th century main building is flanked by two wings at right angles on the side of the main courtyard and by two imposing towers on the side

---

MAINE-ET-LOIRE **LE PLESSIS-MACÉ**

Louis XI stayed in this château which his Chamberlain, Louis de Beaumont, had transformed from an ancient fortress built in the 12th century. This château offers an example of transitional architecture, midway between the fortifications of the middle ages and the palaces of the Renaissance.

which faces the moat. The monumental gateway dates from the 17th century and the romantic gardens from the 19th century. Louis IV, Napoleon 1 and the Duchesse du Berry were among the château's illustrious visitors. Serrant has kept its period furniture, its Flanders tapestries and its pictures.

Open March 20 to Oct. 31 : 9 - 11:30, 1 - 6.
Closed Tuesday except in July and August.
Parking.
Guided tours, pamphlets.
English - German - Dutch - Italian.
Leaflets avaiable.
Tel. : (41) 41.13.01.

La Thibaudière (Château).

Juigné-Bène - 49460 Montreuil-Juigné.
Angers : 12 km.
Bus service.
Private property.

The marquis de Vezins, Governor of Angers, built the main building of the château de La Thibaudière in 1692. It was the scene of fighting during the Vendée, when it was partly burnt down, but was restored and extended by a south wing in 1840, a chapel in 1862 and a north wing in 1864. The furniture dates from the 18th century, the Restoration and the Second Empire. In the middle of an English park designed in 1846 by Choulot you can see a temple in antique style which dates from 1583.

Open by request only, July 15 to Oct. 15 : 3 - 6.
Closed Monday.
Parking.
Guided tours.
English - Portuguese.
Tel. : (41) 91.61.92 or 91.62.02.

MAYENNE

Les Arsis (Château).

Meslay-du-Maine - 53170.
Sablé-sur-Sarthe - Laval : 20 km.
Private property.

This château, on which building was begun in the 16th century, consists of a huge square courtyard enclosed by a main building, outbuildings flanked by a dovecote, and a keep which overlooks the entry to the courtyard. The orangerie, with its Italianate roof was built in 1805 ; the entry pavillion in 1900.

Open by request.
Grounds only.
Tel. : (43) 98.40.17.

Le Bois-de-Maine (Château).

Rennes-en-Grenouilles - 53110.
Lassay-les-Châteaux : 7 km.
Station : Briouze 30 km.
Private property.

The former fortified castle of Le Bois-de-Maine dates back to the 11th century. Occupied by the En-

---

MAINE-ET-LOIRE

SERRANT

The château of Serrant is a large building, severe and sumptuous at the same time, whose symettry is reflected in the waters of the moat.
Philibert Delorme designed the ensemble, and later on, Hardouin-Mansart, one of the architects of Versailles, built the chapel which houses Vaubran's mausoleum. The château next passed to the Walsh family and then in 1830, through marriage, to the Dukes de Trémoille, ancestors of the present day owners.
The rooms are richly furnished, and were decorated at different times. They include a Library, a collection of works of art, pictures and tapestries.
Serrant, the last of the great château of the Loire, is surrounded by water.

glish during the Hundred Years War, it was transformed thereafter. The main building is flanked by two towers, one of which dates back to the 14/15th century, the other of which is 18th century.
Open all year : 10 - 12, 2 - 6.
By request for groups.
Closed Sunday.
Grounds only.
Tours of the interior by request only.
Unaccompanied tours.
Pamphlets.
Lecture tours for affiliated groups.
Tel. : (43) 46.81.05.

Craon (Château).
Craon - 53400.
Laval : 30 km.
Station : Laval.
Bus service.
Property of M. de Guébriant.
  On the crest of a hill overlooking the town, the château of Craon, built for the d'Armaillé family between 1770 and 1775, stands on the site of a medieval fortress rased to the ground by Henri IV. The Toulouse architect, Pommeryol, was clearly inspired by the Antique, as the pediment, friezes, garlands and vases attest. Inside, the rooms have panelling and furniture of the period. The château is set in extensive grounds which include a formal French garden.
Open park : April 1 to Oct. 31 : 2 - 6:30.
Château : July 1 to Aug. 31 : 2:30 - 6:30.
By appointment for groups out of season.
Closed Tuesday.
Parking.
Guided tours of château.
Unaccompanied tours of grounds.
English - Scandinavian languages - Guides.
Lecture tours for school groups only.
Tel. : (43) 06.11.02.

L'Escoublère (Château).
Daon - 53200.
Angers or Laval : 40 km.
Station : Sablé-sur-Sarthe 28 km.
Private property.
  Built in the 15th century and enlarged and fortified by the Salle Family in the 16th, the manor house of l'Escoublère is a small château with a moat. The inner courtyard has a Renaissance well.
Open Aug. 15 to Oct. 1 : 2:30 - 6:30.
Closed Thursday.
Guided tours.
Tel. : (43) 07.16.31.

Foulletorte (Château).
Saint-Georges-sur-Erve - 53600.
Evron : 10 km.
Station : Evron/Sillé-le-Guillaume 14 km.
Private property.
  From 1570 Antoine de Vassé built this severe Renaissance château on the site of an ancient castle destroyed by the English. Two stories, with windows framed by columns support an Imperial cupola. Its staircases and fireplaces are made of local granite and the château has furniture of the Louis XV and Louis XVI period.
Open by request only.
Parking.
Tel. : (43) 01.64.21.

Goué (Château).
Fougerolles-du-Plessis - 53190.
Fougères : 17 km.
Private property.
  Goué consists of an oblong building with a 14th century tower and a monumental staircase. It was transformed by Jean-Baptiste de Goué, cousin of the King of Yvetot and member of the King's Council in 1681. Two of the rooms have decorated pannelling and coffered ceilings in the Renaissance and Louis XIII styles.
Open by request May 1 to Oct. 15, sats and suns : 3 - 7.
Parking.
Guided tours.
Tel. : (43) 05.41.43.

LAVAL
Vieux Château.
Laval - 53000.
Place de la Trémoille.
Rennes : 80 km.
Angers : 70 km.
Bus service.
Property of the commune.
  Built in the 15th century of the foundations of an ancient castle — whose 13th century keep remains in tact — the Vieux Château was enlarged in the 16th century. The Renaissance building is separated from the ramparts and keep by an 18th century gateway. Apart from housing the Museum of Archaeology, this former residence of the Comtes de Laval has a collection of naive painting, including works by Henri Rousseau.
Open June 16 to Sept. 15 : 9 - 12, 2 - 6.
Sept. 16 to June 15 : 10 - 12, 2 - 6.
Closed Mondays.
Parking.
Guided or unaccompanied tours.
Leaflets available.
English - German - Guides.
Pamphlets.
Festivals, concerts.
Temporary exhibitions of painting.
Tel. : (43) 53.39.89.

Magnanne (Château).
Ménil - 53200.
Château-Gontier : 8 km.
Station : Sablé 40 km.
Angers, Laval : 35 km.
Bus service.
Private property.
  Built in 1690 and made a marquisate by Louis XIV in 1701, Magnanne offers a fine example of a Mansart building. The main building is flanked by two pavilions and has an entry framed by two columns and crowned by a triangular pediment. It looks onto a formal garden.
Open on request, July and Aug.
Parking.
Guided tours by appointment.
Theatre, concerts.
Temporary exhibitions of painting.
Tel. : (43) 07.10.02.

La Roche-Pichemer (Château).
Saint-Ouen-des-Vallons - 53150.
Laval : 25 km.
Station : Montsurs 4 km.
Private property.
  Built for the du Plessis family, la Roche-Pichemer is an ancient defensive outpost commanding a basin in a wooded valley. The present day château, with its terraces, was added between the 16th and 17th centuries. In the 17th century, René du Plessis, marquis de Jazé — exiled by Mazarin from Louis XIII's court — decorated the interior, and the boiseries, painted ceilings and marble and granite fireplaces are due to him.
Open by request for groups.
Parking.
Guided tours.
Tel. : (43) 01.01.31.

Le Rocher (Château).

Mézangers - 53600.
Evron : 5 km.
Station : Evron.
Private property.

The de Bouillé family built the château du Rocher from granite in the 15th century. The two buildings at right angles with their towers of various forms were enlarged by a chapel, added in the 16th century, and a pavilion, added in the 18th. A Renaissance gallery, with basket-handle arcades, embellishes the inner courtyard.
Open June 15 to Oct. 15 : 10 - 12, 3 - 6.
Closed Fridays.
Grounds only.
Unaccompanied tours.
Tel. : (43) 01.65.01.

Sainte-Suzanne (Château).

Sainte-Suzanne : 53270.
Laval : 34 km.
Station : Evron 7 km.
Property of the commune.

On a rocky promontory, the medieval city of Sainte-Suzanne, built between the 11th and 15th centuries, is surrounded by ramparts which enclose the 11th century keep. Sainte-Suzanne was the only fortification that William the Conqueror failed to capture, despite a siege which lasted from 1083 to 1087. Fouquet de la Garenne, Comptroller-General of the Post and one of Henri IV's ministers, built a château on this site between 1083 and 1087.
Open June 15 to Sept. 15 : 11 - 12:30, 2:30 - 7.
May 1 to Oct. 1 : sundays 2:30 - 6.
By appointment for groups off season, Sept. 16 to June 14.
Guided tours, pamphlets.
Festivals : theatre, cabaret.
Lecture tours for school groups only.
Tel. : (43) 01.40.77.

SARTHE

Ballon (keep).

Ballon - 72290.
Le Mans : 20 km.
Station : Montbizot 4 km.
Bus service.
Private property.

At the gateway to the Maine, the fortress of Ballon originally protected Maine from the Normans and then became the centre of bloody fighting between the English and the French during the Hundred Years War. The 12th century keep and its connecting walls were gradually transformed until the 17th century. Furnished in Louis XIII style, the château has retained its facade and its inner court, the latter in Renaissance style. It is surrounded by botanical gardens stretching over 2 hectares.
Open July 7 to Sept. 9 : 2:30 - 6:30.
Parking at the town hall.
Guided tours.

SAINTE-SUZANNE
Medieval City

MAYENNE

We offer you our château and its grounds, set in the heart of this medieval city, for your receptions, lectures, seminars and for your marriages, drinks parties, etc. Exhibitions from June to September.

2 1/2 hours from Paris by the motorway A 11, F 11, RN 157.

For information contact Friends of the Château de Sainte-Suzanne.
Tel. : (43) 01.40.77 or 01.40.10.

Guided tours available for groups during June, July, August : 11 to 12:30, 2:30 to 7, except Monday.

Photo J. Pierre

Leaflets available.
English - German - Italian, guides, leaflets.
Lecture tours for school groups only.
Tel. : (43) 27.30.51.

Balluère (Château).

Pirmil - 72430.
Le Mans : 30 km.
Station : Noyen-sur-Sarthe 4 km.
Property of M. R. Martin.
  Built in 1426 Balluère has a main building set at right angles with a large tower attached to one side. Pentagonal at its base, it becomes four sided in its upper stories and is surmounted by sculpted dormer windows.
Open upon request for groups.
Parking.
Grounds only.
Guided tours.
Tel. : (43) 95.75.04.

Bazouges (Château).

Bazouges-sur-Loire - 72200.
Near de La Flèche.
Bus service.
Private property.
  Formerly a fortress and transformed into a residence, Bazouges has a Louis XVI main building which inculdes a chapel, a Guards room with a large stone fireplace and 18th century salons. The entrance has two large towers with parapets and pepper-pot rooves.
Open April 2 to July 1, saturdays : 2 - 5.
July 1 to Sept. 15, tuesdays : 10 -12; thursdays, saturdays : 2 - 5.
April 2 to Sept. 15, for groups by written request only.
Parking.
Guided tours.
Temporary exhibitions.
Tel. : (43) 94.30.67.

Le Bourq (abbey).

Château-l'Hermitage - 72510.
Le Mans : 25 km.
Bus service.
Private property.
  The abbey was founded in the 12th century by the Plantagenets and fortified at the beginning of the 15th century. All that remains of the Renaissance cloisters are five arches, decorated with flower and fruit motifs. The chapter house has ribbed vaulting on the ground floor and a huge fireplace.
Open by request April 15 to Oct. 31.
Parking.
Guided tours.
Tel. : (43) 44.90.91.

Le Lude (Château).

Le Lude - 72800.
Tours or le Mans : 42 km.
Private property.
  Jean Daillon, a friend of Louis XI, was responsible for building this fortress in 1457. The four towers at each corner of the complex and the Louis XII wing date from this period. The south wing built between 1520 and 1530, with pilasters and medallions inspired by the Italian Renaissance, helped transform this fortress into a residence. A last wing was designed by the architect Barré in the 18th century : it has a triangular pediment at its centre. Lude is surroun

---

SARTHE

LE LUDE

Set at the crossroads of Tourine, Maine and Anjou, the impressive ensemble of the château de Lude is mirrored in the waters of the Loire river.
The evening entertainment has been watched by hundreds of visitors from all over the world for over 25 years.

Night show :
June and July, Friday and Saturday at 10:30 pm.
August to 3 September at 10:00 pm.

Reservations and information.
Tel. : (43) 94.62.20 or 94.60.09.

Photo A. Delourmel

Montmirail (Château).

Montmirail - 72570.
La Ferté-Bernard : 15 km.
Private property.

Dominating the village, the fortress of Montmirail is famous as the setting for the meeting that took place between Louis VII and Henry Plantagenet in 1169. In the 15th century the castle was remodelled by Charles d'Anjou, and the Princesse de Conti, Louis XIV's daughter, transformed the main facade in the 18th century. The octagonal tower and the underground rooms, which are on three levels, are all preserved, and the salons are decorated with boiseries and furniture of the Louis XIV period.
Open every day, except tuesdays, July 1 to Sept. 15 : 2 - 6, sundays ; March 1 to Oct. 31 : 2 - 6.
Parking.
Guided tours, pamphlets.
Audiovisual.
English - German, leaflets.
Temporary exhibitions : paintings.
Tel. : (43) 93.65.01.

Poncé (Château).

Poncé-sur-Loire - 72340.
Tours, Le Mans, Vendôme : 45 km.
Station : Château-du-Loir 25 km.
Bus service.
Private property.

Built on the site of the feudal castle of the lords of Poncé in the 16th century by the Chambray family, Poncé has two large pavilions flanking a central tower and a small L shaped wing on the north side. The coffered Renaissance stairway is decorated with floral, animal and human motifs. The dovecote dates from the 18th century. The outbuildings house the Museum of Sarthois. Folklore.
Open April 1 to 10 Nov. : 10 - 12, 2 - 6.
Closed sunday a.m.
Unaccompanied visits, leaflets.
Explanatory pamphlets.
English - German guides.
Temporary exhibitions.
Tel. : (43) 44.45.39.

Saint-Aignan (Château).

Saint-Aignan - 72110.
Le Mans :
Private property.

Saint-Aignan, built in the 17th century, has a classical facade which includes, at its centre, a large pavilion crowned by a dome which houses the staircase. The property of Saint-Aignan was once owned by the Chaource and Craon families.
Open June 1 to Sept. 30 : 9 - 7.
Grounds only.
Château by request only.
Parking.
Tel. : (43) 97.46.04.

Venevelles (manor house).

Luché-Pringé - 72800.
Station : Le Mans 36 km.
Bus service.
Property of M. Dufourq.

Set on an island surrounded by a moat, the manor house of Venevelles has a main building flanked by two 15th century round towers. The northern side of the complex is completed by a 16th century farm and there are four large Louis XIII pavilions at each corner. Two 17th century drawbridges lead to the Regency gateway and to the formal gardens. Inside, the Louis XII and Louis XIV boiseries have been preserved, as have the fireplaces which date from the 15th to the 18th centuries, and the ironwork of the Louis XIII period.
Open upon request during the holiday season.
Parking.
Grounds only (inside by appointment only).
Tel. : (43) 94.43.35.

VENDÉE

Apremont (Château).

Apremont - 85220.
La Roche-sur-Yon : 29 km.
Nantes : 65 km.
Property of the commune.

This 11th century fortress was transformed between 1530 and 1535 by the Admiral Chabot, François I's chamberlain, only to be demolished by Richelieu who intended to retain nothing but the church. Despite this, two high towers, part of the ramparts and a drawbridge remain, and the fortress is in the process of being restored.
Open daily June 15 to Sept. 15 : 10 - 12, 2 - 7.
Palm Sunday to June 15, Sept. 15 to Nov. 11 : 10 -12, 2 - 6.
Parking.
Unaccompanied tours.
Pamphlets.
Information in English and German.
Shows, exhibitions.
Tel. : (51) 55.73.66.

Beaumarchais (Château).

Brétignolles - 85470.
Saint-Gilles-Croix-de-Vie : 10 km.
Station : Saint-Gilles-Croix-de-Vie.
Private property.

Bouyer de l'Ecluse, one of Henri IV's chief supporters and later Treasurer of the Royal Purse, was responsible for modernising the old central building of the Beaumarchais castle. This building is flanked by two L shaped wings and outbuildings which are completed by turrets built during the reign of Louis XIV.
Parking.
Tel. : (51) 90.15.44.

La Bonnelière (Manor house).

Saint-Michel-Mont-Mercure - 85700.
Pouzages and Les Herbiers : 11 km.
Station : Pouzages.
Private property.

Built in the 16th century, the Renaissance manor of La Bonnelière was transformed in the 17th century. The central building with its armorial pediment, is completed by two farm pavilions with bow-shaped rooves. The moat is crossed by a drawbridge.
Grounds only.
Tel. : (51) 57.70.71.

La Chabotterie (Château).

Saint-Sulpice-le-Verdon.
By l'Hébergement - 85260.
Property of M. de Goué.

During the Vendée wars, La Chabotterie witnessed the capture of the famous Vendée leader, Athanase de Charette, in March 1796. Wounded, he was taken care of in the kitchens of this château. La Chabottrie house a Museum of Military history of the period 1780 to 1945

Open daily April 1 to Sept. 30 : 10 - 12, 2 - 6:30.
Oct. 1 to March 31, by appointment for groups.
Unaccompanied visit.
Pamphlets in English, German, Dutch at the Tourist Office.
Temporary exhibitions :
Tel. : (51) 42.81.80.

La Court d'Aron (Château and gardens).

Saint-Cyr-en-Talmondais - 85540.
Luçon : 13 km.
Station : Champs-Saint-Père : 7 km.
Private property.

La Court d'Aron, typical of 19th century Renaissance revival architecture, has two L shaped wings which are flanked on one side by a round tower with gallery, and on the other by arcades. Inside you can see 16th century Flanders tapestry and 17th century monumental fireplaces. The floral gardens extend over some 10 hectares.
Open April 1 to Sept. 30 : 10 - 12, 2 - 6.
Parking.
Guides tours.
Tel. : (51) 30.81.82.

Les Essarts (Château).

La Roche-sur-Yon : 20 km.
Bus service.
Private property.

Of the original castle, built in the 11th century, all that remains is the Tower Sarrazine, the castle's keep which is attached to the entry, itself framed by two 12th century round towers. At the back of the courtyard are the remnants of the seignorial mainbuilding which dates from the 16th century. From the 12th to the 18th centuries many families have succeeded to the title of Baron of Essarts. Henry IV stayed here and attempted to convert the region to Protestantism. From 1621 the region was reconverted to Catholicism by the Countess de Mercœur.
Open all year, 9 - 6.
Parking.
Unaccompanied tours, itinerary suggested.
Pamphlets.
Mary Tudor festival.
Tel. : (51) 42.81.80.

La Grainetière (abbey).

Les Herbiers - 85500.
Station : Cholet 35 km.
Bus service.
Private property of the Priory of the Congrégation Notre-Dame de l'Espérance.

Founded and built by the Benedictines in the 12th century, the abbey of La Grainetière was damaged in the 16th century during the Wars of Religion. The walls and former chapter house — the present day chapel — are from the initial period of construction, as are the remains of the abbatial buildings, and one of the cloisters to which was added a loggia during the 17th century. The interior diplays elements of Gothic decoration.
Open daily 2:30 - 5:30.
Closed Monday.
Parking.
Pamphlets and guides.
English - German.
Tel. : (51) 67.21.19.

Notre-Dame-de-Lieu-Dieu (abbey).

Jard-sur-Mer - 85520.
Les Sables-d'Olonne.
Bus service.
Private property.

In 1197 Richard the Lionheart founded the abbey of Notre-Dame-de-Lieu-Dieu for the Premonstratensian monks. After a long period of prosperity the abbey was ruined by the Protestants in 1676 and then abandoned. The buildings consist of a chapter house, sacristy and little refectory and they are arranged on a rectangular plan around the remains of the cloisters. The main building has kept its large gable decorated with octagonal turrets. The abbey houses a private museum of furniture and objects from the Bas-Poitou.
Open daily July 1 to Aug. 31 : 10 - 12, 2 - 6:30.
Upon request for groups in June and Sept.
Parking.
Guided tours, pamphlets.
Tel. : (51) 33.40.06.

Maillezais Saint-Pierre (abbey).

Maillezais - 85420.
La Rochelle : 46 km.
Station : Niort 25 km.
Private property.

Founded in 1000 by William of Aquitaine and made into a bishopric in 1317, the abbey of Saint-Pierre-de-Maillezais was sequestered by the Protestants and transformed into a fortified centre by Agrippa d'Aubigné in 1621. The impressive ruins of the Romanesque and Gothic cathedral, 95 metres in length, can still be seen, as can two gothic buildings set at right angles to it. Excavations have discovered the remains of the cloister as well as tomb stones. Rabelais lived in this abbey for five years.
Open June 1 to Aug. 31 : 9 - 8.
Sept. 1 to May 31 : 9 - 12:30, 1:30 - 6
Parking.
Guided tours, July and Aug.
Off season, unaccompanied tours.
Guided tours for groups only.
Leaflet available off season.
English - German - Dutch - Spanish pamphlets.
Temporary exhibitions.
Tel. : (51) 00.70.11.

La Métairie (Château).

Le Poiré-sur-Vie - 85170.
La Roche-sur-Yon : 18 km.
Belleville : 7 km.
Property of M. de la Thébaudière.

La Métairie is outstanding for its fine proportions and the excellent state in which it has been preserved. It is one of the few examples of 15th century architecture from the Vendée to have survived. The château de La Métairie should be visited along with the châteaux of Pont-de-Vie and de La Chabotterie.

Open June 1 to Sept. 30 : 2 - 7.
Parking.
Individual acoustiguides.
Information in English.
Tel. : (31) 31.80.26.

MOUILLERON-EN-PAREDS
Birthplace of Maréchal de Lattre and the National Museum of the two victories.

Mouilleron-en-Pareds - 85390.
La Roche-sur-Yon : 50 km.
Station : Chavagnes-les-Redoux 6 km.
Bus service.
Property of the State.

The Museum of the two victories, established in 1961, is dedicated to the memory of two men born at Mouilleron-en-Pareds, Georges Clemenceau and the Maréchal de Lattre de Tassigny. Near the museum you can see the house in which de Lattre was born. De Lattre's life is documented by portraits, furniture and personal belongings.
Open all year : 10 - 12, 2 - 6.
Closed Tuesday.
Parking.
Guided tours.
Tel. : (51) 00.31.49.

NIEUL-SUR-L'AUTISE
Abbey of Saint Vincent.

Nieul-sur-l'Autise - 85240.
Fontenay-le-Comte : 12 km.
Station : Fontenay-le-Comte.
Property of the Département.

Like so many others, the royal abbey of Saint Vincent suffered during the Wars of Religion and during the 16th century. By 1717 it no longer acted as a centre of religious life, yet it has maintained its cloisters which date back to the abbey's foundation in 1068. Four vaulted galleries open onto the chapter house, whose vaults were restored in the 17th century. The church's facade is decorated with fantastical animal designs and geometric motifs. Much if it was restored during the 19th century.
Open all year : 8 - 7, from July 1 to Aug. 31 : 9 - 12, 2 - 6.
Guided tours.
Parking.
Pamphlets available.
Concerts.
Tel. : (51) 00.92.17.

Pierre-Levée (Château).

Olonne-sur-Mer - 85340.
Les Sables-d'Olonne : 4 km.
Property of Mme Avuynet and M. de la Roche Saint-André.

The château of Pierre-Levée (raised stone) takes its name from the two menhirs nearby. Built in the 18th century it seems to have been designed by the architect Jacques-Ange Gabriel : the richly decorated facades and the balustrade of wrought iron which complements the iron gateway are typical of his style.
Open upon request for groups only.
Grounds only.
Parking.
Guided tours by the owner.
Tel. : (51) 95.28.11.

La Preuille (Château).

Saint-Hilaire-de-Loulay - 85600.
Montaigu : 10 km.
Station : Clisson 8 km.
Bus service.
Property of M. Fradin.

On the border between the Kingdom of France and the Duchy of Brittany. La Preuille was originally a strategic fortification and was probably built towards the middle of the 15th century. To the two large towers attached to the central mainbuilding were added new buildings, transformed during the 19th century. One remaining tower has kept its 15th century appearance. The château also has grounds and a basin.
Open July 14 to Sept. 15 : 10 - 12, 3 - 6.
Closed Friday.
Guided tours, pamphlets.
English, German, Spanish, Arabic, guides.
Tel. : (51) 94.04.49.

Le Puy-du-Fou (Château).

Les Espesses - 85590.
Near Cholet.
Property of the Département.

The château of Le Puy-du-Fou consists of the remains of a fifteenth century fortified residence, to which a Renaissance brick and granite château was attached in the following century. The château was burnt down in 1794 and part of the edifice was never restored. An arcaded gallery, which has been preserved, is magnificently restored and now houses the Museum of the Vendée. Le Puy-du-Fou also mounts an impressive play with 600 local inhabitants re-enacting the history of the region.
Open July 1 to Sept. 30 : 10 - 12, 2 - 6.
By appointment for groups.
Closed Monday.
Guided tours of interior and grounds.
Tours of theatre by request.
Grounds cannot be visited while play in progress.
Tel. : (51) 57.03.04.

Saint-Juire (Château).

Saint-Juire - 85210.
La Roche-sur-Yon : 35 km.
Private property.

Built in the 15th century on the site of a former fortress, the château de Saint-Juire, enclosed by a moat, includes a monumental staircase, three fireplaces and a guards room. Inside you can see portraits of Mme de Maintenon and of Louis XIV and Agrippa.
Open July 14 - Sept. 15 : 10 - 6.
Parking.
Pamphlets.
Tel. : (51) 30.03.41.

Saint-Michel-en-l'Herm (Abbey and Château inside Abbey).

Saint-Michel-en-l'Herm - 85580.
Luçon : 15 km.
Station : Luçon.
Bus service.
Private property.

The Benedictine abbey of Saint-Michel-en-l'Herm, founded in 682 by the Bishop of Poitiers, has been restored several times over the centuries. The present day château, designed by the architect François Le Duc, called the Tuscan, dates back to the 17th century. The complex of buildings, including the chapter house and refectory, are perfectly intact. Mazarin held the sinecure of abbot of Saint-Michel-en-l'Herm.
Open July 1 to Sept. 1 : 10 - 12, 3 - 5, Wednesday, Saturday and Friday.
Château, grounds only.
Abbey, interior.
Parking.
Guided tours, pamphlets.
Tel. : (51) 30.20.23.

Saint-Vincent-sur-Jard (Clemenceau's House).

Jard-sur-Mer - 85520.
Property of the State.

After retiring from political life, George Clemenceau rented this fishing lodge in the Vendée in 1919 and spent many summers here. The house has remained exactly as it was when he died. Passing through an avenue of pine trees, you enter this low built house in which you can see the desk at which Clemenceau wrote.

VENDÉE

TALMONT

This 11th century fortress has preserved its three sided surrounding walls, its keep and its inner chapel.

VENDÉE

TERRE-NEUVE

FONTENAY-LE-COMTE

Remember to see the panelling which comes from Chambord and the château's fireplaces.

PAYS-DE-LOIRE — 307 — VENDÉE

the grandeur and misery of victory.
Open April 1 to Sept. 30 : 9 - 12, 2 - 5.
Oct. 1 to March 31 : 9 - 12, 2 - 4.
Closed Tuesday.
Guided tours, pamphlets.
Tel. : (51) 33.40.32.

Sigournais (Château).

Sigournais - 85110.
La Roche-sur-Yon : 40 km.
Station : Chaudonnay 7 km.
Property of M. de Lépinay.

All that remains of this medieval fortress, originally built with nine towers connected by walls, is the entry flanked by two towers with parapets. Bertrand de Goth, archbishop of Bordeaux and later Pope, visited the castle in 1320.

Open upon request only.
Parking.
Guided tour.
Tel. : (50) 94.34.58.

Talmont (Château).

Talmont-Saint-Hilaire - 85440.
Les Sables-d'Olonne : 13 km.
Station : Les Sables-d'Olonne.
Bus service.
Property of the Commune.

Built on a rock and originally surrounded by water, the feudal fort of Talmont was built in the 11th century by William the Bald to protect Poitou against Norman invaders. Extended in the 15th century and then demolished on Richelieu's orders, the château has kept its surrounding walls and keep, the latter with its romanesque facade and chapel inside.
Open March to Nov. 11 : 9 - 12, 2:30 - 7.
Parking.
Unaccompanied tour.
Explanatory panels.
English, German guides.
Pamphlets.
Tel. : (51) 90.27.43.

Terre-Neuve (Château).

Fontenay-le-Comte - 85200.
Niort : 30 km.
Station : Niort.
Bus service.
Property of M. du Fontenioux.

In the 16th century, Nicolas Rapin, poet and Prevost of the Constabulary of France, commissioned the architect Morisson to transform his dwelling into a noble residence. Two main buildings set at right angles and flanked with turrets and large towers on the court side, present facades that are decorated with statues. The famous 19th century watercolour painter, Octave de Rochebrune, decorated the château and assembled an important collection of

---

LA VÉRIE
VENDÉE

Guests welcome ; luxurious rooms available.
Salons available for receptions.

Sound and Light show 14 July, 15th August.
Exhibitions.

paintings and bronzes. Inside you can see two monumental fireplaces from the Renaissance and boiseries dating from the period Louis XV and Louis XVI.
Open daily June 1 to Sept. 30 : 9 - 12, 2 - 7.
Upon request for groups, Oct. 1 to Nov. 30, April 1 to May 30.
Parking.
Guided tours, pamphlets.
English, German guides.
Festival of folklore.
Concerts, theatre.
Tel. : (51) 69.17.75.

TIFFAUGES
Château de Gilles de Rais.

Tiffauges - 85130.
Cholet : 20 km.
Station : Torfou-Tiffauges 3 km.
Property of the Commune.

Gilles de Rais, the first Maréchal of France and one of Joan of Arc's companions, was also the infamous « Blue Beard » who was hanged at the age of 36 for his terrible crimes and orgies. It was here that he lived, and the impressive ruins of his castle include the chapel and crypt, dating from the 11th and 12th centuries, the 12th century keep, the 14th century watch-tower and two towers which date from the 15th and 16th century respectively. The Vidame tower still has many of its 16th century rooms preserved.
Open May 1 to Sept. 15 : 9 - 12, 2 - 6.
Oct. 15 to April 30, Sundays, Holidays : 9 - 12, 2 - 6.
Closed Tuesday.
Parking.
Guided tours, pamphlets.
Tel. : (51) 91.70.51.

La Vérie (Château).

Challans - 85300.
Challans : 2 km.
Private property.

Built to protect the coastline from Norman and Viking invasions, the castle belonged to the order of the Knight Templars of Coudrie in 1100, and then to François de la Vérie, one of Louis XI's most faithful supporters by 1450. Made into a marquisate in 1610, Louis XII stayed at La Vérie which is set in the middle of wooded grounds and has preserved its slate rooves and classical facade. Its chapel, entry hall, stone staircase and dining room have been restored.
Open upon request in the summer season between Easter and All Saints Day.
Guided tour.
Son et lumière.
Tel. : (51) 35.25.43.

PICARDIE

AISNE, OISE, SOMME.

- ■ castle, château, manor house
- ● abbey, priory
- ▲ garden, park
- ★ town house, famous men house, farm, mill...
- ○ city

SENLIS
- ★ Pavillon Sainte-Martine
- ● Abbaye de la Victoire

SOISSONS
- ● Abbaye St-Jean-des-Vignes
- ● Anc. Abbaye St-Léger

● Valloires
■ Regniere
■ Abbeville : ■ Vauchelles
■ Bagatelle ■ Long
■ Bertangles
● Airaines   ■ Guise   ● Saint-Michel
■ Rambures
AMIENS ○
■ Prouzel
■ Courcelles
■ Wailly   ■ Bois-les-Pargny
● Saint-Germain les Verberie
■ Rivecourt   ○ LAON
● Sainte-Croix ■ Plessis-Brion ■ Blérancourt
■ Verderonne ● Abbaye d'Ourscamp ■ Coucy
■ Compiègne ■ Condé-Chivresval
○ BEAUVAIS ■ Pierrefonds ○ Soissons ● Vauclair
● Valgenceuse ● Longpont
★ Neuilly ● Montgobert
■ Corbeil-Cerf ● Morienval ■ Vierzy
■ Boury ■ Chaalis ■ Crépy-en-Valois ■ Fère-en-Tardenois
■ Raray ■ Chantilly
■ Mont-l'Evêque ■ Versigny
○ Senlis ▲ Ermenonville : ■ Condé-en-Brie
parc J.J. Rousseau ★ Château-Thierry
Maison natale de La Fontaine

AISNE

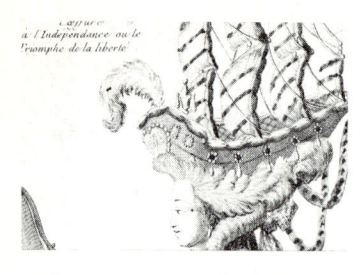

Blérancourt (Château and Franco-American Museum).

Blérancourt - Chauny - 02300.
Noyon : 15 km.
Property of the State.

Blérancourt was built by Salomon de Brosse. The surviving rooms are now a museum thanks to the donations of American and French benefactors. The museum is devoted to the history of Franco-American relations (colonial America, cooperation during the two world wars and portraits of many famous people like Saint-Just, the ducs de Guèvres and others...).
Open daily Nov. 1 to March 31 : 10 - 12, 2 - 4.
April 1 to Oct. 31 : 2 - 5.
Closed Tuesdays.
Temprary exhibits.
Tel. : (23) 39.60.16

Bois-lés-Pargny (Château).

Bois-lés-Pargny - 02270.
Laon : 18 km.
Private property.

Bois-lés-Pargny is a Louis XIII eep as the red brickwalls and wrought iron fixtures mared 1611 attest. It has four turrets of unequal height. The vaulted ground floor rooms have large fireplaces. The abbey belonged to the abbey of Saint Jean de Laon and to the Maubeuge family.
Interiors open on request.
Unaccompanied visits of the grounds.
Parking.
Tel. : (23) 80.81.96.

Château-Thierry (La Fontaine's Birthplace).

Château-Thierry - 02044.
12, rue Jean-de-La-Fontaine.
Staiton : Château-Thierry.
Property of the commune.

In 1621, Jean de La Fontaine was born in this 1559 town house built between courtyard, gardens and ramparts. It is tile covered and has two perpendicular wings and a small porch. Although he had left the towntwon after his marriage he returned here on the death of his father in 1658. Inside are documents and paintings.
Open April 1 to June 30 : 10 -12, 2 - 6.
July 1 to Sept. 3* : 10 - 12, 2:30 - 6:30.
Oct. 1 to March 31 : 10 - 12, 2 - 5 or Sundays, 2 - 5 during the week.
Closed Tuesdays.
Parking.
Guided tours on request for groups.
Lecture tours for school groups.
Tel. : (23) 69.05.60.

Condé (Château).

Conde-en-Brie - 02330.
Château-Thierry : 14 km.
Private property.

All that remains of the original 13th century construction built by Enguerrand de Coucy are a few thick walls. The castle was enlarged by the Bourbons in the 15th century. The present day appea

---

JEAN DE LA FONTAINE MUSEUM

AISNE   CHÂTEAU-THIERRY

Jean de La Fontaine's birthplace is a fine 16th century town house with a collection of documents and portraits relating to the life and work of the author, including information on the various editions and translations of the Fables and their iconography.
The first floor is devoted to French painting from the 17th century to the mid-20th century : Le Nain, Revel, Barthélemy, Daubigny, Guillaumin, Aman-Jean, Valtat, Ladureau, and local history and temporary exhibits.

PICARDIE — AISNE

rance of the château is due to the transformations carried out by marquis Leriget de la Faye who employed the Italian architect Servandoni, the designer of the Farnese palace. The interiors are the work of Servandoni, oudry, Watteau, Lancret.
Open daily July 1 to August 31 : 10 - 12, 2:30 - 6:30.
Groups on request out of season.
Parking.
Guided tours.
English, German.
Concerts.
Temporary exhibitions. Lecture tours.
Tel. : (23) 82.42.25.

Condé-Chivres-Val (Fort).

Chivres-Val - 02200.
Soissons : 15 km.
Property of the commune.
Built in 1877 by General Serré de Rivière, this fort played an important part in the First World War battles that took place around the nearby « Chemin des Dames »... This magnificent buiding covers five hectares in the midst of a wood.
Open all year : 8:30 - 7.
Guided tours on request.
Tel. : (23) 55.50.67.

Coucy (Castle).

Coucy-le-Château - Auffrique - 02380.
Soissons : 17 km.
Bus nearby.
Property of the State.
The ruins of Coucy rise from a propontory overlooing the oise and Ailette valleys. The castle was built in the 13th century by Enguerrand III de Coucy, nicknamed « the Builder ». Its keep is as high as the towers of Notre Dame and the castle was part of a huge fortified complex. It was turned over to the crown in the 16th century and dismantled by Mazarin in 1652. The fortress was restored by Viollet-le-Duc before being badly damaged in the First World War.
Open April 1 to Sept. 30 : 9 - 12, 2 - 6.
Oct. 1 to March 31 : 10 - 12, 1:30 - 4.
Closed Tuesdays and Wednesdays.
Guided tours, brochures.
Tel. : (23) 52.71.28.

Fère-en-Tardenois (Castle).

Fère-en-Tardenois - 02130.
Château-Thierry : 28 km.
Station : Fère-en-Tardenois 2 km.
Property of M. R. de la Tramerye.
All that is left of the 13th century castle errected on an artificial paved mound are the foundations of seven towers. In the 16th century constable Anne de Montmorency turned the castle into a hunting lodge to receive the king. From this period dated the double gallery bridge which spans the dry moat. At the death of the last duc de Montmorency, the castle was confiscated by Louis XIII and finally demolished by the duc d'Orleans the future Philippe Egalité.
Parking.
Unaccompanied visits.
Guided tour for groups.
Facilities for the handicapped.
Brochure.

Guise (Castle).

Guise - 02120.
Saint-Quentin : 26 km.
Station : Saint-Quentin.
Bus service.
Property of the commune.
Guise castle was built on the site of a 10th century fort. It is dominated by a 12th century keep. Most recently restored by Vauban in the 17th century its ruins include part of the 14th, 16th, 17th and 18th century ramparts and bastions. It also comprises a 13th century chapel, fortified doors, underground rooms and galleries. Ruined during the First World War it is being restored by volunteers.
Open June 1 to July : 1 : 9 - 12, 2 - 6.
July 2 to Oct. 15 : 9 - 12, 2 - 7.
Oct. 16 to Dec. 22 : 9 - 12, 2 - 5:30.
Parking.
Guided tours, brochures.
Audiovisual programme.
English, guide.
Lecture tours for school groups.
Tel. : (23) 61.11.76.

Longpont (Abbey).

Longpont - 02600.
Soissons : 15 km.
Villers-Cotterets : 10 km.
Property of M. A.-P. de Montesquiou.
Longpont was a Cistercian abbey founded by Saint Bernard in 1131 and consecrated in the presene of Saint Louis in 1232. It was the size of Soissons cathedral. The vast edifice was partially ruined at the Revolution and transformed into a private residence. The vaulted rooms, 13th century warming room and cloister and cellar salon remain from the Gothic period. In the 18th century the monks remodelled the vestibule and grand staircase which survive.
Open weekends and holidays March 15 to Nov. 15 : 10 - 12, 2:30 - 7.
Groups on request in the week.
English, German.
Guided tours, brochures.
Facilities for the handicapped.
Tel. : (23) 96.01.53.

Montgobert (Château).

Villers-Cotterets - 02600.
Soissons : 20 km.
Station : Villers-Cotterets 9 km.
Private property.
The huge somber 18th century château of Montgobert is situated on the edge of the Retz forest. It belonged to the maréchal de Joyeuse and then to Pauline Bonaparte, Napoleon's sister. The three story main bloc flanked with two perpendicular wings houses a museum of wooden objects and woodworing.
Open daily (except Tuesdays) April 1 to Oct. 31 : 10 - 12, 2 - 6.
Sundays 3 - 7.
Parking.
Lecture tours for school groups of Fridays.
Tel. : (23) 72.51.09 and 96.11.43.

AISNE

MONTGOBERT

Montgobert belonged to the maréchal de Joyeuse and then to Pauline Bonaparte Napoleon's sister who married to general Leclerc, governor general of Saint-Domingue. The château then passed to the marechal Davout, duc d'Auersteadt, prince d'Eckmühl and to the Cambacérès and Suchet d'Albufera families. General Alexander von Klück spent the night before the Battle of the Marne here. The present château is a vast austere 18th century building constructed by Antoine-Pierre Desplasses, royal notary in 1756 and enlarged in 1799. Today it houses a woodworking museum.

Saint-Michel (Abbey).

Saint-Michel - 02500.
Hirson : 5 km.
Station : Hirson.
Bus service.
Property of the commune.

Saint-Michel was founded in 945 by two Irish mons who set up an abbey following the Benedictine rule. It was destroyed and reconstructed between 1598 and 1632 and again in 1715 after a fire. In the church the choir, transept and rose window go bac to the 12th century while the nave, door and belfry date from the 17th century. Other buildings date from the 16th to 19th centuries. The abbey is surounded by a formal garden and a pond.
Open on request.
Parking.
Guided tours, brochures.
English, pannels and leaflets.
Festivals, concerts, recitals.
Theatre, temporary exhibits.
Lecture tours for school children.
Tel. : (23) 98.64.76.

Photo J. Delaplace

Saint-Jean-des-Vignes (Abbey).

Soissons - 02200.
Rue Saint-Jean.
Bus service.
Property of the commune.

Saint-Jean-des-Vignes was founded in 1067 by a repentant nobleman on the advice of the bishop of Soissons. It is a complex of buildings which date from the Romanesque period to the Renaissance and used to house Augustinians. Although it was ruined at the Revolution it still has a decorated façade, a 13th century refectory, a 15th century residence and the remains of a 16th century cloister.
Open March 1 to May 31 : 10 - 12, 2 - 5.
June 1 to Aug. 31 : 10 - 12, 2 - 6.
Sept. to Nov. : 10 - 12, 2 - 5.
Nov. 1 to Feb. 28, weekends and Wednesdays : 10 - 12, 2 - 5.
Closed Tuesdays.
Parking.
Guided tours available.
Brochures.
Concerts.
Temporary art exhibitions.
Lecture tours for school groups.
Tel. : (23) 53.17.37.

Saint-Léger (Abbey).

Soissons - 02200.
2, rue de la Congrégation.
Reims : 57 km.
Station : Soissons.
Bus service.
Property of the commune.

Saint-Léger was founded in 1139 thanks to the influence of the bishop of Soissons. Remains include the abbey church which has been partially destroyed and often remodelled, a 17th century tower, an 13th century chapter house and

---

SAINT-MICHEL-EN-THIERACHE AISNE
Sound and Light   Cultural Centre

Come and visit the 12th and 17th century church, the 17th and 18th century abbey, the 1741 Boizard organ, the 16th century prévot's house, the formal garden, ponds and museum.

a late 13th century cloister. The abbey now houses the municipal museum.
Open all year : 10 - 12, 2 - 5.
Closed Tuesdays.
Parking.
Unaccompanied visits, brochures.
Lecture tours for school groups.
Tel. : (23) 59.12.00.

Vauclair (Abbey).

Bouconville-Vauclair - 02000.
Laon : 20 km.
Station : Laon.
Property of the department.

The first Cistercian abbey was built on this site in 1143 by Saint Bernard. The second was constructed in the 13th century and survived the Hundred Years War and the Revolution only to be destroyed in 1917 during the Chemin des Dames battle. Today temporary exhibits are held here and a garden of medicinal plants has been established on the site of the monk's pharmacy.
Open April 4 to Oct. 31 : 8 am to 10 pm.
Parking.
Guided tours on request.
Pannels or leaflets.

Dutch, English, German : university holidays.
Brochure.
Concerts.

Vierzy (Castle Farm).

Vierzy - 02010.
Soissons : 13 km.
Station : Vierzy.
Private property.

The keep in the midle of the court is all that remains of the 15th century castle of Vierzy. A second residence was errected in 1500 and a gallery for watching toournements was added in 1520. Three rooms are hung with paintings and prints. Henri IV and Gabrielle d'Estrées were guests at this castle which belonged to Jean d'Estrées, Lepeletier de Saint-Fargeau and the princesse de Chimay.
Open on request July 1 to Sept. 30, for groups Sunday afternoons.
(With one month's notice.)
Parking.
Unaccompanied visits.
Lecture tours for school groups.
Tel. : (23) 55.31.48.

OISE

Boury-en-Vexin (Château).

Boury-en-Vexin - 60240.
Gisors : 7 km.
Station : Gisors.
Property of M. Zentz d'Alnois.

This typical Classical styl French château was vuilt betwee 1685 and 1689 by Jules Hardouir Mansart for the marquis de Boury Guillaume Aubourg. The mai block is flanked by two wings an surmounted by a pediment. Th original cut-stone façades are de corated with sculpture by Miche Poissant. The 18th century chape houses a Charles Le Brun alte piece.
Open weekends April 15 to Oct. 1.
daily July 1 to Aug. 31 : 2:30 - 6:30.
Closed Tuesdays.
Parling.
Groups on request.
Guided tours.
English.
Lecture tours for school groups.
Ballets.
Tel. : (32) 55.15.10.

BOURY-EN-VEXIN

OISE

Jules Hardouin-Mansart designed this château for Guillaume Aubourg, marquis de Boury, councillor to Louis XIV, between 1685 and 1689. The sculptures are by Michel Poissant. The chapel contains a Le Brun alterpiece and the iron staircase is the work of Nicholas Duflos (1691).
This is a fine example of 17th century French Classical architecture. The château is still in habited by descendants of the marquis de Boury and has kept its family character.

CHANTILLY

OISE

One of the world's finest museum's in one of the world's finest settings.

Here at Chantilly the Institut de France owns a complex of châteaux and other buildings built between the 16th and 19th centuries by the d'Orgemont, Montmorency, Condé families and by the duc d'Aumale.

The Condé museum is open daily except Tuesdays from 10:30 to 5 or 6 according to season.

(Tel. : (4) 457.03.62.) It includes an extraordinary collection of paintings, drawings, enamels, furniture, tapestries, arms and a very precious library.

The large park comprises a formal garden, an English garden, a hamlet and a number of basins and water falls.

The Institut de France has opened a horse museum in the main stables.

Chaalis (Château and abbey).

Fontaine Chaalis - 60305.
Senlis : 10 km.
Property of the Institut de France.

Romantic ruins are all that remain of this 18th century abbey built by Jean Aubert on the site on a 13th century abbey. The château survived the Revolution to house a collection of Egyptian antiquities and Medieval paintings as well as mementoes of Jean-Jacques Rousseau. Madame Jacquemart-André left the complex to the Institut de France.
Open : Museum : March 1 to Nov. 1, Mon., Wed., Sat. : 1:30 - 6.
Sun. and holidays : 10 - 12, 1:30 - 6.
Closed Tuersdays.
Park daily except Tuesdays.
Parking.
Guided tour of the Museum.
Tel. : (4) 454.00.01.

Chantilly (Château).

Chantilly - 60500.
Station : Chantilly 3 km.
Property of the Institution de France.

Chantilly belonged to the Montmorency family fron 1484 to 1632 and to the princes de Condé until 1830. It then passed to Henri d'Orléans, duc d'Aumale, son of Louis-Philippe who left it and its collection to the Institut de France. The connetable Anne de Montmorency called on the finest artists of the Renaissance, Clouet, Goujon and Bullant, to build and decorate the Petit Château which is intact. The gardens were designed by Le Nôtre for the Grand Condé. The 18th century château of the duc d'Enghien faces the 19th century edifice errected by the duc d'Aumale to replace the 17th century Mansart château destroyed at the Revolution. Across the road lie the magnificent stables designed by Jean Aubert (1719-1740). The château houses a major picture collection from primitives to Poussin, Raphael, Delacroix, Corot and Ingres as well as tapestries, porcelaine and furniture. The park includes gardens, fountains and a hamlet.
Open April 1 to Sept. 30 : 10 - 6.
Oct. 1 to 31 : 10:30 - 5:30.
Nov. 1 to March 31 : 10:30 - 5.
Closed Tuesdays.
Parking.
Guided tours.
TEl. : (4) 457.03.62.

Compiègne (Château).

Compiègne - 60200.
Property of the State.

Louis XV called on Jacques-Ange Gabriel to transform Compiègne into a residence worthy of the king of France. Work began in 1751 and was not finished until 1787 under Louis XVI. The garden façade has a fine portico and the main courtyard entrance has two pavilions linked by a colonade. The royal apartments were decorated for Marie-Antoinette and the Imperial apartments were painted by Redouté and Girodet. Part of the palace houses a vintage car museum and a Second Empire museum.
Open April 1 to Sept. 30 : 10 - 12, 1:30 - 6.
Oct. 1 to March 31 : 10 - 12, 1:30 - 5.
Closed Tuesdays.
Parking.
Audiovisual programmes.
English, German, Spanish, guides.
Facilities for the handicapped.
Brochures.
Lecture tours for school groups.
Tel. : (4) 440.02.02.

Corbeil-Cerf (Château).

Corbeil-Cerf - 60110.
Méru : 6 km.
Station : Méru.
Private property.

This little 16th century château has two mian buildings, one Renaissance, the other Henri IV. It is surrounded by a leafy park.
Open on request.
Parking.
Guided tours.
English, guide.
Tel. : (4) 452.02.43 or (1) 520.23.10.

CRÉPY-EN-VALOIS

Le Valois and L'Archerie (Castle and Museum).

Crépy-en-Valois - 60800.
Rue Gustave-Choppinet.
Station : Crépy-en-Valois.
Property of the commune.

This archery museum, the on of its kind in France is housed the auditorium and 12th centu chapel of Valois castle. These o ginal edifices are situated near t ramparts and have fine woode ceilings. Two towers and the r mains of a 14th century keep s survive along with a museum religious art.
Open March 21 to Nov. 11 : 10 - 2 - 6.
Closed Tuesdays.
Parking.
Unaccompanied visits, brochures.
Pannels or leaflets.
English, German.
Lecture tours for school groups.
Tel. : (4) 459.21.97.

ERMENONVILLE

Jean-Jacques Roussea Park.

Ermenonville - 60440.
Senlis : 12 km.
Station : Plessis-Belleville 8 km.
Bus service.

This park was designed in t English style at the end of the 18 century by the marquis de Gira din. Jean-Jacques Roussea spent the last six weeks of his li here. His tomb is on the Ile au peupliers in the park. Archeolo cal centre.
Main entrance open all year : 9 - 1 5 - 7.
Village entrance, rue Girardin : July 1 Sept. 30 : 2 - 6.
April to May and Sept. to Oct. : we kends 2 - 6.
Closed Tuesdays.
Parking.
Unaccompanied visits, brochures.
Closed Tuesdays.
Pannels or leaflets.
English, German.
Tel. : (4) 454.00.08.

Morienval (Abbey).

Morienval - 60127.
Place de l'Église.
Crépy-en-Valois : 7 km.
Private property.

This Benedictine abbey w founded by Dagobert; rebuilt the 17th century and closed on t king's orders in 1743. The 17 century conventual buildings an abbess's pavilion are built adjc

Mont-l'Évêque (Castle).

Mont-l'Évêque - 60300.
Station : Chantilly 12 km.
Bus service.
Property of M. de Pontalba.

A 13th century façade remains from this former hunting lodge. Most of the castle was built in 1835 in Romantic Troubadour style. The 15th century chapel contains period sculpture.
Open on request.
Parking.
Guided tours.
English, guide.
Tel. : (4) 453.05.34.

Neuilly (Commanderie).

Neuilly-sous-Clermont - 60290.
31, rue de la Commanderie.
Clermont : 5 km.
Station : Clermont.
Private property.

This complex belonged first to the Templars and then to the knights of Saint John of Jerusalem. It comprises a Gothic chapel and cellar and a Renaissance residence surrounded by a formal garden.
Open May 1 to Oct. 15.
Groups by request 1 month's notice by writing to M. Ariès, 19, boulevard Montmorency, 75016 Paris.
Guided tours.
Tel. : (4) 473.00.53.

Ourscamp (Abbey).

Chiry-Ourscamp - 60138.
Noyon : 6 km.
Station : Ourscamp 1,5 km.
Private property.

This abbey was founded by Saint Bernard in 1129 date of the ruins of the choir and infirmary one of the few remaining in France. The abbot's palace with one wing remaining intact was built in the 18th century.
Open all year Jan. 1 to Dec. 12 : 8 - 6. The infirmary is used for religious services Sundays and holidays and is Closed from 9 - 12 on those days.
Parking.
Guided tours on request.
Brochures.
Concerts and organ recitals.
Tel. : (4) 476.98.08.

Pierrefonds (Castle).

Pierrefonds - 60450.
Compiègne : 14 km.
Property of the State.

This castle was built at the end of the 14th century by Louis d'Orléans in a clearing of the Valois forset particulary rich in game. It was dismantled by Louis XIII but its Romantic ruins caought the attention of Napoleon III who asked Viollet-le-Duc to restore it and adapt it to the needs of the court. The result is a fine reconstruction of a Medieval castle and a good example of the 19th century rediscovery of the period.
Open April 1 to Sept. 30 : 10 - 12, 2 - 6.

PIERREFONDS

OISE

The old castle was completely demolished by Louis XIII but Pierrefonds was resurrected by Viollet-le-Duc in 1857. It is an extraordinary example of the Neo-Gothic style popular in the 19th century and much appreciated by the Emperess Eugénie.

le prieuré d'airaines

Airaines Priory prides itself on offering the visitor a variety of cultural activities in which he can be an active participant instead of a passive consumer.

The 16th century priory with its 12th century church is regularly the setting for exhibits and concerts.

For further information write to the Prieuré d'Airaine, 80270 Airaines or cal the « Amis du Prieuré » : (22) 26.05.05.

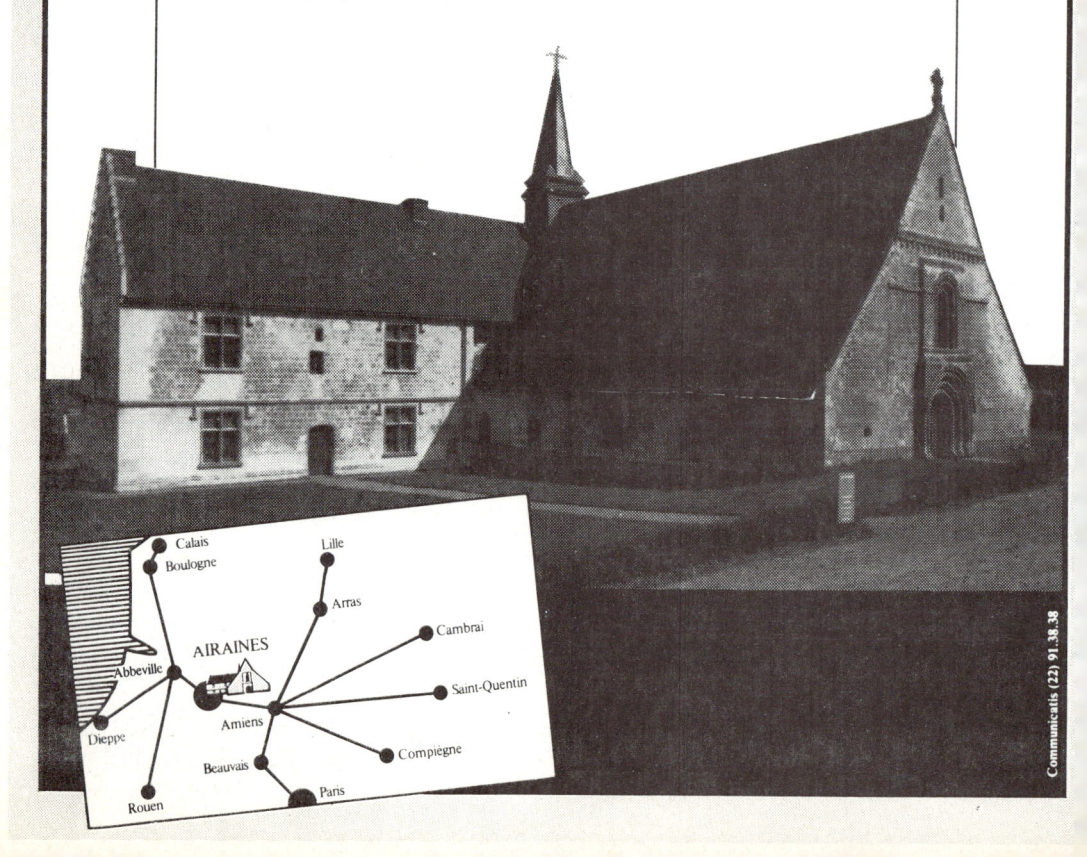

ct. 1 to March 31 : 10 - 12, 2 - 4.
Closed Tuesdays in summer.
Closed Tuesdays and Wednesdays in winter.
Guided tours, brochures.
Tel. : (4) 442.80.77.

Le Plessis-Brion (Château).

Le Plessis-Brion - 60150.
Compiègne : 8 km.
Station : Thourotte 1, 5 km.
Bus service.
Private property.
This brick and stone Renaissance château is one of the few remaining from that period in the region. It was built on medieval foundations and is a fine example of the transition between Gothic and Renaissance style. The monumental gate dates from the 16th century. Inside are period furniture and tapestries.
Open daily July 1 to Aug. 15 : 9 - 12, 2 - 6.
Parking.
Guided tours, brochures.
English, text.
Tel. : (4) 476.09.07.

Raray (Château).

Raray-Barbery - 60810.
Senlis : 12 km.
Private property.
Nicholas de Lancy had a new château built here in 1600. He had it surrounded by walls with small defensive towers. From this period remains the two stories of the North pavilion and main block and the two extraordinary arcades of the main court with their busts and statues of hunting scenes. Around 1760 the marquise des Barres had the château enlarged. Jean Cocteau chose the site for the location of his film « La Belle et la Bête ».
Open weekends and holidays March 15 to Nov. 11 : 1 - 7.
Parking.
Grounds only.
Unaccompanied visits, brochures.
Pannels and leaflets.
Tel. : (4) 454.73.53.

Rivecourt (Château).

Rivecourt - 60126.
Compiègne : 15 km.
Station : Longueil-Sainte-Marie 8 km.
Bus service.
Property of M. and Mme J. Varenne.
Rivecourt was built on the foundations of the ancient castle by the marquis de Maleyssie-Melun in 1643. The building is a pure example of French Clasical style with its main block flanked with two wingws, its slate roof and small paned windows. Set in a vast park the estate has a kennel for hounds.
Open on request for groups.
Parking.
Tel. : (4) 441.17.48.

SENLIS

Saint-Martin (Pavilion).

Senlis - 60300.
93, rue du Faubourg-Saint-Martin.
Station : Chantilly 10 km.
Bus service.
Private property.
This large 18th century house has a ground floor which shows the influence of Ledoux and two salons with period panelling. It is surrounded by a small park and served as maréchal Foch's headquarters during World War One.
Open by request for groups.
Tel. : (40 453.00.71.

La Victoire (Abbey).

Senlis - 60300.
Station : Chantilly 10 km.
Bus service.
Property of Madame de Pontalba.
Founded by Philip Augustus in 1223 to commemorate the battle of Bouvines, La Victoire remained a pilgrimage site until the Revolution. Besides the 17th century convent buildings, a monumental gate and 18th cnetury abbot's residence still survuve.
Open on request.
Guided tours.
English, guide.
Tel. : (4) 453.00.72.

Sainte-Croix (Priory).

Offemont - Saint-Crépin-aux-Bois 60170.
Compiègne : 16 km.
Bus service.
Private property.
This priory was established in 1331 to house a fragment of the True Cross. The ruins give some idea of the establishment : the remains of a Renaissance cloister, and the Henri IV church and cloister.
Open afternoons, Sundays and holidays.
Grounds only.
Parking.
Guided tours.
Tel. : (4) 485.92.31.

Saint-Germain-les-Verberie (Manor House).

Verberie - 60410.
Senlis : 18 km.
Station : Pont-Sainte-Maxence 10 km.
Bus service.
Private property.
The first manor was built here in the 14th century on a Gallo-Roman site. The current building dates from the 16th century with its façade flanked by two towers giving onto a paved closed court with a well and a rare period dovecote.
Open on written request.
Grounds only.
Parking.
Guided tours.
English, Italian.
Tel. : (4) 440.92.37.

Valgenceuse (Château).

Senlis - 60305.
Route de Nanteuil.
Bus service.
Private porperty.
In her château built around 1810, the marquise de Giac held a literary salon in the middle of the 19th century. Her guests included Alexandre Dumas. The seven hectare park is attributed to Le Nôtre and is laid out with three allées and a reflecting pool overlooked by a terrace with a balustrade and stone statues.
Open weekdays and holidays April 15 to Oct. 15 : 2 - 5.
Groups on written request.
Closed in August.
Grounds only.
Recommended itinerary.
Tel. : (4) 453.00.76.

Verderonne (Château).

Verderonne-Liancourt - 60140.
9, rue du Château.

Senlis : 20 km.
Station : Liancourt-Rantigny.
Private property.

Étienne-Louis de l'Aubespine kept the two towers and moat of the 1586 château when he had his edifice built in the 18th century. The out-buildings comprise tax barn, stables and dairy. In 1760 one of te dovecotes was replaced by by a large theatre with a coffered ceiling and cupola. A pond lies near the out-buildings. Helvetius lived here.
Open on request.
Parking.
Concerts.
Temporary exhibits.
Tel. : (4) 473.10.67.

Versigny (Château).

Versigny - 60440.
Senlis : 14 km.
Station : Nanteuil-le-Haudouin 4 km.
Private property.

Richelieu burned down the Philip-Augustus castle which was then rebuilt between 1640 and 1690. Bossuet lived here in 1695 when he was bishop of Meaux. Versigny was restored in 1848 in a style half way between the Venetian and English Palladian.
Open daily May 15 to Aug. 1 : 2 - 6.
Groups on request out of season.
Parking.
Grounds only.
Unaccompanied visits.
Information pannels.
Brochures.
Tel. : (4) 488.04.38.

SOMME

Airaines (Priory).

Airaines - 80270.
Amiens : 30 km.
Station : 10 km.
Bus service.
Property of the commune.

This Benedictine priory was founded in 1110 for the Cluniacs and destroyed by the Burgundians in 1422. It was rebuilt in the 16th century. The church is the oldest religious monument in the department and is an example of the transition between Romanesque and Gothic styles. The 11th century baptismal font survives. Since 1978 the priory has been a cultural centre.
Open daily June 19 to Sept 26 : 2 - 6.
Weekends April 24 to June 6 : 2 - 6.
Parking.
Unaccompanied visits, brochures.
Temporary modern art exhibits.
Tel. : (22) 26.05.05.

Bagatelle (Château).

Abbeville - 80100.
131, route de Paris.
Station : Abbeville.
Private property.

Once a small pavilion, Bagatelle was transformed in the 18th century by Josse Van Robais, the son of a Dutch draper. This harmonious « folly » comprises a rotunda flanked by short symetrical wings crowned by a Mansard roof. The richly sculpted façades blend well with the painted woodwork, wrought iron and formal gardens. Poets and Musicians such as Sedaine, Eric Satie and Vincent d'Indy were guests here.
Open July 1 to Aug. 30 : 2 - 7.
Groups on request from Easter to Nov. 1.
Closed Tuesdays.
Guided tours.
English, German, guides.
Lecture tours for school groups.

Bertangles (Château).

Villers-Bocages - 80260.
Amiens : 10 km.
Station : Amiens.
Bus service.
Property of M. de Clermont-Tonnerre.

A long avenue enclosed by a wrought iron gate decorated with hunting scenes by Jean Veyren leads up to this Regency château built between 1730 and 1734 by Louis-Joseph de Clermont-Tonnerre. The edifice comprises a central block decorated by trophies and a pediment. The panelled rooms contain Louis XV and Louis XVI furniture. The grand staircase occupies the left of the main block. The estate also has a typical regional farm.
Open July 14 to Sept. 9, weekdays 5 pm, Sundays and holidays 3:30, 4:30, 5:30.
Parking at the camp site.
Guided tours.
English, guides.
Tel. : (22) 43.09.01 and (1) 520.32.69.

Courcelles (Château).

Courcelles-sous-Moyencourt - 80290.
Amiens : 22 km.
Station : Poix-de-Picardie.
Bus service.
Private property.

A semi-circular gate with four pillars surmounted by carved flower pots opens on to the formal gardens in front of Courcelles. This brick and stone edifice was built in the 18th century for Pierre Langlois de Septenville. It comprises a main block with a pediment flanked by two perpendicular wings. Maxime de Gome bought the château after the Revolution and planted an arboretum.
Open July 1 to July 31 : 10 - 12, 2 - 6
Sept. 1 to Sept. 30 : 10 - 12, 2 - 6.
Closed Sundays.
Groups on request all year.
Parking.
Guided tours.
English.
Tel. : (22) 90.82.51.

Long (Château).

Longpré-les-Corps-Saints - 80510.
Grand-Place.
Abbeville and Amiens : 18 km.
Station : Abbeville and Amiens.
Private property.

Honoré Charles de Buissy mayor of Abbeville had this château built in 1733. The two story brick and stone main building with its rounded decoration is a rarity in Picardy. The painted Huet panelled rooms contain Louis XV and Louis XVI furniture and a collection of 18th century clocks.
Open daily Aug. 20 to Sept. 30 : 10 12, 2 - 5.
Parking.
Guided tours.
Acoustiguides.
Tel. : (22) 31.82.22.

Prouzel (Château).

Prouzel - 80160.
Amiens.
Bus service.
Property of M. G. de l'Épine.

Prouzel was built in 1699 and 1700 by Adrien Creton, royal councillor and mayor of Amiens. The château comprises a main block with two single story wings. The court facade has a pediment. The carved wood panneled interiors are the work of Jacques Rousseau the 18th century architect builder of the old theatre in Amiens.
Open Aug. 1 to Sept. 30.
Interiors on writen request.
Parking.
Unaccompanied visits.
Tel. : (22) 42.12.81.

ABBEVILLE

BAGATELLE
The fairy tale folly

SOMME

This delicate little brick and stone castle is hidden behind a wall on the outskirts of Abbeville.
The exteriors and the interior decoration of painted woodwork, wrought iron and furniture are a fetching architectural ensemble. Set in its formal garden and park Bagatelle has remained untouched by time. A visit here is a trip into a fairy tale. Poetry and music mingle at Bagatelle : Sedaine, Eric Satie and Vincent d'Indy were guests here.
The museum of contemporary history « France 40 » commemorates the men who fought here in 1940 : Weygand, de Gaulle, Evans, Guderian, Rommel. It includes pictures, models, artillery.
Open Easter and July 1 to August 30, except Tuesdays, 2 - 7. Also weekends in September.
By appointment at other times.
131, route de Paris, 80100 Abbeville.
Tel. : 551.82.83 in Paris.

SOMME

RAMBURES

Six centuries of history in a leafy setting.
A feudal fortress.
A unique example of 15th century military architecture which recieved a visit from Henri IV.

Rambures castle is the most complete and well preserved specimen of military architecture. It was designed in the mid-15th century to resist the new artillery.

Its history is linked to thoat of the end of the Hundred Years War in Picardy where the Rambures family played a crucial role. In 1402 David de Rambures was a member of the royal council ; in 1410 he was one of the twelve knights put in charge of the government when Charles VI went mad. The Rambures family continued in the royal service. The most famous was Charles « the brave » who saved the life of Henri IV at the battle of Ivry in 1590.

Throughout the years Rambures has kept its massive structure rising from the dry moat with its four large towers, machiculations and interiors where past meets present.

Rambures (Castle).

Disemont-Rambures - 80140
Abbeville : 25 km.
Private property.

The fortress built by the Rambures family in the 15th century and transformed in the 18th still belongs to the same family. The four massive towers are set around a square. A white stone gallery surounds the brick castle along the sentry way. A deep dry moat enclosed the castle and the 17th century out-buildings. The interiors have undergone many transformations.
Open daily except Tuesdays, March 1 to Oct. 31 : 10 -12, 2 - 6.
Sundays and holidays, or by appointment, Nov. 1 to Feb. 28 : 2 - 5.
Parking.
Guided tours, brochures.
Tel. : (22) 25.10.93.

Regnière-Écluse (Château).

Reginière-Écluse - 80120.
Abbeville : 23 km.
Station : Rue 6 km.
Private property.

The Renaissance château was restored and transformed in 1830 to turn into a neo-Gothic castle. The park also dates from the 19th century.
Open on request easter to Nov. 1.
Unaccompanied visits.
Tel. : (22) 29.92.64.

Valloires (Abbey).

Near Argoules
Valloires - 80120.
Abbeville : 30 km.
Station : 16 km.
Private property.

This 12th century Cistercian monastery was ruined by war and pillaging between the 14th and 16th century. It was rebuilt in the 18th century under the auspices of Monseigneur d'Orléans de La Motte. The austere exteriors and cloister contrast with the elaborate wood carving of the chapel and the objets d'art of the chapter house and sacristy. The gate is a masterpiece of 18th century wrought iron work.
Open daily, April 1 to Nov. 3 : 10 - 12, 2:30 - 6:30.
Parking.
Guided tours.
Concerts.
Tel. : (22) 29.91.01.

Vauchelles (Château).

Vauchelles-Lés-Domart - 80620.
Abbeville : 14 km.
Amiens : 28 km.
Station : Abbeville.
Bus service.
Private property.

This vast 17th and 18th century brick and stone edifice is set around a paved courtyard. The main building is flanked by a perpendicular wing and two corner pavilions. The château has been passed down in the same family of royal officals since the seventeenth century.
Open July 1 to Sept. 30 : 11 - 3.
Interiors on request for groups.
Parking.

SOMME

VAUCHELLES

A superb 17th a, d 18th century brick and stone edifice.
Tourist environment.
Route Nationale 1 between Amiens and Abbeville.
Tennis, gardens, park.

Near the seaside.
Guest rooms, meals served for groups.
Receptions, weddings, exhibits.
Open in season.
Tel. : (22) 41.62.51 and 51.62.51.

Guided tours.
Pannels or leaflets, brochures.
English, guides.
Festival.
Lecture tours for school groups.
Tel. : (22) 41.62.51 and 51.62.51.

Wailly (Château).

Conty 80160.
Amiens : 18 km.
Station : Amiens.
Private property.

All that remains of the 1630 château is one wing and the arcaded out-buildings dating from 1670. The Louis XVI semi-circular decoration was not completed until 1785. The Louis XIII brick and stone château contains a Louis XVI chapel.

Open on request.
Parling.
Tel. : (22) 42.11.07.

POITOU CHARENTES

CHARENTE,
CHARENTE-MARITIME,
DEUX-SÈVRES,
VIENNE.

- ■ castle, château, manor house
- ● abbey, priory
- ▲ garden, park
- ★ town house, famous men house, farm, mill...
- ○ city

NIORT
- ★ Donjon
- ★ Ancien Hôtel de Ville

LA ROCHELLE
- ★ Tours

ANGOULÊME
- ★ Hôtel d'Epernon
- ★ Hôtel de ville

○ Moulins
■ Champ d'Oiseau
■ Oiron
■ Ternay
★ Loudun
■ La Chapelle-Bellouin
■ La Rye (manoir de)
● Airvault
■ Les Robinières
■ Tennessue
■ Touffou
POITIERS ○
■ La Sayette
● ▲ Saint-Benoît
■ Chauvigny (château d'Harcourt)
■ Marconnay
■ La Roussière
■ Chambonneau ● Villesalem
■ Le Coudray-Salbart
■ Gençay
NIORT ○
■ Epanvilliers
○ LA ROCHELLE
■ Leray ● La Réau
■ Buzay
● Charroux
■ Dampierre-sur-Boutonne
★ Ile d'Aix
■ Beaufief
■ Biracq (tour de)
■ Crazannes
■ Bayers
■ Rochebrune
■ La Roche-Courbon
★ Brouage ■ Panloy
■ La Gataudière ■ Le Douhet
■ Château Chesnel ★ Boisbreteau (logis de)
● Fontdouce (Abbaye de)
■ Cognac
ANGOULÊME ○
■ Villebois-Lavalette
■ Lerse

POITOU-CHARENTES

CHARENTE

ANGOULÊME
Hôtel d'Épernon.

Angoulême - 16000.
60, rue du Minage.
Private property.

This house once belonged to the duc d'Épernon the governor of the Angoumois. It is said to have been the inspiration for Balzac in his novel « Les Illusions Perdues ». The crenelated south face is flanked by an octagonal tower whereas the south face has a crenelated entrance. It was remodelled in the 18th century and the interiors include fireplaces, pannelling and mirrors dated 1794. Numerous historic and literary mementoes are kept here.

Open on request.
Parking.
Tel. : (45) 95.34.64.

Hôtel de Ville.

Angoulême - 16000.
Property of the city.

The Angoulême city hall was built in the 19th century in Renaissance style on the site of the castle of the ducs d'Angoulême. All that remains of the old castle are its two finest towers. Inside are Second Empire salons.

Open July 1 to Aug. 31 : 10, 2:30, 4:30.
Groups on request all year.
Closed Sundays.
Guided tours.
English, German, Spanish.
Tel. : (45) 38.98.44.

Bayers (Castle).

Aunac - 16460.
Angoulême : 38 km.
Station : 14 km.
Private property.

The castle was dismantled at the Revolution and slowly fell to ruin until restoration began in 1979. It comprises a tower and sentry near a 15th century building.

Open on request during the restoration work.
Parking.
Tel. : (45) 20.24.07 and 22.24.07.

Boisbreteau (Residence).

Rouillac - 16170.
Angoulême : 25 km station.
Property of M. Natalis.

Boisbreteau comprises a restored 12th century square tower next to a 17th century pavilion with a Mansard roof. Fine interior staircase.

Open on request July 20 to Aug. 30 : 3 - 7.
Parking.
Guided tours.
Information in English, German, Spanish and Dutch.
Pannels, brochures.
Tel. : (45) 96.78.15.

Chesnel (Château).

Cherves-de-Cognac - Cherves-Richemont - 16370.
Cognac : 7 km.
Property of M. de Roffignac.

Jacques Chesnel, governor of Cognac had the château built between 1590 and 1610. It is a horeshoe-shaped Italian Renaissance style building, flanked by four square towers. The complex is surrounded by the dry moat dug out of the rock which served as quarry for the château.

Open April 1 to Oct. 15.
Groups only, on request.
Guided tours.
Tel. : (45) 83.24.52.

Cognac (Château).

Cognac - 16100.
Angoulême : 40 km.
Property of Cognac Otard S.A.

The Valois family château was embellished by François I and reached its apogee in the 16th century. From this period date the king's balcony and the guard room. The Otard Cognac company has been here since 1795.

Open daily April 1 to Sept. 30 : (July and Aug.; every half hour) : 9:30 - 11:30, 2 - 5:30.
Oct. 1 to March 31 : 10, 11, 2, 3, 4, 5 (except weekends).
Parking.
Guided tours with audiovisual programme.
Information in English and German.
Brochures.
Tel. : (45) 82.40.00.

Lerse (Castle).

Pérignac - Blanzac - 16250.
Angoulême : 30 km.
Station : Montmoreau 7 km.
Private property.

Lerse is a 13th century stronghold built on a square plan around an interior courtyard. It has remained unchanged throughout the centuries. On the side of a hill in Périgord, just south of Angoulême, it was a hostel for pilgrims on their way to Santiago da Compostella.

Open all year 2 - 6.
Parking.

Grounds only.
Unaccompanied visits.
Information in English.
Tel. : (45) 60.32.81.

Rochebrune (Castle).

Étagnac - 16150.
Chabanais : 6 km.
Property of M. de Richemont.

Rochebrune was built in the 11th century by the princes de Chabanais and then belonged to the maréchal de Montluc. It is a example of a Romanesque stronghold, built on a square plan, protected by four round towers and moat. Inside is Renaissance and Empire Furniture.

Open April 1 to June 30, Sept. 16 à Nov. 11 : 2 - 6.
July 1 to Sept. 15 : 10 - 12, 2 - 6.
Guided tours, brochures.
Information in English, German, Dutch
Tel. : (45) 89.00.42 and 89.20.65.

Villebois-Lavalette (Château).

Villebois-Lavalette - 16320.
Angoulême : 25 km.
Station : Charmant 10 km.
Property of MM. B. and P. de Fleury.

Villebois-Lavalette was rebuilt in the 17th century on an ancient Gaulish site. A few towers and the chapel remain from the 11th century structure. The church is Romanesque. A walk around the fortress offers fine views of the surrounding countryside.

Open all year.
Parking.
Grounds only.
Guided tours.
Tel. : (45) 64.90.47.

CHARENTE-MARITIME

Beaufief (Château).

Beaufief-Mazeray - 17400.
Station : Saint-Jean-d'Angély 2 km.
Private property.

This Louis XV folly was built in season. It comprises a main bloc with two circular wings and contains 18th century furniture and a chapel decorated with plaster work.

Open daily Easter to Nov. 1 : 2 - 7.
On request the rest of the year.
Parking.
Guided tours, brochures.
Information in English, German, Portuguese.
Show and concerts.
Picnic area.
Tel. : (46) 32.35.93.

iracq (Tower).

randjean-Saint-Savinien - 17350.
aintes : 10 km.
ation : Saint-Savinien 7 km.
operty of M. Foucher.
This 13th century fortified house typical of the region but its history and origin remain a mystery. It built on a square plan and is nked by a corner tower. Inside a small museum of regional archeological artifacts.
pen all year : 10 - 12, 2:30 - 6.
arking.
uided tours.
cnic area.
el. : (46) 90.25.68.

rouage (Fortified city).

iers-Brouage - 17320.
arennes : 7 km.
operty of the town.
In the 17th century Brouage was ill a major salt exporting port, rilling La Rochelle. The salt flats as abandoned and the port silted p. It was only at the end of the th century that any interes was own in this monumental comex surrounded by two kilometers walls. Today Brouage is one of e finest remains of military architecture. It was the home of Samuel de Champlain.
Open daily 9 - 12, 2 - 7, during Easter holidays and from June 1 to the second Sunday in Sept. and Sundays in April and May.
Guided tours, brochures.
Tel. : (46) 85.19.16.

Buzay (Château).

La Jarrie - 17720.
La Rochelle : 7 km.
Private property.
Buzay has belonged to the same family since its construction in the 18th century. The interiors still have their wood pannelling and fine period furniture. The garden façade is decorated with Ionic pilasters.
Open daily July 1 to Aug. 31 : 2:30 - 5:30.
On request out of season.
Guided tours.
Notices in English and German.
Tel. : (46) 44.28.31.

Crazannes (Château).

Crazannes near Saint-Savinien - 17350.
Station : Saintes 14 km.
Property of M. and Mme de Rochefort.

The current residence was built in the 15th century by the seigneurs de Tonnay-Charente. It comprises a keep and a dwelling with a fine Gothic north face. 11th century Romanesque chapel.
Open school holidays and weekends : 2 - 6.
Parking.
Guided tours, brochures.
Information in English and German.
Tel. : (46) 90.15.94.

Dampierre-sur-Boutonne (Château).

Dampierre-sur-Boutonne - Aulnay - 17470.
Niort : 35 km.
Villeneuve-la-Comtesse : 8 km.
Private property.
This little Renaissance château

COGNAC

CHARENTE

The Valois château and the Otard Cognac cellars.

CHARENTE

ROCHEBRUNE

Set in the heart of the Charente Limousine, between Limoges and Angoulême, Rochebrune is open to the public from Palm Sunday to November 11. It is inhabited and entirely furnished and contains interesting Renaissance and Second Empire mementoes.

Tel. : (45) 89.00.42 or 89.20.65.

...set on an island in the Boutonne ...ver. It has a remarkable façade ...ith a carved double gallery. ...ampierre was besieged four ...mes and visited by François I and ...ouis XIII.
...pen daily June 1 to Sept. 30 : 9:30 - ...2, 2:30 - 7.
...ct. 1 to May 31 : 10 - 12, 2 - 5, Sun-...ays and holidays.
...arking.
...uided tours, brochures.
...annels.
...formation in English.
...xhibitions.
...el. : (46) 33.82.24.

...e Douhet (Château).

...e Douhet near Saintes - 17100.
...aintes : 10 km.
...rivate property.
   This former residence of the bis-...ops of Saintes was built on the ...ite of a feudal castle around 1680. ...was sold at the Revolution and ...nally restored in 1925. A double ...taircase leads down to two ba-...ins.
...pen all year : 10 - 12, 2 - 7.
...losed Monday mornings.
...naccompanied visits.
...annels, brochures.
...emporary exhibits.
...el. : (46) 74.38.14.

...ontdouce (Abbey).

...aint-Bris-des-Bois.
...rizambourg - 17770.
...tation : Saintes or Cognac 15 km.
...rivate property.
   This stopping place on the route ... Santiago da Compostella was ...t its apogée in the 14th century ...ut later suffered in the Wars of ...eligion. The cellar has been com-...letely preserved. The two Roma-...esque Chapels, the chapter ...ouse etc. are open to the public. ...he abbey houses cultural and re-...gious activities while the excava-...ons are still in progress.
...pen July 1 to Sept. 30 : 10 - 12, 2 - 7.
...pril 1 to June 30 : and Oct. 1 to 31 : 2 -

...losed Sunday mornings.
...arking.
...uided tours, brochures.
...el. : (46) 91.55.24.

La Gataudière (Château).

Marennes - 17320.
Station : Rochefort-sur-Mer 22 km.
Private property.

   Once the property of François Fresneau, a pupil of Vauban, royal engineer, mathematician, botanist and explorer, this edifice is an example of 18th century architecture. The sculpted salon is a masterpiece in its genre.
Open daily March 1 to May 31 and Oct. 1 to Nov. 30, Sundays and holidays : 10 - 12, 2:30 - 6.
Parking.
Guided tours of the interiors, brochures.
Tel. : (46) 85.01.07.

Panloy (Château).

Port-d'Envaux-Saint-Savinien - 17350.
Near Saintes.
Private property.
   Restored in 1770, Panloy now offers a fine example of Louis XV architecture set between two Renaissance pavilions. The wood-panneled dining room, the salon hung with Beauvais tapestries, the dovecote and park are open to the public.
Open daily June 1 to Sept. 30 : 2 - 6.
Sundays and holidays Oct. 1 to May 31.
Groups on request in the mornings.
Parking.
Guided tours.
Leaflets in English and German.
Facilities for the handicapped.
Temporary exhibits.
Tel. : (46) 91.73.23.

La Roche-Courbon (Château).

Saint-Porchaire - 17250.
Station : Saintes 17 km.
Private property.
   This large residence was built in the middle of a forest in the 15th century and transformed in the 17th century. It has remarkable 17th century interiors and a formal garden. There is also a small museum of the prehistoric artifacts found on the grounds of the château.
Château and keep open daily March 16 to Feb. 2 : 10 - 12, 2:30 - 6:30.
Closed Thursdays Sept. 15 to June 15.
Park, gardens and grottoes open daily 9 - 12, 2 - 6:30.
Parking.
Guided tours, brochures.
Tel. : (46) 95.60.10.

LA ROCHELLE

Tour de la Lanterne
Tour Saint-Nicolas.

Property of the State.
   These two towers are situated at the entrance of the port of La Rochelle which they used to defend.
Tour Saint-Nicholas : April 1 to Sept. 30 : 10 - 12:30, 2:30 - 6.
Oct. 1 to March 31 : 2 - 5.
Tour de la Lanterne : April 1 to Sept. 30 : 9 - 12, 2 - 6:30.
Oct. 1 to March 31 : 2 - 5.
Closed Tuesdays.
Guided tours, brochures.
Tel. : (46) 41.09.57.

DEUX-SÈVRES

Airvault (Abbey).

Airvault - 79600.
Thouars : 23 km.
Property of the city.
This ancient abbey comprises ramparts, a prison, a chapel, residential buildings and a vaulted

cellar. It now houses a folk museum.
Open daily July 1 to Sept. 15 : 2:30 - 6.
Sundays and holidays Sept. 16 to June 30 : 2 - 5.
Parking.
Unaccompanied visits, brochures.
Temporary exhibits.
Lecture tours for groups on request.
Tel. : (49) 64.71.42.

Coudray-Salbart (Castle).

Échiré.- 79410.
Niort : 8 km.
Private property.

This six towerd fortress dates from the 13th century and occupied a strategic position at the gates of Niort. Its good state of preservation makes it one of the best examples of medieval military architecture. The castle could contain a garrison of 300 men but never seems to have been put to the test.
Open all year : 9 - 12, 2 - 7.
Closed Tuesdays.
Parking.
Unaccompanied visits, brochures.
Temporary exhibits, receptions.
Tel. : (49) 25.71.07.

NIORT
Former Town Hall

Niort - 79000.
Place du Pilori.
Station in town.
Property of the city.

This original building was begun in the 14th century on the pilory site. Today it houses an archeological museum.
Open May 2 to Sept. 15 : 9 - 12, 2 - 4.
Sept. 16 to May 1 : 9 - 12, 2 - 5.
Guided tours avaiiable on request from the Tourist Office.
Tel. : (49) 79.25.97.

Keep and Local Ethnographical Museum.

Niort - 79000.
Place du Donjon.
Station in town.
Property of the city.

These twin keeps were errected by Henri II Plantagenet and Richard the Lionheart. They are joined by a late medieval building and house a museum of local ethnography.
Open May 2 to Sept. 14 : 9 - 12, 2 - 6.
Sept. 15 to April 30 : 9 - 12, 2 - 5.
Closed Tuesdays.
Parking.
Guided tours on request.
Information in English.
Tel. : (49) 28.14.28.

Oiron (Château).

Oiron - Thouars - 79100.
Poitiers : 57 km.
Property of the State.

Oiron rivals in beauty with the finest of the Loirs châteaux. This residence was continuously transformed by generations of the Gouffier family and offers an overview of French architecture from the 15th to the 17th centuries. The north wing is remarkable for its 16th century wall paintings. The south wing is partly the work of Madame de Montespan who acquired the château in 1700. In 1943 the State bought the château and began restoring both interiors and exteriors.
Open all year : 9 - 12:15, 2 - 6:30.
Closed Tuesdays and Wednesdays.
Parking.
Guided tours, brochures.
Tel. (49) 66.71.25.

La Roussière (Château).

Saint-Maixent-de-Beugné
Coulonges-sur-l'Auzite - 79160.
Station : Niort 25 km.
Private property.

All that is left of the original castle is the 15th century gate. The main residence was burnt down during the Wars of Religion. It was rebuilt in the 18th century. The château is in the middle of the countryside, surrounded by formal gardens.
Open daily July 1 to Aug. 31 : 9:30 - 12, 2:30 - 7.
By appointment in June.
Parking.
Information in English, ateau.
Leaflets.
Facilities for the handicapped.
Temporary exhibits.
Tel. : (49) 06.12.11.

La Sayette (Château).

Vasles - 79340.
Station : Poitiers and Parthenay 30 km.
Property of M. de La Sayette.

La Sayette consists of a central 17th century block built between two 13th century towers. Two pavilions and a Neo-Gothic chape were added in the 19th century. There is a park and elm grove with four cut stone and wrought iron gates. The La Sayette family has lived here for seven centuries.
Open Aug. 1 to Sept. 9 : 2 - 6:30 and on request.
Parking.
Guided tours, brochures.
English, German.
Guided tours on request.

Tennessue (Castle).

Amailloux - 79350.
Parthenay : 8 km.
Private property.

This little military edifice, flanked by two towers was errected in the 14th century. A keep and two blocks surround a courtyard Access is by a working draw bridge.
Open daily June 15 to Sept. 15, except Tues. : 2 - 7.
Weekends and holidays the rest of the year.
Groups on request out of season.
Parking.
Recommended itinerary.
Tel. : (49) 94.09.13.

POITOU-CHARENTES — VIENNE

VIENNE

Chambonneau (Castle).

Chambonneau-Gizay - 86340.
La Villedieu-du-Clain.
Poitiers : 18 km.
Private property.

This beautifully restored small 14th century castle is located on the site of a Roman camp. It gives out on to a park. King Jean le Bon is said to have spent his first night in captivity here.
Open July 1 to Sept. 30 : 9 - 12, 2 - 6.
Closed Sundays and holidays.
Parking.
Unaccompanied visits.
Information in English when the owner is present.
Tel. : (49) 42.00.11.

Champ-d'Oiseau (Manor House).

Les Trois-Moutiers - 86120.
Loudun : 10 km.
Private property.

This late medieval manor house was transformed into a farm. It is now in the course of restoration.
Open on request April 1 to Sept. 30.
Parking.
Tel. : (49) 98.00.10.

La Chapelle-Bellouin (Château).

La Roche-Rigault - 86200.
Loudun and Richelieu : 10 km.
Poitiers and Tours : 60 km.
Property of M. Jean-Marie Barillé.

This château was purchased in 1636 by Cardinal Richelieu. Although it is in ruins you can still make out the Renaissance main building, the main courtyard and the double surrounding walls with moat making a picturesque site.
Open daily April 1 to Oct. 30 : 2:30 - 6.
Parking.
Guided tours, brochures.
English, German, Spanish.
Pannels.
Shows and receptions.
Tel. : (49) 98.34.93.

Charroux (Abbey).

Charroux - 86250.
Property of the State.

Set in a valley near the Charente, the octagonal tower of Charroux marks the site of what was once one of the most powerful Benedictine abbeys of medieval France. It was founded in the 8th century by Robert, comte de Limoges and was protected by

---

OIRON

DEUX-SÈVRES

Sixteenth century château and collegiate, acquired by Madame de Montespan be become the « Hospice of the Holy family », Oiron has a ribbed vaulted gallery, a Renaissance grand staircase and fine painted rooms.

Charlemagne. The large 11th century church still has remnants of Carolingian style architecture. The 15th century chapter house contains pieces of Gothic sculpture.
Open April 1 to Sept. 30 : 9 - 12, 2 - 6.
Oct. 1 to March 31 : 10-12, 2 - 5.
Parking.
Guided tours, brochures.

Épanvilliers (Château).

Brux-Civray - 86400.
Poitiers : 40 km.
Station : Épanvilliers 1 km.
Private property.

This inhabited château is decorated with mantel pieces and wood-panneling dating from the XVIII th century.

It contains even older artifacts as it was once the residence of a companion at arms of François I. Special stays are organised for school children.
Open July 1 to Sept. 10 : 2 - 6.
Out of season by request.
Closed Thursdays.
Guided tours.
Information in English, Italian.
Facilities for the handicapped.
Concerts, shows, cultural activities for children.
Temporary exhibits.
Restoration site for young people.
Tel. : (49) 87.18.43.

Gençay (Castle).

Gençay - 86160.
Poitiers : 25 km.
Private property.

This massive fortress is said to have been occupied by the Black Prince who held Jean le Bon prisoner here in 1356. Today in ruins, it comprises the outer walls and a few towers housing a collection of artifacts found during the excavations.
Open Aug. 1 to 31 : 2 - 7, daily.

Sundays the rest of the year and on request.
Parking.
Guided tours.
Tel. : (49) 58.01.82.

Harcourt (Castle).

Ville Haute Chauvigny - 86300.
Poitiers : 25 km.
Property of the State.

The castle gets its name from the Norman family which sold it to Charles d'Anjou in 1447. It then passed to the bishops of Poitiers. The visitor enters through a fortified gate to visit the four stories of the Harcourt tower.
Open June 24 to Aug. 31 : 3:30 - 6:30
Sundays : 3:30 - 7.
Closed Tuesdays.

VIENNE

LA CHAPELLE-BELLOIN
12th and 16th century castle

Open April 1 to October 30.
Receptions, seminars, colloquia, conferences.
Medieval candle light dinners with troubadour entertainment for groups of at least 25.
Concerts, theatrical evenings.
Locations for films and photography.

POITOU-CHARENTES / VIENNE

...arking.
...ance concerts.
...emporary exhibits.
...el. : (49) 46.30.21.

...ayré (Castle).

...aint-Pierre-d'Exideuil-Civray - 86400.
...rivate property.
The castle was ruined in the Wars of Religion and rebuilt in the 7th century. It is inhabited.
Open June 15 to July 31, Sept. 1 to Sept. 15 : 3 - 5:30 by telephonic appointment.
Other times by written request.
Grounds only.
Parking.
Guided tours.
Horse Shows.
Tel. : (49) 87.08.55.

LOUDUN
Théophraste Renaudot's House.

Loudun - 86200.
Rue Théophraste-Renaudot.
Poitiers : 50 km.
Property of the commune.
This is the birthplace of Théophraste Renaudot, founder of the Gazette » and Louis XIII's physician. The interiors have been restored to Louis XIII style and include wax figures tracing the life of Renaudot.
Open Tue., Thurs., weekends and holidays June 15 to Sept. 15 : 3 - 6.
Sundays and holidays Sept. 16 to June 14 : 3 - 6.
Parking.
Recorded information.
Brochures.
Tel. : (49) 98.15.38.

Marconnay (Castle).

Sanxay - 86600.
Poitiers : 30 km.
Station : Rouillé 12 km.
Private property.
This fortified castle is surrounded by a moat. After being abandoned for many years it has recently been opened to the public.
Open daily July 1 to Aug. 31 and holidays Sept. 1 to June 30 : 2:30 - 6.
Closed Saturdays and July 14.
Parking.
Guided tours.
Tel. : (49) 53.53.70 after 7 pm.

Moulins (Commanderie).

Tournand near les Trois-Moutiers - 86120.
Loudun : 6 km.
Station : Saumur 27 km.
Private property.

This edifice probably belonged to the Templars until 1307 before passing to the order of the Knights of Saint John of Jerusalem. Next to the 15th century main building is a western French Gothic style chapel.
Open daily July 1 to 25 and Sept. 6 to 30 : 2:30 - 6:30.
Parking.
Unaccompanied visits, brochures.
Tel. : (49) 22.64.32.

La Réau (Abbey).

Saint-Martin-l'Ars - 86350.
Poitiers : 48 km.
Private property.
This Augustinian establishment had François de La Rochefoucauld as prior and, in 1666 d'Artagnan's brother as abbot. The Romanesque church is the largest building of the complex. Others include the chapter house with its carved keystone and a watch tower.
Open March 1 to Sept. 30 : 10 - 7.
Out of season on request.
Closed Tuesdays.
Guided tours on request.
Information in English and Dutch.
Tel. : (49) 87.84.22.

Les Robinières (Castle).

Le Haut-Clairvaux
Scorbé-Clairvaux - 86140.
Châtellerault : 10 km.
Private property.
This small rectangular two storied castle with a slate roof and turrets is built on a rock. It is surrounded by a dry moat and has a dovecote out-buildings. Inside is a small arms collection.
Open July 1 to Sept. 30 : 2 - 5.
Other times on request.
Parking.
Closed Mondays.
Guided tours.
Information in English.
Facilities for the handicapped.
Tel. : (49) 93.81.28.

La Rye (Manor House).

Vellèches - 86100.
Near Châtellerault.
Station : Dangé-Saint-Romain : 10 km.
Private property.
This 1450 manor house was part of the nearby Marmande estate. Renaissance fireplaces and mullioned windows embellish the four main rooms.
Open on request.
Parking.
Information in English and Spanish.
Tel. : (49) 21.09.51.

Saint-Benoît (Abbey).

Saint-Benoît - 86280.
Poitiers : 5 km.
Private property.
The origins of the abbey are shrouded in mystery. It may have been founded in the 7th century by Saint Auchard. It was damaged by the Vikings and during the Wars of Religion. Religious activity had almost ceased before the Revolution. Very fine capitals remain from the cloister. The highly ornemented chapter house door contrasts sharply with the austere architecture.
Open March 1 to Nov. 30.
Tel. : Tourist office : 742.21.34 or 766.75.10.

Photo M. François

Ternay (Château).

Ternay-les-Trois-Moutiers - 86120.
Loudun : 12 km.
Montreuil-Bellay : 15 km.
Property of M. and Mme de Ternay.
This 15th and 17th century château comprises a fortified keep and a Flamboyant Gothic chapel. It is the birthplace of admiral de Ternay whose fleet carried Rochambeau's troops to fight in the American war of independence.
Open during school holidays.
Parking.
Guided tours.
Tel. : (49) 22.92.82.

Touffou (Château).

Bonnes - 86300.
Chauvigny : 5 km.
Station : Châtellerault-Poitiers 25 km.
Bus service.
Private property.
This monumental complex overlooking the Vienne has kept one of its two 12th century keeps, four 15th century towers and a Renaissance wing. The so called François I room is decorated with early 17th century frescoes. The château now houses a hunting museum.
Open July 1 to Sept. 1 : 9:30 - 12:45, 2 - 6:30.
Closed Mondays.
Parking.
Guided tours, brochures.
Tel. : (49) 46.35.02.

Villesalem (Abbey).

Villesalem - Journet.
La Trémouille - 86290.
Station : Montmorillon 12 km.
Property of the State.

This convent was linked to Fontevrault until the Revolution. Its fine 12th century architecture and decoration has been kept through the ages. Its west wing is particularly interesting and it has a gem collection.

Open Oct. 1 to March 31 : 9 - 12, 2 - 4.
April 1 to Sept. 30 : 9 - 12, 2 - 7.
Closed Tuesdays.
Parking.
Facilities for the handicapped.
Brochures.
Tel. : (49) 91.62.23.

PROVENCE CÔTE D'AZUR

ALPES-DE-HAUTE-PROVENCE,
HAUTES-ALPES,
ALPES-MARITIMES,
BOUCHES-DU-RHÔNE,
VAR,
VAUCLUSE,

- ■ castle, château, manor house
- ● abbey, priory
- ▲ garden, park
- ★ town house, famous men house, farm, mill...
- ○ city

ARLES
- ● Prieuré de Malte
- ★ Hôtel de Laval-Castellanne

AVIGNON
- ★ Palais des Papes
- ★ Petit Palais
- ★ Hôtel de Villeneuve-Martignan
- ★ Hôtel d'Adhémar

GRASSE
- ★ Hôtel de Clapiers-Cabris
- ★ Villa Fragonard

NICE
- ★ Palais Lascaris
- ● Cimiez
- ▲ Arènes parc et jardin du monastère

PROVENCE-CÔTE-D'AZUR

ALPES-DE-HAUTE-PROVENCE

Allemagne (Château).
Allemagne-en-Provence - 04550.
Riez : 7 km.
Gréoux-les-Bains : 12 km.
Station : Manosque 25 km.
Bus service.
Private property.

Built by François de Castellane in 1500 and finished by his son, Mechior, in 1550, this fine Renaissance Château, of rectangular plan, boasts several impressive mullioned windows, some of which are decorated with lions, slate roofs and a spiral staircase. An enormous keep, dating from thre 11th century, remains intact. Seat of the Castellane family, Barons of Allemagne, until the 17th century, the Château was besieged during the Fronde in 1586.
Open May 31 to Sept. 30 : 3 - 7.
Closed Wednesday.
Parking.
Brochures.
Information : German.
Lecture tours.
Guided tours.
Tel. : (92) 74.41.61.

Château-Arnoux (Château).
Château-Arnoux - 04160.
Digne : 17 km.
Station : Château-Arnoux.
Bus service.
Property of the commune.

In the heart of the village. Château-Arnoux is one of the few Renaissance Châteaux to have survived intact in the region. Built in 1510, this qudrilateral, with its mullioned windows, has two round towers and two square towers. Attached to the east face is a hexagonal tower, built later, and with a monumental sculpted staircase. The park has been transformed into an arboretum and has many rare species.
Open all year : 9 - 12, 2 - 6.
Closed saturday and sunday.
Parking.
Unaccompanied tours, Brochures.
Temporary exhibitions.
Tel. : (92) 64.06.01.

Colmars-les-Alpes (Fortress) (called Fortress of Savoy).
Colmars-les-Alpes - 04370.
Digne : 50 km.
Nice : 120 km.
Station : Thorame 12 km.
Property of the commune.

The fortress of Colmars, built in the 17th century by Vauban's pupils, protected Provence from the Piedmontese. To the north, the Fortress of Savoy acts as a pendant to the southern Fortress of France, and both tower above the fortified village of Colmar-les-Alpes. The group of fortifications has remained intact.
Open daily, June 15 to Sept. 15 : 3 - 7.
By appointment, through the Tourist office, Jan. 1 to June 14 and Sept. 16 to Dec. 31.
Parking.
Guided tours, brochures.
English, German, Dutch.
Temporary exhibitions.
Tel. : (92) 83.41.92.

Entrevaux (fortress).
Entrevaux - 04320.
Nice : 70 km.
Station : 2 km.
Property of the commune.

The furthest point in the Kingdom', Entrevaux was built on the top of a cliff by Vauban in 1692. With its fortified bridge, its ramparts and its watch tower, this fortress offers a fine example of military architecture of the early 18th century.
Open June 1 to Oct. 1 : 9 - 12, 2 - 6.
Closed monday.
Parking.

FORCALQUIER

Convent of the Cordeliers.
Forcalquier - 04300.
Manosque : 23 km.
Station : Manosque.
Bus service.
Private property.

The Cordeliers Convent was one of the earliest Franciscan establishments in Provence. It was founded at the beginning of the 13th century and was supported by Count Raymond de Béranger, who endowed the convent with his own property. The complex was ravaged during the Wars of Religion and the Revolution, but the Convent has preserved its cloisters and chapter house, the latter fully restored.
Open July 1 to Sept. 30 : 10:30 - 12, 2:30 - 6.
Apr. 1 to June 30, month of October, sundays only : 2:30 - 5.
By appointment for groups throughout the year.
Parking.
Guided tours, brochures.
Temporary exhibitions.
Tel. : (92) 75.02.38.

Lure (Notre-Dame abbey).
Saint-Étienne-les-Orgues - 04230.
Forcalquier : 22 km.
Sisteron : 39 km.
Station : Sisteron 39 km.
Property of the commune.

The Chalaisien order was responsible for the foundation of this church, on the pilgrim's route some 1 200 metres above sea-level in the heart of a densely forested valley. Lure was built at the moment when the Chalaisien monasteries were integrated within the Cistercian order. The harmony of the abbey's architecture perfectly reflexts the style of the Cistercians.
Open Aug. 1 to Aug. 30 : 8 - 8.
By appointment off season.
Parking.
Guided tours, brochures.
Panels.
Facilities for the handicapped.
Concerts and temporary exhibitions.
Preservation sites.

Salagon (Abbey and Priory).
Mane - 04300.
Station : Avignon 100 km.
Bus service.
Property of the commune.

Formerly the abbey of Saint-André de Villeneuve-lès-Avignon, on the medieval route between Apt and Forcalquier, Salagon was nationalised during the Revolution

PROVENCE-CÔTE-D'AZUR — HAUTES-ALPES-ALPES-MARITIMES

nd finally rehabilitated in 1955. his rural Benedictine priory has reserved its 12th century Romanesque church, its 15th century ain building, the stables and its arn, which dates from the 17th entury. Salagon is also the home f the society for the Patrimony of aute-Provence, where the assoation « Alpes de Lumière » exhits objects and documents relang to daily life in Haute-Provence.
pen all year : 2 - 6.
arking.
uided tours for groups upon request.
naccompanied tours.
anels and leaflets.
emporary exhibitions.
cture tours for school groups.
l. : (92) 75.19.93.

isteron (citadel).

steron - 04200.
operty of the commune.
This fortress has been the site of any battles, and most notably ose of the Wars of Religion hich devestated the region beteen 1560 and 1590. Sisteron's ntry way, flanked by the keep, tes from the 13th century. Thereafter you see a series of surrounng walls which date from the th century and were designed a precursor of Vauban's. In 60 a gothic chapel was erected, d the last modifications were ded in 1645, which enabled the rtress to withstand the kingdom Savoy. The underground stairse, built into the rocks and linng the citadel with the north enof the city also dates from this riod. Of the designs drawn up Vauban in 1692, only the Storeom on the northern side was alised. In 1693 the future king of land, Jean Casimir, was held soner in the citadel. Finally, in 15, Sisteron chose to leave its ns and let Napoleon pass ough on his return from Elba.
en daily, March 15 to Nov. 15 : 8 - 7 in summer).
rking.
corded guides.
nslations in English and German.

Brochures.
Lecture tours available.
Festival in July, August, Theatre, Danse, Music.
Temporary exhibitions in the chapel.
Tel. : (92) 61.27.57.

HAUTES-ALPES

Boscodon (Abbey).

Crots-Embrun - 05200.
Gap : 38 km.
Station : Embrun 10 km.
Property of the Association of the Friends of Boscodon.

In a mountainous region at a height of 1150 metres, Boscodon towers over the lake of Serre-Ponçon. Founded in 1132, the style of its architecture is very close to Cistercian art. Rased between 1579 and 1692, it became a hamlet in 1791. During the 17th and 18th centuries, the monk's quarters were restored. Boscodon has remained a religious centre and still has its own community.
Open all year : 10 - 12, 3 - 6.
Parking.
Tours upon request.
Recommended itinerary.
Panels.
Facilities for the handicapped.
Brochures.
Concerts.
Lecture tours for school groups only.
Tel. : (92) 43.14.45.

BRIANÇON

Salettes (Fort).

Briançon - 05100.
Chemin des Salettes.
Croix de Toulouse.
Station : Briançon 2 km.
Property of the commune.

Situated on an escarpment dominating the fortifications of Briançon, the fort of Salettes, recently restored, provides a fascinating introduction to French defensive architecture during the period of Louis XIV.
Open July and August : 9 - 12, 2 - 7.
Guided tours with audiovisual.
Information, English and Italian.
Brochures.
Temporary exhibitions.
Restoration and programmes organised by the Vieux Manoir club.

Montmaur (Château).

Montmaur - 05400.
Gap : 20 km.
Station : Veynes-Devoluy 5 km.
Bus service.
Private property.

Seat of the fourth Barony of the Dauphiné, Montmaur is set in mountainous countryside and is a medieval fortress transformed during the Renaissance. Its main facade is decorated with mullioned windows and flanked by two powerful towers. Inside you can see beamed ceilings, frescoes and monumental fireplaces. There is also a monument to the Resistance.
Open daily, June 15 to Sept 15 : 2 - 6.
Upon request for groups, June 15 to Sept. 15.
Parking.
Guided tours, English, German, Dutch, Italian.
Panels and leaflets.
Audiovisual.
Music on Sunday afternoons.
Temporary exhibitions.
Tel. : (92) 58.11.42.

ALPES-MARITIMES

Antibes (Fort Carré).

Antibes - 06600.
Station : Antibes.
Property of the State.
Set on the Saint-Roch Hill, a peninsula which divides the bay of Nice from the town of Antibes, the Fort Carré was built by Henri III in 1578 to protect the port of Antibes. The seige of 1592 was the most dramatic event in the history of the Fort Carré. Later on, at the time of the war against the league of Augsbourg, Vauban added a surrounding wall at the foot of the fort. During the wars of the Austrian Succession (1746-1747), Fort Carré withstood an attack from the English fleet which lasted some 46 days. The fort consists of four strongholds at each corner of the quadrilateral ramparts, in the middle of wing a semi-circular building gives onto a rounded courtyard with huge terraces above. Fort Carré is being restored through the offices of the Club du Vieux Manoir.
Open July 2 to August 31 : 9 - 12, 2 - 7.
Parling.
Guided tours.
Information, English, Italian, Spanish, German, Dutch.
Lecture tours, brochures.
Temporary exhibitions.

BEAULIEU-SUR-MER
Théodore Reinach Foundation
Greek Villa Kérylos.

Beaulieu-sur-Mer - 06130.
Rue Gustave-Eiffel.
Nice : 6 km.
Station : Beaulieu-sur-Mer.
Property of the Institut de France.
At the beginning of the century an enthusiastic hellenist reconstructed an ancient Greek palace with great care. In the Library you can see several works of antique art. After a long period of neglect, the villa has been recently restored.
Open Sept. 1 to June 30 : 2 - 6.
July 1 to Aug. 31 : 3 - 6.
Mornings by appointment for groups.
Closed Mondays in November.
Parking.
Guided tours.
Brochures.
Concerts.
Lecture tours for school groups.
Tel. : (93) 01.01.44.

Gourdon (Château).

Gourdon - 06620.
Grasse : 14 km.
Cannes : 31 km.
Private property.
The Saracens who occupied Bar-dur-Loup in the 9th century built a fortress which one of Henri IV's favorites transformed into a luxurious residence several centuries later. Set in grounds which can be visited, the four-sided building flanked with towers at each corner, dominates the Loup valley. Gourdon has period furniture, armour, documents and paintings of the 17th and 18th centuries.
Open July 1 to Sept. 15 : 11 - 1, 2 - 6.
Sept. 9 to June 30 : 10 - 12, 2 - 6.
Closed Tuesdays, Sept. 9 to June 30.
Parking.
July 1 to Sept. 15, tours of the Historical Museum in French and English.
Unaccompanied visit of Museum of primitive painting.
Brochures.
Tel. : (93) 42.50.13.

GRASSE
Hôtel de Clapiers-Cabris (Museum of the Art and History of Provence).

Grasse - 06130.
2, rue Mirabeau.
Station : Grasse.
Bus service.
Property of the town.
Former town house of the Clapiers-Cabris family, built by the Milanese architect Giovanni Orello for Mirabeau's sister in 1770, the Museum of the Art and History of Provence moved into this hôtel in 1921. The Museum has a rich collection of furniture, faience, objets d'art, etc. There is also a Library.
Open Oct. 1 to June 30 : 10 - 12, 2 - 5.
July 1 to Sept. 30 : 10 - 12, 2 - 6.
Closed Saturday and Sunday, except first and last Sunday of the month.
Parking.
Lecture tour for school groups.
Tel. : (93) 36.01.61.

Villa Fragonard.

Grasse - 06130.
Boulevard Fragonard.
Station : Grasse.
Bus service.
Property of the town.
Formerly the hôtel Maubert, Jean-Honoré Fragonard and his family lived here between 1790 and 1791. The paintings he h done for Madame du Barry, whi he hung in this hôtel (and whi are now in the Frick Collectio New York) were replaced by c pies during the 19th century. T stairwell was decorated by h son, Alexandre-Evariste. On t first floor the Musée Fragona has works and memorabilia of F gonard, his family and Marguér Gérard.
Open Oct. 1 to May 31 : 10 - 12, 2 - 5
June 1 to Sept. 30 : 10 - 12, 2 - 6.
Closed Saturday and Sunday, exc fort the first and last Sunday of month.
Parking.
Lecture tours for school groups.
Tel. : (93) 36.01.61.

Lérins (Abbey).

Cannes - 06406.
Ile Saint-Honorat - Cannes : 10 km.
Station : Cannes.
Private property (religious communit
Situated on the southern pen sula of the ile de Saint-Honor the original abbey of lérins wi dates from the 5th century w badly damaged by Saracen a Norman invasions. In 1073 Alc bart built a fortified abbey to p tect the monks. The vaulted cades of the cloister are Roman que ; the 14th and 17th cent vaults are remnants of later rem delling. A new monastery w built around the old cloisters b ween 1880 and 1930.
Open July 1 to Sept. 15 : 10 - 12, 2: 4:30.
Upon request during the rest of the ye
Tel. : (93) 48.68.68.

MENTON
Palais Carnoles (Museur

Menton - 06500.
3, avenue de la Madone.
Property of the Department.
Built by Gabriel and Robert Cotte in the 18th century, this re dence used to be the summer

...ce of the Princes of Monaco. It as since been purchased by the epartment, which has restored e interiors and transformed the alace into a museum of old masrs and modern painting.
pen Sept. 16 to June 16 : 10 - 12, 2 -

ne 16 to Sept. 15 : 10 - 12, 3 - 6.
losed monday and tuesday.
arking.
cture tours for school groups.
oncerts, temporary exhibitions.
el. : (93) 35.49.71.

NICE
Palais Lascaris

ice - 06300.
5, rue Droite.
operty of the town.
This fine 17th and 18th century alace in genoese style has recently been restored to its original ate. The museum's collection inludes decorative arts and ethnoaphy.
pen Oct. 1 to Dec. 31 : 8:30 - 12, 2:30 5.
ly 1 to Sept. 30 : 9:30 - 12, 2:30 30.
n. 1 to July 30 : 9:30 - 12, 2:30 - 6.

Closed monday.
Parking
Guided tours.
Information in English, German, Spanish, Italian (request beforehand).
Brochures.
Lectures.
Concerts.
Temporary exhibitions.
Tel. : (93) 62.05.54.

Cimiez (Franciscan monastery).

Nice - 06000.
Station : Nice.
Bus service.
Property of the commune.
In 1546 the Fransicans established themselves in a former Benedictine monastery which dates from the 11th century. They remodelled the 15th century abbatial church and built two cloisters and a chapter house the following century. One of the cloisters was only completed in the 18th century. The refectory, oratory and sacristy are decorated with biblical frescoes which date from the 17th and 18th century. The monastery has preserved its furniture, sculpture, engravings and manuscripts. There is a Franciscan museum.
Open all year, visits at 10, 11, 3, 4, 5.
Closed sturday afternoon, sunday and holidays.
Texts in English, German, Italian, Spanish.
Brochures.
Lecture tours.
Organ concerts.
Tel. : (93) 81.00.04.

Cimiez Amphitheatre (Park and gardens)

Nice - 06100.
Boulevard de Cimiez.
Town property.
During the Roman occupation some 4000 spectators used to watch the circus which was held in the amphitheatres of Nice. Today the site is a park with facilities

---

HÔTEL DE CLAPIERS-CABRIS
GRASSE-ALPES-MARITIMES

Mirabeau resided in this 18th century hôtel on several occasions during his life.

Visits :
Oct. 1 to May 31 : 10 - 12, 2 - 5.
June 1 to Sept. 30 : 10 - 12, 2 - 6.

ALPES-MARITIMES

VILLA FRAGONARD

GRASSE

The provencal home where Fragonard and his family used to live (18th century).

Visits :
Oct. 1 to May 31 : 10 - 12, 2 - 5.
June 1 to Sept. 30 : 10 - 12, 2 - 6.

for children. You can still see the ruins of the ancient amphitheatre. Matisse used to paint here.
Open daily, Apr. 1 to May 31, and Sept. 1 to Sept. 30 : 7:30 - 7.
June 1 to Aug. 31 : 7:30 - 8.
Oct. 1 to March 31 : 7:30 - 5:30.

SAINT-JEAN-CAP-FERRAT
Gardens and Villa Ile de France; Fondation Ephrussi de Rothschild.

Saint-Jean-Cap-Ferrat - 06230.
Avenue Ephrussi-de-Rothschild.
Nice : 11 km.
Beaulieu-sur-Mer : 3 km.
Property of the Institut de France.

The « Ile de France » Villa and its gardens were built between 1905 and 1912 and form the setting for a collection of objets d'art from the 14th to the 19th century. The exterior architecture is reminiscent of Venetian palaces. The park, which extends over 7 hectares has different sorts of gardens and offers an unusual itinerary.
Open Sept. 1 to June 30 : 2 - 6.
July 1 to Aug. 31 : 3 - 7.
Large groups may visit mornings by request.
Guided tours.
Unaccompanied tours (gardens).
English, German, Italian, Spanish.
Lectures, concerts, receptions.
Tel. : (93) 01.33.09.

VILLEFRANCHE
Saint-Elme (citadel).

Villefranche-sur-Mer - 06230.
Nice : 5 km.
Station : 1 km.
Property of the commune.

Initially built in the 16th century by the Duke of Savoy to protect the port of Villefranche, the citadel witnessed several attacks during the 17th and 18th century, but today houses the Goetz-Boumeester museum, the town hall, and will shortly be the home of an Arts and Crafts centre.
Open Oct. 1 to Apr. 30 : 10 - 12, 2 - 5:30.
May 1 to Sept. 30 : 10 - 12, 3 - 7.
Parking.
Guided tours optional.
English, German.
Brochures.
Concerts.
Temporary exhibitions.
Lecture tours possible.
Tel. : (93) 55.45.12.

BOUCHES-DU-RHÔNE

AIX-EN-PROVENCE

La Pioline (Château).

Aix-en-Provence - 13290.
Bus service.
Private property.

First known as Beauvoisin, this stronghold, with its main building which dates from the 16th and 17th centuries, has received many illustrious visitors, such as Charles Quint, at the time of the seige of Marseille, and Catherine de Medicis, who signed a peace treaty here. La Pioline, so named after the family of magistrats who later lived here, was embellished and transformed during the 18th century ; you can see the two wings framing a main courtyard and a basin all of which were added in the 18th century. Inside, the Louis XVI salon is famous for its columns and faux mabre decoration.
Open upon request for groups of 20 or more.
Guided tours.
Concerts, danses.
Rooms and grounds avilable for hire for receptions, filming.
Tel. : (42) 20.07.81.

ARLES
Grand Prieuré de Malte (musée Réattu).

Arles - 13200.
10, rue du Grand-Prieuré.
Private property.

This ancient outpost of the Knights of the order of St-John of Jerusalem was demolished during the Revolution, but was rehabilitated by the painter Reattu, whose pictures can be seen in the Museum. The museum also has the collection of the museum of Arles : paintings, sculpture, drawings and tapestries.
Open Jan. 2 to Feb. 28 : 9 - 11:50, 2 - 4:30.
March 1 to March 31 : 9 - 11:50, 2 - 5:30.
Apr. 1 to Apr. 31 : 9 - 11:50, 2 - 6:30.
May 1 to May 31 : 9 - 11:50, 2 - 7.
June 1 to Sept. 14 : 8:30 - 12:20, 2 - 7.
Sept. 15 to Oct. 11 : 8:30 - 12:20, 2 - 6:30.
Oct. 12 to Oct. 31 : 8:30 - 12:20, 2 - 6.
Nov. 1 to Nov. 8 : 8:30 - 12:20, 2 - 5:30.
Nov. 9 to Nov. 30 : 8:30 - 12:20, 2 - 5.
Dec. 1 to Dec. 31 : 8:30 - 12:20 - 2 - 4:30.
Closed Jan. 1, May 1, Dec. 25.
Parking.
Unaccompanied tours.
Brochures.
Information in German, English, Italian, Spanish.
Temporary exhibitions.
Education department.
Tel. : (90) 96.37.68.

Hôtel de Laval-Castellane (muséon Arlaten).

Arles - 13200.
Rue de la République.
Town property.

In the Hôtel de Laval-Castellane, a 16th century building with remains of a Roman forum, Frédéric Mistral established a museum devoted to arts and crafts. You can see a gallery of costumes, reconstructed studio interiors and memorabilia relating to Frédéric Mistral.
Open daily from July 1 to Sept. 30 : 9 - 12, 2 - 6.
Oct. 1 to June 30 : 9 - 12, 2 - 5.
Closed Mondays.
Unaccompanied tours.
Guided tours with the Monuments Historiques available.
Education department.
Tel. : (90) 96.37.68.

La Barben (Château).

La Barben — 13330.
Salon-de-Provence : 9 km.
Bus service.

This fairy-tale palace, set in the heart of a forest, has towers, parapets and fortification slits. Once the property of the monks of Saint-Victor of Marseille, it passed to the Pontevés family. During the 15th century it was owned by King René who sold it to Jean II de Forbin in 1474. For almost 500 years, the Château has remained the property of this family, who, in the 17th century, transformed the medieval castle into a comfortable residence. Le Nôtre was responsible for the formal gardens, and inside you can see fine period furniture, Flanders and Aubusson tapestries and Cordoba leather. The damask salon has kept its original ceiling. Pauline Borghese, mistress of Auguste de Forbin, once lived here.
Open daily 10 - 12, 2 - 6.
Closed Tuesdays, except in summer.
Parking.

BOUCHES-DU-RHÔNE

LA PIOLINE
Welcomes you among its age old trees

Whenever you wish, this romantic building can be yours for a day or for an evening : you will not forget its marvellous decor for your parties, marriages, candle-lit dinners.
Just make a reservation by telephone : (42) 20.07.81.

The setting is also suitable for film making, conferences, musical or artistic entertainment, exhibitions, etc.

Salons and gardens may be hired for receptions, advertising and cinema.

PROVENCE-CÔTE-D'AZUR —— 343 —— BOUCHES-DU-RHÔNE

...imal park.
...ided tours.
Tel. : (90) 55.19.12.

...arbentane (Château).
...rbentane - 13570.
...ignon : 10 km.
...vate property.
...Barbentane provides a perfect ...ample of how the classical pari-...n style was adapted in the re-...on of Provence, adding to the ...lm and imposing 17th century ...ilding a charm and seducti-...ness derived from Italian de-...gn. The latter addition was the ...ork of the Marquis de Barben-...ne, Louis XV's ambassador in ...scany. The main salon with its ...t vault has a fine marble interior ...d 18th century furniture. The ...her salons are decorated with ...loured stucco. This fine building ...s remained in the de Barben-...ne family until this day.
...en March 26 to Nov. 1 : 10 - 12, 2 -
...osed Wednesdays, except in July, ...gust and September.
...ided tours.
Tel. : (90) 95.51.07.

...hâteaurenard ...astle).
...âteaurenard - 13160.
...ignon : 12 km.
...s service to the area.
...operty of the commune.
...During the middle ages, a for-...ss was built on an oppidum ...ich dated from the time of Ju-...s Caesar, and this fortress took ...e name of its owner : the castle ...Reynaud. Before it was demo-...hed at the time of the Revolu-...n, Philippe le Hardi, Catherine ...Medicis and Louis XIV stayed ...ere. You can take an accompa-...ed tour of the ruins and see the ...useum.
...en daily 10 - 12, 2 - 6.
...enfor groups on request.
...rking.
...ormation in German.
...cilties for the handicapped.
...ochures.
...ncerts, folk dancing.

Lecture tours for school groups organised by local teacher.
Tel. : (90) 94.07.27.

If (Château).
Outskirts of Marseille - 13000.
Access by boat.
Property of the State.
In 1524 François 1 built a citadel on the island that guards the entry to the city as a means of defence for Marseille. The naturally strategic position was reinforced by the architecture of the citadel, a compact, square building protected by three powerful round towers. Having performed its defensive functions effectively, If became a state prison, and was later immortalised by Alexandre Dumas in his tale of the Count of Monte-Cirsto.
Open : 9 - 6.
Parking.
Brochure.
Guided tours.

Montmajour (Abbey).
Arles - 13200.
State property.
Built in the 10th century on an islet in the midst of swamps, the abbey ne Montmajour still stands on its rocky site, towering above the plain of Arles, though partly in ruin. Of the original buildings you can still see the small church of Saint Peter — a rare example of early Romesque architecture. In the 12th century the major abbatial buildings were constructed around the cloisters — the church of Notre Dame, the chapter house, the refectory and dormitory. Nearby was the abbot's building, of which only the Abbot's tower, built in 1369 in the style of a keep, remains. The remains of a new series of abbatial buildings, dating to the 18th century before the abbey was suppressed by Louis XVI, are to be seen crossing the medieval foundations. Restoration and reconstruction began in the early 19th century, and the abbey is still being worked on.
Open Apr. 1 to Sept. 30 : 9 - 12, 2 - 6.
Oct. 1 to March 31 : 9 - 12, 2 - 5.
Closed Tuesday.
Guided tours, brochures.
Panels.

Saint-Michel-de-Frigolet (Abbey).
Tarascon - 13150.
Arles : 17 km.
Private property.
Founded in the 11th century by the monks of Montmajour, the monastery welcomed several orders until the Revolution. The reverend father Edmond brought the order of the Premonstratensians here in the 19th century and enclosed the abbey with medieval walls. The church of Saint-Michel and the cloister are of romanesque style. You can also see gilded panelling of the 17th century and pictures by Mignard.
Open 9, 10, 2, 3, 4, 5 and 6 weekdays.
9, 11:30, 2, 4, 5, 6 sundays.
Guided tours, brochures.
Leaflets.
Facilities for the handicapped.
Concerts of sacred music, Sundays at 4 in July and august.
Religious festivals.
Tel. : (90) 91.70.07.

SAINT-RÉMY-DE-PROVENCE
Cardinal's tower.
Saint-Rémy-de-Provence - 13210.
Old road to Arles.
Station : Avignon 23 km.
Private property.
Probably once the residence of a cardinal from Avignon, this Renaissance house was built in 1558. The most impressive rooms are the balcony, the square tower decorated with a freize and the large spiral staircase which is sculpted. After being left to ruin, restoration was begun in 1961. You can also see a 16th century columned well.
Open upon request throughout the year.
Parking.
Guided tours.
Leaflets in French, English, German, Dutch and Spanish.
Tel. : (90) 92.15.92.

VAR

ENTRECASTEAUX

Winner of the Prix des chefs-d'œuvre en péril, 1977
Awarded Obelisk of the Conseil de l'Europe, 1980

This magnificent Château, now completely restored, is one of the major historic monuments of the Var.
Set on a rock, it towers above the fine French gardens designed by Le Nôtre and the medieval village of Entrecasteaux. Some of the most illutrious men of Provence have lived here : the Marquis François de Grignan, Lieutenant Governor of Provence who married Mme de Sévigné's daughter. Raymond de Bruni, Treasurer General of France : Jean-Baptiste d'Entrecasteaux, President of the Parlement of Provence. The Admiral Bruni d'Entrecasteaux, one of the heroesof the Franch navy.
The building you see today replaced an 11th century fortress and dates, for the most part, from the 16th and 17th centuries.
Concerts, lectures, exhibitions of painting, receptions, film-making.

The Château is open daily, April to September : 10 - 8, October to March : 10 - 6.
For information call 16 (94) 04.43.95.

SALON-DE-PROVENCE

L'Empéri (Château).

Salon-de-Provence - 13300.
Station : Salon-de-Provence 1 km.
Property of the commune.

One of the three greatest fortresses of Provence, l'Empéri is the oldest. Once the residence of the Lord Archbishops of Arles, under the Holy Roman Emperor (whence the name l'Empéri), it was constructed between the 11th and 13th century on a rocky hill which dominates the city. In the 16th century an arcaded gallery was added. The museum houses the collections of Raoul and Jean Brunon, devoted to military history since the reign of Louis XIV. There are over 10,000 objects exhibited here.
Open Apr. 1 to Sept. 30 : 10 - 12, 2:30 - 6:30.
Oct. 1 to March 31 : 10 - 12, 2 - 6.
Closed Tuesdays, 1 Jan., 1 May, 25 Dec.
Parking.
Unaccompanied tours.
Brochures.
Leaflets and panels.
Music, dance and theatre festival, June 15 to Aug. 15.
Tel. : (90) 56.22.36.

Silvacane (Abbey).

La Roque-d'Anthéron - 13640.
Aix-en-Provence : 30 km.
Property of the State.

Founded in the 11th century the abbey of Silvacane is a perfect example of Cistercian organisation. The oldest section is the church, completed at the beginning of the 13th century. This abuts the cloister, whose cradle shaped galleries follow the monks buildings. To the east, the capter house and the monks buildings have gothic vaults which date from the 13th century. To the north, the large refectory was rebuilt in the 15th century. Despite the various transformations since the Revolution, the abbey has managed to retain its original appearance, largely due to the State which has undertaken restoration since the beginning of the century.
Open Apr. 1 to Sept. 30 : 10 - 12, 2 - 7.
Oct. 1 to March 31 : 10 - 12, 2 - 5.
Closed Tuesday.
Guided tours.
Brochures.
Concerts.
Tel. : (42) 50.41.69.

Tarascon (Château of King René).

Tarascon - 13150.
Property of the State.

On the edge of the Rhône, the Château of Tarascon protected the territory of the Comtes de Provence. Consisting of a forecourt which leads to the Château itself, the new building was constructed in 1400 by Louis II of Anjou and completed 50 years later by King René. With its stark high walls, Tarascon looks more like a fortress than a palace, yet the outer appearance give no hint of the sumptuous and refined palace inside. Transformed into a prison during the 18th century, Tarascon was purchased by the State in 1926. The Château houses the recently acquired tapestry series representing the history of Scipio the African — a unique series which has been acquired by the Caisse Nationale de Monuments Historiques et des Sites.
Open Apr. 1 to Sept. 30 : 9 - 12, 2 - 5.
Oct. 1 to March 31 : 9 - 12, 2 - 6.
Closed Tuesday.
Guided tours.
Brochures.
Festival.
Tel. : (90) 91.01.93.

VAR

Entrecasteaux (Château).

Entrecastreux - 83570.
Draguignan : 25 km.
Private property.

Perched on a rock, this Château dominates the medieval village. The building dates back to the 11th century, but the present day ensemble was built between the 16th and 17th centuries. Wrought iron balustrades decorate this long building. The fief of Entrecasteaux belonged to several families, among whom was the admiral of Entrecasteaux who lead the fleet which went in search of Le Pérouse in 1791. The painter, Mac Garvie-Munn bought the Château in 1974 and has restored it. The gardens are given to Le Nôtre.
Open daily, Apr. 1 to Sept. 30 : 10 - 8.
Oct. 1 ti March 31 : 10 - 6.
Parking.
Unaccompanied tours, brochure.
English, German, Spanish.
Concerts.
Temporary exhibitions of paintings.
Lectures.
Tel. : (94) 04.43.95.

La Moutte (Château).

Saint-Tropez - 83990.
Salins area.
Station : Saint-Tropez 4 km.
Private property.

This provençal dwelling once belonged to Émile Olivier, minister under Napoléon III. Here he received the most prominent writers of the period. The Château consists of a main pavilion linked to the Italianate outbuildings by a veranda.
Open by request.
Guided tours, unaccompanied tours.
English and German.
Concerts.
Seminars.
Tel. : (94) 97.03.26.

Saint-Maximin (Royal Convent).

Saint-Maximin - 83470.
Cooperative property.

From the earliest times, Saint-Maximim attracted pilgrims who came to visit the tombs of the Magdalene and the Bishop Saint Maximim. Following the rediscovery of the crypt in the 13th century, Charles II of Anjou, a nephew

PROVENCE-CÔTE-D'AZUR

of Saint Louis, endowed a Dominican convent on this site. Building then took place over two centuries : the basilica, the monks buildings and the cloisters are important examples of gothic architecture in Provence. Placed under royal protection, the former convent now functions as a centre for exchange-visitors.
Open daily : 10 - 12, 2 - 6.
By appointment off Season.
Guided tours : 10 : 30, 3, 5.
Concerts, temporary exhibitions.
Conférences, brochures.
Tel. : (94) 78.01.93.

Sanary-Bandol (Tropical Gardens and Zoo).

Sanary - 83110.
Pont d'Aran.
Toulon : 18 km.
Motorway : exit Bandol.
Station : Bandol 4 km.
Private property.

In this rocky park you will find tropical plants, rare flowers, all sorts of different animals (monkeys, birds, llamas) in a harmonious and pleasant setting.

Open Oct. 1 to March 31 : 8 - 12, 2 - 6.
Apr. 1 to Sept. 30 : 8 - 12, 2 - 7.
Closed Sunday morning.
Parking.
Unaccompanied tours.
Information German, English.
Panels.
Access for the handicapped.
Tel. : (94) 29.40.38.

Le Thoronet (Abbey).

Le Luc - 83340.
Draguignan : 20 km.
Property of the State.

The abbey of le Thoronet was a new Cistercian monastery built in 1146 by the monks of Tourtour. In a wild setting in the Var valley, the monks buildings are arranged around a cloister which is protected by strong arcades dating from the Romanesque period. All the rooms execpt the chapter house have ribbed vaulting, from the church to the wine press, and including the dormitory whose 18th century decorations have finally been removed. Le Thoronet was purchased by the State from as early as 1854. Major restoration has succeeded in recoverinf the abbey's original appearance.
Open March`1 to Apr. 30, Oct. 1 to Oct. 31 : 10 - 12, 2 - 5.
May 2 to Sept. 30, Nov. 1 to Feb. 28 : 10 - 12, 2 - 4.
Parking.
Guided and unaccompanied tours.
Brochures.
Tel. : (94) 73.87.13.

Valbelle (Château).

Tourves - 83170.
Brignole : 12 km.
Station : Toulon 45 km.
Bus service.
Property of the commune.

Valbelle, a huge palace was built at the end of the 18th century on the site of a feudal castle. Destroyed by fire, the palaces' ruins still attest to the period's passion for greco-roman antiquity : the co-

---

VAR

SANARY-BANDOL
Tropical gardens, zoo

The joyous harmony that has been created among the plants, animals and birds here, distinguishes Sanary-Bandol from many other zoos and botanical gardens. Year after year new species are added, and the grounds and setting are scrupulously maintained.
We offer you a moment of relaxation with a great variety of things to see, of interest to parents as well as children, to dreamers as well as those who come to learn something new.

Location : 18 km from Toulon, 50 km from Marseille.
Open daily except Sunday mornings in winter. (Closed between noon and 2 pm.)
83110 - Sanary-sur-Mer.
Tel. : (94) 29.40.38.

Valmogne (Priory).

Baudinard-sur-Verdon - Aups - 83630.
Draguignan : 48 km.
Station : 53 km.
Private property.
   On the site of a baptsistry of a greco-roman villa, this abbey was founded in the High Middle Ages. The main building is reached through a romanesque gateway.
Open June 15 to July 31 : 10 - 12, 3 - 6.
Open by appointment for individual visits and for groups.
Closed sundays and holidays.
Tel. : (94) 70.18.65.

La Verne (Charterhouse).

Collobrières - 83610.
Toulon : 40 km.
Station : Cuers 20 km.
Bus service.
Property of the State.
   Founded in 1170 by the Bishops of Fréjus and Toulon, this monastery, which is set in the forest of the Maures, was inhabited by members of the Carthusian order until 1792. The buildings you see today, restored in 1968, date from the 16th to the 18th centuries. A monastic community still lives in the charterhouse.
Open March 25 to Sept. 22 : 11 - 6.
Sept. 23 to Dec. 31 : 10 - 5.
Closed Tuesday.
Parking.
Panels.
Brochures.
Pamphlets and leaflets.
Audiovisual.
Information in English and German.
Facilities for the handicapped.
(Restoration sites - voluntary work).
Guided tours in summer.

VAUCLUSE

Ansouis (Château).

Ansouis - 84240.
Aix-en-Provence : 30 km.
Pertuis : 8 km.
Private property.
   This Château was built around a 10th century keep and was later remodelled in the 16th century when gardens were added. It combines the strategic requirements of a fortress on which Vau-ban worked with the refinement of classical decoration : the facades date from the 17th century and the sculpted ornaments are of the rococo period. The Château has remained in the Sabran-Ponteves family for over 800 years.
Open Jan. 2 to Dec. 31, 2:30 - 6.
By appointment for groups.
Closed Tuesday.
Brochures.
Conferences, seminars, receptions.
Tel. : (90) 79.20.99.

AVIGNON

Palais des Papes.

Avignon - 84000.
Property of the State and the town.
   The instability that reigned in 14th century Rome forced Pope Clement V, who was of French birth, to seek refuge in the region of Provence, near the Comtat Venaissin. This initiated a period of prosperity for the city of Avignon where the Palais des Papes was built on the site of the former bishops palace in 1335. With its defence system, the buildings are arranged around the four sided main courtyards. To the north and east, the Old Palace, built by Benoit XII, is flanked by the galleries of the cloister. To the south and the west you can see the New Palace, built by Clement VI, in more severe style. Inside both palaces you will see many enormous rooms : the Consistoire, the Grand Tinel and the main Audience chamber. Of the original painted decoration, the frescoes of the Pope's private chambers and several main rooms decorated by Matteo Giovanetti still remain. After much rebuilding during the 19th century, the Palais des Papes has been the object of important restoration.
Open daily, Oct. 1 to Apr. 1 : 9 - 11:15, 2 - 4:15.
Apr. 1 to June 30 : 9 - 11:30, 2 - 5:30.
July 1 to Sept. 30 : 9 - 6.
Guided or unaccompanied tours.
Leaflets and Brochures.
Avignon festival.
Exhibitions.
Tel. : (90) 86.03.32.

Petit Palais.

Avignon - 84000.
Place du Palais des Papes.
Property of the town.
   The Petit Palais, fomerly the residence of the bishops and archbishops who joined the Pope during his exile in Avignon, offers, along with the Palais des Papes, one of the finest example of late Gothic architecture. After the Great Schism, it was used as a citadel and was rebuilt during the 15th century. Today it houses a remarkable collection of Italian primitives, making the collection one of the most important in France (collection Campana).
Open : 9:15 - 12, 2 - 6.
Closed Tuesday.
Unaccompanied tours.
Brochures.
Temporary exhibitions.
Tel. : (90) 86.44.58.

Hôtel de Villeneuve-Martignan musée Calvet.

Avignon - 84000.
65, rue Joseph-Vernet.
Property of the town.
   This magnificent 18th century French building with characteristic French elegance stands is marked contrast to the other hôtels in Avignon, which are italianate in style. In the museum's spacious rooms you will see a collection of antiquities and examples of French painting from the 16th century to the present day. As early as the 19th century Stendhal wrote enthusiastically about this museum in his « Mémoires d'un touriste ».
Open : 9 - 12, 2 - 6.
Closed Tuesday.
Parking difficult.
Tel. : (90) 86.33.84.

Hôtel d'Adhémar de Cransac.

Avignon - 84000.
11, rue de Taulignan.
Property of Mme L. de Lambilly.

VAUCLUSE — 348 — PROVENCE-CÔTE-D'AZUR

Fine example of 17th century domestic architecture, the hôtel d'Adhémar de Cransac, which has been undergoing restoration since 1971, reflects the elegance and the restraint of the Midi. The monumental inner courtyard is paved with typically provencal stone and has a staircase in Henri II style. It also has a ramp with a balustrade which leads to the three first floor reception rooms, en enfilade. The doors and the marble fireplaces are crowned with decorated pier glass which are set in sculpted and gilded panelling. In certain rooms the beamed ceilings are still in place.
Open on written request only.
Parking.
Guided tours.
Information English.
Brochures.
Tel. : (90) 86.13.26.

Bonpas (Charterhouse).
Caumont-sur-Durance - 84510.
Avignon : 10 km.
Station : Avignon.
Bus service.
Private property.

The convent of Bonpas, whose 12th century romanesque chapel can still be seen, was transformed into a charterhouse by Jean XXIII in 1320. The carthusians made it into a fortified monastery, and from this period date the outer walls and the entryway.
The formal gardens are surrounded by pine trees.
Open all year : 10 - 12, 2 - 6.
By request for groups.
Ground only.
Parking.
Recommended itinerary, unaccompanied tours.
Brochure.
Tel. : (90) 22.54.03.

Buoux (Fort).
Vallon-de-Buoux - 84480.
Near Bonnieux.
Property of the commune.

It is difficult to date Buoux's origins with certainty, just as little is known of the buildings erected in the Middle Ages. You will first see the ruins of the fort, whose towers are bow-shaped. Then you move on to the Guards room, the only room to have remained intact, and the protected residence of the Governor which is situated above an ancient wash place which might have served sacrificial functions. You leave by the pathway which leads to the unusual staircase cut into the rocks.
Open daily, all year : 8 - 7, (8 - 9 in summer).
Parking.
Guided tours by request at the Apt Tourist office.
Brochures.
Guided tours for school groups only.
Tel. : (90) 74.25.75.

Gordes (Château).
Gordes - 84220.
Cavaillon : 13 km.
Station : Cavaillon.
Property of the commune.

The old village of Gordes rises on its promontory which is dominated by the Château. Built during the first half of the 16th century by the de Simiane family, this Renaissance building is closer to a medieval fortress with its round towers at each corner and its rough-cut stone walls. In the large room inside you see two features charactersitic of the Renaissance however : the wooden ceiling with exposed beams and the monumental fireplace which dates from 1541. The Château now houses the Vas arely museum.
Open all year : 10 - 12, 2 - 6.
Closed Tuesday.
Parking.
Unaccompanied tours.
Tel. : (90) 72.02.89.

Loumarin (Château).
Loumarin - 84160 Cadenet.
Aix-en-Provence : 30 km.
Avignon : 55 km.
Station : Aix-en-Provence.
Bus service.
Property of the Academy of Science, Arts and Belles Lettres d'Aix-en-Provence.

At the foot of the Lubéron mountain, Loumarin rises opposite the village. The oldest part of the Château was built between 1495 and 1525 by the d'Agoult family, on the ruins of a 12th century fortress. In 1540 a Renaissance building, called the Château neuf, was attached to the old castle by Blanche de Levis. Robert Laurent-Vibert restored the Château between 1920 and 1925 and received artists and writers there. You can also see 16th century furniture, engravings, paintings, objets d'art and a Library.
Open all year, Oct. 1 to March 31 : 9 - 11:45, 2 - 4:45.
Apr. 1 to Sept. 30 : 9 - 11:45, 2:30 - 6:15.
Closed Tuesdays in winter.
Parking.
Guided tours.
English, German.
Concerts.
Temporary exhibitions of painting.
Tel. : (90) 68.15.23.

Saint-Hilaire (Abbey).
Menerbes-en-Vaucluse.
Cavaillon : 20 km.
Apt : 20 km.
Private property.

Still being restored, the abbey of Saint-Hilaire offers a complete ensemble of monastic buildings that made up this medieval abbey. Medieval chapels, a cloister and monastic buildings of the 17th century can be seen.
Visits possible all year when owners present.
Parking.
Panels.
Illuminations.
Lectures.
Retreats.
Tel. : (26) 09.27.38.

Sénanque (Abbey).
Gordes - 84220.
Gordes : 5 km.
Private property.

PROVENCE-CÔTE-D'AZUR — VAUCLUSE

A few kilometres from Gordes, the abbey of Sénanque is set in a narrow valley. Founded in 1148 by the Cistercians, it enjoyed several centuries of prosperity before falling into a state of diminution in the second half of the 15th century. Despite efforts made during the 17th century, Sénanque never recovered its former vitality. The last group of monks withdrew in 1969 when the building was taken over by the Friends of Sénanque, who have done much to energise this ancient abbey.
Open all year.
Summer : 10 - 12:30, 2 - 7.
Winter : 10 - 12, 2 - 6.
Individual tours upon application.
Guided tours during school holidays.
Audiovisual.
Cultural Centre.
Tel. : (90) 72.02.05.

Sérignan-du-Comtat (Harmas of J.-H. Fabre).

Sérignan-du-Comtat - 84830.
Orange : 7 km.
Station : Orange.
Property of the National Museum of Natural History.

This typical provencal house was lived in by J.-H. Fabre in 1879. He wrote nine of the ten volumes of his « Souvenirs entomologiques » here. In one of the wings of the house you can visit his study and see memorabilia relating to him. In one of the other rooms you will see 300 watercolours of mushrooms painted by Fabre.
Botanical gardens.
Open Apr. 1 to Sept. 30 : 9 - 11:30, 2 -
Oct. 1 to March 31 : 9 - 11:30, 2 - 4.
By request for groups of 30 or more.
Closed Tuesday.
Parking.
Guided tours, brochures.
Italian, English, German.
Tel. : (90) 70.00.44.

The Château de Simiane was built from 1639 on plans by La Valfenière for Mme de Sévigné's granddaughter. It is a classic building, symmetrical and supported by arcades on the ground storey. Inside you can see French ceilings, frescoes, a picture collection and period furniture.
Open Oct. 1 to March 31 : 2 - 4.
July 15 to Aug. 30 : 10 - 12, 3 - 5.
Closed Sundays and holidays.
Guided tours.
Festival : Evening music and theatre in the Enclave of the Popes.
Lectures.
Tel. : (90) 35.04.71 ou (90) 35.00.45.

Photo A. Orhon

Simiane (Château).

Valréas - 84600.
Place A.-Briand.
Montélimar or Orange.
Station : Montélimar or Orange : 37 km.
Bus service.
Property of the commune.

DISCOVER FRANCE AND ITS OLD CITIES
with the guided tours of the Caisse Nationale des Monuments Historiques

When travelling in France during your holidays, discover 100 Old Cities and their art treasures with the guided tours organised by the Caisse Nationale des Monuments Historiques. Daily tours are organised and last one hour or more. Ask for timetable and details in the Tourist Offices of cities like : AIX-EN-PROVENCE, ARLES, ARRAS, AVIGNON, BEAUNE, BEAUVAIS, LAON, LA ROCHELLE, LYON, METZ, MONTLUÇON, MONTPELLIER, NANCY, NANTES, ROUEN, STRASBOURG, VERSAILLES...

ENGLISH SPEAKING GUIDES.

Hôtel de Sully
62, rue Saint-Antoine 75004 PARIS
Tél. : 274.22.22.

RHÔNE-ALPES

AIN, ARDÈCHE, DRÔME, ISÈRE, LOIRE, RHÔNE, SAVOIE, HAUTE-SAVOIE.

- ■ castle, château, manor house
- ● abbey, priory
- ▲ garden, park
- ★ town house, famous men house, farm, mill...
- ○ city

CHAMBERY
- ★ Les Charmettes
- ● Musée Savoisien
- ■ Ducs de Savoie

CHARLIEU
- ● Abbaye
- ● Couvent des Cordeliers

LYON
- ★ Hôtel Gadagne

PAILLE
- ■ Château
- ▲ Arboretum

RHÔNE-ALPES

AIN

Les Allymes (Château).

Ambérieu-sur-Bugey - 01500.
Lyon : 50 km.
Station : Ambérieu-en-Bugey.
Town property.

Allymes is a typical example of savoyard military architecture, and was an arena for the conflict between the Dauphinois and the Savoyards. In 1354 the Château was captured by Savoy and passed into the hands of the Faucigny-Lucinge family. A member of this family, René de Lucinge, ambassador of Savoy at the court of Henry III, negotiated the Treaty of Lyon with Henry IV which made the Ain a part of France. The Château houses a museum of archaeology and local history.
Open daily, May 1 to Nov. 11 : 10 - 12, 2 - 6.
Sundays, March 1 to Apr. 31 : 2 - 6.
Nov. 16 to Dec. 30 : 2 - 5.
Upon request for groups.
Guided and unaccompanied tours.
Panels.
Information English, German, Italian, Dutch, Spanish.
Brochures.
Theatre.
Temporary exhibitions.
Lecture tours for school groups.
Tel. : (74) 38.06.07.

Ambronay (Royal Abbey).

Ambronay - 01500.
Bourg-en-Bresse : 23 km.
Station : Ambronay.
Property of the commune.

This Benedictine abbey was founded in the 10th century by Saint Barnard, one of Charlemagne's captains. It is attached to several priories, the best known being Brou in Bourg-en-Bresse.
Open all year : 10 - 12, 2 - 6.
Closed Monday mornings.
Unaccompanied tours, brochures.
Audiovisual.
Information in German.
Acoustiguide.
Concerts, temporary exhibitions.
Tel. : (74) 38.13.32.

Brou (Abbey).

Bourg-en-Bresse - 01000.
Property of the State.

At the beginning of the 16

AMBRONAY

AIN

The abbey of Ambronay was founded by Saint Barnard during the reign of Charlemagne and for centuries was an important spiritual centre. It was taken over by the Benedictine order of Saint-Maur in the middle of the 17th century.
The abbatial church, the cloisters, the 15th century chapter house and the sculpted jube are of special interest.

Concerts, exhibitions.

AMBÉRIEU-EN-BUGEY

LES ALLYMES

AIN

Medieval citadel, built the 13th to the 16th century, situatat 630 mètres above sea level.
Of great interest are the panoramic view over the Département of the Ain, the mountainous setting, and its strategic importance for the history of the region of the Rhônes-Alpes.
You can also see the exhibitions that are held here throughout the year, devoted to archaelogy, history, art and literature.
This is a rare example of an medieval castle which has remained architecturally intact.

BOURG-EN-BRESSE

BROU

AIN

This splendid 16th century abbey is justly proud of its flamboyant jube and its famous tombs — among which is the tomb of Marguerite of Austria who founded the monastery and made Brou one of the major centres of Renaissance art in France.

century, Marguerite of Austria built the abbey of Brou both to satisfy a now and to honour the memory of her 3rd husband, Philippe le Beau, to whom she erected a mausoleum. Situated on the route that linked Venice to Bruges, brou soon became a centre for artists from all Europe. The north side of the church with its three cloisters is built in a transitional style between High Gothic and early Renaissance. The choir is finished by one of the few jubes that can still be seen in France. The original stained glass windows that are set in the high windows above illuminate the tombs of Philippe le Beau, his mother and his wife. All this ornamentation does not, however, diminish the beauty of the more local art of the sculpted stalls. After much changing of hands, the abbey is now owned by the Service des Monuments historiques which has recovered its original beauty. In the monastery you will also see works of the 16th century that form the collection of the Museum of the town of Bourg.
Open Apr. 1 to Sept. 30 : 8:30 - 12, 2 - 6:30.
Oct. 1 to Oct. 31 : 10 - 12, 2 - 4:30.
Guided tour.
Brochures.
Sound and Light show Thursdays, Saturdays, Sundays, Holidays at 9:30 pm from the last Saturday in May to the last Sunday in September and Easter weekend.

Buenc (Keep).

Hautecourt-Romanèche - 01250.
Bourg-en-Bresse : 20 km.
Station : Villeneuve 5 km.
Property of M. Michel Chomarat.
This keep is the most important remnant of the 13th and 14th century castle of Buenc. Characteristic of Savoyard architecture, it rises to a height of some 30 mètres. It has been part of the fiefs of the House of Savoy, of the Lords of Beaujeu, the Lords of la Baume and the Coligny family.
Open Apr. 15 to Sept. 30 : 10 - 12, 2 - 7.
Parking.
Brochures.
Panels.

Temporary exhibitions.
Lecture tours.
Guided tours.
Tel. : (74) 30.66.18.

Courtes (Farmhouse).

Saint-Trivier-de-Courtes - Courtes - 01560.
Bourg-en-Bresse : 30 km.
Property of the commune.
This regional farmhouse is typical of Bresse architecture with its fireplace and exterior gallery, and its local furniture inside.
Open July 1 to Aug. 31 : 2 - 7, May 1 to Oct. 15, Sundays and Holidays : 2 - 7.
Off season for groups upon request.
Guided tours, brochures.
Entertainment.
Tel. : (74) 30.70.32.

Dortan (Château).

Dortan - 01590.
Oyonnax : 7 km.
Private property.
This fortress was originally one of the furthest outposts of the House of Savoy, protecting the border between Franche-Comté. Rebuilt during the 18th century, the former 14th century kitchen has kept all its character. Dortan is set in expansive grounds, with a river and a spring.
Open upon request for groups of more than 10, all year June 1 to Sept. 30, Tuesday, Thursday, Saturday : 3 - 7.
Guided tours, brochures.
Entertainment, temporary exhibitions.
Lectures.
Tel. : (74) 77.70.01.

ARDÈCHE

Alba (Château).

Alba - 07400.
Le Teil : 9 km.
Private property.
The Château of Alba consists of four towers and a ruined keep. Its chief attraction lies in the main building's facade. Set on volcanic rock it towers over the village and its environs. It was built in 1620 and for a long time remained in the possession of the Montaigu family.

Open June 12 to Sept. 5 : 10 - 12, 3 - ?
April 1 to Nov. 1 : 3 - 7.
Panels.
Information English, German, Dutch.
Concerts, Temporary exhibitions.
Lectures.
Courses in painting and weaving (in preparation).
Tel. : (75) 90.50.96.

Aubenas (Château).

Aubenas - 07200.
Place de L'Hôtel-de-Ville.
Valence : 70 km.
Property of the commune.
This fortress was transforme during the 15 th century into luxurious residence, but it ha kept its military appearance.
Open July 1 to Aug. 31 : 10 - 12, 3 - 6.
Closed sunday afternoons.
Parking.
Guided tours.
Brochures.
Concerts, temporary exhibitions.
Tel. : (75) 35.52.66.

PRANLES
Home of Pierre and Mari Durand.

Pranles - 07000.
Le Bouchet-de-Pranles.
Valence : 50 km.
Property of the Society for the History French Protestantism.
In 1685 Louis XIV revoked th Edict of Nantes. The Protestant r ligion was thereby forbidden, b certain churches continued function clandestinely. In the Viv rais Pierre Durand was behind or such community, and he died 1732. His sister, Larie, was imp soned for 38 years at Aigue Mortes, and on her release she r turned to her home and die there. This period of history keenly evoked by the furniture ar documents to be found in th house.
Open daily, June 16 to Sept. 15 : 10 12, 2:30 - 6.
Saturday and sunday of Apr. 1 to Ju 15, and Sept. 16 to Nov. 1 : 2:30 - 6:3
Guided tours, brochures.
Information English, German, Dutch.
Lectures.
Tel. : (75) 64.22.74.

Le Roure (Château).

La Bastide-de-Virac - 07150.
Montélimar : 55 km.
Private property.
This Château belonged to th counts de Roure, Protestants, an was almost demolished in 162 when Louis XIII and Richelieu s gned the peace treaty of Alès. I

ide you can see the room in which the Duc de Rohan slept in 1628, the rooms with their French ceilings and monumental fireplaces. There is a great deal of informations and documents relating to the history of the Château, as well as a permanent exhibition of silk weaving.
Open from Easter to Sept. 15 : 10 - 12, 2 - 7.
Closed Sundays.
Guided tours.
Tel. : (75) 38.61.13.

Tournon (Château and Museum).

Tournon-sur-Rhône - 07300.
Place Auguste-Faure.
Station : Valence 18 km and Tain l'Hermitage 2 km.
Bus service.
Property of the town.

The counts de Tournon built this Château during the 10th and 11th centuries. The dauphin François, son of François I, died there in 1536. The Renaissance main building has a large tower and chapel which date from the 15th century. Inside, the Museum of the Rhône has prehistoric and etnographic collections, as well as works of regional artists such as the sculptures of Marcel Gimond (1894-1961).
Open Apr. 1 to Oct. 31 : 2:15 - 6.
Sept. 1 to Oct. 1, June 1 to Sept. 1 : 10 - 12, 2:15 - 6.
Off season by request.
Guided tours, brochures.
Shows, tempory exhibitions.
Tel. : (75) 08.10.30.

Ventadour (Fortress).

Lalevade - 07380.
Aubenas : 15 km.
Station : Lalevade 7 km.
Bus service.
Property of the Association to save Ventadour.

This fortress was built between the 11th and the 16th centuries at the confluence of the Ardèche and the Fontaulière, a major medieval vantage point. Once known as Meyras, it was called Ventadour just before it was demolished in the 18th century. Since 1969 groups of young volunteers have been helping on restoration.
Open July 1 to Sept. 4 : 8:30 - 12, 2 - 6:30.
Off season, by request for groups.
Ground all year.
Parking.
Guided tours of interior.
Information by request, English, German, Dutch.
Brochures.
Temporary exhibitions.
Lectures tours for school groups.
Tel. : (75) 38.00.92.

Versas (Château).

Sanilhac - 07110.
Largentière.
Private property.

This Renaissance Château comprises two main buildings joined together by an octagonal tour. The dovecote dates from the same period.
Open Dec. 16 to Jan. 1 (times not given : ring) and July 14 to Sept. 15.
Ground only (in principle).
Unaccompanied tour.
Information in English and German.
Tel. : (75) 39.12.25.

Voguë (Château).

Voguë - 07200.
Place du Château.
Aubenas : 10 km.

FARMHOUSE « LA FORÊT »   AIN
SAINT-TRIVIER-DE-COURTES

Visit the Farmhouse-Museum of « La Forêt » any day during the months of July and August, and every sunday between May and October. It's open all year, by request, for groups. Discover the Haute-Bresse and the Canton of Saint-Trivier-de-Courtes — its farms, produce, chicken and chesses.

Numerous Hotels, Inns, Camping sites, etc.

Syndicat d'Initiative.
01560 Saint-Trivier-de-Courtes.
Tel. : (74) 30.70.32.

DRÔME

MONTÉLIMAR

This impressive military ensemble, built at various times from the 11th to the 14th century, was the work of the Adhémar de Monteil family. You can see fine examples of military, domestic and religious architecture. Montélimar is now being restored and has been open to the public since 1983. Property of the Drôme, it is now a cultural centre and the setting for archaeological activities.

SUZE-LA-ROUSSE

DRÔME

This powerful medieval fortress, set alongside the wine growing region of the Côtes-du-Rhône, is also one of the great examples of French 16th century architecture, due to its main courtyard.

Suze-la-Rousse also belongs to the Département of the Drôme, where it is used for cultural events, seminars, and the activities of the University of Wine.

Photo J.-M. Paillot

Montélimar : 40 km.
Property of M. de Voguë.
Home of the Association « Vivante Ardèche ».
This Château was the home of the de Voguë family, who lost the property during the Middle Ages, but recovered it in the 17th century. By this time it had been completely transformed. Today it serves as the centre for Departmental information.
Open July 1 to Aug. 31 : 3 - 6.
Off season for groups.
Closed sunday mornings.
Parking.
Unaccompanied tours, brochures.
Concerts, temporary exhibitions.
Tel. : (75) 35.22.66.

DRÔME

Aulan (Château).

Aulan - 26570.
Carpentras and Orange : 70 km.
Private property.
According to archives, this Château was already standing by 1240 and has been remodelled many times since. Inside you can see memorabilia relating to the Suarez family, as well as several objets d'art, included Spanish 14th century decoration and pictures by Mignard.
Parking.
Guided tours.
Theatre.
Candle-lit tours.
Tel. : (75) 28.80.00.

Crest (Tower).

Crest - 26400.
Valence : 28 km.
Private property.
You can see two towers : the old tower, built between the 4th and the 11th century, and the new tower, built in the 14th century. Together they form a building some 51 metres high which is all that remains of the château that was demolished in 1632 and which had been built by Aymart VI de Poitiers, count de Valentinois. Inside you can see three floors of well maintained rooms. At the top, the view extends to Mont Gerbier des Joncs.
Open all year : 9 - 12, 2 - 6.
Unaccompanied tours, brochures.
Information English, German, Dutch.
Lecture tours for school groups.
Tel. : (75) 75.00.22.

Grignan (Château).

Grignan - 26230.
Station : Montélimar 27 km.
Bus service.
Property of the Department.
Grignan is one of the most remarkable Châteaux in the Midi, and in France as a whole. Built on the top of an isolated rock and on the site of a fort (some ruins of which can still be seen), Grignan is made up of several buildings, including the « prelates building », given to Jules Hardouin-Mansart and dating to the 17th century. Inside you can see the main chambers and state apartments which have been magnificently restored (the Salle du Roi, the Salle de la Reine), as well as the terraces which Mme de Sévigné immortalised in the letters to her daughter, Mme de Grignan. This famous woman died at Grignan on 17 April 1696.
Open Jan. 2 to Nov. 31, Dec. 1 to Dec. 24, Dec. 26 to Dec. 31 : 9:30 - 11:30, 2:30 - 5:30.
Closed Tuesday and Wednesday mornings.
Guided tours.
Information in English, German and Spanish.
Panels, brochures.
Theatre, concerts.
Temporary exhibitions.
Tel. : (75) 46.51.56.

MONTÉLIMAR

Château des Adhémar.

Montélimar - 26200.
Property of the Department.
This important group of buildings once belonged to the Popes of Avignon and the counts de Valentinois. Its construction spans the 11th to the 14th centuries. The upper level of the main building has a very interesting series of sculpted arcatures which date from the 12th century. You can also see a romanesque chapel.
Open : 10 - 12, 2 - 7.
Closed Tuesday, Wednesday mornings, throughout the month of December.
Guided tours, Wednesday, Saturday and Sunday at 3:00.
Guided tours for groups : telephone either the Château or Grignan (75) 46.51.56.
Brochure.
Summer festival.
Exhibitions.
Tel. : (75) 01.07.85.

Suze-la-Rousse (Château).

Suze-la-Rousse - 26130.
Orange : 20 km.
Pierrelatte : 18 km.
Property of the Department.
Suze-la-Rousse was already owned by the Princes of Orange during the Late Middle Ages. This military building is unusual in not having been destroyed during the 12th and 13th centuries. Richelieu saved it in acknowledgement of the fidelity of the Comte de Suze towards the throne. The first floor which gives onto the Renaissance main courtyard is decorated with frescoes and stucco work.
Open daily July 1 to Sept. 30 : 3 - 3:45, 4:30 - 5:15.
Sundays from June 1 to June 30, Oct. 1 to May 31 (except in Nov.) : 3 - 3:45, 4:30 - 5:15.
Closed Tuesday.
Parking.
Guided tours.
Theatre, concerts.
Tel. : (75) 46.51.56.

ISÈRE

Bérenger (Château).

*Sassenage - 38360.
Grenoble : 4 km.
Property of the International Council of the French language.*

This fine Dauphinois residence, built between 1662 and 1669 in Louis XIII style, offers a rare collection of 17th and 18th century furniture in its several rooms. The Salle des Fêtes is decorated with a serie of pictures representing the story of Psyche. The Château remained in the hands of its original owners until the death of the Marquise de Bérenger in 1971.

*Open July 1 to Aug. 31 : 10:30, 3 - 4:30.
Closed saturday, sunday, holidays.
Guided tours, brochures.
Tel. : (76) 27.54.44.*

Bresson (Château).

*Moissieu-sur-Dolon - Beaurepaire - 38270.
Lyon : 60 km.
Vienne : 25 km.
Bus service.
Private property.*

This Louis XIII Château, built on the remains of an old castle, has a terraced formal garden.

*Open July 4 to Aug. 31.
Ground only.
Guided tour.
Tel. : (74) 84.57.82.*

Crôlles (Château).

*Crôlles-Brignoud - 38190.
Grenoble : 17 km.
Bus service.
Property of M. de Bernis.*

Near a pond, this Château was built in 1340 and has been remodelled since. The most notable addition was the inclusion of windows in the facade. Henri IV, Louis XIII and Richelieu stayed here, and the latter sent his host a portrait by Philippe de Champaigne as a gift for his hospitality.

*Open upon request July 1 to Sept. 30.
Tel. : (76) 08.01.01.*

Grenoble (Priory Saint-Laurent).

*Grenoble - 38000.
Rue Saint-Laurent.
Property of the town.*

This site retains traces of the earliest Christian architecture : chapels, oratories which were destroyed and replaced by the romanesque church. Excavations of the interior have revealed the various stages of this church's construction and include important funerary remains.

*Open July 1 to Sept. 30.
Tours leave from the Tourist office at 10, 2:30, 4:30.
Off season upon request for groups.
Closed Tuesdays.
Tel. : for all information CAHMGI (76) 44.78.68.*

Lautaret (Alpine station).

*Grenoble - 38041.
University of Grenoble 1.
Property of the Medical and Science University of Grenoble.*

This station consist of a garden, two hectares in size, planted with selected species of Alpine plants and other mountainous vegetation from all over the world. There is also a laboratory.

*Open June 20 to Sept. 20 : 8 - 12, 2 - 6.
Closed Friday.
Parking.
Unaccompanied tours.
Brochures.
Tel. : (76) 44.82.72.*

Longpra (Château).

*Saint-Geoire-en-Valdaine - 38620.
Grenoble : 40 km.
Station : Voiron 13 km.
Bus service.
Private property*

Once a fort, defended by Jean Pascalis against the Protestants in 1590, Longpra was rebuilt during the 18th century, and has remained in the same family ever since.

*Open June 15 to Sept. 15 : 2 - 6, Tuesdays, Thursdays and Saturdays.
For groups by request.
Guided tours.
Tel. : (76) 07.50.21.*

Quincivet (Château).

*Saint-Vérand.
Saint-Marcellin - 38160.
Private property.*

This house was initially intended as a hunting lodge for Louis XI. The mullioned windows are intricately worked, and you can visit the tower and the large Arms room whose monumental fireplaces help give the Château the feel of a medieval castle.

*Open July 1 to Sept. 15 : 9 - 12, 2 - 5.
Closed Tuesdays and Saturdays.
Guided tours.
Individual acoustiguides.
Tel. : (76) 38.26.75.*

Septême (Château).

*Septême-PontÉvêque - 38780.
Vienne : 15 km.
Bus service.
Private property.*

An ancient fortress set on the Roman road between Vienne and Milan, the Château's ramparts were built in the 14th century by the Counts of Savoy. The inner courtyard was the former site of the Château which had an arcaded gallery surmounted by Renaissance loggias and an old well.

*Open Saturday, Sunday, holidays March 15 to Nov. 11 : 3 - 6.
Parking.
Tel. : (74) 58.26.05.*

Serviantin (Château).

*Biviers - 38330.
Station : Grenoble 9 km.
Bus service.
Property of M. Jacquemont.*

It is here that Abel Serviem who negotiated the Treaty of Westphalia was born. The Château consists of buildings at right angles flanked by two round towers.

*Open July 1 to Sept. 12 : 9 - 12, 2 to 5.
Closed Saturday, Sunday, Holidays.*

Le Touvet (Château).

*Le Touvet - 38660.
Chambéry and Grenoble : 30 km.
Private property.*

Between Grenoble and Chambéry, in the Chartreuse Mountain, the Château dominates the village and the Grésivaudan valley. The gardens and fountains are very well kept. Inside one can see memorabilia dating from the Monarchy, the Empire and nowadays. The Château is still inhabited by the family.

*Open May 4 to Nov. 1 : 2 - 6.
Saturday, Sunday, Holiday.
Guided tours.
Tel. : (76) 08.42.27.*

VIENNE
Saint-André-le-Bas (Cloisters).

*Vienne - 38200.
Lyon : 31 km.
Property of the town.*

The abbey of Saint-André-les-Bas was founded in the 6th century. The cloister, with its small columns and decorated capitals dates from the 12th century. The cloisters have a collection of Christian epigraphs. Since 1982 photographic exhibitions have been held here.

Open Apr. 1 to Oct. 15 (except Tuesdays) : 9 - 12, 2 - 6:30.

Oct. 16 to March 31 : 10 - 12, 2 - 5 (Sunday 2 - 6).
Parking.
Unaccompanied tours.
Tel. : (74) 85.18.49.

Virieu (Château).

Virieu-sur-Bourbe - 38730.
La Tour du Pin : 12 km.
Station : Virieu 2 km.
Property of Mme de Virieu.

The fort of Virieu was founded in the 11th century by Wilfrid de Virieu and successively extended until the 18th century, when terraces were added beneath the ramparts. You can see the 13th century keep, and the chamber where Louis XIII once slept which has been preserved. Virieu was beseiged on two separate occasions during the Wars of Religion.
Open July 1 to Sept. 30 : 2 - 6.
Closed Mondays.
Guided tours.
Temporary exhibitions.
Tel. : (74) 88.20.10.

Vizille (Château).

Vizille - 38220.
Grenoble : 20 km.
Property of the State.

Situated on the Roman road between Milan and Vienne, Vizille occupied a commanding position over the valley of la Romanche. The ruins of the medieval camp are now overshadowed by the Château which was built at the beginning of the 17th century on a different site by the Duke de Lesdiguières, the last Constable of France. The two wings of the facade which looks onto the garden are completed by a perspective arranged with basin and monumental steps. Framed by a solitary main building, the main courtyard is entered by a gateway that dates from the period of Louis XIII... It was here that the States General of the Dauphiné met in 1788. In the 19th century Vizille became a cloth factory before returning to its status as luxurious hôtel in the 20th century. It was given to the state in 1924 and until recently was used as a presidential residence.
Open Jan. 1 to March 31 : 10 - 12, 2 - 5.
Apr. 1 to Sept. 30 : 9 - 12, 2 - 7.
Closed mondays and tuesdays.
Limited parking facilities.
Theatre festival, June 19-29.
Concerts.
Brochure.
Tel. : (76) 68.00.19.

LOIRE

Les Bruneaux (Château).

Firminy - 42700.
Rue de Chanzy.
Saint-Étienne : 12 km.
Firminy : 2 km.
Bus service.
Property of the Society for the History of Firminy and district.

On the pilgrim's route between Lyon and Le Puy, this old castle was completely transformed during the 18th century. You must not be misled by the stark exterior of this building : inside, the Louis XVI salon and dining room contrast with the medieval kitchen. The Château's museum has a nail maker's studio and a baker's oven.
Open Apr. 1 to Sept. 30 : 2 - 6:30, saturdays, sundays, holidays.
By request for groups.
Parking.
Unaccompanied tours.
Panels.
Exhibitions.
Tel. : 756.04.86.

La Bastie d'Urfé (Château).

Saint-Étienne-le-Molard - 42130.
Montbrison : 12 km.
Bus service.
Private property.

This Renaissance Château, Italianate in style was built by Claude d'Urfé, François I's ambassador to Rome ans grandfather of the author of « L'Astrée ». The triangular courtyard has a mainbuilding with arcaded double loggias. Inside, the « nymphée » — or refreshment room — is a remarkable grotto made up exclusively of stones whose forms are meant to evoke mythological figures. The chapel has a very fine sculpted arch.
Open daily 9 - 11:30, 2:30 - 6.
Closed Tuesday.
Parking.
Guided tours.
Brochures.
Information English, German.
Facilities for the handicapped.
Shows and exhibitions.
Tel. : (77) 97.54.68.

CHARLIEU
Benedictine Abbey.

Charlieu - 42190.
Place de l'Abbaye.
Roanne : 19 km.
Bus service.
Property of the State and the department.

Founded in 872, the abbey still preserves two gateways that date from the 11th and 12th century, and are masterpieces of Romanesque art. The narthex of the church of Saint-Fortunat a colonnade, and the keep-tower Philippe Auguste are also romanesque. The remaining buildings (cloisters, chapter house, Prior's house) date from the 15th and 16th centuries. The abbey also has a museum of gems and religious art.
Open Apr. 1 to Sept. 30 : 9 - 12, 2 - 7 (closed Tuesdays).
Oct. 1 to March 31 : 9 - 12, 2 - 5 (closed Tuesdays, Wednesdays and for annual holidays).
Parking.
Guided tours.
Information English, German.
Brochures.
Shows (concerts).
Exhibitions.
Lectures.
Tel. : (77) 60.08.17.

Les Cordeliers (Convent).

Charlieu - 42190.
Route de Saint-Nizier.
Roanne.
Bus service.
Property of the department.

The Cordeliers convent of Charlieu is famous for its gothic cloisters. This group of monastic buildings includes the monks church and a building known as the Library.

pen Apr. 1 to Sept. 30 : 9 - 12, 2:15 -
15 (closed Tuesday).
ct. 1 to March 31 : 9 - 12, 2:15 - 5:15
losed Tuesday, Wednesday, annual
olidays).
arking.
uided tours.
rochures.
formation German, English.
hows (concerts).
xhibitions.
ectures.
el. : (77) 60.07.42.

outelas (Château).

arcous par Boen-sur-Lignon.
arcoux - 42130.
aint-Étienne : 50 km.
roperty of the Association of the
riends of Goutelas.
   Theis 16th century Château, pur-
hased by Jean Papon and trans-
ormed into a Renaissance dwel-
ng, Goutelas was built in a pictu-
esque setting that was attached
o many legends : It is also called
he Château of the White Lady. It
as restored in 1961 by the Asso-
iation of the Friends of Goutelas.
pen permanently for visit of grounds.
arking.
hows.
el. : (77) 24.09.73.

Les Grands-Murcins (Arboretum).

Arcon-Renaison - 42370.
Roanne : 22 km.
Property of the Caisse d'Épargne of Roanne.
   Established in 1936 by the Caisse d'Épargne as an experiment and renovated and extended in the past few years, this arboretum has over 150 different species of broad leafed and coniferous trees. It is also well worth visiting for its restful location, set as it is in the Monts de la Madeleine at 780 metres above sea level and with a spectacular panoramic view.
Open all year.
Guided tours by request.
Write to Société des Arbres de la Loire, Caisse d'Épargne de Roanne, 33, rue de Brison, Roanne 42300.
Panels, Brochures.
Tel. : (77) 65.80.38.

Montrond (Château).

Montrond-les-Bains - 42210.
Montbrison : 15 km.
Saint-Étienne : 30 km.
Montrond : 2 km.
Bus service.
Property of the Association of the Friends of the Vieux Château.
   Built during the 13th century, this fort once protected the toll gates of the Loire. It was transformed into a domestic Château in the 14th century. At the centre of a circular complex with posterns at the north and south, it has a keep to the East, which rises to a height of 40 metres and joins the horshoe-shaped buildings. Burnt down in 1793, it is currently being restored.
Open July 15 to Sept. 15 : 2 - 6:30.
Closed Tuesday.
By request for groups.
Parking.
Guided tours.
Exhibitions.
Tel. : (78) 28.89.72.

Roche-la-Molière (Château).

Roche-la-Molière - 42230.
1, rue Victor-Hugo.
Saint-Étienne : 7 km.
Bus service.
Property of the town.
   Most of this complex has remained intact since the 15th century.

CHARLIEU

Benedictine abbey (11th - 16th centuries).
Cordeliers Convent (13th and 16 th centuries).
Historic centre (over 30 12th and 13th century houses).
Former Town Hall (18th century - gilded 17th century altar).
18th century Town Hall (Aubusson tapestry).

The interior decoration, which has been restored, is largely 18th century, most notably the parquet floors and fireplaces. The chapel has a painting by Rubens and reliquaries which date from the end of the 15th century.
Open all year, saturdays, sundays and holidays : 2 - 5.
Other times, by appointment.
Guided tours.
Exhibitions.
Lectures.
Tel. : (78) 60.75.19.

Saint-Galmier (« Renaissance House »).

Saint-Galmier - 42330.
24 et 26, rue de Saint-Étienne.
Saint-Étienne : 20 km.
Station : 3 km.
Property of the Association of the Friends of the Old Saint-Galmier and district.

Supporting the door of St-Stephen, part of the old city ramparts, and set in the heart of the interesting old city, this Renaissance house has two large arcades with doric columns and fine mullioned windows on the first floor.
Open on request (except at times of exhibitions).
Guided tours.
Exhibitions.

Saint-Marcel (Château).

Bourg-Saint-Marcel-de-Félines - 42122.
Roanne : 25 km.
Balbigny : 7 km.
Bus service.
Private property.

This 11th century castle was transformed in the 16th century. Access is by a stone bridge which crosses the deep dry moat and you see a fine inner courtyard in Renaissance style inspired by Italian examples. The rooms are decorated with boiseries painted in the 17th century by Italian artists and in trompe l'œil.
Open Sunday, Monday, holidays from Apr. 22 to Oct. 31 : 2 - 6.
By request for groups.
Parking.
Guided tours.
Brochures.

Information English, German.
Panels.
Tel. : (77) 63.23.08.

Sury-le-Comtal (Château).

Sury-le-Comtal - 42450.
Saint-Étienne : 24 km.
Montbrison : 12 km.
Bus service.
Property of Mr. de La Grange Sury.

Formerly the property of the Counts of Forez in the 11th century, then in the possession of the Kings of France, the present day Château was built in the 17th century by the Sourdin family who were responsible for the impressive interiors. There are three salons and a bedroom decorated with wooden and stone ceillings and coffered ceilings of the Louis XIII style. The dining room, with its panels and painting boiseries, is in a more romantic style.
Open Easter to Sept. 30 : 2 - 6.
Guided tours.
Brochures.
Information English.
Tel. : (77) 53.51.58.

Vaugirard (Château).

Champdieu-Montbrison - 42500.
Private property.

Built in the 16th century, the Château is set in an inner courtyard with two belltowers at the front. Two room are of special interest : the Henry IV bedchamber with its wood-carved fireplace and painted ceiling and wall. ; and the Kingt's room which is also painted with frescoes.
Open upon request for groups.
Parking.
Guided tours.
Brochures.
Information in German.
Exhibitions.
Tel. : (77) 58.33.88.

RHÔNE

La Chaize (Vats).

Odenas - 69460 Saint-Étienne-des-Oullières.
Villefranche-sur-Saône : 13 km.

Mâcon : 25 km.
Bus service.
Property of Mr. de Roussy de Sales.

Built a century after the Châte de la Chaize as a result of incr sing wine production, this is unusual « historic monume with its ancient frame (1771) s porting the largest vaulted ce (110 metres) which houses 55 t of the local Brouilly. The ferme tion process was modernised 1978.
Open Apr. 1 to July 31, Aug. 2 Sept. 14, Oct. 15 to Dec. 12 : 9 - 12 5.
Closed saturday and sunday.
Guided tours.
Leaflets.
Tel. : (74) 03.41.05.

Corcelles (Château).

Corcelles-en-Beaujolais - 69220.
Belleville-sur-Saône : 7 km.
Private property.

Built in the 15th century to p tect the Beaujolais region, C celles was acquired by Tircuy d Barre in 1592. In the follwoing c tury the castle was transform into a residence by the Mag leine de Ragny family. A squ keep unites two main buildir both flanked by towers. The co tyard has a Renaissance wood gallery. Utrillo stayed here seve times and painted at Corcelles.
Open all year : 2:30 - 6:30.
Mornings, 10 - 12, by request.
Closed sundays and holidays.
Parking.
Tel. : (74) 66.00.24.

LYON
Hôtel Gadagne.

Lyon - 69005.
Rue de Gadagne et Place du Petit-Collège.
Nearby buses and metro.
Property of the city.

Formerly the hôtel of Anne Pierrerive (16th century) it was quired by the sons of a Florent banker operating in Lyon, Thom Gadagne, in 1545. Since 1921 has been the Historical Muse of Lyon with collections of ly nais archaeological material fr

...e roman period, Nevers faience, ...intings and engravings relating ... the history of Lyon. It also ...rves as the Puppet museum.
...en all year : 10:45 - 12, 2 - 6.
...naccompanied tours.
...nels.
...diovisual.
...glish, German.
...hibitions, lectures.
...l. : (78) 42.03.61.

...ainte-Marie ... la Tourette (Convent).

... Tourette - Eveux-sur-l'Arbresle - ...210.
...on : 25 km.
...Arbresle : 2 km.
... service.
...ivate property.

Designed and built by Le Corbu-...er between 1956 and 1959, this ...ilding was first used as the se-...inary of the Dominicans of Lyon, ...d from 1969 has become the ...me of a Dominican community. ... inner plan follows that of the ...assical Dominican convent. ...ree of the facades of the main ...ilding are loggias with large ...ertures. This is one of the few ...ntemporary buildings to have been listed as a historic building.
Open July 1-Sept. 20 : 9 - 12, 2 - 6.
Parking.
Guided tours.
Brochures.
Information English, German, Spanish, Italian.
Shows.
Tel. : (74) 01.01.03.

Salles (Chapter House of the Chanoinesses-Comtesses).

Salles - Saint-Georges-de-Reneins - 69380.
Villefranche-sur-Saône : 10 km.
Bus service.
Property of the commune.

The ancient Cluniac priory of Saint-Martin was occupied until the 18th century by a group of noble women, which included Lamartine's grandmother, before her marriage. The 12th century Romanesque church is noteworthy for its elegant facade, flanked on its right by an ornate doorway which opens onto the cloisters and the chapter house. The latter is paved and has frescoes from the 15th century.

Open Apr. 10-Nov. 1 : 10 - 12, 2 - 6.
By request off season, Tel. :
Mme Médal (74) 67.51.81 or
M. Bernard (74) 67.57.39.
Guided or unaccompanied tours.
Brochures.
Shows (concerts).
Tel. : (7) 862.65.23.

Vaurenard (Château).

Gleize - 69400.
Villefranche-sur-Saône : 2 km.
Bus service.
Private property.

Vaurenard was originally where the Lords of Beaujeu came to hunt from their neighbouring castle which no longer exists. The property was purchased in 1672 by the Corteille family, and partially transformed during the 18th century. The Baron Richemont, who claimed to be Louis XVII, once lived here.

Open June 1 to Oct. 30 : 2 - 6.
By request for groups on Sundays.
Closed sunday and monday during the wine harvest.
Parking.
Guided tours.
Tel. : (74) 68.21.65.

SAINTE-MARIE-DE-LA-TOURETTE
RHÔNE

Designed and built by Le Corbusier between 1956 and 1959, this building was first used as the seminary of the Domicicans of Lyon. Now it is the home of group of Dominicans but is open to all kinds of groups (those on retreat, researchers students of architecture, international exchange groups).
« This concrete convent is a work of love » (Le Corbusier).
Guided tours from July until the end of September.

SAVOIE

Le Bourget du Lac (Château priory).

*Le Bourget du Lac - 73370.
Place de l'Église.
Chambéry ou Aix-les-Bains : 10 km.
Bus service.
Property of the commune.*

The Château-priory which abuts the church of Le Bourget du Lac was built in the 11th century by Saint Odilon, abbot of Cluny, on a site given to him by the Count of Savoy. The property belonged thereafter to several different religious orders (Benedictines, Jesuits) before it was purchased at the beginning of the 20th century by the Duchess de Choiseul. From the inner courtyard you can see the gothic cloisters with romanesque gallery — an anachronism perpetrated during the 15th century. You end your visit to the abbey with a walk in the formal gardens, where the hefges are cut in the shape of chess pieces.
*Open daily, June 25 to Sept. 5 : 3 - 7.
Parking.*
Unaccompanied and guided tours.
Information in English.
Brochures.
Exhibitions, shows, festival (concerts).
Tel. : (79) 25.01.43.

CHAMBÉRY
Les Charmettes (house).

*Chambéry - 73000.
Chemin des Charmettes.
Bus service.
Town property.*

« Les Charmettes » is a country house built in the 17th century by the Noiray family who where senators of Savoy. The museum displays objects relating to the visits Jean-Jaxques Rousseas made here as the guest of Madame de Warens. The house has preserved its interiors and its 18th century furniture.
*Open Apr. 1 to Sept. 30 : 10 - 12, 2 - 6.
Oct. 1 to Mar. 31 : 10 - 12, 2 - 4:30.
Closed Tuesday.*
Guided tours.
Tel. : (79) 33.39.44.

Museum of Savoy.

*Chambéry - 73000.
Square de Lannoy de Bissy.
Bus service.
Town property.*

This former Franciscan convent consists of a group of buildings disposed around 17th century cloisters. The Bishops residence is an eighteenth century building, and the private chapel dates from 1807. The museum, established in 1864, has a fine historical, archaeological and ethnographic collection.
*Open all year : 10 - 12, 2 - 6.
Closed Tuesday.*
Panels, brochures.
Audiovisual.
Theatre, exhibtiions, lectures.
Tel. : (79) 34.44.48.

Château of the Dukes of Savoy.

*Chambéry - 73000.
Place du Château.
Property of the Département.*

Built in the 11th century by the counts and Dukes of Savoy, the palace has been enlarged over the centuries and is now the seat of the Départment. The east building is medieval, and the Sainte-Chapelle is especially fine, whereas the west building dates from the 19th century. The marriage of Louis XI was consecrated in the east chapel.
*Open daily : 10:30, 2 - 5.
Sept. 16 to June 14, saturdays at 2:30.
Closed sunday morning.*
Guided tours, brochures.
Information in English, German and Italian.
Tel. : (79) 33.42.47.

CONFLANS
Manuel de Locatel (Château).

*Conflans-Albertville - 73200.
Property of Albertville Town Hall.*

Conflans is the historc section of Albertville a fortified town until 1600. The Château was built by Locatel family at the end of 16th century and is in French naissance style. The gardens arranged in terraces, and althou the original furniture has dis peared, the Château has pres ved a fine 17th century ceiling.
*Open June 12 to Sept. 13 and Ea weekend : 10 - 12, 3 - 6:30.
Off season upon request.
Parking.*
Unaccompanied and guided tours.
Audiovisual.
Information German, Spanish, Ital English.
Concerts.
Tel. : (79) 32.00.12, 32.29.93.

Hautecombe (Abbey).

*Saint-Pierre-de-Curtille - Chindrieu 73310.
Aix-les-Bains : 27 km.
Access by boat.
Station : Chindrieux.
Property of a monastic community nedictines).*

Until the 15th century, this C tercian abbey served as the bu place of the Counts of Savoy was fully restored in the 19th c tury by King Charles-Felix of Sa nia, who transformed the chu into a monument to the got troubadour style.
*Open Jan. 1 to March 4 : 10:30 - 11. 2 - 4:25.
March 5 to sept. 30 : 10:30 - 11:25, 2 - 5:45.
Oct. 1 to Dec. 31 : 10:30 - 11:25, 4:25.
Closed mondays (except in winter).
Services 9:30 weekdays, 9:15 Sund (Mass in Gregorian chant).
Parking.*
Guided tours.
Brochures.
Acoustiguides.
Information German, English, Itali Dutch.
Tel. : (79) 54.26.12.

Miolans (Château).

*Miolans - 73250.
Saint-Pierre-d'Albigny.
Chambéry ou Albertville : 30 km.
Private property.*

This medieval fortress was b between the 11th and 16th cent by the Lords of Miolans, on site of a Roman camp which h been on Hannibal's route. Build continued until the 15th cent and thereafter Miolans became state prison under the Dukes Savoy. The Marquis de Sade w imprisoned here in 1772. The C teau has a splendid panoram view over the Grande Chartreu and Mont-Blanc.

RHÔNE-ALPES — HAUTE-SAVOIE

Open June 1 to Sept. 15 : 10 - 11:30, 2 - 6.
Closed sunday morning.
Parking.
Unaccompanied tours.
Guided tours for groups.
Panels, brochures.
Information English, German, Italian, Dutch.
Tel. : (79) 28.50.47.

HAUTE-SAVOIE

Abondance (Abbey).

Abondance - 74360.
Evian and Thonon : 28 km.
Bus service.
Property of the commune.
   The abbey was founded in 1080 by the monks of Saint Augustin and Saint Maurice and later restored bu Saint François-de-Sales and the order of the Feuillants. The cloisters have preserved their frescoes which date from the 15th century, and you can also visit a museum of religious art.
Open, Cloisters, Jan. 1 to March 31 : 10 - 12, 2 - 4.
Apr. 1 to May 31 : 10 - 12, 2 - 5.
June 1 to Sept. 30 : 9 - 12, 2 - 6.
Oct. 1 to Dec. 31 : 10 - 12, 2 - 5.
Parking.
Guided and unaccompanied tours.
Information English.
Facilities for the handicapped.
Light and sound show.
Tel. : (50) 73.00.16.

Les Allinges (Château).

Allinges - Thonon-les-Bains - 74200.
Thonon-les-Bains : 5 km.
   Property of the missionaries of Saint-François-de-Sales. Fortified during the 11th century, Allignes hill is crowned by two feudal monuments — the new and old castle — which were once the administrative, religious and military centre of all Chablais, until they were demolished in 1703. From the ruins you have a fine panoramic view over lower Chablais and the Dent d'Oche.
Open all year.
Guided and unaccompanied tours.
Brochures.
Tel. : (50) 71.46.33.

Beauregard (Château).

Chens-sur-Léman - 74140.
Thonon-les-Bains : 18 km.
Genève : 18 km.
Property of Costa de Beauregard family.
   In an idyllic setting on Lake Geneva, this Château has a large 12th century tower and buildings constructed between the 14th and 15th centuries. Acquired in 1670 by the Costa family, it was restored in the 17th century by Henry Costa de Beauregard and has remained in the same family since that time.
Open July 1 to July 10, Sept. 1 to Sept. 30 : 9 - 12, 3 - 7.
By request for groups.
Grounds only.
Tel. : (50) 94.04.07.

Clermont (Château).

Clermont-Frangy - 74270.
Annecy : 20 km.

MIOLANS
SAVOIE

Miolans is « one of the finest feudal castles preserved today and the most perfect example of 15th century military architecture ».
Previously the site of a roman camp, and on Hannibal's route when he crossed the Alps, this castle was built in the 11th century by the Lords of Miolans who would later gain fame as the crusaders who brought back the three thorns of Christ's crown.

By 1536, through the lack of a male heir, the Château passed out of this family and was used by the Dukes of Savoy as a state prison from 1564 to the Revolution. This terrifying Savoyard fortress has entertained such prisoners as the Marquis de Sade who succeeded in escaping from it.

Seyssel : 10 km.
Frangy : 8 km.
Property of the Department.
   Bishop Gallois de Regard built this Château in 1575, after seeing many Renaissance buildings in Italy. The inner courtyard has arcaded galleries on three sides and the mainbuilding is linked to two tours each attached to the corners of the entry façade. The Département of the Haute-Savoy acquired the Château in 1966.
Open Easter Monday to Oct. 31 : 9 - 12, 2:30 - 5:30.
Closed Tuesday.
Guided and unaccompanied tours.
Information English, Italian, German.
Brochures.
Shows (Light and sound, galas, concerts).
Exhibitions.
Tel. : (50) 77.63.15 and 69.63.15.

Menthon (Château).

Menthon-Saint-Bernard.
Station : Annecy 10 km.
Bus service.
Property of M. de Menthon.
   This medieval castle, with additions made from the 14th to the 19th century, has always belonged to the same family, which issues from Saint Bernard de Menthon, founder of the hospital of Grand-Saint-Bernard in the 10th century. With its spiky towers the château dominates Lake Annecy.
Open thursdays, saturday, sunday, June 1 to Sept. 30 : 2 - 6.
Parking.
Guided tours.
Acoustiguides.

Montrottier (Château).

Lovagny - 74330.
Annecy : 9 km.
Property of the Florimontane Academy.
   A characteristic medieval fortress overlooking the Fier river, the château belonged to the Menthon family for four centuries before it became national property in 1792. Inside you see the rich collection of Léon Marès : 800 arms, 18th century Flemish tapestry, faïences and lace.
Open Apr. 4 to Oct. 15 : 9 - 12, 2 - 6.
Closed tuesdays except July and August.

Parking.
Guided tours.
Brochures.
Exhibitions of painting.
Tel. : (50) 46.23.02.

Ripaille (Château).

Thonon-les-Bains - 74200.
Thonon-les-Bains : 2 km.
Bus service.
Property of the Ripaille Foundation.
   This 15th century Château, with its four remaining towers, was restored between 1892 and 1902 and was once the favorite hunting ground of the Court of Savoy. Bonne de Bourbon, wife of the « Green Count » who built the Château made it a luxurious residence. Amédée VII, first Duke of Savoy and later Pope, founded the order of the monks of Saint-Augustin here. The Château later passed to the Carthusians of Vallon who held it until the Revolution.
Open Apr. 1 to May 31, Oct. 1 to Oct 31 : 2 - 6.
June 1 to Sept. 30 : 10 - 12, 2:30 - 6:30.
Closed Monday.
Off season : For groups upon request.
Shows, exhibitions.
Tel. : (50) 71.84.44.

Ripaille (Arboretum and Forest).

Thonon-les-Bains - 74200.
Ripaille.
Thonon-les-Bains : 2 km.
Bus service.
Private property and property of Thonon.
   This collection of trees was constituted between 1930 and 1934. It includes some 58 different species of coniferous trees. Initially experimental, the trees have adapted well to difficult soil and climactic conditions, and there are some rare examples to be found here. The forest is 53 hectares in size, the arboretum 19.
Open May 1 to Sept. 30 : 10 - 7.
Oct. 1 to Apr. 30 : 10 - 4:30.
Closed mondays except between July 1 to Sept. 15.
Recommended itinerary.
Facilities for the handicapped.
Brochures.
Tel. : (50) 71.02.15 and 41.59.77.

Thorens (Château).

Thorens-Glières.
Annecy : 20 km.
Property of M. de Roussy de Sales.
   Once a fine feudal fortress given to the lords of Compay by the Counts of Geneva in 1060, it then became a hiding place for bandits before belonging to the Sales family who restored the Château in the 16th century. Saint François de Sales often came here. The Château also has a memorial to Cavour and the Treasury of Saint François de Sales.
Open Apr. 1 to Sept. 30 : 10 - 12, 2 - 7.
Parking.
Guided tours.
Brochures.
Panels, Audiovisual.
Information English, German, Italian.
Tel. : (50) 77.42.02.

GUADELOUPE

Fort Napoleon.
Terre de Haut - 97137.
Property of the Département.
　This fort was built between 1844 and 1867. You can visit the sentry way, the tropical garden, and the Diorama of the Battle des Saintes. Regional furniture of the 19th and 20th century.
Open all year : 9 - 12.
Closed New Years Day.
Guided and unaccompanied tours.
Panels, Leaflets.
Carnival, Theatre, exhibitions.
Lecture tours.

MARTINIQUE

Pécoul (Plantation).
Basse-Pointe Martinique - 97218.
Private property.
　This master's residence was bought by Joseph Pécoul in 1780. The building has remained in the family ever since and was open to the public in 1983.
Open by appointment (M. de Wouves).
Tel. : 75.50.32.

La Pagerie (Birthplace of the Empress Josephine).
Les Trois-Ilets Martinique - 97229.
Private property.
　In this tropical park you can see the remains of the home of Joséphine Tascher de La Pagerie who became Empress of France. The house was destroyed by a hurricane, but the cane sugar mill and the outbuildings have been restored and now house a museum devoted to Napoleon's first wife.
Open all year : 9 - 5:30.
Closed Monday.
Tel. : 76.31.07.

INDEX

A

Abondance Rhône-Alpes - 365
Aguts Midi-Pyrénées - 252
Aigues-Mortes Languedoc-Roussillon - 173
Ainay-le-Vieil Centre - 88
Airaines Picardie - 320
Airvault Poitou-Charentes - 329
Aix-en-Provence Provence-Côte d'Azur - 341
Ajaccio Corse - 139
Alba Rhône-Alpes - 354
Albi Midi-Pyrénées - 252
Aléria Corse - 139
Allemagne Provence-Côte d'Azur - 336
Allinges (les) Rhône-Alpes - 365
Alluyes Centre - 96
Allymes (les) Rhône-Alpes - 352
Alteville Lorraine - 238
Amboise Centre - 106
Ambronay Rhône-Alpes - 352
Ancy-le-Franc Bourgogne - 64
Andurain Aquitaine - 28
Anet Centre - 96
Angers Pays de Loire - 291 and 218
Ango Haute Normandie - 280
Angoulême Poitou-Charentes - 326
Anjony Auvergne - 38 and 193
Ansouis Provence-Côte d'Azur - 347
Antibes Provence-Côte d'Azur - 337
Apremont Pays de Loire - 303 and 221
Apremont-sur-Allier Centre - 88
Arbois Franche-Comté - 142
Arc-et-Senans Franche-Comté - 143
Aren Aquitaine - 28
Arcizans-Avant Midi-Pyrénées - 250
Argentelles Basse-Normandie - 270
Argy Centre - 101
Arlay Franche-Comté - 142
Arlempes Auvergne - 41
Arles Provence-Côte d'Azur - 341
Arles-sur-Tech Languedoc-Roussillon - 183
Arras Nord-Pas-de-Calais - 260
Arsis (les) Pays de Loire - 299
Arthous Aquitaine - 23

Arville Centre - 120
Asnières Pays de Loire - 291
Assier Midi-Pyrénées - 248
Aubazine Limousin - 186
Aubenas Rhône-Alpes - 354
Aubichon Basse-Normandie - 262
Aulan Rhône-Alpes - 358
Aulteribe Auvergne - 44 and 196
Auray Bretagne - 82
Autrey Lorraine - 239
Autry-le-Châtel Centre - 127
Autun Bourgogne - 59
Auxerre Bourgogne - 64
Auzers Auvergne - 38
Avezan Midi-Pyrénées - 247
Avignon Provence-Côte d'Azur - 347
Azay-le-Ferron Centre - 101
Azay-le-Rideau Centre - 106

B

Bagatelle Picardie - 320
Bains-les-Bains Lorraine - 239
Balaine Auvergne - 34
Balleroy Basse-Normandie - 262
Ballon Pays de Loire - 301
Ballue (la) Bretagne - 76
Ballure Pays de Loire - 302
Baneuil Aquitaine - 12
Barberey-Saint-Sulpice Champagne-Ardennes - 135
Barben (la) Provence-Côte d'Azur - 341
Barbentane Provence-Côte d'Azur - 343
Barge (la) Auvergne - 44
Barly Nord-Pas-de-Calais - 260
Baronnière (la) Pays de Loire - 291
Bastie d'Urfé Rhône-Alpes - 360
Batisse (la) Auvergne - 44
Baume (la) Languedoc-Roussillon - 181
Baume-les-Messieurs Franche-Comté - 142
Bayers Poitou-Charentes - 326
Bazincourt-sur-Saulx Lorraine - 236
Bazeilles Champagne-Ardennes - 134
Bazouges Pays de Loire - 302
Beaucaire Languedoc-Roussillon - 174
Beaufief Poitou-Charentes - 326

Beaulieu-en-Rouergue Midi-Pyrébées - 255 and 211
Beaulieu-sur-Mer Provence-Côte d'Azur - 338
Beaumarchais Pays de Loire - 303
Beaumesnil Haute-Normandie - 276
Beaune Bourgogne - 52
Beauport Bretagne - 72
Beauregard Rhône-Alpes - 120 and 203
Beauregard Rhône-Alpes - 365
Beauvoir-sur-Besbre Auvergne - 34
Bec Hellouin (le) Haute-Normandie - 276
Belfort Franche-Comté - 144
Belinaye (la) Bretagne - 77
Bellegarde Centre - 128
Bellaigue Auvergne - 45
Belval Champagne-Ardennes - 134
Belvoir Franche-Comté - 142
Bérardière (la) Basse-Normandie - 271
Bérenger Rhône-Alpes - 358
Bernadières (les) Aquitaine - 12
Bertangles Picardie - 320
Berzé-la-Ville Bourgogne - 59
Berzé-le-Châtel Bourgogne - 59
Besançon Franche-Comté - 142
Besne Bourgogne - 58
Beynac Aquitaine - 12.
Béziers Languedoc-Roussillon - 178
Bidache Aquitaine - 28
Bidestroff Lorraine - 238
Bienassis Bretagne - 72
Billy Auvergne - 34
Biracq Poitou-Charentes - 327
Biron Aquitaine - 12
Bitche Lorraine - 238
Bizy Haute-Normandie - 276 and 217
Blancafort Centre - 88
Blandy-les-Tours Ile-de-France - 154
Blanville Centre - 97
Blérancourt Picardie - 310
Blois Centre - 120
Bois-Aubry Centre - 108
Bois-Breteau Poitou-Charentes - 326
Bois-Chevalier Pays de Loire - 288
Bois-de-Maine (le) Pays de Loire - 299

Bois-lés-Pargny Picardie - 310
Boisset-les-Prévanches Haute-Normandie - 277
Bois-le-Roi Bourgogne - 63
Bonaguil Aquitaine - 27
Bonaventure Centre - 121
Bondaroy Centre - 128
Bonnelière (la) Pays de Loire - 303
Bonnemare Haute-Normandie - 277
Bonneval Limousin - 187
Bonneville-sur-Touquet Basse-Normandie - 262
Bonpas Provence-Côte d'Azur - 348
Bontin Bourgogne - 64
Bordeaux Aquitaine - 18
Bories (les) Aquitaine - 12
Bosc (le) Midi-Pyrénées - 244
Boschaud (Notre-Dame-de) Aquitaine - 12
Boscodon Provence-Côte d'Azur - 337
Bosq (le) Bretagne - 77
Bouchat (le) Auvergne - 34
Bouchet-en-Brenne (le) Centre - 101
Bouges Centre - 101 and *197*
Bouilh (le) Aquitaine - 18
Bouillé-Ménard Pays de Loire - 291
Boumois Pays de Loire - 291
Bourbansais (la) Bretagne - 78
Bourbon-l'Archambault Auvergne - 34
Bourbilly Bourgogne - 52
Bourdeilles Aquitaine - 12
Bourges Centre - 89 and *201*
Bourget-du-Lac Rhône-Alpes - 364
Bourgueil Centre - 108
Bournac Aquitaine - 27
Bourq (le) Pays de Loire - 302
Bourron Ile-de-France - 154
Boury-en-Vexin Picardie - 314
Boussac Limousin - 186
Boutissaint Bourgogne - 64
Bouzonville Lorraine - 238
Bouxviller Alsace - 8
Brancion Bourgogne - 59
Brandon Bourgogne - 60
Branféré Bretagne - 82
Brassac Midi-Pyrénées - 255
Braux-Sainte-Cohière Champagne-Ardennes - 135
Brècy Basse-Normandie - 262
Bresson Rhône-Alpes - 359
Breteuil Ile-de-France - 164
Breuil-Yvain Centre - 102
Briançon Provence-Côte d'Azur - 353
Bridoré Centre - 108
Brie Limousin - 187
Briottières (les) Pays de Loire - 294
Brissac Pays de Loire - 292
Brou Rhône-Alpes - 352

Brouage Poitou-Charentes - 327
Bruneaux (les) Rhône-Alpes - 360
Buenc Rhône-Alpes - 354
Buoux Provence-Côte d'Azur - 348
Bussière (la) Centre - 128
Bussy-Rabutin Bourgogne - 52 and *197*
Buzay Poitou-Charentes - 327
By Ile-de-France - 155

C

Cadillac Aquitaine - 18
Cadouin Aquitaine - 13
Caen Basse-Normandie - 262
Calberte Languedoc-Roussillon - 181
Canon Basse-Normandie - 262
Canteleu Haute-Normandie - 280
Cany Haute-Normandie - 280
Caradeuc Bretagne - 78
Carcassonne Languedoc-Roussillon - 172
Carrouges Basse-Normandie - 271 and *217*
Cas Midi-Pyrénées - 255
Cassagne (la) Aquitaine - 13
Castanet Languedoc-Roussillon - 181
Castellas Languedoc-Roussillon - 174
Castelnau-Bretenoux Midi-Pyrénées - 248
Castelnaudary Languedoc-Roussillon - 172
Castres Midi-Pyrénées - 252
Castries Languedoc-Roussillon - 178
Caudeval Languedoc-Roussillon - 172
Caumont Midi-Pyrénées - 248
Caussade Midi-Pyrénées - 255
Cayla (le) Midi-Pyrénées - 252
Cazilhac Languedoc-Roussillon - 178 and *211*
Cenevières Midi-Pyrénées - 248
Cerisy Basse-Mormandie - 266
Cerisy-la-forêt Basse-Normandie - 266
Chaalis Picardie - 316
Chabottière (la) Pays de Loire - 303
Chaise-Dieu (la) Auvergne - 42
Chaize (la) Rhône-Alpes - 362
Châlons-sur-Marne Champagne-Ardennes - 134
Chalus-Chabrol Limousin - 187
Chamagne Lorraine - 239
Chambéry Rhône-Alpes - 364
Chambonneau Poitou-Charentes - 331
Chambord Centre - 121
Champ-de-Bataille Haute-Normandie - 277

Champ d'Oiseau Poitou-Charentes - 331
Champigny-sur-Veude Centre - 110
Champobert Basse-Normandie - 273
Champs (les) Bretagne - 78
Champs-sur-Marne Ile-de-France - 155 and *206*
Chantilly Picardie - 316
Chapelle-Belloin (la) Poitou-Charentes - 331
Chapelle d'Angillon (la) Centre - 90
Charlemont Champagne-Ardennes - 134
Charleville-Mézières Champagne-Ardennes - 134
Charlieu Rhône-Alpes - 360
Charroux Poitou-Charentes - 331
Chartres Centre - 97
Chastenay (le) Bourgogne - 64
Château-Arnoux Provence-Côte d'Azur - 336
Château-Dauphin Auvergne - 45
Châteaudun Centre - 97
Château-Guillaume Centre - 102
Châteauneuf-en-Auxois Bourgogne - 52
Châteauneuf-sur-Loire Centre - 128
Châteaurenard Provence-Côte d'Azur - 343
Château-Thierry Picardie - 310
Châtelier (le) Centre - 102
Châtel-sur-Moselle Lorraine - 240
Chatigny Centre - 110
Châtillon Bourgogne - 58
Châtillon-sur-Saône Lorraine - 240
Chaumont-sur-Loire Centre - 121
Chazeron Auvergne - 45
Chemery Centre - 122
Chêne-Galon Basse-Normandie - 273
Chenonceau Centre - 110
Cherbourg Basse-Normandie - 267
Chesnel Poitou-Charentes - 326
Chevannes Bourgogne - 60
Chevenon Bourgogne - 58
Cheverny Centre - 122
Chevigné Bourgogne - 60
Chevilly Centre - 130
Chevreloup Ile-de-France - 164
Chinon Centre - 110
Chitry Bourgogne - 58
Choix Ile-de-France - 155
Cimiez Provence-Côte d'Azur - 339
Cinq-Mars Centre - 110
Clamart Ile-de-France - 152
Clermont Rhône-Alpes - 365
Clisson Pays de Loire - 288
Clos-de-Vougeot Bourgogne - 52
Clos-Lucé (le) Centre - 110
Cluny Bourgogne - 60

Coarraze Aquitaine - 28
Coatcouraval Bretagne - 72
Coeuilly Ile-de-France - 158
Cognac Poitou-Charentes - 326
Coigny Basse-Normandie - 267
Colaissières Pays de Loire - 292
Collioures Languedoc-Roussillon - 183
Collonges Bourgogne - 52
Colmar Alsace - 9
Colmars-les-Alpes Provence-Côte d'Azur - 336
Colombier (le) Bretagne - 72
Combourg Bretagne - 80
Commarin Bourgogne - 54
Compiègne Picardie - 316
Condé Picardie - 310
Condé-Chivres-Val Picardie - 311
Condres Languedoc-Roussillon - 181
Conflans Rhône-Alpes - 364
Conques Midi-Pyrénées - 245
Conros Auvergne - 38
Cons-la-Grandville Lorraine - 232
Corbeil-Cerf Picardie - 316
Corbelin Bourgogne - 58
Corcelles Rhône-Alpes - 362
Cordès Auvergne - 45
Cormatin Bourgogne - 61 and *199*
Couches Bourgogne - 61
Coucy Picardie - 311
Coudray-Monbault Pays de Loire - 292
Coudray-Salbart Poitou-Charentes - 330
Couiza Languedoc-Roussillon - 172
Courances Ile-de-France - 150
Courcelles Picardie - 320
Courcy Basse-Normandie - 267
Courson Ile-de-France - 150
Courson Basse-Normandie - 263
Cour-sur-Loire Centre - 123
Court d'Aron Pays de Loire - 304
Courtes Rhône-Alpes - 354
Courtivron Bourgogne - 54
Couvertoirade (la) Midi-Pyrénées - 245
Craon Pays de la Loire - 300 and *221*
Crazannes Poitou-Charentes - 327
Creac'h Ingar Bretagne - 74
Crépy-en-Valois Picardie - 316
Crest Rhône-Alpes - 358
Creusot (le) Bourgogne - 61
Crôlles Rhône-Alpes - 359
Cugarel Languedoc-Roussillon - 172
Culan Centre - 90
Cypierre Bourgogne - 61

D

Dampierre Ile-de-France - 166
Dampierre-sur-Boutonne Poitou-Charentes - 327

Demigny Bourgogne - 61
Denacre (le) Nord-Pas-de-Calais - 260
Denainvilliers Centre - 130
Denone Auvergne - 45
Denonville Centre - 100
Deuilly-les-Morizecourt Lorraine - 240
Devinière (la) Centre - 111
Digoine Bourgogne - 61
Dijon Bourgogne - 54
Diors Centre - 104
Domme Aquitaine - 13
Dommerville Ile-de-France - 150
Dortan Rhône-Alpes - 354
Douhet (le) Poitou-Charentes - 329
Dourdan Ile-de-France - 150
Douzon Auvergne - 34
Druyes Bourgogne - 64
Dur-Écu Basse-Normandie - 268

E

Écouen Ile-de-France - 159
Effiat Auvergne - 45
Engarran (l') Languedoc-Roussillon - 178
Entrange Lorraine - 238
Entrecasteaux Provence-Côte d'Azur - 345
Entrevaux Provence-Côte d'Azur - 336
Épanvilliers Poitou-Charentes - 332
Époisses Bourgogne - 54
Ermenonville Picardie - 316
Escoublère (l') Pays-de-Loire - 300
Esquelbecq Nord-Pas-de-Calais - 258
Esnes Nord-Pas-de-Calais - 258
Essarts (les) Pays de Loire - 304
Esternay Champagné-Ardennes - 136
Estier (l') Bretagne - 82
Estignols Aquitaine - 23
Estillac Aquitaine - 27
Ételan Haute-Normandie - 280
Eu Haute-Normandie - 280
Eyzies-de-Tayac (les) Aquitaine - 13

F

Falaise Basse-Normandie - 263
Fénelon Aquitaine - 13
Fère-en-Tardenois Picardie - 311 and *22*
Ferrières Ile-de-France - 156
Ferrières Midi-Pyrénées - 252
Ferté-Imbault (la) Centre - 123
Fervaques Basse-Normandie - 263
Filain Franche-Comté - 145
Fillières Haute-Normandie - 281

Flammarens Midi-Pyrénées - 248
Flaugergues Languedoc-Roussillon - 178
Fleurigny Bourgogne - 65
Fléville Lorraine - 232
Fontainebleau Ile-de-France - 156
Fontaine-Française Bourgogne - 54
Fontaine-Henry Basse-Normandie - 263 and *216*
Fontaine-Guérard Haute-Normandie - 277
Fontcaude Languedoc-Roussillon - 179
Fontenay Bourgogne - 55 and *198*
Fontenoy Lorraine - 240
Fontdouce Poitou-Charentes - 329
Fontevraud Pays de Loire - 295 and *220*
Fontfroide Languedoc-Roussillon - 172
Forcalquier Provence-Côte d'Azur - 336
Fougères Bretagne - 80
Fougères-sur-Bièvre Centre - 123
Foulletorte Pays de Loire - 300
Foux (la) Languedoc-Roussillon - 174
Frazé Centre - 100
Frolois Bourgogne - 55
Fromental Limousin - 188
Frontenay Franche-Comté - 144

G

Gadancourt Ile-de-France - 162
Gageac Aquitaine - 13
Gaillac Midi-Pyrénées - 254
Gaillon Haute-Normandie - 277
Gataudière (la) Poitou-Charentes - 329
Gaudiès Midi-Pyrénées - 244
Gaujacq Aquitaine - 24
Gavaudun Aquitaine - 27
Gencay Poitou-Charentes - 332
Genetay (le) Haute-Normandie - 281
Genissac Aquitaine - 18
Gerbeviller Lorraine - 232
Germolles Bourgogne - 61
Gien Centre - 130
Giry Bourgogne - 58
Gisors Haute-Normandie - 277
Giverny Haute-Normandie - 277 and *218*
Gonneville Basse-Normandie - 268
Gordes Provence-Côte d'Azur - 348
Goué Pays de Loire - 300
Goulaine Pays de Loire - 288
Gourdon Provence-Côte d'Azur - 338 and *223*
Goutelas Rhône-Alpes - 361

Grainetière (la) Pays de Loire - 304
Gramont Midi-Pyrénées - 256 and *214*
Grandchamp Bourgogne - 65
Grandes-Bruyères (les) Centre - 131
Grand-Geroldseck Alsace - 8
Grand-Murcins (les) Rhône-Alpes - 361
Grandpré Champagne-Ardennes - 134
Grand-Pressigny (le) Centre - 111
Grange (la) Ile-de-France - 150
Grange (la) Lorraine - 238
Gran'maisons Ile-de-France - 166
Grasse Provence-Côte d'Azur - 338
Gratot Basse-Normandie - 268
Gray Franche-Comté - 145
Grenoble Rhône-Alpes - 359
Grignan Rhône-Alpes - 358 and *224*
Grignon Bourgogne - 55
Grignols Aquitaine - 13
Grillemont Centre - 111
Grosbois Ile-de-France - 158
Gua (le) Midi-Pyrénées - 254
Guadeloupe Guadeloupe - 367
Gué-Péan (le) Centre - 124
Guerche (la) Centre - 111
Guermantes Ile-de-France - 156 and *207*
Gué-Robert (le) Pays de Loire - 295
Guiche Aquitaine - 28
Guiry Ile-de-France - 162
Guise Picardie - 311

H

Hac Bretagne - 73
Hamyde (la) Nord-Pas-de-Calais - 258
Hambye Basse-Normandie - 268
Harcourt Haute-Normandie - 278
Harcourt Poitou-Charentes - 332
Haroué Lorraine - 233
Hattonchâtel Lorraine - 236
Haute-Combe Rhône-Alpes - 364
Hautefort Aquitaine - 13 and *193*
Haute-Guerche (la) Pays de Loire - 295
Haut-Koenigsbourg Alsace - 9
Haye (la) Bretagne - 80
Hellenvilliers Haute-Normandie - 278
Hérisson Auvergne - 34
Hesdin (Vieil) Nord-Pas-de-Calais - 260
Heudicourt Haute-Normandie - 278
Honfleur Basse-Normandie - 264
Houssaye (la) Bretagne - 73

Hort de Dieu (l') Languedoc-Roussillon - 174
Hugstein Alsace - 9
Hunaudaye Bretagne - 73

I

If Provence-Côte d'Azur - 343
Issoudun Centre - 104

J

Jaillac Aquitaine - 14
Jeurre Ile-de-France - 152
Josselin Bretagne - 82
Jouarre Ile-de-France - 156
Jours Bourgogne - 56
Jumièges Haute-Normandie - 281
Jumilhac Aquitaine - 14
Jussy-Champagne Centre - 90

K

Kerangat Bretagne - 84
Keranroux Bretagne - 74
Kerazan Bretagne - 74
Kergrist Bretagne - 73
Kerivon Bretagne - 73
Kerjean Bretagne - 74
Kerlevenan Bretagne - 84
Kerouzéré Bretagne - 76
Klap Houck (le) Nord-Pas-de-Calais - 258

L

Laas Aquitaine - 29
Labrède Aquitaine - 18
Lafayette Auvergne - 41
Landais (le) Centre - 104
Langeais Centre - 111
Langres Champagne-Ardennes - 137
Lanquais Aquitaine - 15
Lanrigan Bretagne - 80
Lantenay Bourgogne - 56
Lantilly (Côte d'Or) Bourgogne - 56
Lantilly (Nièvre) Bourgogne - 59
Lantheuil Basse-Normandie - 264
La Palice Auvergne - 35
Largouët Bretagne - 84
La Rochelle Poitou-Charentes - 329
Lassay-sur-Croisne Centre - 124
Lastours Midi-Pyrénées - 246
Latte (la) Bretagne - 73
Launay Haute-Normandie - 278
Lautaret Rhône-Alpes - 359
Laval Pays de Loire - 300
Lavardin Centre - 124
Lavaufranche Limousin - 186

Lavault Bourgogne - 62
Lavaur Midi-Pyrénées - 254
La Villeneuve Nord-Pas-de-Calais - 260
Lavoûte-Polignac Auvergne - 41
Layré Poitou-Charentes - 333
Léhélec Bretagne - 84
Lénoncourt Lorraine - 233
Léotoing Auvergne - 41
Lérins Provence-Côte-d'Azur - 338
Lerse Poitou-Charentes - 326
Libourne Aquitaine - 20
Lichecourt Lorraine - 240
Lieu-Dieu (Notre-Dame de) Pays de Loire - 304
Liget (le) Centre - 111
Limoges Limousin - 188
Lisieux Basse-Normandie - 264
Loc-Dieu Midi-Pyrénées - 245
Loches Centre - 115
Londres Languedoc-Roussillon - 179
Long Picardie - 320
Longpont Picardie - 311
Longpra Rhône-Alpes - 359
Longues-sur-Mer Basse-Normandie - 264
Lormont Aquitaine - 20
Losse Aquitaine - 15
Loudun Poitou-Charentes - 333
Lourdes Midi-Pyrénées - 250
Lourmarin Provence-Côte-d'Azur - 348
Louverie (la) Bretagne - 80
Lude (le) Pays de Loire - 302
Lucerne (la) Basse-Normandie - 269
Lygny-les-Charolles Bourgogne - 62
Lunéville Lorraine - 233
Lure Provence-Côte-d'Azur - 336
Lusigneul Haute-Normandie - 278
Luttange Lorraine - 238
Lux Bourgogne - 56
Luxeuil-les-Bains Franche-Comté - 146
Lyon Rhône-Alpes - 362
Lys (le) Ile-de-France - 157
Lys-Saint-Georges (le) Centre - 104

M

Magnanne Pays de Loire - 300
Maillé Bretagne - 76
Maillezais Pays de Loire - 304
Maintenon Centre - 100
Maison-Laffitte Ile-de-France - 166 and *208*
Malans Franche-Comté - 146
Malle Aquitaine - 20
Maillebois Centre - 100

lesherbes Centre - 131
lmaison Ile-de-France - 154
lromé Aquitaine - 20
rais (le) Ile-de-France - 152
nd *205*
rbœuf Haute-Normandie - 278
rcevol Languedoc-Roussillon 183
rconnay Poitou-Charentes - 33
rigny-le-Cahouet Bourgogne 56
mite (la) Pays de Loire - 295
rtainville Haute-Normandie - 33
rtel Midi-Pyrénées - 250
rthonie (la) Aquitaine - 15
rtinanches (les) Auvergne - 46
rtinvast Basse-Normandie - 59
ssebeau Auvergne - 38
udetour Ile-de-France - 162
tray (la) Auvergne - 34
upas Centre - 91
uriac Midi-Pyrénées - 254
uriac Aquitaine - 15
uvezin Midi-Pyrénées - 250
uvières Ile-de-France - 166 nd *207*
uzun Auvergne - 46
age (le) Auvergne - 35
ux Ile-de-France - 157
an Ile-de-France - 166
avy Basse-Normandie - 273
loc (fort) Aquitaine - 20
un-sur-Yèvre Centre - 91
llant Centre - 91
essaire Bourgogne - 56
etou-Salon Centre - 92
thon Rhône-Alpes - 366
ton Provence-Côte-d'Azur - 38
cœur Auvergne - 42
le Limousin - 186
lay Centre - 115
nière-en-Bray Haute-Normandie - 283
nil-Voisin Ile-de-France - 2
poulet Aquitaine - 15
ssac Auvergne - 38
silhac Auvergne - 39
airie (la) Pays-de-Loire - 304
ng-sur-Loire Centre - 131
lans Rhône-Alpes - 364
epoix Midi-Pyrénées - 244
omesnil Haute-Normandie - 3
gère (la) Languedoc-Roussillon - 179
esme Bourgogne - 56
tbazillac Aquitaine - 15
bouan Bretagne - 80
cley Franche-Conté - 142
daye Basse-Normandie - 264
gaston Aquitaine - 29
gey Midi-Pyrénées - 255
sec Aquitaine - 16

Montaigu-le-Blin Auvergne - 35
Montaiguet-en-Forez Auvergne - 35
Montaigu Lorraine - 234
Montaigut Midi-Pyrénées - 246
Montambert Bourgogne - 59
Montauban-de-Bretagne Bretagne - 80
Montauban Midi-Pyrénées - 256
Montbart Bourgogne - 55
Montbrun Aquitaine - 16
Montbrun Limousin - 189
Montcornet Champagne-Ardennes - 134
Mont-de-la-Vigne Basse-Normandie - 264
Montélimar Rhône-Alpes - 358
Montfan Auvergne - 35
Montfleury Auvergne - 46
Montgeoffroy Pays de Loire - 295
Montgeroult Ile-de-France - 162
Montgobert Picardie - 311
Montigny-sur-Avre Centre - 101
Montlaur Languedoc-Roussillon - 180
Mont l'Évêque Picardie - 317
Montléry Ile-de-France - 152
Montmajour Provence-Côte-d'Azur - 343
Montmaur Provence-Côte-d'Azur - 337
Montmédy Lorraine - 237
Montmirail Pays de Loire - 303
Montmorin Auvergne - 46
Montpoupon Centre - 115
Montmuran Bretagne - 81
Montréal (Dordogne) Aquitaine - 16
Montréal (Landes) Aquitaine - 24
Montrésor Centre - 115
Montreuil-Bellay Pays de Loire - 295
Montrond Rhône-Alpes - 361
Montrottier Rhône-Alpes - 366
Montségur Midi-Pyrénées - 244
Mont-Saint-Michel Basse-Normandie - 269
Moret-sur-Loing Ile-de-France - 157
Morienval Picardie - 316
Morlanne Aquitaine - 29
Mortain Basse-Normandie - 269
Motte (la) Basse-Normandie - 264
Motte-Glain (la) Pays de Loire - 290
Motte-Tilly (la) Champagne-Ardennes - 135 and *209*
Moudeyres Auvergne - 42
Mouilleron-en-Pareds Pays de Loire - 305
Moulins Poitou-Charentes - 333
Moulins Auvergne - 35
Moussy Ile-de-France - 164
Moutte (la) Provence-Côte-d'Azur - 345
Moutiers (les) Haute-Normandie - 283 and *219*

Mouzon Champagne-Ardennes - 134
Moyenmoutier Lorraine - 240
Moyre Pays de Loire - 295
Mulhouse Alsace - 9

N

Nacqueville Basse-Normandie - 269
Najac Midi-Pyrénées - 246
Nancy Lorraine - 234
Nantes Pays de Loire - 290
Narbonne Languedoc-Roussillon - 172
Nassigny Auvergne - 35
Navarrenx Aquitaine - 29
Nemours Ile-de-France - 157
Neuilly Picardie - 317
Neuville Ile-de-France - 166 and *209*
Nice Provence-Côte-d'Azur - 339
Nieul-sur-l'Autise Pays de Loire - 305
Nîmes Languedoc-Roussillon - 174 and *212-213*
Niort Poitou-Charentes - 330
Nitray Centre - 115
Nöe de Bel-Air (la) Pays de Loire - 290
Nohant Centre - 104
Nointel Ile-de-France - 164
Noirlac Centre - 92
Nuits Bourgogne - 65

O

O Basse-Normandie - 273
Oiron Poitou-Charentes - 330
Olhain Nord-Pas-de-Calais - 260 and *214*
Opme Auvergne - 47
Orcher Haute-Normandie - 283
Orléans Centre - 131
Ortenbourg Alsace - 8
Ourscamp Picardie - 317
Outrelaise Basse-Normandie - 264

P

Pagerie (la) Martinique - 367
Palluau Centre - 104
Panloy Poitou-Charentes - 329
Palice (la) Auvergne - 35 and *194*
Pange Lorraine - 238
Paraclet (le) Champagne-Ardennes - 135
Parentignat Auvergne - 47
Paris Ile-de-France - 148
Parnot Champagne-Ardennes - 138
Pau Aquitaine - 29
Pécoul Martinique - 367
Pennautier Languedoc-Roussillon - 173
Périgueux Aquitaine - 16

Perpignan Languedoc-Roussillon - 183
Pesmes Franche-Comté - 146
Pesteils Auvergne - 39
Petit-Couronne Haute-Normandie - 283
Petite-Pierre (la) Alsace - 8
Pètre Aquitaine - 24
Pézenas Languedoc-Roussillon - 180
Pierre-de-Bresse Bourgogne - 62
Pierrefonds Picardie - 317
Pierre Levée Pays de Loire - 305
Pimbat-Cruzalet Midi-Pyrénées - 248
Pin (le) Franche-Comté - 144
Pioline (la) Provence-Côte d'Azur - 341
Pirou Basse-Normandie - 270
Plessis-Bourré Pays de Loire - 296
Plessis-Brion (de) Picardie - 319
Plessis-Macé Pays de Loire - 296
Plessis-sur-Thilouze (le) Centre - 115
Plessis-Josso (le) Bretagne - 84
Pompignac Auvergne - 39
Poncé Pays de Loire - 303
Pont-à-Mousson Lorraine - 234
Pont-Chevron Centre - 131
Pontgirard Basse-Normandie - 274
Pontivy Bretagne - 85
Pontlevoy Centre - 124
Portes Languedoc-Roussillon - 175
Port-Royal Ile-de-France - 166
Possonière (la) Centre - 124
Pouancé Pays de Loire - 296
Poudenas Aquitaine - 27
Pouget (le) Languedoc-Roussillon - 183
Poyanne Aquitaine - 26
Prades Aquitaine - 27
Prades Languedoc-Roussillon - 183
Prafrance Languedoc-Roussillon - 175
Prébenoit Limousin - 186
Pranles Rhône-Alpes - 354
Preuille (le) Pays de Loire - 305
Prouzel Picardie - 320
Prunoy Bourgogne - 66
Puy-du-Fou (le) Pays de Loire - 305
Puyguilhem Aquitaine - 16
Puymartin Aquitaine - 16

Q

Quatre-Croix Pays de Loire - 297
Quincivet Rhône-Alpes - 359
Quintin Bretagne - 73

R

Rabodanges Basse-Normandie - 274

Radrets (les) Centre - 124
Ragheaud Auvergne - 39
Raguin Pays de Loire - 297
Rambouillet Ile-de-France - 168
Rambures Picardie - 323
Ramière (la) Midi-Pyrénées - 250
Ranrouët Pays de Loire - 290
Raray Picardie - 319
Rarécourt-la-Vallée Lorraine - 237
Ratilly Bourgogne - 66
Rauzan Aquitaine - 20
Ravignan Aquitaine - 26
Ray Franche-Comté - 146
Réau (la) Poitou-Charentes - 333
Réaux (les) Centre - 116
Reclus (le) Champagne-Ardennes - 136
Régnière-Écluse Picardie - 323
Reims Champagne-Ardennes - 137
Relecq (le) Bretagne - 76
Réole (la) Aquitaine - 21
Revel Midi-Pyrénées - 246
Reverseaux Centre - 101
Reynerie (la) Midi-Pyrénées - 246
Riau (le) Auvergne - 35
Richemont Aquitaine - 16
Riom Auvergne - 47
Ripaille Rhône-Alpes - 366
Riquewihr Alsace - 10
Ristz Auvergne - 36
Rivau (le) Centre - 116 and *202*
Rivecourt Picardie - 319
Robinières (les) Poitou-Charentes - 333
Rocamadour Midi-Pyrénées - 260
Roche (la) Auvergne - 48
Roche (la) Pays de Loire - 297
Rochebaron Auvergne - 42
Rochebrune Auvergne - 40
Rochebrune Poitou-Charentes - 326
Rochechouart Limousin - 189
Roche-Courbon (la) Poitou-Charentes - 329
Roche-la-Molière Rhône-Alpes - 361
Roche-Pichemer (la) Pays de Loire - 300
Rocher (le) Pays de Loire - 301
Roche-Racan (la) Centre - 116
Rochers-Sévigné (les) Bretagne - 81
Rocroi Champagne-Ardennes - 134
Rodemack Lorraine - 238
Romieu (la) Midi-Pyrénées - 248
Roquetaillade Aquitaine - 21
Rosanbo Bretagne - 74
Rouen Haute-Normandie - 284
Roure (la) Rhône-Alpes - 354
Roussière (la) Poitou-Charentes - 330
Roussillon Midi-Pyrénées - 250
Rousson Languedoc-Roussillon - 176 and *209*
Rouville Centre - 131

Royaumont Ile-de-France - 164
Rully Bourgogne - 62
Rye (la) Poitou-Charentes - 333

S

Saché Centre - 116
Sagonne Centre - 93
Saint-Agil Centre - 124
Saint-Aignan Pays de Loire - 30
Saint-Aubin-sur-Loire Bourgogne - 62
Saint-Augustin Auvergne - 36
Saint-Benoît Poitou-Charentes 333
Saint-Chamant Auvergne - 40
Saint-Cloud Ile-de-France - 154
Saint-Cosme Centre - 118
Saint-Denis Ile-de-France - 158
Saint-Denis-sur-Loire Centre 124
Saint-Émilion Aquitaine - 23
Saint-Fargeau Bourgogne - 66
Saint-Félix-de-Montceau Languedoc-Roussillon - 180
Saint-Félix-du-Lauragais Midi-Pyrénées - 247
Saint-Gabriel Basse-Normandie - 265
Saint-Galmier Rhône-Alpes - 3
Saint-Geniès Midi-Pyrénées - 2
Saint-Germain de Beaupré Limousin - 186
Saint-Germain de Livet Basse-Normandie - 265
Saint-Germain-en-Laye Ile-de-France - 168
Saint-Germain-Lès-Verberies Picardie - 319
Saint-Georges-de-Boscherville Haute-Normandie - 284
Saint-Géry Midi-Pyrénées - 25
Saint-Hilaire Provence-Côte d'Azur - 348
Saint-Hippolyte Basse-Normandie - 266
Saint-Jean-Cap-Ferrat Provence-Côte d'Azur - 341
Saint-Jean-de-Luz Aquitaine -
Saint-Jean-des-Vignes Picardie 313
Saint-Juire Pays de Loire - 305
Saint-Just Haute-Normandie - 278
Saint-Laurent Centre - 104
Saint-Léger Picardie - 313
Saint-Malo Bretagne - 81
Saint-Marcel Rhône-Alpes - 3
Saint-Martin-du-Canigou Languedoc-Roussillon - 183
Saint-Maur-de-Bleurville Lorraine - 241
Saint-Maximin Provence-Côte d'Azur - 345
Saint-Michel Picardie - 313
Saint-Michel-de-Cuxa Languedoc-Roussillon - 183

nt-Michel-de-Grandmont Languedoc-Roussillon - 181
nt-Michel-de-Frigolet Provence-Côte d'Azur - 343
nt-Michel-en-l'Herm Pays de oire - 305
nt-Pandelon Aquitaine - 26
nt-Papoul Languedoc-Roussillon - 173
nt-Philibert-de-Grandlieu ays de Loire - 290
nt-Pierre-Église Basse-Normandie - 270
nt-Point Bourgogne - 62
nt-Pont Auvergne - 38
nt-Quintin Auvergne - 48
nt-Rémy-de-Provence Provence-Côte d'Azur - 343
nt-Saturnin Auvergne - 48
nt-Sauveur Basse-Normandie 274
nt-Sever Aquitaine - 27
nt-Vidal Auvergne - 42
nt-Vincent-sur-Jard Pays de oire - 305
nt-Wandrille Haute-Normandie - 285
te-Croix Picardie - 319
te-Enimie Languedoc-Roussillon - 183
te-Eulalie-de-Cernon Midi-yrénées - 246
te-Marguerite Lorraine - 240
te-Marie-de-la-Tourette hône-Alpes - 363
te-Marie-d'Orbieu Languedoc-Roussillon - 173
te-Mesme Ile-de-France - 8
te-Suzanne Pays de Loire - 1
sac Languedoc-Roussillon - 3
gon Provence-Côte-d'Azur - 6
rs Auvergne - 40
es Rhône-Alpes - 363
e-de-Guerre Champagne-rdennes - 137
naise Bourgogne - 58
n-de-Provence Provence-Côte d'Azur - 345
es Languedoc-Roussillon - 4
ary-Bandol Provence-Côte Azur - 346
cé Pays de Loire - 298
at Aquitaine - 16
ay Centre - 106
y Basse-Normandie - 274
nur Pays-de-Loire - 298
ssay (le) Ile-de-France - 152
ve-Majeure (la) Aquitaine -
eterre-la-Lémance Aquitaine 28
eterre-Saint-Denis Aquitaine 28

Saverne Alsace - 8
Sayette (la) Poitou-Charentes - 330
Sceaux Ile-de-France - 154
Schlucht (la) Lorraine - 241
Sedan Champagne-Ardennes - 134
Segange Auvergne - 36
Sénanque Provence-Côte d'Azur - 348
Senlis Picardie - 319
Senneville Haute-Normandie - 278
Sens Bourgogne - 66
Septême Rhône-Alpes - 359
Sercy Bourgogne - 62
Sérignan-du-Comtat Provence-Côte d'Azur - 349
Serrant Pays de Loire - 298
Serviantin Rhône-Alpes - 359
Sèvres Ile-de-France - 154
Seyne-les-Alpes Provence-Côte d'Azur - 337
Sexey Lorraine - 234
Sierck Lorraine - 239
Sigournais Pays de Loire - 307
Silvacane Provence-Côte d'Azur - 345
Simiane Provence-Côte d'Azur - 349
Sisteron Provence-Côte d'Azur - 337
Solidor Bretagne - 81
Sorel Centre - 101
Strasbourg Alsace - 8
Sully Bourgogne - 62
Sully-sur-Loire Centre - 131
Sury-le-Comtal Rhône-Alpes - 362
Suscinio Bretagne - 85
Suze-la-Rousse Rhône-Alpes - 358
Syam Franche-Comté - 144

T

Talcy Centre - 126
Talmont Pays de Loire - 307
Tanlay Bourgogne - 66
Tarascon Provence-Côte d'Azur - 345
Tarbes Midi-Pyrénées - 252
Tassigny Champagne-Ardennes - 135
Tau Champagne-Ardennes - 137
Taverny Ile-de-France - 164
Teillan Languedoc-Roussillon - 176
Tennessue Poitou-Charentes 330
Ternay Poitou-Charentes - 333
Ternes (les) Auvergne - 40
Terre-Neuve Pays de Loire - 307
Tertre (le) Basse-Normandie - 274
Thaumiers Centre - 93
Thibaudière (la) Pays de Loire - 299

Thil Bourgogne - 58
Thizy Bourgogne - 68
Thoiry Ile-de-France - 168 and *210*
Thons (le) Lorraine - 241
Thorens Rhône-Alpes - 366
Thoronet (le) Provence-Côte d'Azur - 346
Tiffauges Pays de Loire - 308
Tilly Ile-de-France - 169
Touche-Trébly (la) Bourgogne - 74
Touffou Poitou-Charentes - 333
Toulouse Midi-Pyrénées - 247
Tour-Blanche (la) Aquitaine - 18
Tour Daniel Auvergne - 42
Tourelles (les) Champagne-Ardennes - 135
Tournoël Auvergne - 48 and *196*
Tournon Rhône-Alpes - 355
Tours Centre - 118
Tour de Vèvre Centre - 93
Touvet (le) Rhône-Alpes - 359
Tramayes Bourgogne - 64
Trébodennic Bretagne - 76
Tréguier Bretagne - 74
Tremblay Bourgogne - 68
Trémilly Champagne-Ardennes - 138
Tremohar-en-Berric Bretagne - 85
Trévarez Bretagne - 76
Trevilit Bretagne - 76
Trois-Fontaines Champagne-Ardennes - 137
Tronjoly Bretagne - 76
Troussay Centre - 126
Tulle Limousin - 186
Turenne Limousin - 186
Turpenay Centre - 118

U

Ussé Centre - 118
Uturbie Aquitaine - 31
Uzès Languedoc-Roussillon - 176

V

Val Auvergne - 40 and *195*
Valençay Centre - 106
Valbelle Provence-Côte d'Azur - 346
Valbonnes Languedoc-Roussillon - 177
Valgenceuse Picardie - 319
Valloires Picardie - 323
Valmagne Languedoc-Roussillon - 181
Valmogne Provence-Côte d'Azur - 347
Valmont Haute-Normandie - 285
Valognes Basse-Normandie - 270
Valprivas Auvergne - 42
Varenne (la) Lorraine - 237

Varennes Centre - 106
Vascœuil Haute-Normandie - 280
Vauboyen Ile-de-France - 152
Vaucelles Nord-Pas-de-Calais - 258
Vauchelles Picardie - 323
Vauclair Picardie - 314
Vaudesir Centre - 118
Vaugirard Rhône-Alpes - 362
Vaurenard Rhône-Alpes - 363
Vausse Bourgogne - 68
Vaux-le-Vicomte Ile-de-France - 157
Vayres Aquitaine - 23
Veauce Auvergne - 38
Veckring Lorraine - 239
Vendeuvre Basse-Normandie - 266
Vendôme Centre - 127
Venevelles Pays de Loire - 303
Ventadour Rhône-Alpes - 355
Verderonne Picardie - 319 and 222
Vergeur (le) Champagne-Ardennes - 137
Verie (la) Pays de Loire - 308
Verne (la) Provence-Côte d'Azur - 347
Verrerie (la) Centre - 93
Versailles Ile-de-France - 169
Versas Rhône-Alpes - 355
Versigny Picardie - 320
Vert-Bois (le) Nord-Pas-de-Calais - 258 and 215
Veuil Centre - 106

Vieil-Hesdin Nord-Pas-de-Calais - 260
Vienne Rhône-Alpes - 359
Vierzy Picardie - 314
Vigne (la) Auvergne - 40
Villandraut Aquitaine - 23
Villandry Centre - 118
Villatre Centre - 96
Ville-André (la) Bretagne - 82
Villebois-Lavalette Poitou-Charentes - 326
Villefranche Provence-Côte-d'Azur - 341
Villefranche-de-Conflent Languedoc-Roussillon - 184
Villefranche-de-Rouergue Midi-Pyrénées - 246
Villegongis Centre - 106
Villemolin Bourgogne - 59
Villemonteix Limousin - 187
Villeneuve (la) Nord-Pas-de-Calais - 260
Villeneuve-Jacquelot (la) Bretagne - 85
Villeneuve-Lembron Auvergne - 49
Villeneuve-lès-Avignon Languedoc-Roussillon - 177
Villeneuve-sur-Yonne Bourgogne - 69
Ville-Prévost Centre - 101
Villequier Haute-Normandie - 285
Viller-lès-Nancy Lorraine - 236
Villersexel Franche-Comté - 146

Villesalem Poitou-Charentes 334
Villesavin Centre - 127
Villette Ile-de-France - 164
Villevieille Languedoc-Roussillon - 178
Villy-la-Ferté Champagne-Ardennes - 135
Vincennes Ile-de-France - 15 and *200*
Virieu Rhône-Alpes - 360
Vitré Bretagne - 82
Vizille Rhône-Alpes - 360
Voguë Rhône-Alpes - 355
Vollore Auvergne - 49
Vove (la) Basse-Normandie - 27

W

Wailly Picardie - 324
Wagenbourg Alsace - 9
Wasigenstein Alsace - 9
Wurtemberg Alsace - 10

X

Xaintrailles Aquitaine - 28

Y

Yèvre-le-Chatel Centre - 131